The boxmaker's revenge

The boxmaker's revenge

'Orthodoxy', 'heterodoxy' and
the politics of the parish
in early Stuart London

Peter Lake

Stanford University Press
Stanford, California
2001

Stanford University Press
Stanford, California

© 2001 by Peter Lake

Originating publisher Manchester University Press, Manchester

First published in the U.S.A. by
Stanford University Press, 2001

Printed in Great Britain

ISBN 0-8047-3717-7 cloth
ISBN 0-8047-4128-x paperback

Library of Congress Card Number: 00-109035

This book is printed on acid-free paper.

Contents

LIST OF FIGURES—vii
ACKNOWLEDGEMENTS—viii

PART I
STEPHEN DENISON

1 Introduction: the occasion — 2

2 The puritanism of Stephen Denison: i. doctrinal and pietistic underpinnings — 11

3 The puritanism of Stephen Denison: ii. ecclesiastical forms and political consequences — 53

PART II
JOHN ETHERINGTON

4 Denison and Etherington or was John Etherington a familist? — 86

5 Another pair of initials? T.L., H.N. and the ideological formation of the young Etherington — 120

6 What Etherington really thought: the 1620s — 148

PART III
THE LONDON PURITAN SCENE

7 The London puritan underground — 170

8 William Chibald and the strange case of *A trial of faith* — 190

9 Doctrinal dispute and damage limitation in the London puritan community — 218

PART IV
DENISON AND ETHERINGTON AGAIN

10 Heading for the high ground: Denison and Etherington on order, authority and orthodoxy — 262

Contents

11 The Laudian style and the politics of the parish-pump 298

12 Retrospective: Denison and Etherington position themselves for posterity 342

CONCLUSION—389

INDEX—416

Figures

1. The title page of *The white wolf*. Reproduced courtesy of the Bodleian Library, Oxford. — page 3
2. 'The woolfe in a sheepes skinne'. Reproduced courtesy of the Bodleian Library, Oxford. — 6
3. 'The woolfe in his owne skinne'. Reproduced courtesy of the Bodleian Library, Oxford. — 7
4. The arms of the city of London, embossed on the roof of St Katharine Cree. — 302
5. The funeral monument of the goldsmith William Avenon. — 305
6. An eighteenth-century view of the church of St Katharine Cree. Reproduced courtesy of the Guildhall Library, London. — 307
7. A view of the nave at St Katharine Cree, showing the arms of various city companies. — 308
8. The upper portion of the offending stained-glass window at St Katharine Cree. — 309
9. The title page of Etherington's 1651 edition of the collected works of T.L. Reproduced courtesy of the Bodleian Library, Oxford. — 381

Acknowledgements

In trying to spread the blame for what follows, I fear I have to name many of the usual suspects. In many ways this book owes its origins to a chance remark of Patrick Collinson's. When I showed him an early version – a typically bloated and overwritten 'article' essentially on the puritanism of Stephen Denison, he suggested, quite rightly, that the thing was too long and thin, too abstract and Denison-centred and that what it needed was more context. I could see that he was right but not what sort of context to provide. Vaguely dissatisfied with the thing and suspecting that I did not understand John Etherington at all, I thrust it back in the drawer. It lay there until I read Christopher Marsh's brilliant book on familism. This made it immediately clear to me that I had indeed got John Etherington seriously wrong and that his first book was amongst other things a lightly coded familist message, which my initial reading of the text had entirely failed to detect. Indeed, when I first read the book I fear that I could not have recognised a familist message, coded or not, had it hit me on the nose. Having read Marsh, however, it became clear that familism and its milieu might well form a good deal of the context for which Pat Collinson had been asking. That led, through Etherington, to T.L. and thence even to some dabblings in H.N., for the study of all of whom Marsh's book has been a constant source of inspiration. Thereafter the thing just grew. That growth owes a great deal to my having an extraordinarily learned and long-suffering collection of friends and colleagues. Michael Winship more than once gave me nuggets of information and made crucial suggestions about where to go for more and still more context, insisting, in particular, that I look in detail at Chibald and Walker and Wotton, and at the end of the project insisting that I look more closely at earlier writers on the relation between justification and repentance. Anthony Milton, Ann Hughes, Ethan Shagan, Bill Jordan, Tom Cogswell, Michael Questier, Ken Fincham and Patrick Collinson all read various drafts of the thing. Bill pronounced it 'dense', not realising, I hope, the full connotations of that word in a London-centred linguistic universe and Tom gave it a sympathetic and astute reading when it really needed one. Paul Seaver read it for the press twice with exemplary patience, care and insight and provided me with many extremely useful pieces of information and a good deal of excellent advice, some of which I even managed to take. Ann Hughes' work on Thomas Edwards and *Gangraena*, which she has allowed me to read and discuss with

Acknowledgements

her over the past few years, provided crucial insights for the analysis of puritan anti-puritanism and the nature of what one might term, sparing her blushes, the 'puritan public sphere'. Anthony Milton shared with me his thoughts on 'censorship' and a good deal else and has been a constant source of encouragement. Julia Merritt gave me various references and very patiently helped to introduce me to the arcana of London records. Her own work on Westminster was a crucial source of ideas on the politics of the parish and on the social, political and administrative contexts in which churches were rebuilt and refurbished during this period. Our understanding of these issues will be transformed by the publication of her book on Westminster and by the completion of her research project on Stow's *Survey*. Eliot Vernon also shared his considerable knowledge of London presbyterianism and parish sources during the 1640s in long chats in the Institute of Historical Research and the Norfolk Arms. Michael Questier, Andrew Thrush and Simon Healey all helped with London Company records and the mysteries of Chancery. Andrew Thrush let me consult his biography for the history of parliament on Martin Bond. Tim Wales talked to me about pardons and checked some references for me at the PRO. Evan Haefeli helped me with – that is, he translated – the Dutch bits and was very helpful indeed in guiding me towards the Dutch works of T.L. Richard Cust very kindly wasted what was, for me at least, a very enjoyable afternoon taking photographs of St Katharine Cree. A variety of archivists in the Guildhall, at several livery companies and what was at the time the Greater London Record Office all answered the idiot questions of a novice in early modern London with great patience. Ariel Hessayon talked at length to me one night at the Skinners Arms about London sources and puritan weirdos and then, very late in the project, he was extremely generous in sharing the fruits of his own research on St Katharine Cree, saving me from several errors and putting me on to several crucial leads. Our knowledge of radical religion in London at mid-century will be greatly enhanced when his own work on Thomas Tanny is published.

My greatest debt, however, is to David Como whose own research on shifting puritan notions of orthodoxy and the challenge of antinomianism provided a crucial context against which to set the current project. He has been a consistent source of advice and support; two or three times he pushed me in what turned out to be just the right directions. He has provided me with some wonderful titbits of information not to mention really informed and engaged readings and critiques of some of the crucial parts of the text. He has, indeed, on many occasions, played the adviser to my student.

In intention this was a 'short silly book', a micro-history that got big on me. It is now too long to be short and too theological to be entertainingly silly. However, it remains a long, thin, story-based book and as such it is designed to serve as an introduction to many themes and developments in the period

Acknowledgements

that have now received an altogether more rounded, not to say definitive, treatment in David Como's Princeton Ph.D. thesis and forthcoming monograph on antinomianism and Ariel Hessayon's study of Tanny.

I need finally to acknowledge three not only scholarly but also financial debts; the first is to the Folger Shakespeare Library where, on a fellowship in 1986–87, I first came upon the very juicy looking writings of Stephen Denison; the second is to the Institute for Advanced Study where in 1989–90 I made my first stab at writing up Denison and little bits of Etherington. That I pushed on into the local sources owed a great deal to a research project on funeral sermons funded by the Leverhulme Trust. I had thought originally that the Denison/Juxon nexus might be one of a number of short case studies of the relations between the subjects of funeral sermons and their pulpit panegyrists. As the reader will soon see, I got both carried away with and sidetracked from that initial intent. But there is a sense in which the current volume is the first published fruits of that project and I should like to thank the Trust for their support when much of the initial work was being done.

Part I

Stephen Denison

Chapter 1

Introduction: the occasion

On 11 February 1627 Stephen Denison, minister of St Katharine Cree church in London, preached a Paul's Cross sermon. Standing in front of the pulpit was John Etherington. On Etherington's chest was pinned a paper 'written with large letters'. Prevented by the physical attentions of a gaoler and a pursuivant from removing his label, Etherington was forced to stand there and listen for three hours while Denison denounced him as a heretic, a familist and an anabaptist. At the end of the sermon Etherington made a public demonstration of his dissent from these claims and, since he refused either to own or to recant the heresies imputed to him, he was thence returned to prison, where he was to languish for another three years, petitioning the parliament of 1628 for a temporary release from gaol so that he might, the more effectively, pursue his appeal in person. This bizarre scene must have attracted a certain contemporary notoriety; certainly the diarist Thomas Crossfield saw fit to note in his entry for February 1627 both Denison's performance at the Cross and the existence in London of a sect of what he called 'Edringtonians', whose leader was one 'Edrington', an ex-boxmaker blessed with 'some skill in the scriptures' whose tenets had some 'affinity with the family of love'. Nor is Crossfield's diary our only evidence for the notoriety of Etherington's bizarre opinions in contemporary Oxford; in his Act lecture for 1626 John Prideaux included, in a list of contemporary radical groups and heresies ('enthusiasts' as he termed them), a casual reference to a group he called the 'Hetheringtinianos'. This was a list which, amongst other contemporary groups, included Saturday sabbatarians and a glance backwards to those dangerous Elizabethan eccentrics and visionaries, Hacket and Coppinger. Clearly Prideaux's audience was expected to catch the reference and accept the almost proverbial association of all of these groups in the single Europe-wide 'historiae enthusiastarum' to which he was alluding.[1]

Not one of Denison's parishioners, Etherington was variously described by

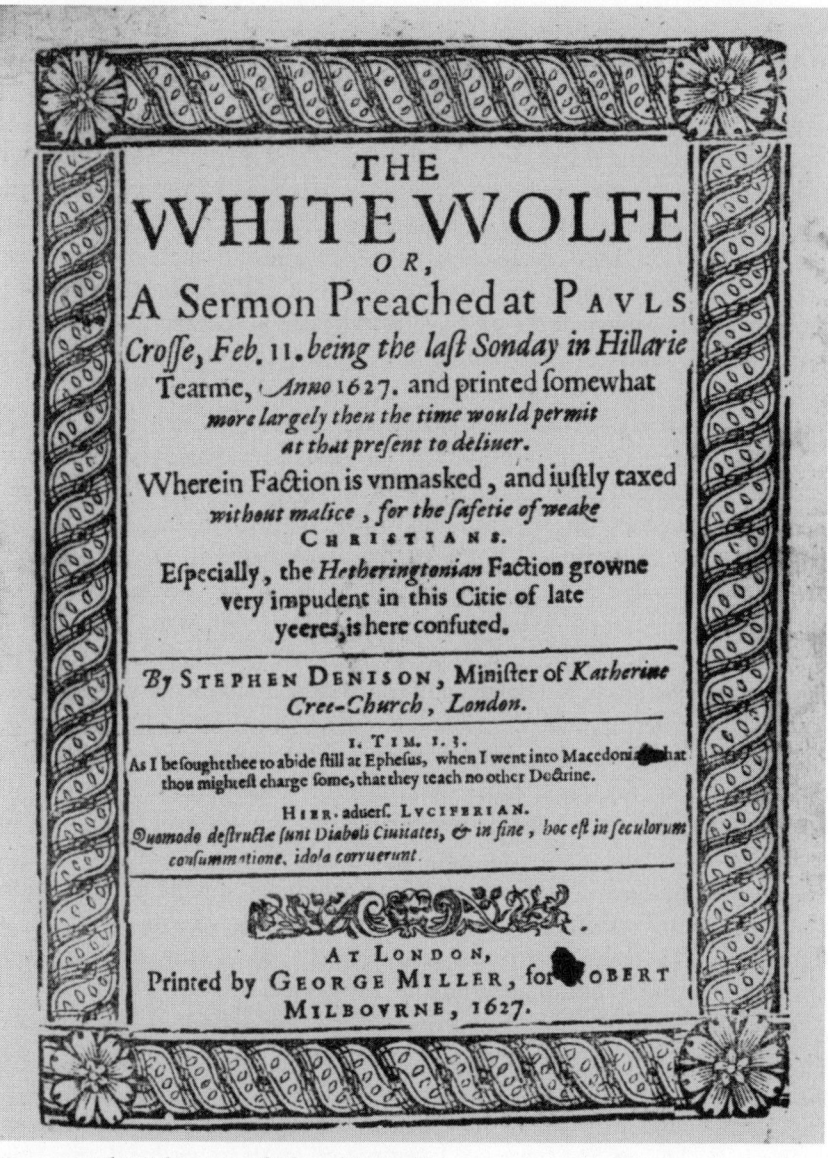

Figure 1 The title page of *The white wolf*

himself as a conventionally pious designer and maker of water conduits and by Denison as an erstwhile boxmaker and semi-professional sect master or prophet. Denison himself was a Cambridge man from Trinity College, who received his BA in 1602–03 and his MA in 1606. Meanwhile he had been ordained deacon and priest in 1603. This places him (perhaps unsurprisingly, given his subsequent career and opinions) slap bang in the middle of the Cambridge of William Perkins and Laurence Chaderton. He disappears from view thereafter until the late 1610s when he resurfaces in the London records as first the curate and then the perpetual curate of St Katharine Cree.

After his showdown at the cross with Etherington, Denison[2] resumed his parish ministry and various London lectureships, publishing his denunciation of Etherington under the title *The white wolf* later that year and dedicating it to the king. By the 1630s, however, the shoe was on the other foot, with Denison in trouble with the High Commission, the same court which had sentenced Etherington. He had been denounced there by various of his parishioners who were rather keener on the Laudian drive to give external architectural expression to the 'beauty of holiness' than was Denison. Denison's harsh manner in the pulpit and, in particular, his ridicule of his parishioners' recent efforts at church decoration had clearly alienated a section of the parish. Then, in 1641, Etherington came back to haunt him, when, taking advantage of the collapse of censorship, the boxmaker replied in print to the fourteen-year-old accusations of heresy, anabaptism and familism contained in *The white wolf*.

Denison appears in various guises in the course of these events; in his own eyes and works, he was a pillar of doctrinal orthodoxy, a defender of the English church against sectarian assault; in the eyes of some of his parishioners, in the 1630s, he appeared a 'puritan' opponent of Laudian reform, an intemperate defamer of his parishioners' morals and intentions and a lascivious womaniser to boot. In Etherington's account, however, he figured as a clericalist tyrant, an enemy of the godly laity, obsessed with crushing the merest hint of lay initiative and criticism.

Etherington, too, inhabited a number of different personae in the course of the affair. In Denison's eyes, he was a sectary, indeed a sect master, a self-proclaimed prophet and successor to the shadowy T.L., who lured away loyal but unsuspecting members of the English church into familist, Arminian and anabaptistical errors and heresies. Etherington, on the other hand, presented himself in an altogether less sinister light. Here, he claimed, was a loyal, albeit enthusiastically pious, member of the national church, who merely shared what ever rays of spiritual illumination he had managed to achieve with his fellow Christians. Not a familist nor a sectary nor an Arminian, Etherington claimed to be a thoroughly conforming member of the church of England, fully committed to the predestinarian theology that both he and Denison were convinced represented that church's doctrinal position.

Introduction: the occasion

This book takes the altercation between this rather odd couple as its starting point and then moves out from there, to place the dispute in the multiple social, cultural, polemical and political contexts necessary to see precisely what was going on here. What forces, what ideological and personal trajectories, brought these two men to their strange meeting at the Cross in 1627? What did their dispute mean? What issues did it raise and what do they have tell us about the religious history of early Stuart England?

To begin with, Denison's eerily protracted altercation with Etherington provides us with an example, almost unique for the period before 1640, of an interaction between a godly minister and an active, critical and relatively humble member of his flock. Putting together clues culled from Denison's peculiarly chatty and discursive denunciation of Etherington with other asides and references in Etherington's own very self-referential printed works, we can learn a good deal about Etherington's own development and ultimate ideological position. And through Etherington, and the even more indistinct figure of T.L., we can gain a glimpse of an arena of lay activism and, at least potentially heterodox, doctrinal debate in puritan circles in London. We can do so, moreover, albeit intermittently, throughout a period that stretches from the 1590s to the 1640s. This is a puritan underground that is all too often obscured from view by the nature of the sources and the political prudence and doctrinal tact, or, to put it more conspiratorially, the self-censorship and self-regulation, of the godly community.

In addressing those questions I have paid particular attention to the most obvious and yet also the most seemingly ephemeral, and least reliable, aspect of Etherington and Denison's protracted shouting match – that is, the names they called each other and the identities they constructed both for themselves and for one another through the process of name calling. How, if at all, are the various versions of Denison's and Etherington's careers and characters, canvassed in the course of the dispute, to be squared with one another? What can these very different identities, polemical labels and claims tell us about the religious scene of early seventeenth-century England?

These are intrinsically interesting questions but they take on a heightened significance given the bad name that polemic and any source taken to be tainted with polemic have acquired of late amongst some scholars. Indeed, things have reached such a pass that a category has only to be shown to be literarily or polemically constructed, and hence subject to rhetorical and political manipulation and change, in order for it to be dismissed as a mere figment of the imaginations of ideologically motivated, and hence entirely untypical, contemporaries. The result has been, on the one hand, the claim that, for instance, the theatre in some meaningful sense 'invented' puritanism, and, on the other, a flight to supposedly purer un- or non-polemical sources in, what seems to me to be, the entirely mistaken belief that

Figure 2 'The woolfe in a sheepes skinne'

Figure 3 'The woolfe in his owne skinne'

they more or less guarantee us a less biased, more objective account of contemporary opinion.[3]

What follows is an attempt to buck this trend. I shall be using here overtly polemical sources and, admittedly, that fact brings with it considerable limitations and difficulties. But it also has advantages. The very polemical intensity of the sources upon which the following account is largely based, allows us a privileged, albeit indistinct, glimpse into a world that we do not usually get to see at all. Since many of the sources are polemical, a good deal of time is spent reading them against the grain, comparing and collating them with one another to overcome the biases, the silences and exaggerations that the polemical mode always produces. That process can only ever be partially successful. And yet polemic and the polarities it reproduces did, in part at least, structure people's lives, their images of themselves and of others. Accordingly, we ignore it at our peril. In the end, the polemical constructs through which the story has come down to us become necessarily a part of the story itself and that is a good not a bad thing. They provide us with our entry point into these events, and it is only by following the clues strewn about these inherently polemical, entirely *partis pris* and self-serving exchanges that we can say anything at all about Etherington or much of interest about that otherwise standard London puritan minister, Stephen Denison.

Certainly, if it were not for the fury of Stephen Denison's polemical assault on Etherington we would be able to find out far less about the boxmaker's eccentric views than we can at present. But if we are to use Denison's polemic, we must study the career and context, the subject-position, out of which it was produced. And Denison, too, is a figure of considerable interest, whose career, for all his success in denouncing Etherington in the 1620s, scarcely enjoyed a stable or univocal relationship to power or orthodoxy. Indeed, Denison's career and his altercation with Etherington raise, and may indeed help to resolve, a number of issues that have emerged in recent writing as crucial to the religious history of the period. The nature of puritanism, the tensions within puritan divinity between lay activism, on the one hand, and clerical authority, on the other – in short, the whole relationship between 'perfect protestants', order- and orthodoxy-obsessed puritans like Denison, and 'the people' and 'popular radicalism', variously defined – all these issues are raised by the tangled web of Denison and Etherington's careers and interactions.[4]

Moreover, in order to pursue these themes the better, the Denison/Etherington dispute needs to be set in a number of contexts; some of them local, involving other disputes within the London puritan brotherhood, conducted both by Denison and other similar representatives of the mainstream puritan tradition, others of them national, involving the highest of high court politics and theologico-political manoeuvre. Here central themes in the religious history of the period will be encountered and interrogated,

Introduction: the occasion

including the much discussed existence or otherwise of a 'Calvinist consensus' in the early Stuart church, a consensus policed and maintained (or not) by an effective system of censorship. Internal centrifugal features of the puritan scene will be related to the issue of 'censorship' and the workings of the resulting 'system', whereby doctrinal dispute and expression were controlled both by authority and by the godly themselves, will be keyed into the attendant political circumstances, both local and national, which in fact determined the outcome of each such dispute.[5]

In short, starting out from their confrontation at Paul's Cross, we will pursue both Etherington and Denison into a number of different contexts, encountering, on the way, many of the central questions and issues raised by recent writing on the early Stuart church. Of course, it is neither possible nor desirable to rewrite the history of English puritanism based on the rather episodic account of two men and a pair of initials that follows. From so peculiar a series of events and so odd a couple definitive conclusions can scarcely be drawn. But it is precisely because both parties were so odd and so obsessive that their altercation can show us aspects of the period that are all but invisible in other more normal, conventional or typical sources. To return finally to the question of polemic, it is certainly true that if the people involved in these events had not come cordially to loathe and resent one another as much as they did, we would know next to nothing of these events and they are events, I will argue below, that, for all their indeterminacy and oddness, have much to tell us about religion in early Stuart England.

NOTES

1 S. Denison, *The white wolf* (London, 1627), pp. 33–5 for the date and site of the performance and the text of Etherington's projected recantation. Also see John Etherington, *The defence of John Etherington against Steven Denison* (London, 1641), pp. 47–8, for a more detailed account of the proceedings, stressing, perhaps predictably, Etherington's heroic resistance to the whole denunciatory labelling process. For Etherington's appeal to parliament, see R.C. Johnson, M.J. Cole and W.B. Bidwell, *Proceedings in parliament, 1628* (New Haven, 1977–83), vol. III, p. 146. F.S. Boas, ed., *The diary of Thomas Crosfield* (Oxford, 1935), p. 9. I owe these references to the kindness of Tom Cogswell. J. Prideaux, *Viginti-duae lectiones* (Oxford, 1648), 'oratio X, inauguralis in promotione doctorum ... 1626', pp. 95–6. I owe this reference to the kindness of Anthony Milton.

2 J.A. Venn, *Alumni Cantabrigienses ... part 1* (Cambridge, 1922–27), s.v., Denison Stephen. For the heavily reformed or Calvinist, moderate puritan milieu that dominated certain sections of the university at that date see P. Lake, *Moderate puritans and the Elizabethan church* (Cambridge, 1982); H.C. Porter, *Reformation and reaction in Tudor Cambridge* (Cambridge, 1958), chapters 10 and 12 and J. Morgan, *Godly learning* (Cambridge, 1986). For the wider role of the university in training the early Stuart generation of moderate puritan divines see T. Webster, *Godly clergy in early Stuart*

England: the Caroline puritan movement, c. 1620–1643 (Cambridge, 1997). Webster's book omits all discussion of London.

3 On the unreliability of 'polemic' and for an account of the religious thought of the period predicated on the supposed dichotomy between theology and polemic see P. White, Predestination, policy and polemic (Cambridge, 1992). For a variety of forays into the constructedness of puritan identity see P. Collinson, The puritan character (Clark Memorial Library, Los Angeles, 1989); 'Bartholomew Fair: theatre invents puritans', in D. Bevington and D. Smith, eds, The theatrical city (Cambridge, 1995); 'Ecclesiastical vitriol: religious satire in the 1590s and the invention of puritanism', in J. Guy, ed., The reign of Elizabeth I (Cambridge, 1995). For the invocation of the entirely unpolemical perspective supposedly provided by catechisms see I. Green, The Christian's A B C (Oxford, 1995).

4 See here Nicholas Tyacke, 'Puritanism, Arminianism and counter-revolution', in C.S.R. Russell, ed., The origins of the English civil war (London, 1973); P. Collinson, The religion of protestants (London, 1982). Also see C.S.R. Russell, Parliaments and English politics, 1621–1629 (Oxford, 1979), pp. 26–32; Russell, Unrevolutionary England (London, 1990), chapter 12, 'The parliamentary career of John Pym, 1621–9' and Russell, The causes of the English civil war (Oxford, 1990), chapters 3, 4 and 5 and appendix. Dr Tyacke has subsequently modified his position in two important articles: the first, The fortunes of English puritanism, 1603–1640 (Friends of Dr Williams Library, forty-fourth lecture, London, 1990) and the second, '"The rise of puritanism" and the legalising of dissent, 1571–1719', in Ole Peter Grell, Jonathan Israel and Nicholas Tyacke, eds, From persecution to toleration (Oxford, 1991). For more in this mode see J. Eales, 'A road to revolution: the continuity of puritanism, 1559–1642', in C. Durston and J. Eales, eds, The culture of puritanism, 1560–1700 (Basingstoke, 1996). Now see T. Webster, Godly clergy in early Stuart England: the Caroline puritan movement, c. 1620–1643.

5 G. Bernard, 'The church of England c. 1529–c. 1642', History, 75 (1990); P. White, Predestination, policy and polemic (Cambridge, 1992) and his 'The via media in the early Stuart church', in K. Fincham, ed., The early Stuart church (London, 1993); Kevin Sharpe, The personal rule of Charles I (London and New Haven, 1993) especially chapters VI and XI. On the more specific issue of censorship see Sheila Lambert, 'State control of the press in theory and practice: the role of the Stationer's Company before 1640', in R. Myers and M. Harris, eds, Censorship and control of print in England and France, 1600–1910 (Winchester, 1992) and 'Richard Montague, Arminianism and censorship', Past and Present, 124 (1989); A.B. Worden, 'Literature and political censorship in early modern England', in A.C. Duke and C.A. Tamse, eds, Too mighty to be free: censorship in Britain and the Netherlands, Britain and the Netherlands, vol. 9 (Zutphen, 1987); Sharpe, Personal rule of Charles I, pp. 644–54. For the rather extreme positions against which much of this literature is reacting see Christopher Hill, 'Censorship and English literature', in Hill, The collected essays of Christopher Hill: volume 1 – writing and revolution in seventeenth century England (Brighton, 1985) and Annabel Patterson, Censorship and interpretation (Madison, 1984). The whole discussion has been raised to a new level of sense and sophistication by Anthony Milton in his 'Licensing, censorship and religious orthodoxy in early Stuart England', Historical Journal, 42 (1998). My remarks on this subject in what follow are deeply indebted to Dr Milton whom I would like to thank for letting me read his paper in advance of publication and for many discussions of these issues over the past few years.

Chapter 2

The puritanism of Stephen Denison: i. doctrinal and pietistic underpinnings

THE PROBLEM OF PURITANISM

Let us start with Denison's own style of divinity, the sources for the reconstruction of which are excellent. Denison preached and printed two Paul's Cross sermons, some lectures on the sacraments and an exposition of the first chapter of the second epistle of Peter (both preached in the parish church of St Katharine Cree), two funeral sermons (one for John Juxon, a merchant, and the other for his wife, Elizabeth, Denison's first and greatest lay patrons) and a catechism dedicated to and for the use of his parishioners which was based, he claimed, on his own catechetical practice. In addition there is in the library of the American Antiquarian Society in Worcester, Mass., over 130 folios of notes taken by one Henry Fleming from a number of sermons preached by Denison between 1637 and 1639. These are frequently very full indeed and are in a good hand, presumably written up later from more hurried notes taken at the time.[1] We have, therefore, a good idea of Denison's views as they were presented in a variety of arenas. We know how he preached when he wanted to show off (at the Cross); we have a taste of his day-to-day preaching style in his own parish; we have (in the funeral sermons) his ideal image of elect sainthood; and, in the catechism, we have a compendium of what he took to be the knowledge necessary for the simplest Christians – 'children and servants' as he put it in the introduction to the book. We can also check what Denison was prepared to print, against what appear to be fairly detailed notes taken from his quotidian pulpit offerings as a London lecturer.

Denison's oeuvre thus provides us with a wonderfully compact body of evidence against which to test a number of recent claims about the existence and nature, and social, ideological and theological timbre of early Stuart puritanism. These claims range from a frank scepticism about whether a distinctive body of thought and feeling deserving the appellation puritan ever actually existed, to full-blown studies of something called 'the early Stuart puritan movement'.[2] Not only are we faced with a number of mutually exclusive interpretations but within each interpretative camp or tendency there are a number of distinct strands. Thus there are hard and soft versions of the sceptics' position running from the typically bracing naysaying of J.C. Davies, to the more nuanced to-ing and fro-ing of Patrick Collinson.[3]

There is, moreover, almost as much disagreement amongst those scholars prepared to admit the existence of something like a distinctively puritan style of divinity or culture (if not of a puritan 'movement') during the early Stuart period. At particular issue here is the ideological valence, the 'radicalism' or 'moderation' of the stance adopted by the entity thus conceived towards the contemporary status quo in church, state and society. For some scholars (Ken Fincham, Nicholas Tyacke and, in certain moods at least, Patrick Collinson and myself) puritanism was merely the most zealous and activist face of far wider bodies of Calvinist or reformed thought, bodies of thought that were in effect hegemonic in the church of Elizabeth, James and during the early part of the reign of Charles I.

There are soft and hard versions even of this position, however, with 'puritans' all but disappearing into a wider 'perfect protestant' consensus in at least some of the accounts of the period produced by Nicholas Tyacke, Patrick Collinson, Conrad Russell and perhaps most recently Ken Parker and Eric Carlson. In some quarters at least the term must be in terminal decline if even so archetypal a figure as Richard Greenham no longer counts as a 'puritan'.[4] Others (Paul Seaver, myself, Ken Fincham, Jacqui Eales, Tom Webster and both Tyacke mark two and Collinson marks three and now perhaps even four, to name but a few) are far happier to concede the existence of a puritan style or attitude, operating within, but certainly not subsumed by, the wider bodies of reformed thought and feeling that did indeed dominate, if not entirely monopolise, the commanding heights of the Elizabethan and Jacobean theological and ecclesiastical establishments.[5] Either way, within this construction of the subject, puritans were integrated, in some sense conforming, members of the national church. For the most part, under James I, puritan ministers subscribed and at least partially conformed to the ceremonial practices of the national church, which, as Ken Fincham has shown, was, in practice, as much as the Jacobean church required of them. But if such 'moderate puritans' predominated, there were also some radicals who refused to conform or whose scruples about conformity or episcopacy had led them to become marked men. But, for the most part, even these 'radical' puritans were scarcely separatists waiting to happen. Such inveterate non-conformists as John Dodd, William Bradshaw, Arthur Hildersham, John Cotton or Julines Herring spent a great deal of time and trouble mobilising lay support, schmoozing well-affected bishops or finding stipendiary lectureships so that they could somehow continue their ministry within the national church. From that position even the radicals – but even more so the conforming, 'moderate' majority – were able, certainly in some areas and at some times, and in some areas nearly all of the time, successfully to present themselves as but the evangelically zealous and activist, the genuinely protestant and therefore genuinely politically loyal, face of the English church.[6]

Other scholars, who are even happier to admit the existence of a distinctively puritan strain of thought, feeling and action in the early Stuart church, dispute this account of puritanism's relationship to that church. Thus for Peter White, George Bernard and Kevin Sharpe puritans were a theologically distinct, socially divisive and at least potentially politically dissident, 'radical' or 'subversive' subgroup within the national church, their allegiance to which was at best conditional. For Sharpe, certainly, the puritans' 'conformity' to the rites, ceremonies and broader unifying assumptions of the national church was at best only partial and their underlying ideological agenda antipathetic to the institutional and ideological structures and assumptions of that church. For Sharpe, White and Bernard the distinctiveness and radicalism of the puritans had theological as well as cultural and political aspects. In the perhaps oversimplifying parlance of recent debate they alone were the true 'Calvinists' in the English church and it was their intermittent attempts to hijack that church for their own narrowly predestinarian and distinctly reformed notions of orthodoxy, that produced the sporadic if intense outbreaks of doctrinal dispute and contestation amongst certain segments of the clerical establishment that punctuated the period. It was similarly their intense interest in the doctrines of election and reprobation and their concomitant vision of a church and society radically divided between the godly and the ungodly that rendered their religious style so socially divisive and politically subversive.[7]

Consequent doctrinal disputes about, amongst other things, predestination were brief but intense. However, Sharpe, Bernard, White and Green are all anxious to argue that interest in such disputes was largely restricted to a cadre of often puritanically inclined clerical intellectuals. For the mass of the laity and even a good deal of the clergy, they claim, such fine intellectual distinctions were not merely beside the point, they were a distinct turn-off. And here what one might term the most extreme version of the revisionist interpretation of the early Stuart period joins hands with the similarly extreme revisionist version of the long English reformation/s of the sixteenth century. Coming at the period under discussion from behind, as it were, scholars like Christopher Haigh, while accepting the puritans' self-description as the only authentic protestants in England, have argued that their religious style – predestinarian, book-, word- and sermon-centred, wedded to an austere notion of what a reformed society should look like and what a true Christian professor should do, heavily iconoclastic, if not iconophobic, in its attitudes to the ceremonies, external fripperies and ritual practices of the national church – was antithetical to the religious needs and expectations of a still largely 'catholic' 'people'. The godly, therefore, were doomed to be an embattled minority, incapable of cultivating a following amongst 'the people'.

Insofar as the godly did manage to speak to a popular audience they did so by 'dumbing down' their message, removing the sharp angles, the conceptual quirks and predestinarian quiddities from their style of divinity and pushing basically the same version of the central Christian verities around which other sorts of protestant (and indeed catholic) clerics organised their instructional literature. The result, Drs Watt and Marsh have both argued, was a distinctly post-reformation but scarcely protestant style of popular piety that had little or nothing in common with the aridities and angularities of the religion of 'the godly'. Organising her analysis around the central theme of providence and providentialism, Alexandra Walsham has produced a subtle but significant variation on this theme. Walsham uses the trope of providence to argue for both continuity and discontinuity; on the one hand, she points out the considerable continuities linking post-reformation beliefs about providence and those prevalent before the reformation, while, on the other, she shows how a new emphasis on providence as the key to divining God's purposes and judgements amongst the protestant godly allowed such people access to the assumptions and beliefs, the anxieties and obsessions of 'the people'. On this basis, she is able to assert the existence of bodies of popular belief and assumption that we can justifiably describe as protestant without collapsing them into the self-consciously perfect protestantism of 'the godly'. In making this case, Walsham oscillates between seeing the resulting cultural and ideological melange as merely an unintended consequence of a series of melds and syntheses between the popular and the hot protestant that took place despite the best intentions of the godly, and as the outcome of a process of self-conscious outreach whereby the godly deliberately dumbed down their otherwise austerely predestinarian world view for popular consumption. Here Walsham is both appropriating and modifying the claims of Professor Green who, taking catechisms to be a sort of lowest common denominator of popular instruction and hence (far more problematically) as an epitome both of what 'ordinary Christians' believed and of what 'the church of England' held to be doctrinally true and important, claims to be able to detect no distinctively puritan or predestinarian style of catechism. Elsewhere Dr Bernard has cast doubt on the sustainability, out in the parishes, of any style of piety which retained the doctrines of absolute predestination or justification by faith alone at or near its centre. On these views, insofar as they were distinctive, the puritans were an isolated, inward-looking group, the carriers of a socially divisive and politically subversive ideology. Insofar as they were pastorally effective, they slipped back indistinguishably into a mass of basic Christian instruction and edification upon which the theological and indeed the confessional conflicts of the period made little or no impact.[8]

Here the diverse but connected revisionisms of both Haigh and Sharpe, Green and White, sit rather neatly if oddly next to the post-Hillian social history of Professors Wrightson, Hunt and Underdown and others, which sees the spread of puritan values as part of wider processes of social differentiation and social control that were dividing an increasingly prosperous and literate middling sort and gentry from an immiserated people. Indeed in the work of Professor Sharpe the wheel seems to have turned almost full circle, resulting in a rather curious revisionist embrace of some of the basic tenets and insights of Christopher Hill. For in his magisterial study of the *Personal rule of Charles I*, Sharpe presents us with an order- and authority-obsessed Anglican mainstream, taken straight out of an 'Elizabethan world picture' presided over by such quintessentially English (and thus necessarily Anglican) cultural icons as Hooker and Shakespeare. In Sharpe's account the inheritors and champions of this position are Charles I and Laud, who are pictured as engaged in a life or death struggle for the soul of the English church and polity with a small, ideologically motivated, socially isolated group of puritan engagés. In this construction of the period the puritans find themselves in a distinctly odd situation. On the one hand, they are pictured as an ideologically and socially marginal group, in the process of being roundly trounced by the 'sensible tendency' within the Caroline regime. On the other, after 1637 they are abruptly thrust to centre stage by a revisionist interpretative mode at its wits' end to explain political conflict by any other means. Now the puritans, in alliance with the Scots and a few dissident court peers, are able miraculously to plunge the kingdom into chaos. Using the inherently contingent crisis created by the king's failure to win the bishops' war, they seize the political initiative and are thus available conveniently to take the lion's share of the blame for the outbreak of the civil war.[9]

Now clearly we are in very deep interpretative waters here and all these issues cannot be resolved through a study of the career and opinions of one man. And yet one way to test and modify the sort of meta-claims being summarised here is through detailed case studies, and Denison's life and works do provide us with a wonderfully well-documented opportunity to conduct just such a test. Professor Green's reliance solely on catechisms can be tested by setting Denison's catechism (which itself scarcely accords to his model) within the context provided by his other works. Again those other printed works can be set against the sermon notes taken by Henry Fleming. We can trace in detail the style of practical piety that Denison teased out of his formal doctrinal commitments and watch how he phrased and pitched that style of divinity both in the press and in the popular pulpit. We can hear him descanting on the role of his sort of ministry in contemporary society, and watch him construct a number of images of social and political order to which that ministry was allegedly central. We can watch him react both to wider events in church and state (the rise of Arminianism, the impact, both local and national, of Laudian reform) and to the varied local responses to his preaching style and personality. We can listen as he defines his formal relationship to the ceremonies, polity and doctrine of the English church and then watch him interact with both local and central, social and ecclesiastical authorities that claimed to epitomise, define and administer 'order' in both the parish and the wider national church. Denison's account of his ministry and its effects can be set against what other sources have to tell us about what 'actually happened' in his parish. A picture, albeit an indistinct one, can be gleaned of both his supporters and enemies there and elsewhere. Moreover, all this can be done in early Stuart London.

This, in itself, is a most welcome opportunity, since, for all its prominence in and importance for the political, religious, cultural and economic life of the kingdom, London has not bulked as large in recent revisionist accounts of the religious and political history of post-reformation England as it might.[10] On the whole, 'the people' with whom reformation and post-reformation revisionists like Dr Haigh have been concerned, have been a notionally rural not an urban, a provincial not a metropolitan, 'people'. Not for nothing was John Morrill's ur-text of civil war revisionism called *The revolt of the provinces*. Again when Patrick Collinson wanted to supplant Paul Seaver's account of the effect of puritan lecturing on the structure of ecclesiastical life before 1640 he countered a book based in large part on London sources with examples drawn from lectures by combination (not stipendiary lectures) in market towns and other centres set in the countryside.[11] At the other end of the historiographical spectrum, when Christopher Hill wanted to find a social and geographical locale for his underground radical and sectarian tradition it was, perversely, to the forests and wastelands that he turned. Clearly, it would be silly (as so many have and continue to do) to treat England as but London writ large. But, by the same token, attempts to explain the course and consequences of the reformation or the causes, outbreak and course of the civil war that, in effect, leave London out of account will not do either. It is to be hoped that the account provided below of Denison's career and, in particular, of his altercation with Etherington, will take its place in what amounts to a flood of recent research that is at last redressing this particular imbalance.

DENISON AND THE DOUBLE DECREE

What, therefore, was Denison's style of piety, his view of the Christian community, true religion and individual Christian profession like? Denison's was a heavily predestinarian view of the world. Having defined the nature of

God ('an eternal spirit who hath his being of himself and is distinguished into three persons') on the first page of his catechism, he proceeded on the second to define 'God's decree'. This was 'an absolute foreknowledge and determination of all things that ever were or shall be, to serve to the glory of God'. It was divided into two parts; the first, election, was defined as 'the eternal and unchangeable decree of God whereby, of his free grace and favour, he hath made choice of some rather then of others to bestow upon them eternal life and happiness and that for the glory of his free grace'. The second, reprobation, he defined as 'also the eternal decree of God whereby he hath rejected others, leaving them, in the fall of Adam, to their eternal destruction and that to the praise of his power and justice'.

Election was a free and gratuitous act of the divine will.[12] Neither election nor reprobation were grounded on the foreseen merits or sins of humankind. Only papists, Arminians, anabaptists and other heretics argued that they were. Their doctrine of free will, Denison maintained, 'denieth the doctrine of the eternal truth of God concerning election and reprobation, maintaining that one person is not elected more than another, except it be for their foreseen faith or foreseen works'.[13] Election, Denison explained, was 'before the foundation of the world'. It was unchangeable, a product of 'God's free grace and not of men's merits foreseen'; an act done entirely for 'the glory of God's free grace ... [God] having predestinated us unto the adoption of children, by Jesus Christ, to himself according to the good pleasure of his will, to the praise and glory of his grace'.[14]

For Denison humankind was utterly and desperately lost in sin. There was, he claimed 'a desperate frowardness in us unto that which is good and a desperate forwardness and proneness unto that which is evil'. Until they were regenerated by divine grace, Denison told his audience at the Cross in 1619, they were 'the very slaves of satan and the best things that you do or can do in your natural condition are abominable and odious to God'. 'Before regeneration', Denison observed in 1637/38, 'the very righteous are totally hardened, they have hearts as hard as stones'.[15] It was only, Denison declared, 'through the radical grace of God's spirit' that 'man, who is by nature a branch of the wild olive, that is of the first Adam, is engrafted into Christ, the true olive tree'.[16]

For Denison, Christ had died only for the elect. 'Christ Jesus was set apart by God, the father, from all eternity, to be the redeemer of the elect.' Christ 'by his sufferings' had wrought redemption for the world of God's elect.[17] The world, he conceded, was a phrase that bore diverse meanings in the scriptures. Sometimes we should take it to mean 'the frame of the world'; sometimes, 'the reprobate people of the world'; sometimes, 'the profits, pleasures and honours of the world' and sometimes 'the elect people which dwell in the world'. That last was the sense deployed in the text 'John 3.16 "God so loved the world", that is the elect, that he gave his only begotten son etc.'[18]

Stephen Denison

On the basis of this firm predestinarian foundation, Denison erected equally unequivocal doctrines of perseverance and assurance. 'It is manifest', Denison boomed at Paul's Cross in 1619, 'that they which are once effectually called and truly regenerate and have received the spirit of adoption, they are forever the children of God.' To a papist or Arminian invocation of the examples of Judas or Damas or of 'many professors that turn carnal', Denison answered that those that finally and totally fell away from the truth '"were never of us, for if they had been of us they would have continued with us." ... These might possibly receive certain common gifts of the spirit, as to be enlightened etc., but they never were truly regenerate.' 'Efficacious grace', Denison explained in 1637/38, 'doth come as a mighty wind that beateth down as it doth go. But the common motions of the spirit are easily resisted by a hard heart.' As for the elect, they could and certainly would sin and might be 'much weakened concerning the degree of saving faith which formerly' they felt. 'There are remainders of all sin in the regenerate after their regeneration. There is remainders of ignorance, of unbelief, of profaneness, of injustice, of rash anger, of malice.' 'The children of God may fall in some measure from some degree of that grace which they have had in former times. They may fall into great errors of judgement ... they may fall from their first love in some degree ... they may fall into gross sin ... they may fall from the sense and feeling of God's grace and they may come to think themselves to be reprobates and castaways, to be utterly deprived of grace and the like' and yet they could not utterly and finally fall. 'They have hardness of the heart but it ... doth not rule in them. Nay, they should not ever be hardened finally.' For 'God's promises are infallible'; 'our marriage with Christ is an everlasting marriage'; 'the father is stronger than all and none can pluck us out of his hand.' His decrees 'are immutable', the 'mighty mountains which stand fast forever'.[19]

Nor was this doctrine of perseverance of only theoretical significance. For Denison it had crucially important subjective, pietistic consequences. For the doctrine of perseverance led straight to that of assurance and all true believers were obliged to search for a settled assurance of their own calling as elect saints. 'It was', claimed Denison, 'the part and duty of every Christian to be well persuaded and assured of the truth of his calling.' 'Give all diligence to make your calling and election sure', he told his auditors in 1639. 'Saith the apostle ... examine yourselves whether you be in the faith, prove your own selves. Know you not that Jesus Christ is in you, except you be reprobates? Effectual calling is absolutely necessary to salvation, for unless a man be born again he cannot see the kingdom of God ... yea, effectual calling is that which God especially respecteth. For circumcision availeth nothing nor uncircumcision, but a new creature.'[20]

Certainly, such a settled assurance was the only true antidote to death. Many Christians, Denison assured his auditory at the funeral of Elizabeth

Juxon, had 'comfortably endured' the pangs of death, being 'assured of God's favour and also privy to themselves of a well spent life'. If we wanted to die well, to resist the temptations of satan even at the last, 'we must endeavour betimes to make our calling and election sure. Thus Simeon departed in peace because his eyes had seen God's salvation. And, indeed, how can we expect to die with comfort while we are unresolved? What shall become of our souls in the world to come?'[21]

If Denison was unafraid to place such expressly predestinarian notions at the centre of his sermons, lectures and, indeed, his catechism, he was equally ready to defend those doctrines from the obvious objections. Did not his very severe doctrine of divine providence and the double decree, which tied all events in the world – including prosperity and affliction, the damnation of the reprobate as well as the salvation of the elect – directly to the will of God, make God the author of sin?[22] Denison posed the question only to dismiss it. God was not the author of sin, he contended, he merely 'disposeth of it that it works in the end (maugre the malice of the devil and all wicked men) to the glory of his justice when he shall come to take just vengeance'.[23] It was true that fallen humanity could not choose but sin, yet no one could be said to have been forced or compelled to sin. 'None doth compel to sin; for howbeit men sin necessarily, they cannot choose but sin, yet they do not sin compulsively. Satan prevails more by enticement than by force ... Every sinner is worthy to be condemned because he sins without compulsion. God may justly say unto a graceless person who compelled thee to swear, to lie, to steal, to be drunken and the like? Might not these things have been avoided?' While fallen humanity could worsen their spiritual condition by hardening their hearts with sin, they were unable, in and of themselves, to improve or reform. 'We being naturally hard by nature, have more hardness gathering to us. A man may easily make himself worse then he is ... but he cannot make himself better. Evil is unto him voluntary; he hath free will to do it, so he may easily find a willingness in himself to harden himself.' It was in terms of this post-lapsarian condition that, Denison explained, God's hardening of the hearts of the reprobate, described in scripture, should be interpreted. This, he claimed, was the 'most fearful punishment that God can lay upon the children of man.'

> God doth not inflict hardness of heart through the infusion of any vicious quality into the heart ... He doth not make man vicious. But God doth it privatively, as the sun in some sort may be said to be the occasion of the night. This is not properly but because it doth withdraw his beams and light from it. So God doth it because he doth withdraw the beams of his grace from the heart. Negatively God doth it by denying the grace that may soften the heart ... God doth harden the heart permissively when he doth deliver a command to a man's particular hardness of heart. God doth harden objectively by propounding some object which meeting with our nature, being corrupt, doth harden the heart. Thus he is said to harden the

heart by his word ... But it doth not harden the heart properly but accidentally, according to the disposition of the object, as the sun is said to make the dunghill stink, but not properly but accidentally. It is not the sun but the dunghill that stinketh.[24]

Again, Denison replied to the claim that, since God was omnipotent and yet still 'doth not restrain men from sin nor prevent them with his grace', he was, therefore, guilty of humanity's destruction. 'For is a man not guilty of a childs death that seeth it run toward a pit and stayeth it not, when there is power in his hand to do it?' That was true enough, but we must not, Denison warned, 'measure God, who is above the law, by man under the law'. In the case outlined above, the man was indeed at fault 'because he is bound by the law to save life if he can, but God is a free worker, it is in him to have mercy on whom he will, it is also lawful for him to do what he will with his own, for he is bound to no man.'[25] What, to us, might appear as mere restatements of the paradoxes, even contradictions, inherent in Denison's vision of the relations between divine omnipotence and human responsibility, for Denison at least, evidently counted as cogent defences of the validity and coherence of his position.

He was equally bold in confronting the argument that his doctrines of perseverance and assurance were antinomian. There were those, Denison conceded, who objected that 'the doctrine of assurance of salvation is a doctrine of carnal liberty or that it makes people secure and negligent'. In fact, the opposite was the case; 'there is no stricter doctrine can be preached than the doctrine of assurance'. Given the enormous spiritual benefits consequent upon a settled assurance of our salvation – its presence brought 'the peace that passeth all understanding', its lack rendered 'our life most uncomfortable and our death most terrible' – it was inevitable that anyone who had once enjoyed true assurance would move heaven and earth to keep it. 'Who is there, that is truly assured of his salvation, but he is careful, above all things, to keep that assurance?' Indeed, once assured 'that there is a crown of glory laid up for them in the heavens' would not the godly face the 'crosses and afflictions' of this life with renewed zeal and determination? Thus, for Denison, far from being an inducement to quietism, complacency or sin, the doctrine of assurance was itself a 'means to prevent falling away' because 'such is the sweetness of full assurance that whosoever hath it, he would not part with it again for any pleasure or profit whereby he is tempted to fall away'.[26]

THE SUBJECTIVE CORRELATIVES OF PREDESTINATION: ASSURANCE AND THE LANGUAGE OF VOLUNTARISM

Denison's works, therefore, provide plentiful evidence that, pace Dr Bernard, Calvinist doctrine could indeed penetrate into catechisms, funeral sermons and the parochial ministry of the early seventeenth-century church.[27] But

Doctrinal and pietistic underpinnings

granted that Denison was a Calvinist and that his Calvinism was prominently displayed in his printed works and, at least judging from Fleming's sermon notes, by no means absent from his day to day preaching, what style of piety did he choose to spin out from these heavily predestinarian foundations? Like many another puritan divine of the period, Denison enlisted the paradoxes, contradictions and tensions at the heart of his position in the service of an activist Christian piety, centred on a community of true believers, united by their common apprehension of right doctrine, their consequent pursuit of a lively, justifying faith and a concomitant sense of their own status as elect saints of God, engaged in a common struggle against the forces of sin, satan, the world and the flesh.

The emotional dynamic for Denison's version of Christian activism came from the individual Christian's desperate search for assurance, a settled sense of the reality and efficacy of his or her own calling. For, granted that the world was divided between the elect and the reprobate, and granted that the elect could and should arrive at a sense of their own election, how was one to be sure that one was elect and not reprobate? How was one really to make one's calling and election sure? Denison turned the emotional screw on this issue even tighter by emphasising just how much like one of the elect the reprobate could look. 'Natural men and women may attain some degree of sorrow, as Judas did, and some degree of outward humiliation, as Ahab did, and some degree of confession, as Pharaoh did.'[28] Again, both elect and reprobate remained subject to sin throughout their mortal lives.[29] Moreover, the reprobate as well as the elect could abstain from sin. Similarly, 'they may attain a kind of desire after the word'. Again, they 'may have a kind of persuasion of God's favour towards them'. 'The very reprobate may also be changed' by the operations of the holy spirit. Both the elect and the reprobate were subject in this world to affliction, persecution and temptation. The true child of God 'may be so sensible of his affliction and his cross may be so irksome unto him as that he may fall thereby into divers dangerous temptations'. Indeed, Denison conceded, sometimes 'God suffers his dear children to die uncomfortably'.[30]

In the light of these similarities it became even more urgent for the true child of God to be able to distinguish between his or her own spiritual estate and that of the reprobate. Denison was only too happy to provide his audience with guidance on this point. To an extent, of course, what separated the elect from the reprobate was good works. 'True godliness', Denison maintained, was 'a sure mark of election.' A true faith must be fruitful. 'As grace is the cause of painfulness in the child of God, so it is of fruitfulness.'[31] 'Faith must be tried by the fruits', Denison claimed, 'for faith without good works is but a carcass of faith ... For howsoever faith alone doth justify the person, yet works must necessarily justify the faith.' 'Where faith is, there is a purging of ourselves, as God is pure so that where there is no endeavour to purge ourselves from filthiness of flesh and spirit, there is no true faith.' 'We must be filled with good works as Dorcas was ... we must labour to be fruitful and to express our fruitfulness to those that are in distress and want.'[32] Here, therefore, was a crucial distinction between the elect and the reprobate. 'The spiritual quickening' of the elect made them 'bear the image and stamp of God himself, being made holy as he is holy'. Similarly their spiritual illumination led them both to hate sin and amend, while in the reprobate such illumination led merely to a deadening despair at the extent of their own sins and a rooted conviction that they could never be forgiven.[33]

However, all this certainly did not mean that the Christian in search a certain sense of election should put all his or her eggs in the basket of good works. Far from it. All such faith in externals was a snare and a delusion. If the pursuit of good works was not to degenerate into a pharisaical and vainglorious religion of external show and outward forms, a sincere and properly introspective faith had to accompany the works of outward virtue. Thus, Denison explained in 1637/38, 'resting on outward performance is a great cause of hardness of heart. Thus many professors do deceive themselves that think they do well and are in a good state because they pray and keep the sabbath, when, in the mean time, he doth never repent himself of his sins and is never regenerate.' If it was true that 'virtue must be added unto faith', it was still more the case that 'it must flow from faith as from the fountain ... because without faith it is impossible to please God'.[34]

In short, the pursuit of external holiness should be bound up with what Denison described as 'a holy and experimental knowledge'. That knowledge, 'wrought in the hearts of the elect by the Holy Ghost and that by the means of God's word', brought us to 'know ourselves, to wit our cursed estate by nature' and to know God, Christ and the Holy Ghost as our father, redeemer and comforter. To know, in short, both God's will and satan and his wiles. Only by maintaining a proper balance between the inner world of faith and experimental knowledge, on the one hand, and the outer world of external righteousness, on the other, could the believer come to true godliness.[35]

The way in which this balance between the internal and external worked showed clearly in Denison's account of the relationship of the godly to their own sins and afflictions. As we have seen, Denison was insistent that both the elect and the reprobate committed sins and were subject to afflictions. The crucial difference between them lay in the attitudes that they adopted towards those actions and experiences. As Denison argued (against both the papists and the familists), 'sin remaineth in the children of God after conversion'. The difference was that in the 'unconverted or wicked men' sin 'is the master of the house ... but in the converted it is but a drudge, being indeed unruly and malicious but wanting power'. Thus when the child of God sinned he did so unwillingly, on the spur of the moment, in lesser matters. His sin caused him sorrow and provided the occasion for futher rounds of self-examination, repentance and amendment. When the reprobate sinned, they did so habitually, with a presumptuous pleasure, or, if they came to repent, they did so in desperation, scared, not by the offence of God involved in any infraction of divine law, but by the punishments threatened by God against sinners. The objective fact of sin was not the point, therefore, rather the crucial issue was the subjective attitude adopted towards it. As Denison explained, the elect should not despair if they found 'corruption in ourselves after conversion'. 'It is not sin but the love of sin that bains the soul.' Sin we must, but if we would be saved, sin must make us miserable.[36]

A similar pattern can be discerned in Denison's treatment of affliction. Both elect and reprobate might suffer precisely the same fate – disease, misfortune, injury, bereavement, loss – but the meaning of their sufferings was completely different. The origins of that difference lay in God's intentions in visiting affliction on the two groups. Misfortunes inflicted on the godly were not judgements at all, but chastisements and corrections, signs of God's love and fatherly concern for the fate of his children. Precisely the same misfortunes, visited on the wicked, were fearful punishments for sin, tokens of the fate which awaited them in hell. But, if the misfortunes used by God to punish and reduce the reprobate to despair were precisely the same as those used to chastise, correct and encourage the elect, how was one to tell them apart? Again, the key lay in the subjective response of the individual to his or her own experience. We should ask ourselves 'whether we have submitted ourselves unto God's correcting hand as gracious children, without murmuring or complaining. Willing submission is a great sign of fatherly chastisement.' Again, 'we must examine what good use we have made of God's hand upon us. If our afflictions have made us better it is a good evidence that they are no other but fatherly corrections.' 'We must submit to God's corrections', Denison told his auditors in 1637/38. 'We must endure and be content to suffer all that God doth lay upon us with patience and humility. For afflictions are able to melt the hearts of the righteous.'[37] For God, affliction was a means to bring his elect back to the path of righteousness. The careers of 'many sound and experienced Christians' confirmed this claim, Denison explained. Afflictions submitted to meekly, as deserved punishments for sin, had indeed brought many erring Christians back to God.[38] It was crucial, therefore, that the true believer submit to affliction, using it as a mirror in which to see his or her sins and as an occasion for repentance and spiritual purging. Thus, for Denison, the Christian's response to affliction was a crucial test of his or her spiritual standing. If Christians remained patient under the rod of affliction, they were elect; if not, it was certain that they were not yet in a state of grace.

In short, the meaning of the sins, good works and afflictions of the elect was in large part a function of the way in which they chose to interpret their own experience. On this view, the elect, the godly, the children of God, invented or fashioned themselves by imposing a set of meanings or interpretations on their own actions and experience – actions and experiences (sin, good works and affliction) which they, in fact, shared with the ungodly but which in their case led them towards a particular view of themselves and of the world, a view provided for them, in part, by the sermons, private counsel and published works of ministers like Denison. In other words, what distinguished the elect from the reprobate, the godly from the ungodly, was not so much their objective condition or external behaviour as their subjective apprehension of the meaning of their condition and actions. Admitting that a 'universal' conformity to the will of God was beyond even the best of Christians in this life, Denison claimed that God would accept 'a sincere desire and conscionable endeavour in the case of his own dear children'. 'God respecteth not so much the thing which we do, as the mind wherewith we do it; a little done, with a good will, is better than a good deal done with constraint.' In the second covenant of grace, won for the elect by Christ's sacrifice on the cross, 'the will passeth for the deed', Denison explained.[39] All of which could be used to dismiss the apparently sincere repentance and considerable good works of those deemed to be reprobate and to underwrite the assured salvation of those deemed godly, however meagre the outward fruits of their profession might be.

It was precisely that potential that won for the puritans a reputation for hypocrisy amongst some of their contemporaries. The position outlined above represented an attempt to avoid that; the emphasis on good works, on the necessary fruitfulness and painfulness of a true saving faith was there to guard against a merely verbal and internal profession of true religion, while the countervailing stress on a properly experimental knowledge of the truths of right doctrine, the correct subjective apprehension of experiences held in common by both elect and reprobate, served to undercut any tendency towards a pharisaical or popish insistence on works' righteousness or human merit.

The tension between these opposite tendencies in Denison's position entered the realm of individual piety through his insistence that truly elect believers should, indeed if they were elect, must, continually grow in grace. 'It is not sufficient to talk of grace, or to profess grace', Denison explained, 'but we must have it in possession.' 'Adding grace unto grace' was itself 'a means to prevent backsliding.' 'Effectual illumination', Denison declared, 'though it be but a small light at the first yet it groweth greater and greater.' For 'true illumination floweth from Christ as from the sun of righteousness'. The first glimmerings of faith might, therefore, be small enough but no truly elect child of God would rest content with that. 'They, therefore, which can content themselves with that grace which they suppose they have received and think they need no more, it is a manifest sign they have received nothing yet as they ought to receive.' Indeed Denison even delivered himself of the opinion that it was permissible for the godly sincerely to want not to die, so long as they did so only in order to maximise their opportunities to grow in grace; 'they may desire to live that they may glorify God and amend what is amiss; that they may repent; that they may show more fruitfulness; that they may zealously give themselves to the hearing of God's word'.[40]

The result of all this was an essentially activist vision of the spiritual quest of the elect saint, hot in pursuit of ever more effectual spiritual graces, ever purer and more exalted standards of personal godliness and profession. That pursuit was fuelled by a series of antinomies or oppositions between fear and joy, repentance and assurance, the law and the gospel, the pursuit of external righteousness and the quest for a properly experimental knowledge of Christ. In the initial conversion of the sinner the first incision of the Holy Spirit into the unregenerate soul was made by the hammer of the law. This convinced the individual of his or her own sinful nature, destroyed any residual faith in human merit or means and drove the Christian into a total reliance on the promises of God in Christ for his or her salvation.[41] Similarly, in the process whereby the elect saint was driven up the ladder of sanctification, the contrasting emotions of sorrow for one's own sins and joy and gratitude for the promises of God and the sacrifice of Christ which rendered those promises effectual, played off one another in a continual oscillation or upward spiral. In the course of that spiral the believer was both forced to externalise his or her profession of true religion in a stream of good works and yet consistently reminded of his or her own corruption and total reliance on Christ for salvation. Thus, describing how the individual should prepare to receive the sacrament, Denison invoked an emotional dialectic or oscillation between sorrow for Christ's sufferings on the cross (and the human sin which had rendered them necessary), on the one hand, and joy and gratitude for the benefits of the passion displayed in and sealed by the sacrament, on the other. 'We must meditate on the passion of Jesus Christ. We must not pass lightly over them [our sins] but meditate upon them and that it was the cause of his passion that we have sinned so against God.'[42]

A clearer sense of how this spiritual spiral worked in practice can be gleaned from Denison's picture of Elizabeth Juxon's last days in his funeral sermon of 1621. Despite the exemplary Christian virtues which Mrs Juxon had displayed after her conversion – her fervour to hear the word preached, her scrupulous sabbath keeping, her charitable benefactions to both poor ministers and the godly poor, the closeness of her spiritual relationship with Denison and other ministers of his ilk – she had been troubled by a certain spiritual dryness. Too often she had failed to experience 'that degree of joy which she had felt in former times'. 'A sound faith', Denison conceded, might be the 'evident mark of a true Christian' but Mrs Juxon, 'our dear sister', had not always felt 'this full assurance at all times, but she groaned many a time under the sense of unbelief'. Likewise Denison recorded 'her complaints in respect of hardness of heart', 'her mourning because she could not mourn as she ought'. Even on her deathbed she had suffered dreadful physical and spiritual pangs. This, Denison contended, had been all to the good. 'Her want of full joy was so sanctified unto her that it was a furtherance to a better grace, namely to repentance and self denial and base esteem of herself.' Thus, even at the last, she had desired to 'hear of her sins and to that end desired me, either in my own person or by some other good minister, to preach a sermon of the cursed state of men by nature and of the uttermost terrors of the law against sin, that so her stony heart might be more and more broken'.

Through the attentions of Denison and other ministers she was finally brought to embrace death in a full assurance of her own eventual salvation. This was due in part, Denison claimed, to his good offices in reminding Elizabeth Juxon of certain crucial marks of her own spiritual estate; her great growth in godly learning and understanding; the resultant change in her will and affections, her life and conversation; her denial of herself and her earnest search after God in Christ. In the light of this evidence,

> not many days before her departure out of this life she made a very excellent, sensible acknowledgment of the goodness of God unto her and how she knew that it should be well with her after this life ended, blessing God withal for the benefit which she had received by the ministry of the word and exhorting her kindred and friends, which were about her, that they should be careful to hear sermons and to meditate of them. Yea, she did so speak with that evidence of spirit as that she drew tears from them which heard her at that time.

Here, at the last, the continual tracking back and forth between the external forms of godliness and the internal, subjective correlatives of those forms in the spiritual sorrow and joy of the individual had done its work. Final confirmation had been conferred on Mrs Juxon's elect status by the quality of her own response to suffering and death and in the tears evoked by that response in the eyes of the godly gathered around her deathbed, tears which themselves set the seal of godly approval on the sincerity of her final profession.

Denison proffered his picture of Mrs Juxon as a model for his readers, who could, he claimed, examine themselves 'by these marks' of godliness set out in the sermon. 'If thou dost find them in thee', he continued, it was safe with a 'childlike boldness and holy confidence' to go to God and claim eternal life. Where the reprobate fell away into presumptuous sin, hypocritical self-righteousness or simple despair, the godly distinguished themselves as elect saints by maintaining the requisite balance between the constituent parts of Christian profession, as Denison described them. With Mrs Juxon they enlisted even their spiritual drynesses and failures, in the upward spiral of alternate introspection and externalisation that led to a settled assurance, a godly death and eternal life.[43]

Thus, for all its explicitly predestinarian underpinnings, Denison's vision of elect sainthood was anything but quietist. Indeed, on the basis of those underpinnings, when Denison took to exhorting his flock to emulate the ideal of puritan sainthood embodied by Elizabeth Juxon, he used a decidedly voluntarist rhetoric. Thus, just having asserted the immutability of the divine decrees, Denison proceeded to claim that all 'the threatenings of God are made with a secret condition of repentance'.[44] Again, having admitted that 'we have an higher cause of standing than our own endeavours, to wit, the divine power or else we should quickly fall for anything we are able to do', Denison observed that 'he that made us without us, will not save us without us. We must work out our salvation ... so that our endeavours are required in this business.' Indeed, the reason that so many professors 'fall off at these days ... is because they never were diligent to make their calling and election sure'. Our salvation, Denison explained, was conditional on our repentance, which he defined as a final forsaking of all sin, involving the heart and spirit, the memory, will, affection and conscience. Repeatedly in his sermons of the late 1630s Denison simply exhorted his auditors 'to labour for the fullness of the spirit'. 'It deeply concerns everyone to be filled with the spirit, to labour for it.' We should, of course, labour principally by prayer to God but we should do more than pray. 'There is nothing that we should pray for at the hands of God but we should diligently use good means to obtain it. If we pray for bread we must use our hands in a lawful calling to get it, if for grace we must be diligent in hearing the word etc. to get grace.'[45]

It was repentance which effected our entry into the church. Of course, none could 'minister an entrance unto themselves but it is ministered unto them by God himself'; 'as a lock cannot open itself, no more can our hearts, without the key of God's spirit'. Yet once God had opened the door of salvation we had to strive to enter in, 'lest wilfully refusing to enter when we might, we provoke the Lord to shut up the gate and never to be entreated to open again unto us'. After all, as he reminded his audience, 'thou mayest be alive and in health today and dead and buried tomorrow'. 'There be ... multitudes at this instant in hell fire for deferring their repentance, notwithstanding that they purposed ... to repent hereafter.'[46]

Again, once entrance into the church had been effected, it was incumbent on the Christian to 'labour to get more rich entrance; let us not content ourselves that we have an entrance, but let us endeavour to grow rich in grace'. For 'by adding grace unto grace you shall more and more find entrance into Christ his kingdom'. Here Denison cited the example of David. David was eminent in grace but 'he was withal very diligent in the use of means. For the obtaining the same he prayed often, he fasted much; he meditated in God's word day and night.' Elsewhere Denison pictured God's saints 'digging for it [saving knowledge] in the mines of God's ordinances. They must prepare themselves diligently for divine worship, for the hearing of the word and the reception of the sacrament.' A Christian, Denison explained, 'may be violent in his calling', wrestling with God in prayer, in search of greater and greater degrees of grace and holiness. Again, Christians should be active in judging themselves by applying the hammer of the law to their own sins. For men were judged according to their works, Denison explained, and, in accepting the rebukes of God's ministers and applying the threats of the law against sin to their own lives, they could pre-empt and avoid the far more awful judgements of God. 'If we acknowledge and confess our sins, God is true and faithful to forgive', Denison reassured his auditors in 1638.[47]

It might be tempting to see in all this the collapse of the rigours of Calvinist orthodoxy before the constraints and demands of an inclusive pastoral ministry. That certainly is what Dr Bernard and others would have us believe as Calvinists in the printed tome and university disputation became, for all practical purposes, Arminians in the pulpit. Thus, even the most severe puritan clergy succumbed to the unifying and homogenising undertow of the great Christian verities and platitudes in their quest to convert the general run of the people to something like orthodox Christianity.[48] There are, however, problems with such a view. To begin with nearly all the passages of voluntarist rhetoric cited above from Denison's sermons were consciously placed by Denison himself in explicitly predestinarian contexts or frames. We are not, therefore, dealing here with a subliminal or subconscious slippage from an exclusivist reformed and rigourist orthodoxy to a laxly 'latitudinarian', 'anglican' practical piety. Denison appears to have known precisely what he was doing in these passages and was clearly aware of no incongruity or intellectual inconsistency in this juxtaposition of the voluntarist language of evangelical exhortation with the rigours of predestinarian Calvinism; something which is all the more remarkable given that we are dealing here with texts prepared by the author himself for the apotheosis of print. On the contrary, Denison seems to have been quite at home using the seeming fatalism of the divine decrees, the objective reality of both election and reprobation, to add both urgency and piquancy to his pleas that his audience strain every emotional and spiritual nerve to experience the fact of election in and through their own spiritual experience and practical conversation.

This tendency was, if anything, even more marked in the manuscript notes taken by Fleming in the late 1630s than in Denison's printed works of the previous decade or so. For there Denison can be found putting even the doctrine of reprobation to evangelical use. He did so by describing the characteristics and spiritual condition of 'sinners' and 'reprobates' in both stark but also very extreme terms. The term 'sinners' he claimed at one point was used in the bible not to refer to the general run of sinful humanity. After all, after the fall, we were all 'sinners'. On the contrary the word was used to refer only to notorious or desperate malefactors. 'The scripture speaks of notorious sinners in this style, sinners: that is great sinners above others, Psalm 1, the latter end, sinners shall not stand in the congregation of the righteous ... John 9.35. God doth not hear sinners. It is not meant sinners as all men are by infirmity but such as are notorious sinners, thus the Sodomites were.'[49]

The reprobate were similarly described as those that are 'totally and finally hardened'. Such were beyond all hope: all the angels in heaven, acting on God's direct command, could not convert them. 'This disease of the stone in the heart', Denison intoned in 1639, 'it is incurable in the reprobate. They never come to melting by saving grace.' This was not because God 'cannot cure them, for God can do it very easily if he please but the wicked they do not so much as desire to be healed and cured but resist all the means that should cure them. They despise all means whereby they should be softened, therefore God doth deliver them up to be totally hardened, so that their hearts come to be like Pharaoh's heart. It is a natural thing for a reprobate's heart to be so hardened that no ordinances of God can enter into it.'[50]

Having thus described the wicked and reprobate in the starkest and most extreme terms, Denison then used the very extremity of that description to open up room for evangelical hope. Thus, he explained, 'hardness of heart, though a disease natural to all men, yet it is curable provided that it is not total and final, as it is in the reprobate'. And here he added the crucial rider that self-consciousness of and worry about our own hardness of heart should be taken as a sign that our hearts had not in fact become imperviously hard.

> For a Christian to be sensible in himself that he doth not profit by sermons as he doth desire to do and that he finds that his corruptions do grow stronger and his graces do grow weaker, this doth not argue a hard heart but rather a tender heart for it is by grace whereby we come to be sensible of a hard heart ... The stony heart is without a sense, it is the fleshly heart that doth feel sin and I believe the most accepted tenderness that we can attain unto in this world it is the sense and mourning of the remainder of hardness that is in us.[51]

Thus was the worried Christian invited to identify him or her self not as a reprobate but as, at least potentially, elect. For over against these stringent definitions of what constituted a reprobate or a notorious sinner, Denison juxtaposed a decidedly generous vision of the extent and potential efficacy of the atonement. Many came not to God, he claimed, because they did not understand just 'how freely God doth save us, not for our own righteousness but for his mercy's sake. Do we take note that God doth save not for our merit but for his mercy?' Denison asked. We should all remember, he told his auditors, how freely and truly Christ is offered to every one of us, that he is offered to every man and woman in the world and therefore it is said Math 15.16 go and preach the gospel to every creature to show to us that there is no man nor woman but Christ and salvation by Christ is offered him in the gospel. Do we take notice of this that Christ is truly tendered and offered to us in the preaching of the word, that he is truly tendered to us in the sacraments? Do we not put him from ourselves and reject him, refusing to receive him when he is truly offered to us and so we cast a stumbling block in our own way? Are not we willing to remain in that opinion that our sins are greater than can be forgiven?

'Entrance into the kingdom of glory', Denison reminded his auditors, came not 'by any mere creature nor by any merit of our own but only by the merit of the Lord Jesus Christ. It is he that hath purchased for us. He is the door by whom alone we must enter. There is no other name under heaven whereby we can be saved, Acts 4.12.' To make his point, Denison cited the figure of the repentant thief on the cross. 'Therefore shaking off all conceit of our own merit, all the dependence on the creature, let us learn with this penitent thief to depend on Christ only for salvation and let us learn to prize the service of Christ.'[52]

Here, then, the extreme example of the heart of Pharaoh, hardened by God himself, through which Denison had figured forth the doctrine of reprobation, was being balanced by the equally extreme figure of the thief on the cross, through whom Denison was in turn illustrating the doctrine of election and salvation through Christ's free grace. There was, he intoned, no sin so great as to overcome or outweigh the mercy of God and the sacrifice of Christ. If we came to believe or even to act as though there were, we were merely putting stumbling blocks in our own way and doing the devil's work for him.

Denison, in fact, took the figure of the thief on the cross as the theme for one of his sermons of the late 1630s and drew a number of lessons therefrom. 'The truth is that God sometimes doth make choice to work upon such and to pass others that seem to be far more honest creatures and indeed are, in respect of civil honesty. God doth sometimes work upon a witch or wizard or whore or drunkard when he doth not work upon civil honest men.' This was no accident for such desperate malefactors, such 'great sinners best feel the work of Christ being truly converted. Those that live so civilly honest do not feel so great necessity of Christ as those that have been great sinners. The whole need not the physician but those that are sick.' By such miracles of grace God was able to show conclusively the complete dependence of sinful humanity on divine grace. For the moral here was clear: 'it is not in him that willeth and runneth but of God that showeth mercy'. God (and, of course, his minister Denison) was also able to use such instances to underline the complete provisionality of any this-worldly, human judgement on the spiritual condition or ultimate destination of other people, however apparently sinful their past and indeed present lives had been and were. He was also, of course, able to hold out the prospect of true repentance and conversion to even the most desperate and notorious sinner, which, given the banality and currency of the sins that Denison counted desperate (usury, sabbath breaking, swearing, drunkenness), was probably just as well. 'We are not to despair', he declaimed, 'concerning the conversion of most notorious and gross sinners ... of idolaters, of blasphemers, of common sabbath breakers, of disobedient to parents, concerning the conversion of common strumpets or of common drunkards, of notorious murderers or thieves or robbers or cheaters or cut purses.'[53]

From all this we must conclude, Denison argued, that 'we must know that faith is bold because it doth not look at man's merit but at God's free mercy and knoweth and seeth that where sin hath abounded there grace doth abound much more and that it is not the multitude of sins that should debar us from laying hold on Christ, if we be truly repentant'. Accordingly, Denison concluded, 'though our sins be manifold and great for measure yet we must not utterly despair but we must labour for true sorrow and repentance for our sin which if we can attain unto, be our sins what they may be, we may say as boldly as this man did "Lord remember me"'.[54]

Now, in their insistence on the total impotence of fallen humanity to work their own salvation, on the depth of human sin, on the power of God to give or withhold grace, on the completely free and gratuitous nature of that gift of divine grace, these passages were entirely true to the 'Calvinist' or reformed tradition in which Denison had been formed. In that sense there was no conceptual or theological gap between what Fleming noted him as saying on a day-to-day basis in the pulpit in the late 1630s and the doctrines to which he had committed himself in print. But if this was a form of Calvinism it was a Calvinism of a vibrantly open-ended and violently evangelical sort. Denison was producing in these sermons a vividly populist style of pulpit oratory; a style which oscillated between the extremes of human depravity and divine grace, between the figures of the thief on the cross, snatched by Christ's sacrifice from the very jaws of hell, on the one side, and that of pharaoh, hardened into reprobation and damnation by a vengeful but just God, on the other. Here is the religious style that allowed some puritan ministers to haunt the gaols, hoping to convert even the most hardened felons on the very steps of the gallows in order to repeat, in their own time, miracles of grace like that which had saved the thief crucified next to Christ.

Nor could the consequences of this heightened evangelical style be confined to the level of the individual. As Denison was only too eager to point out, the exemplum of the thief on the cross had social consequences for a number of different groups and constituencies. For masters and parents it meant that premature judgements about the moral or spiritual standing of their charges were quite out of order and certainly should not be used as an excuse to turn the relevant miscreant out without a penny.[55] As for ministers, they, too, should learn

> not to despair concerning the most wicked of the parishioners, if they should come as the pharisee did to catch the minister or to meet their mates to be drunk or to cut purses, the ministers of the gospel must welcome such to their ministry forasmuch as God is able of great sinners to make great saints, of cut purses, of whores, of common drunkards, of common informers God may please to make of them great saints, though they are great sinners. They must use the means to convert them according to God's ordinance. They should cast out the net of God's word which may bring in great sinners as well as small.

As for the godly, they were likewise taught by such examples to 'receive into the communion of saints not only those that have lived without scandal in the church of God but those that have been notorious sinners, common sabbath breakers, common drunkards, common swearers and common whores and such like if it please God to convert them'.

> This must teach us not to think it so strange as to be incredible when we hear of the conversion of some notorious whore, of some notorious drunkard, of some notorious swearer. When we hear of such and such as they are to become saints and reformed persons, zealous to hear the word of God and to reform, what is amiss? Now such relations seem so incredible that men will not believe it that such are truly converted to God; they may dissemble but they are not truly converted, will some say. But why should we not believe it? God can turn the most wicked sinner that lives on the face of the earth.[56]

All this is not perhaps what we have been led to expect from recent accounts of the religion of protestants produced by scholars like Dr Haigh or Dr Bernard. For on their account the aridities and exclusivities of the version of ('Calvinist') orthodoxy being peddled by the godly should have rendered the development of such a populist style impossible. For them the notion of popular protestantism is an oxymoron; puritan ministers like Denison remained trapped within the iron cage of their own self-righteous, election- (and reprobation-) centred style of orthodoxy, entirely unable to address the religious concerns and anxieties of the people. Others, myself included, have placed an exclusivist sense of the community of the godly very close to the heart of puritan religion; so close, in fact, that it might be thought to have precluded the sort of inclusive style of pulpit rhetoric that Fleming records Denison using during the late 1630s.[57] But just as the evangelical pitch adopted by Denison and noted by Fleming did not so much contradict as enlist and develop the 'Calvinism' of Denison's printed works, so the passages cited here addressed and worked out from a recognisably puritan notion of the godly community. Indeed they took the existence for granted of a social entity, here termed the 'communion of the saints', policed by a heavily moralistic, not to say censorious, godly opinion. In these sermons Denison was, in short, taking the accumulated emotional and social effects of literally thousands of puritan sermons as his starting point, and then seeking to both soften and complicate the application of certain typically puritan assumptions and equivalences to the social experience of the godly. The equation of manifest or outrageous sinfulness with *de facto* reprobation, the intense dislike and distrust felt by the godly towards the ungodly, the tendency for both godly laity and clergy to turn in upon themselves – all of them tendencies to which Denison was himself prone – were all targeted in these passages. Thus, assuming that central features of the style of divinity set out in his printed works had sunk in, in the sermons noted by Fleming, Denison might be seen as addressing and mitigating some of the more evangelically unfortunate effects of his own ministry. It may not be an accident that we find him doing so rather late on in his career. After all, by the late 1630s, London ministers like Denison were not seeking to convert neophytes to the gospel so much as to stimulate lay palates jaded by generations of hot protestant preaching.

That Denison was adopting this tone not in sermons gussied up for the relative permanence of print, but in notes taken more or less verbatim from the preacher's mouth in the day to day conduct of his ministry, may also be significant. For while both Denison's printed works and the sermons of the late 1630s recorded by Fleming were recognisably the product of essentially the same austerely reformed thought-world or theological tradition, it is nevertheless true that there were distinct areas of tension, and even of apparent contradiction, between the two. For example there seems to be a flat contradiction between the version of the salvific effects of the atonement as limited only to the elect, adumbrated in the printed works, and the claim, made in the Fleming sermons, that Christ was indeed offered in the gospel to every man and woman in the world. It is, of course, entirely possible that in the intervening period Denison had merely changed his mind on this subject. After all, from the late teens on, so-called hypothetical universalism was becoming increasingly popular in godly circles as a response to Arminian assaults on hard-core Calvinism.[58]

But it is at least as likely that what we are seeing here is merely a peculiarly pointed example of that creative tension between what one might term formal theology or reformed orthodoxy, and practical divinity that we can observe in puritan piety from at least the last third of Elizabeth's reign. If, as I have argued both here and elsewhere, the puritan exploitation of the anxiety-filled gap between the objective fact of the double decree and the individual's subjective construction and apprehension of his or her own spiritual condition and religous identity, did indeed throw up areas of doctrinal difficulty or contradiction, the transition from manuscript to print, from sermon as preached and as heard, to sermon as edited for the press, provided the author with a wonderful opportunity, if not exactly to censor than at least to check himself. Here was an ideal moment to dot theological i's and cross doctrinal t's. Moreover, if we take the act of printing a sermon or tract as, amongst other things, a self-conscious move to establish a minister's reputation in the public sphere of licensed print, a formal entrance into a charged and impersonal domain of theological and pietistic utterance, then the transition from pulpit and manuscript to print was an extremely charged moment for the aspiring divine. It represented a point in both his intellectual and professional career when a certain care over matters of theological propriety might seem both necessary and appropriate; a moment when the demands of what passed for doctrinal orthodoxy amongst the godly might exercise a peculiarly intense influence over the editing process.

Equally we may be dealing here not so much with a process of self-censorship, as with the difference between two modes of discourse designed for two rather different audiences. Put crudely, is it not at least plausible that the intended or likely market for printed versions of the sermons of divines like Denison was the self-described godly? If so, then presumably those works as printed would be tailored to fit within, to speak to and to strengthen the expectations, self-image and doctrinal prejudices or opinions of that group. Sermons preached to the general congregation in the normal course of a parish ministry, as those noted down by Fleming very likely were, would, however, have had a very different, more promiscuously evangelical purpose. Perhaps that is the reason for the difference in tone between Denison's printed works and the sermons recorded so sedulously by Fleming in the late 1630s.[59]

But however that may have been, whatever the logical strains and contradictions produced by maintaining such distinct levels of discourse – formal theological assertion and debate, practical pulpit divinity and that mix or compromise between the two that was produced when practical pulpit divinity was polished and edited for the press – there remained an underlying emotional logic to the puritan style of practical divinity, a logic that turned on the insistent shuffling back and forth between the objective level of formal theological truth and the subjective level of individual spiritual experience. We can see best how this worked by returning for a moment to the issue of the atonement. Viewed formally, the two positions adopted by Denison on the issue seemed both clear-cut and mutually exclusive; Christ either died for the elect alone or for all humankind. But Denison could hold and defend the former position and maintain his open-ended style of evangelism based on Christ's sacrifice on the cross precisely because he was addressing a situation in which, while we knew that there were reprobate souls, as the figure of the thief on the cross showed only too clearly, we could never be entirely sure who they were. Thus in addressing the sinner desperate for repentance, saving grace and eternal life, it was both necessary and legitimate for Denison to talk as though Christ had indeed died, if not for everyone, then at least for him. In other words, the exigencies of his pastoral position were forcing Denison to talk as though Christ had indeed died for everyone. This was doubly true since the only means available in this life whereby either the sinner concerned or his contemporaries could make even a provisional decision about whether Christ really had died for him was if he personally started to behave as though he believed that to be the case. For, as Denison had explained, for all that Christ's ministers and the godly knew, Christ could indeed have died for even the most notorious and unprepossessing of sinners.

To conclude, whatever the logical difficulties encountered by the modern reader in the face of these pastoral manoeuvres, however dizzy one may become gazing into the vertiginous abyss of God's hidden purposes, struggling to grasp his timeless providence and will as they work their way through the apparently contingent and, to mere mortals, ultimately unfathomable events of human time, the emotional logic of the style of divinity under discussion here remains clear enough. In the face of death, affliction, loss and pain, the individual was called to separate him or her self from the transitory things of this world, to cast him or her self on God's mercy in Christ. Through a dynamic oscillation between joy and fear, anxiety and assurance, objective doctrinal truth and subjective spiritual experience, external piety and the pursuit of good works, and internal anguish and spiritual zeal, the individual professor was to edge towards that settled assurance of eternal life which alone would allow him or her to negotiate the final encounter with death with the grace and certitude ultimately displayed by Elizabeth Juxon. Here, then, for all its dialectically generated internal tensions and potential contradictions, was no mere mish-mash, a theoretical Calvinism laced with and vitiated by a practical Arminianism, but rather a mature and emotionally compelling style of divinity designed to bring the insights of predestinarian piety to bear on the lives and experience of early modern English people.[60]

THE COLLECTIVE CONSEQUENCES OF PURITAN SUBJECTIVISM: DENISON AND THE COMMUNITY OF THE GODLY

In describing this style of piety we have concentrated, thus far, on the eerie shadow world of individual consciousness, but what were the social consequences of this view of true religion? What vision of the Christian community and of the relations between that community and the visible church did Denison draw out from these theoretical and pietistic foundations?

How was the anguished spiral of godly identity formation to be translated into social forms? How did it enter the everyday world of household, street and church?

Unsurprisingly, Denison's vision of the Christian community was fractured by a rigid division between the godly and the ungodly, the holy and the profane. There was, he pointed out, a natural state of enmity subsisting between the two groups. 'The hatred and distemper of the wicked' directed against the godly was built into the very structure of the world. 'For when', asked Denison, 'will the world cease her hatred, or when will she be in true charity towards them which are good in God's sight?' 'Whosoever will live godly in Christ Jesus', Denison concluded, 'must suffer persecution, as the apostle speaketh.' Thus, while Elizabeth Juxon was 'in her carnal estate her carnal neighbours respected her' but after her conversion 'when they observed this godly change in her, they ceased to give her that respect which was due unto her'. Indeed, thereafter she suffered 'the persecution of the tongue and the taunts of carnal friends', enduring the 'hatred of the world for her profession's sake'.[61]

All this was natural enough, Denison explained, because to the carnally minded the religous rigourism of the godly looked alternately threatening and ridiculous. Denison repeatedly denounced those carnal, hypocritical and profane Christians who derided the godly. Such people were 'scoffers at religion' who cried 'down all holiness and fear of God under the colour of a hell invented nick name'. The wicked, he complained, routinely condemned 'holy people' as 'runners to sermons'. If a member of the godly died in pain or despair the profane eagerly spread the news, hoping thereby to demonstrate the impotence of the godly's profession of true religion in the face of the grim reaper. Such people affected to regard the godly person's drive to make his or her calling and election sure as 'mere curiosity and niceness'. They 'laboured to persuade them [the godly] that they are too froward and the like' and routinely accused zealous ministers like Denison of going officiously beyond the demands of their calling. In short, for Denison the godly were 'a sect' 'evil spoken of in every place'; 'the world', he claimed, 'is so far from loving the godly, as that they hate no people in the world more'.[62]

In these passages Denison was dividing the world between those who used the words 'puritan' or 'precisian' as terms of abuse or insult and those against whom that accusation was habitually made. The former he described variously as 'the wicked', the 'ignorant', 'carnal Christians' and hypocrites. It was, he claimed, the habitual practice of drunkards, swearers, usurers and sabbath breakers to 'censure religious people to be hypocrites and the like.' Again, those who opposed the proselytising efforts of zealous ministers like himself, Denison characterised as common swearers, usurers, sabbath breakers, adulterers, the notorious sinners whom even Denison at his most charitable was disposed to regard as very likely reprobate. These were the people who persecuted 'the ministers of Christ'.[63]

In fact, it was the people who derided the godly who were the real hypocrites; these were people 'which will not be counted fools for Christ and therefore will profess no further than will stand with their credits'. It was the ignorant, those who vainly hoped to 'be saved by their good meanings, by their good prayers, by their just dealings' who 'nick name and persecute the dear children of God', 'neglect Christ' and 'hate the powerful preaching of the word'. For Denison, it was the mark of 'proud worldlings' 'to despise sanctified Christians' and to 'exalt themselves above poor Christians'. Such people redefined sin as virtue and lampooned the zeal and moral rigour of the godly as precisian excess and scrupulosity. For such carnal Christians drunkenness was good fellowship; a slavish and ostentatious following of fashion, decency; swearing, grace of speech; covetousness, good husbandry, and whoredom 'but a trick of youth'. Such people 'are proud of their oaths', they 'boast of their cozenage' and 'exult in their drunkenness'. In this way Denison was able to construct an image of an alternately carnal, hypocritical, ignorant and ultimately simply wicked 'world', bent on reviling and persecuting the godly minority in their midst.[64]

Those labelled 'puritan' by the world he described in very different language. These were 'God's dear children', 'professors endued with grace, excellent ones', or simply 'zealous Christians'. The ministers derided by the ungodly were simply 'men of God'.[65] Such people were marked off from their contemporaries both by the zeal with which they approached the public ordinances of the church and by the intensity of their private devotions and personal piety. In describing the road to repentance and regeneration, Denison was also describing the defining characteristics of the godly – prayer, advised reading, frequent hearing, prepared receiving of the sacrament and the avoidance 'of the company of such as have been the instruments of satan formerly to allure us into sin'. In using the public ordinances of the church one should prepare to hear the word with repentance, reading and prayer, go to church fired with a desire to benefit from the experience, pay attention to the sermon, meditate on the word and act on its dictates. The sacrament should be similarly prepared for, taken often and received with reverence and attention. In his funeral sermon on Elizabeth Juxon, Denison compiled a similar list of the ways in which the zealous Christian should work towards eternal life, a list which consisted 'in hearing, in reading, meditating, in the use of the sacrament, in conference, in keeping faith and a good conscience, in prayer and such like'.[66]

Perhaps the most striking aspect of lists like this is the way in which they mix together the public ordinances of the church and the spiritual exercises and self-help of the godly in an undifferentiated continuum of spiritual exercises and means of grace, leading the individual from sin to salvation.

Most obviously, the spiritual self-help of the godly operated on the level of the individual, reading, meditating, taking stock of his or her spiritual condition alone. But Denison's concept of godliness was not solely or even mainly centred on the individual; it did not simply oscillate between the public space of the open congregation and the chamber of the would-be elect saint. The gap between those opposite poles was filled by Denison's vision of the mutuality, solidarity and collective piety of the godly community. Thus, in one of his many lists of the means to achieve godliness, Denison cited prayer, reading, meditation and converse with the godly. Elsewhere Denison exhorted the godly to meditate, beat down their fleshly appetites, examine themselves, repent and associate only 'with such as are godly', that is, those 'who truly fear God unto whom, of all other men, our love and best affections are due'. In the passage cited above, where Denison described the godly 'digging in the mines of God's ordinances' for saving knowledge, he immediately associated that process with keeping company only 'with such as fear God, and by this means we shall be made more wise'. Again, having sung the praises of the pure worship of God in the public congregation, Denison immediately went on to recommend 'vows, fastings and leagues of amity' 'amongst them which fear God'. The regulation of one's social life according to such criteria was, for Denison, a crucial step on the road to godliness. There was, he claimed, much 'increase in godliness' to be obtained from 'Christian society'. And here Denison placed particular emphasis on 'the duty of common Christians to exhort one another'. Such exhortation must be frequent – 'daily and seasonable' – and 'when we are exhorted we should bless the Lord God of Israel for so great benefit given to us and we should thank them that are instruments of restraining us from our evil courses.'[67]

Such mutual exhortation was a crucial sign of our love for our brethren, and for Denison the 'love of the brethren' was a crucial sign of true godliness. 'We must labour for love to our brethren', he claimed in 1637/38, 'for except we have a love to our brethren's souls it will be all one to us whether they go to heaven or to hell; whether they be in a good way or a bad, therefore we must be affected by a true Christian love. We are the children of one father, of one mother; we are fed by the same food; we are redeemed by one and the same blood and means; we shall be partakers of the same inheritance. These should move our hearts to love our brethren that we may be zealous to be the means of Christian exhortation to eternal salvation'. 'By brethren', he explained, 'we are to understand such as truly fear God.' Accordingly, the godly were under a very strong obligation to show love and charity towards one another. 'One brother will have a fellow feeling with another', intoned Denison. That feeling must be felt equally towards all true Christians, both rich and poor, and must take a practical form in works of charity directed towards our brethrens' souls *and* bodies. As for the mutual care of souls, the true professor should pity the spiritual condition of his or her brethren, instruct them and, if they lapsed into sin, at once forgive, reprove, admonish and pray for them. Charity towards the bodies of our brethren should be showed by 'commiserating their estate, to wit in grieving for their affliction', in 'visiting them in their distress', 'in feeding the hungry', in 'lending them sufficient for their need', in 'forgiving them their debts' and in 'standing in the gap to turn away God's judgement from them'.[68]

Thus Denison praised Elizabeth Juxon's love for the godly. 'She loved poor Christians', he claimed, 'as well as the rich; to my knowledge she preferred them before rich kindred. She loved them merely for their graces and not for worldly respects.' 'She was fruitful in goods ... What money she had of her own in the time of her health, she distributed it freely, partly to poor preachers about this city, partly also to poor Christians.' As for her husband's wealth, 'she was a blessed instrument to stir up her willing husband to many secret gifts and bountiful alms deeds, especially unto them which were of the household of faith'.[69]

Indeed, for Denison, the social unity and spiritual mutuality achieved by the godly represented the closest we could approach, in this life, to the pleasures of heaven. 'To be much conversant in God's ordinances, in reading and hearing and meditating God's word, in prayer, in holy conference and the like; these present heaven unto our eye, these lead us into sweet fellowship and communion with God and Christ, these fill us with the joy of the Holy Ghost and peace of conscience.' The godly, to Denison, represented the most lively image of the divine nature available to us in this life. For, as he observed, 'grace comes nearest to the nature of God' and the 'divine nature, the image of God, our true saving grace' were all to be found implanted in the elect, by the living word of the gospel. Here, in 'grace and virtue' not in popish pictures and idols, Denison claimed, was to be found God's image. 'Dost thou', Denison asked his audience of the late 1630s, not 'affect the children of God for their common courtesy but for the graces that be in them, for the image of Christ that is shining in them and apparent in them.' If they did, he assured them, 'this is a sign that the object of thy love is changed' and that therefore they had been truly converted.[70]

In other passages Denison went even further in seeming to identify the godly community with the elect, on the one hand, and with the church, on the other. At one point, he claimed that it was quite vain for the ill disposed to defame 'God's children' for 'God will cast honour upon his servants in spite of satan himself.' 'This may be a reproof to the wicked which labour to dishonour the godly. Let them know God hath a time to honour his children, maugre the malice of satan and all his instruments.' Here, typically, Denison was using the tendency of the ungodly to revile and persecute the godly as a clinching argument for his identification of the objects of that hostility with 'God's own children', a group whose ultimate destination in heaven was beyond doubt.[71]

He performed a similar transaction between the godly and the church in a remarkable passage in his catechism. There, against the claims of the church of Rome, he asserted that 'I am taught not to believe in, but to believe, the holy catholic church. That is, to believe that God hath had in all ages, both at this day and will have to the world's end an universal church that is a selected number out of all nations of such as are elected to eternal life and truly and effectually called.' 'This universal catholic church or selected number', he continued, was 'holy by virtue of Christ, who is made unto it holiness and redemption, yea who doth sanctify it by his spirit'. The defining characteristic of this select company was 'a sweet fellowship or communion between themselves in the partaking of God's ordinances'.[72] In this passage the godly householders of St Katharine Cree took their place in that visible succession of true believers which God maintained in every generation, and which constituted that church which alone deserved the epithets universal and catholic.

THE SOCIAL CONSEQUENCES OF PURITAN PIETY: STEPHEN DENISON AND THE ISSUE OF SOCIAL ORDER

We have here a vision of the Christian community radically divided between the godly and the ungodly. Here was the collective face of experimental predestinarian piety. Here was the holy located in the sanctified souls of the godly, remade by the purging and purifying impact of the Holy Spirit, and made manifest in the personal virtues and interpersonal bonds of charity and goodwill which bound the godly together and served (along with the inevitable ill-will of the profane) to separate them off from 'the world'. It was a view constructed, as we have seen, against a vision of a wider society characterised by hypocrisy, carnality, ignorance and sin, characteristics which the corrupt common sense of the ordinarily ignorant and carnal Christian tried to pass off as normal. The true order represented by the community of the godly was defined against a vision of a corrupt world in which true religion was reviled, the godly hated, and the pursuit of private wealth and gratification was the order of the day. In Denison's terms, covetousness and wastefulness produced a whole series of sins in getting (sacrilege, enclosures, engrossing, usury) and spending (stage plays, the elaborate following of fashion) which threatened to impoverish the commonwealth and undermine both the social and the sexual order.

This very sharp contrast between the spiritual mutuality and charity of the godly, on the one hand, and the atomised, sinful individualism of the wider society, on the other, may have born little resemblance to reality. Indeed, Denison himself all but admitted as much in a series of asides criticising, for instance, those who lived idly off the sweat of other men's brows, yet maintained an appearance of godly zeal by assiduous attendance at sermons. Pursuing the same tack, he denounced others who appeared to think that their charitable duties towards the poor were entirely spiritual in scope and did not demand tangible material care for their bodies as well as for their souls.[73] However, for our present purpose, the correspondence of these ideal types of vice and virtue, true religion and hypocrisy with 'reality' is scarcely the point. We are dealing here with two ideal types of order and disorder, godliness and hypocrisy, types generated by Denison in order to turn the tables on those opponents of the godly who wanted to stereotype them as singular, vainglorious agents of disorder.

By constructing his vision of the mutuality and spiritual unity of the godly against a countervailing image of an atomised, individualistic 'world', riven with the effects of covetousness, idleness and wasteful display, Denison was able to claim for the godly the high moral ground of true order and hierarchy, while at the same time constructing a moral vantage point from which to launch some very pointed critiques of the rich and powerful.[74]

This is not to suggest that there was anything directly anti-hierarchical in his view of the godly community. On the contrary, all Christians had two callings, a general Christian calling and a particular secular calling into which God had placed them and in which they should labour all the days of their lives. Indeed, it was a defining characteristic of the godly to display a consistent diligence in their lawful callings, avoiding both covetousness and wastefulness, which otherwise threatened to ruin and impoverish the commonwealth. Again, in writing of the spiritual guilt and responsibility of the heads of households in which the servants and children were not properly catechised and hence condemned to hell for want of knowledge, Denison was also, by implication, confirming and strengthening the hierarchical social arrangements which defined the duties of masters to servants and of servants to masters.[75]

And yet, the very strictness with which he applied the doctrine of callings to the lives of all Christians, both rich and poor, powerful and weak, allowed Denison to denounce both the pursuit of wealth for its own sake and the idleness of the rich. Again, the bonds of mutual charity, love and support which were to pertain amongst the godly, together with the natural enmity of their relations with the profane, served both to undercut or modify the conventional solidarities and hierarchies of family and neighbourhood – Mrs Juxon was praised for preferring the company of her poor godly brethren to that of her rich relations – and to reinforce the material and spiritual obligations owed by the rich and powerful to their inferiors and dependents.

On this basis, Denison was able to say some very cutting things about the doings of the rich and powerful. Indeed Fleming's sermon notes from the late

1630s reveal Denison to have been something of a specialist in intermittent but intense and sometimes frankly odd diatribes against the lifestyles of the city and parish elite. The subjects of some of these passages were perhaps predictable enough. Thus, he denounced proud worldlings who, puffed up by their possession of worldly office, despised poor Christians; the calling of the poorest Christian, he observed, was greater than that of the greatest secular office holder. No one was too grand to avoid the spiritual examination of the minister as a preliminary to receiving the sacrament. Since their standing in the parish could scarcely render them exempt from sin in the eyes of God, they were as guilty of profaning the sacrament in receiving unworthily as the poorest apprentice.[76]

Elsewhere in his sermons of the 1630s he lamented the popularity of certain debased styles of divinity 'as will judge of heavenly things according to corrupt reason, which is all the divinity that a corrupt reprobate man hath'. 'This', he continued, 'is the cause wherefore corrupt doctrine is so highly embraced because they stand with carnal reason. Hence it is that the false doctrine concerning the lawfulness of usury finds great applause among usurers.' Others of the elite used similar arguments from 'reason' to legitimate the breach of the sabbath if not by themselves then by their inferiors and dependents. 'Some pretend that it is but reasonable, yea a thing necessary, that servants that work hard all the week should, upon the sabbath day have lawful recreations.' Thus, Denison roared, sin often disguised itself as virtue, in this instance the breech of the sabbath masquerading as a 'work of mercy and necessity'.[77]

In these instances Denison was lambasting two of his pet hates, usury and sabbath breaking, and merely pointing out the willingness of the better sort to patronise a divinity that allowed them to indulge in both activities willy nilly. But his critique of elite mores could take altogether more bizarre forms than this. Thus he berated those wealthy citizens who, leaving the city in the heat of the summer, betook themselves into the country with little or no care for the quality of the ministry under which they spent the summer months. 'So it be for their pleasure', he lamented, 'they make little conscience under what ministry they plant themselves and so lose more spiritually in the summer than they get in the winter.' Again he railed against those substantial citizens who repine at 'true Christians', who when they 'come to hear some eminent divine' 'make bold with the church and our pews'. 'This condemns the wicked practice of many that cannot endure to come to church themselves and yet will not have others to possess their pews.'[78] Given the social significance attached to the hierarchies of pew possession there could scarcely be a better example of the potential clash between the values of the godly, pressing to hear 'some eminent divine', their zeal for the word overcoming their comparatively lowly social status, and the conventional notions of social hierarchy and propriety that the distribution of pews in the parish church was supposed both to reflect and uphold.

Others of the elite might come to church but in precisely the wrong spirit. Dilating on the example of Mary Magdalene who had used her own hair to wash Christ's feet, Denison launched himself into a extended riff on the sartorial and, in particular, the tonsorial vanities of the age. Thus he condemned 'the practice of too many men that live in this Frenchified age, for the French men brought in this fashion that they must have their locks like to women. Some will put down very women with their cursed locks.' Now Denison was convinced that both the fashion for long hair amongst men and the obsession with the appearance of their hair amongst women were against the laws of 'nature, grace and religion' and he produced a bizarre argument to clinch the point. 'Hair', he explained, was 'an excrement and an excrement comes *ex carne*, out of the flesh.' While at the day of judgement whole and entire bodies would be raised from the grave, with all their disparate and perhaps amputated or dismembered bits restored to wholeness, this did not apply to the excess hair cut off during life. 'Much of the hair shall perish at the day of judgement', Denison explained. 'Shall not rise up again there that which is cut off by the barber. So the paring of the nails shall not rise up again at the day of judgement because they do not make again to the perfecting of the body.' If, as an excrement, excess hair was thus dispensable in heaven, Denison triumphantly concluded, then long love locks could be no fit cause for pride in this life.[79]

Unsurprisingly given these premises, Denison was particularly severe on what he perceived to be a peculiarly feminine tonsorial obsession and hair-based pride.

> What a trimming is there among proud women and what time do they spend in laying out their hair and in combing of it. What abundance of precious time do they spend by these wicked and unlawful employments, in so much that it is true of them ... as the comedian sayeth, they are, as it were, a year in dressing of themselves. Thus a great deal of time is spent on the sabbath day by a company of proud women in trimming up themselves that spend whole forenoons and are hardly ready to come to the sermon on the sabbath day.[80]

Such people, Denison was convinced, were primping and preening themselves all the way to hell. 'There be some wicked men that will not cut off their locks till the devil puts a candle in them to burn them off in hell.' And, as for women, their teasing and dyeing of their hair went directly against nature. 'Now artificial colours are sought for and they are set above natural colours', he wailed. 'It is a very wonderful thing to see how many fashions they can turn themselves but a great deal more admirable to see how many colours they change their hair.' 'Hair', Denison concluded, was 'not the least monument of women'; an observation from which he went directly into a long disquisition on Revelations 9.6: 'it is said there of the locusts, whose king is the angel of the bottomless pit, that they had hair as the hair of women which pretended a great deal of spiritual beauty, they had great deal of such hair. And thus the whore of Rome doth trick up herself withal to allure spiritual adultery. Even as whores do trick up themselves to allure adulterers, so doth the whore of Rome in these days.' In these passages pride is seen leading to a vain pleasure in sexualised sartorial and tonsorial display and is then associated with whoredom and adultery. Thence, it is directly linked, via the notions of whoredom and adultery, with popery. Mary Magdalene, on the other hand, 'being truly converted had not dyed her hair' but 'wiped the feet of our saviour with that hair which the Lord had given her'. This was a contrast that left the spiritual condition and likely fate of those wealthy, primping city matrons, who spent the best part of the day getting dressed up to go to church, in little doubt.[81]

If feminine and feminising personal display provoked by far the most visceral and vitriolic responses from Denison, he was not much better disposed towards other forms of elite conspicuous consumption and display. Contemporary London he compared to Jerome's time 'when the walls of men's houses shine with gold and roofs shine with gold and tops of the pillars shine with gold. But Christ lies in the poor, being poor and naked before the door.' 'Now if rich men can have all things fine at home and give nothing at all to the poor their sin is aggravated and if they be prodigal in their lusts in spending it on whores, in keeping hawks and hounds and well feeding of themselves and will not spend any thing in pious uses, this doth much aggravate their sin.' Elsewhere Denison denounced the sin of those that 'murmur and complain of taxes. If they pay never so little to the poor or the maintenance of ministers they are ready to complain, when as they will spend an hundred times more ... upon their base lusts, upon their wrangling and their pride and drunkenness and whoredom.' More in hope than expectation perhaps, Denison predicted financial ruin for such malefactors. 'Yet though all are not brought to poverty by serving of lusts, yet no question but many are come to poverty by them; either they have been too contentious at the law or have maintained themselves, their wives and children with too much pride, or else have been addicted to gluttony and feasting, or to drunkenness and intemperance or have consumed their estates by whores and harlots or with gaming and the like or spent it in faction.'[82]

The smooth, indeed seamless, transition effected in these passages from entirely conventional, arguably harmless and seemingly lawful activities and recreations – fashionable dress, long hair, hunting, hawking, feasting, litigation – to the most overtly and unimpeachably unlawful and sinful of enormities – whoredom, adultery, popery – represented a classic move in Denison's (and indeed in the wider puritan) repertoire of moral obloquy and social criticism; a repertoire Denison seems to have been more than at home employing against the peccadilloes and sins of both parish and city elites. Indeed, judging from some of the passages cited above, we might conclude that for Denison the wages of too enthusiastic an espousal of the mores of the city elite was likely to be ruin in this life and damnation in the next. Of course, he might have replied to this that, along with his clerical contemporaries of all ideological stripes, both here and throughout his sermons, he was concerned to denounce human sin in all its forms and that if he seemed to concentrate at times on the sins of the better sort that was because they had more time and money to indulge what were, in fact, corrupt impulses common to fallen humanity. Thus, denouncing the idleness of those who lived off the sweat of other men's brows, Denison produced a list of the leading culprits. This lumped together the idle, pleasure-loving gentry, beggars, usurers, stage players, cheats, drunkards and harlots; a list, be it noted, that included figures from both extremes of the social order.[83]

Here, in fact, was a veritable world upside down of corrupt and deviant characters. These were the moral anti-types of the godly. In this moral universe, the world the right way up was the world of the godly community, while the world turned upside down was that of the profane and the ungodly. In seeking to portray the world as some sort of choice between these two models of social relations, Denison produced an eminently hierarchical and ordered vision of mutuality and community. However, the sort of social relations envisaged by Denison pertaining amongst the godly did not simply reproduce the normal boundaries, solidarities and hierarchies of neighbourhood, family and parish. Indeed, they contained an implicit critique of the mores of the wider society, a critique which allowed Denison and other preachers to say some very cutting things about the lifestyles of the rich and famous. Not that he was condemning the mores of the elite *tout court*. There remained room in his moral universe for fitting differences of display and consumption between rich and poor. He was, he often pointed out, merely arguing for moderation in all things; as he concluded one sermon of 1639: 'we must take heed that while we do avoid prodigality, we do not fall into the other extreme, into the extreme of too much parsimony, but let us labour to find out the way of true liberality'.[84]

But having said all that, there does seem to have been something of a social edge to the running social commentary and moral critique that Denison maintained throughout his sermons, an edge only too likely to alienate and annoy those substantial burghers who recognised themselves and their petty vanities, peccadilloes and pleasures in Denison's diatribes. And that may well prove to be of some significance when we return below to the subject of Denison's relations with the more substantial of his parishioners in St Katharine Cree.

To conclude, historians who comment on the 'conservatism' and respectability of puritan attitudes to the social order are quite correct, but they miss half the point. For ministers like Denison tied their entirely conventional, hierarchical and static image of the social order to their very polarised view of the social world, fractured by the division between the godly and the ungodly. Out of the resulting moral polarities they were able to generate some quite outspoken critiques of contemporary mores and elite behaviour. Similarly, historians who note the polarised picture painted by ministers like Denison of relations between the godly and the profane, the stark contrast they drew between the mutuality and unity of the godly, on the one hand, and the profanity, hypocrisy and atomised individualism of 'the world', on the other, are quite justified when they question whether such a polarised view of the social world could ever have corresponded with 'reality'. Even for Denison, theorising on the subject in the pulpit, the division between the two groups was never watertight. Indeed as we have seen above, having helped to set up the basic godly/ungodly dichotomy in his own preaching, Denison spent a good deal of time softening and blurring the lines between the two groups, warning both the godly laity and the clergy to beware of simply writing off even the most notorious of sinners and bidding them welcome repentant malefactors into the 'communion of the saints' with open arms. He went on to reassure his audience of the late 1630s that social and even festive contact with the ungodly was acceptable. 'It is lawful', he intoned, 'for Christians to eat with wicked men or unbelievers, yea with heathens and pagans.' Had not Christ supped with Simon the leper when he was still an unbeliever and Paul given 'lawful liberty to the church of the Corinthians' 'that were then dispersed among unbelievers' 'that if an unbeliever did invite them to a feast, they might go and eat of those things that were set before'? It was clear therefore that 'it is lawful for a Christian to eat and drink with wicked men'. Of course, Denison conceded, Christians ought to be 'choice of their company' but not out of pride, rather because of fear 'to be with wicked men'. But even as Denison licensed such social contact he hedged it around with caveats and provisos of a sort which served to reintroduce his basic distinction between the godly and the ungodly into the very centre of those social or festive occasions at which those two groups might meet and intermingle. Thus he told his hearers that they must be careful that

> we not partake of the sins of those wicked men with whom we eat and drink; that we do not take guilt of those sins to ourselves either by liking of them or not grieving for them or by applauding them or by not reproving of them. Thus we may take the guilt of other men's sins upon ourselves if we like them and they please us; if we do not grieve when we see their absurd behaviour and hear their foolish speeches and jesting and the like; if we do not grieve and are not inwardly vexed at it. We take upon us the guilt of their sin if we hear the name of God blasphemed as it is in this

city by swearing and cursing, if we do not grieve for it, we make it our own sin. So if we come into wicked men's company if we do not reprove them so much as in our countenance or with our behaviour or do not do it in words, thus if we do not reprove them, we make the sin to be ours, we derive the guilt of it upon ourselves.[85]

If, in theory, such concessions to Christian charity and social reality breached the walls of indifference, hostility and disdain that might otherwise have separated the godly from the ungodly, they scarcely conjure up a picture of easy personal or social interaction. We have here envisioned occasions on which the godly sat scowling at or telling off their companions and generally feeling bad about both themselves and their fellow revellers. Indeed, the passage might be taken to imply that contact between the two groups merely served to heighten and more fully internalise the godly's sense of difference and apartness.

But the passages under discussion here in fact worked in two directions, speaking both to a pharisaical godly pride and self-love that eschewed all contact with the notionally ungodly, and to the opposite impulse that led the godly towards an easy familiarity with and self-forgetfulness amongst the company of the profane. On this evidence we might surmise that the division between the godly and the ungodly was effected at least as much between the ears of the godly as it was constituted in and through their actual social networks and day to day dealings with other people.

It would, however, be a mistake to use such doubts about the social 'reality' of the godly community, the one to one relationship between godly self-consciousness and identity formation and social conduct, either to call the whole category of puritanism into question or to expel it from the realm of the social to that of ideology. Certainly, we are dealing here with a polemical construct, an idealised picture of a social world that could never, in reality, conform to the moral absolutes and manichean contrasts inherent in these polarities. Contemporaries recognised as much when they accused the godly of hypocrisy. But that does not mean that we are dealing here only with literary conceits and conventional moral types. On the contrary, these idealised types and dichotomies were crucial to the self-image of the godly. In using the term puritan at all we are seeking to enter the half-lit, distorted world of individual and collective consciousness and identity formation and we have to accept the limitations and opportunities which always attend that task. At this point it is crucial to remember that the paradigms and ideal types that people use to structure reality are themselves part of the reality they structure. It is being argued here that the use of these opposed models of the social order to shape and maintain their view of themselves and of the world in which they lived was one of the defining characteristics of the godly. Contemporaries, like Ben Jonson, acknowledged that, when, in seeking to lay bare puritan hypocrisy, as they perceived it, they inverted the inversions and antinomies implicit in puritan attitudes to the self and to society. It is, perhaps, time for modern historians to realise it too and to integrate the generation and manipulation by contemporaries of such models and ideal types of godly and ungodly behaviour, hypocritical and sincere Christian profession, into their accounts of the religious conflicts of the period. They can do so in the full knowledge that all such categories and dichotomies were ideologically charged, rhetorically moulded and polemically constructed and yet still avoid reducing puritanism to the status of a mere literary conceit or a polemical convention.[86]

NOTES

1 S. Denison, *The new creature. A sermon preached at Paul's Cross, January 1619* (London, 1619); *The monument or tombstone, or a sermon preached at Laurence Pountnies Church in London, November 21, 1619 at the funeral of Mrs Elizabeth Juxon* (London, 1620); *A compendious catechism* (London, 1621); *The doctrine of both the sacraments* (London, 1621); *An exposition upon the first chapter of the second epistle of Peter* (London, 1622); *Another tombstone, or a sermon preached at Laurence Pountnies church, London, upon the last day of August ... 1626 at the celebration of the funerals of Master John Juxon* (London, 1626); *The white wolf or a sermon preached at Paul's Cross, Feb.11 ... 1627* (London, 1627). American Antiquarian Society, Worcester, Mass., Denison sermon notes. Hereafter cited as Denison sermon notes. I would like to thank David Como for drawing this last source to my attention.

2 J.C. Davies, 'Puritanism and revolution: themes, categories, methods and conclusions', *Historical Journal*, 34 (1991); T. Webster, *Godly clergy in early Stuart England: the Caroline puritan movement, c. 1620–1643* (Cambridge, 1997).

3 Davies, 'Puritanism and revolution' and P. Collinson, *The religion of protestants* (Oxford, 1982). For one of the earliest and certainly the most influential statements of 'the relative disappearance of puritanism' thesis see Nicholas Tyacke, 'Puritanism, Arminianism and counter-revolution', in C.S.R. Russell, ed., *The origins of the English civil war* (London, 1973). Dr Tyacke has subsequently modified his position in two important articles for which see n.5 below. In this mode also see C.H. and Katharine George, *The protestant mind of the English reformation* (Princeton, 1961); C.S.R. Russell, *Parliaments and English politics, 1621–1629* (Oxford, 1979), pp. 26–32; Russell, *Unrevolutionary England* (London, 1990), chapter 12, 'The parliamentary career of John Pym, 1621–9' and Russell, *The causes of the English civil war* (Oxford, 1990), chapters 3, 4 and 5 and appendix.

4 K. Fincham, *Prelate as pastor* (Oxford, 1990) and his introduction to K. Fincham, ed., *The early Stuart church* (Basingstoke, 1993); Collinson, *Religion of protestants*; P. Lake, *Moderate puritans and the Elizabethan church* (Cambridge, 1982); 'Matthew Hutton: a puritan bishop?' *History*, 64 (1979); 'Calvinism and the English church, 1570–1635', *Past and Present*, 115 (1987); Nicholas Tyacke, *Anti-Calvinists* (Oxford, 1987). E. Carlson and K. Parker, *Practical divinity: the works and life of Revd. Richard Greenham* (Aldershot, 1998), pp. 121–6.

5 P. Seaver, *The puritan lectureships* (Stanford, 1970) and P. Seaver, *Wallington's world* (London, 1985); Lake, *Moderate puritans*; P. Lake, 'Defining puritanism – again?' in F. Bremer, ed., *Puritanism: trans-atlantic perspectives on a seventeenth-century Anglo-*

American faith (Boston, 1993); Fincham, *Prelate as pastor*; N. Tyacke, *The fortunes of English puritanism, 1603–1640* (Friends of Dr Williams Library, forty-fourth lecture, London, 1990) and '"The rise of puritanism" and the legalising of dissent, 1571–1719', in Ole Peter Grell, Jonathan Israel and Nicholas Tyacke, eds, *From persecution to toleration* (Oxford, 1991); J. Eales, 'A road to revolution: the continuity of puritanism, 1559–1642', in C. Durston and J. Eales, eds, *The culture of puritanism, 1560–1700* (Basingstoke, 1996); Webster, *Godly clergy*. Also see the articles by Collinson and Lake in Durston and Eales, eds, *Culture of English puritanism*.

6   Fincham, *Prelate as pastor*; Lake, *Moderate puritans*, chapter 10; also see Lake, 'Moving the goal posts: construing conformity in the early Stuart church', forthcoming in P. Lake and M. Questier, eds, *Orthodoxy and conformity in the early Stuart church*. The discussion of puritan debates about conformity in Webster, *Godly clergy*, is also informative on this point.

7   G. Bernard, 'The church of England c. 1529–c. 1642', *History*, 75 (1990); P. White, *Predestination, policy and polemic* (Cambridge, 1992) and his 'The via media in the early Stuart church', in K. Fincham, ed., *The early Stuart church*; Kevin Sharpe, *The Personal rule of Charles I* (London and New Haven, 1993).

8   C. Haigh, 'Puritan evangelism in the reign of Elizabeth I', *English Historical Review*, 92 (1977); 'The church of England, the catholics and the people', in C. Haigh, ed., *The reign of Elizabeth I* (London, 1984) and most recently in his *English reformations* (Oxford, 1993); A. Walsham, *Providence in early modern England* (Oxford, 1999); I. Green, *The Christian's A B C* (Oxford, 1995); Bernard, 'Church of England'. For further critical comment on these issues and this literature see the introduction to Peter Lake and Michael Questier, eds, *Orthodoxy and conformity in the English church, 1560–1660* forthcoming from Boydell and Brewer, Woodbridge.

9   K. Wrightson and D. Levine, *Poverty and piety in an English village: Terling, 1525–1700* (Oxford, 1995); W. Hunt, *The puritan moment* (Cambridge, Mass., 1983); D. Underdown, *Fire from heaven* (London, 1992). All of which works draw on and develop, through local manuscript research, the insights in Hill, *Puritanism and society*.

10 For pioneering both pre- and post-revisionist work on London see Seaver, *Puritan lectureships* and *Wallington's world* and, of course, for the earlier period, Susan Brigden's seminal *London and the reformation* (Oxford, 1989). Crucial here will be Julia Merritt's forthcoming book on early modern Westminister. Nicholas Tyacke's very important Dr Williams' lecture, the *Fortunes of English puritanism*, also contains some pregnant remarks on the nature of puritan networks in early Stuart London. For the period of the civil war the balance has, of course, been massively redressed of late by three books: Keith Lindley, *Popular politics and religion in civil war London* (Aldershot, 1997); Dagmar Freist, *Governed by opinion* (London, 1997) and Robert Brenner, *Merchants and revolution: commercial change, political conflict and London's overseas traders, 1550–1653* (Cambridge, 1993).

11 On the issue of lectureships compare Seaver's *Puritan lectureships* with Collinson's essay on 'lectures by combination' in his *Godly people*. Given the prominence of local studies of Lancashire and Cheshire in the early revisionist assault on both the reformation and the civil war we might conclude that there was something of a 'revenge of the provinces', indeed 'a revenge of Greater Manchester', about early revisionism. I refer here, of course, to Christopher Haigh's path-breaking local study of the reformation, *Reformation and reaction in Tudor Lancashire* (Cambridge, 1976), and to John Morrill's application of Alan Everrit's 'county community' model of local gentry

politics and sociability to Cheshire and then his extrapolation from Cheshire outwards to all England in his hugely influential student text *The revolt of the provinces* (London, 1976) now 'remade' in a third edition as *The revolt in the provinces* (Basingstoke, 1999).

12   Denison, *Catechism*, pp. 2–3, 8.
13   Denison, *New creature*, pp. 15–16.
14   Denison, *Exposition*, p. 84.
15   Denison, *New creature*, pp. 17, 53. Denison sermon notes, fol. 8v.
16   Denison, *Catechism*, p. 11.
17   Ibid., p. 8; Denison, *Sacraments*, p. 136.
18   Denison, *Sacraments*, pp. 190–1.
19   Denison, *New creature*, pp. 74–5; *Exposition*, pp. 93–4. Denison sermon notes, fols 4v., 8v.
20   Denison, *Exposition*, p. 84. Denison sermon notes, fol. 50r.
21   Denison, *Monument*, pp. 71, 75.
22   Denison, *Catechism*, p. 14 where Denison stated that 'providence is a work of God whereby he disposeth and ordereth all things to their proper ends'. Also see *Monument*, pp. 59–60 where Denison claimed that 'all afflictions come by the providence of God and by his decree and determinate purpose'.
23   Denison, *Catechism*, p. 14.
24   Denison, *Exposition*, pp. 40–1. Denison sermon notes, fol. 5r.–v.
25   Denison, *New creature*, pp. 82–3.
26   Denison, *Sacraments*, pp. 195–6; *Exposition*, p. 91.
27   Bernard, 'Church of England'.
28   Denison, *New creature*, pp. 10–11.
29   Denison, *Tombstone*, pp. 13, 19–21.
30   Denison, *New creature*, pp. 64–9; *Monument*, pp. 62, 64.
31   Denison, *Exposition*, pp. 56, 73.
32   Denison, *Sacraments*, p. 146. Denison sermon notes, fol. 45r.
33   Denison, *New creature*, pp. 57–9.
34   Denison, *Exposition*, p. 47.
35   Ibid., p. 49.
36   Denison, *Tombstone*, pp. 18, 20, 23.
37   Denison, *Sacraments*, p. 189. Denison sermon notes, fol. 21r.
38   Denison, *Monument*, p. 29.
39   Denison, *Sacraments*, pp. 110, 131; *Exposition*, p. 56.
40   Denison, *Exposition*, pp. 69, 95, 185, 43. Denison sermon notes, fol. 53r.
41   Denison, *Sacraments*, p. 130.
42   Ibid., p. 126. Denison sermon notes, fol. 22r.

Doctrinal and pietistic underpinnings

43 Denison, *Monument*, pp. 117, 100, 94, 108, 124.
44 Denison, *Sacraments*, p. 137; *Exposition*, p. 95.
45 Denison, *Exposition*, p. 92; *New creature*, pp. 3, 5–6. Denison sermon notes, fols 41v., 46v., 60r.
46 Denison, *Exposition*, pp. 102, 103; *New creature*, p. 33.
47 Denison, *Exposition*, pp. 104, 43, 24–5, 16, 29; *Sacraments*, pp. 180–1. Denison sermon notes, fol. 30v.
48 Bernard, 'Church of England'; Green, *The Christians A B C*; Haigh, *English reformations*, esp. chapter 16 and conclusion.
49 Denison sermon notes, fol. 68r.
50 *Ibid.*, fols 8v., 23r.–v.
51 *Ibid.*, fols 21r., 9v.
52 *Ibid.*, fols 78v.–79r., 99r.
53 *Ibid.*, fols 69v., 68v.
54 *Ibid.*, fol. 98r.–v.
55 *Ibid.*, fol. 70v.
56 *Ibid.*, fols 71r., 72r.–v.
57 P. Lake and M. Questier, 'Prisons, priests and people', in N. Tyacke, ed., *England's Long Reformation* (London, 1998); Bernard, 'Church of England'; Haigh, *English reformations*. P. Lake, '"A charitable Christian hatred"; the godly and their enemies in the 1630s', in Eales and Durston, eds, *The culture of English puritanism*.
58 Tyacke, *Anti-Calvinists*; P. Lake, 'Serving God and the times: the Calvinist conformity of Robert Sanderson', *Journal of British Studies*, 26 (1987); P. Lake, 'The moderate and irenic case for religious war: Joseph Hall's Via Media in context', in S. Amussen and M. Kishlansky, eds, *Political culture and cultural politics in early modern England* (Manchester, 1995).
59 The transition from the spoken and written to the printed sermon is currently the subject of important research by Arnold Hunt, which may or may not confirm the conjectures made here on the basis of what is admittedly a very narrow sample.
60 P. Lake, *Moderate puritans and the Elizabethan church* (Cambridge, 1982), esp. chapter 7.
61 Denison, *Sacraments*, p. 75; *Exposition*, p. 56; *Tombstone*, pp. 90–1, 111.
62 Denison, *New creature*, p. 44; *Monument*, p. 65; *Exposition*, pp. 68, 90, 107, 61.
63 For the words puritan and precisian see Denison, *Monument*, p. 105; Denison, *Sacraments*, pp. 17, 19.
64 Denison, *Sacraments*, pp. 55, 106, 31; *Exposition*, pp. 69, 30. Also see Denison sermon notes fols 31v.–32r.
65 *Monument*, pp. 102–3; *Exposition*, pp. 196, 115.
66 Denison, *New creature*, p. 38; *Monument*, dedicatory epistle, sig. A4r., p. 21; *New creature*, pp. 85–91.
67 Denison, *Exposition*, pp. 26–7, 58, 16. Also see Denison sermon notes, fols 2r.–3r.

68 *Ibid.*, pp. 59, 64. Also see Denison sermon notes, fol. 3v.

69 Denison, *Monument*, pp. 102–3, 114–15.

70 Denison, *Tombstone*, p. 11; *Exposition*, pp. 34–5, 36. 'We must esteem of God's children', wrote Denison, 'which are indued with this divine nature and we must labour for the same image which we see in them; it is worth labouring for, it is no less than the divine nature'. Also see Denison sermon notes, fol. 92r.

71 Denison, *Exposition*, pp. 154, 157.

72 Denison, *Catechism*, pp. 25–6.

73 Denison, *Catechism*, pp. 40–1; *Tombstone*, p. 6; *Exposition*, pp. 62–3.

74 See Lake, 'Charitable Christian hatred'.

75 Denison, *Catechism*, pp. 40–3; *New creature*, dedicatory epistle, sig. A3v.

76 Denison, *Exposition*, p. 30.

77 Denison sermon notes, fols 40v.–41r., 31r.

78 *Ibid.*, fols 67r., 76r., 75v.

79 *Ibid.*, fol. 88r.–v.

80 *Ibid.*, fol. 88r.

81 *Ibid.*, fol. 87r.–v.

82 *Ibid.*, fols 104v.–105r., 116v.–117r.

83 Denison, *Sacraments*, pp. 143, 150; *Exposition*, p. 71.

84 Denison sermon notes, fol. 117v.

85 *Ibid.*, fol. 74r.

86 Lake, 'Charitable Christian hatred'.

Chapter 3

The puritanism of Stephen Denison: ii. ecclesiastical forms and political consequences

THE POINTS OF CONTACT BETWEEN THE GODLY AND THE CHURCH:
I THE WORD PREACHED AND THE POWER OF THE MINISTRY

Potentially, Denison's vision of the godly community was enormously divisive. It threatened to fracture the community of Christians in two and to elevate the private devotions, conferences, conventicles, fasts, prayers and mutual admonitions of the godly to a status equal to the public ordinances of the national church. To the opponents of puritanism this looked suspiciously like the first step on a road which led inexorably towards schism and separation. How did Denison control these dangerously radical tendencies? How did his vision of the community of the godly key into his vision of the visible church?

Perhaps unsurprisingly, Denison's view of the church was dominated by the figure of the 'powerful preacher', gazing down from the pulpit, pronouncing the curses of the law and applying the promises of the gospel to the souls of his flock, cowering below. For Denison, preaching was *the* means of grace. Here was the normal way to come to a saving and properly experimental faith in Christ. In order for the ordinary Christian to experience an effectual calling, God had to add power to the outward calling of the word. While the initiating cause in this process was God himself, his usual instrument was the word preached. The word preached was powerful; it was the means whereby the divine image could be implanted into sinful humanity. Even a carnal and corrupt minister, so long as he preached only the unvarnished word, could transform and convert souls through his preaching. Through preaching, God not only changed individuals; he would also 'by the spirit of his mouth' destroy Antichrist and change the world.[1]

Here was the central function of the ministry of Christ. 'It is the duty of ministers to preach unto God's church', Denison claimed. 'God sent us not so much to baptise as to preach the gospel.' Evaluating the various aspects of the ministry, Denison concluded that 'the word is the principal, and the sacraments are the accessory or appendices'. 'Where should a good minister die but in the pulpit?', Denison asked at one point.[2]

It was true that the word read was still the word of God, apt, with the attendant action of the spirit, to enlighten and convert the soul of the sinner. Thus, the laity could enjoy direct access to the word by reading and meditating on the scriptures. But, asked Denison, 'how shall the people understand without a guide? They may read and beat their brain but unless they have a guide they may come short of sound understanding.' 'The church of God hath need of an interpreter, one of a thousand', he concluded.[3]

Indeed, Denison habitually equated the 'word' with the word preached. 'God's word is not only that which is expressly written in the bible but also the labours of God's servants in expounding and preaching, so far as they deliver nothing but that which hath warrant from the scripture this is also God's word.' The laity should therefore not merely read and meditate on the scripture but attend closely to the words of 'Christ in the ministry'. All Christians must 'frequent the house of God where it [the word] is faithfully taught ... hearken carefully to it while it is delivered and ... examine ourselves by it and ... make conscience to practise it'. 'We are in darkness naturally', Denison intoned, 'and therefore have need of light, and what means is it ordinarily that doth turn men from darkness to light, but God's word truly preached.' Indeed, so central was preaching to Denison's view of true religion that he counselled his flock to doubt the validity of any faith which had not come by preaching. 'If any desire to try the truth of their faith', Denison advised, 'let them examine first how they came by it, or by what means it was wrought in them. For true faith is commonly wrought by the means of hearing God's word preached ... Therefore, if thy faith be not wrought in thee by this means, it is the more suspicious not to be true.' For Denison, 'the hearing of the word' was 'the one thing necessary' for a true believer.[4]

In the pulpit, therefore, lay the ultimate source and affirmation of the power and majesty of the ministry, and Denison gloried in the fact. The minister, he claimed, should be a 'son of thunder', appealing not only to the mind of his hearers but much more to their 'will and affections'. 'Religion is more in the will and affections than in any other faculty of the soul whatsoever.' It was essential, therefore, that the will and affections should be 'stirred up' as well as the mind instructed. 'Doth not zealous preaching especially stir up?' Denison asked. To that end the ministers should apply a simple scriptural message directly to the spiritual condition of their flock. They should do so, moreover, in a very loud voice. Since ministers spoke in God's stead, Denison argued, they should be ready not to 'favour ourselves too much but to strain ourselves, that we may be heard of the people and to extend our voices, if it be necessary, to make them audible. And this the Lord requireth, Esay 58.1 "Cry aloud, spare not, lift up thy voice like a trumpet."' 'Sons of thunder' indeed. Nor, as we shall see below, should we merely limit ourselves to imagining Denison bellowing away in the pulpit; he was also very likely waving his arms about in histrionic gestures as well.[5]

But if the medium ought to grate, so too should the message. It is true that Denison deprecated the preaching style of those ministers who remained fixated on the threats of the law and never managed to apply the saving promises of the gospel. However, his concept of 'powerful preaching' was undoubtedly centred on the stentorian denunciation of the auditory's sins and moral failings from the pulpit. 'Many people live under a flattering ministry, which is a main cause that they never come to the sight of their estate by nature.' 'Flattering ministers therefore do strengthen the wicked that he cannot [turn] from his wickedness. Thus it is a dangerous thing for any people to live under such a ministry.' Denison praised Elizabeth Juxon for fearing 'both the company and doctrine of such ministers as she perceived would give her too much liberty. She was likewise best pleased in the greatest strictness.' If such plain speaking led to division or contention, that was too bad. In that event, 'the fault is not in the word', Denison explained, 'but in the hearers which have not grace to make any better use of it'. 'Ministers are not, therefore, to be censured for their true preaching of God's word, or to be unjustly condemned for their pains in their ministry, as though they had done or committed some great offence, for if any faithful minister preach the word what doth he but that which is just and meet?'[6]

Indeed, such divisive effects were only to be expected, since for Denison the different responses of the laity to the word preached represented crucial proof of their elect or reprobate status. Thus, a defining characteristic of those who had Christ for their head was the possession 'of a sanctified ear, to hear the word profitably'. Christ had 'bored' their ears. 'Zeal and forwardness to hear God's word' was thus a crucial sign of election. 'If we esteem it precious, sure we will press unto it', be thankful for it, enjoy it and spare no efforts to 'keep it safe'. It was a defining characteristic of 'God's people' that they 'are enlightened to see how faithful preaching brings glory to God and how it brings good to the church and how just a thing it is in itself. They can look further unto these mysteries than unregenerate persons can and therefore they have a better faculty to approve the things that are excellent ... than others have.' Elizabeth Juxon, as death approached, had only wanted to listen to the word of God, both expounded and read. Of course, even the godly could and did find themselves sometimes resenting the lash of the minister's tongue, when it was applied to their own sins. But that should only stir up all 'that think themselves to be God's children to approve themselves so by their approving things excellent and by their standing for the same'.[7]

Certainly, the word was hated by the wicked and the hypocritical. 'Lewd and wicked men' 'so hated the word' 'because it is a light and discovereth their naughtiness. What doth the thief or the adulterer hate more than if any come with a candle to reveal his practises?', Denison asked. He invited the ungodly to test their spiritual condition by asking themselves 'first, if thou contemn powerful preaching and wilfully neglect it; secondly, if thou art loath that thy conscience should be pricked with the sense and feeling of thy sin; thirdly, if thou hatest them that would instruct thee; fourthly, if thou shunnest the company and places where knowledge is to be learned'. For Denison, speaking in the late 1630s, it remained a crucial test for would-be true believers whether or not they 'loved a powerful ministry'.[8]

Nor was all this merely theory. On the contrary, we have good reason to believe that these strictures and warnings were grounded in Denison's own experience of a somewhat satirical, even adverse, response to his pulpit performances in St Katharine Cree itself. For, in a church court case of March 1617, a number of witnesses, amongst them Denison himself, testified that the previous autumn, 'at Bartholomew tide last past', after a sermon delivered by Denison to a meeting 'of the company of bricklayers', one Mistress Rose Law had announced her intention of entering the pulpit. Despite the warnings of her more timorous (female) companions that 'you know not whether the wrath of God will fall upon you for it or not', Law entered the hallowed space where, before an audience of five or six other women, one of them a bricklayer's wife from St Mary Aldermanbury, she proceeded to parody Denison's stentorian preaching style, much to the amusement of the onlookers – it was the consequent 'noise and laughter' that attracted the attention of the witnesses, Denison included, who was brought by the commotion back from the vestry into the body of the church. While none of the witnesses claimed to have heard what Mistress Law had said, she clearly addressed her 'flock' – 'her lips moved and she spake somewhat', claimed one, and she 'spread her arms abroad and over the pulpit as preachers sometimes use to do'. Denison missed the main feature, but emerged in time to see Law descending the stairs from the pulpit and at the bottom 'look after the ministers pew' and, 'laughing exceedingly', make 'an immodest and unseemly gesture, not fit to be used in the church', the precise nature of which goes, sadly, unrecorded. Immediate upon his arrival in the parish Denison's overbearing style had elicited a less than reverential response from his audience and while the immediate reaction to Mistress Law's antics had been a mixture of shock – one witness records placing his finger over his mouth to beckon Rose 'to be silent' – and hilarity, the church court case and public penance consequent upon her antics presumably made Mistress Law at least laugh out of the other side of her face.[9] It certainly demonstrated that there was something important at stake in all this for Denison.

Nor did Denison's stentorian histrionics in the pulpit merely provoke derision. When, in 1622, the bishop of London authorised a select vestry to run the affairs of the parish, he unsurprisingly nominated Denison as one of the twenty-four men with whom power was to repose. But in doing so he made the curate's involvement in the vestry's deliberations contingent on his 'giving satisfaction unto our said Chancellor on the behalf of those in the said parish whom he hath wronged and offended'. On this evidence, 'powerful preaching', at least as Denison defined and practised it, provoked an equally powerful, if not always a favourable, response.[10]

There was, of course, more than a certain irony in all this. For, on the one hand, it was precisely the figure of the preaching minister which served most firmly to key Denison's vision of the godly community into the structures of the national church. But, on the other, it was precisely the word preached that provided the crucial element of division, the emotional and ideological cleaver, by which the godly were to be separated off from the ungodly.

A parallel tension or paradox can be observed in Denison's attitude to the standing of the minister himself. Certainly, his vision of the centrality of the word preached to the godly community and true religion conferred great status and authority on the authentically powerful preacher. But there was a sense in which that concept itself was divisive, since not all preaching was equally 'powerful', a quality or epithet which was conferred on the preacher, in part at least, by the lay response to his preaching.

Thus, to begin with, the clergy's standing was a function of their willingness to preach. Denison was clear, for instance, that non-resident ministers 'deserve not the name of brethren in that they suffer the people to perish for want of diligent preaching'. He was almost as damning in his judgement of those ministers who, while they did preach, preached negligently: 'such ministers as make no great conscience what they deliver, so they may fill up the hour ... idle ministers which do the work of the lord negligently, being ready to deliver what comes next to the tongues end, though it be little to the purpose'. Indeed, preaching, even prepared preaching, was not, in itself, enough to validate a minister as a genuinely 'powerful' preacher. It had to be the right sort of preaching. Thus Denison complained that there were too many 'erronious and deceitful teachers which sophisticate the word of God by the mingling of their own crotches and subtle distinctions to deceive'. Such ministers behaved as though 'they never preach or write well unless they invent and broach some newfangled conceit of their own invention; as though known truth were grown too stale for their mouths to utter'. Such men were motivated, as often as not, by the drive to please 'the itching ears' and the 'Athenian like desire after novelties' of the people. They desired to be 'esteemed witty men' and to please 'humorous men that so they might the more deeply insinuate themselves into their purses'. Others were anxious to show off their human learning through a persistent 'citing of authors', but this raised the suspicion that 'a minister seeks himself and affects his own glory'. Certainly, Denison concluded, 'this flourishing preaching, which is so affectedly set out with the enticing speech of man's wisdom, it never proved so profitable for the general good of God's church as the plain preaching of the word; yea, if there were no powerfuller preaching than that vain affected preaching, I wonder what would become of the conversion of souls'.[11]

The remedy against such vainglory, popularity and rhetorical excess lay in the minister delivering to his flock only those doctrines and images that he had received from God in scripture. The minister must 'prove whatsoever doctrine he doth deliver unto God's people' and make 'good his doctrine by canonical scripture'. Indeed, Denison went further than that; ministers were obliged to teach their 'judicious hearers' 'to try the doctrine delivered unto them whether it be of Christ or no'. 'If any come unto you and bring not this doctrine, receive him not to house, saith the apostle ... and it is set down as the commendation of God's people in John 10.5 that they will not follow a stranger, but fly from him.'[12]

Thus, while the centrality of preaching to Denison's view of true religion might provide the crucial ground for his very exalted vision of ministerial authority, it also served to render that authority subject not merely to scripture but to the scripturally informed judgement of the godly laity. For it was a necessary implication of the passages cited above that the performance of the minister in the pulpit, in both its style and content, was to be tested against the word of God by the laity. Admittedly, Denison was silent on what practical recourse was open to lay people unfortunate enough to live under a negligent, non-resident or newfangled preacher. But the criteria by which the laity should judge their minister – as well as their right, indeed their duty, to do so – were all made crystal clear.

Denison attempted to contain the radical potential for lay activism and self-help implicit in his position through an idealised picture of the mutual rights and duties of minister and people. In his catechism, Denison outlined the 'duties of people to their ministers' and 'of ministers to the people'. The people were obliged, firstly, 'to have them in respect and love; secondly, to hear them; thirdly, to obey their doctrine; fourthly, to follow their steps in goodness; fifthly, to maintain them comfortably'. The people should deal with the minister 'as with a brother, that is courteously and kindly; affording him cheerful maintenance, not seeking unkindly to deprive him of his due nor railing upon him or reviling him'. If their pastor fell into trouble the people should, 'in a lawful course' and 'not by tumult', defend him, both 'by their speeches and by their purses and by their friends'. In return, ministers were to be active 'in catechising and instructing' their flock; 'secondly, in administering the sacraments unto them; thirdly, in reading and expounding the scriptures unto them; fourthly, in praying for them; fifthly, in giving a good example unto them'. Thus, while the minister was bound 'to reprove sharply when he seeth just occasion', his 'very reproof must be in love because they have to do with their brethren'. Ministers must learn humility, even as they took the laity to task for their sins. Again, the minister had a duty to anticipate and prevent the objections of the laity to his doctrine.

> This preventing of objections is very necessary; first, in regard of the wicked to prevent sin in them, for indeed it is no small sin to contradict God's truth delivered by God's ministers ... secondly, the preventing of objections is necessary in respect of the godly, as namely to prevent scruples in their consciences. How subject are tender Christians, when they hear the word preached, to take scruple applying that to themselves which belongs only to the wicked.

For their part, the people should 'bear with such ministers as are earnest against the corruptions of the time'. They should be 'less cavillous against the word' than at present they were, thus freeing the minister from answering 'frivolous objections' against his preaching.[13]

Here, therefore, was a perfectly integrated model of lay/clerical relations, a model which Denison saw exemplified in his own relations with the Juxons. He had been their client, even their dependent, living in their house for twelve years, yet at the same time they had been his spiritual charges, consulting him and deferring to him in all matters religious, doctrinal or spiritual. In return, Denison had figured prominently in John Juxon's will. He left 'my special friend Mr Stephen Denison' an income of £10 a year and gave him a leading role in administering the alms houses he was founding in Mortlake in Surrey where he had recently built a new house. Denison was also included in a list of prominent puritan divines from the city, including Richard Sibbes, Elias Crabtree, John Spendloe, Mr Culverwell and others, all of whom were to receive £4 each to attend Juxon's funeral. On this evidence, then, Juxon's obsequies in which Denison was to appear as the star turn, preaching the sermon, was to be something of a godly *fête*, a demonstration both of Juxon's connections with the leading lights of London clerical puritanism and of the city-wide links and solidarities that bound the London puritan community together. Thus, Juxon also left a series of bequests to a number of city lectureships – All Hallows in Lombard Street, St Margaret's in New Fish Street, All Hallows the Great in Thames Street (where Denison was a lecturer), St Mildred's in Bread Street, 'the church at Little East Cheap' and the St Antholin's lecture (which last bequest was settled for life on Spendloe).[14]

On this evidence, Denison had really 'arrived' as a presence in puritan London, and he had done so in part through the Juxon's patronage, first associating himself with the intense personal piety and godly charisma of Elizabeth Juxon and then with the material resources and status of her husband – both connections asserted, first, through the ritual display of the godly funeral, and then, again, through the more permanent medium of print. Denison's pastoral and pulpit style might make him enemies, then, but it also, as we shall see below, won him a considerable following amongst the laity. But even Denison was forced to concede that the ideal combination of subtle reciprocities, of myriad transfers of mutual esteem, and material and spiritual support that he had achieved with the Juxons was unlikely to be often repeated. For the current state of the world ensured that 'ministers should cry shame against the abominations of the times surely much more now, for never was the world more full of corruption'. But that same parlous situation also meant that such rebukes would inevitably meet with opposition and resentment from the laity. Again, while the minister should certainly seek to head off the objections of the people to his doctrine, in present circumstances, 'he had need to be as wise as Solomon, that should be able to prevent all objections which cavillous people will make against the truth at these days'.[15]

It would appear that those last remarks contained an element of special pleading on Denison's part as he struggled to lay the blame for the adverse, as well as the positive, response to his ministry anywhere but on his own shoulders. Indeed, it may be that the somewhat idealised picture of lay clerical relations proffered in Denison's sermons represented an almost perfectly inverted mirror image of his own somewhat less than ideal experiences in St Katharine Cree. We have already noted the adverse response to his powerful preaching of some of his audience. To this evidence can be added certain tensions about the control and finances of the living, which was owned by Magdalene College, Cambridge and leased by the college to the parish, and was run, before 1622, by a general and, after that date, by a select vestry. According to the claims of the vestry men, in a later Chancery case, the curate's pay was a matter for private treaty between the incumbent and the vestry. However that may have been, the curate was clearly not a mere tenant of will for, as we shall see below, even as they suspended and then stripped Denison of his living, the court of High Commission stood by his right to back pay, dating from the period before his formal suspension but long after powerful figures in the parish had turned against him. Certainly, financial arrangements like these were unlikely to foster harmony between Denison and the parish, or rather the vestry, who doubled as his flock and his employers. When in 1639 Denison remarked 'that the best service that a man serves, the best recompense he doth deserve' 'belongs to the ministers of God', he added the observation that when 'ministers speak in this kind they are presently suspected to preach only for themselves, though it be the will of God'. He was no doubt speaking from bitter personal experience.[16]

While no parish records survive from the period before 1640, judging from the vestry minutes and churchwardens' accounts of the 1640s and 1650s, money was always an issue. The minister was paid out of the surplus of the tithe money left after the rent had been paid to Magdalene. There were constant complaints about arrears in payment of tithes. In 1645 an attempt was made to rate the parish at £200 a year, £50 of which was to go to Magdalene and £25 towards the debts of the parish, while the remainder went to the minister. This would almost certainly have both increased and regularised the curate's income, but, probably in part because of that, almost immediately the scheme ran into trouble. 'Not liked by many of the parish', it was swiftly abandoned in favour of a system of voluntary contributions. When in 1655 an assistant was appointed to the curate, the issue of payment again provoked trouble. At first, it was agreed that the surplus of the tithe money and various voluntary contributions would be pooled and then divided equally between the curate Mr Palmer and his assistant Mr Good. However, it swiftly transpired that some parishioners would only pay towards the upkeep of Mr Palmer, while others would only contribute to Good. Thus 'by experience' this set-up was found to 'much obstruct the raising of a competency' for the ministers and it was accordingly scrapped in favour of an arrangement whereby the surplus tithe money (which in 1655 amounted to the princely sum of £28 4s 10d) went to Palmer and the quarterly contributions of the parishioners went to Mr Good.[17]

It is, however, clear, from a number of asides in court records from the earlier period, that the curate was not entirely dependent on the surplus tithe money. Thus, when Denison was suing for unpaid arrears of pay in the 1630s his quarterly income was estimated by the High Commission at £20, and elsewhere, during the dispute over Denison's successor in the living, it was claimed that 'the greatest part of the salary and payment of the said curate or minister doth arise and come, over and above the aforesaid usual tithes, oblations and other profits' from the contributions of the ordinary parishioners. What form these contributions took and how they were collected remains unclear. What does seem certain is that Denison was reliant for a good part of his income on the voluntary contributions of his flock and that the payment of those contributions was not altogether regular.[18]

Luckily, there were other sources of income open to Denison and his successors. There was the parish lecture, given weekly, and a monthly Saturday lecture to be given in preparation for the reception of the sacrament. This last, which brought in £8 a year, had been set up, and indeed settled for life on Denison, in 1621 by a female admirer, one Thomasine Owefield, to whom, along with 'all them which fear God in the parish', Denison dedicated the published version of his sermons on the sacraments. There he hailed her for her beneficence in endowing the lecture 'not for a year or two years, but for a thousand years, if the world continue so long'. In so doing, she had become 'a benefactrice to our parish, to God's church and to my self'. Thus in 1650 and 1651 (when the extant churchwardens' accounts start) we find the incumbent Mr Palmer being paid £8 'for the lecture' and £10 'for the monthly sermons or lectures'. In addition we know that Denison gave a regular lecture at Great All Hallows.[19] There were also the considerable perquisites of pick-up preaching; the going rate for stand-in sermons at St Katharine Cree in the 1640s seems to have been 10s a go. For more prestigious jobs, like the Juxons' funeral sermons, Denison probably received considerably more, as he very likely did for his sermon to the bricklayers that provoked such a derisive response from Rose Law in 1617. Thus, in 1623, the apothecary William Wells left 40s to Stephen Denison to preach his funeral sermon, while in their accounts for 1630/31 the Skinners' Company record paying Thomas Gataker 20s for his sermon 'on the election day', while in the same year the Grocers paid John Oldsworth, rector of St Peter's in Broadstreet, £2 for a commemoration of benefactors day sermon and Mr Thomas Saxby MA another £2 for preaching on their election day.

Certainly, as we shall see below, even after he had lost his major living at St Katharine Cree, Denison was able to keep body and soul together with the proceeds of his other preaching engagements, along with the bequest from John Juxon and whatever other perks and perquisites he had managed to extract from his lay favourers over the years. And these, it seems, may have been considerable; Mrs Juxon had rewarded the 'minister which was the means (under God) of her conversion' – Denison tactfully omitted to say whether he was the lucky man in question – with a gift of £50. When she was desperate on her deathbed to feel the further lash of the law, she had offered to confer on any minister able or willing to provide it 'a large reward in gold'. As Denison informs us, he certainly acted in that capacity, but again he omits to tell us whether or how much he profited from his efforts. Similarly, at their deaths various grateful parishioners left him more modest bequests in their wills. In 1631 the goldsmith William Avenon left Denison, in his capacity as 'the minister of St Katharine Creechurch near Aldgate', a bequest of £6 13s 4d. As late as 1648, Mr Chiverton, one of his former parishioners, arranged for Denison to receive an exhibition of £5 a year from the Skinners' Company.[20]

While living in the crowded world of early Stuart London clearly gave ministers like Denison plenty of opportunity to augment their incomes, it also placed them in an interesting relationship with the various flocks and auditories who also, of course, doubled as their patrons and employers. Certainly, when Denison did fall out with a powerful group of parishioners in the early 1630s, matters turned pretty quickly to money, with Denison not being paid, withdrawing his labour in reply and thus provoking a complaint against him in the church courts where it was alleged in October 1633 that 'he hath and doth neglect his cure and hath left the same unofficiated several sundays and holy days within this last six months last past'. Things had reached a head on the last two Sundays when 'his cure was altogether neglected' and 'no service or sermon was read or preached'. Apparently Denison had embarked on this virtual strike because 'he hath not competent allowance for the officiating the same'. This cut no ice with the court who told him 'carefully' 'to celebrate divine service and also preach and catechise as the canons of the church of England require and command him'. If he had complaints about his wages he was to seek redress through the courts.[21]

Thus, Denison's life, lived in day to day dependence on the goodwill of the laity, both in his own parish and in the wider London puritan scene, reminds one of nothing so much as Richard Bancroft's wickedly satiric portrait of the puritan clergy as 'trencher chaplains', utterly dependent for their living and status on the goodwill of the godly laity and thus virtually forced both to play to the popular crowd and to ingratiate themselves with the puritan gentry/merchant elite. Denison, with his initial dependence on the inherently 'popular' form of a general vestry for his job and on wealthy merchants and female admirers like the Juxons for his perks, seems to have combined both the populist and oligarchic elements of Bancroft's fantasy life in one career.[22]

Nor were the resultant strains only or even mainly a function of money. When in 1622 leading parishioners, with the help of Sir Henry Martin, chancellor of the diocese of London, sought to go from a general to a select vestry, issues of power, of ecclesiastical and secular jurisdiction, were at the centre of discussion. According to the petition from Martin Bond, Edward Lawes, Randall Crew and Martin Hall (one of the churchwardens), parish government was in disarray 'by reason of the dissent of some of the parishioners that resort unto their vestry'. They, therefore, called on the bishop to regularise what they claimed had been the *de facto* system of parish oligarchy that had been 'the usual custom for these 40 or 50 years last past'. They wanted him to appoint twenty-four men (with a quorum of twelve), all, for the most part, former churchwardens or constables, as a formal, self-selecting and self-perpetuating oligarchy to run the affairs of the parish. In acceding to this request, which he described as 'for the peace, good and quiet of the church and parish', the bishop was careful to delimit the areas of church jurisdiction over which the vestry could claim no power. Thus, they were told that they had no jurisdiction over the minister, about whom, if they had any complaints, they should refer themselves to the 'ecclesiastical or temporal magistrate'. They were not to meddle with the churchwardens' presentments or to arrogate to themselves any business 'determinable or punishable' by any ecclesiastical court. These were stock phrases and concerns, used habitually to defang the considerable erastian potential of such vestry jurisdictions. What was not conventional were the next two provisions. The first, as we have seen, made Denison's role as one of the twenty-four dependent on his reconciliation with those in the parish 'whom he hath wronged and offended'. The second insisted that if he 'should hereafter be admitted to join with the said vestry meeting ... then he [was] to have but his bare voice amongst them and not otherwise'.[23] Denison, it would seem, had been making trouble and this raises the question of whether the recent divisions in the parish, to which the request for a select vestry was a response, were in part a creation of the powerful preaching of Stephen Denison, with the truculence of those who 'resort unto the vestry' to cause trouble representing the divisive effects of Denison's pastoral style?

Confirmation that this was in fact the case comes from a deposition given by Denison to the court of arches many years later in 1636. Then, Denison recalled that he had always been opposed to the usurpation of power over the conduct of parish business 'which some of the parishioners, calling themselves by the name of vestrymen, have pretended wholly to belong to them'. Throughout his period as curate he had 'been very much displeased' with the arrangement set up in 1622 and 'hath diverse times told them that he conceived that they had no authority to challenge the choice of the churchwardens and sidesmen to belong only to them and to exclude other of the parishioners ... from having votes therein'. Indeed, Denison recalled, 'about twelve years sithence' (i.e. in 1624, only some two years after the select vestry had been established), 'upon some differences that happened between him ... and some of those that termed themselves vestrymen', he had complained to the bishop of London 'of certain abuses which this deponent [Denison] then conceived some of the said vestrymen had offered to this deponent and some others of the said parish, under pretence of a vestry which, as some of the parishioners affirmed, they had procured to be confirmed by the authority of the bishop'.

Bishop Montaigne, alerted to these abuses, on Denison's account at least, then 'caused some of the said vestrymen to be called before him at his palace in London', where, 'upon the debating of the business and differences between them', he decided that the 'said instrument should be taken away from the said vestrymen'. The offending document was delivered to the chancellor of the diocese, Dr Duck, who, in Denison's presence, in his 'chamber in Doctors' Commons', 'did break off the seal of the said instrument, whereby this deponent conceiveth the same was and is utterly made void and canceled'.[24] There is no record of such a removal of the vestry's powers in the Vicar-general's book and, judging from the subsequent conduct of parish business and indeed the course of the court of arches' case from which the deposition being quoted here comes, the subsequent conduct of parish business did not reflect Denison's view that the powers of the vestry had been dissolved. But what does emerge clearly from all this is that, from the outset, the select vestry had been set up against Denison's wishes, very likely in reaction to his attempts to dominate the parish and the divisive effects of his preaching style. Brought under control by explicit episcopal rebuke and a formal redistribution of power in the parish in 1622, Denison and his supporters continued to challenge the vestry's powers into the mid-1620s. Even by this early date in his ministry, then, Denison had clearly divided or helped to divide the parish. Of course, he claimed only to be at odds with some of the vestry and presumably in supporting the claims of other parishioners to a say in parish government he was able to draw on support from outside the ruling clique as well.

Indeed, there are some asides in his sermons that suggest a certain resentment on the part of Denison and his followers against some of the leading men of the parish. We can almost sense his frustration at his limited powers of spiritual discipline over the parish elite in the following denunciation of those who felt themselves too grand to offer themselves for spiritual examination before receiving the communion. 'Many ancient people, and many masters of families ... think to receive the sacrament without control, by reason of their antiquity, though they remain ignorant and profane. But let such obstinate persons remember, that though they be not turned back according to their just desert, yet they are guilty of the body and blood of the lord, as well as the most ignorant prentice boy that they keep.' 'You think it much', he told his auditory at another point in the same sermon cycle, ' to be reproved at a minister's hand for your sins, especially if you be grown rich and great in the world, but know it for your terror, that God will hamper the proudest of you, and if you come to be judged of him, woe unto you'. The potential levelling effect of powerful preaching and puritan godliness Denison-style on the traditional structures of status and authority in the parish could hardly have been more clearly spelled out. We can, perhaps, guess at the sort of response such reproofs drew from at least some of Denison's flock from his subsequent complaint against 'captious hearers, which repair to the church (the more is the pity), not so much with desire to receive any benefit, as to catch and entrap the minister in his speech'.[25]

Elsewhere, in sermons printed in 1622, he lambasted the

> folly of such as despise sanctified Christians. Many proud worldlings are lifted up, and exalt themselves above poor Christians, because they have borne all offices which some Christians have not. But understand ye, unwise amongst the people, the poorest Christian hath a more honourable calling than yourselves. You have borne office on earth, but a true Christian is set in heavenly places in Christ ... His calling is worth ten thousand of yours; yea, indeed, yours is not worthy to be compared to it.

As a remark dropped into a local context in which Denison and his followers were known to be at odds with certain leading parishioners – men who had indeed 'born all offices', like the haberdasher, vestryman, MP and coming man in the city, Martin Bond – that came very close to identifying and directly rebuking certain of his parishioners from the public pulpit. No wonder Denison had enemies.[26]

But if his antics in the pulpit provoked a reaction, he had the perfect reply. For Denison took it for granted that those most likely to react adversely to powerful preaching were the wicked and the reprobate. The elect, on the other hand, reacted very differently. Their attraction to powerful preaching might not be immediate, but it was certain. 'I doubt not but that many of God's own people may reject and lightly esteem a powerful minister, being carried away with a prejudicate opinion which they have of the person of the minister.' It is hard not to see in these remarks a direct comment on Denison's own experience in St Katharine Cree. Certainly, such a view might account for the initial hostile response of the likes of Rose Law to Denison's pastoral efforts. But such a situation would not and could not last, at least not where the truly godly were concerned. For Denison was sure that 'certainly God will reveal this unto them in time, and then they will repent their prejudice'. There were, however, others, 'tares in the corn field of God's church ... Therein be hypocritical professors as well as sincere professors and it is the brood of hypocrites especially which persecute God's ministers, having itching ears and will not endure wholesome doctrine; it is not the best sort of professors. This puts a manifest difference', Denison concluded in triumph, 'betwixt the children of God and others. God's children approve a powerful ministry, others, for the most part, do not.' All of which, of course, more than put his persistent adversaries in the parish in their place.[27]

On this basis, we can surely envision both pro- and anti-Denison groups in the parish involved in a dispute, in part at least, about lay/clerical relations and the proper distribution of power both between pastor and flock and amongst the laity themselves. Evidently the seamlessly smooth account of lay/clerical relations, the easy balance between lay zeal and clerical authority, achieved at the level of theory, in Denison's sermons, was a heavily idealised picture, even perhaps a piece of wish fulfilment, which, at best, bore only a tangential and perhaps even a symmetrically negative relation to Denison's actual experience in St Katharine Cree.

Whatever its relation to reality, at least at the level of theory, Denison's vision of the powerful preacher served to unite the Christian community, to integrate the community of the godly into the structures and ordinances of the national church and to affirm the status and authority of the clergy. But at almost every turn in the argument, Denison's view of the role of the word preached in constituting the Christian community contained elements and insights which seemed to subvert or call into radical question those same unifying, integrating and hierarchical tendencies.

THE POINTS OF CONTACT BETWEEN THE GODLY AND THE CHURCH:
II THE SACRAMENT

If that was true of Denison's attitude to the word preached it was no less true of the other focal point around which he organised his vision of the godly community – the sacraments. We have already seen that when he was forced to compare the two, Denison rated the word preached above the sacraments. Preaching provided the central task for the minister of the word and the crucial means whereby the godly community was created and sustained. This, however, did not prevent Denison from talking of both the sacraments in the most exalted language. 'By baptising with water', Denison intoned, 'are shadowed out unto us two things, to wit, the blood of Christ and the spirit of Christ.' In the sacrament of the altar Christ was offered to all. 'So verily as the minister reacheth out unto us in the sacrament the outward signs, so verily doth the father reach his son, with his merits, unto every believer, so that, as by the consecrating the elements is meant the action of God the father, ordaining his son to the office of mediatorship, so, by the delivering of the same, is meant the action of the same blessed father in exhibiting his son.' By 'eating the bread and drinking the wine' 'is meant', claimed Denison, 'such a kind of applying of Christ and his benefits unto ourselves as by the same applying our souls are fed and nourished'. Christ *was* present in the sacrament, Denison insisted, but 'representatively and sacramentally'; 'the body and blood of Christ are present in the sacrament virtually'. 'This bread is a lively sign and this wine is a lively representation of my body and blood.' If the covenant of grace, of which all the elect were beneficiaries, could be compared to a will, then the bequests contained in the promises of the gospel could be said to be authorised and activated by the seal of Christ himself present and applied in the sacrament.[28]

For Denison, the sacrament should be administered and received frequently. 'The Lord's Supper ought to be often administered and often to be received ... first, because it is a remembrance of the death of Christ and Christ's death cannot too often be thought upon and considered. Secondly, because it is the means of feeding and refreshing the soul, yea of confirming and establishing it ... Thirdly, the often partaking of the sacrament is a means of the often renewing of our preparation' and 'hereby we are made more careful to shun sin and to keep a clear conscience both towards God and towards men'. Denison's tract on the sacraments was, in fact, a published version of lectures given on the first Saturday of every month to prepare the congregation to receive the sacrament on the following Sunday. It seems likely, therefore, that by 'often' Denison meant at least once a month. Certainly, Denison was very critical of those ministers who allowed the sacrament to be 'hardly administered three times in a year'. 'A shameful neglect' he called that, and he was similarly sharp on the subject of those persons who, living in a parish 'where the sacrament is frequently ministered, yet are exceedingly negligent in repairing to God's ordinance'. 'How many be there', he lamented, 'which repair unto the sacrament at easter, either by custom or else by constraint, which are not for the sacrament all the year after?' To such neglect Denison attributed the fact that 'people live so loosely as they do. For if they knew a necessity of frequent receiving, surely then they would endeavour to keep themselves in a better temper, that so they might be always fit to partake of the sacrament. Yea, hence also it is that people do so much waver in their faith and doubt, because they take not the benefit of the sacrament to settle and establish them.'[29]

But Denison accounted unworthy receiving an even worse sin than infrequent reception. 'Unworthy receivers may be said to be guilty of the body and blood of the Lord'; 'the sin of unworthy receiving, even as rebellion against God, is compared to witchcraft', Denison declaimed. Moreover, for Denison unworthy receiving encompassed anyone who came to the sacrament ignorantly, unpreparedly or unrepentantly. The sacrament, he warned, only benefited Christians who 'come with a spiritual appetite'. If we brought with us 'bad humours' we would 'take away the strength and nourishing power of God's ordinance'.[30]

All this renders extremely dubious recent claims, made by Dr Bernard and others, to the effect that puritans or Calvinists played down or even minimised the role of the sacraments in the life of the church. Relative moderates like Denison, as well as radical puritans and non-conformists like William Bradshaw, paid great attention to the sacrament. This point has been confirmed by a recent article by Arnold Hunt and, as Hunt points out, makes nonsense of the claim that any increase in the frequency with which communion was administered should be taken as a sign of the growth of a non- or anti-Calvinist or even 'anglican' style of piety. But nor is it the case – as Hunt goes on to argue – that the enthusiasm of a Denison or a Bradshaw for the sacraments renders untenable any characterisation of Laudian or avant-garde conformist piety as distinctively sacrament centred. For it is only after a divine's attitudes to the sacrament have been integrated into his broader style of piety, situated within his larger vision of the economy of grace, that we can properly evaluate and characterise the resulting position in terms of the balance struck between the word and the sacrament, the grace of the sacrament and the grace of election. This is a task that is comprehensively shirked in Hunt's discussion of this subject and it is only because of his failure, indeed his refusal, to contextualise their statements about the sacrament into any wider picture of their styles of divinity, piety or affect and indeed into any discussion of their polemical images the one of the other, that Hunt finds it so easy to collapse the attitudes of both puritan and Laudian divines to the sacrament into some sort of undifferentiated 'anglican' soup. It is certainly not necessary, as Hunt seems to think, to regard preaching and the sacraments as 'two different forms of religion' in order to make distinctions between the ways contemporaries related and weighed the relative significance of the two ordinances in their overall view of true religion and Christian worship.[31]

In Denison's case the nature of that balance was made crystal clear throughout his works. For him, the sacraments merely sealed and confirmed the grace already conferred by election and justification. Writing of the believer's duty to make his or her election sure, Denison spoke of the 'confirming and establishing power' of the sacrament. 'Indeed it is a true rule', Denison intoned, 'sacraments do rather confirm grace where it is already, than confer grace where it is wanting.' In the case of baptism, he denied that the sacrament washed away sin *'ex opere operato* or by the work done. For Simon Magus was baptised ... and remained in the gall of bitterness and in the bond of iniquity, notwithstanding his baptism ... The whole multitude of Israel were baptised ... and yet with divers of them the lord was not pleased ... Ishmael was circumcised, as well as Abraham ... and yet remained a scoffer. Judas was a partaker of the passover, as well as Christ himself and yet remained a traitor.'[32]

Baptism, it was true, was the seal upon our entrance into the church and Denison described 'the estate of the church here below as being, indeed, the kingdom of Christ'. But he warned, 'the entrance into this kingdom is no easy entrance, for indeed the gate is straight, as Christ himself saith of it'. True entrance into the church came, therefore, not so much through baptism as through repentance and amendment of life. 'After we are entered into this holy city or kingdom we must not think to live loosely, as in former times, but we must come to a more strict course of life.' Baptism, clearly, was not enough; it had to be activated, rendered effectual by subsequent repentance. And when our baptism was rendered effectual through a true repentance we should thank God for it. But the normal route to repentance, that is, 'an effectual change in mind wrought by God himself in the hearts of the elect', was 'by the means of preaching of the word'. Here, therefore, was the rationale both for Denison's exalted language applied to the sacraments and his decisive ranking of them as secondary, confirming ordinances behind the primary ordinance of the word preached and the grace conferred by election, justification and conversion. Thus, at one point, pursuing his parallel between the covenant of grace and a will or bequest made by Christ and sealed by the sacraments, Denison claimed that 'baptism without the word [that is, preaching] is like a seal without writing; a seal without writing is a strange kind of deed, even so is baptism without the word a strange sacrament'.[33]

Denison performed a very similar manoeuvre in his account of the relations between the communion and the word preached. Just as the effectiveness of baptism was dependent on a repentance worked subsequently in the true believer by the word preached, so a crucial element in the right receiving of the sacrament stemmed from the recipient's knowledge. 'Two things are especially condemned in unworthy receivers', Denison explained: 'first, ignorance and secondly, want of reverence. The ignorant person doth not discern the body of Christ for want of knowledge and the unreverent person doth not discern the body of Christ for want of respect.' Such ignorance was damnable; 'the ignorance which the Holy Ghost condemneth is the not discerning the Lord's body ... and this kind of ignorance is sin indeed, yea, a greater sin then every one takes it to be. Why were the people destroyed but for want of knowledge?' Denison asked. And knowledge, of course, came primarily from the word. If he or she 'wouldst have knowledge', Denison explained, the true believer should seek it humbly, with a true fear of God, praying the while for it and thus, having prepared him or her self spiritually, become actively 'conversant in the hearing and reading of God's word'. In short, knowledge, reverence and faith came usually by hearing and the sacraments served merely to confirm and strengthen those attributes and spiritual gifts, not to confer them. Certainly the sacrament's efficacy would not merely be stymied, the sacrament itself would be rendered spiritually lethal, if it were received without the knowledge, faith and reverence which the word (and especially the word preached) could alone confer. 'It is', he concluded, 'a wretched ignorance to live ignorant under a powerful minister, or in a Christian family.'[34]

The sacraments, then, were enthusiastically enlisted by Denison as necessary aids and appendices to the word preached. Ordained by God himself, they demanded both our respect and our attention. The fact that 'God is the author of the sacraments' 'must teach us highly to prize and esteem of the sacraments; we must not look so much upon the outward elements, which seem to be weak and simple, but we must look upon them as things ordained by God himself and that for excellent ends and purposes'. Elsewhere, having defined baptism in largely symbolic terms – it was, he said, 'a sign and seal of our union with Christ', 'of our regeneration and new birth', 'of the pardon and remission of our sins' and as such certainly not necessary to salvation – Denison claimed that if the negligence of parents in not having their newborn progeny baptised as quickly as possible might not 'condemn the children' yet it would surely condemn them; 'for the willful neglect of any to receive the sacrament, when they might have it, is damnable'.[35]

If baptism could be said to be 'the means of our admission into the congregation of saints', then the sacrament of Christ's body and blood could likewise be said to signify 'the action of faith whereby we lay hold of and apply unto ourselves Christ Jesus and all his benefits'. Approached with the properly 'spiritual appetites', accepted with the 'hands of faith', not those of the flesh, the sacrament would confer a series of magnificent spiritual benefits on the true believer or elect saint. It 'puts us sacramentally in mind of Christ', Denison explained. 'It renews our communion with Christ', 'it nourisheth our souls to eternal life', 'it moveth us to often renew our covenants with God' and it is 'an especial means to nourish love amongst the brethren'. 'It is', he concluded, 'a blessed condition ... to be strong in the Lord and to feel the power of increased strength.' And, if Christians came to the sacrament devoid of the sort of 'bad humours which take away the strength and power of God's ordinance', they should find 'by blessed experience that the body of Christ, sacramentally received, giveth strength like a staff of bread'. Denison was still singing the same song in the late 1630s when he observed 'that the sacrament of baptism is a good means to convey grace where there is none. So the sacrament of the Lord's supper, though it do not confer grace where there is none before, but it confirms grace where it is already begun.'

In this mode Denison could talk of the power of the sacrament in terms almost as exalted (and as carnally explicit) as any Laudian. 'As the wine is pressed out of the grape in the wine press, even so the blood of Christ was pressed out in the wine press of the cross ... so that our blessed lord Jesus thought nothing too dear for his church, not his blood, not his precious blood, no, not the least drop of his dearest heart's blood, he thought it well bestowed, so that his elect thereby might be redeemed'. 'Applied by a lively faith', the 'blood of Jesus Christ' thus 'doth quench the spiritual thirst of', indeed 'doth comfort and rejoice' 'the soul'. Having set the sacrament within the basic parameters of his predestinarian, word-based style of piety and public worship, then, Denison could wax lyrical on the spiritual benefits to be derived from the often partaking of the sacraments. His position was thus far from the logocentric, predestinarian aridities attributed by some modern scholars to the Calvinistically inclined puritan godly. On the contrary, like nearly all his contemporaries, Denison was intent on striking a balance between word and sacrament; it was just that in his case, when all was said and done, his remained a decidedly word-centred balance.[36]

Just how word-centred emerges even more clearly from Fleming's notes from the sermons of the late 1630s. For in a number of passages recorded there, Denison more or less equated the effects of what he termed generally 'God's ordinances' with those of the word preached. Thus he spoke of our 'happiness to stand before the ministers of God in the use of the ordinances to hear God and Christ opened to us'. Again the beauty of the Lord and his presence in his church was made evident, he claimed, by 'faithful preaching'. He spoke movingly of the readiness of the 'tender heart' of a true Christian 'to receive any divine impression from the ordinances of God, of fear, of holiness, of obedience. It is ready to receive any impression from the seal of the word of God. We may receive good by the word of God, by hearing of it, by meditating of it. It is a great blessing if we have a heart so fitted to receive grace and benefit from any ordinance of God.' The move made there, almost subconscious and certainly unacknowledged, from any ordinance of God to the word and in particular the word preached and back again is redolent of Denison's wider priorities and assumptions.

Dilating on the need for all true Christians to obtain the spirit of God, Denison actually ranked in order of importance the means whereby this could be done. Since the greatest obstacles to receiving the gifts of the spirit were blindness and ignorance, he explained, 'we must be conversant in the diligent hearing of the word of God, Acts 10.44'. Ordinarily 'God did breath his spirit from sabbath to sabbath, from time to time, by virtue of the sound preaching of the word.' This, however, was not the only means whereby we could obtain the gifts of the spirit. 'Prayer is an excellent means to get the spirit, as to pray the mind into a heavenly frame, so to possess us of the blessed spirit of God Luke 11.13. So if we were more frequent in prayer we should be more full of the spirit.' Prayer here, of course, included private as well as public, extempore as well as set prayer. Indeed all of Denison's texts are remarkable for their failure to distinguish between these different sorts of prayer. But if prayer was an 'excellent means' to get the spirit, he described the sacraments, which came next on the list, as only 'a good means to obtain it'. At the end of this discussion, Denison came to the fairly anodyne conclusion that 'therefore if we will receive the blessed endowment of the blessed spirit of grace we must be constant in the use of all the ordinances of God'. All ordinances were necessary, therefore, but it is hard to escape the impression that for Denison at least some were more necessary than others.

There was a balance implied in all these passages and indeed throughout Denison's works between the word (both preached and read), prayer (both public and private) and the sacraments, and Denison's version of that balance gave clear and consistent primacy to the word preached. In this, as in so much else, he was entirely typical of contemporary puritan attitudes. Certainly in the light of this evidence, the offhand omniscience of Hunt's claim that contemporaries like Nehemiah Wallington 'would not have recognised' the 'distinction between word and sacraments' seems merely bizarre. If he spent any time listening to or reading the works of ministers like Denison, as we know that he did, Wallington (along with the rest of the London godly) can have been only too familiar with the distinction.[37]

Thus for all the universalist language into which he slipped with such ease, particularly when dealing with the sacraments, Denison was in fact able to enlist the sacraments to confirm and underwrite, rather than to undercut or soften, his potentially very divisive (and word-centred) vision of the community of the godly. Precisely because unworthy receiving was such a heinous sin and precisely because the sacrament could not so much confer as only confirm grace already vouchsafed to the elect, Denison used the reception of the communion as yet another occasion to call the believer to the anxious examination of the self for the tell-tale marks of a saving faith. Here, as so often, the whole thrust of Denison's position was from the external to the internal; Christians were not to content themselves 'with external privileges' – baptism, the reception of the sacrament, the hearing of the word, the title of a Christian – these were 'but the shell as it were'. True professors must not settle for the outward forms but labour inwardly 'for regeneration, for sanctification, for sound faith to apply the blood of Christ unto thyself, for these are the things signified and these are the main'. We are back, therefore, to the anxiety-ridden examination of the self for the tell-tale marks of saving faith and the grace of election. For Denison the sacrament became yet another jumping-off point for those processes of self-examination and spiritual stocktaking whereby the would-be saint pursued a genuine assurance of his or her own salvation.[38]

Such self-examination should take place both before and after receiving the sacrament. To prepare adequately beforehand, communicants should examine themselves 'by the rules which have been set down concerning knowledge, faith, repentance and charity'. Afterwards, since the 'sacrament worthily, preparedly received doth bring great nourishment to the soul', all diligent professors should examine themselves for tell-tale traces of the sacrament's improving effects. Denison posed a series of questions for the zealous Christian who wanted to know whether he or she had 'received Christ or no' in the sacrament.

> Do you find that the strong man is cast out? ... Do you find the image of Christ renewed in you in righteousness and true holiness? Do you find that you walk in Christ, that you live in the spirit, that you follow his directions and not your own foolish spirit? Then assuredly you have received Christ. But if it be contrary with you, that you still follow the lusts of your ignorance, that you still remain destitute of the image of God, that you walk not in Christ but every one doth that which is good in his own eyes, then rejoice not, neither be ye liars against the truth for you never received Christ, though you have received the sacrament a thousand times.[39]

Thus was the reception of the sacrament – ostensibly the central occasion upon which the social unity of the Christian community should be publicly confirmed, celebrated and strengthened – converted into yet another means by which the godly could heighten their own consciousness of themselves as elect saints and thus separate themselves off from their less godly neighbours. Denison seems to have been well aware of the tensions and difficulties inherent in this position and he took active and explicit steps to deal with them in his sermons. Thus, he went out of his way to explain that, despite the natural enmity that pertained between the godly and the profane and the almost inevitably unworthy reception of the ungodly, the godly and the

Stephen Denison

ungodly could and should receive communion together. For, while it was true that the unworthy communicant 'doth pollute the sacrament to himself', it was not the case that his unworthiness could pollute the sacrament 'to all the rest' of the congregation. This doctrine effectively confuted 'those of the separation which refuse our sacraments ... because ... swearers, adulterers, drunkards and such like are admitted to the sacrament'. It also served to 'comfort the tender conscience' of the godly person, alarmed by the presence at the sacrament of 'some whom thou fearest not to be so well prepared as they should'. Here was a fit subject for grief but no reason to abstain from the sacrament, for 'his being there shall not prejudice thee; he eateth and drinketh damnation only to himself'.[40]

This, of course, was to introduce the mutual hostility of the godly and the ungodly into the very act of reception. Denison was well aware that this might seem to contradict the principle (confirmed by the prayer book) that Christians should only present themselves at communion if they were in charity with their neighbours. This, however, was not the case. For, Denison explained, since, in this world, tension between the godly and the ungodly was inevitable, to insist that the two groups be in charity before communion could be administered was to render it effectively impossible ever, in good conscience, to minister or to receive the sacrament. If, therefore, the godly could sincerely assure themselves that 'the wicked do hate us and persecute us, not for any wrong that we have done unto them, but because we follow goodness and for religion sake', then it was all right to ignore this rent in the social body of the Christian community and communicate anyway.[41]

THE POINTS OF CONTACT BETWEEN THE GODLY AND THE CHURCH: III THE SABBATH

If the word and sacraments were the two central public ordinances around which Denison organised his vision of the godly community, they were followed by a close third such ordinance – the sabbath. Denison was a strict sabbatarian, citing the fourth commandment in order to denounce any form of secular recreation on the Lord's day as a sin. 'I am taught [by the fourth commandment]', he wrote, 'to rest upon the Lord's day from mine own worldly thoughts, words and actions and much more from sin and to learn to celebrate that day to God's glory in works of piety and also in works of mercy and that both publicly and privately.'[42] Just how strictly Denison interpreted this injunction is clear from his funeral sermon for Elizabeth Juxon. He did not merely condemn 'men servants and maidservants' for 'haunting taverns and alehouses' and behaving adulterously and wantonly upon 'the very day on which they have been at the blessed sacrament'. On the contrary, for Denison the mere fact of the young Mrs Juxon's habitual 'walking up and down, sitting at her gate', 'talking of worldly matters and such like' on the Lord's day had been a sure sign of her unregenerate state before her conversion.[43] In Denison's view the whole day should be devoted to God; 'the holy keeping of the sabbath is a means to hallow us the better for all the week after, whereas the profaning of the sabbath is the cause of profaneness and ungodliness, if God be not more merciful all our life after'. Keeping the sabbath holy was, therefore, a crucial means of furthering the cause of true religion. The godly 'knew by experience the infinite benefit of God's sabbath', Denison claimed in 1626. Put negatively rather than positively, 'take away the sabbath and farewell all religion'. In his Paul's Cross sermon of 1619 he had included 'depraving the sabbath', along with popery, Arminianism, anabaptism and familism, in a list of heresies and enormities worthy to be suppressed by the magistrate. In the intermittent lists of notorious sins contained in Fleming's sermon notes, sabbath breaking was always at or near the top of the list. Here was a doctrine and a practice of the very essence of true religion.[44]

As with both the word and the sacrament, sabbath observance straddled the divide between the public ordinances of the church and the private devotional practices of the godly. On the one hand, sabbath observance was a publicly enforceable duty; Denison dedicated his first Paul's Cross sermon of 1619 to the Lord Mayor of London in part because of the latter's 'singular care of God's sabbath, that it may not be profaned by the lewdness of men'. On the other, their 'strictness or holy curiosity' in keeping the sabbath was a crucial aid to and mark of the godly's separate status as true saints of God. Denison listed the observance of the sabbath first in a list of 'means to godliness' which went on to include all the various spiritual exercises characteristic of the godly. Conversely, he claimed 'that it is a sure mark of an ungodly person to be a sabbath breaker, as, on the contrary, it is an evidence of godliness conscionably to celebrate it to God's glory'. He cited Mrs Juxon's devotion of the whole day to religion, her rising before six, even in the midst of winter, to attend a sabbath day lecture in the city, as a sure sign of the genuineness of her conversion. Thus, he concluded, 'if we desire to be truly godly, we must be careful to keep the sabbath'.

While, as Dr Parker has usefully pointed out, virtually all English protestants of the period would have agreed that 'keeping the sabbath' was a good idea, as we have seen, what Denison meant by that phrase greatly exceeded what many of his contemporaries meant by it. In that sense, neither contemporaries nor later historians have been wrong to see a Denison-style sabbatarianism as a distinctively puritan trait during this period. For Denison and other puritans the sabbath joined the word preached and the sacraments as one of the three uniquely scriptural ordinances around which both the public life of the national church and the private devotions of the godly community should be arranged.[45]

DENISON AND 'MODERATION'

In Denison's works, therefore, we have an almost perfect example of what I have styled elsewhere a moderate puritan style of piety or divinity. The unabashed Calvinism of his attitude to predestination; his use of the anxiety-filled gap between the objective fact of the double decree and the subjective experience of the individual Christian in order to develop an activist style of piety, combining a stridently voluntarist rhetoric, with an unashamedly predestinarian theology; the dominance of his view of the visible church by preaching; his near obsession with sabbath observance; his view of the Christian community as radically divided between the godly and the ungodly; his *de facto* identification of the godly with both the elect and the church; his inversion of the common use of the term puritan as an insult, so that those thus insulted became the godly and those who used the insult became the ungodly – these are the defining characteristics of the style of piety under discussion, a style of piety put together in the universities and developed by university-trained ministers in the parishes during the 1570s and 1580s, and evidently still going strong in the London of the 1620s. The stability and continuance over time of that style of piety surely allow us, *pace* Dr Bernard, to identify, in both the universities and the parishes, something like a moderate puritan tradition running throughout the period.[46]

Nor was this purely a clerical phenomenon. If puritanism, as described above, can be found perfectly represented in Denison's sermons, we know that at least some of his listeners internalised the full lesson with enthusiasm and even joy. Nehemiah Wallington possessed at least one of Denison's printed works – his funeral sermon for Elizabeth Juxon – to which he appended comments to the effect that he had applied the 'tests and evidences ... that she did belong to God' outlined at the end of that book to his own spiritual condition and that 'upon examination, I find in some measure and can lay claim to them and so I endeavour and strive to follow as they did follow Christ'.[47] Henry Roborough, who served as Denison's right-hand man in his campaign against Etherington, was also Wallington's parish minister at St Leonard's Eastcheap. Wallington and Denison then moved in the same circles and, in fact, Wallington, as he has been described by Professor Seaver, provides us with the perfect lay analogue for Denison's style of piety. Here is the puritan lay person precisely as he or she could now be extrapolated out of, or was indeed constructed at the time by, Denison's sermons.

Wallington's style of piety, his values and priorities, parallel almost perfectly those laid down in the pulpit by Stephen Denison. Wallington's virtual obsession with the word preached, his inveterate sermon gadding and note taking parallel Denison's priorities. So, too, did his liking for 'powerful preaching', the full-throated denunciation of sin on which Denison so prided himself and which Wallington saw as a crucial, indeed, with the failure of presbyterian reformation, as the only way in which the sins of the city could be repressed and controlled and divine judgement averted. Thus he told a new preacher at St Leonard's Eastcheap that, though he personally found the minister's preaching style 'very sweet and profitable', it contained altogether too much gospel and not enough law. 'Some may sleep and die snoring in their sins for many years and scarce ever be awakened by so sweet preaching as yours is.' It behoved God's ministers, he informed another clergyman in 1650, 'to thunder out God's judgements against all horrible covenant breakers'. The results of clerical laxity were only too apparent to Wallington by the 1650s. 'Oh the contempt of the gospel, the breach of protestations and covenants and not a minister's mouth opened to reprove any of these sins, except a few despised presbyterians, as they call them.' Here, at least, was one layman who had internalised Denison's vision of the nature and worth of 'powerful preaching'. On this evidence, we should clearly resist the assumption that attitudes and behaviour in the pulpit like Denison's could only alienate or provoke the laity. For Wallington, at least, nothing could have been further from the truth.

But if Wallington agreed with Denison on the power and importance of preaching – he was certain, as Professor Seaver puts it, that 'sermons, not sacraments, were the ordinary vehicle of grace' – he also shared Denison's exalted view of the sacrament. In the late 1630s Wallington was receiving the sacrament 'as often as occasion is offered' and thereafter received, just as Denison recommended, at least monthly. Again, just as Denison prescribed, the period both before and after communion became yet another occasion for an intense examination of his spiritual state, and during periods of spiritual dryness Wallington found himself much 'troubled in mind' that he could perceive so little benefit derived from his assiduous sacramental devotions. To quote Professor Seaver, for Wallington, 'preparation for the sacrament in fact became simply another occasion for self-examination'. And yet, of course, there was more to Wallington's sacramental devotions than that. As he wrote, describing what he was about in going to communion,

> Lord I am going to that ordinance wherein I expect to have communion with thyself and the communication of thy chief mercies to my soul in Jesus Christ. Yea, I am going to set the seal of the covenant, on my part to renew my covenant with thee. I am going to have communion with the saints, to have the bond of communion with all thy people, to be confirmed to me that there might be a stronger bond of union and love between me and the saints for ever.

For Wallington, then, as for Denison, the sacrament was secondary to the word preached but nonetheless central to his devotional life, linked as it was both to his own style of experimental predestinarian introspection, on the one hand, and to his broader concept of the communion of the saints, on the other. There could scarcely be a clearer object lesson in the need to integrate all the various parts of the puritan world view or style together. Puritan sacramentalism was puritan in large part because it was linked, on the one hand, to puritan subjectivity and, on the other, to a puritan sense of the community of the godly. Abstracted from that context it can no doubt be made to appear conventionally protestant (as, indeed, in many ways it was); what made it puritan was its place in a distinctively puritan synthesis or style.

As for that communion of the saints upon which the sacrament was a seal, Wallington viewed it in precisely the same polarising and dichotomising terms as Denison. The division between the godly and the ungodly was crucial to his view of the world and he tended to see the godly as in effect 'the saints', to worry intensely if any actions of his or his servants brought disrepute on the godly or the puritans, and to salivate with considerable satisfaction over the providential punishments visited by a just God on the sins of the ungodly. And here the need for a punctilious observation of the sabbath, precisely as Denison had defined the issue, bulked very large indeed in Wallington's view of what divided the public profession of the godly from that of the ungodly.

If Wallington's view of the godly community, and its relationship to the ordinances of the visible church and the ministry of the word and sacraments echoed, with almost complete accuracy, the views propagated by Denison in the pulpit, so, too, did the nature of his interior life or style of subjectivity accord with the norms of puritan experimental predestinarianism as Denison had expounded them. Certainly, towards the end of his life, Wallington had not only succeeded in imposing on his febrile emotional life the norms and forms of puritan spirituality, he had even managed to achieve a certain serenity and peace of mind in the process. For Wallington, at least ultimately, predestination, as it was glossed and purveyed by the likes of Denison, in association with the concomitant doctrines of assurance, perseverance and sanctification, was a comfortable and comforting doctrine.

But if his was a life patterned on the tenets and nostrums pedalled in the pulpit by the likes of Stephen Denison, Wallington was anything but servile in his overall relations with the ministry. Even here, of course, he was following Denison's tenets, distinguishing between powerful preachers and those who, through either conformist laziness and self-interest or a lack of moral fibre, failed to fulfil his and Denison's vision of what a minister should be. Here his own sense of his spiritual prerogatives as a godly lay person kicked in and allowed the otherwise rather timorous Wallington to write letters of sharp advice, admonition and reproof to a variety of errant clergy. When ministers were made of the right stuff, however, as was Denison's old ally against Etherington, Henry Roborough, Wallington was prepared to defer to their insight and authority on spiritual matters of the most intimate and personal nature. And yet he, too, as a lay person, experienced in the workings of the spirit, was quite prepared to fulfil the role of doctor of the soul, for which, in distress in 1621–22 he had resorted to Roborough, in his own later dealings with other troubled members of the godly community.[48]

In Wallington, then, we see a satisfied customer, an almost perfect product of ministries like that exercised by Denison. Puritanism as it was exemplified in Denison's works and Wallington's life appears as a stable, integrated system of lay/clerical relations, of formal doctrinal profession and personal piety and subjectivity, and of public profession and religious performance. As the examples of both Wallington and the Juxons show, relations between the puritan clergy and laity could go swimmingly.

But, if the identification of the resulting synthesis as puritan can be accepted as relatively uncontroversial, the extremity and even crudity of much of Denison's thought and language might well seem to call into question his claim to 'moderation'. The application of that term even to a man of Denison's intemperate diction and personality is based on the studiously moderate attitude he took, in public, at least, to the issues of external conformity, obedience and church government which have traditionally been taken to define puritanism. For, on those issues, Denison *was* moderate; more moderate indeed than the likes of Laurence Chaderton whose attitude to both subscription and conformity was a good deal more grudging than Denison's. Matters fundamental to true religion, Denison conceded, God had reserved to himself, 'yet in matters circumstantial he hath left great power to his church'. Thus the Jews had felt free several times to alter the external arrangements attendant upon the celebration of the passover, and the Christian church had similarly changed the manner in which the sacrament was administered since its first institution by Christ and the apostles. In externals and matters of ceremony the church was left free to do as it saw fit, limited only by the scriptural injunction to 'see things done by order'.

Admittedly, the word of God itself prescribed 'the best order and every true church should be ruled and guided thereby',[49] but Denison was careful to add that the examples provided by scripture, down to and including the practice of Christ himself, were only binding if they were accompanied by an explicit precept. 'Where Christ did not second his example with a precept, there he doth not strictly exact our imitation. The consideration of this point must teach us not to contend with our mother the church about matters of circumstance.' On the contrary, it was incumbent upon all Christians 'to study the peace of our mother the church and ... not be enemies to any lawful order established by her'. Elsewhere, Denison associated those who would indulge themselves in vain speculations 'about ceremonies and the government of the church' with papists and anabaptists; all of them enemies of true order in the church, who preferred their own idle speculations and inventions to the well-tried path of 'solid truth'. As one might expect, on this basis, Denison explained that for all his obligation to preach the word in season and out, a minister 'restrained from preaching by authority' must obey, comforting himself with the thought that 'God hath wrought by him and accomplished already the main work whereunto he sent him' and confining his pastoral activities to the writing and publishing of books for the edification of the brethren.[50]

While Denison's attitude on such questions was clearly designed to, at best, avoid and, at worst, cushion any collision between the precisian conscience and the demands of authority, it certainly did not betoken any particular, what one might term, *religious* enthusiasm for the ceremonies of the church as they were currently enforced. In one passage, Denison discussed the different physical postures in which the sacrament had been received in various churches since its first inception 'sitting or rather leaning' in the last supper. He stressed that kneeling was only one of a number of acceptable positions. The others included standing, 'walking, as in Geneva' and 'sitting, as by the Dutch'. Such insouciance was in marked contrast to avant-garde conformists like Lancelot Andrewes, John Buckeridge or the later Laudians all of whom sought to invest kneeling with a peculiar religious charge, as a distinctive and superior outward token of an inner awe and reverence. If Denison conformed, therefore, he did so on the lukewarm grounds of respect for authority and the need for order and obedience, not because he invested the particular ceremonies of the English church with any positive religious charge or significance.[51]

Nor did Denison's claims to 'moderation' end with his conformity. For his position was portrayed, again and again, as occupying a middle ground of orthodoxy; a middle ground which he located between the two extremes of popery, on the one side, and sectarian protestant heresy – familism, anabaptism, separatism – on the other. Predictably, Denison continually juxtaposed the central elements of his view of the world against what he took to be popish abuse and error. His predestinarianism, his insistence on justification by faith alone and his concomitant rejection of all concepts of free will or human merit, his obsession with preaching and identification of a detailed knowledge of scripture as a defining characteristic of a saving faith – all these were consistently juxtaposed against the papists' will worship, idolatry, priestcraft and deliberate perpetuation of lay ignorance. For Denison, popery was the very antithesis of true religion and the pope was Antichrist.

However, the threat posed by popery, on the right, was paralleled, on the left, by the threat of protestant sectarianism. Anabaptist and familist views on predestination, the perfectability of human nature after baptism and justification by works were all reminiscent of popery. Just like the papists, the sectaries were wolves in sheep's clothing; heretics and sect masters, they, no less than the papists, were hypocritical agents of Antichrist bent on leading the little

Ecclesiastical forms and political consequences

flock of Christ astray, all the while posing as good and zealous Christians. Denison pictured himself as a defender of the doctrinal orthodoxy represented both by his own writings and by the official formularies of the English church, against this dual Antichristian threat.[52]

NOTES

1 S. Denison, *An exposition upon the first chapter of the second epistle of Peter* (London, 1622), p. 83, the 'instrumental cause' of our calling 'is the word of God' ... and yet let us not limit the holy one; howbeit God doth most ordinarily call effectually by the preaching of the word, yet we acknowledge he is able to call, and that effectually, by other means; yea even without means, if it please him.' *Ibid.*, pp. 57, 145 on Antichrist; *The doctrine of both the sacraments* (London, 1621), p. 59, 'if a carnal minister stand in God's counsel, and cause the people to hear God's word, he may be the means to convert souls'.

2 Denison, *Sacraments*, pp. 63, 18, 46; *Exposition*, p. 121. In attempting to gauge the relative weight placed by Denison on the word and the sacraments it is notable how many of his most exalted statements on the ultimate superiority of the word come from his treatise on the sacraments.

3 Denison, *Exposition*, p. 190.

4 *Ibid.*, dedicatory epistle, sig. A4r.; pp. 176, 184; *Sacraments*, pp. 145, 212.

5 Denison, *Exposition*, pp. 123–4, 167.

6 Denison, *Exposition*, pp. 142–3, 115; *The monument or tombstone, or a sermon preached at Laurence Pountnies Church in London, November 21, 1619 at the funeral of Mrs Elizabeth Juxon* (London, 1620), p. 97; *Sacraments*, p. 179; American Antiquarian Society, Worcester, Mass., Denison sermon notes. Hereafter cited as Denison sermon notes, fol. 7r.

7 Denison, *Exposition*, pp. 19, 32, 118; *Monument*, pp. 97–8.

8 Denison, *Exposition*, pp. 181, 77; Denison sermon notes, fol. 90v.

9 L[ondon] M[etropolitan] A[rchives] DL/C/314, pp. 42–3, dated 28 March 1617/18. I almost owe this reference to the kindness of Arnold Hunt.

10 LMA DLC/C/341 (Vicar-general's book) fols 262r.–263r., dated 8 May 1622.

11 Denison, *Exposition*, pp. 137, 113; *Sacraments*, pp. 205, 61–2.

12 Denison, *Sacraments*, p. 200; *Exposition*, p. 4.

13 Denison, *A compendious catechism* (London, 1621), pp. 35–6; *Sacraments*, pp. 206, 204, 185, 187.

14 P[rerogative] C[ourt] of C[anterbury] 112 Hele; PRO Prob. 11/150/fol. 22r.–26v.

15 Denison, *Exposition*, p. 38; *Sacraments*, p. 186.

16 See below, chapter 9, 'The Walker and Wotton affair'. Denison sermon notes, fol. 79v.

17 G[uildhall] L[ibrary] Ms 1196/1 (vestry minute book of St Katharine Cree), fols 32v.–33r.; 70r.–v. Also see GL Ms 1198/1 (churchwardens' accounts from St Katharine Cree), unpaginated.

Stephen Denison

18 PRO C2/Chas 1/C81/63/1, dated 25 January 1635/6. *Ibid.*, S.P. Dom. 16/261, fol. 308r.

19 Denison, *Sacraments*, dedicatory epistle; PRO S.P. Dom. 16/281/32, copy of the deed, dated 15 October 1621, whereby Thomasine Owefield set up the lectureship in preparation for the sacrament.

20 For Wells' will see PCC Swan II, PRO Prob. 11\141, fol. 82r.–v.; for Avenon's will, dated 20 December 1631, see PCC St John 135; PRO Prob. 11/160, fols 522v.–524r. For Skinners' Company accounts see GL Ms 30,727/6, p. 416. For the Grocers' Company see GL Ms 11571/11, fols 424v., 425r. Denison, *Monument*, pp. 115, 108. For Chiverton's exhibition see GL Ms 30, 708/3, Skinners' Company court book, 1617–51, fol. 230v. On 1 August 1649, on Denison's death, the exhibition was transferrred to Dr Christian Sherwood. *Ibid.*, fol. 239v. I owe this last reference to the kindness of Ariel Hessayan.

21 LMA DLC/320, fol. 59v., dated 25 October 1633.

22 P. Lake, 'Conformist clericalism? Richard Bancroft's analysis of the socio-economic roots of presbyterianism', in W.J. Sheils and Diana Wood, eds, *Studies in church history*, vol. 23 (Oxford, 1987).

23 LMA DLC/C/341 (Vicar-general's book), fols 262r.–263r., dated 8 May 1622.

24 PRO S.P. Dom. 16/342/87, pt. V, fols 227r.–228v.

25 Denison, *Sacraments*, pp. 143, 181, 185.

26 Denison, *Exposition*, pp. 30, 82.

27 *Ibid.*, p. 117.

28 Denison, *Sacraments*, pp. 25, 111, 122–3.

29 Denison, *Sacraments*, p. 134. Also see *ibid.*, p. 85, 'there is a frequent need of often partaking of the body of Christ, in the sacrament, we must not think it sufficient, with carnal gospellers, to receive the Lord's Supper once or twice by the year'. Denison made the same point in *Monument*, pp. 75–6, 'that we may make our calling and election sure, we must frequently receive the Lord's Supper. What experienced Christian is there, but he is able to tell you that the sacrament, by God's blessing, hath a notable confirming and establishing power and therefore those negligent ministers are guilty of the weakness of the faith of the people, in that they do not, so frequently as they ought, administer the holy sacrament.' *Sacraments*, pp. 134–5.

30 Denison, *Sacraments*, pp. 142, 83–4.

31 Bernard, 'Church of England'; C. Haigh, 'The church of England, the catholics and the people', in C. Haigh, ed., *The reign of Elizabeth I* (London, 1984). For a recent and very sensible brief discussion of puritan sacramentalism see Webster, *Godly clergy*, pp. 112–21. Also see P. Lake, 'William Bradshaw, Antichrist and the community of the godly', *Journal of Ecclesiastical History*, 36 (1985). This makes all the odder Arnold Hunt's assumption that it is conventional wisdom to regard the sacraments and preaching as representing 'two different forms of religion' and to equate the former exclusively with 'Laudians` and the latter exclusively with 'puritans'. Certainly presented, as it is in Hunt's article, as a characterisation of my position, this is entirely inaccurate. See A. Hunt, 'The Lord's Supper in early modern England', *Past and Present*, 161 (1998), quote at p. 75.

32 Denison, *Monument* , p. 76; *Sacrament*, pp. 39–40 'indeed it is a true rule, sacraments do rather confirm grace, where it is already, than confer grace, where it is wanting'.

33 Denison, *Exposition*, p. 100; *Catechism*, p. 12; *Sacraments*, pp. 45–6.
34 Denison, *Sacraments*, pp. 158–62.
35 *Ibid.*, pp. 68, 10, 15.
36 *Ibid.*, pp. 10, 112, 84, 69, 86. Denison sermon notes, fol. 42v. For a control group against which Denison's relatively restrained language on this subject might be compared see the discussion of Lancelot Andrewes and John Buckeridge's treatment of the same issue in P. Lake, 'Lancelot Andrewes, John Buckeridge and *avant garde* conformity at the court of James I', in L.L. Peck, ed., *The mental world of the Jacobean court* (Cambridge, 1991).
37 Denison sermon notes, fols 57r., 53r., 20r., 22r. Hunt, 'The Lord's Supper', p. 55.
38 Denison, *Sacraments*, p. 40.
39 *Ibid.*, pp. 105, 118, 91. Also see *Catechism*, pp. 6–7.
40 Denison, *Sacraments*, pp. 155, 156–7.
41 *Ibid.*, p. 76.
42 Denison, *Catechism*, p. 32.
43 Denison, *Sacraments*, pp. 163–4; *Monument*, pp. 89–90.
44 Denison, *Exposition*, pp. 57–8; *The white wolf or a sermon preached at Paul's Cross, Feb.11 ... 1627* (London, 1627), pp. 53, 70; *The new creature. A sermon preached at Paul's Cross, January 1619* (London, 1619), p. 39.
45 Denison, *New creature*, epistle dedicatory to Sir Sebastian Harvey, Lord Mayor of London, sig. A3v.; *New creature*, pp. 68, 26, 57; *Monument*, p. 90. K. Parker, *The English sabbath* (Cambridge, 1988).
46 See Lake, *Moderate puritans*, esp. chapter 7.
47 Wallington's manuscript notes to this effect are to be found, dated 1648, on the blank page opposite p. 124 of the copy in the British Library, shelf mark BL 1418 i 19. I owe this reference to the kindness of Paul Seaver, Retha Warnicke and Eric Carlson.
48 P. Seaver, *Wallington's world* (London, 1985), *passim*, but see esp. p. 107 for his rebuke to the independent minister; p. 109 for Wallington's role as spiritual counsellor; pp. 35–7, for the Lord's Supper, quote at p. 36; pp. 143–4 on puritans as 'the children of God'; pp. 131–2 on worry about the public image of the godly; pp. 60–1, 56–7 for delight in the bad ends of the profane, particularly sabbath breakers.
49 Denison, *Sacraments*, pp. 70–2, 216–17.
50 *Ibid.*, pp. 73, 217; *Exposition*, pp. 137, 121–2.
51 Denison, *Sacraments*, p. 72; Lake, 'Avant-garde conformity'.
52 Denison, *Exposition*, pp. 137, 112; *Tombstone*, p. 22; *White wolf*, pp. 8, 23–5, 48–9.

Part II

John Etherington

Chapter 4

Denison and Etherington or was John Etherington a familist?

THE MULTIPLE CONTEXTS OF DENISON'S SERMON

It was in his Paul's Cross sermon against Etherington that Denison was most explicit in his equation of the popish and familist threats with 'Arminianism' and it was also in that sermon that he used the figure of the errant boxmaker, Etherington, as a familist firebrand, in order to present himself as a bulwark of order and orthodoxy against the threat of sectarian heterodoxy. Now the nature and circumstances of that sermon's production and publication repay detailed consideration. On the one hand, *The white wolf* needs to be set in the local, almost subterranean, context of Denison's altercation with Etherington and the stresses and strains within the London puritan scene of which that confrontation was a product. That will be done *in extenso* below. But there is also another, altogether more exalted context, in which the sermon needs to be set, one centred on the high politics of the court, the parliament house and the episcopate.

For Denison was a bit player on that stage as well. Two years before he appeared at the Cross to denounce Etherington, Denison himself had been publicly humiliated at the same venue. On 13 Febuary 1625 two books by the recently deceased puritan minister of Bermondsey in Southwark, Edward Elton, were publicly burned at the Cross. The two books in question – Elton's *God's holy mind*, a catechetically organised explication of the ten commandments, and a pendant *Plain and easy exposition of the Lord's Prayer* – were dispatched to the flames as 'scandalous and seditious, tending to innovation and to the subversion of the religion and piety which is received among us'. According to a newsletter to Joseph Mede of 18 February the books had been burned for 'containing schismatical doctrine of the Lord's day and the administration of the sacrament'. The errors attributed to Elton included a denial of the lawfulness of private communion, a number of extreme sabbatarian opinions, a ban on marriage with papists, suspect notions about the validity of infant baptism and a denunciation of the use of the Lord's Prayer and music in the worship of God.[1]

The scene, perhaps predictably, tickled the fancy of Richard Montague and John Cosin, who crowed in their correspondence about the 'goodly fire our sabbatarian heretics made at the cross'. 'It is well the books made a fire, though not all I doubt. But they are not burned that made the books', was Montague's typically acerbic comment.[2] Nor was the affair limited in its effects to the trashing of the posthumous reputation of poor Elton. Thomas Gataker, a leading London puritan minister, was imprisoned in the Fleet for having written a fairly anodyne letter of commendation to Elton's book, a letter that, as Gataker later complained, had, in fact, been couched in the most hedged and general terms. Having secured his release, via the good offices of the earl of Manchester, Gataker found himself placed under house arrest again and suspended from his ministry 'by his majesty's special command'.

This was serious stuff; what appears to have been happening was a court manoeuvre, aimed, as Gataker claimed, at 'others far greater than myself, even the Archbishop himself' or rather his chaplain Daniel Featley. Montague and Cosin certainly both blamed and targeted Featley. 'Were not the Dr's [i.e. Featley's] brains made from the pap of an apple, that would allow such stuff to the press?' Montague jokingly asked his fellow conspirator, Cosin.[3] Predictably, it was Featley who found himself on the carpet in front of the king for having licensed Elton's books and yet another recent puritan publication by one William Crompton. Behind this attack on Calvinist licensing policy were John Cosin, fingered later by the printer as the moving spirit behind the seizure and destruction of almost the whole print run of Elton's books, and Bishops Neile and Laud, who figured prominently in a later account of Crompton's tribulations at court.[4]

We have here an attempt to discredit Featley and, behind him, surely Abbot himself, as puritan fellow travellers, men prepared to connive at the printing of typically puritan errors of the sort with which Elton was charged at the Cross. To find the context which prompted this attempt we need to look at the recent course of theologico-political manoeuvres at court. The charges against Crompton and Elton seem effectively to have linked together the issues and paranoias attendant upon the end of the fuss over the Spanish match and the beginning of the fuss over the allegedly Arminian works of Richard Montague. For, while both men were alleged to have said that it was unlawful for protestants to marry catholics, Crompton's book has the look of a reply to Montague's first effort at Arminian propagandising, the *New gagg*. At stake in all this was the nature of official licensing policy, the conventional parameters of which were being deliberately tested by Montague's activities. Indeed, even as Montague and Cosin congratulated themselves over the events at the Cross, they were also discussing the safe passage through the press and the licensing system of Montague's second 'Arminian' book, his *Appello Caesarem*. In the assault on Elton and Crompton and, through them, on Featley and Abbot, Laud, Neile and Cosin were playing on James' fears of a populist puritanism, opposed to his policies over the Spanish match, determined to start a war with Spain and to disgrace Montague. The objections against Elton and Crompton dealt both with popery, the quintessentially puritan shibboleth of the sabbath and, in Crompton's case at least, the issues of church government and outward conformity. While the doctrine of predestination did not play any part in the charges against either man, it did figure quite prominently in Laud's definition of 'doctrinal puritanism', drawn up as a handy guide to the current ecclesiastical scene for the duke of Buckingham, at exactly this time. Indeed, Laud's 'little treatise' on this subject is mentioned in precisely the same entry in Laud's diary that discusses his reading over Crompton's manuscript answers to the charges laid against him. Crompton emerges from the affair as some sort of client or suitor for the favour of the duke and Laud may have been got in by James to explain to the favourite precisely what was wrong with having such men attached to one's coat tails.[5]

Caught on the edge of these events was none other than Stephen Denison. 'A little book of Mr Denison's' was burnt with Elton's two works at the Cross. According to Gataker, Denison was also suspended from his lectureship at Katharine Cree, 'for maintaining that in Mr Elton's posthumous book about the lawfulness of private communions'.[6] Denison had, it seems, with what we shall see below was a typical pertinacity and lack of tact, horned in on the dispute and, by publicly supporting the doctrine of the departed Elton, merely got himself into trouble with authority. No doubt it did his standing in certain godly circles no end of good – and Denison made a habit of playing to the godly gallery, as we shall see – but insofar as Denison was used to marketing himself and his opinions as the epitome of order, orthodoxy and protestant rectitude, it can have done his public stock and self-image no good at all.

Coming on the heels of this earlier humiliation, Denison's assault on Etherington at the Cross and then in print allowed him to more than regain lost ground. No longer the denounced, Denison could preen himself on this most public of stages as the officially sanctioned denouncer, the very personification of orthodoxy and order in the struggle against sectarian heterodoxy. Nor was Denison's vindication limited to an evanescent, albeit delicious, moment of revenge at the Cross; the printed version of his diatribe was dedicated to the king and contained fulsome praise of both the High Commission and the archbishop of Canterbury, all of whom, Denison claimed, had stood four square behind him in his struggles against Etherington.[7]

As late as May 1628 Denison was still receiving plaudits for his rout of

Etherington, for it was then that he received from his alma mater, the university of Cambridge, the degree of D.D., with the grace book being signed by many of the Calvinist luminaries of that university, including John Preston and Samuel Ward.[8] In short, Denison's altercation with Etherington was the occasion for a complete personal rehabilitation or vindication. Moreover, as we will see below, certainly in its printed version, the sermon at the Cross allowed Denison to revisit his views on both the sacrament and the sabbath, not to mention the relationship between repentance and justification, for all of which he had received public rebuke in the recent past. In short, it must have been very sweet indeed for Denison to visit his revenge on the unfortunate boxmaker in 1626/27.

But *The white wolf* served other than Denison's purely private purposes. In a sermon preached at Paul's Cross, and subsequently printed, dedicated to the king and ostensibly backed by the archbishop of Canterbury and High Commission, Denison was able triumphantly to equate Arminianism with both popish and sectarian error. He did so, firstly, by a process of name calling, listing the several kinds of 'mystical wolves breeding in England', starting with 'popish wolves', and then proceeding through 'Arminian wolves' to 'rosy-cross wolves' before finally arriving at the various sorts of 'familistical wolves' to which Etherington himself belonged.[9] Secondly, Denison embarked upon a process of more precise theological identification – as we shall see, one of the errors of which Denison accused Etherington was a frankly Arminian account of the doctrine of election. Nor was Denison merely freelancing here; we know that he worked hard to get the book dedicated to the king. As we shall see below, Sir Henry Martin, the chancellor of the diocese of London, had played a crucial role in managing Denison's dispute with Etherington, and it was to Martin that Denison turned as he struggled to get *The white wolf* dedicated to Charles. In response to Denison's importunities, Martin wrote to Sir Robert Harley to intercede with his father-in-law, Secretary of State Conway. Harley, of course, was also at this date a client of the duke of Buckingham. In short, the whole episode is redolent of the continuing connections with the establishment that were still open to the godly during the 1620s. Indeed, we have here yet another example of the integration of puritans and Calvinists in the early Stuart establishment. For here are zealous London ministers, like Denison, high-ranking ecclesiastical lawyers, like Martin, the archbishop of Canterbury, the Calvinist George Abbot, and the court of High Commission, prominent parliament men like Harley and royal officials like Conway, all uniting behind the campaign against poor Etherington.[10]

We have here very much the same alignment of forces, the same politico-theological groupings, whose hold on power had been under attack during the Elton/Crompton/Denison affair of 1625, now using the Denison/Etherington altercation to strike back very publicly, affirming the orthodoxy of their

Calvinist doctrinal opinions and their own status as bastions of order, orthodoxy and obedience, against the genuinely subversive sectarian threat represented by Etherington and his allegedly Arminian opinions on the theology of grace. Their ability to do this was a direct function of the course of national politics. For in 1626–27, with hopes of parliamentary supply for the war effort still far from dead (particularly amongst Dr Cust's 'moderate counselors'), there were elements in the regime anxious to put their most reformed face forward, and the opportunity offered by Denison's assault on Etherington to represent the establishment, from Charles himself down, as protecting the doctrinal purity of the English church from the threat of Arminianism – a threat identified here not with the problematically respectable figure of Richard Montague but with the unequivocally subversive person of John Etherington – must have been too good to miss.[11]

On one view, therefore, the whole affair was an astute and carefully stage-managed exercise in anti-Arminian and pro-Calvinist, indeed, even pro-puritan, politicking. To a cursory observer, concerned primarily with national politics, with the rise of Arminianism and the Calvinist reaction to that rise, it might appear that we are dealing here with the exploitation of an obscure local dispute as the occasion for a sidelong but sensationalist attack on Arminianism. That, however, is far from being the whole story. For whatever political and polemical forces dragged the affair into print in the first place, the result was the exposure to very public view of a dispute the nature and significance of which cannot be reduced to national politics and the clash between Arminianism and Calvinism.

In fact, what seems to have happened is that national tensions and controversies about Arminianism dragged into the limelight a dispute between different elements in the London puritan community that in different, 'more normal', circumstances, might well have been kept within the closed world of the conventicle and decided by the unofficial court of godly opinion and rumour. However, what was thus accidentally exposed to view was something that historians of early Stuart religion very seldom have the chance to analyse – a dispute between a puritan minister and a lay member of his flock. We are getting here, I shall argue below, a direct glimpse into the otherwise hidden underworld of London puritanism. But to discover just what was at stake in all this we need to examine more closely the accusations levelled by Denison against Etherington, and the basis of those accusations in Etherington's own position, a position which we can reconstruct, at least in part, from an apologia written in prison in 1627 and published in 1641 and from a variety of books of anti-separatist polemic that Etherington published throughout his life, starting in 1610 and ending in 1645.

CHARGE AND COUNTER CHARGE

Let us start with what Etherington was supposed to have done. According to Denison, Etherington had, five or six years previously, thrown over his calling as a boxmaker and 'frequented private conventicles ... taking upon me, within the time articulated, to be the chief speaker and to instruct others, not being of mine own family, in points of doctrine and matters of faith'. Etherington, Denison conceded, pretended to admonish 'only your neighbours and friends, besides your own family'. But he 'took your neighbours and friends in a very large sense, for did not your followers come out of many parts of the city as duly to hear you upon every thursday and mostly upon the Lord's day, as good Christians come to a public lecture?' Again, while Etherington claimed that these meetings were private ones, held only for prayer and the worship of God, Denison would have none of it. For him they were 'public', open to people not personally acquainted with Etherington who merely wanted to hear the boxmaker expatiate on his dangerously heterodox doctrinal obsessions. 'For were your private meetings only for prayer or to worship God or rather to oppose divine truth and seduce?' 'In your meetings have there not been discussions against the morality of the sabbath, whether the church of England be a true church? Whether our ministers have a right calling? Whether the two books of the apocryphal Esdras be not as holy as any other, particularly as the books of the canonical Ezra? Do any good Christians need to discuss such and the like questions? Or is this your repeating of sermons to edify one another, as you pretend?' 'Instead of being edified' attenders at Etherington's conventicle 'were ... drawn into a faction, speaking evil of the public ministry and only applauding you and such like and did not they not trouble other sound professors and endeavour by all their power to seduce them? Witness those that have been assaulted by you and many others in the city that took notice of you and your proselytes. I verily think hundreds.' Etherington, in short, had used his 'public meetings' and his considerable number of 'followers' to vent 'poisonful doctrine' abroad thus causing 'an altercation in the city' that had become a matter of public knowledge. In short, he had become a sect master or semi-professional prophet. In that role he had encroached on Denison's monopoly within the parish. According to Denison, 'many tender conscienced Christians in my parish have been tampered with ... and solicited to Etherington's conventicles'. Once there, they were brought by Etherington's 'spiritual enchantments to despise the church, to reject the public ministry thereof or, at least, to cease to esteem and believe it'. In other words, they were alienated from Denison and infected with what he took to be 'expositions contrary to the received opinions of this our church of England'. 'They do meet together to censure the ministers, to contradict the doctrine.'[12]

But what particular errors had Etherington spread amongst Denison's flock? To begin with, he had asserted that no true church existed other than 'that which consists of lively stones, meaning by his church of living stones his own factious company, as all schismatics understand none but themselves, whensoever they speak of the true church of Christ'. Secondly, he appropriated to himself and his followers the power of the keys, 'falsely interpreting that in Math 18.7 "tell the church", that is, saith he ... tell it to those little ones born of God'. Thirdly, 'he arrogateth to his church the knowledge of infallibility in judging concerning the members of the same'.[13] In other words, Etherington and his company equated the true church with the elect and claimed that they themselves were elect saints and, as such, able to tell the regenerate from the unregenerate. Moreover, they used that capacity to call in question the authority of ecclesiastical officers of whose spiritual status they were unsure, claiming that 'bishops and ministers, as they are consecrated in the church of England, are not so much as members of the church'. On this basis, Etherington preferred the private meetings of his own conventicle before the public ordinances of the national church. Indeed, in those meetings Etherington cast doubt on whether the church of England was a true church at all.[14]

In matters of doctrine, Etherington and his company confounded 'reprobation and damnation, making the foresight of man's folly and wickedness to be the cause why God preordains any to condemnation'. They denied the sacraments all but symbolic significance. In particular, Etherington spoke 'contemptuously of baptism, terming it elemental baptism ... He holds no other baptism to be of any virtue but that which he calls the baptism of a thousand tears.' In short, Etherington 'allegorised' the sacraments, as all familists did, claiming that 'neither confers nor confirms grace to the heart of any'. Finally, Etherington denied that the observance of the sabbath could be grounded on the moral (rather than the ceremonial) law; for him 'the true morality of the sabbath' consisted 'in a mystical resting from sin'. Accordingly, 'neither Etherington nor his followers make any conscience of working in their ordinary trades upon that day, or of buying and selling and the like'. Etherington also claimed that repentance must precede justification and held that the book of Esdras was a canonical rather than an apocryphal text.[15]

In response, Etherington denied that he had ever abandoned his lawful calling to earn his living as a prophet or minister. He had, he explained, indeed given over his career as a boxmaker some years before, not to become a sect master or prophet but to make his living through the manufacture of water conduits and pipes. While he still made the occasional box to help make ends meet, he had never gathered a sect or conventicle. He did not, however, deny that 'for these five or six and thirty years, since the time that it pleased God, of his gracious goodness, to call me from the pleasures of the sins of my youth to seek him, I have given my mind, with earnest desire of my heart and prayer unto God, to read, hear and understand the word of God to the end that, understanding the truth and way of life contained in the same, I might walk therein all the days of my life, to the honour of God and my own comfort and salvation'. This was a practice that Etherington justified in terms of the fundamental spiritual obligations and rights of every Christian. 'For I remembered that Christ commanded to "search the scriptures" and, foretelling of the abomination of desolation that was to come, warneth his people that who so readeth should understand and how he doth pronounce them blessed that read and hear the words of his prophecy and keep those things which he hath spoken, because the time of his coming is at hand.'[16]

This, though, was not so much a solitary as a collective exercise and, accordingly, Etherington explained, he had felt obliged to share what small elements of spiritual enlightenment he had achieved with others, as indeed all true Christians should. 'As God vouchsafed to show his grace and mercies unto me and give me understanding in the same, his truth and way of life so I have endeavoured to impart that which I understood, with admonition, to my wife and children, neighbour and friend, desiring in my heart and praying unto God in secret that he would vouchsafe the same grace unto them.' This was, however, by no means a one-way traffic, with instruction flowing down from Etherington the prophet or sect master to his followers. Rather, it was a reciprocal process of mutual instruction and edification that took place amongst the godly.

> This I confess I have done, though in great weakness, and so as holding it always a special point of wisdom to be more ready, in this respect, to receive then to give, to hear than to speak. And I confess I have not been in all this time of thirty five years so conversant and sociable with the profane multitude of the world as I have been with the sober and well disposed, the wise in heart. I have desired to converse with such especially above all other, wheresoever I have come to talk and confer together of the word of God, which we have either heard or read, or had in our hearts and memories, edifying one another in the faith and hope of eternal life. This on the first day of the week and so daily as opportunity might permit.

In behaving thus, Etherington explained, he had not thought himself to be doing anything extraordinary or subversive. 'All which I suppose the meanest Christian of the lowest degree or place that is may do and that it concerneth him as much as it doth any other, though never so great.'[17]

Thus Etherington invoked the language of edification and the spiritual growth in grace of the godly – a language that, of course, was central to the world view, rhetoric and day to day activities of puritan ministers like Denison – to justify his own practices, practices that Denison had chosen to excoriate as illegal conventicle keeping. In the face of that accusation, Etherington suddenly went all coy. 'If in this I have offended against the law of the church of England, I have offended it', Etherington conceded. 'But I do suppose, nay, I verily believe there is no law in this Christian kingdom now at this time, forbidding these things.' For such laws were a mark of popery.

> In the times of papistry it was not held lawful for the scriptures to be in the English language nor for the lay people to read the same. But thanks be to God, it is not so now, those days of desolation are shortened in this realm ... the scriptures wherein the light of truth and way of salvation is contained and held forth, which, by Antichrist and his church hath been so long obscured, are, by the laws and authority of this land, translated into our own native tongue and, by the same authority, all men, young and old, have free liberty to read and consider the same, to talk and confer thereof, one neighbour with another.[18]

It was in this same spirit that Etherington glossed his own remark that 'Caesar may command a place for the public [worship of God] ... so he forbid none in private.' Denison had taken that to mean that Etherington regarded the meetings of his own conventicle as of at least equal importance as the public ordinances of the national church. This Etherington denied; he had merely been asserting and defending 'the liberty that every Christian hath to worship God, to pray unto him and do him service at all times and in all places, everywhere, even in our secret chambers, with humble and contrite hearts, lifting up pure hands, as the scriptures speak'.[19]

Etherington similarly denied that he had ever equated his own conventicle or sect with the true church of the elect. He did, indeed, define 'the true church of Christ' as 'the true regenerate servants and people of God, sanctified in heart by faith in Christ Jesus, lively stones, built upon the rock of Jesus Christ, the chief corner stone'. Under questioning by two of Denison's lay acolytes, he had further explained that neither the whole church of England nor any parish in it nor, indeed, any 'private company with myself' could be equated with the true church of Christ. God alone 'knoweth who are his'. 'For although all be not saints that are in the church, as touching the outward estate and society thereof, yet as touching the true spiritual communion, all are saints that are of it and are one body and one bread, being all made partakers of that one bread Christ Jesus and baptised by one spirit into one body and made to drink into one spirit.'[20] This was merely to employ the same distinction between the visible and invisible churches that, as we saw in the previous chapter, was central to the world view and ecclesiology of puritan ministers like Denison.

Thus in England, Etherington continued, 'all of all degrees and callings in the whole kingdom whose hearts were sanctified by faith in Christ Jesus were the true church of Christ here of England'. As for the visible church, he had maintained that 'there was never any church, generally considered as it was outward and visible to the eye of man, but some, yea many times the most part, and of the greatest of them in most eminent place in the church, as well of the lowest and meanest, have been unfaithful, ungodly, unholy and so not of the church, though they were in it'.

But, for all that the church of England could not be equated with the true church, Etherington was in no doubt as to its status as a true church, indeed as a very eminent true church indeed. 'The church of England, as it was by the authority of princes and by law established', he asserted, 'to be the best reformed, so generally considered, this day in the world.' Indeed, he believed that 'God had a special respect unto it above any one nation or kingdom whatsoever and that he had many faithful servants, sons and daughters therein and much people to save, for whose sakes the rest do fare well and are the more happy.'[21] As a practical demonstration of his good opinion of the church of England, Etherington was able to cite his frequent attendance 'at the public assemblies and sacraments' of that church 'for nearly twenty years last past before my imprisonment ... and I never was in any private assembly in my life where I have either received the sacrament myself nor seen it done by others, so that for mine own part I am neither schismatic nor separatist'.[22]

Etherington cited this same conventional distinction between the visible and invisible church to gloss his claim, made in his book of anti-anabaptist polemic, that 'the outward ordination of a minister doth not make a true and faithful minister'. This had not been intended as a repudiation of the orders of the English church. Etherington was only too happy to admit that 'outward ordination' made 'a lawful minister outwardly' 'so as that he may lawfully minister and people may lawfully receive the word and sacraments with him'. It was not, however, enough to make him 'a true and faithful minister inwardly. In God's accounts he may be a deceiver, a false prophet, an Antichrist, notwithstanding which they that are true in God's account, called and sanctified of him by a more special, heavenly, inward calling may not, for they are built upon the rock, the gates of hell shall not prevail against them.'[23]

For the most part, therefore, Etherington simply repudiated Denison's charges of anabaptism and heresy. And he did so, moreover, by invoking doctrines and arguments that were entirely familiar to orthodox Calvinists and mainstream puritans like Denison. But, even on Etherington's own account, this was not *just* a case of maliciously mistaken identities. Etherington did not deny quite all of Denison's accusations. On the contrary, there were certain issues – the relationship between repentance and justification, the efficacy of baptismal grace and the sabbath – upon which Etherington admitted that his opinions diverged from those of Denison and upon which he was prepared to stand his ground. Therein, he claimed, lay his real offence and it was on this basis that Denison and his followers accused him of indiscriminately defaming the ministers of the church of England. Etherington replied that it was not the ministry of the English church that he was attacking but merely some doctrines taught by certain ministers within that church and that certainly there was a considerable difference between criticising the English church or English clergy *tout court* and disagreeing with Stephen Denison and his curate.

This, however, was a distinction that, Etherington lamented, was lost on both Denison himself and his lay acolytes. When Susan Price, 'a woman greatly devoted to Mr Denison' and 'many such women and some men also as unwise as they', accused him of saying that 'the church of England teacheth false doctrine', what they really meant was that he had had the temerity to disagree with Stephen Denison. For that act of defiance Denison had denounced him for months from the pulpit, his lay followers had tried repeatedly to induce him to utter heretical or schismatic opinions before witnesses and Denison himself and his friend Sir Henry Martin had finally trapped him in the toils of the High Commission court.[24]

Thus, where Denison pictured Etherington as a dangerous sectary and familist, Etherington presented himself as an ordinary, zealous son of the church of England, who had dared to question some of the opinions canvassed as orthodox by the public ministry of Stephen Denison. Moreover, in staking out that position for himself, Etherington was careful to cite a good many doctrines that were dear to the heart of Denison himself. Etherington, in short, certainly did not sound like a separatist or an anabaptist. Nor did he behave like one. Both Denison and Etherington agreed that their disagreements were first brought to the notice of the ecclesiastical authorities by Etherington himself. Tired of hearing himself denounced every week from the pulpit, he complained, first, to Sir Henry Martin, the chancellor of the diocese of London, asking him to 'appoint that the things of difference in opinion ... might be heard before some ministers'. Martin brushed Etherington's request aside with the words, 'you have brought me here a strange petition, I know Mr Denison to be a very honest man, I know not you, I will not send for him dic ecclesia'. Etherington then took his case to the bishop of London and thence, fearing that Denison's friendship with Martin would stymie his case again, to the archbishop of Canterbury. On Etherington's account at least, Abbot at first seemed favourably disposed towards him – characterising Denison's complaint against the boxmaker as a 'scrawl of strange things ... so contradictory one to another as never was known to be in any heretic whatsoever'. The archbishop gave similarly short shrift to Denison's claim that he could assemble witnesses to back up his accusations and was about to let Etherington 'clear himself upon his oath'. Accordingly Etherington gave 'unto the register office full answers upon oath to all Stephen Denison's articles'. It was only at that point, Etherington claimed, that Denison, seconded by his friend Martin, raised the spectre of familism, 'affirming that I ... would forswear and deny all things in public which I held and did in private' and repeating his earlier claim that 'he had twenty witnesses that will swear against him'.

In having recourse to the accusation of familism Denison was playing a polemical card of some potency. Familists were members of the family of love, followers of the Dutch mystic Henry Niclaes. As the researches of Christopher Marsh and others have shown, by the second half of Elizabeth's reign there were familists at court as well as in relatively heavy concentrations in parts of rural Cambridgeshire and elsewhere. They were notorious for a variety of doctrinal errors (free will, human perfectibility in this life, mortalism), all of them anathema to the godly, and for their almost complete nicodemism. Concentrating on the inner dynamics of 'the love', members of the family managed to empty of spiritual significance outward conformity to almost any form of public religion and so felt able both to conform to any sort of religious establishment, while keeping their real beliefs and practices an almost complete secret from prying outsiders. All this, together with some rather potent friends in high places, rendered them both extremely difficult, if not to detect, then certainly to convict and they were seen as all the more threatening because of that. By the late 1570s familism had become a byword for sectarian excess and, by the 1620s, as Dr Marsh has shown, the familists' status as such greatly exceeded any very precise sense of what it was that real familists (if any such still existed by this relatively late date) actually did or believed. Thus in deploying the accusation that he was a familist against Etherington, Denison was pulling out the heavy polemical artillery and it worked.

The testimony of Denison and Martin combined to turn even Abbot against the boxmaker and 'his answers to the articles' accordingly 'never came to the view or hearing of the court'. Denison told a much shorter version of the same story, claiming that it was Etherington's complaint against him that had forced him to demonstrate to the authorities 'what just cause I had as a pastor to forewarn my flock of such seducers'. There was some later dispute between the two men as to who had resorted first to the penal sanctions of the law. Etherington claimed that it was Denison who, with the help of his friend Sir Henry Martin, had brought the case before the High Commission. He had merely wanted to 'have things heard in peace and ended without law' before first the bishop of London and then the archbishop of Canterbury but Denison 'prevented me' 'to the Archbishop' and 'got letters missive granted to sue me in the court'. Denison, however, would have none of that, citing Etherington's own works to prove that the box maker had 'complained against me 1. To Sir Henry Martin, the Chancellor to the Bishop of London. 2. To the bishop of London himself. And thirdly to the archbishop of Canterbury.' This, Denison claimed, had left him with no choice; 'being complained of by you for my preaching against your unsound opinions, I could not do less by way of apology for the clearing of my own innocency but show the causes that I had so to preach. And thus I was drawn in by yourself into a cause of law, whereas, if yourself had not begun, I should have thought it sufficient for the safeguard of my flock to confute your opinions in public and to leave you to God and to his ministers of justice to correct you for your errors.' Thus, in effect, both men agreed that it was Etherington not Denison who had first involved the ecclesiastical authorities. Things may then have escalated out of his control but if Etherington was (still) a familist or the leader of an underground congregation of separatists or anabaptists, this was very odd behaviour indeed.[25]

Moreover, as we shall see below, there are very strong hints, dropped throughout Denison's own account of the affair, that many London puritans deeply disapproved of the extremity of Denison's dealing with the poor boxmaker, feeling that he should have interceded with him in private and tried to wean him from his errors rather than denouncing him to the authorities and thus washing the godly's dirty linen in public. Viewed from this perspective, *The white wolf* was as much an attempt to win back Denison's standing in godly quarters as it was an intervention in a national debate about Arminianism in high places.[26]

Finally, if we examine Denison's rendition of his opponent's supposed heresies, there are clear marks of fabrication and exaggeration. Both the books from which Denison culled Etherington's allegedly familist or anabaptist opinions are extant. Ironically both were works of anti-anabaptist and familist polemic. The first had appeared under Etherington's initials in 1610 and he unequivocally accepted it as his own work. The second was ostensibly by one Edmund Jessup, but Denison alleged that Etherington had, in effect, written it, a claim which Etherington seemed to accept, remarking with apparent pride that it had been 'published in print with licence of the bishop of London being first viewed over by himself and, by his appointment, by Master Crashaw, then minister of Whitechapel, who did also approve of the same and subscribe to them, which is well known to be true'.[27]

We can, therefore, check Denison's rendition of Etherington's opinions against what Etherington and Etherington/Jessup actually wrote. The results do Denison little credit. Thus, the passage equating the true church with the godly community built only of lively stones was culled from a long passage in which Etherington used a conventional rendition of the division between the visible church and the elect remnant within it to counter what he took to be the separatists' confusion of the two. Again, Etherington's remarks on the power of the civil magistrate to command a place for public worship were part of a longer defence of the magistrate's authority over things indifferent; an authority which Etherington claimed came from God and to which obedience was owed in God's name.[28]

Similarly, a passage which Denison cited to prove that Etherington would conform outwardly to any church government, even that of the pope, in fact came in the middle of a passage devoted to proving the axiom that all

Christians were obliged to obey the powers that be.[29] Again, the passage Denison cited from Etherington/Jessup's book to demonstrate Etherington's Arminian sympathies was culled from the midst of a long confutation of the quintessentially Arminian claim that God conditionally willed the salvation of all men in return for their repentance and belief in the gospel, and an equally vehement defence of a gratuitous divine decree, made 'before all time', electing a finite number of 'particular persons' 'to grace and life'.[30]

Etherington himself noted Denison and his friends' creative way with a quote. Thus when Denison's 'curate', Henry Roborough, accused Etherington of being the author of a book published in 1588 called *An epistle to the church of Rome* and of holding certain errors contained therein, Etherington replied, firstly, that he could not have been the author, having been 'not eighteen years of age' in 1588 and, secondly, that the quotation upon which Roborough's accusation turned had been torn out of context and then mangled out of all recognition, 'so that Henry Roborough doth here also declare himself to be a very evil minded man in several respects'.[31] On this evidence, there can be no doubt that Denison and his supporters were seriously distorting Etherington/Jessup's views, culling quotations and errant remarks from a variety of sources and glossing them in the most incriminating possible senses. Even Etherington's persistent protestations of conformity to the rites and ordinances of the national church ended up as grist to Denison's mill. By a wonderfully circular logic Denison did not deny the truth of these claims, rather, he enlisted them to support his case against Etherington: what after all could one expect from a familist but a nicodemite conformity in externals? Denison asked.[32]

WHAT ETHERINGTON REALLY THOUGHT

But if we should not simply accept Denison's characterisation of the Etherington of the 1620s as an anabaptist or familist, neither should we merely reproduce Etherington's account of his position as it was written in prison in the 1620s and published in the 1640s. We have a good deal of evidence for the nature and evolution of Etherington's thought over the previous half century, culled from his anti-anabaptist pamphlets of 1610 and of 1623, the reply to Denison of 1626/27 and two later anti-anabaptist and familist pamphlets of the 1640s. Taken together they show us precisely why, for all his exaggeration and logic chopping, Denison might have had good reason to think that he could make the charges levelled against Etherington in *The white wolf* stick. Indeed, they show that Denison's accusations may actually have been, in some rather important senses, 'true'. But more significantly, a close study of Etherington's position/s and, indeed, of his exchanges with Denison, serves to throw considerable light onto the London puritan and sectarian underground of these years; a world of debate and discussion between all sorts of radical sectaries, separatists, familists and lay puritans, all engaged in argument each with the other and, of course, with the great rabbis of London puritanism, ministers and lecturers like Denison himself and their loyal lay followers, rich merchants like the Juxons or more humble professors like Susan Price, who had turned, at Denison's behest, on poor Etherington.

What, then, can we make of Etherington's religion? In his pamphlet of 1610 the centre of his position was to be found where Denison located it, in his vision of a Christian community radically divided between the godly and the ungodly, and in a concomitant tendency to equate the true church with the community of the godly as he defined and recognised it.

> The church that the Lord doth build, [contended Etherington] consisteth of living stones and the gates of hell shall not prevail against that church or any one of the stones thereof ... For this church of Christ and every stone thereof is framed and fashioned from above, he himself is the foundation and chief corner stone. And all the stones of this building are his brethren, reborn and made anew, not in show but in very truth, not for a time but forever, not one of them shall ever fall off. They are all of them everlasting, as is their foundation whereon they rest and whose strength doth stay them up. Great privileges hath this church above all other, for to it he hath given the keys of the kingdom of heaven, to open and shut, to bind and loose. And where two or three of this universal church of Christ, consisting of stones of life, are gathered together in his name he hath promised and will not fail to be in the midst of them ... And where two of them shall agree in earth upon anything, whatsoever you shall desire it shall be given you (saith he) of my father which is in heaven.[33]

Conventionally enough, Etherington held that the individual Christian 'may be certainly assured of reconciliation with God and that his name is written in the book of life and sealed there by an indelible covenant before the moment or hour or day of his death'.[34] As for the spiritual condition of others, that too could be judged by the practical fruit of their profession. Such a judgement must not be superficial or sudden, based on externals, a merely outward profession of Christianity, since reprobates might be 'baptised' and called 'by the names of holy brethren, partakers of the heavenly vocation, etc., insomuch as they were made partakers of the Holy Ghost and consented to that heavenly calling, being enlightened and tasting of that heavenly gift'. On this basis, such people might well be 'called holy in regard of these good beginnings, which was wrought in them whereby their old life was reformed'.[35] They would still, however, end up in hell. For all these were gifts common to the regenerate and the unregenerate. What distinguished the truly saved from their profane or hypocritical contemporaries was, firstly, the intensity of their inner life. Etherington wrote movingly of 'the washing of repentance and the purging of the Holy Ghost through Jesus Christ and faith in him which is indeed the true beginning of every living stone of his church and temple'.

'Whosoever received that word of faith', Etherington explained, 'did first unharden his heart, that is, did first repent, was lost and dead, crying and bewailing, with an unutterable desire of life, his sins and death. And these are the dead, which hear the voice of the son of man and live.'[36]

But, for Etherington, inner convictions and spiritual experiences, however intense, were not, in themselves, enough. The inward must find expression in the outward – in the second defining characteristic of elect saints, in what Etherington termed 'their fruit'. 'And if you ask what fruit that is ... it is love, even that new commandment, the perfection which the Lord commandeth, saying be ye perfect as your heavenly father is perfect. It is the first resurrection which whosoever attaineth is blessed and holy forever. They that attain to this end are blessed at the end of the world and blessed for evermore.' Here was the means 'whereby they know each other to be born of God. As St John saith hereby we know that ye are in him.' But if the godly were known 'either to other by their fruit' and the highest expression of that 'fruit' was 'love', that love itself found its highest and most characteristic expression in their relations with one another.[37] 'Indeed', Etherington conceded, 'many are called but these are they that are chosen, these love one another and thereby do they know each other to be born of God and to be loved of God and that they do love God.'[38]

In short, the love that defined the godly was to be found amongst the godly. At one point Etherington exhorted his readers to

> anoint our eyes with eye salve that we may see, even with the water of a dissolved and broken heart ... that we may discern between those that have but the form of godliness and them that have the power thereof; that we may see and know those little ones whom to receive, is to receive the lord, and to love them, whom to love, is to love the lord and to love the lord, is life for evermore. And this is that love without the which all knowledge and all faith doth but make us as sounding brass and tinkling cymbals. For by this love we shall know that we are translated from death to life and by this love we shall approve ourselves to the little ones to have that one peculiar faith with them, the assurance of the love of God unto us in Christ Jesus and of our reconciliation with God through him.[39]

Vast swathes of the ideological terrain being delineated here were shared between Etherington and Denison. Etherington's diction might differ considerably from that of his clerical assailant – and here the boxmaker's addiction to the rhetoric of 'love' is of particular significance – but in terms of substance a good case could be made thus far that they were in substantial agreement the one with the other.

It is in Etherington's account of the spiritual privileges of 'the little special ones', whose community was 'the New Jerusalem', in which the differences between his position and Denison's begin to show most starkly. 'And this is Jerusalem, that poor little sweet holy city, which hath been trodden under feet of those heathen gentile courtiers and outside Christians, not worth the measuring, these many hundred years.'[40] There was an enormous gulf separating these 'little ones, who are born again, whose love is great for great respects, who know they are translated from death to life' and other, ordinary Christians, 'those unreturned ones that love not nor know whether they go. And as the difference is great in regard of the uncertainty of the one and the certain everlasting happiness of the other, so have they a charter so great and freedom so strong, with so many privileges belonging thereto, as no city in the world nor kingdom can afford the like.'[41]

Amongst those privileges perhaps the greatest was a freedom from sin. Etherington seemed to waver a little on this point. At one point, for instance, he admitted that 'in many things (as one saith) we sin all and love covereth a multitude of these sins and, as it is written, blessed is that man whose iniquities are covered, so that God in his love doth cover the manifold iniquities of his blessed ones'. Yet a mere four pages before he had claimed starkly that 'we know that whosoever is born of God sinneth not, but he that is begotten of God keepeth himself and that wicked one toucheth him not'.[42] Such claims certainly went way beyond anything conceded to the godly by Denison.

Etherington agreed with Denison that just as the love and purity of the saints was a defining mark of their status as a saved remnant, so the hatred of ordinary Christians for the little ones of God was a crucial sign of their damnation. For 'these kind of brethren', 'the unregenerate', 'do often times offend the little ones and despise them: because they are little in their own eyes and poor in their own spirit and are returned and become as little children and because their fruits of love appear beyond theirs, knowing their own works to be evil and their brothers good, wherefore the lord saith to those brethren take heed that ye despise not one of these little ones, these lost sheep whom I have sought out'.[43]

But again on this point Etherington's claims far exceeded those made by Denison. There was, Etherington explained, 'a sin unto death that some of those who are unborn of God do commit'. These were 'sins or trespasses committed against the little ones that are born again, hating them or despising them for that they walk in the light and so, in despising them, they despise the Lord Jesus and his father that sent him and so they sin against that light which should save their souls, which being done wittingly is unpardonable'. Those who were guilty of such sins were 'not to be prayed for', Etherington concluded. They were beyond redemption, doomed to hell.[44]

It was here that the little ones' possession of the power of the keys, the power to bind and loose, really came into play. Etherington outlined certain rules which the godly were to follow in dealing with those 'who do despise or speak evil of any one of you that are returned and revile or persecute you for the light's sake, wherein you walk'. First, the slighted individual was to take his adversary to one side 'and give him to understand that, if he despise, speak evil of, revile or persecute thee, he doth it unto the Lord whom he professeth and exhort him to humble his heart and be converted and walk in that light himself'. If that failed, the offended party was to return with 'one or two of thy fathers own children, of those little returned ones, thy brethren' so that 'if he still resist thy love and utter words of scorn against thee' 'by the mouth of two or three witnesses every word may be confirmed'. If the offending party persisted, even in the face of this collective exhortation to repentance, then the offended party, with his carefully acquired godly witnesses, should

> tell it to the church, that is, to those little ones born of God, being gathered together in my name, who only have this privilege to be my church and pillar of truth, for if there were five hundred brethren more beside the little humble ones yet none can judge this cause but they. This church doth never condemn the innocent and let the guilty go free. This church never decreed lies and condemned the truth. And if he refuse to hear this church, let him be unto thee no longer as a brother and a fellow partaker in the common things of the kingdom ... but let him be unto thee and unto all the church even as a heathen that believeth not the truth of the gospel and as a publican that professeth the practice of sin. Verily, I say unto you, whatsoever you bind on earth shall be bound in heaven and whatsoever you loose on earth shall be loosed in heaven, for to you it is to whom I have given the keys of the kingdom of heaven.[45]

This is a truly remarkable passage. For Etherington's account of the spiritual sanctions at the disposal of the little ones was completely untouched by, indeed it rendered nugatory, the formal powers of excommunication exercised by the church courts. Rather, in Etherington's view, the power to bind and loose resided in the 'little ones of God', who were able, in effect, to curse and damn to hell all those who reviled them or 'the light in them'. 'These are privileges belonging only to those little ones that are born of God who have their parts in the first resurrection, against whom the gates of hell shall not prevail nor yet the second death', he intoned.[46]

All this was entirely typical of Etherington's account of the relationship between the 'new Jerusalem of the little ones' and the ordinances and observances of the visible church. For while he certainly did not portray those relations as antipathetic, or juxtapose the one against the other in a directly polemical way – that, he claimed, was the crucial mistake made by his separatist opponents – he did envision the spiritual kernel of the godly community coming into existence in ways that had alarmingly little to do with the outer husk provided by the visible church. As we have seen, there was a tendency in this direction inherent in Denison's position, but he had taken considerable steps, in his accounts of the powers and perquisites of the clergy, and of the role of the word, the sacraments and the sabbath in the life of the godly, to control them.

These were crucial caveats and controls that Etherington did not merely leave unsaid, but which rather he positively undermined. He did so, typically, by using, for the most part, scrupulously conventional categories and terms. Thus he compared the visible and invisible churches to two houses – the visible church was 'a great house', capacious enough to contain both the regenerate and the unregenerate, while the true kingdom of heaven was 'that little spiritual house whose vessels are all of gold and silver, where is joy in the Holy Ghost and the great rest and peace'. Elsewhere Etherington compared 'the common kingdom of heaven', the visible church, 'to a net which catcheth fish of all sorts, good and bad', 'or a field wherein lay a treasure hid of so great worth that whosoever could get possession of it (though it cost him all that ever he had, if it were never so much) yet should his gain be great and infinite'.[47]

Entry to 'the great house' 'net' or 'field' of the visible church was achieved through outward or what Etherington termed 'elementish baptism'. This gained the Christian access to the general or common privileges, vouchsafed to all the members of the visible church. These privileges included 'receiving the word and believing the truth thereof and of the elementish baptism and the signs of the Lord's body and blood and all other such like common things'. These 'common things should be for the many that are called, but his peculiar things for the few that are chosen'.[48]

In short, entrance to the true kingdom of heaven, the church built only of lively stones, was through the second baptism 'of repentance and of the holy ghost'. The members of that kingdom were not distinguished merely by baptism, which was common to all members of the visible church, both regenerate and unregenerate, but 'by regeneration, the birth of water and of the Holy Ghost'. The first, outward baptism did not confer saving grace. Indeed, many of those baptised by Christ and the apostles themselves had ended in hell. However, the second inward or spiritual baptism of regeneration could and did save and save infallibly. There was some link between the two baptisms – the first was a promise of and figure for the second – but baptism 'is a seal not of every ones salvation that receiveth it but a seal of God's faithfulness, in his covenant of mercy, made to all Abraham's seed, baptised and circumcised in heart like him, which he sealeth unto their hearts by his spirit of promise, not by baptism'. On this view, circumcision under the law was no mere type of baptism under the gospel, rather, they were 'both types of one truth which is circumcision or baptism in heart'.[49] Baptism 'doth prefigure and signify' 'conversion and new birth' but, in and of itself, outward baptism 'is neither able to heal a body nor yet to save a soul'. Thus, if the first, outward, and the second, inward, baptisms were linked, there was no doubt, in Etherington's view, of which was the more important.

Baptism is nothing, nor unbaptism nothing ... compared with a new creature nor yet is able to pollute any, though he had received it in the church of Rome ... it be not worth the contending about, nor yet the speaking of, compared with the doctrine of baptism, which is regeneration, the washing of repentance and the purging of the Holy Ghost, through Jesus Christ and faith in him, which is indeed the true beginning of every living stone of his church and temple, whereof he is the foundation and headstone of the corner stone.[50]

All these claims were made in the context of a refutation of the anabaptist separatism of Smith the se-baptist, a notorious separatist so convinced that there was as yet no true church in the world by which one could be safely baptised that he had baptised himself – hence the name. As Denison was to use him in 1626, so in his tract of 1610, Etherington was using Smith the separatist to contain and control the radical consequences of his own position. Thus, while he might push the division between the godly and the ungodly and the practical equation of the godly with the true church of the elect even further than Denison, he still distanced himself from what he took to be the separatists' use of those same doctrines to justify their own separation from the church of England. He did so on the classic grounds that only God could finally identify his elect and that to second guess the workings of divine grace by trying to give final external form to the division between the saved and the damned in this world (which is what, erroneously as Dr Brachlow has argued, he took the separatists to be doing) was both presumptuous and doomed to failure. 'Good ground or trees, do not appear all at once out of the general field of commoners, but when it pleaseth him who giveth the increase, some sooner, some later. So no more do the evil trees appear all at once but now and then, when their evil fruit is ripe.' This militated against any premature weeding of the garden of the church.

> The servants must not go to weeding at the first sprout of the ear, though some wheat and some tares do evidently appear, lest they pluck up wheat with tares. For some of both shall remain unknown unto them, until the great harvest day. And this is and shall be the condition of the common field and university of Christians until that day and therefore the servants must spare to judge or justify, till their fruits do evidently appear ... so ought also his servants to be kind to the unkind and merciful to all, insomuch as in the first effects, before mentioned, there doth appear little or no difference [between the regenerate and the unregenerate].[51]

Again, over baptism, Etherington used his opposition to anabaptism as a means of controlling the otherwise very radical consequences of his position. Thus, the passage (cited above) in which Etherington so diminished the significance of outward baptism in favour of the second spiritual rebirth of repentance and regeneration came from a defence of infant baptism against the arguments of Smith the se-baptist. Given that outward baptism was merely a sign or figure for that second spiritual rebirth, Etherington asked, why may 'not children be baptised with this hope and to this end, that they might become Christians and be born again'.[52] That conjunction is typical of Etherington's 'defence' of the church of England. He was prepared to defend the outward ordinances of the English church precisely to the extent that he could reduce their status in the overall spiritual economy of the church built only of lively stones to that of mere external forms, outward adjuncts and aids to the inner spiritual realities that alone created and sustained the godly community that remained the true focus of his interest and allegiance.

For it was only once those externals could be seen for what they were – mere externals, incidental to 'the kingdom of heaven which is not meat and drink and apparel but righteousness and peace and joy in the Holy Ghost' – that they could be safely left to the magistrate to order and enforce. Herein consisted the true spiritual liberty of the church, the freedom from externals, which left the godly free to obey the magistrate in things indifferent. 'What he [God] commandeth not, Caesar may forbid, what he forbiddeth not, Caesar may command.' 'If we obey him [Caesar] not, we are guilty of the breach of the moral law ... For although God doth not appoint and command Caesar in all what laws he shall make, yet doth he confirm all those laws which he doth make which are not contrary to his own laws and commandeth obedience thereto at the hands of all subjects to their kings and governors.'[53] Here was the pure conformist gospel as preached by John Whitgift and myriad other defenders of the Elizabethan status quo.

Now at one level, Etherington's position *vis-à-vis* the separatists was very similar to that devised by the presbyterian and radical puritan divines Thomas Cartwright and William Bradshaw. They, too, had stressed the spiritual reality of the godly community, fostered within and through the public ordinances of the English church, to argue that, despite its many faults and shortcomings, the church of England was still a true church. But Etherington parted company with them on two crucial counts. The first was the enthusiasm of his espousal of the cause of outward conformity, a conformity which he grounded, in classically Whitgiftian style, on the magistrate's authority over things indifferent. The second was the extraordinarily exalted spiritual powers and perquisites that he conferred on the godly remnant located within the outward structures of the national church.

Etherington used his own position on the authority of the magistrate and the polemical logic of his engagement with the anabaptists to attack the nonconformist clergy of the day. He told them quite explicitly that they were responsible for the proliferation of sects and schisms in the current age:

> Be it known unto you, your doctrines and proceedings have been the cause of much evil, you have been the breeders of these sects, you have laid the foundations and others build. Their buildings stand upon your foundation and therefore you are no more able to deal with them in this controversy then one is able to deal with his

enemy, when he hath yielded him all the weapons. For, by the same reason you inveigh against the ceremonies (as you call them), will they come against you for going to the assemblies in the temple ... so that if all is true that you say, that is true which they do and so you are the sayers and they the doers. And, therefore, you must of necessity either join with them or change your minds or else hide yourselves for shame; for ye cannot fight with them, seeing you are unarmed and they have all your weapons.[54]

For Etherington there was a clear strand of logical development leading from scruples over ritual conformity to suspension, schism and exile.

Some to ease their consciences, which you had burdened, and to escape trouble, have left their callings, removed their dwellings, sold their possessions, fled their country, separating themselves from the church of England as from idolatry and the abominations of Antichrist. And being beyond the seas (in Holland by name) beholding among the sects of separatists there the wranglings, the brawlings, the divisions, the envy and the gross sins that hath been among them, have been driven to their wits end, running from sect to sect and from error to error, that some of them now at last are become carnal and blasphemous familists, between whom and the worldings there is little difference, but only in their doctrines and blasphemies.[55]

Etherington portrayed non-conformity as a clerically inspired set of scruples, whereby the puritan clergy ensnared the consciences of the laity, won themselves a false reputation for piety and martyrdom in the cause of the gospel and thus attracted a devoted and generous following amongst the godly laity. 'How many hundreds of people (no doubt single and upright in heart, hungering and thirsting for peace and rest to their souls) have been by you seduced and brought to a spiritual bondage?' Etherington asked the puritan clergy. 'As you have troubled many a poor soul with your doubtful doctrines under pretence of abstaining from sin and performing of holy duties, that many of you and of your followers differ but little from the sect of the pharisees.' By their self-willed defiance the non-conformist clergy hoped to prove, by suffering persecution, that they lived 'godly in Christ Jesus'. In fact, they were simply taking up 'a cross of thine own making and because thou wilt be sure to suffer, speak evil of them that are in authority, resist the ordinance of God and so suffer for evil doing'. Their reputation for sanctity thus achieved, suspended ministers too often exploited it for their own gain, bankrupting their poor supporters with collections for the maintenance of ministers who should never have allowed themselves to be suspended or deprived in the first place. 'Through their devotion and bounty unto you' many lay people 'have brought themselves ... into great wants and miseries; some with feasting of you, some with lending, some with giving.'[56]

But if Etherington had it in for the non-conformist clergy, he was scarcely better affected towards 'those that have turned their heat into coldness' in the search for preferment. He excoriated those that can play with both hands, because they will keep their credit with those that are zealous and not lose that neither which they gape for whensoever it falls, who are fed till they are gross with fat, yet gape for more. These are the cunninger sort of subscribing reformers, who speak evil of that in private which they conform to in public, who, under pretence of preaching the gospel for the good of others, preach and plead for themselves and for their own praise and preferment, who reign in their spirits and word, more like lords then many of those whose places and titles and honours they spite and speak against, because it is not theirs.[57]

For Etherington, clearly, moderate puritan divines – men of precisely Denison's stamp, well connected and prepared to accept conformity and yet desperate to retain their authority and reputation for zeal amongst the godly – were no better than their more daring or foolhardy non-conformist brethren.

For all that he used the issue of conformity to denounce the non-conformist clergy, Etherington showed no love lost for those in authority in the church. He might defend bishops but only as some sort of royal commissioners for causes ecclesiastical. 'In former times', it was true 'our bishops received their callings and power from the beast of Rome', 'but now they receive their callings and power from Caesar, our king, who hath authority to determine and appoint every public calling in his kingdoms ... And as the king is bound to see all his great household provided for (to his power) and to place over them the best and fittest for the purpose, I mean for soul and body, so he may give power and authority to all sorts of them, to perform the will of God and to see his own laws kept and executed without resistance and disturbance.' There remained, moreover, distinct limits on episcopal power, inherent in the office and the nature of the Christian community over which the bishop presided. Thus Etherington denied that he would justify or defend 'any that having authority ... do reign as lords over God's heritage, that love salutations and greetings, delighting to be called lords, affecting greatly the title rabbi, sporting themselves with the afflictions of Jacob, that tread the holy city, Jerusalem, under their feet, as the popes and lords of Rome have done and do'. That certainly seemed to open the possibility that there might be such bishops in the Jacobean church. And Etherington saw the normal exercise of authority over things indifferent to be subject to the laws of the avoidance of scandal and the offence of the weak in faith. Thus conformity should not be enforced on weak brethren who 'make conscience for want of knowledge which is offended thereat' or on recent converts from idolatry who 'did yet think that there was some conscience to be made and reverence to be had of it'.[58] On this basis, then, Etherington seems to have had little time for any form of purely clerical authority, be it either puritan or conformist in ideological tone.

ETHERINGTON AND FAMILISM

In a remarkable passage at the end of his *Description*, Etherington ran through the various contenders for the palm of Christian orthodoxy, whose contentions had done so much to disturb the peace of the church, both at home and abroad. 'There is a controversy this day in the world where Christ should be, whereof he hath also foretold us, saying many shall come in my name and say here is Christ and there, but believe them not.' First there were the catholics. 'One saith I am the first and have been of old, I have kept the faith and have not erred to this day.' Then came the protestants. 'Another saith nay, thou liest, thou hast lost the faith and hast erred from the right way and art become a cage of unclean birds this day: but I have recovered that which thou hast lost and I have the right use of the word and sacraments which thou hast polluted; therefore he is here.' Then came the presbyterian-puritan. 'Ye are both liars and harlots and thou that spake last, for thou art not governed by his laws: he is a king, as well as a priest and a prophet and therefore thou liest also: but he is here with us, we have his ordinances and laws, and are ruled by them, we have also the word and sacraments in their right kind and so he is to us a king, a priest and a prophet.' Next came the separatist and anabaptist, 'saying who is this that boasteth thus and retaineth the baptism of the whore? Must they not needs be her children, seeing they hold her baptism sufficient and refuse to be baptised aright? What? Can their baptism be good and their church and government nought? Not possible; wherefore ye are also deceived and he cannot be in the midst of you as you suppose.'

The last claimant to true orthodoxy then came forward.

> Then steps up the fifth, with a high spirit, controlling all, especially the three last, accusing them for wranglers and blasphemers, (saying) ye are all liars, ye are jangling contentious spirits, ye seek Christ without you, seek him within you, you good thinking wise ones, you do not so much as know what Christ is nor yet what Antichrist is; you condemn that holy, ancient father the pope of Rome to be Antichrist, the beast and man of sin, and all the holy orders of their archpriests, priests and offices of good intentions, having all names of good signification and all images, sacrifices and ceremonies of good information to be all blasphemous, idolatrous and superstitious and so blaspheme the holy things used in the catholic church of Rome. Not knowing that as God did teach the world, by the orders, sacrifices and ceremonies used among the Jews till Christ came in the man Jesus, so it pleased him also to teach the world by those orders, images, sacrifices and ceremonies used in the catholic church of Rome until the Christ came again, now in the end of the world, according to his promises, in his obedient man H.N., by whom he hath appointed to judge the world, according to the scriptures. Not with fire and brimstone upon men's heads, as we suppose, but with wise sentences, with dark and parabolous saying, delivering high things with a high spirit; teaching, reproving and condemning the whole world, being the eighth and the last breaker

of the light. The archangel and the last trump, none in this third and last day wherein Christ is perfitted. And is that angel, flying in the midst of heaven, having an everlasting gospel to preach to them that dwell upon the earth, saying Christ is not nor was not a man, as ye suppose, but holiness is Christ. And he that doth believe it is possible to keep all the ten commandments hath the right faith in Christ and they that do attain to the perfect keeping of them are risen from the dead, according to the scriptures, and as holiness is Christ and the son of God, so sin is Antichrist and the son of the devil. Fight, therefore, against the Antichrist in yourselves, overcome the beast which is the sin and put on holiness which is the Christ.[59]

These, he concluded, were 'the contentions of our days, who shall end the controversy?' He answered his own question telling the reader 'to put away therefore all your good thinkings and all your scripture learnedness ... for ... whosoever comes to learn at this school must be as simple and hold himself as ignorant as a little child'. In that state the reader was fit to 'to take this book but keep it close, for H.N. hath many enemies, especially among this wrangling crew'. The truth contained therein 'hath begun to show her face already a little and her voice hath been heard, even in our land, but the wolves come so thick about her that she was glad to retire a little into the wilderness again but, when her appointed time and year is once come, she shall come forth and end this controversy whereby her little ones are much dismayed'. Judging from Etherington's earlier somewhat cryptic remarks in the book, locating the end of the twelve hundred and three year reign of Antichrist in fifty-seven years time, this much to be welcomed event was imminent. 'In the mean time let her poor little children rejoice and be glad, for her light shall shine every day, still more and more, and as light comes in, darkness shall go out, howsoever things seem to go.'[60]

ETHERINGTON AND H.N.

By appending this long passage to his book, Etherington had, in effect, transformed it into a full-blown familist manifesto. We know from an aside in one of his later pamphlets that Etherington, at one point, possessed at least one familist work penned by H.N. himself, the *Evangelium regni* of *c.* 1574.[61] Many of the more distinctive elements of *The description* can be found paralleled or echoed there. Etherington's very catchphrase, 'the little ones', equated persistently by H.N. with 'god his elect', echoed throughout the earlier work.[62] These, in H.N.'s discourse, were 'the holy ones of God; the renewed or godded men upon the earth', 'with whom the living God of heaven hath begun his work, to bring it to perfection'. Like Etherington's little ones, they were evidently without sin, having experienced the spiritual baptisms of both water and fire, of John the Baptist and of Christ, of repentance and the spirit. 'Behold', explained H.N., 'were the man once baptised in such wise, so might he then verily well boast him to be a Christian, but not otherwise. For whosoever is not, in his mind and spirit, one spirit with Christ, he belongeth not unto him.'[63]

Etherington's account of the spiritual privileges of the 'little ones', conceived as the only true church, able to damn their enemies to hell, both echoed and paled into insignificance beside H.N.'s account of the same subject. 'With this same Christ and all his holy ones, which are the true members of his body, will God, now in this day, which he himself hath appointed or ordained, judge the earth with righteousness, according to the scripture.' 'The God of heaven hath now declared himself and his Christ, together with all his saints, unto us, his elect, and also made a dwelling with us and brought even so unto us, out of his holy being, the most holy of his true tabernacle, with the fullness of his garnishing and spiritual, heavenly riches, to an ever-lasting, fast-standing Jerusalem.' While for H.N., the 'little ones' were God's 'Jerusalem', 'a house for God's' dwelling according to the scripture', for Etherington, too, the 'little ones of God' were 'the citizens of the heavenly Jerusalem'.[64]

Again just like Etherington, H.N. contrasted the spiritual insight and true scriptural knowledge to be attained by these little ones with that available to other merely formal Christians and those whom he contemptuously dismissed as 'the scripture learned'. While in this 'day of perfect light, we' 'the little ones and God's elect' 'behold, with naked clearness, the most holy', the same was very far from being true for 'the scripture learned and wise of the world'.[65] The *Evangelium regni* was suffused with damningly dismissive references to 'the discordable or divided wise and scripture learned', such as 'vaunt or give forth themselves for Christians and as illuminated men that are masters of the scripture', who claimed to be 'the expertest or learnedest in the scripture and seemed to be the holiest'.[66] Whatever their pretensions to learning such men could never, 'out of the imagination of their knowledge' or 'the knowledge which they have taken on unto them out of the letter of scripture', even approach a true understanding 'of the clearness of the word of Christ', 'much less of the mind or will of the same'. Such men 'have not kept or passed through with Christ, after the flesh, the pass-over from death into life and from flesh into spirit, nor in the following of Christ attained, through the powers of the holy ghost, unto the clearness of Christ'.[67]

Indeed, H.N. attributed the rise of an Antichrist that, like Etherington's, was far from being entirely or exclusively papal, to the activities of such people. For it was 'unsent preachers' and 'ungodded men' who, cleaving unto 'their goodthinking, according to the imagination of their knowledge, and the earthly ingenious wisdom of the flesh', preached false doctrine to the 'unilluminated'.[68] 'So obtained, then, the nature of sin or the child of the devil and condemnation that contrary-nature or adversary of Christ, which is called Antichrist, his shape in the inward temple of the unbelieving and unregenerated men.' 'This Antichrist hath exalted himself ... above God and above the true God-service ... in the temple of the Lord, namely in the inward part of man, wherein the living God with his Christ ought to dwell and to live and to walk.'[69]

Now such strictures bore more than a passing resemblance to conventional protestant accounts of the rise of the papal Antichrist in the visible church of God. But now the church was defined in entirely internal, spiritual terms and H.N. made it clear that the nexus of error that had driven 'the clear light' out of the world was far from consistently or solely papal or Roman catholic in origin. Indeed, H.N. placed as much, if not more, of the blame for the 'suppression of the light' and the currently divided and persecution-ridden state of Christendom on would-be protestant reformers. Thus H.N. decried 'the wise of the world and scripture learned' who had 'overreached' themselves, forsaking 'the law and the service of the elders' testament and of the priest's office after the ordinance of Aaron'. They had done so, however, prematurely, crying 'Christ, Christ and we are Christians' and attributing to themselves 'much freedom, err ever the time of the appearing of Christ or the anointing of the holy ghost was come to pass or fulfilled with them'.[70] These men claimed great knowledge of scripture but their claims were false; theirs was 'self wisdom, knowledge or scripture learnedness, the which is a false freedom'. 'They spake likewise much of God's word which yet they themselves (like as it is a living and mighty word, that cutteth and pierceth as a sharp sword, into the inmost part of the soul) had never heard nor seen his clearness ... much less understood the mind or will of the same.'[71]

The results of these premature and misconceived attempts at reformation had, of course, been disastrous.

> Many unorderly rejected and blasphemed the services and ceremonies of the catholic church of Rome, rented the concord and nurturable sustentation of the same and turned them away therefrom. And evenso, out of their knowledge, which they took out of the scripture, brought in certain services and ceremonies in an other wise or order and set forth and taught the same for the upright Christian ceremonies unto the people. Howbeit they have procured or obtained little love and righteousness but rather much contention and controversy.[72]

> There was much contention and many divided minds and understandings, which very much reprehended, slandered and judged each other for evil... For the most part they were all divided one against another. For everyone rested persuaded to have right in his cause ... Among all these there have also been certain which were counted of many for sectaries, heretics and seducers of the people and for that cause persecuted and banished and many, for the conscience and faith's cause, were slain and put to death.'

This was an outcome which H.N. bemoaned forcibly and at length; 'oh, what a lamentable thing is the slaying or shedding of blood for the conscience's cause', he wailed. Those who indulged in the practice, he warned, while they were very 'cold' 'towards the love unto the righteousness', were yet 'very diligent in their own enforcements and enterprises'.[73] Here, then, are the general outlines of the particular case made by Etherington against the various strands of English protestant reforming and puritan opinion. Again the boxmaker seems to have been applying the general insights of H.N. to his own experience of the recent bitter history of English intra-puritan, puritan-conformist and indeed puritan-familist debate and denunciation.

Nor was this a mere afterthought on Etherington's part. On the contrary, it enabled him to market his book as a piece of anti-separatist, indeed, of anti-puritan, propaganda. With its assaults on the false claims to purity and principle of both presbyterian, non-conformist and conforming puritans and its vindication of the powers of the Christian prince and his chosen agents, the bishops, over all the externals of religious worship (a category, of course, much expanded by Etherington's 'familist' distinction between the inward things of the spirit, vouchsafed only to 'the little ones', and the outward, external forms of religion, common to all formal Christians and church members), the book appeared for all the world to be a rather eccentric, but nonetheless effective, defence of the ecclesiastical status quo – something that may well help to explain how it came to be printed in the first place.

Not that either H.N. or Etherington had any real time for the papists. In the *Evangelium regni*, popery was presented as a source, if not of Antichristian malignity then certainly of error. It is not hard to discern what many contemporaries lambasted as the soul-killing superstitions of popery within the following description of one source of contemporary error.

> Through this same zeal or diligence ... (wherethrough the figurative services were, in most gorgeous manner, furthered or required and, for to be observed, set forth before the people) many people were therein captived, so that they supposed that the figurative services were the very true God-services and that God was to be reconciled therewith and marked not God his counsel or will because they respected not the clearness of the very true being, whereof the images and figures gave their shadows, wherethrough also they understood not the mystery of those same.

And yet for H.N., while these were errors, they were not damning errors, for those that were subject to them were yet 'bond men and servants of the Lord which were yet bound unto the same services and not as children of God made free through the truth'.[74]

Such a claim made sense when it was set against H.N.'s wider vision of progressive revelation and prophetic history, which saw a gradual movement through a series of outward forms, ceremonies and observances, which had both figured forth and masked the true being of God, until now, in the last days, that true being was finally to be revealed through the writings of H.N. and the activities and example of 'the little ones, God his elect'. Thus the outward forms of popery took their place in a long succession of such services and shadows, which stretched from Moses, through David, John the Baptist and Christ to H.N. and his followers.[75] Under the former dispensation, we had access only to 'the serviceable word which is administered out of the spirit and life of God, with speakable writings or letters and which also figureth forth and expresseth unto us, to wit serviceably and in parables and in images and figures, the new and very true testament which is heavenly, spiritual and living and endureth forever'. The whole movement of human history was thus 'out of the figures into the true being and out of the letter and serviceable word into the revealing of the holy spirit of Christ'. Only now, in these last days, was that movement to be completed. For this was the 'day of love and of salvation of the godly and heavenly clearness, which is revealed and come unto us little ones with whom the living God of heaven hath begun his work, to bring it to perfection'.[76]

The movement here was from the letter to the spirit, from the outward to the inward, from the self-regard and wilfulness of the self-described scripture learned, to the true spiritual insight of the little ones. They were the true church, the true tabernacle, for which all earlier outward forms and ceremonies, both Jewish and catholic, had been mere figures, promises and prophecies. It was through them that 'in this day the most holy be ministered, in his true being, to an everlasting perfection or consummation of all the works of God under the obedience of the love'. And, as we have seen, it was through them that God 'now in this day, which he hath himself appointed or ordained, [will] judge the earth with righteousness, according to the scripture'.[77]

Thus, it had been the error of preceding protestant reformers to have tried to reform the church too soon, before the 'day of love' had arrived and to have presumed to do so outwardly, out of their 'own good thinking', choosing 'this or that or something else' on the basis of the 'literal knowledge' of their own 'scripture learnedness'. Lacking a true inward knowledge and experience of 'the love', having had access only to the mere outward rather than to the two inward baptisms of repentance and of the Holy Spirit, of John the Baptist and of Christ, they had been doomed to error and division. Sharing other reformers' sense that these were the last days, in which Antichrist would fall and the church receive much needed reform and spiritual renewal, H.N. was anxious to convince his readers that it was he and the little ones who had really understood what all this meant.[78]

As for those papists who had faithfully observed the outward forms and ceremonies proffered to them by the catholic church, their earlier addiction to those forms and ceremonies was not to be held against them now in 'this day of love'; for these were practices performed when it was 'yet night with many and the figurative services and sacraments were with diligence set forth' and many 'intended and sought the righteousness therein'.[79] With the arrival of 'the day of love', however, things had changed. Now 'all goodwilling ones to the upright righteousness' had to 'assemble them unto us and our communalty and humble them unto our most holy service of the love and his requiring' or else. For those 'who so refuse this same and they that turn them away therefrom, those shall not obtain the upright righteousness of God, neither presently nor forever'.[80] These really were the last days and it was time to get on the bus of 'the love' or be left behind forever. And it was H.N., although, as he described himself with becoming modesty, 'the least among the holy ones of God', who had been chosen to spread that particular word.[81]

Hence, by recourse to a central familist text by H.N. himself, a text moreover of which we know Etherington had a copy, we can flesh out not only the lineaments of the eschatologically charged, H.N.-centred familist view of the world to which Etherington signed on in the peroration to his *Description*, but also the conceptual underpinning, indeed the, or rather a, very probable source for many of the most central and distinctive features of the overall argument and diction of that book. There, applied to and modified by the recent history of English puritan, sectarian and conformist debate, mixed and miscegenated with the tone, diction and categories of mainstream puritan godliness of the sort purveyed by the likes of Stephen Denison, were many of the central features of familism as they had been defined by H.N. and disseminated in England since the 1570s.[82]

NOTES

1 C[ambridge] U[niversity] L[ibrary] Ms Gg.29, fols 33r.–v. For another copy see CUL Baker Ms Mm 1 43, pp. 513–14 and B[ritish] L[ibrary] Harleian Ms 3142, part 10, headed 'Reasons for burning Mr Elton's book at St Paul's Cross'. I owe these references to the kindness of Ethan Shagan and Michael Questier and I would like to thank Michael Winship for drawing the whole incident to my attention.

2 *The correspondence of John Cosin*, ed. G. Ormsby, 2 vols, Surtees Society, vols lii, lv (Durham, 1869–72), vol. 1, pp. 59, 61. Both letters written from Petworth in Sussex by Montague to Cosin in Febuary 1624–25.

3 T. Gataker, *Discourse apologetical, wherein Lilies' lewd and loud lies ... are clearly laid open* (London, 1654), p. 53.

4 D. Featley, *Cygnea cantio* (London, 1629), *passim*; Dr Williams Library Ms R.N.C.38.34 (nineteenth-century transcripts of J. Quick, *Icones sacrae anglicanae*), pp. 187–224 for the life of Mr William Crompton. For this incident see esp. pp. 188–90.

5 See the entries in Laud's diary for 21 and 23 December 1624 in *The works of the most reverend father in God, William Laud, D.D.*, ed. J. Bliss, 7 vols (Oxford, 1853), vol. III, pp. 155–6.

John Etherington

6 J. Birch, *The court and times of James I* (London, 1849), vol. II, p. 491, letter to Joseph Mede, dated London, 21 January 1624/25; p. 498, letter to Joseph Mede, dated London, 18 February 1624/25.

7 S. Denison, *The white wolf* (London, 1627), dedicatory epistle to Charles I, sigs A2r.–A6v. 'Amongst those worthy and learned [High] Commissioners' Denison picked out for special mention, 'he that is the chief ... [George Abbot, archbishop of Canterbury] whose soundness in the faith, whose singular gravity, whose happy speech, whose excellent parts every way, are the very grace of that venerable court'. Having thus lavished praise on Abbot, Denison turned his attention to Montaigne, bishop of London. 'While I am speaking of ecclesiastical worthies this very duty will not suffer me to be unmindful of him under whom the ministers of London live as children under the care of an indulgent father; his great humility will not suffer him to lord it over the clergy, nor his disposition to tyrannise.' Having started by comparing Abbot to St Basil, he finished by comparing Montaigne to St Cyprian.

8 Cambridge University Archives, Supplications, 1627–29, fol. 130r.; Grace Book Z, pp. 152–3, Doctores in theologia 1628.

9 Denison, *The white wolf*, pp. 37–8, for 'popish, Arminian, Anabaptistical, Rosy-cross, familistical wolves'.

10 BL Loan 29/202, bound between fol. 211 and fol. 223, Martin to Harley, dated 11 April 1627. 'I have observed your good inclination to honest and well deserving ministers, this bearer, Mr Denison, is so, and for the benefit of the church hath been painful to preach and print a book, which he desires to dedicate to his Majesty ... he expects no reward for it, neither are his aims any but the good of our church and the reducing of factious and ill-affected spirits to the truth of religion. My request for him and it, therefore, is that you would favour him herein yourself, or by my Lord Conway, as far as may be convenient.' I owe this reference to the kindness of Jacqui Eales. For the Harleys more generally see J. Eales, *Puritans and Roundheads: the Harleys of Brampton Bryan* (Cambridge, 1990), esp. chapter 4.

11 Richard Cust, *The forced loan and English politics, 1626–8* (Oxford, 1987), chapter 1.

12 Denison, *The white wolf*, pp. 34, 51, 62. S. Denison, *The white wolf* (London, 1641), pp. 84, 86, 80, 90. This is a reissue of the 1627 sermon with a 'brief answer to the defence of John Hetherington alias Etherington by Stephen Denison D.D.' appended. This volume is not listed in Wing but there are copies in Keble College, Oxford and the library of St Paul's Cathedral. I owe my knowledge of this text to Ariel Hessayon and Tom Cogswell.

13 *Ibid.*, pp. 43–4.

14 *Ibid.*, pp. 49–50.

15 *Ibid.*, pp. 45, 46, 49, 53–4.

16 John Etherington, *The defence of John Etherington against Stephen Denison* (London, 1641), pp. 6–7. This last was a printed version of a manuscript vindication of himself written, or, so he claimed (at p. 62), in 'the new prison in Maiden Lane' in 1627.

17 *Ibid.*, pp. 7–8.

18 *Ibid.*, pp. 8–9.

19 *Ibid.*, p. 23.

20 *Ibid.*, pp. 27, 29.

21 *Ibid.*, pp. 27-8.

22 *Ibid.*, p. 46, 'since the beginning of the year 1588, now above these forty years, I have lived in or near unto the city of London and until now that Master Denison and his society had thus persecuted me I was never presented nor once complained of for any neglect or ill carriage towards the church of England in one respect or other'.

23 *Ibid.*, p. 23.

24 *Ibid.*, p. 29.

25 *Ibid.*, pp. 13-15; Denison, *The white wolf*, epistle to the reader, sig. A8v.; J. Etherington, *The deeds of Dr Denison a little more manifested* (London, 1642), sig. A2r. Denison, *The white wolf* (1641), p. 77. On familism see C. Marsh, *The family of love in English society 1558-1630* (Cambridge, 1994); A. Hamilton, *The family of love* (Cambridge, 1981); M.T. Pearse, *Between known men and visible saints* (London, 1994).

26 See below, chapter 7.

27 J. Etherington, *A description of the true church of Christ* (London, 1610); J. Etherington, *A discovery of the English anabaptists* (London, 1623); for Etherington's account of the book's licensing and his seeming acceptance of authorship see Etherington *The defence*, p. 41.

28 Etherington, *Description*, pp. 1-5, 81-3; Denison, *The white wolf*, pp. 43-4.

29 Etherington, *Description*, p. 86; Denison, *The white wolf*, p. 44.

30 Etherington/Jessup, *A discovery*, pp. 1-5; Denison, *The white wolf*, p. 45.

31 Etherington, *Defence*, pp. 43-4.

32 Denison, *The white wolf*, p. 50.

33 Etherington, *Description*, pp. 1-2.

34 *Ibid.*, p. 9.

35 *Ibid.*, p. 60.

36 *Ibid.*, pp. 34, 77.

37 *Ibid.*, pp. 10, 62-3.

38 *Ibid.*, p. 4.

39 *Ibid.*, p. 103.

40 *Ibid.*, pp. 12-13.

41 *Ibid.*, p. 62.

42 *Ibid.*, pp. 70, 66, 67.

43 *Ibid.*, p. 65.

44 *Ibid.*, pp. 73-4.

45 *Ibid.*, p. 76.

46 *Ibid.*, p. 76.

47 *Ibid.*, pp. 31, 58, 61-2.

48 *Ibid.*, pp. 55, 54, 33-4.

49 Ibid., pp. 31, 25, 39.

50 Ibid., pp. 55, 54, 33–4.

51 Ibid., pp. 63, 64. S. Brachlow, *The communion of the saints: radical puritan and separatist ecclesiology, 1570–1625* (Oxford, 1988).

52 Etherington, *Description*, p. 54.

53 Ibid., pp. 77–8, 81, 82.

54 Ibid., pp. 90–1; P. Lake, *Moderate puritans and the Elizabethan church* (Cambridge, 1982), chapters 5 and 11.

55 Etherington, *Description*, p. 92.

56 Ibid., pp. 91, 95, 92, 93, 96.

57 Ibid., p. 97.

58 Ibid., pp. 84–5, 97–8, 88.

59 Ibid., pp. 115–16.

60 Ibid., pp. 117–18, for the date of Antichrist's fall see p. 14.

61 Etherington's tract *A brief discovery of the blasphemous doctrine of familism* (London, 1645) paralleled the teachings of his immediate opponent then, one T.L., with opinions culled from a book by H.N., identified as *The joyful message of the kingdom*, which, of course, was the English subtitle of H.N.'s *Evangelium regni, a joyful message of the kingdom published by the holy spirit of the love of Christ and set forth unto all nations of people ... by H.N.* (?, ?1574).

62 H.N., *Evangelium regni*, pp. 11r., 12v., 55r., 86v., 98r.

63 Ibid., pp. 76r., 86v.

64 Ibid., pp. 46r.–47v.

65 Ibid., pp. 64r., 81v.–82r.

66 Ibid., pp. 79v., 10r., 47v.

67 Ibid., pp. 53v., 53r., 77v.

68 Ibid., pp. 64r.–v.

69 Ibid., pp. 65r.–v., 66r.–v.

70 Ibid., pp. 65r., 34v.–35r. See also p. 58v.

71 Ibid., pp. 65v., 77v.

72 Ibid., p. 77v.

73 Ibid., pp. 78r.–v., 79v.

74 Ibid., p. 40v.

75 Ibid., pp. 87r.–89r.

76 Ibid., pp. 33r., 34v., 86v.

77 Ibid., 87v., 64r.

78 Ibid., pp. 36r., 64v., 47v.

79 Ibid., p. 70v.

80 *Ibid.*, pp. 70v.–71r.
81 *Ibid.*, pp. 81r., 91r., 93v., 94r.
82 Denison, *The white wolf*, pp. 38–9, 46, for the different varieties of familists. Also see C. Marsh, *The family of love in English society, 1550–1630* (Cambridge, 1994).

Chapter 5

Another pair of initials? T.L., H.N. and the ideological formation of the young Etherington

According to Denison H.N. was far from being the only, or even the main, formative influence on the young Etherington. In *The white wolf* Denison had not merely cited passages from Etherington's books against him, he had also quoted and glossed a number of passages from books by one T.L., whom he described as Etherington's 'predecessor' as 'the ringleader of this factious company before Hetherington'. Indeed, throughout his sermon Denison was just as interested in associating his boxmaking adversary with this shadowy figure as with the more notoriously heterodox Niclaes.

Denison identified four books by T.L.: 'the epistle to the church of Rome, ... the tree of regeneration, an exposition upon the 11, 12 and 13 chapters of the revelation, ... the key of David and some other'.[1] Of those 'some other' we can identify one, *Babylon is fallen*, reprinted and attributed to T.L. in 1651, while of those mentioned expressly by Denison, *The tree of regeneration* seems not to have survived. In addition to Denison's attribution of these works to T.L., they were all reprinted in the 1650s and again in 1661, when they were again attributed to the same shadowy author.[2] The surviving books appear to have been first published between 1588/89 and 1597. *To the church of Rome* was printed in 1589 by Edward Allde. *The exposition to the XI, XII, XIII chapters of the revelations* was first printed in 1589 and apparently contained 'An advertisement to the queen, presented to the queen by the author thereof' or so it was claimed on the title page of the first extant edition of 1623. The 'advertisement' does not, in fact, survive from that 1623 edition but was reprinted as a separate item in the editions of T.L.'s works published in 1651 and 1661.[3] In the 1651 reprint the *Exposition* appears with a much shorter dedicatory epistle to James I, which suggests either a lost or a projected new edition during the new reign. *Babylon is fallen*, also printed by Allde in 1597, was dedicated to the earl of Essex. Alone of T.L.'s works this was entered in the Stationer's Register as having been officially licensed ('by master [Abraham]

Hartwell') and was the most frequently reprinted of T.L.'s books, subsequent editions being produced by Nicholas Fosbrooke in 1610 and 1614, under the title of *A prophesy that hath lyen hid for two thousand years*. In 1621 it was reprinted again under the original title, this time by Edward Allde. The *Key of David*, which first appeared in Latin under the title *De fide* in 1592, was also printed by Allde. This was an attack on the proto-Arminian Peter Baro's doctrine of faith which, translated into English, was reissued as *The key of David* in 1610.[4]

THE CHURCH OF ROME, BABYLON AND THE TRUE CHURCH

What, then, can we glean from these texts about T.L.'s position and what were its similarities to that occupied by Etherington? To begin with, T.L.'s interests and tone were heavily prophetic, apocalyptic and eschatological. Two of the four tracts were commentaries on passages from Revelations and the book of Esdras. (Here perhaps is the source of Denison's otherwise puzzling obsession with Etherington's estimation of that book as a canonical, rather an unequivocally apocryphal, text.) In these books T.L. was concerned to identify Rome as the beast, to establish the relations between imperial and papal Rome and hence to read off classical and profane history from the prophetic texts of the bible, thus enabling himself to expatiate on the duration and nature of Antichrist's reign in the church, to date that reign's end, speculate on the timing of the second coming and identify the main agents in bringing about these two much to be desired consummations.

On the issue of dating, T.L. was certain that 'the reign of Antichrist must needs endure 1260 years'. This was a figure that he reached by dissolving the three and a half years of Antichrist's reign in Revelation into months and then days according to the Hebrew calendar. This produced the figure 1260 which T.L. then converted from days into years. Adding that number to the year 406, 'when the egg of Antichristianism was laid in the days of Innocent the first, successor to Anastasius the first', that gave us the year 1666 as the year in which Antichrist, 'this child of perdition and mystery of iniquity', would finally fall.[5]

In *Babylon is fallen* T.L. went further towards making these prophecies good by seeking to tie various oracular texts in the book of Esdras to the history of both pagan and papal Rome, ending with certain cryptic references to what appear to be directly contemporary events in European history. Thus, for T.L., papal Rome represented the natural successor to pagan Rome, her imperium now no longer sustained by tyrannical force but by spiritual stealth. 'When the sinful city saw her feathers so plucked, as the fear of her arms and forces might no longer fly into all kingdoms, commanding them under the pain of imperium Romanum, lying by means of this distress very weak and in danger of falling, her council and body politic devised, by lies and witchcraft (wherein was all her pleasure from her youth), to restore the supremacy and honour of her name, under the colour of ecclesia dei.' Noticing that 'as the world was now so given, as Jupiter with all his idols must needs give place to Christ, because most voices went that way', the dragon (satan) 'thereupon persuaded his ethnic Caesars that, in policy, it was best to play Christians'. Here was a satanic plot against the church of God even worse than pagan imperial persecution. The pagan emperors, 'in whom satan dwelt' 'literally ... in open hostility', did 'fight against the highest, setting before him a God made of a wicked man'. But this overt pagan persecution was less threatening to the church than the covert subversion from within compassed by popery and set in motion by supposedly Christian emperors.[6]

Thus, through the gradual rise of Antichrist, the church was totally corrupted from within, converted, in fact, to a form of paganism.

> The better to bring the mystery of iniquity to pass he [satan] caused his new Christened Caesars to set up a race of sycophantical high and princely priests who, under colour of proctoring the affairs of the lamb, should cunningly clap Jupiter's coat upon the lamb's back and bestow all the ceremonies and rituals of Jupiter and his idols upon Christ that so, by turning Jupiter's worship into Christianism, he might turn the worship of God into paganism and idolatry and that so he might, at the least, profane and desolate the true worship of the true God, whose majesty and truth of deity they could no way blemish.

On this view, popery was a conspiracy to convince all those 'that perish by consenting unto lies that they ought to worship God as the gentiles did worship Jupiter; persuading them that, as the gentiles had their arae, so Christians must have their altars; and, as the heathens had their bloody sacrifices, so Christians must have their unbloody sacrifices, and offer bread and wine to God ... as the pagans had their pontifex maximus, so the Christians must have their pope; and, as ethnics had their sacerdotes, so must Christians have their priests; and, as the gentiles had their gods and goddesses, so must Christians have their he-saints and she-saints; and, as the dragon had his pantheon, so Antichrist must have all his saints; and, as the heathens had their idols, so Christians must have their images' – and so on and on, through a whole series of further parallels between various popish practices and orders and their pagan equivalents.

In all this T.L. was appropriating and at most developing conventional wisdom. The notion of the gradual rise, through stealth, to dominance in God's church of satan's agent Antichrist was a stock protestant trope, as was the idea that the danger represented by this threat from within was far greater than any persecution visited on the true church by the pagan emperors. Similarly, the notion of popery as a mode of idolatrous worship grafted onto Christianity from paganism was common enough. As Glyn Parry has shown, this concept, which he terms gentilism, was a central organising category in the chronological and eschatological schemas developed by William Harrison. What perhaps was less common was the chronological precision of T.L.'s prognostications; for many mainstream protestant exegetes of the period, such claims to accurate foreknowledge of God's plan were at best presumptuous and at worst blasphemous. As we shall see below, what was even more striking was the central role which T.L. gave to even the first Christian emperors in establishing the rise of Antichrist in the church. As Professor Lamont amongst others has pointed out, it was far more conventional amongst mainstream Elizabethan protestant thinkers to laud the role of Constantine and others in rescuing the church from persecution and establishing it on a firm institutional footing. On one view this imperial rescue mission was particularly significant since it prefigured the efforts of those later Christian emperors, Henry VIII and particularly Queen Elizabeth, to rescue the true church in England from popery.[7]

Once established in the church, Antichrist proceeded to invade the state, again acting not by force but by stealth. In Revelation Antichrist was depicted as a beast with 'seven heads and ten horns, and upon his horns ten diadems', 'signifying thereby', T.L. concluded, 'that he should not come to his crown and vainglory by the strength of his sword, his leaders and his legions, as the dragon did, but by the base and voluntary submission of all such Caesars, kings and princes as should, with one counsel and force, deliver up their authority and power secular to the devotion and pleasure of the beast'. The result of all this was satan's masterpiece; 'an extraordinary sovereignty, compounded of such spiritual and temporal claims and jurisdictions as should be equivalent in presumption and profanation to all the transgressions of the seven monarchies which, from the beginning hitherto, have blasphemed God and corrupted his word'.[8]

Throughout his career, in fact, Antichrist enjoyed an interesting complicity with the powers of this world. In *Babylon is fallen*, T.L. explained how the revival of the imperial title in Charlemagne by the pope was all part of the satanic conspiracy to take over the world; 'and the title of dignity imperial which had lain dead above three hundred years was, in this year on Christmas day, thus raised up to life again, to the end it might defend the proceedings of the great adulteress and murderess of the earth'. To the power of the emperor was also added the power of the Spanish and French monarchies, 'whose unhallowed league the prophet foreseeing saith they should be joined with the middle head and like three parts in one accord and agree together, to humble themselves, their authority and power before the beast and for their idol-shepherd should fight against the highest, till by the breath of his mouth they be scattered, like the dust which the wind disperseth'.

And these are the three heads mentioned in the first, fourth and ninth verses of this chapter and are therefore said to finish and determine the last end and wickedness of the whore, because though all other kingdoms hate her and make her desolate and naked and eat her flesh, as England and others have done, yet these three heads shall love her still, and to their dying day shall burn in delight with her, but when those three and every of them shall also forsake her, there shall not be found either kingdom or creature under heaven that shall fall down and worship her.[9]

Such a reading of the prophetical texts served, of course, to link T.L.'s reading of church history and the eschatologically charged progress of the beast to power in the temple of God to the world of contemporary power politics. What else was figured here than the union of the Guise faction and the Holy League with Philip II's Spain, the outcome most feared by both protestant zealots and politiques during the late 1580s and 1590s? In the *Exposition* T.L. applied various prophecies concerning the 'restoration of the true meaning of the scriptures', the defection of 'many kingdoms' from the beast, the concurrent great earthquake, in which the figuratively charged number of seven thousand men were killed, to the disruptions of contemporary Christendom. 'Which broils and bloodshed concerning the institution of religion are so sufficiently reported in the commentaries of Bohemia and Germany and in the troubles of France and Flanders and other nations, as if it were purposefully registered in proof of this prophecy.'[10]

Thus expounding Esdras 4 chapter 11, verse 35 'And I saw and beheld whilst the head on the right side devoured that which was on the left', T.L. commented 'by the right is meant ... the strongest, so as the prophet implyeth that the sword of Spain shall divide the strength of France, that her pride by division made less, may at the least (as every divided kingdom doth) return to nothing. Neither shall the prosperity of this right head be long free from like retaliation but, as the truth foresaith, "he that divideth with the sword, shall perish by the sword." For how may the sword for ever escape him, whom heaven hateth and earth doth persecute?' Clearly contemporary references abound in these passages, with their allusions to the League, the divisions of the French monarchy and Spanish politicking therein and their implicit vision of a special role for England, outstanding amongst the great monarchies of Europe in her opposition to the beast, in the events that now, in this penultimate, sixth age, were about to bring about Antichrist's fall.[11]

It was, perhaps, small wonder that the dedicatee chosen by T.L. for these prophetical ravings was the earl of Essex, a figure increasingly identified as the great hope of godly militarism and the international protestant cause in England. In all this T.L. was scarcely alone. As Dr Bauckham has pointed out, the annus mirabilis of 1588 provoked an efflorescence of apocalyptic optimism; 'in the years after the Armada', he writes, there was 'strong optimism about the defeat of Antichrist within history and ... a new emphasis on the role of

Another pair of initials?

military force in the overthrow of Antichrist'. A number of other authors dedicated books to Essex; George Gifford dedicated his *Sermons upon the whole book of the revelation* of 1596 and John Gibson his *The sacred shield of true Christian soldiers*, of 1599, to the earl. At a more disreputable and openly subversive level, this was the same decade that saw the prophetic ravings of Hacket and Coppinger being addressed to the regime from the very margins of the puritan movement. It was into such company that T.L. thrust himself in his dedicatory epistle:

> Reading of late (my lord) [wrote T.L. to the earl] a chapter of Esdras, folding up in a mystical and dark discourse, a living representation of a long time, whereof the most is past, and some little to come, I thought it no lost labour to take my pen and unfold the same, that therein we may behold (which naturally all desire to see) as well the issues of things to come, as what is past or now in being and thereafter to qualify and moderate our hopes and call our troubled thoughts ... within the circle and limitation bounded and drawn from above. And finding this prophecy written by a man greatly beloved of God and thereto (which rare is) a prince's favourite, high in grace with a king of Persia, I presumed the rather to present this my labour to your honourable Lordship as upon whom God hath vouchsafed like great and rare graces. T'sufficeth that your honour read it, greater favour Esdras seeketh not. He labours not to praise or please, which now-a-days finds many friends, but to admonish and forewarn, which fatally finds none, till't be too late.[12]

Again in applying in both *The exposition of revelation* and particularly *Babylon is fallen* prophetic texts to secular events and indeed even to contemporary power politics T.L. was scarcely alone, although again the directness and seeming precision of the correspondences at which he was surely more than hinting were unusual. And again, even as he plunged into the affairs of kings and emperors, T.L. continued to display a highly ambivalent attitude to secular power. Of course, the power of the papal Antichrist in his account (as in others of the day) expanded at the expense of that of Christian princes, and T.L. could commit himself to what looked like a conventional enough account of the antipathetic relationship between popery and the powers of properly constituted Christian rulers. Thus, in one passage in the *Exposition*, expatiating on the propensity of the beast to blaspheme the name of God, T.L. concluded that it was the 'less marvell then if, like a raging flood, down bearing all before him and overflowing all banks of obedience towards God, he dare extol his cursed head above all that is called or named God, that is to say, all magistracy, authority and power secular, which, by God's own ordinance and commandment, is the only true, lively and immediate representation of his own person, justice and government here on earth, in and over all temporal causes and persons, as well ecclesiastical as civil, of which high treason one apostle also convinceth him, 2. Thess.3.'[13]

But, on the other side, we have the description, quoted above from *Babylon is fallen*, of the first Christian emperors as but 'ethnic Caesars' persuaded only 'in policy' to play the Christian. These, moreover, were the people who actually set up the first springs of the papacy. Thereafter T.L. described papal power as growing by the 'base and voluntary submission' of princes and saw the rise of the Holy Roman Empire and the monarchies of Spain and France as integrally related to the rise and domination of Antichrist. Moreover, even if England was (in the passage cited above) 'mentioned in dispatches' for standing out against the papal monarchy, the purport of T.L.'s letter to Essex was ambivalent. No doubt Spain and France were doomed, together with the beast their master, but they were not doomed quite yet. His was a discourse designed to keep Essex's plans and proceedings 'within the circle and limitation bounded and drawn from above'; he wrote, he claimed, not to 'praise or please but to admonish and forewarn'. And finally, at the end of the passage praising Christian princes as 'the only true, lively and immediate representation of his [God's] own person, justice and government here on earth', we have that tell-tale reference to kingly power over only 'temporal causes and persons, as well ecclesiastical as civil'. That was a phrase which might be taken to leave the issue of royal authority over spiritual questions of right doctrine and Christian practice altogether out of account.

Judging from a passage in the 'advertisement to Queen Elizabeth' that preceded the first and now lost edition of his *Exposition ... of revelation*, T.L. had a vision of temporal magistracy that was almost entirely dependent on the magistrate's response to his (and, of course, God's) message.

> I do not advertise you [T.L. told the Queen] concerning the wisdom of a princess of this world, how to relieve your people if they be oppressed nor how to curb them if fullness make them wanton, nor how to raise a little weal to a great or how to uphold it from falling down again (for all these things you may do and perish) but I advertise you concerning a wisdom from above which, if you understand and do thereafter, then shall your sceptre be a sceptre of continuance and you a princess and queen forever, not like to Babylon nor the monarch of the Turk nor like the rakeshell rout of emperors and kaisers of this world, which for a season flourish and then go down to hell, but like unto his servant David who, in the days of his flesh, performed the duties of a king of this world and yet remained a king forever, for he observed the counsel and wisdom from above which made him so fair in situation, like to Mt. Sion, never to remove.[14]

Taken on their own, some of these phrases might seem to amount to little more than straws in the wind, loose talk or imprecise diction of the sort which someone high on the oracular extremities of the prophetic mode might well produce without thinking through all the possible logical consequences or resonances of what he was saying. And yet it is surely impossible not to detect, certainly in that last passage, a claim to genuinely prophetic status, bringing to the queen a hidden knowledge from above without which even she could not be saved. Viewed from this perspective the average ruler was merely one of the 'rakeshell rout of emperors and kaisers of this world'. Only if enlightened by T.L. could either Essex or his queen hope to play their divinely appointed roles in events and thus be saved.

If we push further into T.L.'s thought we can see that these passages are part of a wider pattern, the product of a rooted propensity to see human history not so much as a struggle between Christian princes, national churches and the papal Antichrist, but far more as a spiritual conflict between what T.L. termed God's two witnesses and the little flock of true believers, on the one hand, and the forces of Antichrist, on the other. For T.L., the two witnesses were God's two testaments of scripture, also referred to in scripture as 'those two olive trees ... which stand and fructify before the ruler of earth for ever and ever. For their leaf, that is to say, their word and judgement shall neither wither nor fade, though heaven and earth should perish and melt away. And they are also two candlesticks which carry in them the light of my truth and power of my spirit, the great moderator of heaven and earth.'[15]

Against these two witnesses the beast waged a constant warfare.

> Antichrist the beast ... shall not only hurt and wound them by slanderous and lying expositions, as his clerks and affects do, but shall set his feet upon their necks and tread down their divine authority by the advancing of his accursed keys and the beauty of his whorish church above them, which the spirit calleth waging battle, inhibiting them to prophesy or teach the words of their testimony vulgarly. And not only putting them to silence, but also reproving and condemning them for corrupters, seducers and sowers of heresies among the people which presumptuous blasphemy and murder the spirit discovereth in saying that he shall overcome them and kill them.[16]

There was, indeed, a sense in which the beast would succeed in killing the two witnesses of scripture.

> And all nations and kingdoms where the beast is worshipped (whom the Holy Ghost for their profanation in life and religion calleth gentiles) shall have, handle and gaze upon the letter and corpse of his two witnesses three days and a half, that is to say, the time, times and half a time, wherein the beast shall reign and persecute ... Neither shall they suffer the word of their prophecy to be read, opened, understood or laid up in the hearts of the people, the true and natural monuments and sepulchres, wherein the testimony of their words ought to be interpreted.[17]

God, however, would not allow his witnesses altogether to be slain and in fact used them to foster and protect a remnant of true believers 'strewed and scattered far and near over the face of the earth', even at the height of Antichrist's persecution. 'Neither was the Lord less loving and provident concerning her food, for he preserved for her diet the two witnesses of his eternal covenant that from their breast she might suck the pure and wholesome milk of grace and life, that so she might be both nobly harboured and princely fed during the tedious and odious reign of the great whore, the church of Rome.'

> If she travel by day, they are her leading cloud; if by night, they are her pillar of fire; if she fly, they lend her wings; if she wander, they harbour her; if she be naked, they cover her; if in prison, they visit her; if captive, they redeem her; if she be weak, they sustain her ... if she doubt, they resolve her; if she err, they direct her; if she thirst, they give her drink; if she hunger, they feed her and make her so strong of constitution that afflictions are rejoicings to her, banishment a haven, dispersion a friend, loss and death advantage. And by these comforts (as by hands) they convey her to her solitude and restless place of rest ... where, ever since her primitive dispersion, she hath lived, strewed and scattered far and near over the face of the earth, seen and known by her lord, by whom she is protected and of the children of wisdom of whom she is justified and so doth and must remain hidden and retired into the privy chambers of God's providence and her own conscience during the reign of Antichrist.[18]

For during that reign the church thus defined was subject to constant persecution and harassment, both by the papal church and by the secular powers in thrall to the pope. For, explained T.L., the 'proctors of Antichrist so baffled and blinded the princes and protectors of their synagogues that they enzealed them to authorise and erect inquisitions, executions and torments against all such as refuse to honour and adore the idol-service and desolation of their Antiochus and that all such as do but mutter against the magnificence of their church and her worship, which all the world adoreth, should be accounted as ... weeds, lollards, heretics, excommunicates and sons of death.'[19]

THE TRUE CHURCH AND THE LITTLE ONES OF GOD

It was the church thus called together and preserved by the two witnesses that constituted the centre of T.L.'s attention. In his *The key of David* T.L. defined the church thus – 'the lord Jesus Christ did, for supplying his own place, send down from heaven the powerful efficacy of his holy spirit to guide and govern his church, which past question is nothing else but the company and society of his holy ones in all places, here and there scattered over the whole world ... this company of God's own people is sanctified by the laver of repentance and the word of faith to be an holy nation forever to the Lord himself'.[20]

Here was the true church against which Antichrist raged and by whose adherence to the testimony of the two witnesses the beast was finally to be brought low. T.L. opened both his *Exposition* and his earlier *To the church of Rome* with long passages detailing the relationship of this hidden true church of believers to the visible, institutional church. 'The kingdom of God', T.L. intoned on the third page of *To the church of Rome*, 'is likened to a field, containing corn and weeds: to a net, enclosing fish of all sorts, good and bad; to a wedding, whereunto all were bidden, those that refused, those that came prepared and those that came and were not appareled ... and this is the kingdom whereof it is written "many are called".'[21]

Within this greater community or kingdom were to be found 'two special differing companies':

> the one that hearing the voice and obeyeth and doth it; the other, that hearing transgresseth and doth not, called in scripture 'hated, bond, forsaken, cast out, children of evil, vessels of wrath' and such like ... But they that, hearing the commandments of God, observe and do them are called in scripture 'beloved, free, chosen, beautiful, children of promise, vessels of mercy, Israel, Jacob, his people, his heritage, a holy nation, a holy city, a kingly and holy priesthood, his house, his temple, his tabernacle, saints, Sion, Jerusalem from above, the pillar and upholder of truth, his vine, his church, his body, his spouse' and such like; ... And this is the generation of them that seek him, the portion and kingdom whereof it is written 'but few are chosen'. And of this company and no other speaketh the scripture, which saith: 'where two or three be gathered together in my name, there am I in the midst of them'. And again: 'And behold I am with you from day to ever, even to the world's end' ... And this is the city and house spiritual built upon the head of the corner, which, through the strength and glory of the foundation, remaineth and liveth for ever, as it is written 'and upon this rock will I build my church, and the gates of hell shall not prevail against her'. And this is the church and sanctuary of God, the stones of life and glory everlasting, disdained and trodden under of worldly builders, prepared notwithstanding from above and appointed to serve for his tabernacle and place of his dwelling ... And this is she which erreth not, dissenteth not, for all her children are endued with a tongue and taster of truth; all are prepared with one and self same water; all are purged with one and self same fire.[22]

Here, then, is a (predestinarian) rhetoric of the little ones as exalted and an identification of them with the true church as complete and explicit as anything produced by Etherington in 1610.

This was a vision of the church of the little ones that T.L. directly contrasted to all the other visible churches of the present age. 'This is the church and city of God not like unto the shameless and adulterous congregations of these times, pure in skin and foul in heart, which boast to be that they are not, each discovering others spots, themselves full of ulcers, daily squaring and falling out like thieves about the treasures and riches of God, which appertain to truer men than they.' If there was more than an echo here of H.N.'s denunciations of the mutually exclusive claims of the era's premature reformers, T.L. went on to produce an almost perfect prefiguring of Etherington's denunciation of 1610 of 'those foolish and irreformed reformers' the puritans, who 'in all this time have not learned to discern between the image of God and the inscription of Caesar'. Using terms very similar to those employed by Etherington, T.L. excoriated Christians who did not realise that, for all the benefits of Christian liberty, they were still born under authority, obliged to obey the magistrate, 'giving to a prince the obedience which to a prince belongeth'. In what was a patent reference to contemporary puritan/conformist debate, T.L. claimed that the resulting controversies had led both sides into potentially damning error. 'As we see everywhere this day', he lamented, some are 'so drunken with the primacies and prerogatives of Caesar as that they fear not to revile the freedom appertaining to the kingdom of God. Others so headlong carried with a false pretended liberty and freedom of a Christian, that they care not to deny the lawful sword and authority of Caesar so that amongst so many, some few, from time to time, are found that can discern how saints are free and yet subject to Caesar.' And, as we might have expected from our previous reading of both Etherington and H.N., these, of course, were the little ones.[23]

Here, then, is surely a, if not the, source for Etherington's vision of the little ones of God and for his equation of that group with the true church. As Professor Collinson has remarked, this was a basic and by now rather old protestant saw; 'shared', as Collinson observes, 'by one of the earliest protestant bishops William Barlow' who 'defined "the trewe church of God" as "where so ever ii or iii simple personnes as ii coblers or wevers were in company and elected in the name of God"' 'with the simple Cornish woman who told her own bishop that the true church was "not your popish church" but "where two or three are gathered together in the name of God"'. Expressed in such anti-papal contexts, where T.L. was ostensibly still exclusively expressing them, such views did indeed lead to separation, but only from the church of Rome. As Collinson argues, their 'longer term implications were anti-separatist. There could be no separation from the true church where it had separated itself against the false. Gathered church and universal church are, as Troeltsch perceived, congruous.'[24] And so, no doubt, T.L. would have told the Elizabethan authorities, as indeed Etherington was to tell Stephen Denison in 1627, when Denison accused him, on the basis of such sentiments, of being a separatist. But, by deploying such raw and unqualified versions of arguments drawn from the radical early years of protestant protest, T.L., and Etherington after him, were surely inviting such suspicions. Moreover, for T.L., as for Etherington, the origins of these true believers were spiritual rather than ecclesiological. If they were produced by baptism it was not by baptism conceived as an outward rite or sacrament but rather as a type or symbol for certain actions of the spirit. For the denizens of this true church, the little ones of God, were initially marked off from their fellows, T.L. explained, by the depth and efficacy of their 'repentance'. They must be prepared by the baptism of water, purveyed by John the Baptist, if they were subsequently to receive the baptism of the Holy Ghost, purveyed by Christ.[25]

Here neither the works of the Jewish law nor the outward forms of popish 'repentance' would do the trick. 'This is he that is poor and bruised, that laboureth and is heavy laden, sick, lost, dead and liveth no more; this is he that travelleth, like a woman that laboureth, that weepeth while the world sporteth, devising pleasantly to pass the time away, and this is he that is turned, begotten by water, prepared by the mourner, and unto whom God hath sworn by the honour of his name, "he shall not die".'[26]

Sometimes this conviction came relatively quickly, sometimes more slowly. But eventually, T.L. assured his readers,

> to this man God maketh answer, early or late, delivereth him; how much the longer withholdeth his countenance, retiring, as it were, his pity from him, so much the more intendeth to advance his love and mercy towards him, to make him great and a pillar of his house, a comforter of the weak and broken knees of others and, in his time, sendeth down his promise, the rich and hidden treasure which, from the beginning, dwelled with himself, and with his holy one, who day by day laboureth, washeth and bindeth up his broken one, not leaving to apply unto his stripe, until he have wrought and shaped in him a full and perfect assurance that God hath given him unto his son: in him and through him, forgiven and covered all those his transgressions which cried out too justly against his blood. And whereas in the day of his trespass, was a stranger and an enemy, now, in his son and for his sake, is reconciled and beloved and is unto him as a son and he to him a father.[27]

Now the true believer was as 'assured that his sins are forgiven' as he was 'sure and persuaded that his lord and redeemer [who] was once dead, now liveth and never dieth more'. 'God being with him, nothing may prevail against him; as it is written "God justifying, who may condemn?" This man is now so assured God loveth him as that he is sure and fully persuaded neither fire nor sword, neither death nor life, neither angels nor powers nor principalities, neither things present nor things to come, neither natures above nor depths below nor any creature other whatsoever may separate him from the love which God beareth him, in Christ Jesus his lord.'[28]

Thus assured that his sins were remitted, the justified sinner was led to bring forth a stream of good works.

> The assurance of mercy and forgiveness of his sin, worketh in him such a true and perfect hatred of sin, as no man knoweth but he that is baptised in Silo with him: and this hatred dwelleth not idle, hidden up and sleeping in him, but as a city built upon a hill, showeth his bastions and beauty to the passers by, so breaketh forth this fire within him, making known to all his members the power and strength thereof, retiring them from their old and wonted ways, remembering unto him with what a precious bath and price he is washed and brought from the unclean and vain conversation wherein once he walked, now and ever after to be holy, as he is holy that hath chosen him.[29]

This hatred of sin was balanced by an equally powerful love of the God who had justified and saved him. 'The assurance that God loveth him worketh in him ... such a love of God and of his lord and redeemer as no man knoweth but he that hath it.' Nor could this love be limited to God alone. '"He that loveth God loveth his brother also" ... And this is the love which the world can neither give nor receive, the love which forebeareth and is gentle, void of envy, vaunteth not, whose countenance is humbled, whose steps are modest, always seeking good to others ... beareth all things, believeth all things, hopeth all things, endureth all things.'[30]

Here, then, was the defining characteristic of the true believer, the truly justified Christian, and T.L., like Etherington after him, talked of it in the most exalted language available. 'And this is the perfection, the new commandment, the garment dipped in the precious price.' 'Love', T.L. intoned, in his advertisement to Queen Elizabeth, is the

> light and perfection of the whole estate and travail of a Christian ... This is that love and that new commandment whose often praise shineth in the two lights and lamps of God which burn before his throne, day and night, and no man can attain thereto or have his part therein that hath not first been cleansed by the promise of the father, which is the spirit of adoption wherein he crieth Abba, father. And this is that holiness and newness of life which the scripture so commendeth unto us, by the names of vivification, renovation spiritual and the first resurrection. Blessed and holy are they that have their parts therein for on such the second death shall have no power, as it is sealed in the book of life.[31]

We *could* be dealing here with no more than an emphatic, indeed a positively ecstatic, rendition of what remained common enough doctrinal positions in late Elizabethan England. Here, albeit stated in T.L.'s own peculiar, exaltedly, even overheatedly, scriptural style, were versions of the doctrines of absolute election, justification by faith alone, assurance and perseverance entirely recognisable from the works of mainstream puritan divines like Stephen Denison and the puritan elders (Perkins, Chaderton *et al.*) who were training Denison and his contemporaries at Cambrige during precisely the same period that T.L. was writing these lines. On the other hand, there is something distinctive about the sheer intensity and insistence of the language in which T.L. formulated and evoked these doctrines. Distinctive, too, was the fondness for the rhetoric of 'love', the insistence on the completeness of 'the first resurrection' which are all redolent of something other than what passed for orthodoxy in the Cambridge of the 1590s. Indeed, as we shall see below, in T.L. (as, indeed, with his alleged follower Etherington) we may be dealing with some sort of synthesis between some of the central commonplaces of late Elizabethan 'perfect protestantism' and a number of crucial insights, doctrines and locutions drawn from the writings of H[enry] N[iclaes] and the beliefs and practices of his English followers in the family of love.

Another pair of initials?

FAITH, REPENTANCE AND THE MAKING OF 'THE LITTLE ONES'

In his *De fide* of 1592, T.L. was at pains to defend this vision of the Christian's progress to true justifying faith against certain assertions of Peter Baro, the Lady Margaret professor of divinity at Cambridge, who, three years later, was to become embroiled as one of the central figures in the predestinarian disputes that culminated in the Lambeth Articles. On the one hand, this book can be placed in a very tight polemical context, provided by concerns and disputes canvassed in puritan circles in Cambridge and London, during the early 1580s. For then a whole series of puritan divines, most of them (William Charke, Laurence Chaderton and Walter Travers) centrally involved in the classis movement, had ganged up on Peter Baro for precisely the same opinions – that our first love of God was of the nature of justifying faith and that justifying faith was commanded in the decalogue – for which T.L. attacked Baro in his *De fide* of 1592. On the other hand, his dispute with Baro merely provides us with another perspective from which to view the central features of T.L.'s thought.[32]

At issue in the dispute was, first, the origins and nature of justifying faith and, second, whether or not that faith was commanded in the law. T.L. defined the faith in question as 'a certain full and firm confidence, engraven by the power of the holy ghost in the heart of such a one as is penitent, whereby he assuredly believeth that all his sins are remitted and that he is reconciled and made one with God, in an everlasting love, through Jesus Christ'.[33]

> The matter of this faith is a sure, full and undoubted trust or confidence and the form is the favour or grace of God the father and of the Lord Jesus Christ. The efficient cause is the finger of God, viz. the Holy Ghost, who alone imprinteth this confidence of grace in the hearts of the elect. The end subordinate is the salvation of the saints, but the main and chief end is the glory of God and of our lord Jesus Christ to whom, with the father and the holy spirit, one God, blessed forever, be all power, praise and honour, throughout all times and ages.

The point at issue between them T.L. defined as 'how this so precious faith is wrought and ingrafted in men and by what degrees we must attain unto it'.[34]

Unlike what he took to be Baro's position, T.L. wanted to distinguish hard between justifying faith itself and the necessary preliminary steps or stages towards its achievement. Of these, he discerned two. The first was 'the gift of illumination or the faith of knowledge'. Despite the fact that Baro admitted that 'the same is incident to unclean spirits and wicked men into whom the faith of Abraham can no way come', Baro erroneously insisted that this knowledge was 'an essential part' of a true justifying faith; further arguing that 'the end of this faith of knowledge is to enjoy God and his righteousness, even the grace of Jesus Christ'. For T.L., to affirm as much without setting down any due and reasonable difference is an impious falsehood. For God vouchsafeth not this faith of knowledge to satan and to reprobates to this end that he may bring them unto his Christ (viz.) to righteousness of life ... God very often granteth the benefit of the word and the fruit of that benefit, which is to believe the truth, even to those that perish, yet not to this end, that he may sanctify them, but that, insomuch as they would not obey the known truth which they plainly understood, he may take vengeance upon them in greater rigour of his justice and severity; for he that knoweth and doth not shall be beaten with more stripes and to whom more is committed, of him more shall be required.[35]

Here T.L. was letting his predestinarian presuppositions show. It was only in a scenario in which God offered salvation to all, and the believer's ultimate fate was in part a function of his or her response to that offer, that it made any sense to present the faith of knowledge as an integral part of justifying faith. That universalist tenet was, of course, central to Baro's overall position. But T.L. simply assumed that Baro's universalism was false, that is, he took it as a given that God did not offer salvation, and hence a true justifying faith, to all. His argument proceeded on the unexamined and undefended assumption that from the first God knew who were his and who were not, whom he had chosen and whom he had left. In the light of that sovereign act of divine choice, the fact that the faith of knowledge was often granted to reprobates meant that such a faith could not constitute any part of justifying faith, for those whom he justified God invariably saved and since reprobates were inevitably doomed to hell they could not be offered any part of a true justifying faith. This, of course, was not an argument that a person of Baro's opinions would have found convincing.

Elsewhere in the book T.L. approached other issues linked to both earlier and later predestinarian assaults on Baro's orthodoxy. In particular Baro's claim that faith was enjoined to the believer in the decalogue, that it was, in fact, part of the law, seemed, both to T.L. and others, fatally to confuse the law with the gospel and so to undermine certain absolutely central elements in what passed for English reformed orthodoxy in this period. For T.L. the law was what brought people to acknowledge the need for faith. 'For the decalogue requireth that piety of the faithful which none of them can fulfil.' It applied, moreover, equally to all, the elect and the reprobate, those blessed with justifying faith and those devoid of it. 'Neither doth it, by the righteous sentence thereof, condemn that righteous man that falleth seven times a day, less than any wicked one that never believed, for the law is delivered to the delinquent and transgressor, not to this or that particular but to all, of what mold so ever thou art made, that sinnest; of what stock, virtue, piety, faith, in what favour with God, it passeth not; if thou fault never so little, it adjudgeth thee to death for the law of the decalogue is that, a spiritual law. Contrarywise every one, even the most holy, is sold under sin.'[36]

In short, the decalogue condemned all, the pious and the impious, the elect and reprobate. It had nothing to do with faith, with the inward spiritual state of the believer, but dealt only with his or her outward works. The moral law provided a balance in which the works of all would be found wanting when weighed in the scales of divine justice against the enormous burden of human sin.

'God in his decalogue', explained T.L., 'hath enjoined that righteousness to us alone which the worthiness of the worker obtaineth, as it is written "the man that doth these things shall live in them."' Of course, since the fall, no one could achieve salvation through such means and the moral law existed simply to bring this depressing fact home to fallen humanity. In short, the threatenings of the law served to drive believers to the promises of the gospel; the moral law existed first and foremost to force believers to rely on the law of faith. 'If God had not found out another law of grace and promise', T.L. continued, 'by which he might freely give inheritance to holy Abraham and his seed, then blessed Isaac should as well have been disinherited as abject Ishmael, and Jacob, beloved, had perished with Esau, that was hated.' This law was, therefore, of an altogether different sort from the decalogue. 'By the law of grace he hath first, twice, thrice, yea always, commended to us that righteousness which is only obtained by the faith of the believers, as it is written "he that believeth in him shall not be ashamed".'[37]

Of course, Christ and the need for a justifying faith in him had, T.L. explained, been shadowed under the law, but only in the *ceremonial* law of the Jews, now abrogated by Christ's sacrifice, and not in the *moral* law of the decalogue. By confusing these categories Baro was disrupting the opposition between law and gospel that shadowed forth the real relationship between a fallen humanity and a just but merciful God and thus, on T.L.'s view at least, Baro was undermining the very basis on which salvation was offered to a sinful humanity through faith in Jesus Christ.

Despite what we know was going to happen to Baro in Cambridge in 1595/ 96, however, T.L. did not develop these points into a full-scale predestinarian, what we might term a 'Calvinist', attack on Baro. Indeed, while, as we have seen above, parts of his argument were drenched in predestinarian assumptions, the explicit statement or defence of the doctrine of predestination was anything but prominent in this text. T.L. clearly had altogether different fish to fry and he pushed onto the real nub of his case – the issue of repentance. For T.L. repentance represented the all-important second preparatory stage before justification could take place. Baro himself referred to a 'second effect or work of the holy ghost' but described it very differently, sometimes calling it 'assent, sometimes a certain putting forward of the will or a kind of love and good liking of this happiness which is offered'. Sometimes, indeed, Baro spoke of this second state as a sort of preliminary love of God, an emotion of which he proposed two sorts, one to be experienced before and the other after justification. This, according to T.L., was to put the cart a long way before the horse. A true love of God was an effect not a cause of justification. 'None can love God', T.L. argued, 'unless he be first sanctified by faith and by that very means do indeed possess God, whom he loveth; for until thou art persuaded in thine own heart that all thy sins are remitted and that thou art eternally beloved of God, thou canst not possibly love God again, as it is written "therefore we love God, because he loved us first".'[38] As we have seen above, for T.L. 'love' was 'the first and last, the beginning and end of the counsel and wisdom of God, even his secret, hidden, eternal and only ordinance'. It was 'the light and perfection of the whole estate and travail of a Christian' and as such it must stand at the end not at the beginning of that process whereby the believer came to a saving faith in God.[39]

The sort of trust or confidence in God, which alone could provoke a true love of God, was, of course, 'the last and highest stone of our regeneration' and thus an effect of justifying faith and not, as Baro typed it, the third and last preparation for justifying faith. According to T.L., this was a doubly ludicrous conclusion, since Baro had reached this point in his argument without any mention of repentance, which, for T.L., provided the very 'foundation' of our regeneration. Baro, in short, 'bestoweth faith upon his elect without so much as once naming repentance'. This was quite wrong, for just as the faith of knowledge was a necessary prerequisite for repentance, so repentance itself was a necessary prerequisite for justifying faith. T.L. proceeded to explain the stages through which the true Christian passed on his or her way to a true justifying faith. 'The first benefit ... which God vouchsafeth ... is the seed and ministry of the word. Unto this outward benefit and ministry of the word there is sometimes added a certain inward virtue and efficacy of the holy ghost, who, as he leaveth some in unbelief, so he inclineth others and causeth them to cleave fast unto the truth, with the whole assent of their minds and to believe it.' This was our old friend 'the faith of knowledge'. 'Now after this the holy ghost, causing his wheel, as it were, to run about the second time, goeth to his work again and of those which are believers, some he reformeth and maketh new creatures, others he reserveth to their more just condemnation because the truth which they knew they obeyed not.' Here was effected the crucial dividing line between the 'little ones of God' and mere outward Christians.[40]

In effecting this division, however, God always observed a very particular order. 'First he mollifieth or softeneth them and causeth them to bewail their sins by earnest prayer, to make suit for pardon and, with restless and unspeakable desire, to seek the favour of that God whom without all reason they have offended.' This even Baro identified as 'the second effect of the spirit' but he 'unfitly and philosophically' insisted on describing it as but 'a certain motion or action of the will'. But, T.L. insisted, 'the scripture contrarily calleth it repentance, which is not only a certain motion of the will but a full change altogether of the whole man'.[41] Repentance was

> an effectual operation of the Holy Ghost whereby a man returneth from his own ways and converteth himself unto God. Now to return from his own ways is to bewail his sins and the transgressions of his life in which, as in wandering paths, he hath gone astray. Wherefore his returning comprehendeth the mollifying of his heart or contrition; and to be converted unto God is to confess our sins unto God and most earnestly to seek peace and reconciliation with him. Therefore conversion unto God containeth in it confession, detesting and praying against the offence and a certain incredible desire or longing after peace.[42]

Here, in T.L.'s and later Etherington's terminology, was the baptism of water, the baptism of John the Baptist 'wherewith except a man be first washed he can by no means put on Christ'. For it was only after this first baptism of repentance that 'he that cometh after [Christ] shall baptise you with the spirit and with fire, viz. shall sanctify you with faith'. For, T.L. claimed, 'the joyful and happy embassage of the free grace and favour of God, for Christ's sake' could only be vouchsafed to 'the captives, the poor, the broken, viz. the penitent. For the kingdom of heaven pertaineth to none but the humble, the poor, the lowly and the little ones, viz. the penitent.'[43]

For it was only to the Christian now 'like a woman with child labouring of sorrow' that 'the Holy Ghost doth the third time reach forth his hand and administreth unto him comforts according to the multitude of his sorrows'. 'And this is that third effect or work of the holy ghost, viz. the sanctification of faith which finisheth or maketh up our regeneration.'[44]

This manner of proceeding, T.L. concluded, was 'God's steadfast and immutable order, whereof he will neither repent nor change it forever'. Thus was the work of regeneration, that had started with repentance, perfected in the gift of true faith. 'For repentance is the first beginning and, as it were, the entry of our regeneration ... but faith is the very perfection and, as it were, the very highest top of our regeneration, viz. the insculpture or engraving of the Holy Ghost whereby the repentant doth assuredly believe that all his iniquities are forgiven and his sins conquered and that he is united with God in an everlasting love of Christ Jesus only.'[45]

TEXT AND SUBTEXT

Ostensibly the targets for all T.L.'s invective in these books were either the errant opinions of Peter Baro or more generally the church of Rome. These, of course, were conventional enough targets. Baro, it was true, had not yet been forced out of Cambridge by the predestinarian broadside of 1595/96 but, as we have seen, he had already been subjected to an assault by London puritans and Cambridge divines on precisely the same doctrinal grounds for which T.L.

was attacking him in *De fide*. Attacks on popery, of course, were ten-a-penny. But there were hints dropped throughout all his books that T.L.'s claims and arguments were not intended to be limited in their resonance or implications to the initial polemical contexts provided either by his debate with Baro or his assault on popery.

To take the book against Baro first; this was strewn with dark hints that it was not only Baro who had misconstrued the proper doctrine of justifying faith. Thus, at one point, T.L. claimed that 'if our divines had walked so uprightly as they ought to have done in so weighty a cause, peradventure we might have had this powerful faith upon earth, the true nature whereof being now (as it were) utterly lost, we do retain nothing of it but the bare shadow only'. He was speaking, he reminded his readers, of 'the faith whose worth and fairness so clearly shineth throughout scripture that, as it is to be wondered however it could be so grossly darkened by the unskilfulness of some wise divines of this our age, so much more marvellous is it that the ignorance of such a great benefit (especially in this clear light of all things) should not hitherto, by God's most righteous judgement, be severely punished'.[46] This was strong stuff, of an intensity not easily explained by the errors of Peter Baro. Who precisely these 'wise divines' were and what precisely the errors that had so hidden the nature of true faith from contemporaries T.L. did not say and it is hard for us, at this distance, to tell. There was more than an element of a coded message in all this. One thing, however, emerged very clearly – T.L. was sanguine about neither the spiritual condition of his countrymen nor the reception likely to be accorded to his own opinions.

We can perhaps detect something of the same covertly subversive, both pessimistic and yet prophetically optimistic, tone in T.L.'s ostensibly anti-papal writings. Anti-popery was, of course, by far the most common form of late Elizabethan protestant writing. If English divines produced anything like systematic theology in this period they did so almost entirely in debate with the church of Rome. Here was a conventional and inherently respectable mode of writing, a polemical code in which one might hope to both disseminate and conceal all sorts of messages. Thus many of the most potent passages quoted above on the spiritual prerogatives of the little ones were culled from a diatribe formally addressed (and entitled) *To the church of Rome*. Throughout his works the 'covenant and mercy and love' was described by T.L. as opposed to the old covenant of Jewish and now *popish* works. In a series of long passages towards the end of his missive *To the church of Rome*, T.L. juxtaposed the true love and virtues of the justified little ones, baptised from above by both water and the spirit, against the false claims to repentance and works righteousness advanced by the papists. Again when T.L. asked bitterly 'what wilt thou do to this man to take his love from him? Wilt thou revile him, charge him with the names of heretic, sectary, private spirit, devil?' he might be taken to have been addressing the notional popish interlocutors to whom the tract as a whole was directed but such remarks had a potential resonance wider than attacks on popery. After all, the propensity, in Elizabethan England, to upbraid the godly as private spirits, sectaries and heretics was far from being limited to papists.[47]

Indeed, the basic polarity around which T.L.'s case was organised had other than merely anti-papal resonances and implications. For the basic theme of T.L.'s thought was the contrast between the inner kernel of true believers and the far greater numbers of merely outward Christians, who made up the vast majority of the membership of any and every visible church. This was a distinction to which T.L. returned again and again, and it was one that simply could not be construed as applying only to the church of Rome. On the contrary, it applied to any and every visible church. It was not, after all, merely the papists who failed to recognise or, still worse, reviled the elect remnant in their midst. Many seeming Christians, who enjoyed the outward privileges of the word and sacraments, in fact belonged to the same reprobate category as the gentiles who 'opposed' and denounced the 'true and sanctified Christian' 'as melancholy, mad, new, factious, schismatical, heretical'. Such people were described at one point by T.L. as 'Christian catholics, politicians, atheists, carnal gospellers and such heathenish protestors like to these.'[48]

In a passage near the end of *To the church of Rome* T.L. again enumerated and labelled the different types of Christian 'whose stink is everlasting and [who] shall not enter into the rest of God forever nor see his holy city'. First, inevitably, came the papists, those 'that shall be found to have worshipped the beast' or 'received the print of his name'. Next came those who peddled false and damning doctrine in the church of God such as 'Arians, ubiquists, libertines, familists, coinonists and any such other antichrists like to them'. And finally came 'all those that follow and shuffle themselves in companies, marching under names and titles whatsoever as Hussites, Lutherans, Calvinists, evangelists, protestants, precisians and any such other like to these and have not their parts in great sorrow and fear, the preparation and beginning of the wisdom from above, shall stand without, among the dogs, the covetous, the murderer, the adulterer and him that is defiled with unspeakable uncleanness and shall not enter into the rest of God forever nor see his holy city'.[49] Here, then, was proof positive that while T.L. might appear to deploy the contrast between the hypocritical and reprobate majority of merely formal Christians and the justified minority of true believers in a primarily anti-papal context, he could not, and did not attempt, to limit the reach and significance of that distinction to discussions of popery or the church of Rome. Of course, at one level, the contrast between the false church of Rome and the true church constituted by scattered groups of true believers was a staple of sixteenth-century anti-papal polemic and ostensibly, in adopting these arguments, T.L. was doing nothing extraordinary or even unconventional. After all, in the 1580s and 1590s, such concepts and argumentative moves were central to the dominant Foxeian mode of defending the catholicity of the English protestant church. However, the way T.L. *insisted* on the equation of these scattered minorities of justified Christians with *the* true church and then juxtaposed the church thus described against a whole slew of contemporary visible churches and confessional groups went far beyond the conventional use of that doctrine. Indeed, it positively invited subversive, indeed, potentially separatist, readings of his position.

To begin with, on T.L.'s account, the true church of justified Christians was a product of the interaction between those chosen by God and God's two witnesses, the two testaments of the bible. The room left for clerical activity and authority in these transactions seems to have been very small indeed. Of course, God's word was often assumed by Elizabethan protestants to be coterminous with the word preached but T.L. made very little of such arguments. When all this is put alongside what has been revealed above as T.L.'s less than adulatory account of the role of the Christian prince, both in the process whereby Antichrist rose to power in the church and, indeed, in the processes whereby he was being induced to fall, we are left with an account of sacred history dominated by the interaction between the two witnesses of scripture and the little ones of God, with precious little stress placed on any of the mediating institutions of the visible church or Christian commonwealth. If Jane Facey is right and there was an inherent tension in the Foxeian account of the relations between the true church of the godly remnant and the national church, between, if you like, the imperial/magisterial and the populist elements in Foxe's account of the process of reformation, then in T.L.'s thought we have a clear example of what happened when that latent populism was played up and Foxe's balancing concern for the overarching structures of royal and clerical power were played down.[50]

Moreover, T.L.'s eschatological (and ostensibly anti-catholic) musings can be linked with his writings on the nature of a true justifying faith and hence on the nature of the community of little ones, who alone constituted the true church in this life. To do so is to gain a clearer insight into his ultimately prophetic purposes and aspirations than his own deliberately illusive and oracular writings usually allow. In a passage at the very start of his tract on the *The key of David*, T.L. expressed a very pessimistic view on the contemporary response to his views on true faith and justification:

> As for this my labour, such as it is, I bequeath it to posterity, for I neither seek after nor reckon of such common patrons as these days afford. Because I have hated, even with perfect detestation, the nice untowardness of these dainty times, running after each palpable error of former ages with strong emulation but denying to

themselves, with envious folly, all benefits of things present, be they never so good, and being daily and continually advertised by the plain and sensible proof of so many mischiefs, coming in troops upon them yet nevertheless ... they still remain sottish and without understanding. Therefore I appeal unto the age next following; not this now, consisting of fleshly minded and worldly men that will be set to sale and corrupted, but that succeeding after this which shall be filled with the spirit and good conditions. This small treatise do I betake unto that age, whereof, seeing that I have no fear lest it should give partial sentence, forestalled with favour or impoisoned with malice, I am come to this assured hope to think that it will entertain this work with all readiness. And (if truth deceive me not) will preserve and keep it safely from time to time.[51]

Here T.L.'s pessimistic estimate of the spiritual temper of the present times met his rather precise and apocalyptically informed periodisation of church history. We know from both his *Exposition of the revelation* and from *Baylon is fallen* that he thought the final fall of Antichrist imminent and conceived of himself as living in the sixth age before the advent of the seventh in which that much to be wished consummation would take place. In thus bequeathing his work on *The key of David* to the next age 'that shall be filled with the spirit and good conditions', T.L. might be taken to have been doing rather more than indulging in a conventional denunciation of the mores and spiritual backsliding of his contemporaries. Rather, he was positioning himself as a prophet of better times, times in which the condition of the little ones, who constituted the true church, and, in particular, their relations both with the false church of Antichrist and with their lukewarm, hypocritical and hostile contemporaries, would be transformed.

In another passage, at the very end of the book, T.L. gave a final hint as to what he meant:

The book of God is a book indeed, full of eyes within and without and written on both sides but withal sealed, so that there are many hard things in it which you Barrowists do not understand. But if you desire to open your closets to enter into the inwards of it you had need of a key. I mean not that which Rome rejoiceth in, which openeth the bottomless pit and bringeth out monstrous lies and blasphemies. Neither do I mean that key B[aro] which laith up for thee a great heap of silver, which bringeth great increase to the dropsy of thy covetousness. Neither do I mean that key which openeth the smokes of sophistry and the mere froth of words and of divine Plato and the sophisters or such like builders of darkness and made wisdom. But I mean B[aro] the key of David that searcheth out the most secret things of the truth and the hidden things of God's wisdom and so openeth them that none can shut and so shutteth them that none can open. Which by your writing, I am sure you are without.[52]

This was, as the book's subtitle announced, 'the key that openeth the gates to the city of God' and was presumably the key of faith. It was a key that T.L. was sure that he possessed, just as he was sure that Baro, because of his erroneous opinions, lacked it. It was a key that had enabled him, in his expositions of Esdras and Revelations, to open both the past and the future to the gaze of the faithful, a key, too, to which all the little ones could lay claim but which the surrounding population of merely outward Christians and formal professors utterly lacked.

Elsewhere in his 'advertisement' T.L. spoke of the 'counsel and wisdom from above' in still more explicit and exalted language. 'The wisdom is called in scripture the new covenant, the covenant of Levi, the everlasting ordinance, the truth, the light, the life, the reward, the promise, the power, the salvation, the redemption, the sanctification, the justice, the counsel, the correction, the hidden purpose, the secret intent, the mystery and the kingdom of God' and it was to this, presumably, that the 'key of David' gave the believer access. It was called the 'wisdom from above', explained T.L., 'because it is not a virtue engendered or begotten by any grace or benefit of nature, growing to perfection by long study and large experience, but a mystery and secret from above, which God determined before all worlds and hath revealed it to the glory of those whom he hath chosen and this is the nature whose wisdom we advertise, not in the terms and eloquence of the theological discourses of this age, but in the power and strength of God, able to raise from death to life the soul that understandeth it.'[53]

Here then was a claim, if not to divine revelation, then at least to privileged insight, that, once let off the leash and deployed promiscuously by the little ones against those who attacked or even disagreed with them, would prove profoundly divisive and subversive. And it was to the next age, when presumably there would be more true believers in possession of this key, better able to make their knowledge and insight count, that T.L. bequeathed his works.

Of course, other than the toppling of the papal Antichrist, T.L. gave virtually no hints as to what visible, institutional consequences might follow from such an intensification of the spiritual temperature. Certainly, if T.L.'s *was* some sort of coded separatist message, it was in very deep code indeed. Indeed, T.L. seems to have used the same divisions between inner and outer realities and authorities, the same expansive definition of Christian liberty combined with a smothering obligation to obey the powers that be in things in themselves indifferent, that Etherington was to deploy in his tract of 1610. Thus, in a passage in *To the church of Rome*, contrasting the true holiness of the little ones to the false works righteousness of the papists, T.L. handled the subject of fasting. On the one hand, he spiritualised the whole notion of bodily abstinence, proclaiming that to 'this man all the days of his pilgrimage are a continual fast'. But, when he turned to the realm of outward observance and bodily comportment, he claimed that 'as concerning meats and bellies', unlike the papists, this man is taught of God that besides the person of a Christian (in which respect all the creatures of God are clean unto him, received in godliness, moderation and thanksgiving), he sustaineth the person of a citizen and knowing his king, his governors or state, whereunder he is placed, for good and probable causes, tending to the peace and maintenance of the many (which God especially will have preserved), have authority to command and forbid in meats, in drinks, in cloth, in days and such like, so eateth, so drinketh, so weareth, so keepeth he, as his prince commandeth, giving to his prince the obedience that to a prince belongeth and honoureth his God with the honour, which to God appertaineth.[54]

Whatever their spiritual prerogatives, insights and liberties, therefore, the little ones lived under authority in their outward temporal lives and, judging from this passage, for T.L. as for Etherington, that was a category that included the outward government and observances of the national church.

Like many of the passages cited above from Etherington's book of 1610, that might sound calmingly conformist enough for anyone. As with Etherington, one could indeed gloss much of T.L.'s position as merely a series of rather overheated and confused recapitulations, overstatements and distortions of what remained recognisably traditional Elizabethan protestant nostrums and doctrines. Thus the traditional Foxeian defence of the church of England from papist attack through recourse to an underground succession of true believers keeping the true church alive, even at the height of Antichristian tyranny, can be seen lurking behind T.L.'s equation of the true church with the scattered groups of little ones. Again, that same equivalence might be seen as an outcrop or development of the general tendency of puritan ministers to confuse or elide, in their practical pulpit divinity, God's elect with the godly community and, in their ecclesiology, both presbyterian and anti-papal, to slip and slide promiscuously between the visible and invisible churches, as their polemical and political needs dictated.[55] The entirely conventional protestant habit of applying the testimony of the prophetic books of the bible to the history of the church clearly lay behind T.L's eschatological and apocalyptic musings, only in his case that habit was now considerably extended to include a precise dating of the fall of Antichrist and a whole series of detailed parallels between biblical texts and the politics of the present and near future.[56] Finally, his vision of the spiritual prerogatives and liberties of the little ones was derived straight from what remained a vigorous but not obviously unorthodox rendition of that quintessentially protestant doctrine – justification by faith alone. Purveyors of the mainstream puritan and Calvinist doctrines of sanctification, assurance and perseverance said almost as much. Even his vision of the epistemological privileges conferred on its bearers by the key of David had parallels, and perhaps origins, in standard protestant accounts of the role of the testimony of the spirit in validating and interpreting scripture and in the prevalent puritan tendency to relate the efficacy and insight of both the clergy's ministerial efforts and, indeed, of the laity's own scriptural and pietistic self-help, to their status as elect saints.[57]

And yet we are left with a sense that there was considerably more going on in T.L.'s works than a mere restatement or even a simple development or extension of orthodox or conventional tenets and tendencies. As we have seen, throughout T.L.'s works there was always a potentially subversive subtext, a message behind the ostensibly anti-papal or anti-Baro message. The details of that subtext were never clear – the messages were so obviously coded and indeterminant that they appeared all the more suspicious and threatening for being indistinct – but they clearly amounted to something a good deal more than even a garbled version of standard protestant or even puritan opinions.

Here the modern commentator's relation to these enigmatic texts and subtexts resembles that of Stephen Denison, who, desperate to 'prove' that the dead 'sectmaster' was indeed a would-be prophet and separatist, combed through some of the more enigmatic or suspicious passages of his works looking for evidence of heterodoxy. In the course of that search, he seized on an aside in the preface to the now lost first edition of *To the church of Rome* in which the contents of the book were announced as 'the best news that ever thou hast heard'. 'Now the best news that ever we have heard', fulminated Denison, 'is the gospel and I appeal to the consciences of this factious company whether they have not in contempt all the writings since the apostles' time in comparison of T.L. his writings; yea, whether they do not equalise them to the very scripture itself, accounting T.L. a great prophet?' Again he homed in on a phrase from the end of the same pamphlet where the author, in addressing the church of Rome on the subject of her coming fall, described himself, in his usual oracular fashion, as 'thy brother' 'in Babylon mourning over thee and it and there will tarry notwithstanding the rage and violence of all thy spades, thy spades and arcu buzadoes this day and tomorrow and the third will pay my vows'. Whatever all that meant, Denison was sure that he detected in it a subtle assault not on Rome but on the church of England. For while T.L. described himself as being 'in Babylon', 'yet he lived in England at Queen Elizabeth's time ... I think I do not guess amiss at this meaning and what was his but to call our church Babylon in the very times of the gospel'. Denison pounced, too, on the passage cited above 'girding at Hussites, Lutherans, Calvinists, evangelists, protestants and precisians' which he claimed showed clearly that 'this railing epistle be pretended only to be written to the church of Rome yet it is intended also against our church'.[58] Denison was arguing here with a typical lack of nuance and subtlety. But while we might hesitate to concede that he had clinched his case against T.L. the sect master, would-be prophet and separatist, it remains the case that Denison was not merely making it up as he went along, simply

Another pair of initials?

inventing a sectarian, heterodox bugbear with which to berate Etherington. There was, in short, both from Denison's perspective and from ours, something distinctly fishy about T.L.

NOTES

1 S. Denison, *The white wolf* (London, 1627), pp. 43, 47.
2 [T.L.] *A voice out of the wilderness* (London, 1651); *A voice out of the wilderness* (London, 1661).
3 T.L., *An exposition* (London, 1623).
4 E. Arber, *A transcript of the register of the company of stationers of London, 1554–1640* (London, 1875–94), vol. III, p. 17, entered 3 January 1597.
5 T.L., *Exposition*, pp. 7–8, 110.
6 T.L., *Babylon is fallen* (London, 1651), pp. 5–6; *Exposition*, p. 88.
7 T.L., *Exposition*, pp. 88, 94–7.
8 Ibid., pp. 60, 64, 69.
9 T.L. *Babylon is fallen*, pp. 19, 20.
10 T.L., *Exposition*, pp. 18–21.
11 T.L., *Babylon is fallen*, p. 23.
12 Richard Bauckham, *Tudor apocalypse* (Abingdon, 1978), chapters 9 and 10. For Gifford's dedication to Essex see pp. 352–8. T.L., *Babylon is fallen*, dedicatory epistle. For the most recent and comprehensive account of the Hacket and Coppinger conspiracy see A. Walsham, '"Frantick Hacket": prophecy, sorcery, insanity and the Elizabethan puritan movement', *Historical Journal*, 41 (1998).
13 T.L., *Exposition*, pp. 77–8.
14 T.L., 'An advertisement to queen Elizabeth' in *A voice crying* (1651), pp. 41–2.
15 T.L., *Exposition*, pp. 11–12, 5, 8.
16 Ibid., pp. 11–12.
17 Ibid., p. 15.
18 Ibid., pp. 40, 53–5.
19 Ibid., p. 100.
20 T.L., *The key of David* (London, 1610), pp. 15–16.
21 T.L., *Exposition*, pp. 1–2; *To the church of Rome* (London, 1651), p. 3. No earlier full version of this tract survives, see RSTC entry 21309.
22 T.L., *To the church of Rome*, pp. 3–5, 36.
23 T.L., *Advertisement to Queen Elizabeth*, pp. 49–51.
24 P. Collinson, 'Sects and the evolution of puritanism', in F. Bremer, ed., *Puritanism: perspectives on a seventeenth-century Anglo-American faith* (Boston, 1993), quote at p. 152.
25 I should like to thank David Como for many discussions of this material.

26 T.L., *To the church of Rome* (London, 1589), p. 15.

27 *Ibid.*, p. 20.

28 *Ibid.*, pp. 20–1.

29 *Ibid.*, pp. 24–5.

30 *Ibid.*, pp. 26–7.

31 *Ibid.*, p. 27. T.L., *An advertisement to Queen Elizabeth*, pp. 47–8.

32 For Baro's opinions and fortunes in the 1590s see H.C. Porter, *Reformation and reaction in Tudor Cambridge* (Cambridge, 1958), chapters 13–17. For Baro, see esp. chapter 17. Also see P. Lake, *Moderate puritans and the Elizabethan church* (Cambridge, 1982), chapter 9. For the earlier altercation in the 1580s see my 1978 Cambridge Ph.D. thesis, *Laurence Chaderton and the Cambridge moderate puritan tradition*, chapter 6.

33 T.L., *The key of David*, p. 19.

34 *Ibid.*, pp. 21–2.

35 *Ibid.*, pp. 24–6.

36 *Ibid.*, pp. 52–3.

37 *Ibid.*, pp. 53, 57.

38 *Ibid.*, pp. 27, 29.

39 T.L., *Advertisement to Queen Elizabeth*, pp. 47–8.

40 T.L., *The key of David*, pp. 31, 32–3.

41 *Ibid.*, pp. 34–5.

42 *Ibid.*, p. 41.

43 *Ibid.*, pp. 39, 38.

44 *Ibid.*, pp. 35–6.

45 *Ibid.*, pp. 36, 45.

46 *Ibid.*, pp. 22–3, 20.

47 T.L., *To the church of Rome*, pp. 10, 27.

48 T.L., *Exposition*, p. 4.

49 T.L., *To the church of Rome*, pp. 36–7.

50 J. Facey, 'John Foxe and the defence of the English church', in P. Lake and M. Dowling, eds, *Protestantism and the national church* (London, 1987); A. Milton, *Catholic and reformed: the Roman and protestant churches in English protestant thought, 1600–1640* (Cambridge, 1995), chapter 1.

51 T.L., *The key of David*, pp. 2–3.

52 *Ibid.*, pp. 76–7.

53 T.L., *Advertisement to Queen Elizabeth*, p. 42.

54 T.L., *To the church of Rome*, p. 34.

55 P. Lake, *Anglicans and puritans? English conformist thought from Whitgift to Hooker* (London, 1988), pp. 28–34; Lake, *Moderate puritans*, chapters 5 and 6; Milton, *Catholic and reformed*, chapter 1.

56 Bauckham, *Tudor apocalypse*; F. Firth, *The apocalyptic tradition in reformation Britain* (Oxford, 1979).
57 Lake, *Moderate puritans*, chapters 6 and 7; J. Morgan, *Godly learning* (Cambridge, 1986), chapters 3–7.
58 Denison, *The white wolf*, pp. 47–8.

Chapter 6

What Etherington really thought: the 1620s

THE REPUDIATION OF FAMILISM

Having examined the thought of his alleged mentor T.L., let us return to Etherington where we left him, in 1610, when, on the face of it, he either *was* a familist in the full Marshian sense or had, at the very least, been heavily influenced by familist thought. Surely, therefore, we need look no further for the roots of Denison's attack upon the boxmaker. There was, however, both more and less to it than that. Etherington's pamphlet of 1610 seems to have attracted no immediate contemporary notice. Etherington was denounced not in 1611 or 1612 but in 1626, and when Denison attacked him, he did so not only or even primarily for things he had said in *A description of the true church of Christ* but rather for things that he had said and done to Denison and his flock in the much more immediate past. Indeed, Denison, presumably like the authorities and the puritan thought police at the time, missed the long familist postscript and some of the most overtly familist claims in the *Description*, none of which figured in *The white wolf*.

Why? One answer is that for all the fanfares and trumpets of *The white wolf* with its distinctions between the Castalian familists, the Gringltonian familists and the familists of the mountains and of the valleys, Denison, in fact, knew a good deal less about familism than he claimed. Perhaps, as Dr Marsh has suggested for a good many other contemporaries, Denison's notions of familism owed more to the stereotypes of puritan polemic and theatrical satire than to the works of H.N. and that, therefore, the coded messages of the *Description* flew way over his head. Or perhaps, at least in the *immediate* altercation between Denison and Etherington, 'familism' was never really the point at all. It is surely not without significance that, having spent pages denouncing Etherington as a familist and an anabaptist, Denison chose not to engage with or confute any of Etherington's supposedly familist

What Etherington really thought: the 1620s

opinions. 'Herein I do not mean to insist upon the refutation of every dotage which he is known to hold, for so I might be infinite. I will not stand to prove against him that the church of England is a true church, for this were to hold a candle to see the sun by ... neither will I insist upon his dotage concerning the perfect purity of the soul ... but that which we shall stand upon shall be 1. the sabbath and 2. the books of Esdras.'[1] This was a surprisingly tame outcome for what purported to be a full-scale exposé of the white wolf of familistical heresy then stalking the streets of London. Denison almost certainly chose these topics for detailed treatment, firstly, because the first, at least, was an issue about which he and Etherington were known recently to have disagreed and, secondly, because both topics – the status of sabbath observance as binding under the moral law and of the apocryphal books as something less than canonical scripture – were subjects upon which Denison could hope to win relatively easy victories before a heavily scripturalist and sabbatarian London puritan audience.

On this basis we might suspect that Etherington's opinions had changed considerably since the publication of his book of 1610 and such, it seems, was indeed the case. Etherington's publishing career did not end in 1610; in 1623, as Denison claimed and Etherington made no effort to deny, he either authored under the *nom de plume* Edmund Jessup or co-authored with Jessup another piece of anti-anabaptist and separatist polemic, *A discovery of the errors of the English anabaptists*. There in the 'advertisement to the christian reader' the author outlined something of his own spiritual development. If we read these passages against other autobiographical asides in works definitely written unaided by Etherington there is a remarkable both chronological and substantive fit.

As in the text of 1610, Etherington/Jessup began by lambasting the separatists for 'following after a form of godliness ... without the power thereof, contenting themselves in the outside of religion, blessing themselves in what they can do and measuring the love of God to themselves by their own doings'. They pursued, in short, an outward separation in the flesh 'when alas it is much to be feared that, with many of them, there is little or no care at all for a separation of the soul from sin'. 'After this manner do they follow the vision of their own hearts, deceiving and being deceived, running and flitting from one opinion unto another, being unstable in all their ways.' This was a process that led all such people 'who have not their hearts established with true saving grace' to toy with a whole series of 'strange and different opinions'. Chief amongst these was now ranked 'that poisonable heresy of the familists'. This was a 'destroying and damnable' nexus of error, the last stopping place on the road to ruin regularly traversed by the sectarian religious flibbertigibbets of the age.[2]

This was the first of several extended passages of anti-familist invective, sometimes as detailed as they were virulent, that studded the pamphlet. One extended piece of vituperation is worth a close look, since it parallels very closely the entirely approving summary of familist doctrine with which Etherington had concluded his *Description*. The familists, Etherington/Jessup maintained, viewed their 'author' 'one Henry Niclaes or H.N. for so they will have him called, that is, (as they expound it) homo novus' to be 'the new man or the holy nature or holiness, which they make to be Christ and sin they will have to be Antichrist, because it is opposite to Christ'. Familists thus spiritualised and universalised the persons of both Christ and Antichrist. 'They say that when Adam sinned, then Christ was killed and Antichrist came to live.' For them Antichrist rose and Christ came again with the soul of the individual. Hence came their belief in the perfectability of the soul. 'They teach that the same perfection of holiness which Adam had before he fell, is to be attained here in this life and affirm that all their family of love are as perfect and innocent as he and that the resurrection of the dead spoken of by St Paul in I Cor.15 ... is fulfilled in them and deny all other resurrection of the body to be after this life.'

On this basis they erected their own distinctive eschatology. There had, the familists held, been 'eight through-breakings of the light ... from Adam to the time that now is, which ... have each exceeded other; the seventh he [H.N.] alloweth Jesus Christ to be the publisher of and his light to be the greatest of all that ever were before him and he maketh his own to be the eighth and last and greatest and the perfection of all, in and by which Christ is perfected, meaning holiness'. Accordingly, Etherington/Jessup explained, 'they will have this blasphemer H.N. to be the son of God, Christ, which was to come in the end of the world to judge the world and say that the day of judgement is already come and that H.N. judgeth the world now by his doctrine so that whosoever doth not obey his gospel shall (in time) be rooted out of the world and that his family of love shall inherit and inhabit the world forever, the world without end'.

It was on this basis that the familists asserted their belief in their own spiritual and moral perfection. They held 'every one of his family of love to be Christ, yea and God, and himself God and Christ in a more excellent manner, saying that he is Godded with God and codeified with him and that God is hominified with him. These horrible blasphemies, with divers others, this H.N. and his family teach to be the everlasting gospel which the angel is said to preach in Revelation 14.6 and himself to be the angel, yea, the archangel which is said to sound the great and last trump, Revel.11.15.'

The familists' spiritualised, entirely internal, vision of the identity and rise of Antichrist allowed them to take a far more favourable view of the church of Rome than Etherington/Jessup found acceptable.

What Etherington really thought: the 1620s

They profess greater love to the church of Rome and to all her idolatries and superstitions then they do to any church else (whatsoever) except themselves ... And they dare compare all the whole religion of the church of Rome to the law of Moses, affirming that as God did teach his people by those shadows and types till Jesus Christ came, so he hath taught the world (ever since) by the images, sacrifices and filthy heathenism of the church of Rome, till this wretch H.N. came and now he must be the only chief teacher, God's obedient man, yea, his son, as they blasphemously call him; he (by his gospel) must make all perfect.

Again rooting their definitions of true religion in the mystical teachings of H.N. and concentrating all their attention on Christ as he was risen within the souls of the little ones, familists felt able to

outwardly submit to any kind of religion and to any idolatrous service whatsoever, pretending it is not the body that can sin but the soul. They will be priests in the church of Rome ... and, as satan can transform himself into an angel of light, so they can thrust themselves (likewise) to be public ministers and preachers in the church of England ... and so close and cunning they can carry themselves ... that ye shall hardly ever find them out. They will profess to agree in all points with the church of England, as also with the church of Rome, if they should be examined by them, only this they will not (lightly) deny their master H.N. nor speak evil of him or his writings, if they should be put to it and there is no way but this whereby to discover them.[3]

There was more than an element of tabloid true confessions about this elaborate account, with the pointed hint on how to discover a familist at the end lending an extra touch of piquancy and authenticity to the whole performance. It was, moreover, an account of familist error which tracked and repudiated, with remarkable fidelity, the tenets of familism as Etherington had espoused them at the conclusion of his *Description* of 1610 and as we have tracked them above through H.N.'s own *Evangelium regni*. We can almost certainly, therefore, take this passage as a formal disavowal, a veritable recantation of familism precisely as Etherington had embraced it at the end of his book of 1610.

Now, all this inside information was based on what the author claimed was direct personal experience. 'Of these things', Etherington/Jessup told the Christian reader, 'I can in some measure best advertise you.' For he himself had spent a good deal of time 'through want of true learning, knowledge and understanding of God and his truth caught and entangled by' a variety of sects. He had wasted years 'wandering up and down amongst the airy hills and mountains, conceiving comfort when, alas, I was far from it and the farther I wandered up and down in that Egyptian darkness, the more intricate labyrinth of error and darkness my soul was plunged into'. He seemed to have hit rock bottom when he joined 'the anabaptists' whose tenets and practices not only overturned and razed 'the foundation of all Christian religion but also' destroyed '(in as much as in them lieth) ... the faith of Jesus Christ'. Things, however, could have been worse, for he had almost become a familist. He had, he claimed, come 'very nigh unto it, having one foot entered therein whiles I walked with the people aforesaid' [the anabaptists]. It was only 'the power and providence of God' that had saved him 'from being seduced and led into that destroying and irrecoverable way of death ... until at last the lord, in his appointed time, was pleased to give me a true sight of the misery wherein I was plunged'.[4]

Here, then, was Jessup, along with his ghostwriter Etherington, producing a recognisable account of the milieu in which the author of the *Description* of 1610 had been moving as well as that out of which Jessup himself was emerging under Etherington's tutelage in 1623. Like Etherington in 1610, on the brink of a full-scale commitment to familist heresy, Jessup had been brought back from the brink by pondering the simple question of whether any of their increasingly bizarre religious opinions 'would any whit avail me unto salvation or whether it would minister comfort unto me in that great and terrible day of the lord'.[5]

The answer to that question had been a resounding no, but the immediate effect of that realisation had been anything but liberating. On the contrary, Etherington/Jessup had been plunged into a prolonged spiritual crisis, where, deprived of the outward props of his singular religious opinions, he had come to despair of his chances of salvation. 'Within a short time after I was so far from having or enjoying true peace and comfort that instead thereof my poor distressed soul was accompanied with nothing but strange fears, terrors, and guiltiness of conscience, crying out against me for nothing but vengeance, the misery whereof was such as caused me to lament the time wherein I was born, not regarding wife, children or any friends whatsoever that came to visit me.' 'The primary and first cause' of this predicament, Etherington/Jessup retrospectively concluded, 'was that original guilt which I drew from the loins of my first parents'.[6]

Thus stripped of familist fantasies about the sinlessness of true believers, Etherington/Jessup was left to confront his own sinful nature alone.

> And so being confounded and utterly lost, yea oft times in despair, fearing there was no mercy with God for me, my sins being so heavy a burden upon my soul then (even then) when I was in greatest despair God, by his spirit, was pleased to work in me a contrite and broken heart whereby it was turned from being a stubborn and stony by dissolving it into a heart of flesh as soft as water and therein, through his infinite love and goodness, did, by a more special working of his spirit, write his everlasting covenant of love and mercy which it so much sued, sought and longed for, with full assurance of the remission of all my sins, whereby I stand sealed until the day of my redemption is accomplished in the second resurrection.[7]

The language of that passage is ironically redolent of the rhetoric of Etherington, writing in his familist phase in the *Description*, but it was a

What Etherington really thought: the 1620s

language being applied now to a conversion worked by the predestinarian doctrine of the church of England.

This, of course, was no accident, since, according to Etherington/Jessup, such a transforming evangelical experience had been unavailable during their separatist and familist phases precisely because the doctrines of both sects obscured the true grounds upon which lasting spiritual comfort and assurance were available to the believer. Etherington/Jessup could gain no peace

> until the lord was pleased to open the eyes of my understanding by hearing the word and doctrine of truth which is maintained by and in the church of England, as namely the doctrine of repentance, free justification by faith, God's eternal predestination and election from the foundation of the world, that no man hath free will or power to obtain his own salvation and that original sin to be in all the posterity of Adam ever since we fell from that happy and blessed estate which once we had in him, with many other excellent truths, all which is such a certain and sure foundation that whosoever can attain to walk in the power thereof the gates of hell shall never overcome nor destroy him.[8]

One major purpose of the 1623 tract was to dot the i's cross the t's of the strongly Calvinist doctrinal position implied by those remarks and, indeed, to defend it against what the author/s took to be the heretical errors of the anabaptists, whose 'first point' was described as the contention 'that God did predestinate all men to be saved, upon condition that they repent and believe the gospel' and 'their second' that God did not predestinate persons but qualities 'and then finding these qualities in men he doth elect their persons for their qualities sake'. Both claims were rejected out of hand. Foreseeing human sin, God 'of his own mere goodness ... and being exceeding willing, not for any thing he could foresee in them, but for his own good pleasure and glory's sake, to save and glorify the same ... did determine by election ... to sustain of the one sort, I mean the angels, and to redeem of the other sort, I mean mankind, such a complete sufficient company of both as himself pleased to be at his right hand, to behold his glory and to partake of his pleasures for evermore'. This he did 'before the foundation of the world, not for [their] qualities sake, which then were not, but for his own good pleasure'. The object of God's decree was man fallen; 'God's election was not of man considered in his innocence but of men foreseen fallen and therefore they are said to be chosen in Christ who was to be a reconciler and mediator for sinners and not for innocent persons.'[9]

From all this it followed that 'election is before calling and justification' . Thus 'the purpose of God according to election, his free love in choosing us first in Christ, is the true ground and principal cause of all spiritual blessings in heavenly things, which in time we come to enjoy in him. For doubtless there was no cause in Jacob more than in Esau, why God should have this respect unto him more than to Esau; the seed of evil was sown in him also and their natures were both corrupt even from their conception, yea from Adam in whose loins both they and their parents were when he transgressed.'[10]

All this was enough effectively to overthrow what Etherington described as the next two errors of the anabaptists: the belief 'that all men have free will in themselves as well to repent of their sins, to believe the gospel and obtain salvation as they have to remain in hardness of heart and unbelief and in the estate of damnation' and that 'the steadfastness of man's justification and salvation doth depend upon his own will in continuing in the act of believing and the works of righteousness'.[11] All, Etherington conceded, were offered salvation, yet if 'God should not vouchsafe (according to his eternal purpose and promise) to call to a more special manner them whom he foreknew and had predestinated to be conformed to the image of his son ... they would and should have perished with the rest, notwithstanding any free will or power they have in nature ... to attain to these things'. On this basis Etherington was able to argue that it was quite impossible that 'such as have faith in Christ, regenerate persons, having their names written in the book of life, may fall away from all, become unregenerate and have their names razed out of the book of life and perish'.[12] For that would mean that 'God doth alter his purpose and promise of mercy and love and come to hate and reject such as he hath formerly loved and justified' to argue which 'is to deny the very foundation and to make God unfaithful'. Thus, while the godly could experience a sense of assurance about their own salvation and were under a perpetual obligation to 'be always walking in and working the works of righteousness', yet 'the steadfastness and certainty of their estates in Christ, their life, salvation and glory everlasting dependeth on the steadfastness, certainty and unchangeableness of God's purpose, promise, love'.[13]

All this marked a distinct shift away from both the sort of positions on predestination usually held by 'familists', as Dr Marsh and others have described them, and, indeed, from many of the opinions at which Etherington had sometimes more than just hinted in the *Description*. In short, the author/s of the 1623 polemic presented themselves as failed sectaries and partial familists, saved from the spiritual despair, into which their errant search for religious truth and assurance of salvation had plunged them, by the settled predestinarian theology of the church of England.

That Etherington chose to produce such a heavily predestinarian version of his position three years *before* his altercation with Denison strongly suggests that such an explicitly anti-familist, predestinarian reading of his position was not merely a short-term expedient, the result of the polemical exigencies of his showdown with Denison in the mid-1620s and as such a manoeuvre typical of a familist nicodemism, only too ready to hide a familist message behind a seemingly orthodox, predestinarian facade. Such an interpretation is confirmed, as we shall see below, by Etherington's subsequent behaviour during the 1640s, when, if he had wanted to, he could at the very least have reverted to the lightly coded message sending of 1610. That he used the relative freedom of the revolutionary decade to publish a further piece of explicitly and fervently anti-familist polemic[14] suggests that his position really had changed since 1610. The definitive transition had very likely taken place at some point between 1610 and the publication of *A discovery* in 1623 and may even have taken something like the form of the spiritual crisis and conversion experience described by Etherington/Jessup in the epistle of *A discovery*. That Denison had noticed this shift can surely be surmised from the way in which, while he was happy enough in *The white wolf* to lambast Etherington as a familist, those claims operated at a fairly high level of generality. For the most part, when Denison staked out the specific issues upon which he wished to confront and confute the boxmaker, he retreated to considerably more limited and specific doctrinal terrain.

Further confirmation for this rough chronology comes from Etherington's penultimate publication, an anti-familist tract of 1645. There he recounted earlier conversations and consultations with a variety of familists. 'There have been and are', he wrote, 'great doctors of divinity, so called, yea and some great peers and persons of quality and estate in this land ... that have taught and entertained the same [familism] with great affection and high applause', a fact of which he claimed personal knowledge 'having had speech with some of them forty years ago and sundry times since'. This would locate his most intense contacts with the familists some time around 1605 in what he now characterised in retrospect as his zealously wayward youth. 'I being, in my youth, zealously affected, was very inquisitive into those several sorts of religions which I heard of then professed and was as apt naturally as another to be seduced some way or other from the truth and had been but that the lord of his goodness, he having by his free grace showed mercy unto me in giving me repentance and forgiveness for my sins.' At this distance of time, engaged in a denunciation of recent outbreaks of old familist heresies, Etherington took the opportunity to go beyond even his claim of 1623 never to have succumbed fully to familist temptation. In the 1645 rendition of his youth, at least, Etherington had 'never had any the least inclination in my mind toward' the errors of H.N.[15]

TRACES OF T.L. AND ECHOES OF H.N. IN ETHERINGTON'S MATURE POSITION

Nothing would seem to be clearer than that. And even if we allow a now very aged Etherington a certain creative editing of his own past, his repudiation of the major tenets of familism would appear to have been pretty complete by the early 1620s. There remain, however, considerable echoes of or, to mix the metaphor, overlaps between his earlier and later positions. Even T.L. was not free from familist associations and by triangulating between T.L., H.N. and the stance adopted by Etherington in his works of the 1620s, we can discern serious traces of T.L. and echoes of H.N., even in the very text in which the boxmaker met Denison's accusations of familist heresy full on, his apologia of 1627.

In the discussion of T.L. in chapter 4, one late sixteenth-century context for his thought – that provided by familism – was largely omitted. For, as Dr Marsh has argued, there are certain 'suggestive phrases' in T.L.'s works that are more than a little reminiscent of the exalted language of the familist sublime. Nor is this insight of an entirely modern provenance. In an anabaptist assault on familism of 1622, *A discovery of the abominable delusions of ... the family of love*, T.L. was identified as one of those who 'while they will not be called familists' 'are deeply tainted with divers of these things; some called the scattered flock who agree with the former "that they may remain in babylon and there mourn and tarry". And what they account the Lord's ordinances may appear by what they write of baptism, which they say is "tears, tears is the water of baptism etc."', which last two snippets were identified by marginal notes as direct quotations from T.L.'s writings.[16]

Nor were these anything like the only verbal echoes to be found reverberating through the writings of the three men. In this context, T.L.'s talk of the 'renovation spiritual and first resurrection' constituted by the rise of 'love' in the justified sinner's soul and his addiction to the rhetoric of 'that love that the world can neither give nor receive' were, indeed, in Dr Marsh's phrase, suggestive. The same applies to Etherington even as he was denouncing 'familism' in his tract of 1623.[17] There he described the true godliness of the elect Christian as 'the first resurrection'. 'These are they that be risen with Christ and seek those things that are above, where Christ sitteth at the right hand of God ... these are not of the world, neither do they love the world nor the things of the world but the love of God, the father, is in their hearts.'[18] Elsewhere, evoking and describing the nature of the 'regenerate, true hearted Christians', Etherington explained that 'they believe to the saving of the soul; they eat the flesh of the son of man and drink his blood, spiritually by faith and have eternal life abiding in them; they dwell in Christ and Christ in them; they are borne of God and therefore draw not back, sin not to perdition for the seed whereby they are begotten remaineth in them, neither can they sin because they are borne of God'. 'On such the second death shall have no power', Etherington intoned.[19]

One might, once again, gloss these merely as peculiarly exalted descriptions of the spiritual prerogatives of God's elect. However, the language in which Etherington chose to describe these spiritual privileges remained, as Dr Marsh has pointed out, heavily tinged with familist associations and resonances. Even more 'suggestive' was Etherington's continuing addiction, even in the expressly anti-familist tract of 1623, to that phraseology of 'love', beloved of both H.N. and T.L., which had suffused his own *Description* of 1610. For Etherington, even in his 1623 incarnation, it was here that the real difference between the merely outwardly Christian, to whom the common gifts vouchsafed to all members of the visible church were granted, and those who had undergone the second baptism of the spirit was to be found.

> Admit thou hadst all faith so as thou couldst move mountains and that thou shouldst give all thy goods to the poor and thy body to be burned and that no man could tax thy heart by any evil fruit that yet appeared, nor thy self perceive thine own heart to be evil, yet if thou hast not that faith which worketh by love, that love with her natural properties which the apostle describeth ... thou art nothing, thou art but as a sounding brass and as a tinkling cymbal notwithstanding all thy gifts of knowledge, faith, prophecy, righteousness or whatsoever.[20]

And here, as it had been in 1610, love amongst the children of God was of the essence. If the godly community was a spiritual temple, its joints and ligaments were clearly held together by love. 'For the love that is showed to the children of God, the brethren of Christ, because they belong to him, of all the fruits and works of righteousness that can be performed by man to man, is of greatest esteem with God and hath the promise of reward above them all, not by reason of any worthiness of desert that is therein, but only for his promise's sake and because it pleases him for his son Christ's sake.'[21]

There was, of course, nothing explicitly or particularly familist in the assertion that it was the mark of true Christians to love both God and one another but the language is surely (in Dr Marsh's phrase) 'suggestive'. So, too, was the marked tendency of all three men (clearly exemplified in many of the extended passages quoted here and in the last chapter) to express themselves in outbursts of the scripturalising rant of the familist sublime: long passages in which a whole series of scripture phrases were run together to describe or evoke the entity or doctrine under discussion.

But we can go further than amassing verbal and stylistic echoes and parallels between the works of H.N., T.L. and the Etherington of the 1620s. Whole swathes of the substantive doctrinal opinions of the two English authors seem to have been either predicated on or remarkably similar to those of the Dutch sect master. This is true both at the most general and at the most particular levels. Most obvious is the domination of all three men's discourse by 'the little ones'. Here T.L.'s insistence on the epistemological privileges, the spiritual insights vouchsafed to the little ones as against the ignorance and error of the surrounding mass of formal believers closely parallels that of H.N. For both men, as indeed for Etherington, there was a sense in which the little ones simply were the church, which last insistence was as prominent in Etherington's pamphlets of the 1620s as it had been in his tract of 1610. As

John Etherington

late as the anti-anabaptist polemic of 1623, Etherington could describe the 'little ones' thus:

> for as they were not of Abraham's seed which came of Abraham after the flesh, not they (all) Israel that came of Israel, and as that was not circumcision which was outward in the flesh, nor that baptism which washeth away but the filth of the flesh, so neither is that the true heavenly and spiritual succession which is outward, by an external ordination and succession in the rooms and seats of the righteous servants of God. But the true and heavenly succession (which have all those heavenly treasures belonging to it) is that which Christ hath built upon the rock, as they that have the faith of Peter, of John and the rest of the apostles, even those lively stones which St Peter speaketh of, who are by faith built upon Christ, the chief cornerstone, like as Peter was, and so are made a spiritual house by this means and do offer up spiritual sacrifices, acceptable to God by Jesus Christ, and are that chosen generation, that royal priesthood, holy nation and peculiar people, which he describeth, who have received spiritual gifts from above.[22]

Here the language of puritan edification and spiritual building met the language of Etherington's earlier familism in a common reliance on the same Pauline texts and phrases; texts and phrases that were used in both Etherington's books to describe the spiritual unities and mutualities of a godly community that, even as late as 1623, Etherington continued to equate with the true church. Here, at least, was one point where Denison's accusations at the Cross had some substance.

Again, as we have seen, both H.N. and T.L. were equally hostile to the misguided efforts of the would-be reformers of the contemporary church. Both denounced the rival claims to an exclusive possession of religious truth advanced by a whole series of confessional or denominational groups in ways that were echoed by Etherington not only in 1610 but, as we shall see below, in his polemics of the 1620s as well. Thus all three agreed that it was the little ones who really knew the truth, a knowledge based not on human learning or study but on a spiritual insight vouchsafed to, in H.N.'s phrase, 'the little ones, God his elect' by God himself.

But perhaps most tellingly of all, for an argument that is at bottom about explicit doctrinal influence, all three men shared a common account of the two spiritual baptisms whereby God created his little ones, both of which they distinguished from the merely outward baptism conferred on even formal Christians by the sacrament. Men should not, warned H.N., 'run forth with an handful of water and so persuade themselves, when they have the elementish water, that it is therewith enough for to be a Christian'. On the contrary, they must first be baptised by John the Baptist with 'the water of repentance, in Jordan, which signifieth unto us a river of judgement. For unto such, where the water of repentance floweth inwardly in the heart, came the mercy or grace of the Lord and they were baptised or washed with the same water of repentance, in the river of judgement, to the knowledge of salvation and to the forgiving and purging of their sins.' This baptism of repentance, purveyed by John the Baptist, was then followed by a second, purveyed by Christ. 'And evenso after that came Messias or Christus ... unto them to the safe-making of their souls; where-through they were baptised under the living waters of the Holy Ghost to the re-edifying of the tabernacle of the living God.' H.N. was peculiarly proud of this doctrinal breakthrough, remarking on 'how great contention and disputation hath there been among many, touching the baptism ... whilst it was yet night with them, so hath no man been able, before this day of love, which is the true light and glory of God himself, to understand nor distinct the baptism of John nor the baptism of Christ'.[23]

And yet we have found precisely the same doctrine and form of words deployed in T.L.'s works and, indeed, at the very centre of his account of the conversion of the true believer to a genuinely saving faith, as he set it out in his dispute with Peter Baro. Etherington, too, remained committed to precisely this form of the doctrine. Thus, in his anti-anabaptist tract of 1623, Etherington continued, in the most explicit language, to contrast the outward baptism of water with the two inward baptisms of water and spirit. Christ

> and his apostles [had] baptised those that did believe and acknowledge him and submit themselves to be informed by his word, though they had not yet either true repentance or justifying faith. For they knew that such a belief and profession, as made men meet for outward baptism, might be where justifying faith was not and that both, that belief, profession and baptism, did but make a Christian outwardly, as the outward profession and circumcision of the Jews did but make a Jew outwardly and no better did they judge or conclude of any but when they saw better cause.

This claim underpinned a rather downbeat defence of infant baptism that closely echoed the position adopted in Etherington's *Description*. Baptism was merely an 'outward sign' to put some difference between the children of the faithful and the children of infidels 'and what can they have less than baptism which can give no man any more then the outward name of a Christian as circumcision did the outward name of a Jew. It doth neither confer nor confirm grace to the heart of any, no more than circumcision did. It proveth that a man is a Christian outwardly and it teacheth that he should be so inwardly and so did circumcision.' In what he again presented as a stark contrast to both the anabaptists' and papists' insistence on outward forms, all of Etherington's emphasis went on what he termed the inward 'baptism of the holy ghost and the birth of the spirit'.[24]

THE SPIRIT AND THE LETTER: I THE SACRAMENTS

Indeed, elsewhere in his reply of 1627 to Denison's accusations at the Cross, Etherington, here again closely echoing both H.N. and particularly T.L., went further in his efforts to allegorise or spiritualise baptism, representing the spiritual progress of the individual to justification, remission of sins and hence salvation as a progression between two baptisms – neither of which, we should note, was coterminous with outward baptism. The first was the baptism of John the Baptist. This Etherington characterised as the 'baptism of repentance'. The second was 'to be baptised with the Holy Ghost and with fire'. This was to be baptised by Christ and followed the first baptism of repentance. For Christ had sent John the Baptist into the world with the words 'the blind do see, the lame do walk and the poor have the gospel preached unto them', words which Etherington glossed as meaning 'the humble repentant sinners, the poor and contrite in heart' – in the parlance of his 1610 tract 'the little ones of God' – shall 'have the glad tidings of peace and remission of sins preached unto them and ministered unto their souls'. Etherington defined to be baptised of repentance as 'to repent, to weep and mourn for our sins, washing them, as it were, in the first laver', a stage in our spiritual development he described as an essential prequisite or preparation for the second baptism by the spirit which justified and saved us.

'God first published his gospel and all do enjoy some benefit thereby' but only some were fully 'enlightened by it' and 'made partakers of those [spiritual gifts] which are special and peculiar.' This special call, wrote Etherington, typically running together a whole range of scriptural phrases, was '"the baptism of the Holy Ghost, the birth of the spirit, the renewing of the Holy Ghost, the spirit of Christ, the spirit of the son which crieth abba, father, the spirit of adoption, the spirit of life, the spirit of truth, the comforter, the anointing of the Holy Ghost" and such like. And it is so called in regard of the special effects it worketh in the hearts of the repentant beyond those that are common to others, as faith, righteousness, peace, joy in the Holy Ghost and other unspeakable comforts and treasures of life.' This, he claimed,

> is the special administration of the word and that gift of the spirit, whereby Christ is formed in the heart of the poor repentant sinner through faith, by which he is justified from all his sins and his heart sanctified and is the second part and finishing of the new birth and these are always together in the act of justification, the word, the spirit and faith; so that a sinner cannot be said to be actually justified till the covenant of remission of sins, which God hath made to the repentant sinner, be applied by the spirit to his broken heart and that he believeth in his heart that his sins be forgiven and that God loveth him in Jesus Christ and this administration of the word, gift of the spirit and faith are expressed in scripture and distinguished from all other administrations of the word, gifts of the spirit and kinds of faith whatsoever by several distinct names.

Thus baptism ceased to be a literal sacrament in these passages and became instead a figure, or rather a series of figures, for the stages through which the individual must pass to salvation. For what he described here under the rubric of two different baptisms Etherington also called 'the true parts of regeneration, the special and most necessary principles of Christ, the foundation, as St Paul calleth them, the brief or sum of the gospel as Christ declareth'.[25]

If Etherington used an allegorised version of baptism to discuss the process of regeneration, he used an equally allegorised or spiritualised version of the sacrament of the Lord's Supper to discuss the prerogatives and blessings of the elect once they had fully entered Christ's mystical body, the church, through the second baptism of the spirit. Thus for Etherington both sacraments were but outward symbols for inward spiritual realities. Without 'some powerful administration' of the 'death and resurrection of Christ, the sacrifice of his body, the value, virtue, price and purchase thereof', 'there is', Etherington admitted, 'no salvation'. 'The sacraments of baptism and the Lord's Supper have both respect unto this. Baptism to the new birth, wherein we are set in the estate of life thereby; the Lord's Supper to the continual communion which every one that is once made alive by it hath therein to eternal life and so the flesh of Christ "is meat indeed and his blood drink indeed" to them, according to the word of Christ.'

This spiritual feeding did not work through the sacrament 'as if any man did or could eat the very flesh or drink his blood carnally ... nor that the bread of the sacrament or the wine is turned into the flesh or blood of Christ either before we receive them or after and so conveyed into us, as some would make us believe'. 'For although the very body and blood of Christ be the price of the purchase and, in that respect, the only mediate cause of our life and salvation, yet doth not his body and blood enter into us to revive and save us.'

> Neither do we, by the acts of eating the bread or drinking the wine of the sacrament, eat or drink the grace of God, purchased by the body and blood of Christ, neither is grace conferred or any way secretly conveyed to our hearts in the bread or wine or by them nor by anything inferior unto itself but it is conferred to the heart of man by the spirit of God, through the word of his promise, therefore called the word of his grace. And the instrument, hand or mouth wherewith we do receive the same is faith in the heart ... so that to believe in Christ is to eat his flesh and drink his blood, according to his meaning and therefore a sinner is sometimes said to be justified by grace, sometimes by the blood of Christ, sometimes by faith because in the act of our justification all these do concur and are together, the grace of God bring the prime and chief cause thereof; the body and blood of Christ the second principal or mediate cause and faith the instrumental and inferior cause.

For Etherington, therefore, the sacrament was not so much a channel of grace as a symbolic means of communication. Here was a God-enjoined and God-designed way 'to show forth and give us to understand the communion that is between Christ and his church and every member of it. How he hath purchased it and life and eternal salvation for it with his own body and blood and that although the members thereof be many, yet they being, by faith, made partakers of him, the true and living bread, are all, in a spiritual manner, one body with him and one bread and do live by him.'[26]

THE SPIRIT AND THE LETTER: II THE SABBATH

For Etherington both sacraments had become and, indeed, remained – even as he defended himself against the accusations of Stephen Denison in 1627 – a source of imagery through which to describe the life of faith, the spiritual pilgrimage or progression undergone by the elect on their way to salvation. External forms and observances, even the sacraments, thus remained just that, mere forms and signs, outward symbols for inner spiritual realities. The same was true of the sabbath.

The accusation that he held 'the sabbath day or that which we call the lord's day' to be 'no more a sabbath ... than any other day' had, as we have seen, enjoyed a peculiar prominence in Denison's indictment of Etherington's views. It was an accusation that Etherington did not so much deny as reformulate. 'I am sure I never said to any man living that the sabbath was of no force but do hold that it is in force and the commandment also, according to the spiritual intent thereof; I mean by the sabbath the true and perfect rest of God which he did rest the seventh day, having finished all his works, therefore called his rest, as he saith "if they shall enter into my rest".'

This 'rest of God' 'and this ... which the faithful do enter into is one and the same rest, and that it is preached unto us in the gospel, as it was to the Israelites in David's time and in the wilderness'. Those that had entered this rest had 'turned from seeking their own pleasures and speaking their own words, from all their corrupt, carnal and sinful pleasures and delights of the world' and 'their delight is now in the Lord and in his holy and heavenly ways, seeking his face continually and honouring him'. Thus, truly to observe the sabbath was to live the life of faith. 'And so I hold the sabbath spiritual and eternal to be in force and that the outward rest of man and beast commanded the Jews of the seventh day was but a shadow thereof and is now ceased to Christians. So that as we are not bound to circumcision nor other ceremonies of the law ... neither are we to the strict observation of any literal sabbaths of years, times, months or days, as the Jews were by the law, but are free as St Paul saith.' All of which was more than a little reminiscent of T.L.'s spiritualised version of fasting. Christians, Etherington concluded, as had T.L. on the issue of physical abstinence from food, 'are free as touching their consciences in all such respects'.

If this was true then 'the first day of the week used in the apostles' times and ever since in the Christian churches for the assembling together of the people of God to breaking of bread and prayer and preaching and hearing the word of God for exhortation, spiritual communion, edification ... was taken up freely and is a free observation and not by force of any commandment of the law or of the gospel'.

Now in the limited sense of accepting that Christians were bound to dedicate time to God's service and to follow the arrangements for that purpose made by the authorities in the church and state in which they lived, Etherington professed himself entirely in favour of keeping the sabbath.

> Although Christians be now free in these things, as touching the conscience in respect of the law and are not bound, yet they not only may observe a day to the Lord ... and forebear therein their common worldly affairs but ought, it being so ordained and appointed by the state and church wherein they live, and so far are we bound by the command of the word of God in all good and lawful things to obey. And some day or time is needful and the more time the better and he that makes the most use of the same time to the same ends doth the best and the first day of the week may very well be the day rather then any other, because it was for some reasons, no doubt, taken up and used for those ends in the apostles' times, whether because they might be more free therein in respect of the Jews then on the sabbath day or for what reason else, it is not written, being not so needful to be known. And so in respect of this spiritual use and end, it hath been and is appointed and employed unto, it may be called a sabbath day, though not by force of the commandment.[27]

Here, remarkably, Etherington was enunciating what was to become the Laudian view of the sabbath as a human or ecclesiastical ordinance, based, perhaps, on apostolic precedent, but not on apostolic, and still less on divine, precept or command, and therefore resting on ecclesiastical and/or royal rather than on divine authority. This, of course, had been precisely T.L.'s position on fasting, where the godly had remained bound by the determinations on outward observance reached by the relevant human authorities. Like other outward forms of worship and external arrangements in the church, sabbath observance, as both Etherington and the Laudians understood it, represented the application to the particular circumstances of the English church of general scriptural nostrums or moral laws. Viewed as such, but only as such, Etherington was quite happy both to respect and observe the sabbath but that was as far as he would go on the subject.[28]

Certainly Etherington repudiated Denison's claim that he was a habitual sabbath breaker, a claim based on one incident 'many years before' when Etherington 'had once ... done some small work upon a needful occasion on the first day of the week, which [when] he had heard of, he brake out against me vehemently, affirming that I could not be of God and saying for proof thereof (using the words of the pharisees against Christ) "we know (as it is written) this man is not of God because he keepeth not the sabbath day"'.[29]

There was, in all this, a certain parallel between Etherington's attitude towards the sabbath and his attitude towards the sacraments. For all that he might spiritualise or, in Denison's accusatory phrase, 'allegorise', such outward observances, Etherington still maintained that we should retain an attitude of diligent observance and respect towards them. 'We may not limit God, neither hath he tied himself to any time or estate of nature in us, nor to any one outward action performed by man unto us, although he hath ordained sundry excellent, holy, outward means whereby he doth direct and lead us (as it were by the hand) to the things that are spiritual and indeed necessary, which we are bound to embrace with much thankfulness to God and to use with reverence and not to despise the least of them, nor in any part willfully to neglect them, in pain of God's high displeasure.'[30]

In short, outward signs, symbols and observances were all very well; they had their place and should be treated with respect, but they should not be mistaken for or confused with the true inner realities of individual and collective spiritual growth and edification. Of course, on one level, there was scarcely a contemporary Christian, and certainly no puritan, who would have disagreed with that bald claim; self-consciously empty formalists were in short supply in this as in, arguably, any age.[31] What set Etherington apart from many of his contemporaries, puritans and Calvinists as well as Laudians, were the very sharp distinctions that he drew between the inward and the outward, the inner spiritual reality and the outer form or shell and the ruthless way in which he applied those distinctions to his account of how the church actually sustained itself in the world. Here, too, we can perhaps detect the spiritualising, or, in Denison's hostile terms, the 'allegorising', afterglow of his earlier familism as well, of course, as the abiding influence of T.L.

THE SPIRIT AND THE LETTER: III THE MINISTRY

We can see the same emphases and priorities being applied in Etherington's discussion of the ordination of ministers, a discussion prompted by what he claimed was the separatist argument that the church of England was an Antichristian church because its 'bishops and ministers have had their first ordination from the false Antichristian church of Rome, whereof Antichrist is head'. This, Etherington claimed, was to place a veritably popish faith in outward forms. 'Neither is it the bare outward ordination, received of the best church that ever was in the world and in the best outward form that is, that can make either him that receiveth it a true faithful minister of God or the church to which he ministreth a true church of Christ but he may be both a false teacher, an Antichrist and his church false and anti-Christian notwithstanding.' It was inward spiritual realities not mere outward forms that determined who was a true minister and who was not. 'If he had kept the first faith, if he had lived the first life, if he had succeeded the apostles and elders (in faith, in doctrine, in exhortation, in patience, in temperance, in meekness, in mortification, in love, in good works, in feeding the flock of Christ and giving them their meat in due season) as he did succeed them in outward place, he had then been a scribe well taught in the kingdom of God.'[32]

Of course, all this could be passed off as a mere rerun of the conventional hot protestant response to catholic arguments about visible succession and institutional continuity as marks of the true church. The church of England was a true church, this argument ran, not because of any visible institutional succession running from the church of the apostles through the church of Rome to the present but because it had succeeded to the purity of the apostles' doctrine and example. Mainstream puritans, too, held that the efficacy of a preacher's ministry was a direct function of his own spiritual status. Ungodly or reprobate ministers could still deliver a valid sacrament and preach God's word, but the truly elect saint would always be a more pastorally effective and genuinely edifying presence in the pulpit or at the communion table.[33]

When challenged by Denison on this point it was to such glosses that Etherington reverted. His claim that the relation between the inner and outer baptisms that made a true Christian was paralleled by the relations between the inner and outer ordinations that made a true minister could indeed be presented as a mere extension or restatement of these priorities and assumptions.

> As they only are the seed and children of Abraham that have the faith and works of Abraham, and as the circumcision of the heart is the true circumcision and as to have the heart sanctified by faith, through the spirit, is to be baptised with the baptism which saveth, to put on Christ by baptism, and to be a true Christian, so likewise to be a true pastor or elder is to enter in by the door first, even through Christ by faith, for he is the door and the way whereby every true pastor must enter and to be called and ordained of God, by those heavenly gifts of Christ whereby they are made able ministers of the new testament and then, in the second place, to be approved and justified of his church and children of wisdom. For the calling of a true minister of God and that which maketh him so to be is as heavenly and spiritual as that which maketh a true Christian, else every true Christian had a greater privilege then every true minister of Christ which (doubtless) is not so, but rather every true minister hath a greater.[34]

We are back here, perhaps, to T.L.'s version of 'the key of David' which only some ministers, those blessed with a true justifying faith, possessed, and which only others, blessed with a like faith, could recognise. Perhaps, too, we are back to H.N.'s diatribes in the *Evangelium regni* against what he termed 'unsent' and merely 'scripture learned' ministers and preachers.

Not, of course, that any of this proves that either T.L. or the Etherington of the 1620s were familists in the straightforward Marshian sense of the word.

On the contrary, there were great swathes of T.L.'s thought (and by the 1620s of Etherington's too) that were entirely incompatible with anything that Dr Marsh would recognise as familism. For all H.N.'s repeated equation of the little ones with 'God his elect', English familism has been characterised by Dr Marsh and others as explicitly and vocally anti-predestinarian. And yet as we have seen, T.L.'s account of the little ones was casually yet deeply predestinarian. In the 1620s Etherington's espousal of a staunchly Calvinist account of the theology of grace was even more stringent and his horror at what he took to be Arminian error utterly explicit.[35]

Again, in marked contrast to H.N., who was after all Dutch, both T.L. and Etherington displayed an engagement with current English politics and in particular with the contemporary debates between puritans and conformists, quite unlike anything to be found either in H.N.'s translated works or indeed in English familism *tout court*, at least as Dr Marsh has described it. Both men aggressively appropriated some of the central arguments and claims of English conformist thought as they denounced the English puritans for not understanding the true nature and limits of Christian liberty and for consequently abusing the legitimate powers of the magistrate.

There were even starker differences between familism and the opinions espoused by Etherington and T.L. on the subject of eschatology. Of course, H.N.'s writings were scarcely innocent of eschatological excitement; these were most definitely the last days; his own activities and those of the little ones presaged the fall of Antichrist. And yet, as we have seen, the Antichrist in question was certainly not equated with the papacy nor, indeed, with any visible institution or church. On the contrary, it was thoroughly spiritualised, conceived as a miasma of error occupying a temple of God also conceived entirely spiritually as the souls of Christians. For H.N., while the church of Rome had some responsibility for this state of affairs, the protestant reformers were at least equally to blame. As we have seen, Etherington, at least in his 1610 incarnation, had bought heavily into this familist eschatology; defending the church of Rome against protestant attack and hailing the world-historical importance of H.N. in ushering in the eighth and last age.

T.L. and the Etherington of the 1620s, however, both demurred from all this. It is true that T.L. occasionally indulged in H.N.-style sallies against various contemporary reformed or protestant groups. But unlike H.N., T.L. and the Etherington of 1623 both included the familists in these diatribes. Most significantly, T.L.'s version of the Antichrist that was about to fall was resolutely papal, entirely identified with the church of Rome, the downfall of which he was extremely anxious both to date and plot, as precisely as possible, against the course of contemporary events. By the 1620s and (as we shall see below) still more explicitly by the 1640s, this was a view which Etherington had come to endorse with a vengeance.

NOTES

1 S. Denison, *The white wolf* (London, 1627), pp. 52–3.
2 J. Etherington, *A discovery of the errors of the English Anabaptists* (London, 1623), 'advertisement to the Christian reader'.
3 *Ibid.*, pp. 88–91.
4 *Ibid.*, 'advertisement to the Christian reader'.
5 *Ibid.*
6 *Ibid.*
7 *Ibid.*
8 *Ibid.*
9 *Ibid.*, pp. 1–4, 44–5.
10 *Ibid.*, pp. 5–6.
11 *Ibid.*, pp. 7, 10.
12 *Ibid.*, p. 8.
13 *Ibid.*, pp. 11, 13, 14.
14 Etherington, *The defence of John Etherington* (London, 1641), pp. 8, 43, 46. For the upsurge of radical and sectarian activity in London in the early 1590s following the collapse of the classis movement see B.R. White, *The English separatist tradition* (Oxford, 1971); P. Lake, 'The dilemma of the establishment puritan: the Cambridge Heads and the case of Francis Johnson and Cuthbert Bainbrigg', *Journal of Ecclesiastical History*, 31 (1978).
15 John Etherington, *A brief discovery of the blasphemous doctrine of familism* (London, 1645), pp. 10–11.
16 *A discovery of the abominable delusions of ... the family of love* (1622), 'to the reader'.
17 C. Marsh, *The family of love in English society, 1550–1630* (Cambridge, 1994), pp. 239–45.
18 J. Etherington, *A discovery of the English anabaptists* (London, 1623), p. 33.
19 *Ibid.*, pp. 37, 46. In 1623 Etherington immediately gave these sentiments a predestinarian gloss: 'this have we proved that whosoever is born from above, by water and the spirit, justified by faith in Christ, whose names are written in the book of life, from the foundation of the world, shall never fall away nor have their names razed out of the book of life again'.
20 *Ibid.*, pp. 21–2.
21 *Ibid.*, p. 31.
22 *Ibid.*, p. 82.
23 H.N., *Evangelium regni* (?, ?1576) pp. 46 r.–v. I should like to thank David Como for drawing the significance of this point to my attention.
24 Etherington, *A discovery*, pp. 57, 61, 58.
25 John Etherington, *The defence of John Etherington* (London, 1641), pp. 56, the longer discussion is at pp. 54–8; Etherington, *A discovery*, p. 25, 26–7.

26 Etherington, *The defence*, pp. 58–60.
27 Ibid., pp. 32–5.
28 K. Parker, *The English sabbath* (Cambridge, 1988), chapter 7; P. Lake, 'The Laudians and the argument from authority', in Bonnelyn Kunze and Dwight Brautigam, eds, *Court, country and culture* (Rochester, New York, 1992).
29 John Etherington, *The deeds of Dr Denison a little more manifested* (London, 1642), sig. Br.
30 Etherington, *The defence*, pp. 57–8.
31 J.C. Davies, 'Against formality: one aspect of the English revolution', *Transactions of the Royal Historical Society*, sixth series, 3 (1993).
32 Etherington, *A discovery*, pp. 69–70, 72.
33 P. Lake, *Moderate puritans and the Elizabethan church* (Cambridge, 1982), chapters 4 and 5; A. Milton, *Catholic and reformed* (Cambridge, 1995), chapter 6.
34 Etherington, *A discovery*, pp. 82–3.
35 Marsh, *Family of love*, pp. 59–60, 244.

Part III

The London puritan scene

Chapter 7

The London puritan underground

MICROCOSM: ETHERINGTON'S SPIRITUAL PILGRIMAGE

What, then, are we to make of all this? There are two main areas of enquiry at stake here. The first is very particular, involving the precise outlines of John Etherington's rake's progress through the sectarian and heterodox fringes of London puritanism in the period between say 1590 and 1627. The second is more general and concerns the light thrown by Etherington's eccentric career and opinions on the wider milieu of what one might term the London puritan underground.

Let us start with the first area of enquiry. In the section that follows, the analysis proceeds on the assumption that the frequent autobiographical asides, with which Etherington's works are studded, are largely true. Since the incidental details let drop in these passages play no significant role in his overall polemical strategy, there is no reason to suppose that he was lying or even systematically misremembering. Of course, he may have been making it all up, but, as we shall see, very often disparate remarks and asides in different works, works whose publication was often years apart, seem to confirm one another. Certainly, if we collate the information he gives us about himself with material taken from Denison and other sources we can produce something like a consistent, if admittedly rather sparse, outline of his career. Given both the interest and obscurity of Etherington and his views, the attempt seems at least worth making.

It seems clear that the Etherington of 1610 can legitimately be called a familist, in the full Marshian sense of the word. We are dealing here, after all, not only with verbal and doctrinal echoes of H.N. but, by the end of the *Description*, with a full-scale endorsement of Niclaes' status as a prophet, an eschatologically charged harbinger of the end of the world. The same was surely never true of T.L. (at least as he expressed himself in print) nor was it true of the Etherington of the 1620s. But having said that, the precise role of T.L. in Etherington's ideological development remains difficult to trace. Judging from the publication dates of his books, T.L. was at his most active during the late 1580s and 1590s and, on Denison's account at least, was dead by the late 1610s. This coincides with what we can identify from a number of autobiographical asides in Etherington's books as his earliest seeking phase, as a young man newly arrived in London.

As we have seen, in his reply to Denison's accusations Etherington claimed that it was 'five or six and thirty years since the time it pleased God ... to call me from the pleasures of my youth to seek him'. 'I confess', he wrote elsewhere in the same apologia of 1627, 'I have not been in all this time of thirty five years so conversant and sociable with the profane multitude of the world, as I have been with the sober and well disposed, the wise in heart.' This would date the beginning of Etherington's religious quest to the early 1590s when, if he was not quite eighteen in 1588, he must have been in his early twenties.

Of course, the early 1590s were a time of intense eschatological excitement, consequent upon the defeat of the Armada and of considerable separatist activity together with much puritan soul searching, consequent upon the final collapse of the classis movement. It is perhaps significant in this context that elsewhere in his reply to Denison, when he was denying any hint of sectarianism in his conduct, Etherington claimed that it was only for the 'nearly twenty years past before my imprisonment' that he had regularly attended the services of the national church.[1] There is therefore a gap here of something like fifteen or sixteen years between the start of Etherington's religious quest in the early 1590s and his consistent attendance at the services and sacraments of the national church, which on his own account only started around 1606–07.

Admittedly, we do know, because he tells us, that he was in contact with real separatists at least at the end of this period of his life. For Etherington himself presents the *Description* as the result not only of a polemical engagement with Smith the se-baptist's printed text but of actual conversations with real anabaptists. 'It fell out of late that I, being in company with some of them, had some conference with them wherein they seemed very well affected to the things that I spake unto them. One of them answering me in these words, I could willingly let all these things which you have said go down in to me, but only the going to the assemblies. Another of them answered him instantly, you heard what he said for that. And so they requested me that I would set the things down in writing which had been said and they would either answer or subscribe unto it.'[2] It was this paper that Etherington had only later decided to publish.

But if Etherington knew anabaptists and separatists there is good reason to

The London puritan scene

doubt that he was himself ever a member of a separatist church or congregation. There is indeed that suspicious fifteen-year gap between the start of his religious quest and the beginning of his regular attendance at the sacraments and services of the national church, but during his later altercation with Denison he also claimed that he could not be called a sectary because he '*never* was in any private assembly where I have either received the sacrament myself, nor seen it done by others'.[3] Never, of course, is a strong word and hard to reconcile with the fifteen years before he started regularly attending the national church, unless, of course, the circles in which he moved neither administered nor received the sacraments.

Moreover, we know both from Etherington's own testimony and from other corroborating sources that such groups existed in the London of the day and indeed were known to Etherington. All Etherington's books were studded with references to and asides about the wilder reaches of the London puritan scene. Thus in the 1623 Etherington/Jessup volume the author made passing mention of John Wilkinson, an 'ancient stout separatist'. At another point in the same book, he confronted his anabaptist interlocutor with the following conundrum: if all Europe were sunk in Antichristian darkness and 'God should call one of the bishops of that church out from them' where could the poor unfortunate go for a new and decently un-popish ordination? 'Wither wouldst thou have him to go for it, or where wilt thou find an eldership to ordain him? In Europe there be none, all are Antichristians. Wilt thou have apostles again, to lay a new foundation?' This, Etherington/Jessup used as the starting point for an extended excursus on recent London sectarian history. For, he explained, this was not only the logical consequence of the anabaptists' position, it had been the actual opinion of 'some of thy predecessors':

> There were (among others) three brethren, ancient separatists from the church of England, living sometimes in the city of London. Their names were Legat. These held it stiffly that there must be new apostles, before there could be a true constituted church and they drew it from this ground. The one was called Walter Legat, who about twenty years since was drowned, with one of his brethren, washing himself in a river called the Old Ford. Another of them called Thomas Legat, died in Newgate about sixteen years since, being laid there for the heresy of Arius. The third, called Bartholemew Legat, was burnt in Smithfield about ten years since being condemned for the same heresy of Arius; for they all held and stood stoutly for the same also. These Legats had a conceit that their name did (as it were) foreshow and entitle them to be the new apostles that must do this work but you see what became of them.[4]

Confirming evidence on the existence and activities of the Legat brothers comes from Henoch Clapham's polemical satire of the separatist and semi-separatist fringe, his *Error on the right hand* of 1608. Clapham had once been a renegade separatist and was now a conformable Kent clergyman. The book took the form of a spoof dialogue dedicated to unmasking the absurd and pernicious opinions of those (to adopt modern parlance) on the puritan 'left', who opposed the middle way of the English church. It was ideologically balanced by another volume of the same year entitled aptly enough *Error on the left hand. Through a frozen security howsoever hot in opposition when satan so heats them*. There a personification of the English church, identified as ever as Mediocrity, engages in a series of dialogues with such interlocutors as Romanistus, Atheos and Libertinus.[5]

Error on the right hand, however, describes another set of exchanges between one Flyer, the archetypically flighty and unsettled religious seeker, and a number of spokesmen for sectarian extremism. Flyer starts off on the road to Gravesend intending to join the English separatists on the continent. *En route*, he falls in with a number of eccentric fellow travellers and is converted successively to a series of increasingly extreme sectarian positions ranging from anabaptism to familism before falling, exhausted, into the arms of the church of England, still personified by a character called Mediocrity.

The two middle dialogues in the book involve a representative of a group called by Clapham the 'Legatine-Arians', whom Clapham describes as believing that, since the church under Antichrist had been so 'latent and invisible for many years' that 'her place was no more to be found', there could be 'no more a visible church till some notable men were stirred up of God to raise it again out of the dust'. 'There is no church', Clapham has Legatine-Arian say, 'nor visible Christian in the world as yet, seeing no miraculous apostles have yet been sent to baptise people and call them into communion'. On Clapham's account these people believed that the situation would remain the same until miracle-working new apostles were sent from God with special warrant to baptise Christians afresh. Clapham also attributed eccentric opinions about Christ's nature to Legatine-Arian. 'He is to be held a mere man, as was Peter, Paul or I, only whereas we have the spirit in measure and were born in sin, he had the spirit beyond measure and was born free from sin.' This was a position he justified on the grounds that since it was 'a mere man that sinned it must be a mere man that must satisfy God's justice'.[6] Nor was this the first time Clapham had mentioned such beliefs. In an earlier anti-separatist work, his *Antidoton or a sovereign remedy against schism and heresy* of 1600, Clapham had mentioned in passing 'our English Arians' who 'deny all baptism and ordination, till new apostles be sent to execute those parts to the gentiles and Elias the Thisbite do come for that end unto the Jews'.[7]

Similar beliefs were described in an anti-separatist tract, *The profane schism of the brownists*, by Christopher Lawn. There Lawn claimed that during his own separatist phase 'I was once half persuaded that Mr Johnson and Mr Ainsworth had been the two witnesses that should prophesy in sackcloth Rev.11, 3,4.' These illusions had since been shattered, Lawn explained, by the subsequent bad behaviour and acrimonious fallings out of the two separatist prophets. Likewise, in *Error on the right hand*, Henoch Clapham had the familist identify the two prophets 'slain by the beast' as faith and love, 'their carcasses only remained in the streets of the harlot's city'. Again, Lawn identified other sectarians and separatists who denied that there was any visible church left in the world at all and claimed that new prophets or apostles were needed to plant new churches. 'John Wilkinson and his disciples will have apostles, Thomas Lemur will have no churches', wailed Lawn. Such beliefs were later at least associated with Etherington. As he himself admitted, one John Okey claimed that he had heard Etherington say that 'he was as Elias, left alone, and that he knew none of the visible church of God but himself'.[8]

The existence of such notions circulating in London and clearly familiar to Etherington is interesting to say the least. For a link with a group who believed that there was no visible church in the world and whose meetings were not those of a gathered church or separatist congregation so much as of a conventicle of like-minded people meeting together to expound scripture and be instructed in the thoughts and insights of some sect master or illuminatus might explain where Etherington had spent those missing fifteen years between the start of his religious pilgrimage and his entry into communion with the national church. And if this was the case, the most obvious candidate for the role of Etherington's prophetical mentor or *éminence grise* was, of course, T.L.

But who was T.L.? The new Short Title Catalogue makes the passing suggestion that it was none other than the Thomas Legat described by Etherington as having died in Newgate in 1607. The two men certainly shared initials and if this identification were to prove correct it would set up some remarkable chronological parallels between the careers of the two men. As we have seen, on his own testimony, Etherington's break with sectarianism and entry into regular contact with the church of England can be dated to around 1606/07. On Denison's account, writing in 1626, it was about twenty years since various ministers of the church of England had started to try to reduce Etherington the sect master to something like orthodoxy. And it was again somewhere around 1607 – 'sixteen years since' as Etherington/Jessup had said in their book of 1623 – that Thomas Legat had died in Newgate. Was it this event, that jolted Etherington into familism and through familism into conformity? If the suggestion made in the previous chapter and confirmed by the 1622 anti-familist pamphlet cited above is right and T.L., while bridling at the name of familist, travelled in familist circles and was heavily influenced by familist ideas, then a transition from his position to H.N.'s might have seemed natural enough to Etherington. On this view, familism served several functions for Etherington. Perhaps most obviously it allowed him to replace one dead prophet – T.L.– with another – H.N. But in adopting familism,

Etherington was able to justify both to himself and to others that conformity to the national church which his attachment to the now notorious figure of Thomas Legat had perhaps rendered prudent. But if familism with its spiritualising and nicodemite tendencies prompted Etherington to conform, it did so in ways which allowed him to retain intact great swathes of T.L.'s position within his own. He could preserve in short what was essentially T.L.'s opinion of the spiritual standing and prerogatives of the little ones and of the centrality of the inner baptisms of water and the spirit, while yet accepting the legitimacy of the outward baptism administered by the national church.

But if this identification of T.L. with Thomas Legat is intriguingly convenient it is also probably untrue, since we know from other scattered sources enough about T.L. to make it unlikely in the extreme that he was one and the same with the unlettered London Arian Legat. To begin with, there was no trace of Arianism in T.L.'s works. Of course, given that one could be burned for Arianism it might be asking a bit much to find such traces in print. Even ignoring Arianism, there was one crucial issue upon which we know that both T.L. and Etherington differed from the likes of the Legat brothers or Lemur or Wilkinson and that concerned the eschatologically charged trope of 'the two witnesses'. Both T.L. and Etherington were very clear that the two witnesses did not refer to concrete individuals or prophets, like, for instance, Enoch and Elias returned, but rather to the two testaments of scripture. In this they were subscribing to what had emerged by the 1580s as the mainstream reformed and respectable puritan position on this issue. Thus, in his *Confutation of the Rheimists' translation*, Thomas Cartwright had explained that just such an interpretation of this passage in Revelation was crucial if the overliteral, indeed Judaising, exegetical tendencies of the papists were to be withstood. For papists, desperate to overthrow the standard protestant identification of the pope with Antichrist, tended to argue that Antichrist could not yet have risen, precisely because the two witnesses (in this reading the prophets Enoch and Elijah) had not yet returned. But if Cartwright's was the mainstream reformed, anti-papal position, as we have seen, there is good reason to suspect that on the familist and separatist fringe things were not so straightforward. It may well be, then, that the insistence of both T.L. and Etherington on what they clearly saw as a key interpretation of a crucial prophetical text was in fact a contribution to some now lost intra-sectarian debates on this issue; an intervention designed as a clear marker to distinguish between their own position and claims and the spiritualising tendencies of the familists, on the one hand, and the Judaising, scriptural literalism that, on this subject at least, united some of the more eccentric figures on the sectarian left with the papists.[9] It was, in short, a tenet which, while it served to key them into the same milieu and concerns as the Legats, also served to distinguish their views from those of Legat and his ilk.

The London puritan scene

Again the Latin critique of Baro points to an educated man, connected to Cambridge as well as to London puritan circles. Moreover, in two crucial, albeit much later, asides in Samuel Hartlib's *Ephemerides*, T.L. is described in terms which key him into the learned world of the university rather than the relatively unlettered milieu of London sectarianism, inhabited by the Legat brothers and by Etherington himself. In two remarks of 1635, Hartlib refers to the views of one Mr Brook on the best way to train 'both scholars and laics' in divinity, citing in the process as examples of the sort of 'complete paraphrasis' necessary for the task two books, one 'upon Ezra called Babylon is fallen' and another 'upon the 12, 13 et 14 of the Revelation'. Brook apparently prized these as 'rare books and masterpieces of learning'. Both were written by one T.L., Hartlib noted, as were 'a letter to Queen Elizabeth' and 'a treatise to the church of Rome'. This, then, is demonstrably Etherington and Denison's T.L., something which Hartlib went on to confirm when he observed that all these works were under a cloud because they had been 'fathered upon Hetherington, a boxmaker' who was 'so much cried down by Dr Denison'. This, Hartlib claimed, was a mistake, since the real author was not Hetherington at all but 'an excellent scholar of Clare Hall', active, we can assume from the dates of the first publication of his books, in the late 1580s and 1590s. This same shadowy figure was also said to have 'made also a new translation upon the whole bible with a commentary upon the revelation' the contents of which were 'in some men's hands and will come forth in better times'.[10]

Some of these claims were if not confirmed then at least repeated in two subsequent editions of T.L.'s works in 1651 and 1661. In 1651 T.L. was described as having 'lived (as appears by his books) in the days of Queen Elizabeth and was once a student at the university of Cambridge, which afterwards (rejecting all expectation of preferments in this world) he forsook and purposely obscured himself in a mean and low estate of a shepherd, as divers patriarchs and the renowned prophets Moses and David and other holy men have sometimes done, that so he might with greater freedom study the scriptures and contemplate heavenly things'. In 1661 he was more laconically described on the title page as 'sometime a student in the university of Cambridge in the days of Queen Elizabeth'.[11] This would seem to rule out the probably unlettered London Arian Thomas Legat and certainly I can find no Thomas Legat attending Clare Hall during the right period.

But if we rule out Legat, there remains another rather more promising candidate, the Thomas Lemur mentioned above in the passage from Lawn's anti-anabaptist tract. A man of that name was active in London separatist circles during the 1590s. His name occurs in the midst of a list of barrowists arrested in 1590.[12] That puts a Thomas Lemur in the right place at the right time both to have written T.L.'s books and to have known and influenced the young Etherington. Thomas Lemur, a London merchant, left England for the

Low Countries in the early seventeenth century. This is the Lemur of the Lemurists, the heretical group mentioned both by Lawn and by Ephraim Pagitt in his *Heresiography*.[13] This Lemur was in frequent trouble with the Dutch authorities for his eccentric doctrinal views and wrote two decidedly odd pamphlets during his stay in Holland. Lemur emerges from these works as an autodidact, who, having taught himself to read Hebrew, then set himself up as an authority in the interpretation of some of the obscurer chronological and numerological aspects of the Old Testament. In the case of the second of these pamphlets these involved his alleged success in devising a scripturally based method for calculating longitude. This keys in with the eschatological and chronological aspects of T.L.'s works. Again, Lemur made very approving remarks about the levels of toleration to be found in Holland and begged the stadtholder's patronage while addressing him as 'lord of hosts', in ways that bear comparison with T.L.'s address to Essex. All this might fit with the information we have about the learned, scripture-translating T.L. Again a departure for the Low Countries around the turn of the century might explain the drying up of T.L.'s works after 1599, while the relative freedom to be found in the United Provinces would have allowed Lemur's ideas to ascend to ever greater heights of heterodox eccentricity, passing through both separatism and anabaptism on his way to his own eccentric brand of heresy – what Pagitt termed 'the monster of Lemurism'.[14] Was it his former mentor, Lemur's, rake's progress, in exile in the Low Countries through a variety of increasingly eccentric sectarian and heretical positions that Etherington was lamenting in the passage from the *Description* quoted above?

But what of the continued reissuing of T.L.'s works during the early seventeenth century? Here it seems likely that this process owed a good deal to Etherington himself. As we have seen, according to Denison, T.L. was dead by the late 1610s. And certainly, as we have seen, his books were all *livres de circonstances*, direct products of the intellectual milieu and concerns of the 1590s. And yet *De fide*, translated by one T.S. as *The key of David*, was reissued in 1610, surely long after the last ripples of Peter Baro's theological squabbles of the 1580s had died away. The printer was Nicholas Fosbrooke, the same man who printed Etherington's *Description* in that very same year. Fosbrooke also produced two further editions of T.L.'s *Babylon is fallen* under the title of *A prophecy that hath lyen hid for two thousand years* in 1610 and 1614. Again its dedicatee, Essex, was long dead and the eschatologically charged atmosphere engendered by the collapse of the Armada and the world-historically significant war with Spain long dissipated. A third edition came out in 1620. Again, the first surviving edition of T.L.'s *The exposition* dates from 1623, by which time, certainly, anti-Spanish and anti-popish war fever might be thought to have created a market for such ravings. This was also, of course, the same year that Etherington's *A discovery* was published, probably by the same printer, one William Jones. Jones was a man with radical connections, having run a secret puritan press back in 1604–08. As we shall see below, Etherington continued to usher his erstwhile mentor's books through the press during the early 1650s.[15]

Even at his cagiest, replying in the 1620s to Denison's allegations that he regarded T.L. as some sort of prophet, Etherington let slip that he did indeed think there was something extraordinary in T.L.'s prophetical writings. For he defended his high opinion of the book of Esdras as a 'holy and true' prophetic text by citing the like opinions of 'sundry divines', the only one of whom he mentioned by name being T.L. whom he identified by a passing reference to his book *Babylon is fallen*. This tome, the boxmaker darkly remarked, contained 'matters of great moment ... worthy, I dare say, to be regarded by every true Christian that desires understanding'.[16] Here, at least, Stephen Denison appears to have been right; a good many of the central elements in T.L.'s thought did indeed live on in Etherington's position, as it was articulated in 1610, during the 1620s and even, perhaps especially, during the 1640s, when, as we shall see below, Etherington at last felt able to reveal the full extent of his admiration for the prophetic powers of the long-dead exegete.

On this view, then, after a long seeking phase, lived in close contact if not open communion with separatists and anabaptists (and perhaps under the either personally or textually transmitted influence of the familist-tinged, predestinarian apocalypticism of T.L.) around 1606–07, Etherington's contacts with familist nicodemism convinced him of the virtues of outward conformity as they were outlined in his anti-separatist book of 1610 and thus provided the ideological bridge across which he progressed into that full communion with and membership of the national church from which he was to confront Denison in the 1620s. But if familism got him into the church of England it did not represent his final ideological resting place. There followed his subsequent conversion to Calvinist orthodoxy which presumably took place sometime after 1610 and before his second excursion into anti-anabaptist polemic of 1623, when he added a predestinarian gloss to his earlier vindication of conformity on the basis of a conversion narrative that might well have applied as much to Etherington as it did to Jessup. It is possible, of course, that it was during this last transition that T.L. entered Etherington's life, providing a familist tinged but in other ways more conventionally reformed, even puritan, body of doctrine, on the basis of which Etherington could leave familism behind and reinvent himself, with T.L., as a fully conforming and predestinarianly orthodox member of the church of England.

The result, it seems, was a synthesis, comprising elements of H.N., T.L., and more mainstream puritan and indeed conformist thought. Certainly, in T.L., at least as much as in H.N., we can find anticipated Etherington's equation of the little ones of God with the true church, his language of the two baptisms of water and of the Holy Spirit, his obsession with repentance as a preparation for justification, and with love as its major effect. Here too may be a, if not the, source for Etherington's very austere version of the subjection owed even by the little ones to the authority over externals wielded by the magistrate and for his slighting opinion of 'puritan' reformers and non-conformists. Here, too, is an explanation for Etherington's stray (decidedly unfamilist) and very precise estimate of the length of Antichrist's reign in the *Description* and for Denison's obsession with Etherington's views on the canonical status of the book of Esdras. And yet even if T.L.'s position was, as Denison proclaimed, the precursor of Etherington's, very likely as he proclaimed it in 1610, let alone as he came to define it in the 1620s and after, we have, I think, on the evidence of the book of 1610 alone, to posit a more direct exposure certainly to H.N.'s works and very likely to the opinions and activities of real, Marshian familists.

MACROCOSM: THE LONDON PURITAN SCENE

Given the limitations of the evidence, any attempt to reconstruct the nature and particularly the sources and precise development of Etherington's views must always remain tentative and provisional. However, if we can never be certain about Etherington, we can I think be rather more confident about the light cast by his eccentric career and opinions on the larger London puritan milieu in which he lived. For by triangulating between the works of H.N., T.L. and Etherington we can, I think, say for certain that there was a milieu in late Elizabethan and early Stuart London in which ideas, texts and individuals of a distinctly familist bent could meet, mingle and miscegenate with other ideas, texts and individuals from more mainstream traditions of hot protestant and puritan thought and feeling. Here was a space where familists, separatists of various stripes and a variety of puritans (both conformist and non-conformist, presbyterian and more quiescently accepting in their attitudes to at least *iure humano* episcopacy) met and debated their rival claims to ideological purity.

The positions espoused in print by T.L. during the 1590s and, in 1610 and during the 1620s, by Etherington are perhaps best seen as the result of that process of mixing and matching; syntheses comprised of radical protestant eschatology and ecclesiology, a conventionally predestinarian account of the theology of grace, key elements of the conformist defence of the status quo and critique of puritan and presbyterian schemes for further reformation, all combined with certain central features of authentically familist thought and diction, as they were to be found exemplified in the ur-texts of H.N. himself.

Given what Dr Marsh has characterised as the almost entirely hostile, adversarial relationship between familism and mainstream puritanism this might at first sight seem surprising. But in dealing with Etherington we are

The London puritan scene

dealing with the very period after about 1610 when, according to Dr Marsh, the family of love as a hermetically sealed group in the world was ceasing to exist. As it did so, it seems reasonable to conclude that familist texts, opinions and claims leaked out into the wider puritan underground. As the familist traces in T.L. show, such leakage was scarcely new but presumably the breakdown of the familist networks and communities sketched by Marsh must have accelerated the process. (Moreover, it may well be that, in his Spuffordian zeal to assimilate the familists to the humble piety of the humbly pious English, Dr Marsh has exaggerated their distance, both ideological and social, from the puritan godly, here taking the polemical stances of the two groups a shade too literally as pictures of social and cultural reality.) However that may be, we should certainly entertain the possibility that, as familism broke up, a variety of different groups – influenced by H.N. and his followers, or themselves perhaps members or rather ex-members of the family – produced different versions of familism, each defined in part against the other. That might explain Etherington's capacity, even at the height of his familist phase in the *Description*, to denounce the errors of familists even as he embraced the central tenets of H.N.

Certainly, by the 1620s Stephen Denison thought that there were rival groups of familists, each with their defining doctrinal quirks and quiddities to be found both in London and around the country. In *The white wolf* Denison was careful to distinguish between what he described as the 'Gringltonian familists', the 'familists of the mountains', the 'familists of the vallies', the 'familists of the cap' and, shades of T.L. as he had been described in 1622, the 'familists of the scattered flock, which seduce by pretending to be of them which fear the lord, when they are nothing less'. It would be tempting to dismiss this as so much polemically inspired myth-making were it not for a later document from the 1630s, a fascinating listing by an ex-familist, Giles Creech, of various familists 'of the mount' and 'of the valley' living in and around London.[17] We might, therefore, entertain the possibility of different groups, sharing a common familist heritage or influence, existing on the fringes of London puritan society throughout the early Stuart period. That certainly is a possibility that renders a career and ideological trajectory like Etherington's altogether explicable.

For we are dealing here not with Dr Marsh's rural East Anglia, but with events and developments in the melting pot of early Stuart London. And Etherington's was a spiritual progression that affords us a fleeting but fascinating glimpse of something that might best be termed a radical protestant or puritan London underground. Certainly it is precisely such a milieu that is constantly being evoked and invoked in Etherington's works. Of course, such hints and asides cannot be used as value-free reportage, transparent evidence for the nature of contemporary social reality. Etherington's works were polemically crafted, rhetorically constructed literary artefacts. Thus, there was almost certainly an element of polemical convenience, even opportunism, in Etherington's choice of not just any old separatist but Smith the se-baptist as the opponent against whom he set out to define his own position. Smith's act of self-baptism represented an almost perfectly Jonsonian parody, a veritable *reductio ad absurdum*, of the separatist impulse. Here was the perfect straw man for Etherington, the closet familist, to rip limb from limb, thus proving his reliability as a defender of the church of England and providing a sufficiently dense screen of flying straw behind which to hide his own covertly familist message.[18] Can we, indeed, really believe Etherington when he claims that the *Description* was a product of actual meetings with real separatists?

In the absence of corroborative evidence we cannot, of course, finally know. But happily that does not much matter for our purpose in this section which, unlike its predecessor, is not exclusively Etherington-centred. For our purpose here in using Etherington and his works as a way into a wider London puritan scene, the very fact that all of Etherington's texts were drenched in 'casual' references to, indeed set against a backdrop of, a skilfully evoked 'London puritan scene', takes on a significance that transcends the literal truth of any of the individual (autobiographical) claims made or encounters described therein. For those references were surely intended to be all too recognisable to the notional reader of Etherington's texts as those texts constructed him or her. As such, they represented so many markers or flags set down to alert his audience to the fact that Etherington was a *habitué* of this world, a man who knew whereof he spoke. As such these asides could only hope to work if the reader was assumed to be able to recognise the people and ideological entities being invoked. We are being confronted here with what amounted to a sediment of 'common knowledge' about this milieu which Etherington was invoking to confirm his bona fides as a teller of truth. For in displaying his own casual conversance with this cast of characters, Etherington was also assuming/expecting his readers to be equally well informed.

Thus in the *Description*, in addition to all those hints and asides about Wilkinson and the Legats, there are mentions of a variety of separatist polemical works and rumours about the fate of Smith's congregation in Amsterdam – all presumably designed to enhance the reality effect of the book[19] – and all of which can be confirmed from a variety of other sources. As we have seen, in drawing out the roots of separatism in puritan non-conformity and presbyterianism in the *Description*, Etherington talked bitterly of simple men who had been led astray into separatist exile abroad or penury at home by false scruples planted in their untutored consciences by puritan ministers. Etherington and his notional readers may well have known such people (amongst whom we might perhaps number Thomas Lemur), for these are all phenomena the existence of which has been confirmed by recent scholarship: puritan doctors and lecturers maintained by the charity of the godly; poor deprived ministers looked after by a doting laity; the integral links between separatism and the presbyterian attack on the allegedly Antichristian government of the English church; the increasingly fractious, febrile and eccentric behaviour of English separatists in the Low Countries – all these are central features in the standard accounts of London puritanism.[20]

Thanks to Christopher Marsh's brilliant research we now also know that there really were familists in London and even at court with whom Etherington could have associated. Indeed, there are even a couple of broad hints in Etherington's own books to confirm Dr Marsh's surmises on that score. At one point in his 1623 tract, he remarked on the familists' capacity 'to thrust themselves ... to be public ministers and preachers in the church of England, yea, into the king's chapel and to be of his officers and messengers', all places where Dr Marsh has detected a palpable familist presence.[21]

Throughout the rest of a publishing career, which, as we shall see, lasted well into the 1640s, Etherington continued to advertise his conversance with the London puritan underworld. And again the names and dates he cites can be confirmed from other sources. In his later response to Denison of 1627 Etherington referred tantalisingly to his continued contacts and debates with sectaries, separatists, familists and lay enthusiasts. At one point he told Denison that 'there be sundry can witness that I have been a means of the withdrawing and dissuading some from schism, separation, anabaptism, familism and other corrupt opinions and unlawful practises'. This was a claim that Denison himself grudgingly confirmed when he admitted that Etherington had indeed converted Edmund Jessup from anabaptism, although he denied that he had converted Jessup to 'the church of England' but rather merely to the tenets of his own 'Hetheringtonian faction'. Elsewhere Etherington replied to the accusation that he had established a conventicle or sect with himself as 'the chief speaker or expounder of the scriptures' surrounded with 'many adherents, disciples and followers of his doctrine', with the claim that not only had he never taken such things upon himself but that he had 'opposed and reproved such as have so done and been so affected, as some can witness'.[22]

Nor did Etherington's resort to and disputes with the radical fringe of the London scene end with his imprisonment in the 1620s. When he returned to the fray of anti-familist polemic in 1645 he did so bragging of a familiarity with that world that stretched back over forty years and was only too ready to prove that he was up to date with the latest developments there by shamelessly dropping names. Having recounted recent debates he had had with a sadly nameless peer about the enormities and blasphemies of H.N.'s doctrine, Etherington vouchsafed to the reader the following account of his more recent

The London puritan underground

contacts. 'There have been doctors and others, that have taught the doctrine of H.N., as one Dr Everet [probably John Everard], one Shaw [probably Peter Shaw, for whose activities see below] and at this present one D. Gill, publicly in the midst of this city of London and one that went from hence to Reading, D. Pordage [almost certainly John Pordage] ... all of whom I have both heard and spoken with and know that they have usually taught the same doctrine.'[23] Even if Etherington was only name-dropping here, recent scholarship has confirmed that he certainly knew which names to drop, which, as ever, was the whole point of the exercise.

INTERROGATING HOSTILE WITNESSES: THE TESTIMONY OF CONFORMIST AND PURITAN COMPLAINT

We are in a world here of godly seeking, where conversations with and rumours about a variety of more or less sectarian experiments and claims were commonplace. It is the same world as that hinted at by such separatist renegades as Peter Fairlambe and Henoch Clapham. In his 1606 tract *The recantation of a brownist* Fairlambe told war stories about his treatment at the hands of the godly in Stepney after he had abandoned the separatist cause. Under the influence of Bancroft and others, Fairlambe had abandoned his opinion that 'my mother (this church) was an harlot' and, on that basis, had entered into a manuscript controversy with one Mr Barnhere, a minister in Barbary where Fairlambe had gone to ply his trade. News of his apostasy from the godly cause passed back to his home parish of Stepney and rumours were spread there that he had 'articled against two churchwardens, for suffering certain brownists to live in the parish with their children unbaptised and that the men were undone by me', all of which was a 'malicious untruth'. Fairlambe had known about the brownists all right but 'I was so far from troubling them ... being honest simple people, that when they were by the officers discovered I went twice to' Archbishop Whitgift 'in their behalf'. By now, however, Fairlambe was in deep disfavour with the godly. When he showed 'my private dislike of certain seditious doctrines delivered at that time in the church of Stepney by one who, for divers horrible, beastly and notorious misdemeanours, was suspended and silenced', he was denounced for his pains. Local puritans spread the rumour that Fairlambe 'was the cause of his [the minister's] troubles and so continued plotting my overthrow ... accounting me worse than Julian the apostata, maliciously beating my children in the streets, not shaming to say that they hoped to see my children seek their bread out of the dirty channels in the streets for driving (as they said) that good man away'. Others had 'railed upon me in the open streets of London with most opprobrious speeches, bidding me go tell their Antichristian holinesses the Bishops, my new masters, that they were enemies to the truth of God and all good preachers, though these impure railers do submit themselves to all the orders of our church as I do, with what conscience let the wise judge'.

Fairlambe, in part through his friends in high places, had struggled to clear himself from these false accusations and rumours. The story about his betrayal of the brownists had been scotched by a 'letter written by Sir Edward Stanhop' at Whitgift's behest 'unto Mr Thomson the minister and the churchwardens of the said parish of Stepney'. As for the rumour of Fairlambe's having denounced the suspended puritan minister, the minister himself had denied that 'publicly in the pulpit and washed his hands (that were so filthy before), though his flatterers give out that he recanted for fear, only to keep himself within the safety of the ministry from irregularity, yea, albeit he subscribed most largely and would have done more than that if he had been urged'.[24] With their rumours and counter rumours, their allegations of ideological links and practical collusions between mainstream puritans and brownists and their undertone of resentment and disgust at the hypocrisy of conforming puritans, Fairlambe's complaints are reminiscent of nothing so much as the picture of the London puritan scene delineated in Etherington's *Description*.

While Fairlambe's account purported to be a straighforwardly factual narration of his own treatment at the hands of the godly of Stepney, Clapham's dialogues were self-consciously satiric and fictional. However, the exchanges they pictured between separatists, moderate puritans, half-conforming presbyterians, anabaptists, familists and 'Legatine-Arians' reproduced, with uncanny accuracy, the cast of characters assembled by Etherington. Indeed the satiric career of Clapham's character Flyer, converted in turn to separatism, anabaptism, Legatine-Arianism and familism, before returning exasperated and exhausted to the fold of the church of England, bears an uncanny resemblance to Etherington/Jessup's account of his own spiritual journey from one errant opinion to another until spiritual crisis and the predestinarian certainties of the English church came to his rescue.

Such similarities and echoes between such ostensibly different types of source invite a variety of interpretations. On the one hand, when they wrote their books both Fairlambe and Clapham were ex-separatists, renegades, who had, as it were, turned Queen's evidence and were now, if not in the employ, then certainly under the wing, of Archbishop Bancroft. Produced in 1607 and 1606 respectively, their texts can be read in part as the down-market, true-confessions end of the conformist propaganda campaign following the Hampton Court Conference and the subsequent subscription crisis. These, then, were distinctly tainted sources and certainly cannot be accepted as anything approaching value-free reportage of the London puritan scene. Pursuing this line of argument, the similarities between the career imputed to Flyer in *Error on the right hand* and the spiritual rake's progress described in

The London puritan underground

Etherington/Jessup's *A discovery* could be construed as merely literary or generic: a function of the increasing currency of certain essentially polemical conventions or narrative tropes. And yet Etherington, for one, was not in the pay of Richard Bancroft. His books came out in 1610 and 1623 and clearly served immediate polemical purposes rather different from those of Clapham and Fairlambe. Stephen Denison was surely right to suspect that there was more to Etherington than an espousal of the simple conformity being pushed by Clapham and Fairlambe. That Clapham's fictionalised and satiric dialogue, written to serve openly conformist polemical purposes, was echoed so closely by the asides and hints that studded Etherington's two pamphlets of 1610 and 1623 should, therefore, give us pause for thought.

We should pause again when we find nugget-like anecdotes that confirm this picture in sources whose polemical purposes had nothing to do with painting some lurid picture of a puritan/sectarian threat to all order. One such was Thomas Gataker's account of the dispute between George Walker and Anthony Wotton. There Gataker's purpose was to acquit himself and several of his friends and colleagues from charges of favouritism and corruption in the handling of the affair and to convict Walker of an extreme and unreasonable level of polemical aggression in his dealings with Wotton. In the process, Gataker told two stories, both of which were designed to show how easy it was to trap the ignorant, the unwary or the loose tongued into the (quite erroneous) appearance of heretical error when in fact at most they were merely confused.

The first was based on personal experience.

> I remember that while I abode at Lincoln's Inn [Gataker recounted] the night before Legate the Arian appeared in the Bishop's consistory at Paul's (of whose being in trouble I then knew nothing) there came to my chamber there, at a very unseasonable hour, a gentlemanlike man who, having knocked at the door, asked to speak with me and, entrance afforded him, reached me a little scroll wherein were these words written 'Whether was the godhead of Christ begotten of the Godhead of the father from all eternity' and withal desired me to give mine opinion whether that were not an error? I required to know first what the meaning of the party was that held or affirmed it. He answered me 'according to that in the creed, God of God, light of light'. I told him that these were not the words there used and that 'to speak properly the God head was not said either to beget or to be begotten. If the party's meaning were that Christ, being God, was begotten of the father, who is likewise God from all eternity, the sense were sound, but the speech improper. 'Then belike as it is there written,' quoth he, 'it is an error'. 'As the words sound', replied I, 'it is: yet it may be not, in his sense that spake it'. He requested me to give him that under my hand. I craved his name. He told me I must excuse him for that. I told him he should likewise excuse me for this. And so we parted. But the next day, hearing Legate in the consistory, as I past through Paul's, I began to surmise that this party might be some friend of his and that some divine or other, in conference

with him, having let some such speech slip from him, this party, his friend, might beat about to get under some other divines hand the censure of it as an error.[25]

The second story concerned not Gataker himself but his close friend, the notorious puritan William Bradshaw, who was taken along to Newgate by some friends to interview 'a busy separatist' incarcerated there who was 'arrogantly challenging to dispute with all comers and scornfully playing upon and gibing at such as dealt with him'. Bradshaw decided to take the man down a peg or two, telling him

> that for all his prating so much of the constitution of a church (the common subject of such men's disputes) yet his skill peradventure might be but mean in the main principles of religion. And being by him provoked to make trial, if he pleased, he demanded of him whether 'Christ's deity assumed the person of man or no.' To which question the bold bayard, without stop or stay, returning an affirmative answer that 'it did', Mr Bradshaw told him 'it was a gross heresy'. And so left him. And indeed, if the words be regarded, so it is, even the heresy of Nestorius, who maintained two persons in Christ and not two natures in one person. And yet neither do I, nor did Mr Bradshaw, hold the silly fellow to be an heretic.[26]

Gataker told these two stories in the course of his condemnation of the polemical manners and mores of George Walker but for our current purposes both anecdotes serve a quite different end. They show, first, the close dialogic relations between various currents of heterodox and sectarian thought and practice and more mainstream puritanism. In the first, doctrinal shock waves, drawn from Legat's Arianism, can be heard reverberating around the puritan scene. In the second, the continuing very personalised contacts and contests between mainstream puritanism and separatism are equally clearly illustrated. In both, the performative, charismatic elements in the reputation of leading puritan ministers are clear. In the first, resonant names were being collected to muddy the doctrinal and ideological waters surrounding Legat's Arianism. In the second, Bradshaw was vindicating not only the church of England against separatist attack, but also establishing that mainstream puritanism, of even his relatively radical sort, was openly and utterly antiseparatist. He was, in short, defending and augmenting his own reputation as the hammer of the sectaries and as an effective public performer and disputant. In Bradshaw's at once underhand and arrogant put-down of the separatist we can also see the considerable tensions between the claims to authority of the learned clergy and the pretensions to autonomy of the godly laity. Finally, in both instances, we can see precisely the sorts of anecdotes, one-liners and stories through the circulation of which reputations were made and points scored amongst the London godly. Here certainly was a world in which Etherington's account of his own career seems entirely credible.

This is, moreover, a version of the London puritan scene that can be confirmed from other contemporary puritan sources. A passage in Robert Bolton's book, *Some general directions for a comfortable walking with God*, quite remarkably confirms the picture being drawn here. Bolton was warning the godly against spiritual pride, a sin to which those whose consciences had never been 'illightened with sight, sense and acknowledgment of the foulness of sin, their own vileness, the exactness of God's law, purity of his most holy nature, severity and certainty of his judgements' were peculiarly subject. Such people, Bolton warned, 'God, in his just judgement, gives over ... sometimes to fantastical opinions, odd and absurd tenets, swerving brainlessly and senselessly from the holy harmony of confessions and our blessed pure orthodox articles of religion.' Prompted by 'superficialness and its ordinary consort self-conceitedness', once these errors had been brought into the world,

> be they never so monstrous and misshapen, yet some giddy heads will harken and hanker after them, so that many times many weak, ungrounded, unstable, young beginners in profession are limed and woefully entangled, as we see too often *in our chiefest city*, whence ensues an incredible deal of prejudice, hurt and hinderance even to the common state of goodness, to the honour and acceptation of Christianity. For thereupon is raised a cry in all conventicles of good fellowship and consistories of worldly wisdom that these forward professors will all turn fantastical familists, anabaptists, Arians, any thing. Which cry awakes the eye of state-jealousy and so, by an unworthy consequent, draws upon those who are true of heart, even God's best servants and the king's best subjects, discountenance, suspicions, if not molestations, unnecessarily, causelessly.[27]

Here, then, is a remarkable confirmation of the picture that we have extrapolated thus far from both Etherington's own works and the entirely hostile polemical assaults of Clapham and Fairlambe. Bolton's passage echoes with eerie accuracy Etherington's own account of his spiritual progress between anabaptism and familism, T.L. and H.N. Bolton's equation of sectarian error with spiritual pride, consequent upon never having experienced a properly piercing sense of sin, even parallels Etherington/Jessup's account of the spiritual crisis that had weaned him/them away from sectarianism and familism and settled him/them in the predestinarian tenets of the national church. Here too, from a leading mainstream puritan, is a chagrined acknowledgement of the polemical advantage which hostile conformist observers could extract from such careers, and the damage that they could inflict on the reputation of the mainstream godly. Finally, here is proof positive that contemporaries (albeit in Bolton's case provincial contemporaries) perceived such phenomena to be particularly prevalent in London.

To conclude, we might surmise that certain anti-puritan and anti-sectarian tropes became conventional, and that certain stereotypes and caricatures became current, because they were in part based on common experiences, oft

The London puritan scene

repeated spiritual or emotional progressions and life stories. Neither spontaneous expressions of first-hand experience nor merely polemically generated myths and stereotypes, such tropes and narrative conventions occupied a middle ground. They were neither value-free terms of art nor heuristic ideal types nor merely polemical or theatrical falsifications. While they should therefore never invite an easy or automatic acceptance of their literal truth, neither should they elicit a straightforwardly sceptical rejection as mere fictions or fantasies. Polemically tainted, literarily and rhetorically constructed, even (as with Clapham) overtly fictional in form, they remain far from valueless as historical sources. They should, in fact, pique our curiosity and interest, prompting a process of collation and comparison in which accounts written from a number of ideological and/or subject positions are read against one another. It is in that spirit that the preceding discussion has been conducted and in which the enquiries which follow are undertaken.

NOTES

1. J. Etherington, *The defence of John Etherington* (London, 1641), pp. 8, 43, 46. For the upsurge of radical and sectarian activity in London in the early 1590s following the collapse of the classis movement see B.R. White, *The English separatist tradition* (Oxford, 1971); P. Lake, 'The dilemma of the establishment puritan: the Cambridge Heads and the case of Francis Johnson and Cuthbert Bainbrigg', *Journal of Ecclesiastical History*, 31 (1978).

2. J. Etherington, *A description of the true church of Christ* (London, 1610), sig. A2v.

3. J. Etherington, *The defence*, p. 46.

4. J. Etherington, *A discovery*, pp. 76–7.

5. Henoch Clapham, *Error on the right hand through a preposterous zeal* (London, 1608) and *Error on the left hand. Through a frozen security howsoever hot in opposition when satan so heats them* (London, 1608). I should like to thank Patrick Collinson for drawing these texts to my attention and for putting me straight on Clapham's overall polemical agenda.

6. Clapham, *Error on the right hand*, pp. 30, 38, 44. W. Lamont, *Godly rule: politics and religion, 1603–60* (London, 1969); G.J.R. Parry, *A protestant vision: William Harrison and the reformation of Elizabethan England* (Cambridge, 1987).

7. Henoch Clapham, *Antidoton or a sovereign remedy against schism and heresy* (London, 1600), p. 33.

8. C. Lawn, *The profane schism of the brownists* (?, 1612), pp. 44, 55; Clapham, *Error on the right hand*, pp. 49, 38.

9. For Cartwright and the mainstream reformed and puritan position see Rodney L. Petersen, *Preaching in the last days: the theme of the two witnesses in the sixteenth and seventeenth centuries* (New York, 1993), pp. 190–1.

10. Sheffield University Hartlib papers 29/3/39B and 29/3/44A, both taken from Samuel Hartlib's *Ephemerides* from the second half of 1635. I owe these references to the kindness of Anthony Milton and David Como.

11 T.L., *A voice out of the wilderness* (London, 1651) in a section headed 'the days of Noah and the coming of Christ mentioned, Math. 24 and Luke 27, compared and referred to the readers consideration' printed in the 1651 compilation after *De fide*; *A voice out of the wilderness* (London, 1661), title page.

12 Champlin Burrage, *The early English dissenters in the light of recent research* (Cambridge, 1912), 2 vols, vol. I, p. 132 and vol. II, p. 22.

13 E. Pagitt, *Heresiography or a description of the heretics and sectaries of these latter times* (London, 1647), p. 77.

14 K.L. Sprunger, *Dutch puritanism* (Leiden, 1982), p. 82; R.B. Evenhuis, *Ook dat was Amsterdam*, 4 vols (Amsterdam, 1965–74), vol. II, pp. 237–8. Lemur's two pamphlets are listed in W.P.C. Knuttel, *Catalogus na de pamphletten-verzameling berustende in de Koninkijke bibliotheek*, 8 vols (The Hague, 1889–1926), nos 2030 and 2085. The details given here are culled from the first (Campen, 1612), fols 1r., 1v., 19r. I should like to thank David Como for bringing this material to my attention and Evan Haefeli for translating the material in Dutch.

15 See *Revised short title catalogue* for printing history; for Jones' career as a printer and puritan connections see *ibid.*, vol. III, p. 94, s.v. Jones, William. For Etherington's later activities see below, chapter 10.

16 Etherington, *The defence*, p. 38.

17 S. Denison, *The white wolf* (London, 1627), pp. 38–9; PRO S.P. Dom. 16/520/85, fols 126r.–127v.

18 B.R. White, *The English separatist tradition* (Oxford, 1971).

19 See, for example, Etherington, *Description*, p. 94, 'and for you, master Smith and your company, here is news come to England already that you are divided'.

20 See, for instance, P. Collinson, *Godly people* (Hambledon, 1983), chapters 1 and 13; N. Tyacke, *The fortunes of English puritanism* (London, 1990); P. Seaver, *The puritan lectureships* (Stanford, 1970); P. Lake and D. Como, '"Orthodoxy" and its discontents: dispute settlement and the production of consensus in the London (puritan) "underground"', *Journal of British Studies*, 39 (2000).

21 Etherington, *A discovery*, pp. 90–1.

22 Denison, *The white wolf*, p. 45; Etherington, *The defence*, pp. 47, 39.

23 Etherington, *A final discovery of ... familism* (London, 1645), p. 10.

24 Peter Fairlambe, *The recantation of a brownist* (London, 1606); for Bancroft's role see the dedicatory epistle, sig. A3v.; 'To the Christian reader', sigs Bv.–B2r.

25 Thomas Gataker, *An answer to George Walker's vindication* (London, 1642), pp. 38–9.

26 *Ibid.*, pp. 39–40.

27 Robert Bolton, *Some general directions for a comfortable walking with God* (London, 1626), pp. 349–50. I should like to thank Michael Winship for drawing the significance of this passage to my attention.

Chapter 8

William Chibald and the strange case of *A trial of faith*

Thus far we have concentrated on what we might term the radical sectarian elements within the London scene from which Etherington's mature position emerged. But, if we want to understand the internal dynamics of that milieu, we need to attend to disputes and tensions within far more respectable puritan and perfect protestant circles. One such, which also enables us to explicate the one area of doctrinal disagreement between Etherington and Denison upon which we have hardly touched – the relations between repentance and justifying faith – is a series of controversies and disputes surrounding the published opinions of the London minister William Chibald, the rector of St Nicholas Cole Abbey in Old Fish Street.[1]

In his 1627 sermon Denison chose not to give this issue detailed treatment but merely denounced Etherington's opinion that repentance preceded faith as 'a damnable error, a familistical point of doctrine', a position that 'none but familists hold'. But in the additional material appended to the 1641 edition he was slightly more forthcoming. 'I confess faith and repentance are twins of a burden but that faith is the first born. It is in this as between the sap and the bud, the fire and the heat; though the bud be first seen yet the sap is first in nature and though the heat be first felt, yet the fire is also first in nature. Even so, though repentance be first seen and first felt, yet faith, as the cause, doth necessarily go before it in nature.' As for the sort of repentance that did indeed precede faith, that was but 'the wicked man's repentance. For that repentance which is before faith is not acceptable to God, "for without faith it is impossible to please God", as the apostle speaks.' As for Etherington's (and, of course, T.L.'s) definition of repentance, that too, with its obsession with 'a true and deep sorrow and mourning' for sin, was quite wrong. True repentance also involved a turning to 'a new life, sorrow being but an accessory but not any integral part of repentance'.[2]

From these short and fragmentary remarks it is difficult to work out quite what was going on here. Luckily, however, the relation between repentance and justification was at the centre of a series of disputes in London provoked by Chibald's books and opinions in the early and mid-1620s, that is, immediately prior to the outbreak of hostilities between Etherington and Denison. A close examination of the consequent exchanges will allow us to set Denison and Etherington's altercation in its immediate local context and to say something about the ways in which developments and tendencies in the sectarian or radical underground were connected to, indeed in dialogue with, more mainstream currents of puritan thought.

In 1622 Chibald published a book called *A trial of faith by the touchstone of the gospel*. Ostensibly this was a fairly standard piece of moderate puritan practical divinity in the Denison mould. The book marketed itself as a guide with which humble Christians could test whether they enjoyed a true saving faith or not. It was designed to bring succour both to the godly, who would be confirmed in the comforts consequent upon the possession of such a faith, and to 'carnal gospellers', who, stripped of their false pretensions to a true justifying faith, would both be confronted with the dire spiritual straits in which they found themselves and be advised on how they might set about achieving the true faith which alone would save them. There was, however, more to the book than these conventionally pietistic aims might imply. It was, in fact, a critique of what Chibald took to be all too prevalent errors amongst the godly concerning saving faith and its relations with assurance, on the one hand, and with repentance, on the other.

Chibald defined true justifying faith as 'a grace of God whereby a sinner doth trust unto Jesus Christ for heavenly and eternal blessedness, according to the gospel'. It was a definition he defended, again in classically moderate puritan terms, as a mid point between two extremes, the first provided by the definition of the papists and the second by that of the Lutherans. The papist position was quickly dispatched for, at least according to Chibald, they equated saving faith with a mere historical faith, that is to say, with a bare intellectual assent 'to all those things that God hath propounded to be believed'.[3]

What Chibald described as the Lutheran position, however, proved more controversial. According to Chibald, the Lutherans held that 'a saving faith is a full assurance and certain persuasion of salvation by Christ and that to believe in Christ is to be fully assured and persuaded of salvation by him'. For Chibald, this was seriously to put the cart before the horse. Assurance was an effect of justifying faith, not a constituent part of that faith. 'A man must be saved before he can be assured of his salvation', Chibald argued, 'and a man must have a saving faith before he can be saved ... therefore he must have a saving faith before he can be assured of his salvation.' By the covenant of grace, Chibald pointed out, salvation was promised 'under a condition and the condition is faith in Christ ... so that he must first perform the condition of the covenant, by believing in Christ, before he can obtain the thing promised in the covenant, which is salvation. For as it is true that he which believeth in Christ by a saving faith is justified as soon as he believeth, so is it as true that before he believeth he is not justified. For till then, he hath no reason to lay hold on the tree of life or to lay claim unto salvation or the assurance of it.'[4]

These, however, were not merely points of scholastic interest. Chibald was not dealing with the conceptual confusions and logical lapses of the Lutherans just to show off his own doctrinal dexterity and orthodoxy. On the contrary, as he went out of his way to point out, such doctrinal errors could lead and were leading to very serious spiritual and pastoral effects. Such mistaken views 'have ... shaken the faith of many weak Christians, who, reading that a saving faith is an assurance of salvation and that to believe in Christ is to be fully persuaded of the forgiveness of sins by Christ, and withal finding to themselves either no assurance at all or (at least) not so full an assurance and persuasion of their salvation, have hereupon concluded (to the great discomfort, as well they might, if their definition of a saving faith were true) that they have not a saving faith, though indeed and in truth they had, as long as they believed in Christ, trusted in him and rested on the merits of his death and righteousness for salvation'.[5]

> For what will such be ready to say against themselves, through the accusation of their own consciences and the suggestion of satan? I am not a child of God, because I have not a saving faith; and I have not a saving faith, because I have not an assurance of salvation. For (will they say) I have read in treatises and catechisms, yea I have heard and been taught in sermons, that to believe in Christ is to be assured of salvation by Christ and that a saving faith is a full persuasion of the heart, grounded upon the promises of God, that whatsoever Christ hath done for the salvation of man, he hath done it as well for me as for any other. Now, alas, I know well enough to my grief that I have not this assurance, for because I want it, I am thus afflicted in mind.[6]

The inherent circularity of these arguments trapped believers inside the maze of their own subjective doubts and fears, searching desperately within their own consciousness for evidence of an affective state – assurance – that could alone provide the basis for the affective state – assurance – for which they were in desperate search. Here was a veritable labyrinth of circularity and contradiction, in which believers were, in effect, committed to the proposition that 'we are justified by being assured of justification'. This, of course, made no sense 'because that whereby we are justified must needs go before our being justified, in as much as it is the means and cause of it, and we must first be actually justified in God's sight before we can be assured of our justification ... wherefore either assurance of salvation must go before salvation itself ... or it cannot be true that we are justified by being assured of our justification'.[7]

On his own account, at least, Chibald's position offered the afflicted

Christian a way out of this spiritual cul-de-sac of doubt and despair. For, since it was logically necessary that justifying faith and consequent justification in the sight of God and salvation must precede our assurance of salvation, it was quite possible that 'many of God's dear children may want the assurance of their salvation, and that for a long while in some cases, and yet, for all that, trust in Christ and hang upon him for salvation'. Faith was a duty by which, under the covenant of grace, we were justified and saved; assurance was a spiritual comfort, a fruit or effect, consequent upon that faith and must under no circumstances be confused with it. 'The comfort of faith is assurance of salvation and assurance of salvation ariseth from peace of conscience and joy in the hope of heaven, both which follow faith in Christ or our being justified by faith in Christ.'[8]

Of course, it was true that such comforts had an important part to play in the life of the Christian, so important that all Christians were obliged to seek them out with zeal. Seeing the 'comforts' of 'a saving faith' are 'possible to be attained' and 'being attained, they are worthy to be enjoyed' and 'being enjoyed they are permanent and may be kept', 'therefore', Chibald concluded, 'are we most worthy of sharp reproof, if we labour not for them'.[9] And yet we should beware of setting so high a premium on them as to, in effect, if not in theory, make our salvation depend upon their attainment. For not every believer experienced these comforts to the same extent. Consequently we 'should not make trial whether we feel them in us or no at all times, or at all times in like measure, for this would deceive many weak Christians, who, though sometimes they want the feeling of these comforts of faith, yet may have a saving faith for all that'. God did indeed vouchsafe these comforts to his elect but he did so to varying degrees. 'Faith doth bring assurance ... to the faithful' but only 'in that measure and at that time, that the Lord, in his wisdom and goodness, sees fit for each of his children'.[10]

But if, on the one side, 'Lutheran' fallacies about the relationship between faith and assurance brought spiritual turmoil to 'weak Christians', on the other, the same doctrinal mistakes had equally destructive effects amongst what Chibald termed 'carnal gospellers'. The definition of faith against which Chibald was arguing 'doth nouzel up men in profaneness and formal profession' since it induced in them 'a strong persuasion they have saving faith and ... a vain presumption of their salvation ... because it makes them, who indeed have not a saving faith, to persuade themselves they have it and them, who as yet are not justified, that they are'. It did so by equating the possession of a saving faith with the possession of a strong subjective conviction or persuasion that one was saved and thus gave such people an incredibly strong incentive to nurture and maintain such a subjective conviction.

The effects of all this were entirely circular and self-confirming and led such carnal professors straight to hell.

The London puritan scene

For when such men do read in books and are taught what a saving faith is, namely an assurance of salvation, and what it is to believe in Christ, namely (as they say) to be assured of forgiveness of sins by Christ, and withal do know and feel that they have an assurance, yea a full assurance, (as they persuade themselves) of their salvation (for they would not doubt of it, say they, for all the world) how can it be but this definition of a saving faith, through the deceitfulness of their proud hearts and satan's craft, must needs nouzel them up in this strong persuasion, that they have a saving faith; especially when they can allege for themselves that they have learned it so by the ministry of the word of their pastors? For, if a saving faith be an assurance of salvation (as their definition imports), then an assurance of salvation is a saving faith and if an assurance of salvation be a saving faith, then why should not their assurance of salvation be a saving faith, as they think?[11]

Such fallacious and self-confirming subjectivism was, Chibald claimed, a necessary consequence of the 'Lutheran' definition of a true faith since 'if a saving faith be nothing else but an assurance of salvation and to believe in Christ be nothing else but to be fully assured of salvation by Christ and to be certainly persuaded that whatsoever Christ hath done for the salvation of others he hath done the same for them in particular and for their salvation, then must it follow that he which hath this particular assurance of his salvation must needs have a saving faith'. This situation was compounded by the propensity of the people Chibald was attacking (still at this point operating under the label of Lutherans) to claim that 'faith in Christ (that is ... a full assurance of salvation by Christ) is the first grace that is wrought in Christians'. For this meant that 'there is no means left to try whether their assurance of salvation be true or counterfeit or whether they have any sound grounds in them of this their assurance of salvation'.[12]

In addressing this problem Chibald switched his main doctrinal objective from the relationship between justifying faith and assurance to that between repentance and assurance. For the other common fallacy against which he organised his argument in *A trial of faith* was the notion that repentance came after faith. Thus Chibald devoted a long section of his treatise to arguing the opposite position; that since 'saving faith is not wrought in men all at one instant before the spirit of God work any other work of grace in them',[13] a crucial part of deciding whether one had a real saving faith or not lay in examining oneself on the preparatory steps necessary to produce such a faith. For, if one had not gone through the necessary preliminaries and preparatory stages, it was reasonable to assume that one did not have a true justifying faith, whereas if one had, the opposite (and altogether more welcome) conclusion became equally compelling.

Chibald described the stages through which the believer would probably go on his or her way to a true saving faith. First came the grace of illumination whereby, through his word, God inculcated a historical faith in the believer.

Then, through the preaching of the law and then the gospel, the believer was led to repentance for his or her sins, which represented the crucial preparation before a genuinely saving justifying faith could be achieved. It was here that Chibald located what he called 'a beginning of repentance'. He broke down the process by which repentance itself was achieved into stages, describing it thus: first came 'a smaller beginning of purpose to forsake former sins, upon the preaching, understanding, believing and laying to heart of the commandments and threatening of the law broken, which convince them of their sin and misery'. Then came a 'greater work thereof, upon the preaching, believing and laying to heart of the promises and comforts of the gospel, which offer grace and mercy'.

> And when people are thus wrought upon by God's spirit, when their mind is enlightened with the knowledge and belief of these points of the gospel and their hearts affected with necessity of having, the possibility of getting and the excellency of enjoying so worthy a thing as is salvation by so worthy a person as is the lord Jesus and for such ungracious persons as themselves are, how is it possible but they should be more fitted and prepared for salvation by Christ and, by this belief in the gospel, more forwarded to believe in Christ and drawn thereunto in hope of pardon.[14]

Chibald did not want to be too dogmatic about the precise nature and invariable order of the spiritual graces preparatory to a true faith.

> I do not say that this preparation is wrought in all men in the same degree but men are made to feel their need of Christ, according as God is pleased to make them sensible of their sins and misery; for some are more subject to be cast down and troubled in mind than other are and consequently more forward to hunger and thirst for Christ and for salvation by him ... Neither will I contend so eagerly about the order of this preparation as to go about resolutely to determine that this grace is always wrought in the first place and that in the second, in every Christian; nor yet to dispute and decide whether or no they be all wrought in one instant time, in every particular man or woman always.[15]

Under pressure from his critics, Chibald even conceded that the precedency of repentance over faith for which he was most concerned to argue was not so much temporal or chronological as categoric or logical. He was, he claimed, more concerned to argue for 'a precedency in nature rather than in time'. God could not be bound. He could infuse 'the gifts and graces of the spirit needful to salvation', at once, 'in an enthusiasm' 'and sudden rapture', as he had done with St Paul. But, Chibald observed, 'Paul's conversion was extraordinary', of a sort not at all 'usual in all men and women in these our days' when the process of conversion and the infusion of spiritual graces worked incrementally, 'one after another, successively, sermon after sermon, week after week'.[16] But having conceded all this, Chibald retained, as a basic sediment of assertion, the claim that the preparatory graces he was describing, up to and including the beginnings of repentance, 'are all wrought in men in some kind or other, in one measure and degree or other, before they can or will be fit and able to trust in Christ for salvation'. Chibald was sure, in short, that 'all Christians are thus prepared, more or less, to faith in Christ before they can or will believe in him'.[17]

Such a view of the origins and nature of justifying faith Chibald then proferred as a sovereign remedy for the spiritual ailments of both the carnal gospeller and the weak Christian outlined above. 'I know by good experience', Chibald, the practical pastor, intoned, 'that the understanding, believing and laying to heart of the truth of God, which I have written in this matter, will be beneficial unto many, in that those that have not this repentance begun in them shall, hereby, be convinced plainly not to have a saving faith, to the end they may labour to get both and in that order that I have said, and those that have, shall be soundly and undoubtedly assured they have a saving faith and may boldly go to Christ for salvation, namely because they have begun to repent and therefore are persons qualified for it.'[18]

Chibald's formal doctrinal claims were thus proffered as a solution to, and almost certainly had their roots in, various pastoral difficulties and dilemmas that Chibald had experienced in dealing both with the weak in faith, broken by their failure to achieve a sense of assurance settled enough to convince them that they had a true faith, and with a sort of carnal gospeller whose simple reiteration of their settled confidence in their own salvation served as a legitimation for a level of spiritual indifference to Chibald's best efforts in the pulpit that had clearly driven him to distraction. There was more than a hint of impatience and relief in Chibald's claim that, since, 'in the common order of God's working generally and in his ordinary course, God prepares men to believe in Christ' through a regular progression of spiritual graces infused through preaching, 'a minister of the gospel, knowing that preaching is the way and means to work faith in Christ (viz. ordinarily)' may 'reprove carnal gospellers that neglect and contemn hearing of sermons and yet think they have faith in Christ'. 'Why, then, may I not say', Chibald defiantly asked the reader, 'that the faith of carnal gospellers is not true saving faith, seeing they were never prepared to believe in Christ by the dispositions which God's Holy Spirit works ordinarily in those in whom he begets a saving faith'.[19]

Chibald thus presented his book as response to and solution for what were common enough puritan pastoral problems. The result, he claimed, was not so much doctrinal innovation, a head-on clash with the opinions of many of his fellow ministers, as an exercise in fine tuning, a more precise definition of terms, through which certain unfortunate tendencies and popular fallacies could be redressed and removed. It was true, Chibald conceded, that the claim that faith went before repentance was regarded as a truism by many of his fellow ministers and that seemed directly to contradict his own opinion on the matter. However, this was only an apparent clash of views; in fact, as he tried hard to explain, the differences between his position and that of other puritan ministers were more apparent than real, a question of semantics rather than of substance. For, on most of the occasions on which other divines committed themselves to the proposition that 'faith goes before repentance', on closer inspection, their position could be in fact be glossed and refined to bring it into line with Chibald's.

Thus, sometimes, when other ministers made the claim they could be construed as meaning that faith, defined as mere 'belief in the gospel', went before repentance. This Chibald had never denied; his concern had been with the relations between repentance and justifying not historical faith. Again, when some ministers claimed that 'faith goes before repentance', they could be glossed as meaning that it was only through a true justifying faith 'that repentance can be acceptable to God' to salvation, which again was a position that Chibald was only too glad to endorse. 'And where I say "repentance goes before faith" I do not mean that this begun repentance can be acceptable unto God to our salvation, before we believe in Christ but that it is only begun as a preparation to make us fit persons to believe in Christ and, by believing, to crave pardon of our sins for his sake.'[20] Finally, those who maintained that 'faith goes before repentance' could be construed as saying that justifying faith 'goes before repentance be fully wrought, perfected and accepted'. That, too, Chibald gladly accepted; he was talking about the beginnings of repentance not its end. It was enough, in order to maintain his position, to argue that 'a true (though a weak) measure of repentance is begun in men before they can trust in Christ for salvation'.[21]

Chibald's defence turned on two crucial distinctions. The first was that between two sorts of faith; the first, historical faith, defined by Chibald as a mere belief in the gospel, did indeed precede repentance, while the second, true justifying faith, did not. Chibald's second distinction was that between the two senses in which the word repentance was most commonly used. On the one hand, repentance could be taken to mean merely 'hearty sorrow for sin past and a true purpose to leave it'. That was its proper and primary meaning, an accurate encapsulation of the true virtue of repentance. On the other hand, the term 'repentance' could be, and often was, used more loosely to refer to 'the practice of amendment of life and new obedience'. That, properly speaking, was not so much repentance itself as 'the practice of repentance or the bringing forth of fruits of worthy amendment of life, which is the putting off the old man and putting on the new man in the actions of our lives and whereby the repentance of the heart is manifested'. This was to equate repentance with the wider process of sanctification, a process that, of course, was only completed after and not before justifying faith. Chibald, on the other hand, was only concerned with repentance taken in the first sense, as sorrow for sin and a determination to avoid it in future. It was only that repentance – in Chibald's terms repentance proper – that preceded justifying faith. 'Where I say "repentance goes before faith" my meaning is that repentance is begun in the heart: and that a true purpose and resolution of heart to leave our former evil ways and to serve God in a new conversation for time to come is begun in men before they can go to Christ to be eased of their sins or trust in him to be saved.'[22]

Addressing his critics, Chibald observed that 'as for repentance I speak for the virtue itself, they of the fruit of that virtue' and that fruit, he was only too pleased to admit, was an effect not a precursor of justifying faith. Thus Chibald freely stated that 'refraining of sin for conscience sake in sincerity and in a settled and constant course is a fruit of faith and requires virtue from Christ's death and resurrection to be drawn down by faith in Christ, and so doth power to mortify our corrupt nature in the lusts of it and to quicken us in our new man to cheerful constant and conscionable new obedience require and presuppose this faith in Christ's death and resurrection'.[23]

Chibald thus presented the differences between his position and that of many of his contemporaries as largely semantic. 'So that however, at first sight, there may seem to be some difference in judgement betwixt myself and some of our divines that speak generally and indefinitely of faith's going before repentance, yet by applying the distinctions that I have made of faith and repentance, there will be no contradiction indeed in this point betwixt me and them, but an easy way of reconciliation and consequently of consent therein.' The only group whom Chibald excluded from this happy consensus were those 'Lutherans' who persisted in equating a true justifying faith with assurance of salvation.[24] That, Chibald remained clear, was an error, but it was not, at least on the account proffered to the reader in *A trial of faith*, an error of which he was prepared to accuse any of his English contemporaries. He restricted his strictures on that score to foreign Lutherans. As we shall see, on that point at least, Chibald was almost certainly being disingenuous.

There is, however, no reason to think the same of his wider claims to belong to what one might term the mainstream of English puritan or advanced reformed opinion. After all, we have been taught by a generation of historians to believe that the general run of puritan divines were by the early seventeenth century, in some sense, 'preparationists' and 'covenant theologians' and here was Chibald using both a version of preparationism and arguments based on the true nature of the covenant of grace to rectify what he saw as prevalent loose or mistaken talk about the relationship between repentance and faith. Indeed, when he came under pressure from certain nameless critics, Chibald cited preparationist passages from the works of William Perkins, Paul Baynes, William Whateley, Edward Elton and Thomas

Rogers (amongst others) to back up his own position in exactly the way one might expect.[25]

Again, when those same critics accused him, with the papists and pelagians of, in effect, locating the origins of true faith, and hence of justification and salvation, in human efforts made before the gift of faith, and of thus overthrowing the basic protestant tenet that held all human actions undertaken before or without faith to be sinful, Chibald replied by exposing what he took to be the entirely orthodox predestinarian underpinnings of his position. In *A trial of faith* he had only been speaking of the elect, he explained. 'I speak of working of those preparations in the elect only (in whom only a saving faith is wrought because they only are to be saved ...), so that, as long as it is evident that the preparations to faith that I speak of be ordinarily wrought in all the elect ... it is no matter though some of them be common to reprobates with the elect.' It was merely that, in the elect, these preparations, wrought by the spirit, always infallibly led to a saving faith in Christ while, in the reprobate, they never did. 'The reprobate have but some of them but the elect have all ordinarily ... by God's appointment they do not tend to the salvation of the reprobate (because God never intended their salvation) but of the elect they do.' 'Those preparations do not, in the event, draw all men to believe in Christ, in whom they are wrought, yet do they, at one time or other, draw all the elect so to do, that are ordained unto eternal life and to believe in him, for that end.' 'In the elect coming follows drawing necessarily in respect of the event.' 'In the elect they which have this wrought in them as a preparation to faith shall, in time, have faith wrought in them also, to the end they may be saved, for God will perfect his work in them when he begins it.'[26]

The preparations of which he was talking, Chibald reminded his readers, were none of them 'sufficient to salvation', even in the elect. 'If a man could truly be imagined, being elected, to die in that estate', that is, not having achieved a justifying faith, he would be damned. Such a thing was, of course, impossible, since the elect were always saved, but it was useful as a thought-experiment to show that Chibald was not halfway to pelagianism and popery. His point was merely that these preparations, the chief of which was the first stages of repentance, 'are appointed as preparations to regeneration in the elect, who, because they are ordained to that end, which is eternal life, and to the means of that end, which is faith, therefore are they also predestinate to the means of this faith, which are these preparations'.[27] Thus, this first beginning of repentance before faith might fail in some people but never in the elect. Considering these preparations 'in relation to the ground from whence they proceed, which is election; to the end for which they are wrought, in the elect, which is to make them persons capable of salvation, unto which they are elected, or to the efficient cause, which is the spirit who perfects his graces begun, so they cannot fail totally or finally. For in the elect this purpose of repentance is seconded with practice accordingly in the event.'[28]

Chibald simply could not see how his position on repentance preceding and preparing for justifying faith 'hindered any duty or comfort of the faithful, or discountenanced the sincerity of profession, or disparaged the perseverance of the elect, in the estate of grace, or derogated from the free grace of God in Christ, or lifted up man in any proud conceit of his own free will, as long as it is affirmed that repentance is but begun only; that it is wrought by the spirit only, and by the word only, and in the elect only, and only as an effect of their election, and only as a means to work God's will on them, by disposing them to faith in Christ, whereby they may be brought to that supernatural end, to which they are ordained in him'. 'As long as the beginning of repentance and sanctification in the preparations (though before faith in Christ) be not attributed to the work of nature or good use of our free will, but only to the work of the spirit, in the elect (which yet is not sufficient to salvation nor acceptable thereunto without faith in Christ) I can see no inconvenience in holding a beginning of repentance or sanctification in the dispositions thereunto before faith.'[29]

On his own account, following the publication of *A trial of faith*, Chibald was excoriated from the pulpit, and lists of his errors on both justification and repentance were drawn up in manuscript and circulated around London until he was forced twice to reply in print to clear his name. While Chibald refused to name his accusers in print, we know from much later remarks in the correspondence of Richard Baxter that one of them was George Walker. In the same exchange, Baxter's correspondent Robert Abbot quite accurately identified Walker as having polemically mugged 'heavenly Mr Wotton' in an earlier dispute, also about the issue of justification. Walker's conduct then had marked him down as a doctrinal attack dog of quite outstanding tenacity and viciousness, which makes his inflammatory role in the Chibald affair entirely likely. While the main focus of the dispute between Wotton and Walker had lain elsewhere, the question of the relationship between justification and repentance had been a side issue and it is reasonable to assume that, at least for Walker, the fuss over Chibald's book represented a continuation or coda to the previous dispute. Thus it should come as no surprise to find in a letter of July 1650 Robert Abbot identifying 'my old learned and godly friend Mr [George] Walker' as the leading assailant on 'my dear Mr Chibald, now with God'.[30]

Certainly, the range of insults and labels used to excoriate Chibald closely paralleled those deployed by Walker to discredit Wotton and his favourers. Thus, on his own account, Chibald was accused of being, amongst other things, a closet and equivocating socinian, pelagian and papist. Walker's earlier assault on Wotton had turned on charges of socinianism, based, so

Walker claimed, on his 'reading of the controversies between Junius and Arminius, Lubertus, Bertius, Gomarus and others of the remonstrants' in the light of which the similarities between Wotton's views and those of Servetus and Socinus had become crystal clear.[31] Yet for all these echoes of the earlier dispute, the claims of popery, socinianism and pelagianism, lodged against Chibald, retained another, more directly contemporary resonance, for all were terms of abuse regularly deployed by the godly against Arminianism, an association registered indeed by Walker himself, who, in his subsequent accounts of his exchanges with Wotton, published in the 1640s, was very free with the accusation of Arminianism as a tag with which to discredit those in authority who had either favoured Wotton or prevented Walker from airing his denunciations of Wotton in print. Thus the pattern of vilification deployed against Chibald almost certainly points to increased anxiety about the need to police and defend orthodoxy in the face of an insurgent Arminianism as, if not an underlying cause, then at least an exacerbating factor in the campaign against Chibald.[32]

But, just as there is no need to agree with George Walker that John King's or George Abbot's chaplains were parties to an Arminian conspiracy to suppress his views, so, judging from the passages quoted above, it seems clear that Chibald himself was no Arminian. This judgement is amply confirmed by a set of near contemporary marginalia (probably dating from the later 1640s) in the copy of Chibald's second reply to his critics in Dr Williams Library. For there, in a series of biting asides, a nameless critic attacked Chibald from a genuinely Arminian point of view. The author of the marginalia equated the elect with those whom God foreknew would believe, adding, at one point, the comment 'by elect let's understand those whom God foreknew would believe, for we must not destroy the foreknowledge of God'. 'Understand elect here', he added in another place, 'such as God foreknew would believe and continue to the end.'[33] He stressed the need for the co-operation of human free will with divine grace in the process of conversion and justification, observing at one point that 'the will of man must comply with God's drawing and grace tendered, else the person will never be brought over unto Christ'.[34] Of course, a Calvinist might say as much, but our nameless critic made his purpose clear when he contradicted Chibald's account of the process whereby God called humankind to repentance and faith with the comment 'it's not then a forcible and irresistible drawing', adding next to a passage claiming that 'God's cords do draw and have always irresistably coming joined with them' the remark that 'here they deceive themselves'. Similarly, he ridiculed Chibald's unwillingness to admit that Christians could fall away from a true faith, adding the comment in the margin: 'note here how loath this man is to grant a departing from faith because he supposes repentance and faith to be effects of election and not the cause'. Next to a passage on Paul's conversion, where Chibald claimed that all 'the gifts and graces of the spirit needful to salvation were (in all likelihood) wrought in him at once and together, in an enthusiasm', our critic commented laconically in the margin 'mere enthusiasm'. In the margin, by a passage in which Chibald outlined the gradual process whereby 'Christ doth frame the church and make it perfect not all at once and together, but successively, by calling one member after another and adding them thereunto', our critic acidly remarked 'that the saints are not perfectly born till the resurrection'. Again, next to a paragraph speculating on the relationship between, and proper order of, election, justifying faith and sanctification, we find the remark 'this thing can possibly be known to none but to God'. And, finally, in the margin beside an account of the order in which the believer should lay hold on God's promises, repent and then achieve faith, our critic inserted another, sacramental, stage, omitted by Chibald, writing 'and being baptised for the remission of sins' against the crucial passage.[35]

While these marginalia show that Chibald's works were perceived by Arminians, as well as by Calvinists and puritans, as having an interesting or ambiguous relationship to contemporary predestinarian dispute, they also serve conclusively to clear Chibald of the accusation of pelagianism or Arminianism; here, after all, was a genuine Arminian picking holes in his work for being unduly Calvinist, not to mention too suffused with a puritan enthusiasm and a potentially antinomian perfectionism. However, they also show why Chibald's work might attract the critical attention of Calvinist and puritan divines, newly sensitised to the Arminian issue. For in two places in Chibald's text our nameless Arminian critic approvingly noted that his arguments clashed with central Calvinist tenets; remarking in one place that 'here is the absolute decree overthrown' and, in another, that 'here the picking or particular election of persons out of the lost lump of Adam is overthrown'.[36]

Let us accept, then, that Chibald was no closet Arminian. Let us accept, indeed, that he was what he said he was, a member of the fraternity of London godly ministers, whose bona fides could be judged from 'my carriage in my ministry and conversation these twenty years in the city and parish where I dwell', as well, as we shall see below, by the clerical company he kept in London.[37] Let us assume, too, that he was indeed a product of, and was still working within, the recognisably puritan or perfect protestant intellectual and pastoral tradition that he continually constructed and appealed to through the authorities that he both quoted in his text and cited in his margins. These ranged from the book of homilies, through John Foxe and William Perkins to Thomas Rogers, Paul Baynes and Bishops Morton and Francis White (the latter in his reformed rather than his Arminian phase) and included, remarkably, T.L. whose *The key of David* was quoted at some length, albeit as an anonymous tract, to prove that many English divines before Chibald had indeed held that repentance preceded justifying faith.[38] Finally, let us accept that Chibald himself really believed that he was merely fine tuning and refining the doctrine of faith, in the process modifying only slightly the semantics of puritan preparationism. On this basis, we can perhaps take his hurt surprise at the hostility that his intervention provoked as genuine. But surprised or not, he was surely being more than a little disingenuous when he claimed that only Lutherans would object to his sharp distinction between faith and assurance.

The Laudian William Forbes expressed himself frankly bemused by that claim. Reviewing what was in many ways the same affective and theological terrain, later in the century, the puritan divine Giles Firmin agreed. For Firmin took it as axiomatic that what he termed variously 'Mr Perkins, Mr Rogers and the ancient divines' or 'our fathers', a group which included his own father, who had catechised him closely on this point, had all 'defined faith by a particular persuasion and assurance'. On this view, 'the essence of saving faith doth lye in a particular persuasion and assurance that Christ, with all his redemption, is mine, that I shall have life and salvation by his means'. 'Thus we have been catechised', Firmin admitted, 'thus we read in eminent, holy men, master builders'.[39] Admittedly, from Firmin's perspective, on the issue of assurance at least, Chibald's was the voice of the future. As he observed, 'divines of late years have cleared up the nature of faith more than ever', replacing the equation of saving faith with assurance – asserted with such confidence by Perkins or John Rogers (or indeed by Stephen Denison) – with the view that Firmin himself adopted, when he defined 'saving faith in Christ' as 'that grace whereby we receive Christ as he is offered to us in the gospel, and so resting upon him, salvation'. 'It is by grounded assurance', Firmin observed, echoing Chibald, 'that thou art comforted, but it is by faith thou art saved.' Firmin reached and defended these conclusions through arguments remarkably similar to those adumbrated over fifty years earlier by Chibald.

On this evidence, we might see Chibald's claims as part of the beginning of a sea change in puritan divinity, the end of which was being signalled by Firmin. On Firmin's account, later generations of puritan doctors of the soul and theological practitioners (himself included), in confronting the pastoral and affective consequences of the doctrinal formulations and edificational, soul-altering techniques of the founding fathers or 'masterbuilders' of the puritan tradition, had been forced to re-examine, refine and even to revise the doctrinal claims and formulations of their predecessors. This, of course, was precisely what Chibald was trying to do in as deliberately an unconfrontational way as possible. Firmin's book *The true Christian* represents his attempt, much later, to codify, summarise and apply the results on a topic virtually identical to the one addressed by Chibald half a century earlier.[40]

But Chibald's was not only the voice of the future of puritan divinity but also that of its immediate past. If, on assurance, his position prefigured that picked out as now dominant by Firmin, so, on repentance, he could be said to have been merely reverting to an earlier position, assumed as natural by puritan preachers of the late sixteenth century as popular and prominent as Arthur Dent. For Dent had habitually talked as though repentance did indeed precede the gift of true, justifying faith and even for Perkins that had been a question upon which orthodox and godly men of good will could and did disagree.[41]

But Chibald's new-found insistence that repentance must precede justification was not merely a revival of the urgent tub-thumping, repentance-centred evangelism practised by Dent or Perkins. Rather, it was a response to his own somewhat different pastoral situation. For, as we have seen, Chibald found himself confronted not with an auditory for whom the perfect protestantism purveyed by the likes of Dent or Perkins retained the shock of the new, but rather with jaded formal Christians, all too superficially familiar with what had become, by the 1620s, in London at least, the dreary mantra of an assurance-centred puritan practical divinity. Developed in the first flush of puritan evangelism, during the central years of Elizabeth's reign, according to Chibald, that style of piety and evangelism had, at least where the word was most plentifully preached (as it most certainly was in London), started to run into the law of diminishing returns, its emotional force blunted by the superficial familiarity of the average carnal gospeller with its central claims.

In theory, the doctrine and experience of assurance was the ultimate goal of the elect soul in search of salvation and spiritual comfort, the pursuit of which was supposed to goad the Christian professor on up the spiral of sanctification to greater and greater heights of spiritual exertion. Now, however, Chibald lamented, the equation of the possession of a saving faith with a settled sense of one's own salvation, in and through Christ's sacrifice, had become part of the repertoire of the carnal gospeller and the routine Christian. It had become a mere cliche, an easily learned and repeated stock response. Thus, what had started out as a major weapon in the destabilising, defamiliarising arsenal of the puritan evangelist had now become part of the carapace of habit, of learned indifference and routinised response, which ordinary Christians used to turn aside the urgent promptings of the godly clergy. In short, what had started out as a central element in the solution had become, through the deadening effects of continual repetition from the pulpit and in the catechism class, part of the problem.

Chibald wanted, in effect, to use his newly revived principle that repentance must generally precede saving faith to shock the carnal gospellers in his auditory out of their spiritual complacence. Here, then, was an old doctrinal tenet being revived and reinserted into a new pastoral situation. In so doing, Chibald's position looked towards and in some ways prefigured the preparationism of divines like Thomas Hooker and Thomas Shepherd. For both men, at least on Firmin's account of their divinity, had come to adopt their preparationist stance in part to shock even practised puritan professors out of what was in danger of becoming a routinised, indeed complacent, assumption that Christ had indeed died for them.

It is crucial here to remember that such theological issues and debates almost never arose in a social, emotional or cultural vacuum. We are not dealing here only or even mainly with the internalist history of formal doctrinal argument, but rather with the cultural, social and intellectual history of puritan religion. Thus, the key question is not just which doctrinal cruxes were at stake in any given argument and how that argument or exchange played out, but also the way in which specific doctrinal claims were inserted and reinserted into a number of polemical, emotional and cultural contexts and clashes. One point of setting Chibald against Firmin's account of the progression of puritan doctrinal insight and pietistic practice, is to provide Chibald's thought with an admittedly lightly sketched long-term context. But more importantly, it serves to re-emphasise the way in which in different contexts, at different points in the dialectical development of the puritan tradition, essentially the same pastoral and emotional imperatives and doctrinal materials could be combined in very different ways, leading to very different both conceptual and affective outcomes.

Thus, it was typical of the dialectical dynamic of the puritan tradition, the continual dialogue, the give and take between the practical exigencies of the pulpit, the demands of formal doctrine and the spiritual experiences and dilemmas of the godly laity themselves that it was against the extremities and asperities of Hooker and Shepherd's preparationism that Firmin himself claimed to have been in reaction from at least the late 1640s. Just like Chibald, Firmin legitimated his excursions into formal doctrinal debate and definition in terms of the deleterious practical and experiential effects of the doctrines he was opposing. He had decided to take on certain central claims advanced by Thomas Shepherd (and Thomas Hooker) about the necessary nature and progress of preparation for saving grace because 'I hear that book hath caused much trouble to gracious Christians'. Indeed what he took to be Shepherd, Perkins and Hooker's claims and errors had 'been a trouble to myself, as to my own state', Firmin admitted.[42]

In making these remarks, of course, Firmin was not concerned primarily with the general run of formal Christians whom Chibald had been trying to frighten out of their spiritual torpor with his newly sharpened sword of preparatory repentance. Rather Firmin was chiefly concerned with a generation of godly persons who, he thought, had been too much affected and afflicted by the strenuous preparationism of divines like Hooker and Shepherd; these were people liable to fear that they were damned if they had not gone through the wrenching experience of repentance, (in Firmin's parlance) 'the dreadful legal horrors' of 'conviction and compunction', invoked in relatively modest terms by Chibald and then described and prescribed with increasing ruthlessness and severity by the likes of Hooker and Shepherd. Such people had been known, Firmin claimed, in their despair, 'almost to quarrel with God for want of legal sorrows and fears'. Firmin's priorities, then, were very different from Chibald's. While he admitted that there were indeed 'proud, high flown, self conceited protestants' and vain carnal gospellers who both stood in need of 'a rousing and sharp pen' to apply the demands and dictates of the law and force them to Christ, there were also a good many 'poor, trembling, laden Christians' and the last thing they needed was more blocks and scruples placed between them and the comfort of a saving faith.[43]

The result of all this was that while, on assurance, Firmin might be thought to stand at the end of a trend started by Chibald, on repentance the tenor of their two positions was very different. Just like Chibald, Firmin was anxious to claim that assurance, although desirable, was not a necessary sign of a saving faith. Certainly, we were obliged to seek for it, but the bitter experience of many thousands of good Christians had shown that it was an experience or state that could not be attained by everyone nor indeed consistently sustained by many. On repentance, however, Firmin's emphasis was very different. For there, while he was prepared to admit that what he termed 'conviction and compunction' were usual preparations for and, by the order of nature, preceded the gift of a justifying faith, he also emphasised that not all Christians had to experience 'dreadful legal terrors' in order to be able to lay claim to a saving faith. 'Illumination, conviction and compunction' might all be consecutive in order of nature but not necessarily in order of time. They could happen, for instance, all at once. 'How often have men come home from one sermon with these works wrought?' asked Firmin. God could save his elect in myriad ways and no one person's passage to or experience of saving grace could or should be taken as normative for another. Certainly, the spiritual prodigies who often dominated the puritan ministry should never make the mistake of converting their own experiences into rules or norms for the generality even of true believers. Speaking of assurance, Firmin denounced those Christians who 'must have their settling and assurance come their way ... they must have their comfort and evidence as such a Christian had it'. This was 'to chalk out God's path for him' and Firmin would have none of it.[44] There were, in short, many routes to a true saving faith; some believers could identify precisely the moment when their conversion had started or happened, others could not. Some suffered extreme legal woes, others did not. Many people, brought up by godly parents under a preaching ministry, never experienced the pangs of repentance in the extreme form apparently posited by Shepherd or even Chibald; 'many ... of a more tender spirit, watchful in their lives and that keep up to a gospel conversation, they go off the stage of this world knowing little or nothing of these afflicting terrors of first to last'. 'There are many Christians who have not found the tenth part of these legal, hellish terrors, yet have proved sound and got to heaven', Firmin reminded his readers. There was much here that must remain a mystery. 'We may certainly conclude such and such things must be wrought before regeneration can be effected but how God works them is a great secret', Firmin claimed. It was all very well to talk of necessary preparations for grace, but how did we know precisely when the process of preparation had stopped and the act of justification been effected? 'May not the lord, at the very first stroke, convey an immortal seed of grace into the soul?' Firmin asked. How could anyone be certain when their new birth had started? 'Some Christians finding, at some time, more stirrings or higher workings or new convictions of some sin, under the ordinances, than they did before, will, from thence, reckon the time of their new birth; when they are much mistaken, God hath begun it before.'[45]

On this basis, it is clear that Chibald's excursion into doctrinal dispute and definition could be located within certain long-term trends, and dialectical exchanges within the puritan tradition of thought and experience, stretching from the formative period of the late sixteenth century, represented by 'our fathers', Firmin's 'master builders', Perkins and Rogers, through the assurance- and sanctification-obsessed experimental predestinarianism purveyed by the likes of Denison, to the preparationism of the early to mid-seventeenth century of men like Shepherd and Hooker and beyond to the sort of reaction against that awesomely demanding style of divinity represented by Firmin. At stake was a continuous debate or conversation between formal doctrine, the exigencies of pastoral and pulpit practice and spiritual experience. Throughout, basic tensions, paradoxical oppositions or antinomies within the reformed tradition of thought and feeling between, say, the law and the gospel, fear and hope, anxiety and assurance, were always in play, the precise balance between them being decided, at any given moment, by a multiplicity of factors, social, cultural, political, intellectual and indeed personal. Reared within the long traditions of Essex puritanism, exposed to the tribal lore of the godly preachers of that county and in particular that of the almost numberless Rogerses who dominated that society, living hard by one such Rogers (Daniel), Firmin both preached against his doctrine and conferred with him about it. Having to deal, in general, with a godly laity and, in particular, with his own psyche, scarred by the pulpit and pamphlet asperities of Thomas Shepherd or Thomas Hooker, Firmin wrote to and disputed with Shepherd about what he took to be his more dubious doctrinal claims. These exchanges all began in the 1640s and 1650s but Firmin only finally sought to codify and disseminate the results in print in 1670.[46]

Chibald, on the other hand, was confronted by a rather different situation. Like Firmin, he had to deal, on the one hand, with the assurance obsessed anxieties of the godly and, on the other, with the routinised and anaesthetising formulae of habitual protestantism. If Chibald's efforts to come to terms with these problems in some ways look towards both opinions and positions that Firmin and his ilk would come to regard as entirely conventional and to preparationist tendencies and positions that Firmin would come to reject, at the time, Chibald was challenging what Firmin would come retrospectively to characterise as a settled consensus about the equivalence of assurance and saving faith and what had emerged by the 1620s as an equally firm, anti-Arminian, conviction, that 'repentance' must follow and not precede justifying faith. Thus, whether he knew it or not, Chibald was taking on more than the errors of a few Lutherans; he was seeking seriously to modify assumptions central to the style of experimental predestinarian piety and divinity being pushed by many of his colleagues in the ministry and internalised by many a godly lay person across the city.

We can gain some sense of just what was at stake here by comparing Chibald's claims with Denison's catechism, which, after all, represented an account of what he took to be the basic elements of true religion that every Christian, however simple, should both know and understand. There Denison posed the question 'what kind of faith is required of those' about to present themselves at communion? Denison replied that 'a true, living, justifying faith' was required and proceeded to define such a faith as 'that radical grace of God's spirit, whereby a man, who is by nature a branch of the wild olive, that is, of the first Adam, is engrafted into Christ, the true olive tree'. Denison then went on to explain that this did not mean that every communicant had to have 'a full persuasion of God's favour'. 'It is indeed to be desired that every receiver were fully persuaded of God's love in particular unto themselves, but this high degree of faith God exacteth not of all.' Asked the logical next question 'what is the weakest degree of faith without the which none must adventure to partake of the sacrament', Denison then replied that 'it is a sense of our own unbelief and sorrow for the same, and a fervent desire to believe'. This picked up his earlier remark that God could always distinguish between 'babes and strong men in Christ' and that 'in babes God accepteth the desire of faith for faith, taking the will for the deed'.[47]

Here, then, was a subtly different view from that put forward by Chibald. For Denison, in the elect, the first stirrings of repentance were not preparations for, but the first signs of, a true justifying faith. In the formulation he was to adopt in 1641, these were the buds, for which a saving faith provided the life giving sap, the heat which emanated from and betrayed the presence of a pre-existing fire of saving faith. 'Babes in Christ' or, in Chibald's terms, 'weak Christians', were thus drawn into the puritan view of true religion by being asked to interpret their basic religious impulses, the first stirrings of repentance in their souls, as at least potential signs of a true saving faith. Reprobates, of course, very often felt those same spiritual stirrings and so, if the individual wanted to find out if his or her first glimmerings of repentance were indeed a sign of a true justifying faith, he or she was plunged directly into the anxious examination of their own conversation and growth in grace in search of that sense of assurance that constituted the central theme and organising principle of puritan practical divinity as it was espoused by the likes of Stephen Denison. In other words, the attention of the would-be godly person was shifted away from the divine act of justification and onto the subsequent process of sanctification. Objectively, in the sight of God, justification occurred as soon as the individual was granted a true justifying faith. God, of course, knew precisely when that had happened and from that moment on the person in question's salvation was certain. Viewed subjectively, however, since the first glimmerings of repentance and desire for divine comfort could be a sign of both a justifying and a hypocritical faith, the only way to find out whether one's faith was a true saving faith was to pursue the course of puritan godliness through the conventional means, seeking to establish one's elect status through a variety of uses of what Dr Kendall has termed the practical syllogism.[48] Thus the process of sanctification, whereby the action of the Holy Spirit remade the soul of the justified sinner, became the prime object of attention. In this approach, the doctrine of justification by faith alone retained very considerable theoretical and polemical importance, but on the level of individual religious subjectivity, the way in which the believer came to perceive him or her self as an elect saint or justified sinner, it had rather a minor role to play compared to the search for signs of elect status in the conversation and interior life of the believer which the puritan stress on assurance placed at the centre of the spiritual lives of the godly.

Chibald's position short-circuited this system; indeed, whether intentionally or not, it potentially transformed it. For it was of the essence of Chibald's argument to distinguish hard between the act of justification and the process of sanctification. Justification was Christ's work, while sanctification was the work of the spirit. It was justifying faith in Christ which worked our 'justification or forgiveness of sins or saving from hell' and this was quite distinct from that sense of 'salvation which comprehends sanctification'. For 'when we say Christ is our saviour, we do not mean he is our sanctifier but one that keeps us from hell and brings us to heaven'. Christ saved us from the punishment of sin (eternal death) which 'is a distinct thing' from 'the power of sin' which was 'taken away by sanctification only'.[49] Thus justification was a divine act, worked by faith in Christ, and its effects were immediate upon the achievement of a true faith. 'For no sooner can a sinner believe in Christ, but immediately he hath remission of his sins and is justified.'[50] Christ was our saviour, he was the object of that saving faith whereby we were justified in the sight of God. This was a transaction with which the subsequent course of our sanctification and experience of assurance of salvation could have nothing to do.

Sanctification, on the other hand, was a process which started with the gift of certain spiritual graces before justifying faith was achieved, but which was only completed after justification. 'Justification goes in nature before the perfection of our sanctification, in all the parts of it, and before the acceptance of it to salvation, but justification doth not go before any or every measure of sanctification can any way be begun.'[51] Where sanctification was a partial and always, in this life, imperfect, process, and the experience of assurance often fleeting, justification was a finite, once and for all divine act. 'Upon saying we are justified by faith, it will thereupon follow that we are totally unjustified ... before we believe in Christ but in saying we are sanctified by faith it will not thereupon follow that we are totally unsanctified before faith come and the reason is because faith, by its office, doth more properly justify than sanctify and justification doth not *suspicere magis et minus* as sanctification doth, neither is wrought by parts and degrees as sanctification is.'[52]

The divine act of justification entered believers' consciousness through their possession of a justifying faith, a faith which, according to Chibald, they could best identify in themselves through their experience of a preparatory repentance rather than through the anxious examination of the subsequent process of sanctification and the subjective sense of assurance that sometimes accompanied it. Thus the crucial before and after transition from unsaved to saved, and the existential relief and comfort to be derived therefrom, turned, on Chibald's account, not on sanctification but on justification. And the route to a proper subjective apprehension of justification turned not on the present and future, but on the past; not on the anxious examination of one's present consciousness, and present and future conduct, but on the recall of the process whereby one had come to Christ in the first place. The finished act of justification supplanted the inherently unfinished, inherently imperfect and thus subjectively unstable process of sanctification as the prime focus of attention.

Thus, when Chibald asked Christian professors to examine themselves to discover whether they possessed a true saving faith, it was not first or even mainly to the process of sanctification that he referred them but rather to the process whereby they had prepared themselves to receive a justifying faith. In short, they were to ask themselves whether they had achieved repentance before they had come to Christ for salvation. If they had, they were invited to assume themselves justified, that is saved. If not, they were to go back to the drawing board and follow Chibald's instructions on how to achieve a saving faith through the normal means and ordinances provided by Christ in his

The strange case of A trial of faith

church. Of course, Chibald did not ignore or omit the issue of sanctification in his instructions to the godly on how to try their faith. If repentance started before justification, it always, in the elect, led afterwards to sanctification; in the elect, repentance proper always had its effects and Chibald was quite happy to refer true believers to those effects as they tested their faith. He did so, however, almost as an afterthought in the last three chapters of the book where he posed the questions: 'whether dost thou find in thy self that thy faith is effectual and lively to the amending both of the heart and life and to the bringing forth of the fruits of faith in new obedience?'; 'whether dost thou labour in the use of the means to feel in thy soul the comforts of saving faith?'; and 'whether dost thou use the means to grow in faith and to strengthen it?' These, however, were questions the answers to which accounted for only fifty-five of the books 349 pages.[53]

This clearly represented a serious shift of emphasis within the standard puritan way of dealing with the problem of assurance and Chibald, for all his claims only to be disagreeing with Lutherans, must have known it. Indeed the intensity with which those claims were made can itself probably be taken as a sure sign that he was up to something. The potential instabilities within puritan practical divinity were however considerable and the stock way of talking about these things represented, in many ways, a carefully calibrated mechanism, a system of checks and balances, designed to keep those instabilities under control. Mess around with one bit and others were likely to be thrown out of kilter. Thus, for all his good and no doubt limited intentions, Chibald's tinkering could be construed as bringing with it some really rather radical, even potentially subversive, implications, implications which, whether Chibald intended them or not (and almost certainly he did not), may help to account for the extreme reaction to his book in certain quarters. I refer here to the potential, within Chibald's position, to generate an antinomian critique of puritan legalism, a repudiation rather than a Chibaldian modification of the process whereby the godly sought a sense of assurance through the contemplation of their own efforts to obey God's law, the success of which, construed as the gradual progress of the spirit's work of sanctification, was taken to validate their elect status.

On the one hand, puritan experimental predestinarianism had been developed to meet the pastoral needs of the laity who, confronted with the inscrutable impersonality of the double decree, had wanted a means to come to a settled sense of their own salvation. On the other, of course, it had been devised to overcome the potentially antinomian effects of the core protestant doctrines of justification by faith alone and absolute election by forcing the godly continually to validate their faith and their calling through their works. As we have seen in the discussion of Denison's position above, the whole elaborate edifice had been structured around an oscillation or transaction between anxiety and confidence, doubt and assurance, and this was a delicate balance that Chibald's position threatened to destroy. For justification was a once and for all event and once, through an examination of their preparations for justifying faith, the godly had been brought to think that they had experienced it, their relationship to the anxiety-filled search for assurance in sanctification and the introspective application of the practical syllogism would or certainly could be definitively changed.

The dispute with Chibald dealt with issues taken from the very centre of puritan practical divinity and trembled on the edge of questions of the utmost importance for that system of thought and feeling's continued stability. It is surely this earlier spat that explains the presence in Denison's assault on Etherington of the claim that the boxmaker held that repentance came before justifying faith. As we have seen above, Denison's was precisely the sort of position on this issue that Chibald had been attacking, and the attacks on Chibald, as he himself described them, were reminiscent of nothing so much as Denison's attack on Etherington. Whether or not the rebarbative perpetual curate of St Katharine Cree was personally involved in the assault on Chibald, he and others in the city had almost certainly been sensitised to this issue by the Chibald affair. As we have seen, T.L. had taken a position on this question, albeit in a very different polemical context in the 1590s, and that may well have predisposed Etherington to take Chibald's side.

Since Etherington was scarcely more explicit on the issue than Denison, it is difficult to be sure how this issue played out in the disputes between the two men. We do, however, have Etherington's rather garbled account of his conversations on the subject with Denison's clerical ally, Henry Roborough. According to Etherington, Roborough had denied 'repentance to be before justifying faith' but acknowledged it

> to be before justification and remission of sins; for he maketh repentance and sanctification (meaning a holy and new life) to be both one and will have them to fall in and come between justifying faith and justification ... as if justifying faith could be one moment in time without or before justification or remission of sins, which are, in effect, both one, for to have one's sins forgiven is to be justified from them and so of necessity it will follow that if repentance be before remission of sins and justification it must be before justifying faith, because where remission of sins is not there can be no justifying faith.[54]

These are admittedly somewhat cryptic, one-sided and probably garbled remarks but, seen from the perspective of the Chibald affair, they become easier to interpret. It is extremely doubtful whether either Denison or Roborough had in fact divided justification from the gift of justifying faith in the way that Etherington claimed. To have done so would have flown in the face of the entire reformed tradition in which they had been raised. We are almost certainly dealing here with a misreading or misconstrual of what

Roborough was saying, a misreading grounded on the terms in which Chibald had couched his critique of puritan practical divinity. For Etherington's account of Roborough's position becomes thoroughly intelligible once we assume that he was imputing to Roborough that confusion between justifying faith and assurance that Chibald attributed to 'the Lutherans'. Thus Roborough was presumably arguing conventionally enough that repentance (used here as a synonym for sanctification) came between justifying faith and assurance, which last term Etherington either heard as or translated into the experience of justifying faith for what were essentially Chibaldian, polemical purposes. To Etherington's ear, at least, such ministerial efforts to maintain a proper balance between faith and works in the life of faith seem to have constituted a lapse into a legalism or moralism, a works theology, that burdened the consciences of the would-be godly with the demands of the moral law in ways entirely inappropriate to souls saved by the free grace of God. Thus, as he explained in the passage quoted above, to Etherington such puritan pastoral emphases confused the once and for all divine *acts* of justification and remission, which were always coterminous and coincident with the first grant of justifying grace, with the subsequent *process* of sanctification, a process that always followed justification in the elect and in and through which, in the conventional puritan view, the elect believer could alone make his or her own assurance sure.

Etherington, of course, was a layman, with a dubiously sectarian past, horning in on an argument that had previously been conducted amongst learned ministers. The very fact of his espousal of Chibald's position must have raised the stakes considerably. Indeed, viewed through the screen of Etherington's 'familism' and 'Arminianism', Chibald's claims about repentance must have looked even more threatening. As we have seen, by appearing to cede too great a role to human effort, unaided by justifying grace, in the run up to justification Chibald's position had invited accusations of Arminianism or pelagianism. Now, in the mouth of an alleged 'familist' like Etherington and, in particular in combination with his crypto-familist emphasis on the transforming effect of the second baptism of the spirit on the elect, it could be linked to familist notions about the perfectibility of the little ones of God and thus to frankly antinomian tenets which, freeing the justified from the thraldom of the law, removed any need for repentance after justification and remission had once taken place.

What we have here, therefore, is not a debate between puritan, predestinarian orthodoxy and familist heterodoxy but rather an intra-reformed, indeed intra-puritan, dispute, centred on issues about preparationism, the *ordo salutis*, the proper relations between justification and sanctification, which were central to contemporary puritan concerns. T.L.'s position on this issue, developed in the 1590s, in the course of a critique of the proto-Arminian Peter

Baro, had clearly been internalised by Etherington as a central tenet. The heart-breaking experience of repentance before the uplifting realisation of justification and remission had become for him, as for T.L., one of the central defining characteristics of those little ones who stood at the centre of both men's views of the world. Now that tenet was reintroduced into another set of concerns, anxieties and accusations, redolent of the 1620s. Chibald's raising of the issue had arguably been prompted by pastoral, edificational and doctrinal dilemmas and cruxes that were entirely internal to the mainstream puritan tradition.

The point here is not to paint Chibald as some underground disciple of T.L., a clerical Etherington. On the contrary, there seems no reason to doubt that he had taken his own autonomous path to this position. That Chibald had read *The key of David* is interesting and may be significant. It is certainly a striking illustration of the circulation and availability of a wide variety of texts in puritan circles and of the permeability of the puritan canon, but it is scarcely either a sufficient or even a necessary explanation for Chibald's stance on the issue. Once espoused, however, the tenet was now canvassed in a political and polemical scene increasingly dominated (as it most certainly was for both Etherington and Denison) by the threat of Arminianism. The fuss involving Chibald in the early 1620s made the issue a current one. Etherington, the lay barrack-room lawyer, then stuck his oar into what had been hitherto a largely ministerial dispute and the issue became incorporated into his wider altercation with Denison. There could scarcely be a better example of the ways in which different intellectual strands and ideological trajectories, divergent career paths and polemical contexts, mixed and merged in the London puritan scene.

NOTES

1 J. Foster, *Alumni Oxonienses, 1500–1714* (Oxford, 1891), s.v., Chibald, William. Of Magdalene College, Chibald received his BA in 1595–96 and his MA in 1598–99. He gained his post at St Michael's Cole Abbey in 1604 and remained there until his death in 1641.

2 John Etherington, *A defence* (London, 1641), pp. 9–10. Also see John Etherington, *The deeds of Dr Denison a little more manifested* (London, 1642); S. Denison, *The white wolf* (London, 1641), p. 83.

3 William Chibald, *A trial of faith* (London, 1622), pp. 96, 116. The section dealing with the popish position runs from p. 115 to p. 137.

4 *Ibid.*, pp. 138, 146–7.

5 *Ibid.*, p. 141.

6 *Ibid.*, p. 154.

7 *Ibid.*, pp. 148–9.

8 Ibid., pp. 149–50.
9 Ibid. p. 331.
10 Ibid., pp. 318, 142.
11 Ibid., pp. 156–7.
12 Ibid., pp. 158, 159.
13 Ibid., p. 219.
14 Ibid., pp. 229, 225.
15 Ibid., p. 228.
16 W. Chibald, *An apology for a trial of faith* (London, 1624), pp. 21–2, 169, 171, 143.
17 Ibid., pp. 228–9.
18 Ibid., p. 234. Also see *ibid.*, pp. 292–3.
19 Chibald, *Apology*, pp. 169–71.
20 Chibald, *Trial*, pp. 289–91.
21 Ibid., pp. 289–90.
22 Chibald, *Apology*, p. 165; *Trial*, p. 290.
23 Chibald, *Apology*, pp. 70, 33.
24 Chibald, *Trial*, p. 291.
25 On preparationism and covenant theology see, for instance, J. von Rohr, *The covenant of grace in puritan thought* (Atlanta, 1986) and N. Pettit, *The heart prepared* (Middletown, 1989); for the citation of Perkins see Chibald, *Trial*, p. 235 and for the others see Chibald, *Apology*, pp. 15–17.
26 Chibald, *Apology*, pp. 11, 12, 18, 19, 57.
27 Ibid., p. 9 and also see *ibid.*, pp. 53–5.
28 Ibid., p. 45.
29 Ibid., pp. 24, 128.
30 N.H. Keeble and G. Nuttall, eds, *Calendar of the correspondence of Richard Baxter* (Oxford, 1991), vol. I, p. 58, a letter from Robert Abbot to Baxter, dated 21 July 1650. Also see *ibid.*, pp. 49–50, for a letter from John Tombes to Baxter of 11 September 1649, again condemning Walker for his polemical antics in denouncing Wotton, Bradshaw and Gataker for holding 'Socinianism' and 'damned and damnable heresy'. I owe these references to the kindness of Michael Winship. Also see T. Gataker, *Mr Anthony Wotton's defence against Mr George Walker's charge* (Cambridge, 1641), pp. 28–31; T. Gataker, *An answer to Mr George Walker's vindication* (London, 1642) pp. 94–6.
31 For the charge of socinianism see *Wotton's defence*, p. 10 and G. Walker, *A true relation of the chief passages between Mr Anthony Wotton and Mr George Walker* (London, 1642), pp. 5–6. Also see chapter 7 above, 'Macrocosm'.
32 Walker, *A true relation*, pp. 19, 24–5.
33 Chibald, *Apology*, the annotations are to be found in the copy in Dr Williams Library; pp. 8, 54. Also see p. 19 the 'elect, that is those whom God foreknew'.
34 Ibid., p. 10. Also see p. 128, 'yet must our free will comply with the motions of the spirit'.

35 Ibid., pp. 13, 17, 45, 143, 29, 60.

36 Ibid., pp. 38, 35.

37 Ibid., p. 187.

38 Ibid., pp. 61–6; for the citation of T.L. see pp. 64–6.

39 Giles Firmin, *The real Christian or a treatise of effectual calling* (London, 1670), pp. 5, 153, 285, 185. I should like to thank both Michael Winship and Patrick Collinson for drawing my attention to the importance of Firmin's work for the present discussion.

40 Ibid., pp. 182, 184. For the same point see also p. 239, where Firmin lamented that for all the recent advances on the doctrinal cutting edge – 'ministers of late have cleared the nature of faith in Christ better than it was before' – many Christians still clung to and were afflicted by the consequences of 'the old doctrine' 'being not yet forgot of many and the latter not so clearly understood by most'.

41 See here A. Dent, *A sermon of repentance* (London, 1583). I should like to thank Michael Winship for many discussions on this point and for pointing me towards Dent and Perkins.

42 Firmin, *The real Christian*, p. 226.

43 Ibid., pp. 75 , 82, 309. For the rooted conviction of hypocrites and formal believers that 'Christ is mine, forgiveness mine' and the almost impossible task of shifting them from that conviction see p. 189.

44 Ibid., pp. 2, 25, 283. On the necessary disqualification of many sound Christians from true belief if assurance really was a *sine qua non* for saving faith see also *ibid.*, pp. 191–3, 239–40.

45 Ibid., pp. 13–17, 78, 81, 18.

46 Ibid., p. 225; for his correspondence of 1647 on these issues with Shepherd see *ibid.*, p. 214.

47 S. Denison, *A compendious catechism* (London, 1621), pp. 11–13. This passage, of course, exposes a contradiction within the position being expressed here by Denison, a contradiction noted later by Firmin. To actually have insisted that all those who had a true saving faith experience a full sense of assurance would have been, Firmin claimed, 'to cut off the greatest part of the generation of sound believers'. This the previous generation of puritan divines, men termed by Firmin 'our holy ancient doctors' (whose insights and assertions Denison was for the most part parroting) had noticed. 'Their experience and trading with souls' could not help but bring this fact to their attention. Accordingly they had made 'several degrees of faith', 'the weakest and least measure of which' had 'no assurance in the believer, and yet inseparable fruits and tokens of faith'. On this point Firmin quoted p. 71 of that seminal early text of puritan practical divinity, the *Seven treatises* of Richard Rogers. 'Yet in p. 23', Firmin triumphantly observed, Rogers 'had set out faith by assurance and said that is the faith that uniteth to Christ. Now how can these things possibly hang together? When as he, and so holy Perkins, will own many sound believers in whom there is no assurance and yet it is that assurance, as he saith, by which men do apply Christ to themselves and which uniteth men to Christ.' Firmin, *True christian*, p. 191.

48 R.T. Kendall, *Calvin and English Calvinism to 1649* (Oxford, 1979), see esp. pp. 8–9 and *passim*.

49 Chibald, *Apology*, p. 141.

50 *Ibid.*, p. 102.
51 *Ibid.*, pp. 147–8.
52 *Ibid.*, p. 124.
53 Chibald, *Trial*, chapter IX, pp. 294–317; chapter X, pp. 318–33; chapter XI, pp. 334–49.
54 John Etherington, *The defence* (London, 1641), p. 11.

Chapter 9

Doctrinal dispute and damage limitation in the London puritan community

THE CASE OF WILLIAM CHIBALD

This was a world, moreover, into which we are offered further insight, firstly, by the course of the controversy surrounding Chibald's *A trial of faith*, secondly, by that of a dispute between Anthony Wotton and George Walker and, thirdly, by both Etherington and Denison's accounts of their altercation of the 1620s.

Let us start with the stirs provoked by Chibald's book. These began with an attack on Chibald in the pulpit by another minister. 'The doctrine therein delivered concerning justification by faith', Chibald complained, 'hath been published to be heretical and blasphemous.' The attack had come not from some jesuit or carnal gospeller but from 'a brother in the sincere profession of Christianity and the ministry'. Speaking of himself in the third person, Chibald explained that 'if it had been laid unto his charge only in a private house, he should have digested it. Or if in public, indefinitely only, the auditors had been warned to take heed of such a doctrine wheresoever they found it ... he might have born it, but the book was named, the page quoted and the doctrine therein contained charged.'[1] Nor was this a lone attack. Elsewhere in his works Chibald mentioned circulating manuscripts and position papers, at one point excusing himself from dealing further with certain points 'because I expect an answer from a learned godly brother, which when I shall have perused ... the lord will either give me ability to defend the truth or humility to recant the error, in that point'.[2]

Chibald spoke less respectfully of other such documents. At the end of his second defence he explained that 'there came to my hands very lately certain papers, containing an accusation against me concerning my first book ... and my second ... The things laid to my charge are no less than perjury, lying and contradiction, heresy, blasphemy and equivocation, as if my book were a mirror of errors and absurdities and myself a monster of ministers.' He had, therefore, taken the opportunity to add a few leaves to the end of his second reply in order to answer this critic 'for the credit of my ministry'.[3]

As we have seen, in the course of these exchanges Chibald was accused, amongst other things, of socinianism, pelagianism and popery. As far as Chibald was concerned these charges could only have been based on a mischievously deliberate misreading of his work.[4] In short, the attack on Chibald clearly mushroomed from the initial pulpit denunciation to incorporate a number of ministers articulating a variety of different doctrinal critiques and charges, both in the pulpit and via circulating manuscripts, at least some of which were couched in the language of polemical denunciation rather than that of scholarly debate. Indeed, Chibald explained his second printed defence not as an attempt to make up for the deficiencies in the first but by the simple fact that the number of attacks and objections had snowballed. 'For now I stop three or four gaps with one bush and answer the exceptions of more than one man.'[5]

Chibald justified his recourse to print by dwelling on the violence and unfairness of the attacks upon him. He was clearly desperate to avoid the imputation of faction or lack of charity and thus imputed all 'the hot fire of indiscreet zeal, passion and prejudice blowing the coals of contention with the bellows of ambition' wholly to his opponents, whom he decorously (but infuriatingly for us) refused to name.

Nor was this mere disingenuousness on Chibald's part. Certainly, he seems to have taken to print as a last resort, recounting in passing at least one meeting arranged by some nameless third parties between him and his critics. This 'conference' had been 'intended by some learned divines for pacification', but had not succeeded 'according to intent'. There, in the presence of two divines acting as referees, moderators or honest brokers, Chibald had attempted to clear his book from the imputations laid upon it 'in the presence of him that made the objection'. Given that his second and far more extensive attempt at self-vindication was printed with two letters to the Christian reader by Henry Mason and Daniel Featley, both coming men, episcopal and archiepiscopal chaplains and inveterate licensers of godly books, it is tempting to identify them as the two 'learned divines' who arranged the conference in a perhaps quasi-official attempt to end the dispute amicably.[6]

That was certainly the spirit in which they both endorsed Chibald's book. Mason, in an epistle to the author, found the book 'sound and orthodox and, as you explain it (to my thinking), not much different from theirs who in words seem to speak contrary'.[7] Featley agreed, reducing the message of the book to an anodyne sediment of uplifting platitude. For Featley 'the modest and learned author of *The trial of faith* and this apology' had sought merely 'to inforce the necessity of repentance as to give it a kind of precedency to faith in

Christ, not any way to detract from the dignity and excellency of faith ... but to keep men from bearing too much on the right hand and sailing too near to the dangerous rock of presumption'. If all the parties to the dispute concentrated on this central point agreement would easily be achieved. 'As for many incident or consequent questions, which the nice handling of this point may breed in refined wits ... I say for these and the like subtleties, I hold it needless and unprofitable' to dwell on them. 'It sufficeth that we ministers of the gospel, in our preaching, and God's people, in their hearing, and all of us in our practice, follow the method used by the Holy Ghost and begin with John Baptist and proceed to Christ, begin with terror and proceed to comfort, begin with sorrow for sin and proceed to joy in the Holy Ghost.'[8]

Having thus attempted to defuse the doctrinal content of the dispute, Featley and Mason proceeded to urge both sides to charity and restraint. Mason urged Chibald not to expect 'that all men should presently yield to be of your opinion, for sober minds may dissent from you and you from them, without breach of charity or love and fiery spirits will dissent from you, if it be for no other cause but only for that salamanders cannot live out of the fire'. Having said his piece, restraint now behoved Chibald as well as his opponents. 'There will never be an end of quarrelling', Mason told him, 'if you labour to get the mastery of him that is contentious, because, though he be a hundred times foiled, he will never be wearied.' Featley ended with a yet more general plea for restraint. 'I earnestly beseech my brethren in the ministry not to interfere nor hinder one another in their holy courses, much less virulently detract from the persons or labours, one of another, but to set aside all prejudicate opinion and allay all heat of passion and contestation.'

And there, as far as we can tell, the affair ended, aside, of course, from its walk-on part in the altercation between Denison and Etherington. In this instance, the internal self-regulating mechanisms of the godly community, the manuscript exchanges and conferences, had failed to satisfy all the parties. But Chibald's recourse to print had not been designed so much to exacerbate the affair and start a more formal and public process of printed dispute as to put both a calming gloss and a quasi-official imprimatur on his own position. In the process, a rebuke was sent to the more intemperate and vocal of his critics, who remained unnamed but were presumably widely known to the London audience to which the books were most obviously addressed.

It is hard not to see the moderation of Chibald's tone and his refusal to name, and thus directly to confront and excoriate, his critics, as the price Chibald paid for the overt support of Featley and Mason, who, having failed to shut Chibald's critics up in private, now allowed both themselves and Chibald recourse to the 'public' medium of print to make his and their point; a point that amounted to an endorsement of Chibald's right to be regarded as 'orthodox', part of the perfect protestant or puritan mainstream that he had invoked so consistently in the margins of his two apologias, and a construal of the points at odds between him and his critics as inherently disputable between protestants of good faith. 'Orthodoxy', in this instance, was being both policed and widened as Featley and Mason, in effect, told both sides to put the best possible construction on their opponent's position and then agree to differ. Clearly such an outcome was more acceptable to Chibald than to some of his nameless critics.

Although even here it seems clear that Chibald's links to the wider godly or puritan fraternity of Caroline London survived more or less unscathed from his run-in with Walker. Robert Abbot's reference in his letter to Baxter (cited above) to 'my dear Mr Chibald' certainly implied that Chibald remained in good odour with the godly in and around London, an impression confirmed by the presence of his name appended to a 'certificate written and subscribed by Ignatius Jurdaine' (the quite frighteningly zealous puritan mayor of Exeter) in June 1627. The document in question was found on the person of one John Haydon when he was apprehended in Norwich in October 1628. Haydon, the certificate explained, was a man of 'great zeal and undertakings ... against the vices of the times' whose 'sufferings, by prosecution in the Star Chamber, for the same and deliverance from it by God's providence, weakness of his estate and several debts' was attested by Jurdaine and a number of leading puritan ministers, including Thomas Taylor, William Gouge, John White, Ezechiel and Richard Culverwell and, third on the list, William Chibald. All the signatories were in effect authenticating Haydon as a deserving object for the charitable donations of the godly. In short, it seems clear from the inclusion of his name in so resonant a list of puritan ministerial worthies that Chibald was and remained very much *persona grata* in puritan circles in the capital.[9]

THE WALKER AND WOTTON AFFAIR

The interpretation of the Chibald affair essayed above is both confirmed and deepened by the course of a previous dispute between Anthony Wotton and George Walker about which, thanks to the later exchange of pamphlets between Walker and Thomas Gataker, more details are available. This again started with an attack on the doctrinal probity of one minister, Anthony Wotton, by another, George Walker. Wotton was an established London puritan minister, while the younger man Walker was newly arrived from Cambridge and seeking a career for himself in London. Even on his own account Walker seems to have been spoiling for a fight. Claiming to discern socinian tendencies in certain papers of Wotton's on justification then 'dispersed in this city', Walker turned first to Alexander Richardson. Richardson was renowned for the unofficial seminary that he maintained in his household in Barking where he trained towards young men from Cambridge for the ministry. Viewing Richardson as some sort of arbiter of orthodoxy, Walker almost certainly hoped to mobilise Richardson's standing amongst the godly against what he took to be Wotton's heterodox opinions. On his own account at least, Walker succeeded in convincing Richardson of the error of Wotton's ways and Richardson 'sent to Mr Wotton to meet him in a conference before some judicious hearers, which Mr Wotton promised but did not perform'. Walker himself also 'sent and desired that he would admit me to come to him and confer with him but, as he was afraid to meet Mr Richardson, so he despised my youth and years and referred me to one Spenser a tradesman, a factious disciple of his'.[10]

Thus spurned, Walker turned to open denunciation in the pulpit and preached two sermons against Wotton in London. This affront finally gained Walker an audience with Wotton, arranged by 'some of Mr Wotton's friends who, being startled' by the ferocity of Walker's assault approached him the day after his second sermon. The subsequent meeting did not go well. On Walker's account 'Wotton welcomed me coldly in words', used various means, including a scandalous miscitation of Luther, to obfuscate the issues which he consistently refused to debate 'in strict form of disputation, which I desired'. Wotton, in short, tried to fob the young upstart Walker off with the claim that although 'my doctrine which I taught concerning imputation of Christ's righteousness was sound and saving truth, able to save believers though they went no further' yet 'he [Wotton] had dived more deeply into the points of justification and did go further but not a contrary way'. Walker expressed himself entirely unsatisfied with this form of words, telling Wotton bluntly that 'his opinion ... was as contrary to my doctrine and faith as darkness is to light'.[11] With that the meeting broke up, and Walker, who had almost certainly, as one of Richardson's protégés, been auditioning for a London living – preaching the two sermons against Wotton 'in the church of which I am now pastor' – returned to Cambridge for the next three months. In his absence, he claimed, Wotton's disciples 'thinking I had quite left the city, did most falsely and abominably report abroad that you [Wotton] did so put me down by arguments that I, with tears, acknowledged my error and vowed to live and die in your opinion'.[12]

If the attack on Wotton was part of an ambitious young man's attempt to make a name for himself and get a job in London it evidently worked, for the next year found Walker 'settled in my pastoral charge' at St John the Evangelist, Watling Street. Once ensconced, however, Walker refused to let the matter drop, although he was careful to provide a properly pastoral, rather than a merely personal, justification for his pertinacity. Finding 'some in my parish much inclining to Mr Wotton's opinion out of respect to his person more than any knowledge, being not able to give any reason for it at all',

Walker explained that he felt called upon to spend 'many sabbaths in preaching the doctrine of justification out of the fifth chapter of the epistle to the Romans'. Despite his claim that what was involved here was not some *ad hominem* assault on a personal rival but a pastorally necessary confutation of 'all errors contrary to the truth professed in the reformed churches' on the subject of justification (with particular reference to those of Socinus), it is clear, even from his own account, that Walker had declared open war in his own pulpit against Anthony Wotton, whom he proceeded to denounce as a socinian and vorstian heretic.[13]

Wotton was a figure of some stature among the London godly; he enjoyed a reputation for learning and had established his credentials as a man of genuinely puritan principle during a run-in with Bancroft (and subsequent period of suspension) at the start of James' reign. Perhaps predictably, therefore, Walker's attack on him went down in some circles like a lead balloon. Some weeks after he had finished his sermon cycle on justification in his own parish Walker was asked to fill in for William Gouge at a Wednesday lecture at Blackfriars. This was a long-standing puritan auditory – in Walker's words 'in that assembly there were many ancient professors of religion' who, because of his recent arrival on the metropolitan scene, could not recognise Walker by sight. They had, however, heard of him by repute, for having been 'so taken with my sermon that they were very inquisitive to know my name', upon being told that this was none other than Mr Walker from St Evangelists, the whole tenor of the meeting changed. 'They were so possessed with an evil opinion of me by the slanders and railings of Mr Wotton and his disciples that they cried, hang him, he will be hanged before he come to preach such a godly sermon as this is, we will never believe that this is that Walker that hath preached against that man of God, Mr Wotton and belied him in the pulpit. My clerk being well acquainted with them', continued Walker, 'and, over hearing, did affirm to them that I was the man and told them that they themselves might easily come to be hanged in hell if they did not repent of their wicked railings against me.'[14]

Nor, on Walker's account at least, was this an isolated incident. Indeed, as he told Wotton in a letter of challenge and complaint, 'in many men's mouths I hear your outrageous exclamations in which you call me an ass, a sot, a boy, an impudent and brazen-faced fellow; yea, your disciples have not been afraid to make mows at me, preaching in the pulpit, as mine eyes and the eyes of divers others did often see and can testify and oftentimes they have cried out in the church and derided me, and scoffed at the word of God, by me delivered and that so loud that all round about have heard and been offended'.[15]

Wotton, for all his hostility, still refused to deal directly with Walker. 'You will neither confer before any of our learned brethren, godly ministers, privately, nor publicly before the reverend bishop of London.' To explain his reluctance in that regard Wotton had put it about that the bishop was 'a wicked judge and will respect persons in judgement' and that 'my [Walker's] friends are too potent with him' to allow the case a fair hearing. Rather than pursue the affair though official channels Wotton preferred to have it tried by the court of godly opinion where his long-standing connections and enthusiastic lay following gave him an unfair advantage. He continued to use his disciples to spread his version of the dispute amongst the godly and to employ his lay follower Spencer as an intermediary and spokesman, claiming before witnesses that 'you did me no wrong in affirming that Spencer understands the doctrine of justification better than I'. Indeed, according to Walker, Wotton actually encouraged Spencer to take Walker on in dispute by writing and circulating a manuscript confutation and challenge. 'You go about by your disciple Spencer to challenge me and to debase my calling and ministry by laying false imputations upon me as ignorance, slander and the like.' This Walker took to be a calculated insult, part of a self-conscious campaign to deny the younger man a parity of respect and ministerial authority by meeting him in open dispute before witnesses.[16]

Indeed, it was the straw of Spencer's continued involvement in the dispute that finally broke the camel's back and elicited from Walker a formal challenge to Wotton either to have the differences between them heard by a panel of eight divines – four to be chosen by each party – or else face the consequences of a formal complaint and articles drawn up against him and presented to the archbishop of Canterbury and the court of High Commission. According to Walker, Wotton's response was to approach the bishop of London, through his chaplain Henry Mason, in order to have any such semi-official hearing amongst the godly banned.[17] Here, however, Thomas Gataker, defending Wotton and himself from Walker's later allegations, had a rather different story to tell. According to Gataker, Wotton's first impulse had been to call Walker's bluff, turning down his offer of 'a private conference' in preference for a 'public trial', which he repaired to the bishop of London, John King, to effect, importuning King to set up 'an open and judiciary trial'. It was only after the bishop himself demurred at such a prospect and 'pressed' Wotton 'to condescend to the course by Mr Walker propounded' that Wotton agreed to the hearing and then only after King had agreed to associate himself with the proceedings by allowing Mason his chaplain to take part.[18]

A jury was then assembled, comprising some of the leading London puritan ministers of the day. Lewis Bayly (who came to take the place of the Walker's first choice Dr Westfield), William Gouge, Richard Stock and John Downham were chosen by Walker, while Thomas Gataker, James Balmford, John Randall and William Hickes were Wotton's selections. Mason, it was later claimed, was unable to attend. After a good deal of argy-bargy and point scoring, at Gataker's suggestion, in order to prove that Wotton was socinian,

Walker presented the panel with a series of parallels between Wotton's words and those of the Dutch heresiarch. Given a copy of this document in advance, Wotton produced a reply in the form of a further exposition of his own opinions in order to distinguish them from those of Socinus and to vindicate himself from the charge of heresy. After examining this document, the eight divines all subscribed to the effect that 'we, whose names are underwritten, do differ from Mr Wotton in some points of the former doctrine of justification, contained in these expositions, yet we do not hold the difference to be so great and weighty as that they are to be justly condemned of heresy and blasphemy'.[19]

Predictably, Wotton and his friends responded to this verdict by (in Walker's words) presently reporting 'through London that I could prove nothing against him nor bring anything out of his books or writings to convince him of socinianism and that the eight learned ministers had justified him and condemned me for a false accuser'.[20] Gataker, too, admitted as much, claiming that, since it was true that the eight ministers had cleared Wotton of heresy and by implication condemned Walker as a false accuser, Wotton was entirely within his rights in so doing.[21] Walker, on the other hand, reacted very differently: when it was clear that the ministers were not going to vindicate him and condemn Wotton, he stormed from the room and immediately began to question the legality and propriety of the proceedings; proceedings, of course, that had been set in motion at his instigation. First, he challenged the legal standing of the inquiry, telling the eight ministers that 'we did more than we could answer in taking upon us to determine heresy'. 'Afterward', in Gataker's words, 'he endeavoured to have us called in question for our meeting, though by himself procured, insomuch that the bishop of London, in regard of his importunate exclaiming against us, did at first pretend to doubt of, yea, in a manner deny, his giving way to it, until, being minded of the motion made by one of chaplains to be a party in the business and his condescending thereto, he could not but agnise it'.[22]

Bishop King's queasiness in the face of his own involvement in the affair becomes more explicable in view of claims made by Lewis Bayly. According to Gataker, Bayly (a future bishop) had opened his involvement in the hearings by attacking Wotton, a non-conformist lecturer, for not wearing proper clerical dress and throughout the proceedings he remained the participant most openly hostile to Wotton. Bayly had been given charge of (or in Gataker's phrase it had been 'detained by him ... in favour of Mr Walker') the signed verdict but then refused to show the document to Wotton or indeed to anyone else. He defended this apparent act of blatant favouritism to the other 'jurors' on the grounds that 'he held it not safe to do, for that, having been lately at the High Commission, some (I know not who) had cast out some words there to him concerning our meeting and that we might peradventure be questioned for it as a conventicle, especially if our subscription should come abroad under our own hands and use made of it as an evidence against us'.[23]

In truth, Walker's refusal to bow to the consensus of learned London puritan opinion, epitomised in this case by the eight ministers, operating under an umbrella of vague episcopal encouragement and approval, had left all concerned in a very exposed position indeed. The affair is reminiscent of nothing so much as Archbishop Whitgift's predicament after the failure of the Lambeth Articles to shut Peter Baro up. Baro's intransigence revealed the archbishop's attempts to enforce a *de facto* doctrinal consensus to be devoid of legal standing and left poor Whitgift exposed to the ire of the queen who threatened him (perhaps jokingly) with a praemunire for seeking to define the doctrinal position of the church of England without royal authority. Here, too, Walker's refusal to accept the verdict of his peers revealed the complete absence of official or legal standing for the proceedings. Conceived initially as a means to suppress what was clearly a *cause célèbre* in godly circles in the capital, the hearings operated in a liminal space halfway between the public and the private, the official and the unofficial.[24]

It was an ambiguous standing registered in the terms in which Thomas Gataker described the proceedings years later. On the one hand, he could write of the divines' 'judiciary sentence' 'considerately signed ' 'and that after serious debate and advice taken with other grave divines', and yet, on the other, liken the proceedings to a form of private arbitration in a normal civil dispute. He compared Walker's attitude to the outcome of the hearings to 'a party appeaching his neighbour of wrong doing and, having pressed him to refer the matter between them to arbitrators jointly agreed on', 'when he perceived them inclining to acquit his neighbour of the pretended wrong', demanding 'of them whether they should take upon them to decide right and wrong'.[25]

Thus, in one sense, the meeting of a panel composed of men chosen by the two ministers involved provided a perfect example of the self-regulating aspirations of the puritan community. The whole proceeding was redolent of the doctrinal authority that was assumed to inhere in the collective judgement of the godly clergy. In that sense it was, by implication if not in intention, a crypto-presbyterian exercise; in the eyes of a certain sort of conformist, anti-puritan observer a conventicle indeed. However, viewed from a different perspective, this was not a simply private meeting at all. Here was no unofficial, introspectively 'puritan' attempt to arbitrate and diffuse an embarassingly public quarrel before it could be brought before the prying eyes of conformist authority. On the contrary, Bishop King had been offered the chance to hear the case formally by Wotton and had turned it down. King clearly preferred that the affair be settled, as it were, 'in house' by the godly. His reasons for that preference must remain a matter for surmise. Of course, charges of socinianism were a very hot potato – people had been very recently burned in England for such opinions – and a formal hearing in which the right to decide the doctrinal position of the church of England (particularly on an issue as central as justification) was not lightly to be entered into. Moreover, the issue of Christology had been the subject of a good deal of royal attention during the Vorstius affair and a public fuss about Wotton's alleged socinianism might attract altogether too much royal attention to King's diocese. Better by far to let the London clergy take care of the matter themselves. The storm, if storm it was, could that way be kept firmly in the teacup of clerical *amour propre* and professional jealousy, and the peace of the church preserved without making too much fuss.

Such a move accorded with a style of evangelical protestant or Calvinist churchmanship that Patrick Collinson and Kenneth Fincham have identified as central to both the Elizabethan and Jacobean churches. Here what was at stake was a form of *de facto* reduced episcopacy whereby the bishop delegated power or associated himself formally or informally with the leading preaching ministers of his diocese in the discharge of various pastoral and jurisdictional functions.[26] Such an approach to ecclesiastical governance was central to the Elizabethan prophesyings and later to lectures by combination as Collinson has described them. Here King was doing precisely the same thing in somehow countenancing and associating himself with the arbitration procedure suggested by Walker and Wotton. However, as Archbishop Grindal could attest, such attitudes and policies did not always enjoy royal approval. It was almost certainly no accident that it was John Reynolds' less than inherently presbyterian suggestion to formalise such arrangements with respect to ordination and ecclesiastical discipline that provoked the famous dictum 'no bishop, no king' from James himself at Hampton Court. By lending his authority to the arbitration process, urging Wotton to eschew formal proceedings against Walker and defer to the collective judgement of his colleagues in the ministry and by allowing his chaplain Mason to be associated with the hearings, King lent the whole affair an air of episcopal approval and authority. There were, however, limits to how far such unofficial means could take you. All the tacit approval in the world could not alter the legal status of the proceedings and when that status was challenged by Walker, King's efforts to distance himself from the whole affair can almost certainly be seen as a sign of the bishop's discomfort at his own complicity in an extralegal if not illegal attempt to regulate the public doctrine of the English church by underhand means.[27]

Insofar as the dispute had its roots in a young man's search for respect, attention and charisma in the intensely competitive clerical market of London, the success of the whole venture turned on a gamble that Walker's need for the approval and regard of his peers in the ministry would exceed his (both existential and political) need to vindicate himself in the struggle with Wotton. Since it was the extremity of his own recourse to the rhetoric of heresy, blasphemy and the potentially deadly accusation of socinianism that had raised the stakes so high in the first place, the chances of Walker deferring to the collective judgement of his peers was probably never as great as many of the participants hoped. Certainly, when the whole affair blew up in their faces, while Gataker accused Walker of breaking clerical ranks and behaving in an entirely uncollegial and unreasonable manner, Walker accused the arbitrators of cliquish favouritism. He was a young man and a relative newcomer to London, while the jury was composed mostly of friends of Wotton who bent over backwards to favour the older man. Personal and generational differences provided the transforming agent that turned what looked to Gataker and his friends like the collective wisdom of the godly learned London clergy into what appeared to Walker to be the cliquishness, corruption and lack of conviction of an ageing, self-satisfied and self-selecting elite.

Certainly, it was the dissemination of this latter version of the proceedings that provided Walker with his second means of repudiating the decision. Gataker's account makes it clear that Walker was as adept at exploiting the gossip networks of the godly community, as Walker's account had shown Wotton and his friends to have been in their attempts to discredit him. Walker's commentary on the affair was swiftly disseminated around the bush telegraph of London puritanism. 'I have formerly been informed', intoned Gataker, at one point, 'that Mr Walker oft in his table talk should not stick to give out that we are all of us ashamed of what we then did.' It is clear from passages like this that certain remarks made in 'private' – the table talk and gossip of the major players in the London puritan scene – reverberated around godly circles in London and were no doubt intended to do so. Hence, on another occasion, Gataker responded to Walker's threat to refute his book on lots with the remark that 'I do not believe ... that he is able to make his word good, though I am not ignorant what he hath bragged of his abilities so to do.'[28]

From Walker's later printed account we can reconstruct something of the sorts of rumours, anecdotes and accusations that he put out about the hearings. According to Walker, in private many of the divines involved had been prepared to criticise Wotton's doctrine. 'Dr Bayly ... condemned Mr Wotton for an heretic and his errors for blasphemy. Mr Downham heard his censure uttered at Mr Westwoods table and by silence assented to it. Mr Randal did argue very hotly against Mr Wotton's opinions ... Dr Gouge hath publicly confuted them ... Mr Stock did ever abhor them, as he often told me in private.' Of course, if all this was true it was by no means clear why the assembled company had not simply condemned Wotton as the heretic they thought him to be. Here Walker had recourse to his claim that many of the judges were in fact 'familiar friends' of Wotton's, whose first instinct was not to defend the truth but rather to fudge and obfuscate the issues in order the better to protect their friend. Thus when Walker asked them to make good their disapproval of Wotton's doctrine with a formal condemnation he was told that 'they desired to convert, not to confound Mr Wotton, that they perceived him to be afraid of shame like to fall on him and that, if I would yield to let him expound himself, he would, by a wrested exposition, gainsay and contradict his former words and opinions and run from them, which being gotten from him under his hand, they would either hold him to it or shame him for ever, if he did fall back again'. Again he quoted Richard Stock as saying that they had only agreed to exonerate Wotton from heresy on the understanding that he would 'silence himself and his disciples in these points' and 'write a large declaration whereby he would purge himself fully from socinianism'. They had done so 'for the suppressing of clamours' but Wotton had gone back on his word and left Stock and the others with egg on their faces.[29]

Needless to say, Gataker strongly contested Walker's version of events and, in particular, objected to his habit of citing unattested private dinner conversation as somehow more significant than the ministers' formal subscription to a written verdict exonerating Wotton from heresy. However, without simply taking Walker at his own word, we can surely detect here arguments and claims used by the participants in their dealings with both the main parties as they strove to end the dispute without formally condemning or vindicating either side. Silence or, failing that, at least tact on the issue and a tacit agreement to live and let live, to agree to disagree, was clearly what was being aimed at and in pursuit of that goal various assurances, euphemisms, concessions and half-truths had been peddled to both Walker and Wotton in an attempt to get them to kiss and make up. The result was that both men had plenty of anecdotal material out of which to construct self-serving versions of what had really happened. That clearly was what Walker was doing here in what emerges as really quite a clever publicity campaign, as he broadcast his own version of events through a series of anecdotes and tableaux. It is also very probably what Gataker was doing too in his later printed account of the affair.

Two examples show how this worked. The first story involved what Walker termed a 'pretty strategem' whereby Walker had exposed the hypocrisy of Mr Stock's position to an audience of lay people. At a dinner party held one Sunday night at Mr Thomas Goodyear's (a parishioner of Walker's) house, Walker had shown Stock an epitome of Wotton's opinions, telling him only that it was 'a paper of new and strange opinions'. When asked what sort of opinions, he read out part of Wotton's self-defence. Stock, 'not knowing that it was Mr Wotton's exposition ... did answer that it was popery or worse. I asked him whether he did not think it to be the heresy and blasphemy of Socinus; he answered, yes, verily. I asked him then what he thought of certain learned

The London puritan scene

divines who had subscribed to this and other such speeches that they were neither heresy nor blasphemy. He said he thought none but mad men would do it and asked who they were.' Walker then read out the text of the verdict and the list of names appended, including Stock's own. At that 'Mr Goodyear laughed heartily and said to Mr Stock "O master, our parson is too cunning for you, I never saw any man so finely taken in a snare as he hath taken you in your own snare. I have ever told you that in this controversy you were too partial to your old friend and familiar Mr Wotton."'[30]

The second anecdote involved not one of the direct participants in the case but that same Alexander Richardson to whom the young Walker had first turned for advice about the unsoundness of Wotton's opinions. Richardson's was evidently a name to conjure with amongst London puritans and Walker recounted the story as one 'which was a strong motive to move divers godly people in London to abhor Mr Wotton's opinions'. On his deathbed, Richardson was attended by, amongst others, one Mr John Barlow 'who had often before resorted to him [Richardson] for direction in his study and resolution of doubts in many points of divinity'. Barlow told Richardson that he had recently heard Walker preach on justification and asked Richardson his opinion of Wotton's views on that subject. 'Mr Richardson answered and said, take these words of me, a dying man. I have read and well weighed Mr Wotton's papers and opinions and I know them to be so pestilent and dangerous that whosoever liveth and dyeth in the belief of them shall never enter into the kingdom of heaven. Commend me to Mr Walker and desire him from me (as being my last request to him) to be courageous in the cause of God and for that saving truth which he hath undertaken to maintain against those dangerous and deadly errors, lately set on foot by Mr Wotton.'[31] Here the charisma of the famous godly preacher was combined with the aura of the deathbed and the last dying speech to enlist the departed Richardson, and all those of the London godly who revered his memory, to Walker's party. Both stories have the feel of well-established anecdotes, rolled smooth, according to the conventions of the jest book and the godly life, by frequent reiteration. It was surely through the word of mouth transmission of such verbal tableaux that Walker's case against Wotton and the process that had exonerated him was made to the wider godly community.

Thus the process of semi-formal, pseudo-official arbitration, far from ending the dispute, merely produced two rival versions of what had taken place. Wotton continued to formulate and disseminate his views in manuscript essays on justification, which Walker just as furiously refuted.[32] Official attempts at damage limitation, however, did not end with the abortive meetings in Lewis Bayly's church. Just as with the Chibald affair, the wider resonance of the dispute, the extent to which it became genuinely public and the limits on acceptable speech on the subject, were all to be regulated and controlled through the licensing process for the press. It was, for instance, surely no accident that the only book printed in England before 1640 that reflected on the contents of the dispute between Wotton and Walker was not written by either of the participants nor by any of the panel of divines that had unsuccessfully tried to end the affair but by William Bradshaw, a close friend of Thomas Gataker and a notorious non-conformist.

Bradshaw's *Treatise of justification* struck an irenic, consensus-building pose. The epistle to the reader immediately grasped the nettle of the recent dispute and without naming names placed Bradshaw's treatise in the midst of the altercation between Wotton and Walker. 'Thou canst not be ignorant (good reader)', Bradshaw opined, 'what special differences have been (and yet are) amongst ourselves in some points about justification of a sinner before God. Whence many weak minds have been somewhat perplexed and some strong ones (at least in their own deceits) exceedingly distempered, as though there were amongst us which over turned foundations, teaching blasphemous heresies about this matter'. That, of course, was Walker's contention and it was one which Bradshaw moved swiftly to deny. 'All of us', Bradshaw proclaimed, 'with one mouth profess' what he described as the fundamental truth of the matter, leaving only differences 'in certain circumstances, wherein nothing is derogated either from the mercy of God or merits of Christ or arrogated to our own works'.

Bradshaw then went on to summarise what he took to be the various positions at stake to locate himself in the middle ground, allowing himself to conclude that 'our differences then ... are not so great but there is both possibility and hope of reconciliation and no such cause of any fiery oppositions one against another, especially seeing that they who herein are out of the way may seem to have been put out thereof only by the blocks that ourselves have laid therein'. Lest his intervention further ruffle the already disturbed feathers of the participants, Bradshaw was quick to disclaim whatever pretensions to authority or superior learning and judgement might be implied by his taking on the role of mediator. 'I take not upon me', he wrote, 'to be a moderator between so many learned men of all sides or to see further than they into so great a mystery.' It was just that in such circumstances, during the heat of polemical battle, 'it was not unusual for those who are standers-by (though simple by comparison) to see some things which the cunningest gamesters sometimes oversee'.

Bradshaw's book, he was careful to explain, owed its origins not to any desire on his part to enter the public dispute between Walker and Wotton. Rather, it had started out as a private exercise, a position paper through which he tried to make up his own mind on the subject. Having written it, he had several manuscript copies made and distributed them 'to sundry reverend and learned divines, submitting the same to their censures, from whom I received (out of their love) divers material animadversions and doubts'. While these had not led Bradshaw to change his mind in 'any material point', they had led him to 'explain matters more fully then otherwise I should have thought had been needful' and he went on to appeal to the learned community for any other comments and criticisms on his position as set out in the body of the treatise. But if the text of Bradshaw's pamphlet was in some sense a collective exercise, so too, he rushed to inform the reader, had been the decision to publish. 'That it dares thus boldly come forth in public, it is not so much from any heartening it hath had from me, as through some private encouragement from others, far more learned and judicious than myself, whom thou must blame if it prove of no use to the church of God.'[33]

In other words, the reader was being left in no doubt that Bradshaw's book was not the product of some rogue puritan trying to make a name for himself by horning in in print on somebody else's argument. Rather, in coded language, those in the know were being told that it was the outcome of a collective attempt, probably inspired by some of the divines involved in the failed arbitration and, at the very least, connived at, if not instigated by, the arch episcopal chaplain (John Sanford), who licensed the book for the press, to bring the Walker and Wotton dispute to a peaceful and irenic conclusion. For, by seeking to position himself rhetorically in the middle ground, by making it clear that he had taken widespread soundings amongst the godly and that in publishing the book at all he was only responding to the advice of his learned friends, Bradshaw was presenting his book as something more than his own private opinion. Rather, it was an embodiment of the collective judgement of a hazily defined godly learned community. That collective judgement, Bradshaw was saying, saw the issues at stake in the Walker/Wotton dispute as inherently disputable circumstances, doctrinal appendages of central truths upon which everyone, in fact, agreed. That, of course, was precisely what Gataker claimed the initial panel of divines had thought. It was also precisely the same line that Featley and Mason were to take in their endorsement of Chibald's reply to his critics.

In short, in both cases the control of the press lodged in the chaplains of the archbishop of Canterbury and the bishop of London was being used to take the heat out of the debate and to restore peace and order to the church. This was done not by deciding the substantive doctrinal debate definitively in one direction or another but by glossing the issues at stake in ways that made continuing disagreement acceptable. The stakes, which in each case had been raised by Walker's (and others') use of the rhetoric of heresy and blasphemy, their invocation of the spectres of socinianism, popery, pelagianism and Arminianism, were being systematically lowered as the questions at issue were recategorised under the rubric of inessentials or, in Bradshaw's terms, 'circumstances' rather than fundamentals.

OBSERVING THE RULES OF ENGAGEMENT

Given that we have become accustomed of late to regard the early Stuart church as being characterised by some sort of doctrinal, reformed or Calvinist, consensus, and given that, not without cause, on the issue of predestination at least, the most vocal and aggressive defenders of that consensus have come to be regarded as the puritans, these are perhaps rather interesting findings. For, in both the Walker and Wotton and the Chibald disputes, we can see godly opinion seeking to maintain unity, order and consensus not by enforcing a unitary and narrow version of orthodoxy but, rather, by constructing room for disagreement and dispute; and doing so, moreover, in close collaboration with the ecclesiastical authorities, personified by episcopal chaplains like Mason and Featley. This, surely, is a subject worthy of further attention and in Thomas Gataker's reply to Walker we have a text in which many of the assumptions and attitudes that underpinned this approach were rendered explicit.

The first step when seeking to defuse such a dispute was to locate the particular point at issue within the broader parameters of reformed orthodoxy, usually defined in terms of some general tenet concerned with the issues at hand to which all the participants could be said to accede.[34] Once the area of disagreement had been located under an overarching umbrella of reformed consensus, it was more than permissible to stress the range of opinions available on the subject within the reformed tradition. This was most easily done by citing an array of resonant names from that tradition as occupying either one's own or a variety of different opinions of the subject at hand. We have already seen Chibald perform that task by citing a number of impeccably puritan and/or reformed authorities in his own defence. Gataker did the same for Wotton and Bradshaw. Hence he located opinions which Walker identified as heretical in Wotton's mouth in the works of a whole array of luminaries including Bucer, Foxe, Perkins, Paraeus, Piscator, Ursinus, Olevian and Pemble. In defence of Bradshaw's book he cited 'writings of some others publicly allowed and generally well esteemed of among us and by name, Mr Pemble's large *Treatise on justification* ... and Mr Torshel's briefer discourse of the same subject'.[35]

Having thus established that the issue at hand did not call into question doctrines fundamental to Christian or reformed orthodoxy and that, in fact, the reformed tradition contained a variety of different positions and opinions, it became possible to accept with relative complaisance the fact of diversity of opinion and even of quite sharp disagreements and stark changes of mind. In his defence of Wotton and himself against Walker, Gataker described a plethora of 'disputes passed in writing, with objections and answers, replies and rejoinders' involving exchanges on the subject of justification between

Bradshaw and Wotton, Bradshaw and Gataker, Wotton and Gataker, and a Mr Woodcock of Chesham and Wotton. Bradshaw himself admitted that his own treatise represented a shift of opinion and Gataker described a long process of consultation and argument with Bradshaw whereby his own mind had been changed on the subject.

> True it is [conceded Gataker] that in this point of justification I went sometime another way then now I do, the same that Gomarus and some other still do and before me did, until, upon occasion of some lectures by Dr Grey, who succeeded Mr Wotton at Gresham College, I fell into conference and disceptation with Mr Bradshaw about it and after many disputes, that passed to and fro in writing between us, wherein I strove stiffly to maintain what I then held, being at length by force of argument beaten from my hold, I yielded not so much to my friend as to truth (as I was then and am still certainly persuaded) which to be overborne by, I shall ever account the best valour, to be overcome by, the fairest victory.[36]

But if diversity of opinion, disagreement and changes of mind were all allowable within the reformed consensus, it followed necessarily that error, contradiction and confusion could all be found within that consensus too. This Gataker freely admitted. His point against Walker was merely that all error or contradiction was not tantamount to heresy. 'How many men's writings may more then seven times seven errors be found in whom it were yet most uncharitable therefore to censure' as a 'blasphemous heretic?' asked Gataker.[37] It was not, he claimed, 'sufficient to prove a man a heretic because he contradicts somewhat contained in God's word, since that every error whatsoever in any point of divinity must of necessity so do and Mr Walker therefore, unless he dare profess himself free from all error, must, by the same ground withal granted, confess himself to be an heretic.' Perhaps there were contradictions in Wotton's position, Gataker conceded. What of it? 'Am I or any man else bound to reconcile whatsoever contradictions are, if any be found, in Mr Wotton's writings? Or is every one that is taken in gross contradictions, of necessity, thereupon, to be condemned for an heretic?'[38] The purpose of the eight arbitrators had not been to vindicate Wotton from all charges of error or contradiction. They were not in the business of simply endorsing his views but rather of weighing Walker's charges of heresy against Wotton's replies to them. 'Nor did either I, or any of those that were joined with me in the meeting related, undertake to defend Mr Wotton as one free from all error, but delivered only what we thought of Mr Wotton's own defence of himself in regard of ought that Mr Walker had laid to his charge.'[39] Besides, if it came to endorsing or recommending a book one could do so without necessarily underwriting every view expressed therein. To prove the point Gataker cited his own unfortunate experience over his commendation of 'Mr Elton's catechetical work' for which, as we have seen, he had been briefly incarcerated – despite his care in noting, even as he recommended the book, that he did not personally agree with every position and opinion contained within it.[40]

For Gataker, then, diversity of opinion, disagreement and error went with the territory. Moreover, he was more than prepared to follow the logic of his own arguments and articulate a vision of doctrinal truth that was incremental and of revelation that was in some sense gradual and progressive.

> Howsoever since that in these latter times it hath been, by God's spirit, foretold that knowledge should increase, yea, reason itself, besides daily experience, telleth us the self-same; for notwithstanding the diligentest searches of all foregoing ages, truth, much of it, still remains undiscovered and it is an easier matter to add to former discoveries than to discover things at first. They may see most that come last and we find it in all other learning and knowledge that those things which have, in these latter days, been brought to light, which, in former ages, for ought that can be descried, were utterly unknown. I suppose, under correction, that it ought not to be deemed any just cause of aspersion if a man shall, with modesty, rendering at least some reason of good probability for his so doing, profess himself compelled, in some things, to depart from all those that, to his knowledge, have dealt in some argument before him.

Certainly, Gataker concluded, the mere profession of dissent, 'in some particulars, from all other orthodox divines' was not sufficient proof to convict a man of heresy. Indeed, he quoted 'a divine as well of good as of great note', who was reported to have said, 'in the council of Dort, when it was objected unto him that something spoken by him differed from some clause in the catechism, "we are taught many things when we are young, that we make doubt of when we are old"'.[41]

Given such a view of the incremental nature of doctrinal truth, it followed that, for Gataker, dispute and argument amongst divines were not merely inevitable, necessary evils to be avoided as far as possible, they were or could be positively beneficial – if, that is, they were conducted in the right way. And that, judging from Gataker's remarks, meant in private conversations or in manuscript discussions between men of learning and good will. That was certainly the nature of Gataker's discussions with Bradshaw that had caused him to change his mind on the topic of justification. It was precisely the same with the discussions amongst the eight divines who heard Wotton's case in 1614. Where Walker alleged that one of them, Mr Randal, had been violently opposed to Wotton's views on a particular topic, Gataker replied with a very different version of the proceedings.

> True it is that there was that day a dispute among us about a nice question ... concerning the work of redemption performed by Christ and the work of our insition into Christ and our union with him, whether of the twain had the precedency in the order of nature. Wherein some were with Mr Wotton on the one side ... some were on the other side (among whom Mr Randal) ... But neither was

the point argued with any heat at all on either side amongst ourselves at least. Nor did either Mr Randal or any of the company, no not Dr Bayly himself ... at any time that ever I can remember during our whole meeting, use any such distasteful speeches unto Mr Wotton as Mr Walker is here pleased to attribute to Mr Randal.[42]

Here, then, was the nub of Gataker's critique of Walker who, on Gataker's account, had throughout the affair displayed such a lack of moderation and decorum, such an excess of polemical aggression, that rational discussion had proved all but impossible with him in the room. Gataker persistently complained of Walker's manner and demeanour, condemning Walker's 'either revilings of him [Wotton] in public or baitings of him in private'. Wotton, he claimed, 'had demeaned himself very moderately throughout the whole hearing, with great patience enduring much reproachful and despiteful language, whereof Mr Walker was no whit sparing'. If Gataker, along with the other arbitrators, had intervened to control the excesses of Walker's language, that had been no mark of favouritism towards Wotton, as Walker alleged, but rather an inevitable product of Walker's bad behaviour. 'I suppose it was fit that those whom that office was committed unto should endeavour to repress such clamorous ballings and barkings as neither beseemed him that used them nor did any way further but hinder rather the issue of that for which we met. In which kind, not I alone, but the rest also laboured with Mr Walker what they could, though to small purpose. But that I "snarled at him" otherwise, is altogether untrue.' As a parthian shot, at the end of his pamphlet, Gataker wished Walker 'a little more sobriety and modesty toward his Christian brethren, that have not so ill deserved either of him or of God's church as to be thus scandalously taxed, traduced, railed upon and reviled'.[43]

Nor was this merely a question of temperament, of outward demeanour and overheated language. For Walker's deployment of the rhetoric of blasphemy and heresy brought with it a wholly polemical mode of argument and interpretation in which phrases and assertions were wrenched out of context from Wotton's works, and juxtaposed to similarly excerpted passages from Socinus. All this Gataker denounced not merely as unseemly and out of place, but as a fundamentally illegitimate way to argue. 'I desire to have it considered', wrote Gataker in his most magisterial tone, 'whether it were equal to censure a man for an heretic upon bare positions or sayings extracted out of his writings, without any regard had to or notice taken of his own expositions of them or his reasons alleged to prove his dissent in them from the errors of those whom he is charged to concur with; confirmed by collation of place with place in his writings and by consideration of the main scope and drift of the dispute, course and tenor of the discourse and the different sense and meaning of the words and terms used by either.' This, of course, echoed very closely Chibald's similar recourse to arguments about context and the different usage of key terms to defuse many of the allegations lodged against him. As Gataker concluded, 'take away all benefit of exposition and who almost may not be condemned of heresy and blasphemy?'[44]

Gataker made a similar point about Walker's tendency to argue not about what Wotton had said but what Walker took Wotton to have meant. Walker consistently drew various implications from Wotton's works and then proceeded to denounce as heretical his own gloss on the passage rather than Wotton's own words or opinions. 'Walker', claimed Gataker, 'maketh Mr Wotton speak not what he doth, but what himself pleaseth and then pronounceth him a heretic, not for what he saith, but for what himself would have him say.' He spoke sarcastically of what he termed Walker's 'chemical faculty, by which he is able to extract everything out of anything.' 'Sure, the mistaking of another man's meaning and thereupon supposing therefore or pretending that some absurdity follows what he saith, doth not, in my weak apprehension, make a man guilty of heresy.'[45] Indeed, Gataker asked, even if it could be shown that 'a denial of Christ's deity might be necessarily deduced from some positions by Mr Wotton maintained, would it thence follow that Mr Wotton denies the deity of Christ?' For his part he thought that 'no good consequence. For some thing may follow truly and necessarily from what a man holds and yet he not hold it, but deny it, yea strongly and stiffly, not in dispute only but even in judgement oppose it, because he deems the consequence whereby it is thence deduced, unsound.'[46]

In short, for Gataker, Walker was a 'restless spirit', whose habitual resort to the language of heresy marked him out as factious.

> If the words heresy and heretic [Gataker intoned] were rightly understood or if they be so taken (as I suppose them to be constantly used in the scripture, nor do I think that the contrary can be easily evinced) the one for faction, the other for a factious person; none, I fear, will be found more truly guilty of heresy, or better to deserve the title of heretic, then those who (therein concurring with the papists, whom yet they profess most to abhor) are so prone to condemn all as heretics and tainted with heresy in their sense, that is, as men cut off from Christ and having no interest in him, who do not, in all matters of practice, comply or, in all points of doctrine, concur, with themselves.[47]

Against this popish arrogance and presumption, Gataker proffered a far more charitable, truly protestant approach. 'I could have wished more charity and less presumption concerning other men's estates', opined Gataker, commenting on Walker's (and Alexander Richardson's) apparent certainty that Wotton's errors would damn him to hell.

> That Mr Wotton lived and died in some errors I doubt not. Nor do I make account but that I do live, and look to die, in many myself. If Mr Walker deem or hope otherwise of himself, he presumeth of and promiseth more to himself then I suppose ever befell any son of Adam, our blessed saviour alone excepted. But that any opinion which Mr Wotton held was so pestilent and pernicious as to cut him

The London puritan scene

wholly off from Christ and all interest in Christ, who shall affirm had need to look to himself, lest he bring thereby a greater guilt upon his own soul, than Mr Wotton contracted by any error that he held. Meanwhile, well it is, that the keys of heaven are not either in Mr Richardson's hands or at Mr Walker's disposition.[48]

By thus labelling Walker factious, presumptuous and uncharitable, Gataker was, of course, staking his own claim to the moral high ground of moderation, irenicism, charity and unity. Far from being, as Walker alleged, 'Thomas of all sides', Gataker proclaimed himself to be 'Thomas of no side, for I love not siding in God's church: among Christ's ministers especially ... Hence proceed schisms and factions and uncharitable censures, many times, of those as unsound, that are, it may be, more sincere, have at least as good a share in Christ, as those that so censure them.'[49] For all the apparent transparency, purity and attractiveness of these claims we need to remember that such a pose was hardly ever polemically innocent. Nor was it in this instance. After all, in replying to Walker at all, Gataker was undertaking a fundamentally polemical task, the immediate agenda of which was largely personal and circumstantial. Gataker wanted to vindicate himself and his departed friends and colleagues, Wotton and Bradshaw, from the vilification visited on them in print by George Walker. Certainly, in analysing the dispute we need to remember its roots in the particular personalities and situations of the main participants. It seems safe to assume that neither the Wotton nor the Chibald affairs would have taken the course they did but for the involvement in them of George Walker who emerges even from his own account (let alone Gataker's) as a prickly, difficult and contentious character. Perhaps, too, Gataker's attitude to the conduct of theological argument and the containment of theological disagreement and error, as it was adumbrated in 1642, was a good deal more coherent and liberal than that espoused by other divines of his ideological and generational stamp. But more is at stake here than a contrast between an irascible and hysterical Walker and a saintly and moderate Gataker. Still less are we dealing with a contrast between the hysteria and unreason of one rogue minister (Walker) and the norms of civilised debate and disagreement maintained by the godly mainstream (personified here by Gataker and his friends). Of course, it was entirely in Gataker's interests in 1642 (just as it had been in Bradshaw's in 1615 and in Chibald's in the early 1620s) to present the matter in that light. But here we need to remind ourselves that Gataker's analysis of Walker's conduct towards Wotton in fact applied with equal accuracy to that of Chibald's enemies (of whom Walker was only one of a number) towards Chibald and of Denison towards John Etherington and others. In fact, in Gataker's portrait of Walker we are confronted with a caricature and a critique of a whole mode of polemical debate, a theological style which was far more prevalent in the cultural milieu in which Gataker and Walker both lived than Gataker's account might lead one to believe.

Doctrinal dispute and damage limitation

For this was a period when political and religious polemic was conducted by assimilating the position of one's opponent to that occupied by an individual or group of unimpeachable unsoundness and corruption. This was the role played in Walker's assault on Wotton by socinianism and Arminianism and in much other contemporary polemic by such terms as puritan, pelagian, Calvinist and papist. The process of assimilation was often undertaken through precisely the sort of logic-chopping, context-blind reading and indeed misreading of one's opponent's position that Gataker ascribed to Walker.[50] It was no accident that while Walker wanted, throughout the affair, to visit the full rigour of formal syllogistic disputation on Wotton, this was a luxury that neither Wotton himself (during their first interview) nor the panel of arbitrators would allow him.[51] The point at which amicable disagreement, strenuous yet collegial discussion (of the sort described by Gataker as operating amongst the puritan clergy over the details of justification), became open conflict, arrived when that process of assimilation and name calling, and the systematic syllogistic terrorism that went with it, was loosed by one side upon the other. That was the pandora's box that Walker had opened with his intemperate assaults on Wotton in private, in the pulpit, before the authorities and now in front of his erstwhile colleagues in the London ministry. And it was that same box that those colleagues, with the connivance of the bishop of London, his chaplain Henry Mason and indeed Archbishop Abbot's chaplain John Sanford, were now desperately trying to force shut again.

Where Gataker's account invited his readers to see a contrast between the hysteria and presumption of Walker and the moderation and charity of Gataker and his friends we can, in fact, discern two very different, but equally common and acceptable, approaches to the fact of theological disagreement coming into conflict the one with the other. Both had a central and complementary role to play in the maintenance of what historians have come to call the Calvinist consensus of the early Stuart church. Of late, a good deal of heavy weather has been made of this phrase. Did the ideological constituents of this consensus come mainly from Calvin? How consensual does a consensus have to be to be a genuine consensus? These and other questions have displayed a capacity to generate terminological pedantry of an intensity and pointlessness rivalled only by that occasioned by similar scruples over the term puritan. But insofar as the phrase merely denotes that the assumption that English protestants were essentially agreed about the central doctrines of predestination and justification and that the English church was essentially at one on these issues with her reformed sisters was crucial to the self-image of the post-reformation English church and, in particular, crucial to the intellectual and emotional processes whereby the perfect protestant and puritan elements within that church maintained and expressed their identity as loyal members of the church of England, there is nothing wrong with it. However, insofar as the phrase can be taken to imply that, even amongst the godly, English attitudes to these doctrines were static; that the sense of consensus was maintained by the simple imposition of a unitary and commonly acknowledged reformed or Calvinist orthodoxy; and that the only danger to that orthodoxy came from an insurgent Arminianism, introduced into the situation from outside the reformed tradition, we should beware. On the contrary, the all-important sense of agreement both amongst English protestants and between the English church and her continental neighbours had to be continually produced and reproduced, maintained and sustained in the face of the continuous tendency of these inherently difficult and unstable issues to generate debate and disagreement.

The trick in controlling such disputes and disagreements lay not in imposing some simple univocal orthodoxy of opinion, but rather in channelling them within certain rhetorical and doctrinal limits or parameters and then conducting them in an appropriately scholarly and moderate tone. The areas off limits were marked with some very threatening and sinister signposts, whereon could be read words like popery, pelagianism, Arminianism or socinianism. These terms operated both as real conceptual limits, marking intellectual positions definitively beyond the reformed pale and as symbolic markers, the ultimate epithets of disgust and rejection. Accordingly, it was all but impossible to conduct a polite intra-reformed discussion when they were in regular play. On the other hand, almost any theological dispute of real seriousness raised issues which bordered on the areas of difficulty and heterodoxy denoted by those terms and, in a situation where the ideological or personal stakes were deemed to be high, the polemical advantage to be gained from attaching one or more such label to an opponent or rival was hard to resist.

Not that the deployment of these terms was always merely rhetorical or instrumental. These were words which meant something to contemporaries; they represented ideological tendencies and ideas of which people were genuinely afraid and the more scared people became the more they had recourse to the use of these labels in order to protect their notion of orthodox belief and practice from pollution. At the same time, while all could agree on the identity and rough location of these markers, in any given polemical confrontation, their precise meaning and configuration were almost always up for grabs, almost infinitely glossable and contestable. Anyone wanting an illustration of that need only refer themselves to Anthony Milton's brilliant explication of the multiple meanings, contradictions and resonances contained in contemporary notions of popery. This meant that those who approached too close to the limits of the acceptable always ran the risk of finding themselves assimilated to one or more of these symbols of deviance. Once that happened they could expect their works and opinions to be read and scrutinised with the systematic lack of sympathy, the syllogistic aggression displayed by Walker towards Wotton. If, however, they managed to make deep enough genuflexions towards the icons of reformed purity and suitably rude gestures towards the concomitant anti-types of impurity, they might hope that further debate about their opinions would be conducted in the ways in which Gataker claimed he and Bradshaw, or Bradshaw and Wotton, had conducted their discussions of the intricacies of the doctrine of justification.[52]

Here the point was to contain and control, rather than to exacerbate, disagreement, by paying elaborate attention to context, to the precise use of key words and by making elaborate obeisance to the vast areas of doctrinal agreement within which the particular disagreement was occurring. As we have seen, this was precisely the sort of reading for which Chibald appealed in his replies to his critics and which Featley and Mason endorsed when they approved his books. Within those limits, in private manuscript and conversational exchange, dispute could be vigorous and disagreement thorough, but the limits of form and genre had to be maintained lest the affair spin out of control, as it clearly had in both Wotton and Chibald's cases. Thus the process whereby the appearance and, indeed, the experience, of consensus was maintained required both the responses to disagreement detailed here. Both the polarising, polemically aggressive approach, adopted with such tiresome consistency by Walker, and the self-consciously moderate, charitable, consensus-building approach, espoused by Gataker, were essential. Here were the carrot and the stick, the promise and the threat, whereby doctrinal disagreement and debate were to be controlled and limited.

On this basis, one might conclude that Walker's fault lay not so much in the argumentative methods he used – they represented nothing more than a vigorous and vociferous adoption of the overtly polemical mode as it has been described here – as in the persons against whom he chose to use them. Wotton (even more than Chibald) was 'one of the boys', an established member of the London puritan clergy who, as he explained to the young Walker at their first meeting, put forward what he clearly acknowledged were novel or eccentric opinions on justification not as opposed to but as developments out of and improvements on the more conventional wisdom on the subject. Of course, such doctrinal innovation and claims to greater insight than one's peers and predecessors, particularly on a subject as central as justification, always created a certain nervousness and tension. What appears to have happened was that the young Walker, anxious to make a name for himself and secure employment in the city, and perhaps feeding off existing suspicions and animosities between Richardson and Wotton, decided to take Wotton on. Having approached the older man, only to be insulted by the insouciance of Wotton's manner, Walker went public with his denunciation; a daring act in itself, which almost required the most serious accusations of error and heresy to justify itself. While in Gataker's account the affair seems to be a largely intra-clerical one, if Walker is to be believed, almost from the outset, this was an altercation that engaged the attention and partisanship of the laity. Early meetings between the two men took place before lay witnesses, Wotton's lay follower Spencer played a central role in the early exchanges and even the scene between Stock and Walker was played out in a parishioner's house before a largely lay audience. Moreover, the pointed anecdotes such incidents became, presumably circulated just as widely amongst the laity as the clergy. Finally, if Walker is to be believed, Wotton's wider reputation amongst the godly laity was used to turn them against the younger man and the resulting outbreaks of visible dissent at his sermons, together with the extremity of Walker's own language, represented a serious challenge to the authority of the ministry and the order of the church. Here, then, was a serious breakdown in the internal mechanisms of hierarchy, co-operation and control that sustained the peace and order of the London puritan community.

'CENSORSHIP' AND THE POLICING OF THE 'CALVINIST CONSENSUS'

What was perhaps most notable about the resulting attempts to bring the affair under control was the degree of collaboration that was achieved between the hierarchy of the church and the unofficial control mechanisms of the godly community. From the outset, with Bishop King's unwillingness to take official cognisance of the altercation, while yet associating himself with the pseudo-judicial arbitration attempt, the authorities connived at and encouraged the efforts of the godly to bring the affair under control. For all of Bayly and Walker's talk of the High Commission, Bishop King's tact, stiffened by his chaplain's rather more acute memory on the subject, prevented any formal enquiry into the proceedings as an illegal conventicle. Nor did official intervention in the affair end with the debacle of the arbitration tribunal. For, as we have seen, the massaged publication of Bradshaw's book represented an attempt to establish, in the public record of print, what was, in effect, the collective verdict of the clerical jury who had heard the case, now officially sanctioned by the exercise of the licensing power. This, of course, was the same tactic that Featley and Mason were to use to fix their own irenic reading on the Chibald affair. In both cases, the divisive, polarising version of the case (Walker's version) was silenced, the passions and denunciations consequent upon full-frontal polemical conflict suppressed and at least the surface appearance of peace and collegiality restored to the London puritan scene. In both cases, no names were mentioned, no reputations sullied. By the same token, both sets of pamphlets were clearly addressed to audiences who were assumed to know all about the issues at stake and presumably a good deal about the identity and track record of the participants.

In view of all this it is perhaps unsurprising that, for all the irenicism, tact and self-conscious moderation of Bradshaw's treatise, it elicited a distinctly dusty answer from the ever aggressive Walker, who both denounced it in a Paul's Cross sermon as 'a book full of contradictions and heresies of the same nature as he had before averred Mr Wotton's writings to be' and wrote a full-scale response under the appropriately lurid title of *A wolf in sheep's clothing*. Walker had earlier also written a reply to Wotton's manuscript essays on justification but found that he could get neither text published. The attack on Bradshaw was described by Gataker as 'so vile and so virulent' that 'tendering it for allowance at London House, he could not obtain passage for it to the press'.[33] As for the reply to Wotton, Walker himself admitted that, when he presented it to Archbishop Abbot's chaplain, Dr Nidd, for licensing, Nidd let the matter drop. Not that Wotton fared much better in the search for vindication in print. On Walker's account, just as Nidd was ignoring his request to license his attack on Wotton, Wotton was 'being admonished by his friends of the danger in which he was unless he and they did forebear to justify and maintain his errors and further to provoke me by their false reports and calumnies'. Even seven years after the hearing, when Wotton presented a volume *De reconciliatione* to Henry Mason for licence, claiming that it cleared him once and for all of socinianism, Mason told him that he would only consider it if Wotton could prevail upon two or more of the divines before whom he had been 'tried' in 1614 to attest that Walker 'did not convince him of heresy before them'. On Walker's own account, Gouge and Downham were happy to do so, while Stock and Bayly refused. Whatever the truth of that, the book was never published in England but was printed instead in Basel.[54] Indeed, Bradshaw's book apart, it was not until the 1640s that the breakdown of censorship combined with Walker's seemingly bottomless desire for vindication and Gataker's wounded pride to get the details of the dispute into print.

The full extent of the puritan/episcopal co-operation and collusion at work here is made clear by the pivotal role of William Bradshaw in the affair. For Bradshaw was a long-standing and principled non-conformist, who had been suspended from the public exercise of his ministry for his pains. He was also a dyed-in-the-wool proto-independent whose standing in the godly community as such was notorious. Here was no official stooge but a man of unimpeachable puritan principle, an epitome of 'English puritanism', to quote the title of his most famous tract. As such he was surely an ideal candidate to win over godly opinion to a right and proper understanding of the affair. Bradshaw got to serve the good of the church and the peace of the puritan community in ways other than the exercise of a public ministry (from which he was banned) while the authorities got the perfect spokesman for their view of the matter. The fact that Bradshaw, while a close friend of Gataker (who wrote the extensive life of Bradshaw in Clarke's *Martyrology*), was not a London figure, with no obvious personal and factional connections in the city and with a track record of disagreement with Wotton on at least some of the questions at issue, was obviously an added advantage. Bradshaw represented an ideal 'honest broker', through whose intervention the ruffled feathers of the participants might be smoothed and order restored.[55]

In short, we have a number of connections, personal, ideological and political, linking the bishop of London to the suspended puritan minister William Bradshaw, all being employed to defuse the feud between Walker and Wotton and restore order and the appearance of consensus to the London puritan scene. We have the power to control what got printed and what did not being used not as a blunt instrument to censure puritan pamphlets, but as a subtle means to gloss and interpret events through the public record of print. The issue here was not so much to prescribe one set of doctrinal opinions and to back another, to impose uniformity of opinion, but rather to use the symbolic power of licensed print to establish one view of both what was at stake in the argument and how such arguments should be conducted. Certainly the main point was not to keep Wotton's views or the points at issue in the dispute out of the public domain; that was a lost cause, since they had already been widely canvassed in manuscript and were summarised, in part, in Bradshaw's book. Anyway, as Wotton's case was subsequently to show, publication abroad was always an option. Rather, the aim was to use the licensing process as a symbolic means of withholding approval or sanction; in this case, to continue to close down rather than reopen the affair, by avoiding even the appearance of giving Wotton the last word, even seven years after the event.

Here, then, are two wonderful examples of the inner workings of the 'Calvinist consensus' of the early Stuart church. In both the Chibald and Wotton cases the challenge to consensus was internally generated from within the puritan community, not artificially inseminated into the reformed scene by an insurgent Arminianism. Disagreement having broken out, however, order and the appearance of consensus were restored through an essentially co-operative process of control, advice and censorship. We can add to all this Daniel Featley's claim to have worked virtually as Edward Elton's editor, cutting, with Elton's full approval, what he took to be difficult, dangerous or misguided from Elton's works, so that they could be safely printed. On this view, then, 'censorship' in this period appears not so much as the imposition of a rigid set of rules and norms downwards from authority onto a subversive puritanism but rather as a series of negotiations and trade-offs, in which the interest of the godly in order, agreement and decorum (which as these cases show could be considerable) was as much at stake as that of the authorities. In the process some opinions – Crompton's views on episcopal authority and ministerial parity, for instance, – were undoubtedly effectively proscribed, but both sides clearly benefited from the exchange. Elton and Bradshaw got their works printed and were thus able to serve the godly commonwealth with their pens. In that sense the access of puritanism defined as a world view, a religious style, to the wider public was facilitated, and the public careers even of radicals like Bradshaw furthered. Episcopal chaplains like Featley and Mason operated within this system as mediators, conduits who might stop some opinions and books getting printed but who, on the whole, worked as much with, as against, the grain of godly opinion and self-interest.[56]

As the Chibald and Wotton/Walker disputes show, this cosy symbiosis was not always maintained without hurt feelings, but it is in these sorts of relationships and their capacity to control and contain a wide range of personal and doctrinal tensions and rivalries that we are confronted with the sociocultural consequences of the 'Calvinist consensus' of the English church. Here, in the personal and ideological links maintained between the likes of Bishop John King and William Bradshaw, through such intermediary figures as Daniel Featley and Henry Mason, ambitious episcopal chaplains and bishops in waiting, and Thomas Gataker, the quintessential moderate puritan minister, or Anthony Wotton, the learned lecturer with puritan scruples, were the means through which puritanism was both tamed and preserved, integrated and perpetuated within the structures of the English church.

And it is in the disruption of these links and connections that the transformative effects of the rise of Arminianism were most obvious. Here the effects of the rise of Arminianism operated on a number of levels. Firstly, Arminianism (in the shape of the Montague affair) raised the stakes and the anxiety level in domestic theological dispute by threatening to move several of the crucial markers by which such disputes had been controlled. Now it seemed indisputable to the godly that there was a genuine internal Arminian/ pelagian/ popish threat to the doctrinal integrity of the English church. In that atmosphere, recourse to the polemical mode as George Walker had wielded it against Wotton and Chibald and as Thomas Gataker had excoriated it in his attack on Walker, became both more likely and more legitimate; for now there really were fundamental doctrinal truths at stake. Secondly, the heightened tensions and anxieties of the mid-1620s pushed men like Featley – who in the Chibald or Walker and Wotton affair had spent their time defusing the explosive potential of the polemical mode – to themselves have recourse to that mode as they turned to confront Arminianism. (Interestingly, Mason went off in the other direction, very likely becoming an Arminian.) Thus, in the mid 1620s it was Featley, the irenic, calming influence of the Chibald affair, who himself set about assimilating the opinions of Richard Montague and the Arminians to pelagianism and who used his powers as a licenser to ease the progress into print of puritan books like that of Crompton, books which were calculated to raise the ideological temperature through their overtly anti-Arminian bent. Thirdly, the rise of Arminianism saw the transfer

The London puritan scene

of more and more power and influence in the church to men whose own ideological presuppositions rendered the sorts of easy collegiality and collaboration between licenser and puritan author, that Featley described in his relationship to Edward Elton, almost entirely sinister. Instead of means whereby puritanism could be de-fanged and integrated into the church, they saw a sinister fifth column, with fellow travellers like Featley easing the progress into print of what Laud termed doctrinal puritanism. As the political and ideological tensions of the 1620s heightened, each side took full advantage of the risks taken and gestures made by the other to pose as the party of orthodoxy and order.[57]

DENISON AND ETHERINGTON

And, as we have seen above, it was in a polemical and political situation dominated by the rise of Arminianism that Stephen Denison had taken on John Etherington. Not only did Denison approach the boxmaker after the humiliations of 1625 had been visited upon him by the activities of Arminians in high places, it is also worth considering the possibility that Denison was amongst the nameless opponents of Chibald silenced and implicitly rebuked by Featley and Mason in 1622. As we have seen, he clearly occupied the positions on assurance and justifying faith that Chibald was criticising and the sort of attacks that were launched on Chibald in return were entirely typical of Denison's distinctly Walkeresque style. And finally there is the overlap of theological substance between the Chibald affair and Denison's dispute with Etherington, in the course of which, as we have seen, Denison was able to denounce what had been Chibald's central contention – that repentance preceded faith – in the most violent possible terms as familist heresy.

But it was not merely the more highly charged personal and general political circumstances that marked off Denison's dispute from the earlier Wotton and Chibald affairs. For in both those cases the main protagonists had been university educated clergymen, respected or emergent figures on the London puritan scene. Certainly, the Chibald fracas appears in the surviving sources as a storm in a largely clerical teacup. Even if we extrapolate back from the greater narrative detail available for the Wotton/Walker dispute and impute the same level of lay interest, partisanship and passion to the Chibald business as appears to have attended Walker's show-down with Wotton, these remain largely intra-clerical disputes and disagreements. This, of course, was not true in the case of Etherington, a fact which on its own seriously altered the balance of power in the dispute. It was far easier for Denison, the established minister, to vent his spleen on Etherington, the ex-familist boxmaker, then it had been for Walker publicly to call out and humiliate established clerical figures like Wotton or Chibald. Intra-ministerial disputes,

Doctrinal dispute and damage limitation

conducted in the pulpit and through the gossip and manuscript reading networks of London were scandals; they represented serious breakdowns in order and decorum, rents in the seamless web of godly unity and clerical respectability that large numbers of people had an interest in mending. Seeing off odd laymen with eccentric doctrinal notions and largish lay followings was, however, a very different proposition. Here the rhetoric of order, uniformity and the maintenance of clerical authority and doctrinal orthodoxy ran entirely in Denison's favour.

Thus, while Bishop King had proved unwilling to intervene officially in the Wotton/Walker business and Mason and Featley had tried throughout to hush things up and protect both Wotton and Chibald from the hostile attentions of George Walker, when Etherington turned to the bishop of London and then the archbishop of Canterbury for help against the polemical aggression of Stephen Denison, the outcome was very different. Now there was no *sotto voce* attempt to heal the breach and smooth things over. On the contrary, Denison was able simply to raise the stakes, doing successfully what Walker had merely threatened to do to Wotton, in unloading the full force of the High Commission on Etherington's head. In the process, of course, he was able to stage, both at the Cross and in print, the sort of public demonstration of his own orthodoxy and power, that Walker could only dream about during his altercations with Wotton and Chibald.

In this case we can see even more of the lay involvement and initiative, that, judging from certain asides by both Walker and Gataker, may also have featured prominently in the two earlier disputes, but which, because of the personal and polemical positions and agendas of the clerical authors describing the events, do not feature prominently in the surviving sources. According to both Etherington and Denison, their confrontation did not start with any direct contacts between the two men themselves. Although, as he claimed in the late 1620s, Etherington had lived in or near the city of London since 1588, or 'for now above these forty years', as he put it elsewhere, he was not, at the time of the dispute, one of Denison's parishioners. Indeed, in *The white wolf*, Denison described him as 'late of the city of Westminister and now of Putney in the county of Surrey'. As we shall see below, Etherington was at pains to maintain that, throughout the affair, Denison refused to have any personal contact with him at all. Rather the dispute seems to have begun with complaints against Etherington made to Denison by his parishioners and followers, some of whom had got into conversation with Etherington and his friends and either had their faith in Denison's doctrine shaken or their sensibilities upset by the heterodoxy of the boxmaker's claims. Denison's complaint that some of his parishioners had been 'tampered with' has already been cited and indeed his major accusation against Etherington was not that he attacked Denison's doctrine or authority as a minister but that he 'hath seduced and withdrawn many, as well men as women, from the church of England, in the famous city of London'. By implication, Etherington confirmed this version of the origins of the dispute when he wrote of Denison's 'associates and devotaries which first set him on'.[58]

All of which, of course, is reminiscent of Walker's claim to have been called to the public refutation of Wotton's errors by the prevalence of half-baked versions of the latter's views amongst his own flock. Indeed, at one point, Walker claimed that he had first heard of Wotton's errors 'by one of your near disciples' in whom 'I observed ... such forwardness to publish them before me, being to him a stranger' and such 'courage in urging and maintaining them, with no other arguments than your authority, whom he so odiously compared with all learned and godly divines, chief pillars of our church, as Calvin, Beza, Whitaker, Perkins and others, that he was not ashamed to call them foolish boys in comparison to you, not worthy to carry your books'.[59] Perhaps, therefore, Walker's claim to have been forced to address the issue of justification by the adherence of some of his parishioners to the peculiar opinions of another man was not a mere excuse for him to pursue his vendetta against Wotton. Certainly, it should draw our attention to the way in which clerical reputations depended on the attention and affection of the laity and the extent to which all such differences of opinion amongst the clergy were played out before interested, indeed, potentially partisan, lay audiences.

We should, then, probably think of the pulpit campaign against Etherington and subsequent legal case as the culmination of tensions that first sprang up amongst the laity. Thus, in one telling aside about John Okey, a clothworker and another of Denison's witnesses against him in High Commission, Etherington hinted at the sorts of tensions and interactions that lay behind the dispute. In reply to Okey's accusations, Etherington explained that Okey was in no position to know anything of his opinions since he had never been 'in his company, to my knowledge, one half hour together in my life, nor spoken two words with him these twenty years at least, but only about three or four years ago I, having heard that he had threatened me, spake to him at a bookseller's stall in Cheapside, who heard what I said unto him'.[60]

But if the origins of the dispute lay in discussions amongst the godly laity, once Etherington had been drawn to his attention, Denison deployed all the cultural capital inherent in his position as a godly minister to bring the boxmaker to heel. On Etherington's account, Denison had set out purposefully first to denounce and then to build a legal case against him. Thus Etherington accused his adversaries of defaming him 'not only in their private talk and conferences together but publicly, in pulpits and printed books and in the open streets and parts both of city and country'. At one point in the legal proceedings between the two men, Denison had launched an appeal from the pulpit for witnesses against Etherington, playing on his credit with the godly as a minister of the word now under attack. According to Etherington, he had broadcast an appeal that 'whosoever hath anything against John Etherington, let him come to my chamber tomorrow by eight o'clock. As ye love the ministers of God now stand for them, for they go about to silence all the good ministers in the city.' In this way, Etherington claimed, 'by his diligent search and inquiry through the city, partly by fair persuasions, partly by threatenings', Denison managed to assemble a case and witnesses against him.[61] Again, this is reminiscent of Walker's account of Wotton's use of his established standing in the city and considerable lay following to turn opinion against the younger man.

Elsewhere Etherington told how almost as soon as Denison had started to revile him in the pulpit, Etherington had used 'all means, both by writing and friends of his and my own to speak with him, to inform him rightly of things concerning my self and my mind in matters of religion before some men of understanding that they might hear and discern truly thereof and so pacify him and stay his violent course'.[62] In other words, through mutual friends and contacts, Etherington had tried to have the dispute mediated and concluded within the social and ideological structures of the godly community, just as Featley and Mason had tried to do with the Chibald affair and just as Wotton had tried to do by meeting with Walker immediately after the young firebrand had first attacked him in the pulpit. The 'men of understanding' were very probably, at this early stage in the proceedings, as likely to be laymen as clergy. When Walker had first gone to see Wotton he had been accompanied by someone he described as 'Mr Standish, one of the witnesses who went along with me' and whose response to the interview Walker recorded with great relish. For 'no sooner were we entered into the street', then Standish 'brake out into speeches of dislike against Mr Wotton's fraudulent dealing', protesting 'that he would never harken to his opinion and doctrine in these points any more'.[63] Presumably such witnesses were to be chosen by both parties, not merely for moral support but also to see fair play and prevent either side from distorting or falsifying their opponent's position, either at the time or later. Certainly, to judge from the very different versions of a whole variety of such meetings, both formal and informal, produced by Walker and Gataker in their rival accounts of the Wotton affair, in such charged circumstances, such an outcome was only too likely.

Denison consistently resisted Etherington's advances and instead chose to deal with Etherington either through lay intermediaries or via Henry Roborough, described throughout Etherington's account as Denison's curate. Thus, after Denison had started his suit in High Commission against Etherington he sent two of his lay followers, Rowland Thomson and Thomas Rogers, both joiners, to seek a conference with the boxmaker. They used as a go-between Saloman Seabright, 'being of his [Denison's] acquaintance and one that knew me'. A meeting was arranged at Seabright's house in Aldgate. Etherington also mentioned another such conference held at the house of one Master Pike in East-cheap. These meetings were offered to Etherington ostensibly as a means to conclude the dispute. Thomson and Rogers and (on the second occasion) Peter Worcester, another lay follower of Denison's, along 'with some other of Master Denison's favourites' told Etherington that 'if they might speak with me and should find things to be otherwise than they had conceived, they would inform Mr Denison thereof and cause him to cease his course and proceedings against me'.[64]

Etherington agreed to the meetings but with grave suspicions, since he had been forewarned 'by one that knew some of their secrets' that, far from a bona fide attempt to get at the truth of his opinions and end the dispute, this was merely a manoeuvre to 'get matter against me, either to prove a conventicle or otherwise to entrap me in my words'. And so it proved, for it was only these meetings, arranged ostensibly to end the dispute, that allowed Thomson and Rogers to accuse Etherington before the High Commission of conventicle keeping, by deposing that 'I have often times taken upon me to expound sundry places of scripture and to instruct many persons in their presence and hearing'.[65]

On the first occasion, at Seabright's house, 'in the hearing of sundry persons, they moved many questions unto me, concerning repentance and faith, the church and other things, to which I did answer them according as I did understand and believe'. The second time, at Pike's house in Eastcheap, Etherington proved more circumspect, refusing to be drawn into a discussion of either repentance or of the sabbath, 'being forewarned of their conspiracy'. For his pains, Worcester and his friends roundly defamed Etherington, 'one saying it is a pity that he liveth, he deserveth to be burned, another, I will never leave him till I make him fry and others to the like effect'. As was typical of his defensive posture against Denison, Etherington presented this hostility as a product of his own essentially peace-loving refusal to dispute. Worcester and the others reacted so badly, he claimed, only 'because I held it not a thing fitting to make a controversy of this matter of the sabbath, which they most desired to have me speak of with them, neither did I ever contend with any man about it until Master Denison had begun to revile me in his pulpits'.[66] Again there are parallels here to be drawn with the Wotton affair, where Wotton had first tried to deal with Walker through a low-status lay intermediary (Spencer) and where, too, meetings were called to end the dispute the purposes of which were viewed very differently by each side. Where Wotton/Etherington wanted mediation and an end to the campaign of vilification in full swing against them, Walker/Denison were preparing for judicial proceedings and the formal condemnation of their miscreant opponent.

We can gain confirmation of the general outlines of this picture of the workings of the London godly community from Denison's account of the same interactions. Interestingly, in *The white wolf*, Denison repeatedly complained of the lack of support amongst the godly for his campaign against Etherington. 'For howsoever there were many which disliked the Hetheringtonian faction, abhorred their opinions, complained of them to ministers in secret and murmured against them ... yet for any that would lend their helping hand to set forward this matter of so great importance for the common safety of the church, I found none.'[67] Indeed, not only had no one been prepared to help Denison, many had criticised him for his zeal. 'I met also with many discouragements', Denison complained. 'Some in their ignorance would be ready to say that, though this faction held some absurd points, yet that they held nothing against the foundation.' Indeed, because of his outward appearance of piety, Etherington and his kind 'are less suspected and less shunned and opposed; yea, with some they find kind entertainment and obtain a good report. I speak this to the shame of many in our times which have not learned to put difference ... between a palliated wolf and a true orthodox sheep of Jesus Christ.' Indeed, Denison lamented the credulity of the people in the face of Etherington's pretended zeal for true religion. 'If error come but masked with a pretence of zeal and a thundering voice, it is readily received for truth by the common multitude. Yea, I would there were not many that make a great profession of religion and yet are thus silly.'[68]

Others clearly thought that it was 'a mere private controversy' which did not concern them. By implication Denison might be thought therefore to be pursuing a private grudge against the unfortunate boxmaker. This was an impression Denison was desperate to deny – hence the enthusiasm with which he denounced Etherington as a familist, a real heretic, rather than merely as a misguided or eccentric godly person with odd views on a variety of disparate subjects. For, if Etherington were merely mistaken, Denison's behaviour was disproportionate, to say the least, and tyrannical and overbearing, to say the worst. But if Etherington were a 'familistical wolf', then 'many hundred souls' were at stake and this was a 'public controversy' that integrally concerned 'the common safety'. Thus, it was only Etherington's status as a fully paid-up familist that allowed Denison to justify his own behaviour in terms of the duty of all ministers to repress heresy 'for the common safety of the church' and to conclude bitterly that, to judge by his experience over the Etherington affair, 'the cause of God may sink or swim ... for any help or countenance that the forward men of our time, for the most part, will give unto it'.[69] The same dynamic applied, of course, to Walker's set-to with Wotton; it was only if Wotton really was a serious heretic, a socinian in puritan clothing, and if the prevalence of his views really did represent a serious threat to the faith and orthodoxy of the London godly, that the extremity of Walker's methods and diction could be justified.

The London puritan scene

Others, however, had argued that Denison should have reasoned privately with Etherington, 'that I ought to have instructed them before I had complained'. This was a sore point at which Etherington himself picked insistently in his reply to Denison's charges, claiming (as we have seen above) that, after the campaign of vilification against him had started, he had tried repeatedly to meet with Denison and have the dispute amicably settled or mediated. But his best efforts had failed; 'I could by no means obtain either the one or the other but that he still persisted, both at Cree Church and at All Hallows, for near half a year together, reviling me by name in most bitter manner, calling me viper, serpent, heretic, familist and many other vile, reproachful and scandalous names, unseemly to be spoken and shameful to be uttered by a minister in a pulpit and charging me with many very false and wicked things and saying to the people, this is one Etherington a boxmaker, whether he be dead or alive, with God or the devil, I cannot tell, I know him not if I meet him in my dish.' Not only did Denison refuse to meet with his adversary, he actively boasted about it in the pulpit saying 'must I speak with every heretic before I may reprove him openly: nay it hath been told me by the household of Chloe and I believe it to be true'.[70] The clerical hauteur of such displays was clearly in part the point. Just as Wotton's refusal to meet Walker on equal terms as a fellow minister had proved a red rag to a bull, so the whole point of Denison's treatment of Etherington was to emphasise the vast gulf in status and cultural power that separated the powerful preacher of Katharine Cree from the humble boxmaker. It was a stance reminiscent of Bradshaw's use of the intricacies of Christology to demonstrate the ignorance of the separatist with whom he was disputing in Newgate. Pulling clerical rank always formed a central part of such exchanges.

However, perhaps what is most remarkable about these rather defensive remarks of Denison's is the clear implication that there were many in puritan London by whom, for all the eccentricity of his opinions, Etherington was seen as far enough within the magic circle of godliness and zeal to deserve far better treatment than he was receiving from Denison. In short, it seems clear that precisely the same sorts of arguments that Gataker used to defuse the points at issue between Wotton and Walker, to excoriate the methods of denunciation and argument adopted by Walker and to preserve a view of the spectrum of respectable opinion and godly society inclusive enough to incorporate Wotton, were being deployed on behalf of Etherington and against Denison by some godly Londoners. Given the vast difference of status that separated Wotton, the university educated and widely respected minister, from Etherington, the unlettered ex-familist boxmaker, this sheds a really remarkable light on the latitude of the godly community in London – at least as it was conceived and maintained by some of its members.

In *The white wolf* we can watch Denison struggling to come to terms with these criticisms. Thus he tried to present his pulpit campaign as an exercise in pastoral concern. Once a week for a whole three months he had denounced the errors of Etherington and his followers from the pulpit in an effort 'to reduce them from their pernicious opinions'. Not only that, but at least three other ministers, Henry Roborough and a Master Cleaver and a Master Stephens, had all met with Etherington and his followers in private. This, at least, is confirmed in Etherington's account of the same events where he recounts discussions with one Master Cleaver on the issue of the sabbath, instituted after Denison's pulpit campaign had started, although, perhaps significantly, Etherington described the exchange with Cleaver as ending amicably. 'We seemed to part friends and not so disagreeing as there need to be any enmity between us for the difference.' Denison took a rather different view of these same meetings, observing that many ministers 'have lost their labour for above these twenty years together in private reasonings with Hetherington and his factious company'.[71] Clearly, what Etherington presented as a process of public denunciation and private entrapment, Denison wanted construed as a fraternal attempt to win the boxmaker back to the truth. Anyway, to judge from his own remarks on the subject, Denison's campaign against Etherington had not gone down uniformly well with the London puritan community – 'the forward men of our time' as Denison himself described them.

From the list given by Etherington of the witnesses arrayed against him in High Commission it seems that Denison's complaints about the reaction of the godly were justified. Apart from Roborough, Denison seems to have enlisted no other clerical backing for his campaign. No other ministers, not even Cleaver or Stephens, testified against the boxmaker and the list of those who did appear was composed of artisans and their wives, quite humble lay people, scarcely leading members of the parish. This seems to have been a campaign conducted by Denison and 'his favourites', as Etherington contemptuously called them, an inner circle of godly laity who hung on Denison's every word. The wider godly community clearly washed its hands of the proceedings in High Commission.

We have here a remarkable picture of the internal dynamics of the London puritan community or underworld. To begin with it is clear that the whole dispute, from its earliest inception up to and including Etherington's imprisonment and humiliation at the Cross, was played out far more before the court of godly opinion than the court of High Commission, just as, according to George Walker, Wotton had initially wanted to conduct their dispute. Certainly, it is hard not to believe Etherington when he wrote that 'it is so well known to many in this city of London how … my adversary … hath dealt and proceeded against me' or indeed Denison, when he claimed in 1641, that 'the altercation' made 'in the city' by Etherington and 'your followers in venting your unsound opinions' was public knowledge (i.e. 'noted by many that would not acquaint themselves with you').[72] It was only when it was clear that they were overmatched in that arena that both Etherington and Walker started to involve or threaten to involve the authorities. Clearly as with the Wotton/Walker dispute, the case for and against Etherington passed to and fro amongst the godly and there were a number of different verdicts registered amongst them, ranging from the fervent partisanship of Susan Price or Peter Worcester to the more measured and even sharply disapproving opinions recorded with such scorn by Denison himself. But while there was clearly a sort of general godly public sphere, an arena of common knowledge and divergent opinion constituted by a whole series of rumours and counter rumours, those rumours passed along discrete and overlapping personal networks, more defined and limited webs of acquaintance, friendship and partisanship.

Denison's friends talked to Etherington's, mutual acquaintances like Saloman Seabright arranged or accommodated meetings in their houses. At times, Etherington challenged his enemies in the street or, in the case of John Okey, in a bookseller's stall on Cheapside. The same pattern emerges in the Wotton and Walker affair, with different networks carrying different versions of the same events, and the same people giving different versions of their conduct to different audiences. Even the prominence of booksellers' premises in the conduct of such exchanges is common to both cases. When Walker wanted to pull Gataker into his dispute with Bradshaw, he sent a message 'by a stationer whose shop I frequented', attributing the real authorship of Bradshaw's treatise to Gataker and challenging him to an open disputation; 'if I would undertake the defence of it, he would prove it to consist of contradictions and heresies'.[73]

We can surely discern within both Etherington and Denison's accounts of these interactions some of the mechanisms whereby the godly community usually defused such tensions; private meetings of instruction and admonition between the parties; relatively informal private chats, ending perhaps in friendly agreements to disagree of the sort that Etherington thought he had had arrived at with Master Cleaver or that Wotton tried to achieve during his first interview with Walker; more formal mediated discussions to establish the points at issue and explore the possibilities of agreement or compromise of the sort held at Seabright's house or Pike's, or more formally in the presence of the eight clerical mediators in Lewis Bayly's church. All these were supposed to precede recourse to official channels, which was clearly regarded as a last resort, if, that is, it was ever really legitimate to rat on a fellow godly person to the authorities. For some, at least, what appears to have mattered here (as it had in the Chibald and Wotton and Walker disputes) was not so much the achievement of complete agreement or consensus but the maintenance of decorum and social peace amongst those loosely defined as in some sense godly people who, because of their pious affect and conversation, could be deemed to belong to the social and ideological universe in which such disputes were best, if not settled, then at least contained. It is, of course, difficult to gauge the full range of doctrinal and ecclesiological positions that could be contained within what was always a potentially shifting notion of insiderhood, but it seems safe to conclude that it was far wider than the relatively narrow definitions of orthodoxy pushed in the pulpit by the likes of Stephen Denison. It is certainly remarkable that the same assumptions and arguments that extended the protection of the charmed circle of godliness and ideological acceptability to Anthony Wotton should also have been applied (in some circles at least) to the very different figure of John Etherington.

Not, of course, that such attitudes were without precedent. In the highly charged atmosphere of the 1590s, it was remarkable how a whole series of respectable presbyterian divines, when approached by the visionaries Hacket and Coppinger, men who were genuinely mad, bad and dangerous to know, while they kept their distance and refused them personal interviews or endorsements, did not inform the authorities.[74] Claims to spiritual charisma and insight, generated from within the charmed circle of puritan godliness, clearly demanded a certain respect and circumspection. Judging from Etherington's own career, separatist, anabaptist and even familist elements moved fairly freely in these circles. Certainly, for many London puritans, Etherington, whatever his doctrinal eccentricities, belonged within the pale of godly respectability and it was Denison's treatment of him that represented the more serious failure to observe the forms of godly interaction and self-regulation.

The decision to break off such interminable fraternal contacts and to invoke the formal stereotypes of heresy and heterodoxy – to move, that is, from the stance adopted by Gataker during the Wotton/Walker altercation, to that adopted by Walker himself – was obviously a very serious one indeed. In taking it, Denison had put his own reputation, as well as that of Etherington, on the line, hence the manic enthusiasm with which he flung around his accusations of familist and Arminian heresy. For the logic of the situation that his own accusations had created was quite clear and quite vicious; either Etherington *was* a heretic or Denison himself was a tyrannical pharisee, prepared to loose the fury of the High Commission on a humble godly layman and all in the pursuit of what remained a purely personal feud.

Finally, what is really remarkable in many of the interactions described by both Denison and Etherington is the prominent role played throughout by quite humble lay people. Denison's representatives at the meetings at Seabright and Pike's houses and later his chief witnesses in High Commission, his 'favourites', as Etherington witheringly called them, were joiners, drawers, a porter's wife. Again, the crucial meetings at which Etherington's position was discussed took place in private houses and before lay audiences. Admittedly, Etherington did have other, private, interviews with ministers like Cleaver and Stephens, and Henry Roborough was involved throughout, but these were occasions by no means dominated by the clergy. They were, moreover, completely innocent of any official ecclesiastical standing.

As with Etherington's account of the exercise of the power of the keys by 'the little ones of God' in 1610, we can see here groups within the London puritan community seeking to regulate their own affairs and to enforce their own codes of doctrinal orthodoxy and spiritual discipline. Ironically, there is a considerable resemblance between Etherington's account of the way in which 'the little ones' should exercise their powers of excommunication and the treatment meted out to Etherington himself by Denison and his followers in the early 1620s. Alerted by some spiritual offence, the little ones should admonish the offending party, before assembling witnesses to make his continued pertinacity in error patent and then 'telling the church', that is, the godly community, which would then proceed to that process of ostracism that constituted, for Etherington, the genuinely spiritual excommunication of offending Christians, by the true church built only of lively stones. In the 1620s, however, when similar procedures were used against him by Denison and his followers, that same process now seemed to Etherington rather more like persecution and entrapment than brotherly admonition. Of course, the parallels between his precept and Denison's practice broke down precisely at the point where Denison involved High Commission and the end of the affair was taken out of the hands of the godly. Even here, however, it is worth remembering that it was Etherington not Denison who had first sought to short-circuit the workings of the godly community by involving the authorities. Denison's removal of the case into High Commission was designed to trump Etherington's appeal to the bishops of London and then of Canterbury, which in turn had been prompted by a desire to stop the trial by public denunciation and private excoriation initiated by Denison and his followers in the London puritan underground.[75]

There is one further link holding together the three disputes under review here – John Etherington. Etherington, of course, was a major protagonist in the third, but he was also, it appears, very likely a bit player in the first and very possibly even in the second. When he returned to the polemical fray against Etherington in 1641 Denison did so desperate to claim that Etherington had not been attacking only his opinions or those 'of some two ministers and some other of their corrupt humour' but 'the doctrine of minister's publicly delivered', the 'teaching of the most reverend ministers amongst us', the opinions 'of all orthodox divines'. To drive that point home he cited an earlier exchange between Etherington and Richard Stock over the issue of repentance

Doctrinal dispute and damage limitation

and justification. 'Did you not,' he asked the boxmaker, 'oppose also Mr Stock in the same doctrine many years ago, witness a manuscript of yours written to him with your hand to it?' Stock, of course, had been a participant in the Wotton/Walker dispute, which had touched on the relations between repentance and justification. The reverberations of that affair around the London puritan scene had thus provided an opportunity for Etherington to continue his career as a 'busy contradictor of ministers', entering the arena thus opened up for doctrinal dispute and inquiry not only through the means of rumour and verbal communication used by most of the interested laity but by actually committing himself to paper in the sort of formal intervention usually reserved for ministers of the word. That a major protagonist in that dispute, George Walker, was also a major player in the Chibald affair, which, of course, also centred on the same doctrinal crux, merely emphasises the continuities in play here and surely increases the likelihood that Etherington himself stuck his oar into those troubled waters too. And, of course, the Chibald furore itself provided a crucial backdrop for Etherington's later run in with Denison. All of which certainly confirms the claim, made above, that the Etherington/Denison dispute represented the working out of a series of long term doctrinal, personal and political strains and tensions within the worlds that constituted London puritanism.[76]

NOTES

1 W. Chibald, *A defence of the treatise called a trial of faith* (London, 1623), 'to the reader', sigs. A2v.–A3r.
2 *Ibid.*, p. 37.
3 W. Chibald, *An apology for a trial of faith* (London, 1624), p. 163.
4 Chibald, *A defence*, p. 15.
5 Chibald, *An apology*, 'to the courteous reader', sig. A4r.
6 Chibald, *A defence*, p. 31; *An apology*, 'To the Christian reader' signed by Daniel Featley, sigs A6v.–a2r.; 'To the author' signed by Henry Mason, sigs a2v.–a3v. *The trial of faith* and Chibald's two subsequent defences of it were all licensed by Daniel Featley. See E. Arber, *A transcript of the register of the company of stationers of London, 1554–1640* (London, 1875–94), vol. IV, pp. 28, 52, 67.
7 Chibald, *An apology*, sig. a2v.
8 *Ibid.*, sigs A6v., A8v.–av.
9 *Ibid.*, sigs a2v.–a3v.; sigs av.–a2r. For the certificate for Haydon see PRO S.P. Dom. 16/119/22, fol. 27r. I owe my knowledge of this document to the kindness of Paul Seaver and David Como.
10 George Walker, *A true relation of the chief passages between Mr Anthony Wotton and Mr George Walker* (London, 1642), pp. 1, 6.

11 Ibid., pp. 6–7.
12 Ibid., pp. 6, 14.
13 Ibid., p. 8.
14 Ibid., pp. 8–9.
15 Ibid., p. 14.
16 Ibid., pp. 15, 13, 17, 14, 12.
17 Ibid., p. 19.
18 Thomas Gataker, *Mr Anthony Wotton's defence against Mr George Walker's charge* (London, 1641), pp. 5–6.
19 Walker, *A true relation*, p. 21.
20 Ibid., p. 24.
21 Thomas Gataker, *An answer to Mr George Walker's vindication* (London, 1642), pp. 64–5.
22 Ibid., p. 47.
23 Ibid., pp. 63–4.
24 P. Lake, *Moderate puritans and the Elizabethan church* (Cambridge, 1982), chapter 9; 'Calvinism and the English church, c. 1570–c. 1635', *Past and Present*, 114 (1987), p. 47, fn. 35 quoting Bodleian Library Tanner Ms vol. 72, fol. 161r.–v., Andrew Byng to Samuel Ward, dated 3 November 1626.
25 Gataker, *An answer*, pp. 58, 47.
26 F.J. Shriver, 'Orthodoxy and diplomacy: James I and the Vorstius affair', *English Historical Review*, 85 (1970); P. Collinson, *The religion of protestants* (Cambridge, 1982); also see his 'Lectures by combination: structures and characteristics of church life in seventeenth-century England' and 'Towards a broader understanding of the dissenting tradition', both in P. Collinson, *Godly people* (Hambledon, 1983); K. Fincham, *Prelate as pastor* (Oxford, 1990).
27 P. Collinson, *Archbishop Grindal* (London, 1979); for Reynolds' comment at Hampton Court see W. Barlow, *The sum and substance of the conference*, as reprinted in E. Cardwell, *A history of conferences ... from the year 1558 to the year 1690* (Oxford, 1840), pp. 183–4, 201–3. Also see K. Fincham and P. Lake, 'The ecclesiastical policy of James I', *Journal of British Studies*, 24 (1985), pp. 173–4.
28 Gataker, *An answer*, pp. 62, 88.
29 Walker, *A true relation*, pp. 22, 20, 23.
30 Ibid., pp. 22–3.
31 Ibid., pp. 25–6.
32 Ibid., p. 24.
33 William Bradshaw, *A treatise of justification* (London, 1615), 'to the reader' sigs A4r.–A9r. This work was entered in the Stationers' register on 3 April 1615 and licensed by 'Master Sandford', see E. Arber, *A transcript of the register of the company of stationers*, vol. III, p. 260. On the role of the censor as both a gatekeeper of orthodoxy and a facilitator of certain sorts of respectable puritan publication see Anthony Milton, 'Licensing, censorship and religious orthodoxy in early Stuart England', *Historical Journal*, 41 (1998).

34 *Ibid.*
35 Gataker, *An answer*, pp. 36, 58, 90, 80.
36 *Ibid.*, pp. 66, 83–4.
37 *Ibid.*, p. 54.
38 *Ibid.*, pp. 103, 100.
39 *Ibid.*, p. 89.
40 *Ibid.*, p. 105.
41 *Ibid.*, pp. 134–5, 82.
42 *Ibid.*, p. 56.
43 *Ibid.*, pp. 53, 136.
44 *Ibid.*, pp. 36–7, 38.
45 *Ibid.*, pp. 59–60.
46 *Ibid.*, pp. 127, 110, 118–19.
47 *Ibid.*, pp. 85–6.
48 *Ibid.*, pp. 67–8.
49 *Ibid.*, p. 85.
50 On this point see P. Lake, 'Calvinism and the English church, 1570–1635', *Past and Present*, 114 (1987).
51 Walker, *A true relation*, p. 21.
52 From a vast literature see esp. N. Tyacke, *Anti-Calvinists* (Oxford, 1987); A. Milton, *Catholic and reformed* (Cambridge, 1995); Lake, 'Calvinism and the English church' and 'The moderate and irenic case for religious war: Joseph Hall's *via media* in context', in S. Amussen and M. Kishlansky, eds, *Political culture and cultural politics in early modern England* (Manchester, 1995).
53 Gataker, *An answer*, pp. 73–4.
54 Walker, *A true relation*, pp. 24–5, 33–4.
55 On Bradshaw's career see Lake, *Moderate puritans*, chapter 11.
56 D. Featley, *Cygnea cantio* (London, 1629). The preceding discussion is much indebted to Milton, 'Licensing, censorship and religious orthodoxy'.
57 Tyacke, *Anti-Calvinists*, chapters 5, 6, 7; also see the articles by P. Lake and D. Como, '"Orthodoxy" and its discontents: dispute settlement and the production of "consensus" in the London (puritan) "underground"' and 'Puritans, antinomians and Laudians in Caroline London: the strange case of Peter Shaw in context', respectively *Journal of British Studies*, 39 (2000) and forthcoming in the *Journal of Ecclesiastical History*.
58 S. Denison, *The white wolf* (London, 1627), dedicatory epistle, sig. A3r.; John Etherington, *The defence of John Etherington* (London, 1641), p. 16.
59 Walker, *A true relation*, pp. 11–12.
60 Etherington, *The defence*, p. 43.
61 *Ibid.*, pp. 2, 16.

62 *Ibid.*, p. 13.
63 Walker, *A true relation*, p. 7.
64 Etherington, *The defence*, pp. 26, 31.
65 *Ibid.*, pp. 26, 11.
66 *Ibid.*, pp. 26–7, 31–2.
67 Denison, *The white wolf*, 'to the Christian reader', sig. A7r.
68 *Ibid.*, sig. A7r., pp. 22, 14.
69 *Ibid.*, p. 31.
70 *Ibid.*, sig. A7v.; Etherington, *The defence*, pp. 13–14.
71 Denison, *The white wolf*, sig. A7v.; Etherington, *The defence*, p. 32.
72 Etherington, *The defence*, p. 2; S. Denison, *The white wolf* (London, 1641), p. 80.
73 Gataker, *An answer*, p. 74.
74 On Hacket and Coppinger see R.J. Bauckham, *Tudor apocalypse* (Abingdon, 1979), pp. 191–204. The most recent account is now to be found in Alexandra Walsham, '"Frantic Hacket": prophecy, sorcery and the Elizabethan puritan movement', *Historical Journal*, 41 (1998).
75 These notions are further canvassed in Lake and Como, '"Orthodoxy" and its discontents'.
76 Denison, *The white wolf* (1641), pp. 83, 87.

Part IV

Denison and Etherington again

Chapter 10

Heading for the high ground: Denison and Etherington on order, authority and orthodoxy

ETHERINGTON, DENISON AND THE LOGIC OF ANTI-PURITANISM

As Dr Marsh has pointed out, when the stresses and strains inherent in the puritan relationship with the social, cultural and political status quo became too much, one of the ways in which the godly responded was through a species of anti-puritanism. That is to say, they attempted to externalise much of the tension in their own position through the production and polemical excoriation of other stereotypes of deviance and dissent, through the ritual destruction and reviling of which they hoped to re-establish themselves as pillars of orthodoxy, normality and order. At one crucial moment in the history of the Elizabethan puritan movement, when the puritans were being denounced by conformist authority as themselves a sect, a subversive excrescence on the body politic of the Christian commonwealth, the role of scapegoat, of polemically necessary ritual victim or 'other' was played (in part at least) by familism. In the late 1570s and early 1580s several puritan divines turned on the familists, denouncing them in polemical works designed to play up their own doctrinal and political orthodoxy in stark contrast to the threat presented by familism to all order in church and state.[1]

It was presumably to such efforts that Etherington was in part replying in his book of 1610, with its denunciation of the puritan clergy – conforming, non-conforming and presbyterian – as subversive and duplicitous in their dealings both with authority and 'the little ones of God'. But, for all its prominent anti-puritan subtext, that book was primarily a work of anti-anabaptist polemic, a fact which points to a central structural similarity between Etherington and Denison's positions. For both men were seeking to construct themselves and to control their equally (albeit differently) strained relationships with orthodoxy, order and the national church, in essentially the same way – by defining themselves against a polemically constructed other, an ideal type of sectarian, separatist and, indeed, heretical excess. Here Smith the se-baptist and anabaptism in general were to Etherington as Etherington and familist anabaptism were to Denison.

It is this common propensity to construct oneself against a deviant other – on and through which all the errant, inconvenient, un- or only partially acknowledged tendencies and trends within one's own position could be projected and repudiated – that explains an otherwise rather bizarre element in Etherington and Denison's altercation: their struggle to see who could deploy with the greater enthusiasm against the other the stock anti-puritan stereotypes and caricatures of conformist polemic. Certainly, the claims, made by Etherington in his tract of 1610, that non-conformity was merely a pose, a way of attracting a false reputation for zeal and the adulation of a credulous laity; that puritan ministers cultivated the support of the people, feasting on the contributions of the godly and glorying in the support of the wealthy; that puritan and presbyterian scruples about the ceremonies and government of the church were but a resting place on a road that led inexorably to schism, heresy and anabaptism, all these were stock conformist conceits, developed and disseminated by the Elizabethan opponents of the classis movement. As for Etherington's denunciation of 'subscribing reformers', who hid their real opinions behind a mask of conformity in order to combine the regard of the godly with the pursuit of ecclesiastical preferment, that echoed the claims of avant-garde conformist polemicists like William Covell and looked forward to the polemical style of Lancelot Andrewes and Richard Montague and, indeed, of myriad spokesmen for the Caroline church.[2]

Nor did Etherington's appropriation of the discourse of conformity stop there. As his dispute with Denison and his supporters developed, it would appear that Etherington started to deploy the term puritan with its attendant associations of a formal pharisaical outward godliness acting as a mask for all sorts of inner corruption and vice. Accused by Denison's supporters of railing against the ministers of the church of England as pharisees, Etherington replied, 'I would it were not true that there is a generation of pharisees among the ministers, as well as among the people and, although it be not an usual thing with me so to speak of any minister *by name*, yet I might well say it of these two [Denison and Henry Roborough] ... and do them no wrong at all and no doubt they have more fellows, elsewhere [in] the church of England, the rarest church that ever was in the world.' We might surely construe that passage as an implicit admission that Etherington commonly deployed the language of pharisaical hypocrisy against a certain sort of minister. As for Denison's supporters, Etherington remarked that he had been attacked in the vilest terms 'by persons professing a strictness in religion above others, as well preachers as professors of that kind'. And here he permitted himself the observation that 'men may profess strictness in religion, as the pharisees did, and yet be no better than they that bare false witness against Christ and persecuted him'.[3] And if that was what he said minding his ps and qs in print, no doubt he was a good deal more forthright in private. We are here very close to confirmation from the horse's mouth that Etherington did indeed (as Denison claimed) traduce 'good ministers and good people, terming them puritans though they be conformable'.[4]

For his part, Denison mobilised a whole series of stock conformist allegations of puritan popularity, greed and pharisaical pride against Etherington. For Denison, Etherington was a typical hypocrite, 'such as seem to be converted, which mourn for their sins, and desire to know the right way to heaven, having been, in some measure, wrought upon by the public ministry of the church'. Such men approached the people 'in the name of zealous Christians' 'with an outward expression of holiness, with a seeming contempt of the world, with prayers, fastings, tears, alms deeds, seeming zeal, comely gestures, seeming love, seeming patience, seeming conformity, seeming humility, seeming harmlessness and the like'. But while 'a mere outside in religion is not sufficient in God's sight', the people were more susceptible and Denison lamented the capacity of men like Etherington to win a following. As for Etherington, he was motivated by a combination of pride and greed. Despite his ignorance of the original tongues, Etherington retained an overweening and baseless confidence in his own interpretation of scripture.[5]

As for his covetousness, this led Etherington to present himself as a wise and holy man 'in order to advance his own gain' at the expense of his misguided followers. Indeed, at the Cross, Denison was forced to admit that 'it is true he will seem to maintain some of his erroneous opinions to this day'. This, Denison claimed, was not because he believed them or 'for any conscience he makes of denying what he holds' but as 'it were to enrich himself in prison by drawing money from his numerous multitude of proselytes, as some other besides himself have been known to do'.[6] But using a pharisaical display of obstinate and self-serving 'consistency' to batten off their misguided lay followers had been precisely one of the charges levelled by Etherington against the non-conformist puritan clergy in his tract of 1610. There could scarcely be a better example of the way in which both men determinedly, even obsessively, shuffled the pack of existing conformist anti-puritan tropes and conceits to one another's detriment.

LAY ACTIVISM AND CLERICAL AUTHORITY

Thus by the 1620s both Denison and Etherington had become rival claimants for roughly the same ideological terrain. For all their readiness to throw the stock epithets of anti-puritan insult at one another they are both probably best seen as products of a social, ideological and geographical milieu that, for want of a better term, we might want to call 'London puritanism'. But if that was the case, they also clearly represented rather different strains and tendencies within the puritan synthesis. For all his quiescence, in his familist phase and beyond, in the face of the formal symbols of outward conformity – the usual shibboleths of puritan radicalism – Etherington retained, throughout his career, an abiding suspicion of all clerical claims to authority in matters of the spirit or of doctrine. This scepticism was a function of his very high sense of his own calling and prerogatives as an informed, even spiritually inspired, lay person.

The intensity of his vision of the true church as a temple built only of lively stones greatly enhanced the area available for lay initiative and spiritual self-help, and Etherington himself took eager advantage of the opportunities for activism thus offered. As he admitted in the *Description*, Etherington himself lacked formal learning and his writings lacked method. Such qualities, however, did not guarantee the possession of the truth. Those anxious to find 'the little ones of God' too often searched for them in the wrong places. 'They sought them among the great, but they were of the little ones. They sought them among the learned and men of great study and long experience, but they were sitting among the little children, weeping with the tender babes.' There can be little doubt that Etherington saw himself as one such. Devoid of 'the skill of the learned disputers of this world', he fought armed only with 'the sword of the spirit' and Christ's 'word and promise for my shield'. 'Method I did forget, matter only was in my mind ... truth I hope hath kept me company, though I could not garnish it with rhetorical compliments.'[7] It was not, he claimed 'that I despise learning but reverence it and do acknowledge myself to be unworthy thereof'. It was merely that learning 'must not be so proud to think that truth should learn of it nor to think that reason must not rule it'. Of course, in defending right doctrine, the godly could always rely on the aid of the spirit and Etherington himself felt able to inform his anabaptist opponent of 1610 that 'the lord my God ... hath assisted me against you and your lies and I have received so much more assurance of the truth of that which I have written unto you than you have of what you have said, as there is difference between night and day'. Certainly in 1610, at the height of his familist phase, Etherington saw himself, in some sense, as a divinely inspired instrument of God, telling his opponent at one point that, for all his errors of doctrine, his chances of salvation were really rather good, since 'God hath enlarged my heart and opened my mouth unto you, which putteth me in great hope that you are of that remnant which shall be saved.'[8]

And yet such attitudes were far from limited to his period of self-conscious familism. In his tract of 1623, he produced an almost equally exalted rendition of the spiritual duties incumbent on the ordinary Christian, enlightened by the spirit, to edify his brethren and hence to build the temple of lively stones that constituted the true church. Etherington was still singing the same song in 1627 when he told his accusers that 'the gifts of God, as to prophecy, if in a man of the lowest degree, place or calling in the church of God, shepherd, clown, carpenter or other, ought not to be despised or envied at for his low estate or meanness of his person's sake'. His accusers forgot 'that they were but envious scorners, though scribes and pharisees, who once upon such terms so slighted and despised the Lord himself, his works and words'.[9]

In all this Etherington was claiming, at the very least, equality with the learned clergy as a scriptural exegete and defender of right doctrine. As he himself readily admitted, he was more than prepared to subject the doctrines delivered from the pulpit by Stephen Denison to a closely argued scriptural critique. On Etherington's account and, indeed in many ways, on Denison's too, there was nothing wrong with such behaviour. Things had come to a pretty pass, Etherington complained in 1627, when it was assumed that 'a man may not reason or dispute with a minister, nor speak or write of religion or of the scriptures but he therein taketh upon him to as a teacher or instructor'.[10] If the clergy's monopoly power to expound and interpret the scripture were expanded to this extent, what room was left for the spiritual liberties and insights of the laity? Of course, Denison might have replied by asking, if the spiritual autonomy and authority of the laity to define right doctrine and challenge ministerial pronouncements were expanded as far as Etherington wanted, what rights, powers and prerogatives were left to the clergy? Clearly, the two men had very different views of the appropriate division of labour and authority between the clergy and the laity. Indeed, when Etherington's definition of schism as attendance at any private meeting at which the sacraments were administered is recalled, it appears that the only spiritual prerogative he left solely to the clergy was the administration of the sacraments and, as we have seen, in his account of 'elementish baptism', his view of the role of the sacraments in the creation and sustenance of the godly community was scarcely exalted.

As one might expect from all this, Etherington remained, throughout his career, suspicious of the clergy's claims to wide-ranging spiritual, jurisdictional or doctrinal authority. For all his 'conformity' in ceding control over the external government of the church to the Christian prince and his representatives, the bishops, Etherington retained a very strict sense of the limitations that remained on any legitimate exercise of episcopal power. Replying to Denison's claims that by ceding, in his 'familist' book of 1610, the power of the keys to the 'little ones of God' he had effectively denied the spiritual jurisdiction of bishops over the church, Etherington reformulated the question in the act of responding to it. First, he reiterated his definition of the true church as 'the little ones born of God, the lively stones built on the head corner-stone, Jesus Christ', and then addressed himself to the rather different question of whether bishops could ever be members of the true church thus defined. It was true, he observed, that 'the places and jurisdictions of bishops be now great, and great and high places be dangerous and slippery places, as the scriptures speak, and experience (lamentable) hath a long time and often proved'. For every Christian, and particularly those in authority in the church, was bound to 'bear with his weak Christian brother and not to constrain him with any kind of violence, either in words or deeds, to do things against his conscience, which he is not, nor can be yet persuaded of, though otherwise lawful, because whatsoever is not of faith is sin'.

The combination of those two remarks did not seem to rate very high the chances of salvation of any bishop who enforced conformity across the board, as the law currently required him to do. It was true, Etherington conceded, that a bishop 'so ruling in wisdom and judging always righteous judgement, instructing with truth in the spirit of meekness and love, showing mercy with good works of charity', 'may receive double honour of his Christian brethren and, so continuing, be found one of those to whom Christ sayeth "blessed is that servant whom his Lord when he cometh shall find so doing."'. However, 'if one so entrusted in place of authority shall begin to smite his fellows ... the same servant's Lord will come in a day that he is not aware of and will hew him in pieces and give him his portion with hypocrites'. 'Yet notwithstanding I undoubtedly believe', Etherington concluded, perhaps more in hope than expectation, 'that bishops have been, or may and shall be, found to be of the little ones born of God, and so be of Christ's true church, against which the gates of hell shall not prevail.'[111] This was scarcely a ringing endorsement of episcopacy or of the clerical power and authority vested in that institution.

Nor, as we have seen in the analysis of his book of 1610, was Etherington necessarily any better disposed towards the puritan clergy; with their false scruples about mere externals, details of outward worship and church government, they, too, were guilty of oppressing the consciences of the little ones of God and gulling them into false positions and penury to boot. We can see precisely the same tendency towards the emancipation of the godly from the false scruples and legal niceties, imposed upon their consciences by an overbearing clergy, in Etherington's critique of what he portrayed as Denison's absurdly strict sabbatarianism. As we have seen, for Etherington the sabbath was a human and ecclesiastical ordinance, improperly equated with the legal sabbath of the Jews. He was so keen to assert this position because, he claimed, strict sabbatarianism had been the occasion of a spiritual tyranny exerted by ministers like Denison over the weak and wavering consciences of the laity, 'charging the people, upon heavy curses and condemnation, to do and not to do such and such kind of things as they prescribe'. The ministers had asserted the duty of the Christian to spend the full twenty-four hours of the sabbath in religious observance. In effect this was to claim that 'those kind of things or actions which, although you may lawfully do them on any other day and not sin, you are bound not to do any of them in this day on pain of condemnation'. On this basis, the ministers bruited it about that 'whosoever doth not conscionably so observe the day cannot be a true Christian, wherewith they have so enthralled the minds of many people, some of tender consciences zealously affected towards God and have brought them to such distraction and unquietness of spirit, by reason they are not nor can be satisfied in every particular action, what they are so bound to do and what not to do upon that day, when to begin and when to end, that there is more talk and questioning among them and [more] and more resorting to ministers for satisfaction about the same than about any matter of religion whatsoever'.[12]

In Etherington, therefore, we see a figure whose position was designed to maximise the autonomy and authority of the laity and minimise both the authority of the clergy and the significance of the external forms and observances of the visible church in the affective and collective life of the godly community, a community that remained the true focus of Etherington's attention and loyalty throughout his career. As we have seen, Etherington had retained the familist tendency to spiritualise the external forms of religious worship, in particular the sacraments, and here his 'familism' served to compound what Geoffrey Nuttall has described as the insistent spiritualising tendency within the entire puritan project.[13] Thus Etherington's familist-tinged position changed the balance between the word, the spirit and the external ordinances of the church that mainstream puritans like Denison were struggling so hard to maintain. In Etherington's hands that balance was shifted sharply away from the forms and authorities of the church and ministry and sharply towards the triad of word, spirit and individual believer out of which was constituted, in Etherington's view, the community of the godly, a group that he did indeed equate with the true church. As Denison discovered, this had unfortunate effects for the authority and status of even the puritan clergy.

Paradoxically, however, what one might at first take to be a radical move towards what Professor Davis has called, writing of a somewhat later period, anti-formalism, did not have conventionally 'radical' puritan consequences.[14] On the contrary, it was precisely the radically desacralising, spiritualising impact of his familism on the external forms and structures of the visible church (up to and including the sacraments) that cured Etherington of his separatist or puritan scruples about conformity and allowed him to leave all such outward things to the authority of the Christian prince and his episcopal agents. In short, in Etherington's case, familism pushed him towards conformity and allowed him to adopt wholesale not only the limited, moderate puritan, but the full-scale Whitgiftian case for conformity, a case conceived in terms of the inherent indifference of the outward ceremonial and institutional forms of the church and the inherent legitimacy of the public authority which defined and enforced those forms. Here was a position which allowed him to outbid even conforming puritans like Denison as a loyal conformist son of the English church and yet left him ample room to challenge their opinions whenever he felt they had gone beyond the warrant of scripture or encroached on the spiritual prerogatives or liberties of the godly.

In so doing, Etherington was able to muster basic assumptions and arguments and to exploit and exacerbate major tensions and contradictions within Denison's own position. Since, for all Denison's fuss about the anabaptist and familist nature of Etherington's thought, it seems clear that, throughout his career, Etherington's own position had been developed in constant tension and dialogue with, had indeed, in some sense, been developed out of, ideological materials supplied by the mainstream puritan tradition purveyed by the likes of Stephen Denison.

In Etherington, then, Denison was confronted with some of the unwanted and unintended consequences of his own position, or rather of that position as it had been assimilated and adapted for his own particular purposes by an active, assertive and ultimately antagonistic member of the laity. For in launching his critique of Denison's doctrine Etherington was, in fact, marshalling arguments and assumptions taken from the very centre of Denison's own position. And he did so in the the 1620s, at least, not as some self-proclaimed familist outsider but as, in the eyes of many, a member of the charmed circle of puritan godliness, a rival claimant for the very ideological terrain within the English church that Denison had come habitually to regard as his own. In Etherington many of the points of tension, ambiguity and potential contradiction, inherent in Denison's own structural and ideological relationship both with the English church and with the godly community, had come back to haunt him. Etherington's sceptical gaze fell, in particular, on precisely the three areas where Denison had tried hardest to attach his potentially very divisive vision of the godly community to the overarching structures of the national church. For Denison habitually sought to perform that task through his insistence on three scriptural ordinances – word, sacrament and sabbath – that he placed at the centre of his vision of true religion. Now here was Etherington undermining those crucial controls and containments. He pushed Denison's view of the sacraments just one step further – now they not only did not confer, they did not even confirm grace. He challenged the clerical monopoly on the definition and dissemination of right doctrine and he directly assaulted Denison's version of the role of sabbath observance in a properly regulated church and a balanced style of piety.

In so doing, Etherington was also addressing wider tendencies and tensions within puritan thought and experience. Here the paradigmatic case was Etherington's treatment of the sabbath, which, as we have seen, he directly related to a crisis of conscience caused amongst at least some of the laity by the extremity of Denison's sabbatarianism. We know, from other sources, that extreme sabbatarianism was a disruptive force amongst the godly of London. On the one hand, Nehemiah Wallington salivated over the awful ends visited upon those who broke the sabbath. On the other, Edward Brerewood and Richard Byfield debated the supposedly subversive effects of extreme sabbatarian doctrines like Denison's on relations between masters and servants. Etherington's position cut through all these difficulties in what seemed to Denison, admittedly writing in 1641, to be dangerously antinomian ways. First, like the closet familist he was, Etherington had spiritualised the sabbath, mistaking a physical and a temporal rest for an eternal and spiritual one. Then, by applying a number of scriptural texts (Acts 15, Gal. 4, Col. 2) to the moral instead of to the ceremonial law, he had left 'Christians free as touching their consciences in all such respects'. This rendered the sabbath a merely human ordinance; 'the observation of the Lord's day was taken up freely and then it is a free observation and not by force of any commandment of the law or the gospel'. To view the sabbath thus was to bring 'in a plain will worship' and to set up Etherington's ultimate claim that 'the observation of the sabbath as pressed by our divines' was 'a burden like them in Amos 8 "when will the sabbath be past"'.

In thus taking up the issue of the sabbath Etherington was addressing an area of disturbance and discord caused amongst the godly by the strenuous style and rigorous legalism of puritan preaching. True here at least to his familist phase, Etherington was offering to free the godly from the rigours of that legalism, offering them instead the spiritual liberty of Christians freed from the toils of Jewish servitude to the ceremonial law. The result for Denison was licence not liberty, antinomian chaos not Christian order. 'You would have no duties pressed for the observation of the Lord's day, neither prayer nor preaching nor coming to the sacrament and the like; neither any outward work to be forbidden, but Christians to be left free to do what they list'. 'Is this your sabbath?' Denison asked contemptuously. 'Then keep it to yourselves and to your faction's company. Christians have not so learned Christ.'[15]

It was as though Etherington were holding up a subtly distorting mirror to Denison's own opinions and practices. Confronted with the result, Denison clearly did not like what he saw there one little bit.

ETHERINGTON, DENISON AND 'ANTINOMIANISM'

One might, indeed, see Etherington's position on repentance and justification in a precisely similar light. As we have seen, for Etherington (following here both T.L. and William Chibald) repentance was a prerequisite for, a necessary precursor of, justification and remission of sins, both of which, he insisted, were once and for all divine acts, instantaneous and coterminous with the first gift of justifying faith. On Etherington's view, justification and remission were entirely separable from the subsequent process of sanctification or repentance (as some divines persisted in calling it) and his insistence on this point, made against what he took to be Denison and Roborough's very different view of these issues might be construed as a move to free true believers from the rigours of an excessive puritan legalism and moralism; a legalism which made assurance dependent upon the ethical endeavours, the good works and repentance, of the individual, during the long-drawn-out process of sanctification. If such people did, in effect, equate assurance with saving faith (as Chibald and Etherington clearly thought that they did), then, at least on the existential level, on which the individual believer experienced the affective consequences of these doctrines, this rendered the conviction of justification, and hence of salvation, entirely dependent on the experience of sanctification. Was Etherington responding here to the same crises of faith and spiritual despair induced in the laity by the demands of Denison's style of practical divinity that had prompted Chibald's book of 1623? Have we, perhaps, found a clue here to the identity of those nameless divines whose explication of the doctrine of true justifying faith had so upset T.L. in 1592? It was, after all, extremely unlikely that he had been referring then to a battery of Peter Baro lookalikes. Attacking Baro, who was already under considerable pressure from the godly for his predestinarian opinions, may have been a way of at once disseminating and disguising T.L.'s real message and real target, in much the same way as Chibald used a nameless group of Lutherans to disguise the real objects of his later polemic on the same subject. Was that target, in fact, the misplaced legalism of puritan divines, who in the 1580s and 1590s, were in the process of developing the very style of practical divinity now being pumped out so assiduously through the pulpit and press by men like Stephen Denison?[16] As with the sabbath, Etherington may well have been seeking once again to free the consciences of justified Christians from yet another aspect of puritan legalism.

Was there, in fact, just a hint here of an emergent 'antinomian' critique of puritan legalism? Such a development would fit well enough with Etherington's own intellectual history and in particular with some of the trajectories inherent in both T.L.'s thought and in familism as Etherington had espoused it. Moreover, it would also speak to what we know of the immediate polemical and intellectual context of the later 1620s, when other critics of the legalist strand in puritan divinity were becoming increasingly vocal and aggressive and consequently coming under attack as 'antinomians' or 'familists'.

And here, Denison's heresy-hunting proclivities provide us with some other key examples of these connections and developments. Sensitised, by his contacts with Etherington, to the presence of sectarian heterodoxy in the godly's midst, it would appear that Denison went on to make something of a career as a heresy hunter. There is, in the state papers, endorsed on the back by Laud himself, a two-page epitome of opinions supposedly expressed in the pulpit at St Michael's Cornhill in December 1630 by one 'Mr Nye' (almost certainly Philip Nye). The opinions were of a decidedly antinomian tinge. Thus Nye was at least alleged to have said that sins 'unmortified and unpardoned' may yet 'stand with our claim and interest in God. For a man must claim God to be his God, before his sins be mortified. And lay claim to Christ whilst he is in sins.' 'For God is not our God because we believe in him, but he is first our God and therefore we believe in him'. Admittedly 'in qualification' of these claims Nye had added that 'a man must be turned in heart from his sins, though he be in his sin and have newly acted it' before he could thus call on Christ. However, this merely meant that he should 'want to be reformed, though he be not reformed'. Was this one reading of the way in which repentance could be said to come before justification? As Nye explained in a follow-up sermon, 'if thy heart be turned against sin, thou mayest come with as much boldness to the throne of grace as if thou hadst not sinned'. 'After conversion', Nye went on, 'a man may sin again and again and carry his sin to his grave, and never be able to shake it off, and yet be the child of God.' 'A man may call God his God before his sins be pardoned, for his sins may be said to be pardoned in respect of God's decree.' 'Look upon the justice of God as thy justice', Nye allegedly told his auditory, 'that being one with Christ, whatsoever God hath done by Christ, thou hast done.' Nye had professed in the initial sermon that 'I dare say one act of faith brings more honour to God, than performing of that virtue which is opposite to that sin which he doth admit.' 'Though thou dishonourest God by sins, yet thou makest recompense by trusting and believing in him.' He followed this up with the subsequent remark that 'if thy sins be never so many for number or great for nature, yet let them trust, for faith is like the ark, though the waters be never so high, it will rise above the top of all'.

As with so much antinomian-sounding rant, if one were being charitable, one might gloss much of this as merely a rhetorically overblown or extreme statement of core protestant doctrines like justification by faith *alone* or *absolute* predestination. But if not flagrantly heterodox, in a London puritan scene now echoing to the sound of genuine antinomianism, and in a wider context of alarm at the rise of Arminianism, this was, at the very least, inflammatory. And certainly Nye's performance seems to have attracted the opprobrium of the godly, Denison amongst them. For at the bottom of the document a note was appended to the effect that 'these things and such like delivered by Mr Nye were so foul and so much disliked that Mr Dr Denison, an able and worthy divine, did preach diverse sermons against them'.[17] The role of a freelance monitor of orthodoxy, a sort of unofficial censor without portfolio, that Denison had taken on in the campaign against Etherington, was clearly one to which he was now wedded.

And we can see him pursuing the same career in a campaign waged the previous year against a preacher called Peter Shaw. His signature (followed by the large letters DD – it was clearly an honour of which he was quite inordinately proud) appears appended with two others at the end of a series of articles headed 'positions of Mr Shaw'. Shaw, who, it was claimed, 'preaches in Crooked Lane on Wednesday at five o'clock at night', was charged with a melange of assertions and doctrines, all of them of an antinomian, and some even of a familist, tone and tendency. At a sermon on 26 November 1628 he was accused of claiming that 'a believer is dead to the law as a ... servant which is made free from his master is no longer under his command or power'. 'He that thinks his disobedience or not observing any of God's commandments makes him farther from God or can stand between him and life, he puts Christ from him and is a legalist, a moralist, no Christian.' 'Sanctification and holiness is no part of the form of a Christian.' 'A believer is not bound to do anything as the way to life for he is quite free from all doing in that respect because Christ hath fulfilled all the law for him.' Even more sensationally other witnesses claimed to have heard Shaw maintain that 'what sin soever a believer commits, as adultery, murder etc., or how oft soever iterated, yet he is no further from God but hath as much interest in God and right to heaven as the most sanctified man in the world'. It was presumably on this basis that Shaw felt able to claim that 'they are idiots and fools that are not assured of their salvation at all times'.

On 4 Febuary 1628/29 Shaw was accused of saying that 'a believer hath the same holiness with Christ and that not imputed holiness only but inherent' and that 'there is no special difference betwixt the holiness of Christ and a believer'. Indeed two other witnesses claimed that they had heard Shaw assert, in typical familist style, that 'a Christian is so Christed with Christ and Godded with God that he is as Christ before God'. On the issue of the authority and meaning of scripture, Shaw distinguished between 'the material and the formal parts'. The former was 'the letter or bare words as they are written in our bibles which, he said, was not the word of God, nor was it able or powerful to be the rule of sanctification'. 'The formal part only was the word of God and this contained the mind and meaning of Christ, expounded as he was a prophet.' From hence he concluded that 'unless a man had the full and perfect understanding of the mind of Christ, the scriptures were not the word of God' and 'the words of scripture pronounced by a divine without the mind of Christ were none of his word, no more than the words of a philosopher were'. Thus 'the reading in the bible, hearing of sermons or meditating upon the matter of the word was unable, insufficient etc. to do a man any good or comfort, but it was only the knowing of the mind of Christ that did it'. Preaching these singular doctrines, complained the puritan divine Nathaniel Walker, Shaw 'hath begot such a faction that, if he preach not, his followers have refused upon the Sundays to hear either sermons or divine prayer, but rest at home'.[18]

There was, moreover, something of a familist tinge to all this. As we have seen, looking back from the 1640s, Etherington had claimed that there had been an intermittent familist presence in the city throughout the early seventeenth century, with familist views being preached by, amongst others, one Shaw. There was that tell-tale reference, in the views attributed to Shaw's followers, to being Christed with Christ and Godded with God.[19] There was a decidedly perfectionist tinge to some of the rhetoric imputed to Shaw and his alleged tendency to spiritualise the scripture, restricting true understanding to those who knew the mind of Christ, was surely reminiscent of familism.

But, by the same token, it is clear that Nye and Etherington's, and certainly Chibald's, positions were all logical extensions and developments of stock puritan and Calvinist notions and arguments. The same might be said of many of Shaw's opinions, albeit in his case the process of development had clearly been carried to distorting extremes, as even a cursory comparison between the opinions attributed to Nye and those attributed to Shaw reveal. While there were distinct affinities between the two men's doctrinal claims and indeed between the tone and locution of their statements, Shaw had clearly gone far beyond the pale of orthodoxy in ways that Nye had not. Similarly, Shaw's reported views far exceeded in the crudity and extremism of their antinomianism anything that can be attributed to John Etherington. As we shall see below, in the 1640s, Etherington went out of his way to close down this sort of familist or antinomian reading of his own position. Nye, too, provided a reading of his preaching style that enabled him plausibly to escape from the more extreme conclusions implied by his somewhat inflated language. 'We must be logicians in our doctrines', he intoned, 'but orators in application for the scripture use to imply impossibilities'.[20]

The point here is thus not to argue that Etherington, Nye and, still less, Chibald *were* antinomians, as were say Traske or Eaton or Shaw. Thus, just like T.L., Etherington and Chibald, Traske argued that repentance preceded justification but he then went on to insist that repentance ceased with justification, freeing the justified Christian from the toils of the law. Here was the crucial move and not even T.L. or Etherington, let alone Chibald, made it. Etherington and Chibald's preoccupation with the impact and affective consequences of puritan legalism and their consequent concern with the relations between repentance and justification and justification and sanctification certainly did not render them antinomians. But it did speak to, indeed was part of, precisely the same emotional and cultural conjuncture within puritan piety that was producing genuine antinomians. Thus what Chibald,

Etherington, Nye and Shaw did have in common was a reaction against, perhaps even an exploitation of, certain pastoral and spiritual tensions induced in the godly community by the extremities of puritan legalism as it was being preached by ministers like Denison. And on this basis one could surely posit a line of development running from say T.L., Chibald and Etherington's account of the relations between repentance, justification and remission to Shaw's altogether more radical claims that 'sanctification and obedience ... is no part of the form of a Christian' or that 'faith is not a grace nor any part of sanctification'.[21] And behind Etherington and T.L., of course, lurked the spectre and influence of H.N. As Professor Bozeman and David Como are in the process of proving, what was at stake here was the emergence, out of a godly reaction against puritan legalism and moralism, of a fully fledged antinomian critique of reformed orthodoxy; a critique composed, in part, of familist and other impulses and ideas brought in from outside the mainstream puritan tradition and grafted onto concepts and debates intrinsic to that tradition, to form a new, radically antinomian synthesis.[22]

On this view, then, the extremity of their reaction to Chibald, Etherington and Nye, was not only a function of the paranoid aggression of Stephen Denison and George Walker (paranoid and aggressive though they undoubtedly were). On the contrary, it was an entirely understandable response to a gathering challenge from within the godly community to what such men took to be orthodox doctrine and true religion. On this view, therefore, in Etherington we are not just dealing with the peculiar insights and claims of a natural eccentric or barrack-room lawyer, the ravings of a lone, last torch-carrier for the insights of T.L. or the inflamed language of H.N., but with issues and questions that spoke to the wider concerns and worries of the London godly.

Spats like those between Etherington and Denison, between Chibald and his critics or Shaw and his accusers, need, in short, to be seen as parts of a wider dialectical process of challenge and response that was inherent to the puritan impulse. There was a continual tracking back and forth here between formal doctrinal cruxes and debates, various pastoral devices and pulpit poses, and the personal and spiritual responses and crises of the laity. Here the *locus classicus* was, of course, Chibald's critique of central strands in puritan practical divinity which, if Chibald is to be believed, was prompted by certain pastoral dilemmas and spiritual crises consequent upon the standard puritan rendition of the doctrines of assurance and sanctification. Etherington's critique of Denison's sabbatarianism, of course, followed precisely the same pattern. Where, on the one hand, godly professors had been driven to despair by their inability to keep the sabbath, as the likes of Denison claimed it should be kept, so, on the other, weak Christians had been driven to a like distraction by their failure to achieve or sustain an assurance of salvation of the sort equated by the likes of Denison with a true saving faith. Of course, many puritans (both clerical and lay) sought to respond to the resulting angst within the conventions, the emotional forms and theoretical formulas, that made up puritan practical divinity and doctrinal orthodoxy. But, it seems, the spiritual experience of the godly was beginning regularly to push up against the limits of conventional wisdom, confronting the arbiters of orthodoxy with what came to appear, to some observers, as the unacceptable subjective or emotional consequences of reformed orthodoxy and puritan practical divinity. In short, the internal spiritual dynamic of puritan religion was posing questions for the godly – ministers and lay people alike – that were increasingly difficult to answer within the confines of what passed, in puritan circles, for doctrinal orthodoxy. This led both Chibald and Etherington to enter the realm of formal doctrine where they began to modify and mitigate the content of 'orthodoxy' itself. They did so in order to remove what they had come to see as the basic theoretical mistakes that were causing the spiritual sufferings of the laity. And where they had led, others like Nye and eventually Shaw, a true antinomian if ever there was one, proved all too ready to follow.

STEPHEN DENISON AND THE LOCAL (DOCTRINAL) EFFECTS OF THE RISE OF LAUDIANISM

If, throughout the 1620s, Denison continued to pursue the same polemical strategy that he had employed against Etherington at the Cross, continuing to act, in his attacks on Nye and Shaw, as something of an arbiter of orthodoxy in the city, the attendant polemical and political circumstances did not remain anything like as congenial as they had been when he had started his campaign against the boxmaker in 1625. It was, after all, one thing to pursue Etherington through the early 1620s when Denison still had friends in high places, like Sir Henry Martin, who were able both to ease his way through the church courts and, through the good offices of Sir Robert Harley, to intercede in his favour at court. These, after all, were events that took place in a church presided over by George Abbot, a man whose doctrinal views were very close to those of Denison himself. A doctor of divinity, with friends in high places in the city – his first Paul's Cross sermon of 1619 had, as we have seen, been dedicated to the Lord Mayor – an intimate of wealthy merchants like the Juxons, Denison was well connected in both the local and national establishments, almost a perfect example, in fact, of that integration of really quite aggressively puritan attitudes and mores into the power structures of Jacobean society that has featured so prominently in recent accounts of the early Stuart church. Given all this, it is small wonder that Denison won his altercation with Etherington.

It was, however, an open question as to whether tactics which had carried all before them in the church of George Abbot would prove as successful in a church now ruled by Charles I and increasingly dominated by William Laud.

For as the Jacobean ecclesiastical dispensation gradually gave way to the Caroline in the late 1620s, the political and ideological climate became decidedly colder for the likes of Stephen Denison. We can see how this worked if we look more closely at the nature of the proceedings against poor Peter Shaw. The documents in which these are recorded consist of a set of court articles, some sermon notes taken by William Watts from two of Shaw's sermons and a letter which purported to have been written by one of Shaw's supporters. These were all put together in a file of papers that may well constitute the formal charges lodged against Shaw in High Commission.[23] Though the records of that court do not survive, we can infer that Shaw was tried and suspended by High Commission from Laud's comments during later proceedings against another antinomian preacher, Samuel Pretty, in 1631. Then apparently Laud explained that he 'spake the less in this cause (as he intimated) because there had been so much said against these same and the like tenets in the causes of one [Robert] Townes and one Mr Shaw'.[24]

Each article or opinion was attested to by a number of witnesses, many, but not all of them, London clergymen. The names appended to the charges represented a remarkable coalition of moderate and radical puritan divines and up and coming Laudians. It is perhaps unsurprising that we find at the forefront of the campaign against Shaw the ministers Brian Walton, William Brough, William Watts and Christopher Dow, all of whom were to emerge during the 1630s as enthusiastic supporters of Laudian policies and rabid anti-puritans. For these Laudian clerics, Shaw's eccentric opinions were simply extrapolations outward from the central pieties and platitudes of puritan divinity. Accordingly, these men appear to have been the most eager witnesses in the case. Walton personally signed eight articles, while William Watts provided detailed notes of two separate sermons.

Strikingly, however, the forces aligned against Shaw were not limited to such men. Denison himself figured amongst the deponents as did his lay henchmen from the campaign against Etherington, the joiners Rowland Thomson and Thomas Rogers. Also involved were Andrew Castleton, rector of St Martin Ironmonger Lane; Richard Culverwell, rector of St Margaret Moses and Nathaniel Walker, a career London lecturer. All these men came from puritan stock and carried godly associations, but there were others involved in the campaign whose puritan credentials were even more striking. Thus Cornelius Burgess, the incumbent at St Magnus, James Nalton, curate of St Mary Colechurch, and Elias Crabtree, perpetual curate of St Lawrence Pountney all shopped Shaw to Laudian authorities. And yet, within a year or two, all three of them, together with Denison, were to be in trouble with those same authorities for a variety of overtly non-conformist and anti-Laudian actions and gestures.[25]

Alongside these prominent puritans turned informers we can set the more obscure figure of one 'A. Grame', who is identified in the dossier as the recipient of an anonymous and threatening letter from one of Shaw's lay followers. This Grame appears to be the Abraham Grame alias Grymes, identified as a lecturer in Denison's parish of St Katharine Cree, and suspended by Laud in October 1630 for derogatory comments, made in the pulpit at St Martin-in-the-Fields, against bowing at the name of Jesus. Grame's suspension was relaxed in December 1630, but this was merely the beginning of his legal woes. In May 1633 he and three others were fined £20 by the High Commission for failure to appear to answer certain unspecified articles. The nature of Grame's offences can be surmised from certain later articles against him preserved in the Tanner Manuscripts. There he was accused of endorsing statements made by his brother Samuel against the surplice and to the effect that 'if it were in his power he would throw all the bishops of this land out of their places and put honest men in their stead'. He was also accused of retelling a story in which Laud was called to his face 'the tail of the great beast'.[26]

These, then, were decidedly odd bedfellows for the likes of Dow, Walton and Watts. Admittedly, the puritan divines played a less prominent role in the official proceedings against Shaw than did the Laudians. Nalton signed off on only two articles, Culverwell and Walker on three each; Burgess was only responsible for one and, unlike many of the more enthusiastic of Shaw's accusers, never signed any of the articles. Grame opted not to produce articles against Shaw and limited his involvement to turning over the threatening letter to the authorities. Denison, Crabtree and Castleton did not, in fact, provide any damningly detailed information against Shaw, instead attesting vaguely that, in addition to his doctrinal 'errors', he was a 'very unprofitable preacher', who affected 'uncouth and strange phrases' unfounded in scripture.[27]

Compared to the heinous heresies of which Shaw was accused elsewhere in the document this was anodyne stuff. But if there was a marked contrast between Denison's rather weedy one article of complaint against Shaw and the multiple articles and sermon notes assembled by Watts and his friends, there was almost as great a contrast between Denison's distinctly muted performance before the High Commission against Shaw and his stentorian denunciation of Nye's far less overtly heterodox views in the 'diverse sermons', reported in the state papers. Just as in the case of Etherington, it would appear that Denison's preferred mode was the pulpit diatribe, his favourite milieu the godly community and his judicial authority of choice the court of godly opinion rather than the court of High Commission.[28]

Indeed, there is evidence, contained within the articles against Shaw, to imply that the official proceedings undertaken by the High Commission were something of a last resort, the culmination of a long-standing intra-puritan effort to discipline and control, if not to silence, Shaw. Thus, at several points it was noted that 'after admonition' by William Boswell, the vicar of St Lawrence Old Jewry, Shaw 'delivered the same again'. But, as in the earlier cases involving Etherington, Wotton and Walker, these meetings were by no means solely clerical affairs. Several of Shaw's more heterodox statements on Christ's nature were recorded as 'gathered from his mouth at home' by one John Wilson and countersigned by Mr Palmer in Pater Noster Row. Particularly significant here was the role of Denison's two joiners, Thomson and Rogers, both veterans of the campaign against Etherington. As their involvement might be taken to imply, Denison's behind-the-scenes role in the intra-puritan effort to ride herd on Shaw may well have been considerably greater than his own rather indeterminate article in the court papers suggests. For, in addition to Thomson and Rogers, others of those active against Shaw had connections with Denison. Richard Culverwell was shortly to appear as a clerical compurgator for Denison in his own showdown with the High Commission. And, as we have seen, Abraham Grame, who had himself denounced Shaw, Denison-style, from the pulpit of St Helen's near Bishopsgate, was serving as a lecturer at St Katharine Cree at precisely this time.[29]

But if Denison and his friends were prominent in the puritan efforts to control Shaw they were far less so in the High Commission case, which was left, as we have seen, in large part to the likes of Watts and Dow. In short, Denison's rather equivocal, arguably pusillanimous, behaviour here may be a product of his attempt to square a particularly difficult polemical circle. For, on the one hand, the repeated claims made by Laudians and anti-puritans that all Calvinist doctrine was antinomian in its effects and implications, made ganging up on Shaw a relatively attractive proposition. What better way to vindicate oneself from such claims, while yet retaining one's credibility with the mainstream godly, many of whom were themselves the subjects of Shaw's contempt for their supposed legalism and moralism? And yet, as he had presumably learnt from his dealings with Etherington, there was a certain price of disapproval, of decreased standing amongst at least some of the godly, to be paid for denouncing one of their number, even when in error, to the authorities. Indeed, the situation was rendered the more delicate by the fact that if Arminians accused Calvinists of antinomianism, antinomians, like Shaw, tended to present their position as the only really reliable way to oppose Arminianism. Those legalist puritan preachers who would not go the whole hog with the antinomians were thus open to the charge of being closet Arminians, godly sell-outs to the prelatical party now in control of the church. Thus, at one point Nathaniel Walker noted that Shaw's 'followers vilify and defame all other ministers, clamouring that because Mr Shaw cuts off the root of the Arminians, ergo it is, that all the ministers of the city oppose him, for they are all tainted with Arminianism'.[30] And, insofar as opinions like those attributed to Shaw, and to a lesser extent even to Nye, did indeed represent a sort of hyper-Calvinism, a super-predestinarian inflation of common doctrines of perseverance and sanctification, of free grace and justification by faith alone, there was something to such claims.

The words cited by Walker had been, it was claimed, 'spoken by Mr Joseph Smith in Bishopsgate street' and it was presumably the same Joseph Smith of Bishopsgate Street who wrote an anonymous and threatening letter to Abraham Grame. The letter is a remarkable document that reveals just how divisive these affairs could be for the London godly.

> Since my coming to town [Smith claimed] I understand that a great quarrel is most cunningly contrived and fomented between you and one Shaw, who is a man strangely reported of. And that you begin to article against him and he the like against you. The truth is I am solicited to be a witness against you. I profess myself to be none of his disciples for, so far as I can judge by your sermons, he is a most erroneous fellow. But, accidentally hearing you at St Ellen's near Bishopsgate, I happened afterwards to repeat some passages which you had delivered and now I am told that I must justify the report which, in regard it is against a minister I conceive so well of, I am loath to do and yet know not how to avoid. Therefore, I give you this private advertisement beforehand, as a cordial friend, to wish you to be very cautelous in the managing of this business. You may, perhaps, do him a displeasure, if all be true that I hear, but be sure ... you will be called to an account, not only for breach of a canon which forbids pulpit's opposition, but also for far greater things, laid to your charge, which, if they should be proved, would crush you to pieces. And, if they be not proved, you must expect to be crushed for the other, whereof I would God there were not proof too much. Sir, mistake me not, I am no bugbear, set on by art to give you a false alarm. If I might safely do it, you should not only have known my name but have seen my face err this, but I cannot yet safely do it, unless I could meet you in some private place, where neither of us are known. I do profess that I love you, as you may one day know. There is no creature under heaven privy to this act of mine, nor shall be, if you be wise for yourself. Therefore, let me tell you, the plot is laid for you. You shall have all fair audience until you have done your utmost against Shaw and, so soon as that is done, you shall be the next man that shall taste of the severity of justice, as some in great place have already discussed and professed. Your best and safest course will be instantly to retire out of the city, either for health's sake or to pursue some preferment, as may fairly be pretended, so you may come off fairly enough if you please. You want not a wit to direct you to plausible excuses for your desisting. If you have interest in any that can prevail with your adversary, Shaw, use them and make a peace, for he is set on as well as you and both by common envyings to the gospel. Count it not wisdom to run on because you have engaged yourself. Reserve yourself for better times ... Tis that Arminians and papists gape for, to see the puritans, as they term you, to dash themselves in pieces one against another. If you surcease and leave the town for a while fools perhaps may cast it in your teeth but wise men will commend you. I could willingly disclose more to you, but I dare not. A word to a wise man is sufficient.[31]

Heading for the high ground

All in all, this was a remarkable performance. In many ways it confirms the picture of the internal workings of the godly community that can be gleaned from the proceedings against Etherington and Shaw, described above. A suspicious prowling around a man's doctrine, a consequent growth of suspicion and animosity between the parties, eavesdropping on sermons to fish for doubtful statements and pronouncements, drawing up lists of errors or articles of denunciation and challenge, tentative contacts between friends of the main principles, worries about tearing the delicate fabric of puritan unity and fellowship and the use that might be made of such indiscretions by the enemies of the godly, consequent attempts to use mutual friends and contacts to manufacture 'a peace' – all these were in evidence here, just as they were in the interactions between Denison and Etherington and indeed between Shaw and at least some of his accusers.

But in this case the intervention of the authorities, the 'plots' of 'some in great place' and the malign purposes of 'Arminians and papists' in seeking to exacerbate and exploit the divisions of the godly were invoked as a strong disincentive to proceed further with the case. Here the authorities are no longer represented by Denison's friend Sir Henry Martin and George Abbot, the sterlingly Calvinist archbishop of Canterbury, but by other nameless but altogether less sympathetic figures, represented on the ground, no doubt, by the very well-connected likes of Christopher Dow and Brian Walton. Instead of a necessary defence of the canons of Calvinist orthodoxy against sectarian excess, of the sort Denison claimed to have undertaken against Etherington and no doubt thought that he was repeating in his efforts against Shaw and Nye, we have a machiavellian attempt by a hostile Arminian authority to divide and rule the godly, exploiting their divisions for polemical purposes, while picking off their leading ministers one by one. If the recipient of this letter wanted to preserve his job and his reputation with the godly he was left in no doubt as to the appropriate course of action – he should skip town and wait for 'better times'.

With its cloak and dagger asides – the recipient was told at one point to 'burn this letter' – Smith's missive was a wonderfully crude attempt at intimidation. As such, the letter's current provenance in the state papers strongly implies that it failed; a judgement much confirmed by the observation scribbled on the bottom of the document to the effect that 'Mr Joseph Smith in Bishopsgate Street is conjectured to be the author or factor in this letter because his wife proffered 20s to one to steal it out of my study.' However, if the missive's transparently intimidatory purpose means that we cannot accept its claims about official conspiracies to exploit the internal divisions of the godly as simply true, the very fact that a letter couched in these terms was sent at all, and that the author felt that the subtle and not so subtle hints and nudges about official plots and Arminian conspiracies were at all credible, tells us much about godly perceptions of the changed political and polemical circumstances of the late 1620s. The shift in the balance of power in the church was changing fundamentally the circumstances in which such exchanges amongst the godly were taking place. The rise of Arminianism placed considerable pressure on puritans, confronting them with an overtly hostile authority armed with an aggressively conformist and coherently anti-Calvinist ideology that forced them to define their own doctrinal position more clearly against a series of anti-Calvinist accusations and caricatures, just as it made such self-definition an altogether more politically dangerous position.[32]

For, as we have seen, antinomianism was not merely a key Arminian caricature of puritan predestinarianism, a polemically motivated fantasy, it was also one way, albeit an extreme one, to respond to Arminian theology, cranking up the rhetoric of free grace, gratuitous election, justification by faith alone in order definitively to close down any Arminianising tendencies in one's own position. In other words, the impact of Arminianism served greatly to increase the impulse within certain sorts of puritan divinity towards antinomianism at precisely the same time that it accused all such divinity of being, at bottom, antinomian.

Even Denison himself, while no antinomian, appears not to have been immune to the distorting effects of the rise of Arminianism on his own position. We can gain some idea of how this worked from a list of really rather extreme opinions on predestination that Etherington had culled from Denison's sermons preached at 'Creechurch and Great All Hallows while he was reviling and scandalising of me', that is, in the mid- to late 1620s. Denison had said, Etherington alleged, that 'God did preordain that Adam should fall and break his commandment'; that 'God is not only a spectator but a powerful agent in sin'; 'that when God, to prove Abraham, commanded him to offer his son for a sacrifice, he commanded him to murder him and to break the sixth commandment'; 'that the Israelites, in taking such things of the Egyptians as they in favour let them have, did steal from them and break the eighth commandment and that God did approve of the breach thereof'.[33]

Of course, not all puritans or Calvinists responded to the challenge of Arminianism by coarsening their position in this way. Some divines, like Joseph Hall, Robert Sanderson, John Davenant, Samuel Ward and, on the puritan side, even John Cotton, responded by modifying and softening their doctrines of divine sovereignty and providence, of election and reprobation.[34] But others, like some of the Dutch Contra remonstrants and, on this evidence at least, Stephen Denison (and in a rather different way, Philip Nye), replied by simply restating the central facts of divine sovereignty and human impotence with ever greater brutality and directness. In this view of the world, since the law itself was a product of the divine will, that will could not be bound by the dictates of the law and apparent infractions of the moral law by God's sovereign actions could occasion no complaint or demand any explication or explanation. The correct human response to the brutal exercise of divine sovereignty was, on Denison's account, awe and worship not complaint or moral queasiness, while, on Nye's, it was a desperate yet joyfully immediate recourse to the throne of grace. In such statements Denison (and Nye) were surely, in part at least, flexing their doctrinal muscles against the Arminianism now notoriously present in a variety of high places. In so doing they were clearly pushing the paradoxes at the heart of the reformed position to breaking point, and, in the process, if Etherington's complaints against Denison and Denison's against Nye are anything to go by, alarming sections of the very godly constituency that they were trying to reassure with these bullish displays of Calvinist machismo. On this account, Denison's propensity to act as the Calvinist thought police, enforcing what he took to be orthodoxy, even as some of his own statements pushed against certain constructions of 'orthodoxy's' edges, represents a classic instance of what one might term transference – a process whereby difficulties and dangers in one's own position could be read into the performances and utterances of others, where they could be safely excoriated and denounced, all the while leaving the central tenets and features of one's own position relatively untouched. This, I have argued, was what Denison had been doing to Etherington and he was surely doing it again to Nye and even to Shaw.

In the short term these changes to the London puritan scene do not seem to have worked to Denison's detriment. Indeed, in the context of his immediate confrontation with Etherington, they even operated to his advantage. At first, things had looked less than promising. After all, in the late 1620s that same national struggle for power to which *The white wolf* had been intended as a contribution was being decided in favour of the very Arminians whom Denison had attempted to equate in his sermon with both the papists and the anabaptists. Etherington was entitled to hope that the changing balance of power at court might operate to his advantage and at least get him out of jail where he was still languishing even after his humiliation at the Cross. Of course, as his book of 1623 showed, he himself was a Calvinist with nothing but contempt for Arminianism but he could at least hope that the enemy of his enemy would be his friend and, anyway, he had a personal connection to Bishop Richard Neile, whom he had been advising on the construction of a water conduit for his episcopal palace at Bishop's Auckland immediately before his arrest.

Their initial discussions completed, Etherington had just arranged another interview to discuss the scheme further with Neile when 'this unexpected sentence was passed against me' and his subsequent imprisonment prevented him from keeping the appointment. Etherington now wrote to Neile giving him to understand the cause thereof (for he was not at the court when I was censured) and requesting his favourable help to relieve me, who hereupon, with the Bishop of Rochester [John Buckeridge], took the matter into their consideration and began to commiserate my case, so that when my petitions of complaint came to the court they were willing to have them read and moved for me to the archbishop that things should be yet further examined according to my request. Whereupon the matter was referred unto them and I acknowledge they took pains therein and were very willing to relieve me, perceiving that I was wronged and, as they found the falsehood of the accusations and of the depositions of the witnesses, caused the register to write them down.[35]

In judging Etherington's case the likes of Neile and Buckeridge were subject to contradictory ideological pressures. On the one hand, they were likely to have little sympathy for 'Etherington the sect master' and if Denison could convince them that the boxmaker really had kept a conventicle and earnt his living as some sort of lay prophet, Etherington's goose would be well and truly cooked. On the other hand, given the recent tribulations of their friend and client Richard Montague, Neile and his friends had very personal reasons for scepticism when confronted by the sort of puritan/Calvinist heresy hunting that suffused *The white wolf*.[36] Moreover, given their own doctrinal preferences, Denison's charges of Arminian heresy were unlikely to cut very much ice with Neile and Buckeridge who, on this basis, might prove only too willing to believe Etherington's presentation of himself as a victim of the sort of puritan extremism and high-handedness that equated the errant Calvinism of a narrow faction with the official doctrinal position of the church of England. On that issue, at least, Etherington's critique of Denison and his followers' pretensions echoed very closely the broader analysis of the contemporary theological scene put forward, amidst such controversy, by Neile's client Richard Montague.

But just as the commissioners, led by Neile and his friend John Cosin, were on the point of releasing Etherington from jail, Denison 'moved the bishops with another point, not in the sentence, concerning baptism'. The point at issue, Etherington conceded, 'I could not deny but endeavoured to maintain for a truth and they much opposed me in and alleged the words of the book of common prayer, that God had sanctified the flood of Jordan and all other waters to the mystical washing away of sin and said unto me, "as thou dost convey water away in thy pipes, so is grace conveyed in the act of baptism and so it was by circumcision"'.[37]

This occasioned an exchange between Cosin and Etherington which persuaded the assembled company to return the unfortunate boxmaker to prison. In the course of that conversation, according to his own account, Etherington had claimed that Cosin's commitment to the universality and efficacy of sacramental grace aligned him with 'the anabaptists, Arminians and papists'. For they, too, held that baptism conferred saving grace on all those baptised, 'from which doctrine ... falling away after regeneration from the estate of salvation to everlasting condemnation, doth necessarily follow free will and other absurd and unsound points of doctrine, which they, likewise, hold and teach, contrary to the doctrine of the church of England'.[38]

Things went from bad to worse at this point, for having started with baptism the conversation naturally turned to the sacrament of the Lord's Supper upon which subject Cosin affirmed that 'the very flesh of Christ was eaten with our teeth, which I could not but say was gross popery'. Etherington then embarked on the ferociously 'Zwinglian' reading of the sacrament, outlined above. As one might expect, that was enough for Neile, Buckeridge and Cosin. 'Upon these occasions', lamented Etherington, 'the bishops' displeasures were kindled against me, things were left without any further examining, and I was sent again to prison.' Etherington's account of this meeting was later confirmed by Denison who admitted that at first Etherington had 'had more favour showed unto you by the means of the two bishops, Dr Neile and Dr Buckeridge, than possibly some orthodox teachers could have found', until, that is, the subject of the sacraments had come up when 'the displeasures of the bishops were occasioned against you' and the boxmaker was thrown back in gaol.

Denison's own position on the sacraments was, if anything, closer to Etherington's than to the one espoused by Cosin, Neile and Buckeridge. As we have seen, Denison denied that the sacrament conferred grace, insisting only that it confirmed and strengthened the grace of election. Knowing, however, that Etherington's opinions on the sacraments were far more extreme than his own and knowing, also, that nothing was more likely to outrage the sensibilities of the assembled Arminian company than the boxmaker's vision of the sacraments as mere signs – showing forth but not actually communicating the grace of God – Denison deliberately introduced the topic into the conversation just when the tide was turning against him. The irony of the resulting situation was considerable. We have the ardent Calvinist, Denison, mobilising a now largely Arminian ecclesiastical authority against his local enemy Etherington, whom he had previously denounced as himself an Arminian, on a doctrinal issue on which his own position was at least as close to that of Etherington as it was to that of John Cosin. Denison's verdict on this outcome in 1641 was that it was 'a providence'. Small wonder.[39]

Denison was no doubt pleased to have pulled off this coup but it was unlikely that a man of his relatively extreme Calvinist opinions and intemperate disposition would escape the consequences of the Laudian takeover of the church forever and so it proved. As we have seen, Etherington's views on the sabbath, that Denison had found so offensive in the 1620s, had amounted to little more than the position that was beginning to pass for orthodox amongst the Laudians in the 1630s. The reissue of the book of sports, combined with the decidedly Etheringtonian gloss on the nature of the sabbath now emerging from high places, put diehard sabbatarians like Denison in a very difficult position, a position which Denison negotiated with what seems to have been a habitual lack of tact. In a newsletter of December 1633, one of Strafford's regular sources of English news, Mr Garrard, reported the current state of play on the book of sports. 'Here begins to be much difference in opinion about the book; for, though it be the same verbatim that was published in King James' time, yet it is commanded to be read in all the churches here, and in the country. In some churches of London it hath been read; one Dr Denison read it, and presently read the ten commandments, then said, "dearly beloved, you have heard now the commandments of God and man, obey which you please".' While Denison's response fell short of the outright refusal to read the book that Garrard attributed to those two other prominent London preachers, 'Mr Holdsworth and Dr Gouge', his was scarcely a conciliatory gesture.[40]

Also in 1633 Denison was a leading signatory of a petition on behalf of none other than George Walker who had recently fallen foul of Laudian authority. The petition came from 'parsons, vicars and curates of divers churches in and about London' all of whom attested that they had known George Walker 'some of us for the space of twenty years and upwards and others during our abode here in the city, to be a man of honest and peaceable life and conversation, a zealous maintainer of the doctrine and discipline established in the church of England and a strong opponent of all sects, schisms and heresies and one who hath reduced many opposites to a peaceable conformity in the church'. The document was signed by many leading London puritans including William Gouge, John Downham, Elias Crabtree and Richard Culverwell. The names appended were listed in terms of rank with Doctors of Divinity coming first, and proudly displayed second on that list was the name of Stephen Denison. When all this is combined with Grame's denunciation of bowing to the name of Jesus of 1630, it begins to make St Katharine Cree look something like a centre of opposition to Laudian ceremonialism in the early 1630s.[41]

THE REMAKING OF A FAMILIST: ETHERINGTON AS DENISON'S POLEMICALLY CONSTRUCTED ALTER EGO

Etheringtonian insubordination and insurrectionism had obviously not been the sort of outcome that Denison had expected or wanted when he had exhorted the laity to cultivate an active, scripturally based piety and, on that basis, to check and, if necessary, to criticise the sermons of the clergy. Be that as it may, within the terms which he himself had set, it was not immediately apparent just what Etherington had done wrong in challenging Denison's authority and doctrine. Denison's own denunciations of other inferior, careless, pluralist or showy preachers all implied that mere ordination did not a powerful preacher make. As he argued, even in the *The white wolf*, the response of the laity had a considerable role to play in validating the claims to authority of the true prophet of God. 'The sheep of Christ will not hear the voice of a stranger, but fly from him', he explained. Such presuppositions about how the authority of powerful preachers was constituted made it hard for Denison simply to pull rank as an ordained minister of the national church. Thus, even as he claimed that one sign of false prophets was that 'they have no calling from the church', he almost at once conceded that this was an argument that 'I will not insist upon'.[42]

One eminently logical outcome of such ideological pressures and qualms would have been to lay all claims to spiritual or doctrinal superiority aside and simply to debate the substantive points of disagreement between the two men, either in private or indeed in the sort of semi-public, semi-private meetings with which, as we saw in the last chapter, the godly often sought to defuse such disputes. But that would have been to cede the boxmaker an implicit parity of authority and standing that, in fact, Denison was desperate to deny him. For in Denison's eyes it was precisely his pretensions to deal with the learned ministry on equal terms that constituted one of Etherington's greatest crimes. 'You magnify your own wisdom', he told the boxmaker at one point. 'You disable the ministers of the church, as though they knew nothing in comparison of you and this knowledge of yours, or rather this proud conceit of your own knowledge, causeth you to err.' Denison denounced 'foolish and ignorant men which take upon them to be teachers of divinity, being unseen in the very grounds thereof'. They were 'much like to presumptuous quacksalves, which take upon them to be great surgeons and physicians, being ungrounded in the art of surgery and physic, and so instead of curing men, do indeed kill them'. Adverting to an earlier difference of opinion between Etherington and Richard Stock, Denison asked how did 'it become you, a poor ignorant man, to contradict so learned and worthy a minister as Mr Richard Stock was?' Having recounted again Etherington's errors on the sacraments he concluded 'and thus we see how grossly divinity is abused when it comes to be dispersed by such ignorant, proud sotts as you are'.[43]

This is the language of the vested interests and privileges of the learned professions being deployed against an upstart lay challenger to clerical authority. Instead, therefore, of debating discrete points of doctrine with Etherington, Denison chose systematically to ignore Etherington the man while attacking his own version of the boxmaker's opinions in the pulpit as familist, anabaptist and Arminian. In so doing Denison was hoping to dismiss Etherington's challenge to his authority as a minister by assimilating him to established anti-types of religious deviance and radicalism. This was a tactic designed to allow Denison to redraw and indeed to strengthen the line separating the authority of the clergy from the rights and prerogatives of the laity, without appearing to make too exalted or overbearing general claims about clerical authority. As we have seen, the delicate balance between the authority of godly ministers and the spiritual autonomy of the activist laity lay at the heart of puritan religion and Denison could not afford to appear to be upsetting that balance. As long as he could sustain his claim that in going after Etherington, he was not so much disciplining an uppity lay person as denouncing a dangerous heretic, Denison could hope to see off the challenge to his ministry represented by Etherington's activities, subtly to strengthen his own position of authority as a godly minister, to maintain indeed enhance his own credentials as a bastion of orthodoxy in the eyes of the authorities in church and state while at the same time retaining his status as a good thing in the eyes of the London godly.

It is this dynamic that explains Denison's unwillingness, throughout their dispute, ever to acknowledge any personal acquaintance or familiarity with Etherington. His refusal to meet or even to speak to the boxmaker was a symbolically charged attempt to establish or rather re-establish the proper distance between the powerful preacher of St Katharine Cree and the unlearned boxmaker, Etherington. In 1642 Etherington gave a fascinating account of his attempts to speak with Denison in the street. Replying to Etherington's charges of clericalist tyranny and bullying, Denison had claimed that 'they had met divers times in the streets of London' and that he (Denison) had often tried to engage Etherington in conversation. This Etherington denied. Throughout the opening stages of their dispute, while the matter lay before the bishop of London and 'all the while that you scandalised and reviled me by name in your pulpits', Etherington had 'often sought and could never obtain to speak with you'. They had met on the street years later, after Denison had 'gotten sentence passed against me and that I had endured three years' imprisonment'.

> I met with you [Etherington wrote] at the end of Cornhill by the stocks and I spake to you and requested that I might now speak with you once, after all my troubles, and your answer or words first were 'I am glad thou hast renounced thy errors' and I answered you, nay, not so, but I disclaimed before the court those false and evil things which you and your witnesses had charged me with, I renounce nothing that I held; and so we went together up Cornhill and into the exchange, where I told you of your false and evil dealing toward me and of your false and wicked sermon, full of bitterness, malice and lies, which you had published and preached against me; and you took me up short, I confess, and reproved me for my boldness, saying 'dost thou speak thus to a doctor'. And upon some words of reproof that I used unto you for your wicked dealing, you told me 'thou hast not the keys, I have the keys etc.' and then after other words you flung away in a fury, threatening me.[44]

There, in those two ejaculations by Denison – 'dost thou speak thus to a doctor' and 'thou hast not the keys, I have the keys' – a central aspect of the confrontation between the two men was encapsulated. The reference to the keys of spiritual discipline recalls Etherington's claim in 1610 that these belonged in reality to the little ones of God rather than to the clerical hierarchy. Denison's proud claim to his new-found status as a doctor of divinity clearly adverts to the gulf that should separate the authority of the learned clergy from the claims to be heard in the church of the unlettered laity. Challenged as to his conduct towards Etherington, Denison instinctively had recourse to these two central symbols of clerical power and authority, waved now in the very face of the disgraced boxmaker.

It was, all in all, a remarkable display for a puritan minister to put on in the streets of London. Denison had, after all, been vindicated by the arbitrary and draconian sanctions of a court (High Commission) that was coming increasingly to symbolise for the godly all that was tyrannical and popishly inclined in the English church. Denison was only able to get away with it because, in his eyes and in those of his followers and sympathisers, Etherington was not some errant but worthy member of the godly community but a heretic, a familist and a sect master. That was why Denison had put so much effort into forcing Etherington's opinions into those stereotypical categories of deviance and otherness. That same manoeuvre enabled Denison to address and dissipate the tensions in his own position between the private observances and spiritual exertions of the godly and the public ordinances of the national church. For if what Etherington was doing constituted heresy and schism, the godly laity must take care to avoid it. Such an approach enabled Denison to tighten his definition of what constituted a conventicle to include any private meeting for the worship of God containing the members of more than one household. And, on this basis, he proceeded to denounce those lay persons 'which are never satisfied with any true teachers, especially in public but have a lusting after the onions and garlic of private errors, preferring anything done in a private conventicle (though it be never so unwholesome) before that which is done in the public congregation'. 'It is just with God', Denison concluded with typical charity, 'to leave such curious persons to be seduced by false prophets, to their own eternal destruction.'[45] Thus, while he was apparently only attacking Etherington's familism, Denison was, in fact, considerably constricting the area for lay autonomy within the workings of the godly community. Indeed, on the issue of conventicles and household worship he was buying into the definition of what it was to keep a conventicle that Laudian authority would shortly mobilise against precisely the sort of godly self-help usually fostered and encouraged by ministers like Denison.[46]

Similarly, in his instructions to the laity on how to avoid false prophets like Etherington, Denison started, conventionally enough, by exhorting them to spiritual self-help and activism. The laity were, first, to 'labour to be well instructed in the grounds and principles of true religion'. Second, they were to 'receive the truth in the love of it' for 'men are hardly drawn from that they love'. Third, they were to 'labour that your knowledge in religion may be experimental' for 'a man is hardly persuaded by any art against his own experience' and, lastly, 'to be practical in religion: be doers of the will of God and then ye shall know of the doctrine, whether it be of God'. These, of course, were the conventional signs of a true faith, the product of the sort of spiritual activism and self-help that preachers like Denison and Chibald habitually enjoined to the laity.

But now Denison joined them to two rather more negative injunctions. The godly were first to 'beware of reading schismatical books, though they be offered unto you as a friendly gift' and to 'beware of frequenting the company and conventicles of seducers, though you be never so kindly invited by false friends'. But how, one might ask, were the godly to know who was a seducer and what was a schismatic book without some personal acquaintance with the persons and texts involved? Should not their knowledge on this score be experimental too? Here Denison's implicit reply was openly authoritarian – they would know because the godly learned clergy would tell them, as Denison himself was doing at such length, in both the preached and printed versions of *The white wolf*.

And here Denison's last piece of advice on how to 'remain sound in the faith' takes on a particular importance. For finally the laity were instructed 'when you have any scruple in your consciences, repair not to seducers for resolution but, according to God's ordinance, ask the priests concerning the law, Agg.2.11, and seek the law at their mouths, Malach.2.7. Go to your faithful ministers and let them resolve you and, if you be tempted by seducers, acquaint them with your temptations, that they may strengthen you'.[47]

In short, while Denison might present himself as merely repelling an assault on God's flock by the wolf of heresy, he was, in fact, taking the opportunity, offered by his campaign against Etherington, to tilt the balance between the authority of the clergy and the primacy of the public ordinances of the national church, on the one hand, and the autonomy, self-help and collective religious observances of the laity, on the other, in a decidedly clericalist direction. Taking each strand of his position in isolation there was certainly nothing novel or unusual in any of Denison's claims; there had always been a certain clericalism latent within puritan divinity but that clericalism was more often than not held in check by contrary ideological forces, forces which Denison was here playing down by holding the line against sectarian heresy. He could hope to effect this manoeuvre, while still retaining his standing in the eyes of the godly, only if his claims that Etherington was a familist and a sectary were accepted and Denison himself was consequently construed as attacking schism and heresy rather than trenching on the rights and prerogatives of the godly laity.

We can see the same process of externalisation and control at work if we look more closely at some of the doctrinal errors with which Denison tried to associate Etherington in *The white wolf*. At one point he listed and denounced the alleged errors of the 'Gringltonian familists' of Yorkshire, amongst which were the beliefs 'that to pray for pardon for sin, after one is assured of God's love, is to offer Christ again' and that there was no reason 'why ministers should speak against the sins of the wicked, seeing the wicked man can do nothing but sin'.[48] Both of these positions could be read as fatalist and antinomian caricatures or distortions of Denison's own uncompromising rendition of the doctrines of election, assurance and reprobation. In precisely this period, while genuine antinomians like Shaw and the Gringltonians themselves were deploying such doctrines to excoriate the empty legalism of mainstream puritans like Denison, at the other end of the ideological spectrum, various Laudians were claiming that such extreme positions were the natural products and progeny of Denison's own style of Calvinism.[49] Attacked from both sides, Denison, through his picture of Etherington as a familist and anabaptist radical, was able safely to vindicate himself from Arminian and Laudian attack – enemies of familist and anabaptist sectarianism were, after all, *ipso facto* defenders of order and orthodoxy – while still retaining the sympathy of the godly, who were themselves no friends to sectarianism and still less to the Arminianism that Denison imputed with such enthusiasm to his boxmaking adversary.

But perhaps the clearest example of this syndrome is provided by Denison's treatment of the sacraments and, in particular, of baptism. As we have seen, Denison's attitude to the sacraments was ambiguous. His own position that the sacrament could not confer but only confirm grace was similar to that expressed by Etherington. On occasion, Denison himself had come close to Etherington's stance in claiming that not baptism but repentance and regeneration marked the believer's real point of entry into the church. Indeed, it would not be going too far to see Etherington's view that baptism neither conferred nor confirmed grace but merely signified and promised it, as a simple extension, a relatively obvious logical development, of Denison's position. Moreover, this was a question of some moment since the aura of significance and spiritual potency with which Denison had contrived to surround the sacraments provided a key point of contact between the word-based godly community and the national church.

Denison repeatedly claimed that, while Etherington might attend the sacraments of the national church, his doctrinal position, by 'allegorising' the sacraments,[50] denied them any true force or efficacy. By thus distancing himself from Etherington, Denison was able to efface or mask some of the similarities between his and Etherington's view of the sacraments. Again, we know from other sources, that at precisely this time the nature and efficacy of sacramental grace was becoming a subject of lively intra-puritan debate. It was also, of course, an issue upon which the Laudians were even then exerting considerable polemical pressure on the godly, by, in effect, conflating Denison's position with that of Etherington in order to convict all Calvinists and puritans of contempt for the sacraments and sacramental grace.

These claims were, as we have seen above and Arnold Hunt has amply demonstrated, erroneous: if puritans and Calvinists had rather different views of the nature of sacramental grace, of the role of the sacraments in the life of the church and, indeed, of the proper balance to be struck in public worship between prayer, preaching and the sacraments, from those purveyed by the Laudians, that did not mean that they did not value the sacraments and that, accordingly, any expression of sacramental zeal or imagery betokened a movement away from 'Calvinism' towards 'Laudianism'. Indeed, for all his alleged (and actual) allegorisation of the sacraments, as we have seen, sacramental imagery, centred on baptism but also involving the Lord's Supper, bulked quite large even in Etherington's thought. And, as Hunt has reminded us, much of the vast literature written during the early Stuart period on how to prepare to receive the sacrament was of a decidedly puritan provenance. Here, as elsewhere, Denison was anything but original.

The claim, then, is that in choosing to produce the polemical image of familist doctrinal error, contained in *The white wolf*, Denison was in fact seeking to address and exorcise difficulties inherent in his own position. Those ambiguities and difficulties had, indeed, been laid bare by Etherington's appropriation of central elements of Denison's world view for his own purposes and were, even then, providing the Laudian critics of puritan Calvinism with some of their juiciest targets. In effect, what Etherington by implication pictured as the natural conseqences of Denison's position, while seeking to displace or challenge him from within the puritan milieu, the Laudians also identified as the necessary consequences of moderate puritan orthodoxy, while challenging that orthodoxy from without.

Thus, in denouncing Etherington, Denison was fending off two major threats to the integrity and stability of his own position. Both were a good deal more dangerous than anything a genuine familist could have done to him. *The white wolf* is best seen as an attempt to kill these two rather predatory birds with one polemical stone. For in that sermon he projected a vision of some of the unacceptable consequences, the radical tendencies in his own thought, onto the unfortunate Etherington. Etherington, as he was pictured in the *The white wolf*, became, in effect, Denison's polemically constructed *alter ego*. By denouncing the resulting image as anabaptist, familist and Arminian, Denison was able to construct himself against that projection as, once again, the representative of an orthodox golden mean, located between the two extremes of familist and popish/ Arminian heresy.

But the fact that Denison's image of Etherington was polemically constructed, produced and conditioned as much by Denison's own position and relationship to the wider political and polemical contexts of the 1620s, as by anything Etherington had ever said or done, does not mean that it was simply false. On the contrary, for all the distortions, hyperbole and downright lies that went into Denison's portrait of Etherington, many of his central assertions have emerged, in the course of the preceding discussion, as, if not 'true', then, at least, as far from devoid of basis in fact. Etherington had been, in some sense, a familist; T.L. had been and, indeed, remained a crucial influence on his thought; however one wants, ultimately, to characterise it, T.L.'s thought had not been altogether orthodox; Etherington had, on his own admission, toyed with some sorts of sectarianism; and his own characterisation of himself as just another loyal, albeit spiritually concerned and active, member of the national church did not really do justice to the intricacies and implications of his position, even as it had evolved by the 1620s. Moreover, on his own admission, on the sabbath, on the sacraments and on the relationship between repentance and justification, Etherington did disagree, sometimes fundamentally, with Denison.

Denison, then, was not just making it up, anymore than was Etherington. Both men were peddling partial, polemically conditioned and personally convenient, versions of what remained recognisably the same events. For, while at first sight their very different accounts of one another might seem mutually incompatible, on closer examination they appear as but different versions of what emerges as essentially the same story. The limitations of the evidence make it impossible to give anything but an incomplete and conjectural account of what really happened, at least to Etherington, during this period. It would, as always, be nice to know a whole lot more about T.L., about Etherington himself, about their friends and associates, their reading patterns, social networks and daily rounds and their relations with other members of the godly community. But the very incompleteness of our knowledge here, our reliance on the heavily polemical projections and images produced by the participants to these disputes, stands nicely for a rather more general feature of the religious history of the period. For, on a whole variety of issues, however much one 'knows' – and 'knowledge' in these matters is always at best provisional and incomplete – it is impossible to escape the polemically constructed and conditioned images in terms of which contemporaries viewed each other and events in the wider world. Moreover, even if we retain a no doubt old-fashioned, and perhaps even epistemologically naive, desire to understand 'what really happened' (and for historians such antediluvian aspirations are happily part of the territory, not to say constitutive of the discipline), it is not desirable for us to effect such an escape, even if such a manoeuvre were possible. Since these were the categories and argumentative moves and manoeuvres, the images and assumptions, through which contemporaries viewed and in terms of which they acted upon the world, our first impulse should be to recover, revivify and imaginatively inhabit those categories and images, not to criticise or reject them for being inadequate, partial or inaccurate. Thus the most fruitful response to this situation is not, realising that claims and images like those mobilised by Denison against Etherington were polemically tainted, to dismiss them as simply unreliable and inaccurate. Nor, it goes without saying, can one (in this instance, with Christopher Hill) simply accept them as more or less true. Rather, we should seek to interrogate them, by reconstructing both the immediate contexts – personal, polemical, political – within which they were manufactured and deployed and the wider discursive structures, the ideological materials within and from which they were constructed. And, if the evidence fortuitously preserved both by Denison's remarkably chatty sermon and by Etherington's extraordinarily pertinacious determination to clear his name is anything to go by, we should also view our initially sceptical response to such overdrawn, exaggerated and patently 'false' images and claims with a certain scepticism. For, as the preceding analysis has shown, while Denison's image of Etherington as a familist, an anabaptist and a sect-master has a great deal to tell us about Stephen Denison, carefully handled, it also has a lot to say about John Etherington, T.L. and the social and ideological milieu that produced and sustained them as well.

NOTES

1 C. Marsh, *The family of love in English society, 1550–1630* (Cambridge, 1994), chapter 5.
2 P. Lake, *Anglicans and puritans? Presbyterianism and English conformist thought from Whitgift to Hooker* (London, 1988); 'Conformist clericalism? Richard Bancroft's analysis of the socio-economic roots of presbyterianism', in W.J. Sheils and D. Wood, eds, *Studies in church history*, vol. 23 (Oxford, 1987); 'Lancelot Andrewes, John Buckeridge and "avant garde" conformity at the Jacobean court', in L.L. Peck, ed., *The mental world of the Jacobean court* (Cambridge, 1991); 'The Laudian style', in K. Fincham, ed., *The early Stuart church* (Basingstoke, 1993).
3 John Etherington, *The defence of John Etherington* (London, 1642), pp. 45–6, 1–2; J. Etherington, *The deeds of Dr Denison a little more manifested* (London, 1642), sig. A2v.
4 S. Denison, *The white wolf* (London, 1627), p. 51.
5 Ibid., pp. 14, 21, 25–6, 71–2.
6 Ibid., pp. 71–2, 50.
7 John Etherington, *A description of the true church of Christ* (London, 1610), p. 113, dedicatory epistle 'to the citizens of the heavenly Jerusalem', sig. A3r.

8 Ibid., pp. 111, 59.
9 John Etherington, *A discovery of the errors of the English anabaptists* (London, 1623), p. 43; Etherington, *The defence*, pp. 12–13. Also see Etherington, *A description*, pp. 58–9.
10 Etherington, *The defence*, p. 12.
11 Ibid., pp. 41–2.
12 Ibid., pp. 35–6.
13 G. Nuttall, *The holy spirit in puritan faith and experience* (Chicago, 1992).
14 J.C. Davies, 'Against formality: one aspect of the English revolution', *Transactions of the Royal Historical Society*, sixth series, 3 (1993).
15 P. Seaver, *Wallington's world* (London, 1985) p. 47; Edward Brerewood, *A learned treatise of the sabbath* (London, 1630); Richard Byfield, *The doctrine of the sabbath vindicated* (London, 1631). S. Denison, *The white wolf* (London, 1641), pp. 8–9.
16 On the origins of this style of 'practical divinity' and religious subjectivity see P. Lake, *Moderate puritans and the Elizabethan church* (Cambridge, 1982), chapter 7. Also see T. Webster, *Godly clergy in early Stuart England: the Caroline puritan movement, c. 1620–1643* (Cambridge, 1997), pp. 105–12, which carries essentially the same story into the early seventeenth century and includes a useful brief survey of the voluminous secondary literature on the subject, particularly in its New England context.
17 PRO S.P. Dom. 16/177/68, fols 135r.–136r. This document is printed as document 4 in the documentary appendix to D. Como and P. Lake, 'Puritans, antinomians and Laudians in Caroline London: the strange case of Peter Shaw in context', forthcoming in the *Journal of Ecclesiastical History*.
18 PRO S.P. Dom. 16/139/91 fols 174r.–177r. The articles and papers concerning Shaw appear as documents 1, 2 and 3 in the documentary appendix to Como and Lake, 'Strange case of Peter Shaw'. Document 2 and document 1, charges, 18, 15, 10.
19 John Etherington, *A brief discovery of ... familism* (London, 1645), p. 10.
20 Como and Lake, 'Strange case of Peter Shaw', document 4.
21 Ibid., document 2; document 1, charge 12.
22 T.D. Bozeman, 'The glory of the "Third Time": John Eaton as contra-puritan', *Journal of Ecclesiastical History*, 47 (1996); our knowledge of these issues has now been transformed by David Como's 1998, Princeton Ph.D. dissertation 'Puritans and heretics: the emergence of a an antinomian underground in early Stuart England'.
23 PRO S.P. Dom. 16/139/91, fols 174r.–177r. These papers are printed and commented upon, as documents 1, 2 and 3, in the documentary appendix to Como and Lake, 'Strange case of Peter Shaw'.
24 S.R. Gardiner, *Reports of cases in the courts of Star Chamber and High Commission*, Camden Society, new series, vol. xxxix (1886), p. 185.
25 For a full account of these men's backgrounds and associations see Como and Lake, 'Strange case of Peter Shaw'.
26 G[uildhall] L[ibrary] Ms 9531, fols 21v.–22r., 23v. For later appearances before the High Commission see PRO S.P. Dom. 16/261/ fol. 2v, 9 May 1633 and C[ambridge] U[niversity] L[ibrary] Ms Dd ii 21, fol. 121r. Also see Bodleian Library, Tanner Ms, vol. 114, fol. 115r.–v., headed 'additionals to other articles against Abraham Grymes' and

dated 1633. I owe these references to the kindness of David Como.

27 Como and Lake, 'Strange case of Peter Shaw' document 1. Smith's letter, discussed below, is printed there as document 3.

28 PRO S.P. Dom. 16/177/68, fol. 135r.–136r., printed as document 4 in Como and Lake, 'Strange case of Peter Shaw'. It is also discussed above in chapter 8.

29 Como and Lake, 'Strange case of Peter Shaw' document 1. For home visits by Palmer and Wilson, see charges 4, 7, 11, 12, 13, 22, 27; for admonition by Boswell, see charges 2, 8, 33.

30 Ibid., document 1, Walker's charge is the last.

31 Ibid., document 3.

32 Ibid. The best account of the impact of Laudianism on the behaviour and mentality of the godly clergy during the 1630s is now T. Webster, *Godly clergy in early Stuart England: the Caroline puritan movement* (Cambridge, 1997), part III, which develops and to some extent modifies the position first mapped out in N. Tyacke, *Anti-Calvinists* (Oxford, 1987), chapter 8. On the impact of Laudian doctrinal regulation see the crucial remarks in Anthony Milton, 'Licensing, censorship and religious orthodoxy in early Stuart England', *Historical Journal*, 41 (1998). All these accounts to my mind both falsify and supersede those provided in K. Sharpe, *The personal rule of Charles I* (New Haven and London, 1992), chapters 6 and 12; J. Davies, *The Caroline captivity of the church* (Oxford, 1992); and P. White, *Predestination, policy and polemic* (Cambridge, 1992). For a critical evaluation of which see N. Tyacke, 'Anglican attitudes: some recent writings on religious history ...', *Journal of British Studies*, 35 (1996) and P. Lake, 'Predestinarian propositions', *Journal of Ecclesiastical History*, 46 (1995).

33 On the rise of antinomianism see T.D. Bozeman, 'The glory of the "Third Time": John Eaton as contra-puritan', *Journal of Ecclesiastical History*, 47 (1996) and Como and Lake, 'Strange case of Peter Shaw'. The definitive account is now to be found in Como, 'Puritans and heretics'. Also P. Lake and D. Como, '"Orthodoxy" and its discontents: dispute settlement and the manufacture of "consensus" in the London (puritan) "underground"', *Journal of British Studies*, 39 (2000). For Denison's alleged opinions see John Etherington, *The deeds of Dr Denison a little more manifested* (London, 1642), sigs A5r.–v.

34 On Hall, see P. Lake, 'The moderate and irenic case for religious war: Joseph Hall's *Via media* in context', in S. Amussen and M. Kishlansky, eds, *Political culture and cultural politics in early modern England* (Manchester, 1995); on Sanderson, see P. Lake, 'Serving God and the times: the Calvinist conformity of Robert Sanderson', *Journal of British Studies*, 27 (1988); on the 'hypothetical universalism' of Ward and Davenant, see N. Tyacke, *Anti-Calvinists* (Oxford, 1987), chapter 4 and P. Lake, 'Calvinism and the English church 1570–1635', *Past and Present*, 114 (1987). On John Cotton, see the article by David Como in P. Lake and M. Questier, eds, *Orthodoxy and conformity in the church of England, 1560–1660*, forthcoming from Boydell and Brewer, Woodbridge.

35 J. Etherington, *The defence of John Etherington* (London, 1641), pp. 49–50.

36 Tyacke, *Anti-Calvinists*, chapter 6, for a later run-in between Neile himself and the Commons see pp. 109–12.

37 Etherington, *The defence*, p. 50.

38 Ibid., p. 51.

39 Ibid., p. 50.
40 W. Knowler, ed., *The earl of Strafford's letters and dispatches*, 2 vols (London, 1739), vol. 1, p. 166.
41 PRO S.P. Dom. 16/414/23, fol. 40r. I owe my knowledge of this document to the kindness of Paul Seaver and David Como.
42 Denison, *The white wolf*, pp. 14, 20.
43 Ibid., pp. 72, 47. S. Denison, *The white wolf* (London, 1641), pp. 83, 91.
44 Etherington, *The deeds of Dr Denison*, sig. A3r.–v. In 1641 Denison denied these claims. 'I have met you divers times on the streets of London and have said unto you, John Etherington, I pray you let me speak with you, but you have passed by grinning with your teeth at me and answering, I scorn it.' S. Denison, *The white wolf* (London, 1641), p. 81.
45 Denison, *The white wolf*, p. 68.
46 Looking back from the perspective of 1641, Denison modulated his position. Lay meetings 'for prayer and the worship of God', for 'the repeating of sermons to edify one another', were fine. Even his ally against Etherington, the ecclesiastical lawyer Sir Henry Martin, had 'laboured in my hearing to free some that have been complained of in the court for the repeating of sermons only'. Indeed, 'for this, to my knowledge, he hath suffered much from some great men'. What Etherington had been doing had, however, been something quite different and like the great man and 'favourer of all just causes' that he was, Martin had, quite rightly, let the law take its course against the heretical boxmaker. Those remarks, however, were made in 1641; in 1627, with the Laudian take-over of the church still to come, Denison had entered no such caveats. Conventicles were any meeting for household worship attended by members of more than one household and that was that. Denison, *The white wolf* (1641), pp. 84, 86.
47 Denison, *The white wolf*, pp. 79–80.
48 Ibid., p. 39.
49 Como and Lake, 'Strange case of Peter Shaw'.
50 Denison, *The white wolf*, pp. 46, 63.

Chapter 11

The Laudian style and the politics of the parish-pump

THE PAROCHIAL FACE OF THE LAUDIAN STYLE?

By 1633 Denison had problems of his own with Laudian authority. Again in dispute with various of his parishioners, this time it was he who was in trouble with the High Commission. Once again the problem was 'invective and uncharitable speeches' delivered from the pulpit against erring members of his flock. The occasion of this clash was the refurbishment of St Katharine Creechurch. In the words of the sentence of the court, 'the parish church of Katharine Creechurch, being in great decay, was recently re-edified by the parishioners thereof'.[1] In March 1624 the parishioners petitioned the House of Lords to prevail on the Master and fellows of Magdalene to rebuild the chancel of the church. They also approached the Earl of Suffolk with the same end in view. As they told the Lords, both church and chancel were 'in extreme decay through age, so as upon view thereof it is conceived by divers workmen and by his majesty's commissioners for building very needful forthwith to be reedified not being able to stand unless it is propped and shored up with divers great pieces of timber as it is'. While it was the chancel that was in the worst state, the parishioners explained, both church and chancel had to be 'raised and built together in respect the ground of them are very low, descending seven steps, causing it thereby to be very damp and noisome'. The parish's attempts to coerce Magdalene to pay up evidently failed and by December 1625 they were preparing to go it alone. For in that month the viewers of the city of London were examining the 'sufficiency and strength' of the church to decide whether it 'might stand without danger to the ... curate and parishioners, resorting thither to divine service and sermons'. Their verdict was that, despite the fact that the roof was out of kilter with the walls in certain places by as much as four and a half inches and that in the chancel certain rafters and beams had decayed and one pillar and arch cracked, the building 'was not in any danger of falling but may safely stand though not with conveniency seven or eight years at the least'. Judging from the will evidence, on the basis of this at best ambivalent report, plans to start the process of repair were being mooted as early as 1625, for in that year a cordwainer named Lawrence Williamson left £8 'towards the re-edifying and repairing of the parish church of St Katharine Creechurch' to be used for that purpose within six months of his death. In August of the same year, John Hough, evidently a close friend of his fellow haberdasher and leading light in the parish, Martin Bond – who was addressed repeatedly in the will as 'my brother Martin Bond' and named as Hough's sole executor – left £10 'towards the re-edifying of the said church ... to be paid within three months after the same shall begin to be re-edified'. In January 1626 a widow named Christiana Wells left £6 13s 6d 'toward the repairing and rebuilding of the parish of St Katharine Creechurch, whereof I am a parishioner'.[2] But if the project was being mooted and money was starting to come in in 1625/26, according to Anthony Munday's continuation of Stow's survey, work did not in fact begin until 1628. The project seems to have been initially conceived as a repair of the existing structure. In a begging letter to Sir Henry Martin, dating from relatively early in the process, that was certainly how the leaders of the parish were still describing it. After 'particular survey' the costs of the 'repair' were estimated at £800. The parishioners, however, were quite unable to raise such a sum on their own. Theirs, they explained, 'as it is the greatest [parish], so it is the poorest within the walls of London, having above 400 poor people in it which receive relief, the charge whereof (in regard they have no stock and now want their collections at lectures which yielded them above £40 per annum) lyeth very heavy upon these parishioners, as the most part of them are not able to undergo the same, far less to contribute towards the repairing of the said church.' Those parishioners who were able had already '(according to their abilities) both voluntarily lent and freely contributed towards' the project, 'yet nevertheless they cannot raise above 400 pounds.' They were, therefore, approaching Martin for a contribution, believing that 'your own piety, the parishioners' poverty and the church's necessity' would move him to an act of beneficence 'for which, as your soul will receive reward in heaven, so your name shall remain on earth amongst their best benefactors and in perpetual memory to your eternal praise.' However what started out as a repair swiftly became the almost complete reconstruction of the church. As the Clothworkers' Company put it in giving £20 to the parish, the church was, in fact, being 'new built from the foundation'.[3] Such ventures did not come cheap and the costs of the project evidently rapidly spiraled upwards.

In the absence of either vestry minutes or churchwardens' accounts for the relevant period it is very hard to say anything very definite about either the costs of the project or the sources from which the very considerable sums involved were raised. Some hints, however, do survive, notably in a Chancery case of 1635 and in a petition to the bishop of London for permission to levy a parish rate to pay for the final costs of the project. According to the former source 'the cost and charge' extracted from 'the parish for building up of the said church and chancel of St Katharine Cree ... which were utterly ruinated and decayed' had been 'to the value of £1000 and upward'.[4] When some parishioners approached the East India Company in November 1630 with begging bowl in hand the figure of £1000 was repeated only to be precisely doubled when, having been rebuffed the first time, they returned to the same potential donors a week later, claiming that they needed a full £2000 more than they had already raised to complete the project.[5] This was an estimate repeated in a suit of February 1630 to the court of common council of London who were told that the parishioners had 'contributed the sum of 1000 over and above which and what they have collected by virtue of his majesty's letter' and still needed a further £2000 to complete the project.[6] The Fishmongers' Company – Sir John Gayer's company – were given an even higher estimate. In March 1630 they were told that the parish had already spent £3000 'and that the finishing of it would cost 2000 more'.[7] On this basis, a figure well in excess of £3000 seems to be a fair guess for the total costs of the rebuilding. Certainly, the outlay for a similarly ambitious building programme at All Hallows Barking was of precisely that order of magnitude. The social, administrative and political strains created by the rapidly increasing scale and costs of what had now become a full-scale rebuilding of the church almost certainly go at least part of the way to explaining the polarisation and faction fighting that broke out in the parish during and immediately after the rebuilding process.[8]

According to the petition to the bishop, money had been raised in a number of ways, from a number of sources.[9] Of these, the first was the parishioners themselves. As we have seen, bequests for the purpose seem to have started in 1625 and continued into the early 1630s. In February 1630 another widow, Grace Woodliefe, left £5 'towards the building of the said church'. Many of the more substantial of such bequests were personalised in some way, the donor intending to have his or her beneficence recorded in the fabric of the refurbished church. Thus in December 1631 a goldsmith and citizen of London, one William Avenon, left '50 pound in money' 'for no other end, intent or purpose', than the 'making and building of a gate between the east end of the said parish church ... and the house wherein Mr James Croft now dwelleth'. When put up, the resulting doorway was indeed adorned with an inscription recording Avenon's generosity, which still survives. Likewise, the font cover was decorated with the personal coat of arms of one of the leading parishioners, Sir John Gayer, and another leading parishioner and member of the select vestry, the merchant John Dyke, personally contributed a pulpit and communion

The Laudian style

table, both of 'pure cedar'. When the foundation stone was laid in 1628 by Sir Martin Bond, clearly a leading figure in the whole project, Munday's continuation of Stow tells us that 'many of the parishioners (following this worthy leader) laid every man his stone with which they laid something else, which the workmen took up very thankfully'.[10] In short, both the process of building and the finished structure were designed to show forth the piety and beneficence of the leaders of the 'parish community', or, perhaps more accurately, to construct in bricks, mortar and ritual observance a version of that community presided over by its natural leaders, as ever a self-selecting group, in this instance coterminous with those who had planned and financed the rebuilding of the church.

As well as the personal gifts of individual parishioners there was a broader collection under letters patent granted by the king and a number of 'voluntary contributions' from 'the chamber of London and from several companies and particular persons in the city of London'. Approached, as we have seen, in March 1630, the city gave the munificent sum of £500.[11] This represented something like the start of a fund-raising drive which saw representatives of the parish approach a whole series of livery companies for donations throughout 1630 and 1631. In March 1630 the Fishmongers – Sir John Gayer's company – after considerable debate, gave the hefty sum of £100 and, in April, the Merchant Taylors gave £21.[12] The Ironmongers gave £25 and, after a vote, the Goldsmiths gave £50, also in April 1630.[13] The Skinners gave £30 in the same year, while the Grocers' Company handed over £66 13s 6d.[14] In May, at the personal request of Martin Bond, who was himself a prominent member of the company, the Haberdashers gave £50[15] and in the same month the Vintners gave £20 and the Mercers and Drapers £50 apiece.[16] The collection of funds went on through the summer as some of the poorer companies were approached. In July the Leathersellers gave £15 and in August the Tilers and Bricklayers gave £10[17] to be followed in September by the Salters who donated £40.[18] Indeed the begging bowl was still out even after the new church had been consecrated and open for business for some months. As late as April 1631 the Clothworkers parted with £20 towards the parish's 'charges in new building the said church'.[19]

Like private donors, the companies were to receive an outward sign of their beneficence inscribed in the very fabric of the new church. 'The company's arms' were 'to be set' in the roof, the Bricklayers proudly remarked, and indeed even today the coats of arms of the various corporate donors to the rebuilding remain embossed in the roof of the nave and side aisles.[20] Such donations by livery companies to 'so charitable' or to 'so godly and pious a work', 'tending much to the glory of God and the good of many souls' and representing 'an ornament to the city', as the Drapers', Goldsmiths' and Fishmongers' Companies respectively put it, were far from unique.[21] At

Denison and Etherington again

Figure 4 The arms of the city of London, embossed on the roof of St Katharine Cree

roughly the same time that representatives from St Katharine Cree were out fund raising, the parishioners of St George's Southwark were doing the same rounds for much the same purposes; only they were repairing rather than rebuilding their church and thus received substantially smaller sums for their admittedly more modest project.[22]

In St Katharine Cree the group of parishioners in charge of the operation doubled as both the lessees of the living from Magdalene College and, in their own minds at least, the members of the select vestry which, since 1622, had had sole control of the parish's affairs.[23] Prominent amongst them were two men of considerable clout in the city – Martin Bond and Sir John Gayer. Bond was a deputy-alderman and a prominent member of the Haberdashers' Company, while Gayer was a future Lord Mayor and sheriff of the city and a leading member of the East India, Levant and Fishmongers' Companies.[24] It was these two who were almost certainly behind the contribution of the East India Company to the rebuilding. Bond and some others first approached the company on 19 November 1630 only to be told that, while theirs was a 'pious and godly' work, the governors of the company had no power to donate company funds for such purposes but would still 'further the same to the generality as best they can'. Presumably this rebuff led to some behind the scenes string pulling by Bond and possibly Gayer, because when another application was made a mere seven days later, this time on the back of a considerably inflated estimate of the cost, it received a far more positive response. The company gave 100 marks for glazing the east window of the church from what amounted to the petty cash (which sum was duly disbursed the following March).[25] Does this mean that the glazing of the window, which, as we shall see, was to cause considerable controversy, was a pet project of Bond's and possibly Gayer's? Perhaps.

What is more certain is that even such zealous fund-raising efforts as these could not, finally, do the job and recourse had to be had to a parish rate. In June 1630 a group of parishioners, led by Bond and Gayer and including Bartholomew Elnow, John Duke, John Crossfield, Robert Parsons, William Thomson, John Weller, William Webb, Martin Hall, Richard Blackwell, William Smith, Richard Andrewes and Nicholas Sheldon, told the bishop of London that there was still a shortfall of some £360 on the cost of completing the rebuilding. They, therefore, asked the bishop to authorise a parish rate to raise this sum. Clearly, burdening the general run of parishioners with financial exactions for such a purpose was not something to be entered into lightly; as the petitioners claimed, there were many in the parish who were unwilling to stump up and they asked for the rate only as something as a last resort.[26]

This, then, was a major effort at refurbishment, involving wide-ranging fund-raising efforts led by the best-connected men in the parish. It appears to have been a project with the full support of the select vestry. None of this was in itself very unusual. As the pathbreaking researches of Dr Julia Merritt have revealed, throughout the early seventeenth century, the parish churches of London were undergoing refurbishments and repairs sometimes so elaborate and expensive as to amount almost to a rebuilding. As Dr Merritt has shown, it is impossible to attribute the motivation for such improvements and beautifications to any one style of churchmanship. There was no 'bare-ruined-choir' or 'leaky roof' faction amongst post-reformation English protestants. Attention to church fabric, seating and, indeed, the physical extension of church buildings to accommodate larger audiences for sermons, were all priorities entirely compatible with puritan and evangelical Calvinist styles of piety. There was nothing to which even Stephen Denison could object in a larger, more handsome and physically secure church in which to exercise his ministry. Godly parishes could spend a great deal on such projects, as Dr Merritt's detailed study of St Martin-in-the-Fields, Westminister has shown. As in the case of St Katharine Cree, the sums of money involved in these schemes could be considerable and when these could not be covered by parish rates and donations from members of the parish, wider collections across the city were sometimes held.[27]

Thus, the mere existence of an elaborate refurbishment/rebuilding project tells us nothing about the ideological complexion of the parish. Certainly Dr Merritt's work has made it clear that there was no necessary connection between even large-scale efforts at beautification and extension and 'Laudian' or 'proto-Laudian' styles of churchmanship. The beauty of holiness was, of course, a Laudian catchphrase and Laudians tended to present themselves as reacting against decades of profane, even sacrilegious, neglect of the outward forms of worship and the fabric and property of the church. This was an argumentative move that helped the Laudians play down the ideological novelties inherent in their programme, at the same time as they played up its significance and necessity. Here, they were saying, was no novel pattern of churchmanship but rather a sensible and long overdue return to proper standards of decency and respect after decades of lay sloth and neglect and puritan sacrilege and disorder. While such a self-presentation clearly served the immediate polemical purposes of the Laudians, it did not necessarily represent an accurate account of the pattern of church repair and rebuilding in the early Stuart church, and historians should beware of simply taking such claims at face value.

Nor, as Dr Merritt has also shown, should they lurch to the other extreme, asserting that, here as elsewhere, Laudian concerns and activities represented merely the continuation of business as usual, at most a peculiarly zealous pursuit of what remained (except amongst a small minority of subversive puritans) largely consensual and conventional concepts of order, decency and uniformity. On the contrary, as Dr Merritt and I have both argued, there *was* a distinctive Laudian concern for 'the beauty of holiness' with concomitant and equally distinctive notions of sacrilege and of the holy. These, however, cannot be assumed to be present wherever contemporaries showed concern for the appearance, integrity and capacity of church buildings. On the contrary, Laudian notions of the holy and of the appropriate liturgical and architectural responses to, and settings for, its presence in the world took very particular liturgical, iconographic, sacerdotal and sacramental forms and it is only where those forms were present that we can assert or assume the influence and power of Laudianism.[28]

However, arguably at Katharine Cree at least, some of such forms were indeed present. According to the admittedly *parti pris* William Prynne, the church was done up in the best Laudian style, complete with altar rails, steps up to the altar and a stained-glass window at the east end depicting 'the story of Abraham offering up his son Isaac'. As Dr Tyacke has shown, there was a strong correlation between the reintroduction of images into the church and Laudian notions of the beauty of holiness and many of the churches new modelled by laymen close to Laud did feature stained-glass windows. But stained glass was far from being a Laudian phenomenon. Bishop John Williams, a man of eclectic churchmanship but no Laudian, was responsible

The Laudian style

> THIS GATE WAS BVILTE AT THE COST
> AND CHARGES OF WILLIAM AVENON
> CITEZEN AND GOVLDSMITH OF LONDON
> WHO DIED IN DECEMBER ANNO DNI 1631

Figure 5 The funeral monument of the goldsmith William Avenon

for elaborate windows in Lincoln College chapel, Oxford. When the neighbouring church of St James, Duke's Place had been rebuilt and consecrated in the early 1620s, an elaborate stained-glass window had been set in the east end. Indeed, throughout the building, stained glass had been a prominent focus for conspicuous donation. The description in the continuation of Stow's *Survey* dwelt lovingly on the glass.

> The main and great east light, in the chancel, Sir Edward Barkham [the prime mover in the church's construction] undertook ... The other sideling by it, but inclining southerly more, the two worshipful gentlemen, Mr George Whitmore and Mr Nicholas Rantan, worthily performed. And the third, standing northerly in the same chancel, Mr Walter Leigh ... did likewise, at his own charge, perform. The two western lights, at the bottom of the church, being (indeed) very fair lights, the honourable Company of Drapers effected the one and the Woodmongers worshipful Society finished the other. Beside, the two southerly windows, the one done at the charge of Mr Cornelius Fish, Chamberlain of London and the other by Mr Waldron.[29]

In a very different theological key, but with almost as much intensity as their late medieval predecessors, such refurbished or rebuilt churches were clearly intended to stand as monuments to the individual and corporate donors who had planned and financed them. Thus, when the goldsmith William Avenon left money for the construction of a gate in the new church at

St Katharine Cree, the resulting structure doubled as a funeral monument for the donor, with a rather ghoulish momento mori and inscription nestling within the neo-classical pediment that completed the gateway. Indeed, the various continuations of Stow, even when they were written by such strongly protestant figures as Anthony Munday, who produced the expanded 1633 edition of the *Survey*, were clearly intended as in part further, literary, memorialisations of these acts of beneficence towards the church and 'the Christian community' by parish and city luminaries, as the passage cited above so clearly illustrates.

Judging from the evidence discussed above, the construction of St James, Duke's Place was no clericalist, still less a Laudian, project; heavily funded by the city, the consecration service was arranged and attended by 'the Lord Mayor and aldermen ... in their scarlet gowns'. At the corporation's invitation, both the bishop of London and the archbishop of Canterbury, that arch-Calvinist George Abbot, attended and the rather elaborate consecration service was conducted by Abbot himself.[30] We know that when parishes were thinking of improving or refurbishing their churches they did the rounds to see what neighbouring parishes had done in the same line.[31] So when Katharine Cree came to be done up, it may have seemed only natural to try to emulate, indeed even to outdo, the church next door; a church, incidentally, with which there had been a certain amount of rivalry and tension, St Katharine Cree at one point making legal objection to the creation of a separate parish just up the road.

Thus, there may have been an element of keeping up with the Joneses at work here. The architectural style adopted in the new church was avant-garde, its use of the Corinthian order unprecedented before Wren, according to Dr Newman. Again, if St James, Duke's Place had elaborate and expensive glass, so should St Katharine Cree. There might even have been some influence exerted on the design of the windows in St Katharine's by the arrangements in St James. According to Stow's *Survey*, in St James there was 'a fair monument in the east end of the chancel, made in resemblance of a golden sun, with beams and rays very ingeniously formed, characterising these verses in and among them: "The rising here/ of the clear gospel sun,/ is through the senates/ free donation/ the globe of that bright sun/ the God of might/ Christ Jesus is the rising/ and the light/ the heat the blessed spirit/ of truth and right/ as these three/ the globe, the light, the heat/ are all one sun/ so three one God complete/ thrice allelujah/ speaks about the rays/ that three in one/ may only have the praise."' That glossed the glass in the east window, which seems to have lacked any figurative elements, in an explicitly word- and Christ-centred sense. It is also, however, very reminiscent of the design of the surviving east window in St Katharine Cree, which, though traditionally identified as a Catherine wheel (to go with the church's patron saint), could

The Laudian style

Figure 6 An eighteenth-entury view of the church of St Katharine Cree

just as well be seen as representing the rays of the sun emanating outwards from the central roundel in which stand the letters IHS. If so, here is the same motif and potentially the same word-based Christocentricity as that to be found in St James, Duke's Place.[32]

However, the beautification of the east window in St Katharine Cree did not end here. While stopping short of a direct figurative depiction of the divine presence, the window there adverted to that presence through the typology of the Old Testament. For in the panels below the sun window was depicted Abraham sacrificing Isaac, which sacrifice was conventionally taken as an Old Testament type for or prefiguration of the sacrifice of Christ for the sins of the world, described in the New Testament. Now, while the window's restriction of figurative representation to the Old Testament could be used to squeeze it past the iconophobic proclivities of the godly, the changing ideological circumstances of the early 1630s made such a transaction increasingly unlikely. For the representation of Abraham's sacrifice of Isaac, with its transparent, typologically explicit message in a window at the east end, directly above a railed-in communion table or altar, might certainly be taken by contemporaries on the look-out for popish, Arminian or idolatrous innovation (as Denison most certainly was), to have had a notably Laudian symbolic and sacramental resonance. Here, on one view at least, was Cosin's notion of the universality and efficacy of sacramental grace, as he had expressed it to Etherington in High Commission, being given material and symbolic form.

Indeed, it would appear that, by the time it was finished, the refurbished St

Figure 7 A view of the nave at St Katharine Cree, showing the arms of various city companies

Katharine Cree had become the epitome of a new model Laudian church, a fit object for the admiration and emulation of the rest of the capital and indeed of the nation at large. Its status as such owed a great deal to the direct intervention of Laud himself, who, as bishop of London, proceeded to make an almighty fuss over the new church's consecration. According to Prynne, since the church had been 'repaired only by the parishioners, not new built from the ground', Laud's predecessor as bishop, George Montaigne, had thought it 'holy enough without any new consecration, not requisite in such a case by the very canon law'. Here, then, was an episcopally sponsored exercise in parish pride and architectural one-upmanship of the sort that Dr Merritt's work has revealed to have been fairly standard in early Stuart London. Laud, however, was having none of such laxity and laziness. Instead, he seized this opportunity to demonstrate Laudian notions of sacred space and the beauty of

Figure 8 The upper portion of the offending stained-glass window at St Katharine Cree

holiness. He 'suspended this new repaired church for a time from all divine service, sermons and sacraments till it was reconsecrated by himself', a process he effected through a magnificently staged and carefully choreographed consecration service.

Prynne's account is, of course, hostile but such was the distance between his and Laud's notion both of the holy and of the liturgically appropriate response to the holy that his critique of Laud's behaviour seems to have amounted to little more than a description of what Laud did, albeit one couched in alternately lurid, scathing and dismissive language. Laud, Prynne wrote,

> on the 16 of January 1630/31, being the Lord's day, came in the morning, about nine of the clock, in a pompous manner to Cree Church, accompanied with Sir Henry Martin, Dr Rive, Dr Duck and many other high commissioners and civilians, there being a very great concourse of people to behold this novelty. The church doors were guarded with many halberders. At the bishops approaching near the west door of the church the hangbies of the bishop cried out with a loud voice, 'open, open ye everlasting doors, that the king of glory may enter in' and presently (as by miracle) the doors flew open and the bishop, with three or four great doctors and many other principal men, entered in and, as soon as they were in the church, the bishop fell down upon his knees, with his eyes lifted up and his hands and arms spread abroad, uttering many words, and saying 'this place is holy and this ground is holy. In the name of the father, the son and the holy ghost I pronounce it holy'. And then he took up some of the earth or dust and threw it up into the air ... This was done in the great middle aisle several times as they came up eastwards towards the chancel, which chancel was then paved. When they approached near to the rail and Lord's Table, unto which was an ascent of two or three steps, the bishop lowly ducked and bowed towards it some five or six times and returning went round about the church in procession on the inside thereof.

The 100th psalm and the 90th psalm were then said and then a prayer which ended with the invocation to God to 'accept we beseech thee, this our holy service, who do give and consecrate this beautiful church unto thee and we separate it unto thee and thy church, as holy ground, not to be profaned any more to common use'. After more readings and prayers, Laud

> betook himself to sit under a cloth of state in an aisle of the chancel near the communion table and, taking a written book in his hand ... he pronounced many curses upon all those which should hereafter any way profane that holy and sacred place, by any musters of soldiers, or keeping any profane law courts or carrying burdens through it. At the end of every curse ... he bowed himself lowly towards the east or table (saying 'let all the people say, amen'). When the curses were ended, he then pronounced the like number of blessings to all those that had any hand in the culture, framing and building of that holy, sacred and beautiful church and pronounced blessings to all those that had given any chalices, plate, ornaments or utensils and that should hereafter give any. At the end of every blessing he also bowed down himself towards the east, saying 'let all the people say amen.'

The Laudian style

After this, there followed a brief sermon preached by Denison and then the celebration by Laud 'and two fat doctors' of the sacrament, a ceremony described with a good deal of satirical bile by Prynne who dwelt lovingly on every bow performed by Laud – and on Prynne's account there were a good many of these – towards the altar and the consecrated elements.

In this way what might may well have started out as a relatively routine, albeit lavish, exercise in church extension and refurbishment was appropriated as a showcase for Laudian notions of sacred space, centred, as we have seen here, on the sacramental presence of God within his church and the proper liturgical forms whereby that presence should be acknowledged and worshipped. These were not the sort of procedures likely to recommend themselves to Stephen Denison, and Prynne tells us that his sermon, which 'was but short', wedged in between the consecration of the church and the celebration of the sacrament, 'bitterly inveighed against setting up pictures and images in churches, saying it was popish and heathenish superstition and idolatry'.[33]

DENISON RETURNS TO THE COURT OF HIGH COMMISSION

Denison evidently continued to harp on this same theme, denouncing, in his normal round of preaching at St Katharine's, the images in the church as 'a whirligig, a crow's nest and more like the swaggering hangman cutting off St John the baptist's head', all of which, it was complained, contributed 'to the great affront and discouragement of the parishioners that took care for the beautifying of the said church'.[34] Since there were clearly those in the parish who had helped to pay and raise money for the refurbishment and presumably approved of the window, Bond and Gayer amongst them, this was scarcely a diplomatic stance to adopt. In part, we may be seeing a replay of Denison's earlier efforts as minister to exercise a disproportionate influence over the affairs of the parish in the face of the lay vestry, efforts that had earned him the bishop's rebuke back in 1622. Having lost a debate in private and been humiliated by the Laudian tableau assembled at the consecration service, Denison was now clearly getting his own back in the pulpit.

Predictably enough, Denison's pulpit provocations started a dispute in the parish in the course of which, for a full year before the case reached the High Commission, Denison had 'reviled some of his parishioners, comparing them to frogs, hogs, dogs and devils and called them by the manner of knaves and villains, rascals, queens, she devils and pillory whores'. Nor need we suppose that Denison's attempts to revile and browbeat his local enemies were restricted to the pulpit. John Etherington, for one, recalled exchanges in the street; one, 'in Cornhill, by the conduit', when Denison had accused him of having 'a hand in my business' and then had threatened 'me with something you would do if I had'. As we have seen above, as early as 1617 Denison's pulpit manner had succeeded in provoking an adverse reaction from his auditory and so perhaps the current outbreak of opposition to his ministry was not only the product of his alienating 'the stained-glass window faction' in the parish but also a working out of more general and long-term tensions and animosities. So much is certainly implied by the claim, made in High Commission, that, 'for these ten years last past', Denison 'had there given cause of scandal and offence, as well to his parishioners as the holy function of the ministry'.[35]

In the May of 1633 Denison complained from the pulpit that

> he was persecuted by a company of base fellows and rascals in that manner that it took him from his studies, for that was enough to look after them that were so wicked and conspired against him and thereupon exhorted his auditory to stand by him and not only to pity him, as some said they did and others prayed for him, but they should go further, for St Paul said that his auditors were ready to lay down their neck for him and wished them not to be worse than hogs, for if a hog be hunted after and be bitten, all the rest of the hogs will run after him and encompass him and cry with him, but many come short of these beasts, though they would not be compared unto them.

In a funeral sermon of October of the same year, Denison had praised the departed and 'told his auditory that he had converted the said woman and that she was not like to the damned crew nor the sort of these cursed conspirators that were ready to thrust out their powerful minister, if all the wit of their knavish pates could do it'.[36] Here he may have been referring to rumours, circulating in the parish, concerning his sexual mores or perhaps to the failure properly to pay him which led to his work to rule of the summer and autumn of 1633, described above. Either way, at this point some of his enemies in the parish turned to formal litigation, complaining to the church courts about Denison's non-performance of his pastoral duties and preferring a case against him in the Lord Mayor's court.[37] This initial recourse to a civil metropolitan authority may be significant, an instance of the parish trying to bring Denison to heal without calling in the potentially hostile attentions of Laudian episcopal authority.

That having failed to shut him up, in December 1633 Denison's opponents complained to the bishop of London who admonished Denison not 'to inveigh and nor tax any in his sermons nor to glance at any man particularly therein'. The next Sunday, however, Denison repeated his offence, responding directly in the pulpit to rumours about his sexual harassment of several married women of the parish and claiming that there was a conspiracy 'to take away the good name of their powerful minister, which they could not restore but they would be hanged before they could do it' – a point he reiterated just for good measure in his prayer after the sermon. This campaign of vilification

The Laudian style

was continued through public confrontation and citation in the church courts. In June 1634 a public altercation broke out during the communion service between one of the church wardens, the vestry man Martin Sheldon, and Denison. According to Denison, Sheldon had failed to consult with him or the other church warden (Denison's supporter John Bill) and then failed to provide 'sufficient measure of wine' so that more had to be sent for at the tavern, while Denison and the congregation twiddled their thumbs 'until it came, to the scandal and offence of the present communicants'. In August of the same year Denison himself publicly denounced William Cordall as an excommunicate 'in the time of reading divine service' and then presented him in the courts for his 'contempt of ecclesiastical authority' in refusing to leave, 'to the great offence of the congregation then and there assembled'. One vestryman, Aldridge Halsey, was presented as 'reputed a common drunkard and was seen drunk in the street and railing on a day the last week in November'. Martin Bond, John Dyke, John Offield, William Smith, and Martin Sheldon (all leading vestrymen and parish office holders – Dyke was a collector for the poor and Offield and Sheldon churchwardens) were cited for alleged financial malpractice in handling funds collected for the relief of the poor and the rebuilding of the church. In response, certain leading parishioners and members of the vestry appear, at about this time, to have simply withdrawn from the parish. Thus Martin Bond, as we have seen, a leading figure in the rebuilding effort, was cited in the church courts in June 1634 for 'refusing to receive the holy communion at his parish church at easter last, nor since'. This was swiftly followed by another even more damning presentment for having 'absented himself from divine service and sermons and the holy communion at his parish church for the space of a year and upwards'. Sir John Gayer's wife was also presented for 'neglecting to come to her parish church to give God thanks after childbirth'. Another parishioner was presented for taking his child for baptism not to Creechurch but to St Andrew Undershaft and several more were presented for their 'frequent absence from church'. A cryptic remark in the same court book may imply that Bond, Sir John Gayer and John Dyke (vestrymen all) had, in the face of Denison's hostility, also repaired to and been admitted at St Andrew Undershaft to receive the communion. Clearly things could not go on like this for long, and at this point, Denison was told not to preach again in the parish until the case against him was heard in the High Commission. In the meantime the bishop of London was deputed to find a substitute preacher.[38]

Denison, however, would not shut up. 'Under pretence of catechising', Denison returned to the pulpit and repeated his offence. He was now suspended from all ministerial functions (save his lecture at Great All Hallows).[39] Still, however, he would not leave off. On the contrary, he did his best to obstruct the substitute preacher appointed by the bishop by, on one occasion, persuading his curate to hold evening prayer an hour earlier than usual and 'by reason hereof children have been brought thither to be baptised at divers times and, the curate being gone and divine service ended, the said Dr Denison would not permit the preacher, authorised by the said reverend father, to baptise the said child, by reason whereof the company, having tarried at the church till five of the clock ... were fain to carry the child home unbaptised'.[40]

This is recognisably the same Stephen Denison who had gone after the luckless Etherington with such polemical fury. Now, however, the authority of 'the powerful preacher' of St Katharine Cree was being used to denounce leading parishioners for doing precisely what the ecclesiastical authorities wanted them to do, that is, to beautify their church according to Laudian notions of the beauty of holiness. Moreover, this time around, unable to type his opponents as either doctrinally unsound or potentially schismatic, Denison's abrasive temperament led him to defy authority.

Now it was his character and doctrinal orthodoxy that were being dragged through the mud. Relatively late in the day, as the dispute spun ever further out of his control, Denison was formally accused of having 'attempted the chastity' of four married women of the parish, all of whom deposed against him in court.[41] And, finally, various passages from his printed works were cited against him. Again, the subject was baptism but now the point at issue was his claim that the sacrament was only fully effectual when conjoined with the word preached. This charge is almost certainly related to Denison's refusal (noted above) to allow children to be baptised except in the context of full divine service. Thus doctrinal positions he had long been maintaining in the pulpit and press became newly offensive and controversial when attached to such openly provocative actions aimed at some of his own parishioners. No doubt these complaints were also encouraged, perhaps even prompted by, that same concern with the universality of sacramental grace amongst the Laudian or Arminian authorities that had earlier prompted Denison's assault on Etherington's views on baptism in the High Commission. Now, with a delightful irony, the biter himself was being well and truly bit.[42]

Confronted by this melange of alleged moral, professional and doctrinal excesses, lapses and misdemeanours, the court tried hard to be fair. The 'erroneous points of doctrine by him divulged in his book' were to be 'considered of by some divines commissioned judges by the court and are to be desired to report their opinion thereof the next court day'. These then disappear from view. Whatever was going on here, it was certainly not an Arminian doctrinal purge. On the accusations of sexual impropriety, 'upon consideration of his defence and exceptions', the court decided, 'their depositions being singular', that the case against Denison was not 'of sufficient validity to convince him thereof, yet inasmuch as six of them had deposed directly to the fact and some others to the public fame thereof' neither did they feel that Denison's defence of himself and exceptions against the witnesses were 'sufficient to annihilate and take away the proofs and depositions taken against' him. Reading between the lines, it would appear that Denison had made a strong case that the parish was divided, that he had virulent enemies there and that these stories were merely lies spread by those enemies to ruin him. Weighing these claims and counter claims, the court took the Solomonic way out. Neither convicting nor merely exonerating him, they made Denison purge himself in public. Accordingly, he was to appear 'the next court day to purge himself with his corporal oath and the oath of six compurgators, ministers of his own rank and quality, dwelling near unto him in the city of London'. This fell a long way short of vindication and, if it did not constitute a perfectly symmetrical replication of Etherington's experience at the Cross, it must still have given the boxmaker a certain frisson of vengeful pleasure. In effect, Denison's fate was referred back to the collective judgement of his peers, the London puritan clergy. And, however extreme and ill advised his recent behaviour and diction may have been, he was still enough of an insider to elicit the requisite support from his colleagues, six of whom duly turned up to help him purge himself. Having (partially at least) removed that stain from his character, there remained the major charges against him and on these the court found him comprehensively guilty of 'making the pulpit the place for revenge of his malice'. He was suspended from the ministry and removed from his post at St Katharine Cree.[43]

THE LOCAL FRIENDS AND ENEMIES OF STEPHEN DENISON

Clearly, then, Denison had his enemies in the parish. From the outset, his personality and style of divinity had shown a capacity to polarise and divide his parishioners, and indeed, on his own account of the Etherington affair, the wider London godly community. But if Denison had always demonstrated a propensity for making enemies, he had also always shown a capacity to attract a loyal personal following amongst the laity. There was his intense pietistic relationship with Elizabeth Juxon and her husband, described with some pride in his funeral sermons for the Juxons and confirmed by the generosity of John Juxon's will. There was the setting up by Thomasin Owefield of a monthly lecture before the communion specifically attached to Denison's person. He was still receiving bequests from parishioners well affected to the rebuilding project as late as 1631. Even Etherington's account of the campaign waged against him during the 1620s admitted that Denison had a devoted lay following. Indeed, he listed those who had testified against him, many of them quite humble lay people. The list comprised Rowland Thomson and Thomas Rogers (both joiners); Christopher Nicholson, a chandler; Peter Worcester, a drawer; Susan Price, a porter's wife; John Okey, a clothworker; George Dunn, a surgeon; and Thomas Stephens, a clerk. The only clergyman mentioned was Henry Roborough, whom Etherington slightingly described as a curate, about which misdescription Denison, ever touchy on issues of clerical status and no doubt wishing to surround himself with the powerful aura of clerical collegiality, complained vociferously in 1641.[44] As we seen, the two joiners, Thomson and Rogers, joined Denison in his campaign against Peter Shaw in 1629. Even after the 'stained-glass window affair', at least eleven parishioners and six neighbouring ministers appeared before the High Commission to support him, amongst whom, again, were some of his clerical allies against Shaw.[45] As we shall see below, even at the end of the case, the court was prepared to admit that there remained some parishioners anxious to hear the pulpit performances of their powerful preacher.

Denison, in short, had, by 1634/35 if not before, effectively divided the parish. We can catch a glimpse of how deep those divisions ran in two subsequent court cases, the one pursued in Chancery, the other in the court of arches. At stake in both of them were the powers claimed by the select vestry over the affairs of the parish. As we have seen, there had been trouble about this before and it seems reasonable to assume that a combination of the financial burden of refurbishing the church, the controversial nature of the refurbishment itself and the fuss caused, first, by Denison's very adverse reaction to the window and, second, by his eventual removal from the parish, had all served to reopen and exacerbate old wounds.

At the centre of the court cases was a very curious document – the parish's answer to Bishop Juxon's 1636 survey of London vestries. The authors of the return were very emphatic, even shrill, in their account of the local vestry's powers. These they initially founded on the bishop's grant of 1622, only immediately and bizarrely to concede that this, 'being abused', had been cancelled by Dr Duck, Sir Henry Martin's successor as chancellor of the diocese. They continued, however, to assert, in the strongest possible terms, the earlier exercise of episcopal prerogative as the basis 'for the maintenance of the power for the ordering of the business of the parish'. If this were not strange enough, they were quick to add, as had their predecessors in 1622, that, whatever the bishop or his chancellor had decided in the recent past, a select vestry represented 'the use and prescription [of the parish] for many years past and beyond the knowledge and memory of man'. Moreover, the terms of the lease of the living from the Master and fellows of Magdalene College had ceded control of the living to a group of lessees, who acted partly in their own right and partly 'as they are feoffees in trust for the generality of all the parishioners'. If this did not sound fishy enough, the churchwardens then proceeded to outline, in detail, the sweeping powers claimed by the vestry.

They claim and challenge power to make choice, out of their own number only, churchwardens from year to year and all other church offices, to make assessments and taxes upon the generality and to act all other business of the parish at their sole will and pleasure and, upon occasion of vacancy, to provide a minister or curate and to order and capitulate with him for his means of entertainment for the church's service and likewise, upon occasion of dislike, to warn him out again and compound with the parish clerk for his wages and to dispose of the rest and also they claim and take power and exercise to choose and supply of their number whom they think fit, at any time.

Rather than a defence of the status quo this passage sounds almost like a denunciation of misgovernment by an overweening oligarchy. Certainly, powers were being claimed here – to levy parish rates and to 'warn out the minister at will' – which the bishop's initial grant had never conferred, indeed had expressly ruled out, and which the author/s must have known neither ecclesiastical authority nor recent precedent would uphold. After all, as recently as 1630, the vestrymen themselves had applied to the bishop for permission to levy a rate towards the rebuilding of the church. Moreover, as we shall see below, far from being able to hire and fire the minister, the parish elite were entirely dependent on the authority of High Commission in ridding themselves of their 'powerful preacher'. And, as we shall see, even as they relieved Denison of his living, the ecclesiastical authorities were very careful to protect his rights to backpay from the depredations of his now very dissatisfied lay paymasters.

The document concluded, at a fever pitch of apparent righteous indignation, with the claim that these powers were to be exercised 'howbeit the administration of this their doings are disliked by the generality of the parish and controverted by suits now depending both in the court of arches, before his Lord's Grace of Canterbury and also in the high court of Chancery, before the Lord Keeper'.[46] While the court of arches records for this period have been destroyed, certain cause papers from the case are preserved in the state papers and we can trace the Chancery case. This last was brought against the vestry by a number of parishioners – John Stonehill, Robert Hill, John Witham, Abraham Nicholas, George Thorpe, Edward Meredith, John Bloyes, John Davies, John Smith, John Fields, John Gibbons and Archibald Cumber. Interestingly, while none of these men were members of the vestry, there was an overlap of four names between this list and the people who had been prepared to bear witness for Denison in the High Commission.[47]

On the view put forward by Stonehill and the others, the powers of the vestry were a function solely of their status as the feoffees who had leased the living from Magdalene College. On their account, in part because of the high cost of the recent rebuilding, the college had agreed to renew the existing lease, when it fell in, with the existing lessees, for a further ten years. By implication, this located the apparent stability of the parish elite as contingent, a function of a particular negotiation with Magdalene, rather than a reflection of some settled or customary distribution of power in the parish. In conducting such negotiations, it was stressed, the lessees were only acting 'in trust for the good ... of the rest of the parishioners' and certainly their powers in disposing of whatever surplus revenue was left over from the tithe money, once the rent on the living had been paid to Magdalene, was a product only of the need to manage 'the great, extraordinary and burdensome charges in erecting and building of the said church'. Such powers, it was again insisted, existed solely 'for the good and benefit of the rest of the parishioners'. In short, insofar as the vestry did enjoy certain 'prerogative' powers over parish finance, they did so only for very specific, short-term, emergency purposes. Moreover, the vestrymen's status as lessees was a function of a finite legal agreement between the parish, more generally construed as the generality of the parishioners, and Magdalene College. As such it could provide no basis for any long-term usurpation of the right of the generality of the parish to govern its own affairs.

With the theoretical issues settled, at least to their own satisfaction, Stonehill and the others concluded the first part of their bill of complaint with dark hints about possible financial malfeasance, noting that no surplus funds were to be retained 'in the hands of any of the said lessees', but all available money was to be 'employed in and about the reparations of the said church'. These hints about financial ill doing and mistrust can be amplified by material drawn from the church courts, where in June 1634 Martin Bond found himself presented because 'the church stock or some part of it is in the hands of the said Mr Bond and is not brought into the treasury of the church, neither any just account hath been made to the minister and parishioners thereof'. These claims against Bond were paralleled by simultaneous charges levelled against other members of the vestry and parish officers. John Offield, it was alleged, 'hath not given any account in the time of his churchwardenship to the ministers and parishioners of the receipts (?) and the disbursement for and concerning the building of the said church'. Similar malpractice was also attributed to another vestry man, John Dyke, who, it was claimed retained £20 meant for the poor of the parish in his own hands. William Smith was presented by Denison 'for not bringing the account of [his] churchwardenship for the last year notwithstanding he hath been sent unto divers times and wished to bring in the said account'. In addition to his dilatoriness over the communion wine Martin Sheldon was also presented by Denison for refusing 'to open the chest wherein the money received at the communion ought to be kept under three locks, insomuch that the minister was constrained to entreat the other churchwarden to keep [the money] until such order might be taken for the keeper of the common chest'.

The Laudian style

Smith's and Sheldon's replies to these charges are instructive. Smith first claimed that he had cleared his accounts before a team of 'auditors' composed of 'Mr Bond, Mr Ellner, Mr Gayer and Mr Offield' and called 'a meeting of the parishioners and vestrymen to certify of his accounts'. Nor had Denison been excluded from these proceedings; on the contrary, attempts had been made to set 'a day and time and place of meeting' 'with his consent and privity'. But all to no avail. He would not attend. Sheldon told a similar story. He had advised with Denison about 'the bread and wine at communion'; Denison had a key to the poor chest and he, Sheldon, 'had the consent of the parish about the distribution of the poor money'. Again, like Smith, he had 'desired' 'Denison to be present at the distributing of such moneys as have been collected at the communion' but 'he hath refused'. Having put the money in a poor box and placed it in the parish chest 'with three locks and keys', he had sent one key to Denison but 'he hath refused to receive the same'. Here the parish chest moves to the centre of the story, for this dispute appears to have transmuted itself from a squabble about whether, how and by whom the money collected at communion should be distributed to the poor of the parish into a symbolically charged disagreement about the placement of and control of access to the plate, ornaments, books, deeds and documents, all of which were kept in the parish chest.[48] In short, the showdown between Sheldon and Denison epitomised in parvo a wider dispute about who controlled, who truly spoke for, 'the parish' that had been going on since at least the foundation of the select vestry in 1622. Ever since then the precise relationship between the self selecting oligarchy of vestrymen and 'the generality of the parish' had remained an issue; appealed against and allegedly repealed by Dr Duck, the vestry's powers had still been much in evidence during the rebuilding project, the great costs and management of which had clearly created ructions in the parish and served to call the vestry's claims to authority into radical question; a question we can watch being fought out in the attempts of the vestry (or perhaps of an activist group within the vestry) to speak and act for the parish in the teeth of the refusal of Denison and his as yet nameless lay supporters to recognise the legitimacy of their position or claims.

The court of arches case involved precisely the same issues, only approached from a different angle – the monopoly claimed by the vestry to appoint parish officers (churchwardens and sidesmen) without reference to the rest of the parish. The suit was brought by one Richard Newberry against John Brewer, Richard Glover, James Parker and James Smith, men elected by the select vestry as churchwardens and sidesmen during Easter week 1636. The case represented a direct challenge to the powers of the select vestry, the bill of complaint alleging that the right to appoint parish officers lay, and had lain from time immemorial, in the curate and parishioners and not in some special self-selecting group termed vestrymen. That group's claim to elect parish officers without the knowledge, consent or approval ('*noticia, consensu, assensu, approbatione et voto*') of the rest of the parishioners, was a recent usurpation, made without either the consent of the rest of the parish or ratification by the bishop (done '*temere, inconsulto, absque ... ratificatione ordinarii*'). Moreover, their claims to such power had been explicitly repudiated by the bishop of London. Despite all this, Henry Parker, James Croft and others of the vestry had proceeded to elect Glover, Brewer and the others as churchwardens and sidesmen during the Easter week of 1636, recommending all of them to the relevant ecclesiastical judge as the choice of the parish. All of this had, moreover, been done without the knowledge or consent of the curate ('*absque omni consensu, assensu, noticia, approbatione, voto vel scientia vicarii seu curati*'). Their requests to have this confirmation process stayed having failed, Newberry and his allies in the parish had now turned to the court of arches for redress.[49]

The reply of the defendants to these allegations is instructive. They, predictably, asserted that from 'time out of mind and memory of man now living, the use and custom' of the parish 'hath been and is that the minister of the said parish and four and twenty of the ancienter and graver sort of the parishioners there, commonly called vestrymen or the maior part of them, have yearly, from time to time in or about Easter week, made choice of the churchwardens and sidesmen'. Their choices had habitually been ratified by ecclesiastical authority and appointed to the office. Similarly ancient was the vestry's right to perpetuate itself; whenever one of the vestry 'had died or departed out of the parish', the 'rest of them have chosen and, by custom, ought to choose others in their rooms or places'. Moreover, the events of Easter week 1636 had been conducted according to this ancient model. Upon 'warning given of the certain time and place for their meeting', the vestry and curate did 'accordingly meet together, according to the ancient custom of the parish' and 'with joint and unanimous consent did elect and choose' Brewer and Glover to be churchwardens and the others to be sidesmen. Then, on 28 May, the curate had appeared before the relevant ecclesiastical authority and 'in his own name and in the names of the rest of the said electors' did present the chosen men and they were 'admitted to the said offices' and 'sworn for the due execution of the said places according to law'. They then actually took office and were in 'quiet and peaceable possession of the execution thereof' and 'did many or some acts as churchwardens and sidesmen there before the said 28th day of May aforesaid'.[50]

Here, then, was a smooth and simple claim to normality; a unanimous election, punctiliously held according to the customs of the parish, ratified by ecclesiastical authority, a smooth transfer of power from one set of office holders to the next and a *de facto* acceptance of the legitimacy of these actions by the parishioners at large. On this view, the claims of Newberry and his backers were utterly baseless. However, even Brewer and his supporters had to admit that of late the exercise of parochial government, the workings of vestry oligarchy, had not been entirely smooth. For years, the vestry's choice of parish officers had been effected 'without contradiction or opposition of any person or persons whatsoever, until now of late time viz. about two or three years last past'. 'These three years last past', they continued, 'and not before, some few of the meaner sort of the parishioners of Katharine Creechurch (but not the maior part of them, as they believe) have dissented and been unwilling that the older sort of the parishioners there, commonly called vestrymen, should, according to the ancient use and custom, choose the churchwardens and sidesmen of the said parish.' 1636 had been no exception. For, while the choice by the curate and 'two of these men William Smith, George Parker and also James Croft and many others of the ancienter and better sort of the parish' of the parish officers had met 'with the goodliking and consent of the greater part of all the other parishioners there', it had also lacked 'the approbation and consent of some others', although 'not the greater or better part, as they believe'.[51]

In other words, three years before, that is, in 1633, the very year in which Denison had started to upbraid some of his parishioners over the window and other issues, there had been outbreaks of dissent, implicit, and finally explicit, legal challenges, to the monopoly powers of the select vestry, of precisely the sort that Denison himself had, on his own admission, instituted in 1624/25 and intermittently encouraged throughout his tenure as curate. The plot, moreover, thickens when we add in some further information from a petition from John Brewer and Richard Glover, writing in their capacity as churchwardens of the parish, to Sir John Lambe. There they laid the blame for the recent outbreak of litigation about the vestry on the return, made in the parish's name, to Juxon's enquiry about the powers of London vestries. This, Glover and Brewer maintained, had been made by John Bill, who, despite being suspended from his office as churchwarden by Lambe himself, had made the return in terms which 'hath, as is conceived, occasioned a suit long depending before your worship about the vestry of the said parish, as whether all the men of the said parish or but some be a vestry'.

Bill, in his own deposition before the court of arches, admitted that he 'cometh to testify in this case being requested thereunto by Mr Newberry whom he favoureth in respect of the truth and not otherwise'. While he confirmed that during his twenty-four years as a resident of the parish it had been customary for the curate and vestry to elect the parish officers and that 'the said officers so chosen have been allowed of the ordinary', he also claimed that the 'order or faculty for the vestry' issued by Montaigne had been 'dissolved and cancelled'. He had personally heard Robert Cook, one of the deputy registrars of the diocese, tell the Chancellor Duck as much.

Accordingly, Bill delivered himself of the opinion that the election of Brewer and Glover *et al.* 'was not legal in respect they were chosen by a vestry which was dissolved'. On his own account, Bill appears as one of those excluded from the election process; for 'albeit he were a parishioner there and had born the office of churchwarden the last year yet he was [word illegible] by some of the said vestrymen that he ... had no vote in the election or nomination of a churchwarden for that he ... was not one of the vestry'.[52]

Here, it seems, is the explanation for the extraordinarily intemperate language and inflated, indeed patently false, claims made on behalf of the vestry in the return to Juxon. This was a set-up, a deliberately inflated version, indeed on one reading an implicit denunciation, of the vestry's powers and recent behaviour, deliberately pitched at a level of intensity that would render the vestry's position vulnerable to legal challenge and episcopal disapproval. Bill's return was part, then, of a concerted attempt by a group within the parish to challenge the powers of the vestry in both the ecclesiastical and secular courts – hence the needlessly inflammatory assertion of the overweening powers of the vestry, whatever the outcome of the cases in arches and Chancery, with which the return had concluded. It was this that Glover and Brewer were hinting at in their claim to Lamb that it had been Bill's return that had provoked the suit in the court of arches, a suit they were trying now to short-circuit by a direct appeal to the arbitration of the Council. We can gain some confirmation of the concerted, planned nature of these manoeuvres from an admission by Denison himself, in his deposition to the court of arches, that 'some of the parishioners of St Katharine Creechurch do join with ... Mr Richard Newberry in this cause and do defray part of the charges thereof but who they are for certain this deponent cannot tell'.[53]

The fuss over the window, Denison's falling out with some of his parishioners, the case against him in High Commission had been accompanied in the parish by outbreaks of popular dissent against the decisions of the ruling oligarchy, dissent which had culminated in what looks like a concerted and collectively funded set of legal challenges to the powers of the vestry. It was a challenge that Brewer and Glover at least hinted had social causes or consequences, as they complained to Lamb of the 'unquietness that hath been and is still like to be' in the parish. For should there be a general and not a select vestry 'the relieved [i.e. the poor, recipients of parish relief] in short time will, being many, be sessors of the relievers, if all be a vestry'. This was a stock contention in such disputes and, while it does recall the earlier dispute between Denison and Sheldon over the fate of the money collected for the poor after communion, it probably does not reflect any particularly striking social divisions pertaining to this case. However, its deployment here may well betoken the members of a closed parish elite, under sustained pressure from certain excluded elements immediately beneath them in the parish and social hierarchy, having recourse to the order card in order to retain their position of local dominance and the support of the wider authorities in church and state. Similarly, the polemical logic of the position of the Denison group as 'outsiders', opponents of an exclusive and corrupt clique, made claims to be defending the poor and the disenfranchised a natural tactic.[54]

Moreover, the issues at stake here were ones over which Denison had long been in conflict with at least some of the parish elite. Even as he was being driven out, it seems, Denison and his supporters in the parish were trying to get their own back on the vestry. And here the claim that the vestry had the right to hire and fire the curate as they saw fit, represented no part of the positive claims of the vestry but was an extrapolation from their recent behaviour towards Denison – whom some in the parish were indeed trying 'to warn out again' – of what were utterly illegitimate and unlawful powers over the clergy.

This picture is confirmed by the course of the Chancery suit, the real beef behind which concerned the appointment of Denison's successor. This was a choice, the petitioners claimed, that was only to be made 'with the mutual consent, approbation and good liking of your said orators and the rest of the parishioners ... for whom the said lessees were only entrusted and from whom the greatest part of the salary and payment of the said curate or minister doth arise and come, over and above the aforesaid usual tithes, oblations and other profits'. In other words, on the complainants' view, the members of the vestry were just lessees, that is to say merely the legal representatives of the rest of the parish, who happened to have signed the lease with Magdalene and it was implicit in that arrangement that the vestrymen's right to choose the minister was dependent on the 'consent, approbation and goodliking' of the rest of the parish, who, since they, in fact, paid the clerical piper, should retain more than a residual say in calling the tune.

Here lay the rub, for when it had come to replacing Denison, at the suggestion of Sir John Gayer, it had been decided to hold a vote amongst the vestrymen in order to choose between the two candidates – a Mr Richard Lee, MA, prebend of Wolverhampton and a Mr Thomas Rhodes, clerk. The winner, Gayer proposed, would then be presented to the bishop as the unanimous choice of both vestry and parish. According to Stonehill and his friends, the meeting was held at Martin Bond's house and Lee had won the vote, but at that point the vestry had reneged on their promise, refusing 'to ratify and confirm their election and to establish the aforesaid Richard Lee in his office and place of curateship ... or to present or tender him to the said Lord Bishop of London'. The vestry had compounded their offence by refusing to make any 'of the rest of the parishioners' privy 'to the knowledge of their proceedings'. Lee, however, remained the minister of choice for the parish which was now 'utterly destitute of any elected minister', the place 'being officiated by one not elected and chosen thereunto'.[55]

Denison and Etherington again

This was the situation that had provoked the suit in Chancery. The defendants' reply to Stonehill and the others gave, however, a very different account of the affair. For them the 'pretended trust' from the rest of the parish, by which they held their powers as a ruling elite, was a chimera. In this local playing out of the great constitutional questions of the age, the difference between notions of absolute as opposed to limited office holding or monarchy clearly did mean something and the participants to this parish-pump dispute were all getting an extended practical training in precisely what might be at stake in such seemingly abstruse and abstract questions. In their reply to the populist, consent-based version of the distribution of power in the parish between 'the generality' and the lessees or vestry, the vestrymen took an uncompromisingly unconditional, even 'absolutist', view of their powers. They ruled the parish by a right neither derived from nor subject to the consent of the rest of the parishioners. Their powers were based rather on a mixture of immemorial custom and episcopal fiat that brooked no populist challenge from 'the generality of the parish'. Uncompromising on the issue of theory, the vestrymen simply dismissed out of hand their accusers' innuendoes about financial malfeasance.

As for the issue of Denison's successor, they explained, they had indeed held an election to decide the issue and had agreed that whoever won would be presented to the bishop as the parish's choice. If the bishop found their man acceptable that would be it, but if not, they decided to proffer the other candidate as an alternative. Sixteen lessees or members of the vestry attended and the vote went 8–7 to Lee with one abstention. Gayer 'suspended his voice until the Lord Bishop of London was acquainted with what was done'. When the bishop was so acquainted, 'for reason best known to himself', he roundly rejected Lee. According to their prior agreement, the vestry then reverted to Mr Rhodes as their candidate who this time proved acceptable to Juxon and 'was accordingly admitted' 'to be curate of the said parish'. This was an outcome for which the vestry took almost no responsibility, a denial for which their proceedings, from the closeness of the initial vote, through Gayer's abstention and elaborate gesture of deference towards the veto of the bishop, may well have been a calculated preparation. Since, they claimed, 'the whole scope of the plaintiffs' bill is but to have Mr Lee their curate, which matter is proper for the said Lord Bishop to determine and neither the said Lord Bishop nor Mr Rhodes, the present curate are made parties to the suit', they asked that it be dismissed. Their tone here was both peremptory and dismissive – clearly tempers at this point were more than a little frayed – so much so that they earned the reprimand of the court for the curtness of their reply.[56]

Rhodes had been the minister brought in to replace Denison upon the latter's suspension – the victim presumably of Denison's guerrilla tactics described above. So perhaps in the Stonehill group – the group who opposed

The Laudian style

Rhodes' appointment and stood up for Lee – we can see the outlines of a pro-Denison group. (And here the overlap of four names between the instigators of the case in Chancery and those bearing witness for Denison in High Commission would be particularly significant.) As we have seen above, Denison had throughout had his supporters as well as his opponents, a situation that seems to have pertained to the bitter end. Whatever else it was, even by 1635, the parish was not united against him. Indeed, the High Commission itself noted that the parish was divided between 'adverse parties' opposed to Denison, which included 'some of the principal of the parish' and others who supported him. This was a version confirmed later by John Etherington who referred to Denison's feud 'with *some* of the chief of your parish'.[57] We have, then, leading parishioners taking against Denison, and some others, perhaps of less standing in the parish, siding with him. Was there a popular puritan faction in the parish, opposing a crypto-Arminian or Laudian elite?

Lee was described by his supporters as 'a very honest, able and sufficient minister and really conformable to all the rites and commands of the church of England'.[58] Of course, in the 1630s the phrase *'really conformable'* had a range of meanings from stalwartly Calvinist, even moderately puritan to rabidly Laudian depending on the presuppositions and polemical purposes of the speaker. Certainly, Juxon's distaste for Lee's candidacy makes the last option unlikely and what we may be seeing here is a residual pro-Denison group, resisting the imposition of the quisling Rhodes, who had replaced their beloved powerful preacher and now attached to the more ideologically sympathetic figure of Mr Lee, that very fact providing the rationale for Juxon's rejection of Lee as curate.

Given the relatively lowly social status of Denison's supporters in the Etherington affair, and his own long-standing opposition to the monopoly powers claimed by the select vestry, it is surely significant that it was the Stonehill group who espoused the more populist reading of parish government against the oligarchical absolutism of the vestry, the same vestry, of course, that had presided over the rebuilding of the church and raised the money for the window. Certainly, the composition of the vestry must have remained an issue in the parish because, in 1640, when the vestry minutes pick up, we find not a select but a general vestry in place. We know, too, from the vestry's petition to the bishop for permission to raise a parish rate, that the rebuilding project had not been universally popular in the parish. Thus the vestry complained that 'divers of the parishioners of the said parish have not contributed anything towards [the rebuilding project] and are still unwilling and backwards in giving and contributing herein'.[59] Whether that represented ideologically or, more likely, financially, motivated disaffection is impossible to say. But, on this basis, we can surely conclude that these disputes of the mid-1630s represented either a continuation or perhaps a rekindling of tensions in the parish which went back at least to the foundation of the select vestry in 1622 and probably to the very beginning of Denison's ministry there.

These divisions had been exacerbated by the financial and ideological strains of the rebuilding project, which had been taken over by Laud in his consecration service as an object lesson in 'the beauty of holiness', as Laud and his friends conceived it. Denison's response to that and his assault on the window placed at the centre of the new church served further to polarise the parish and to turn some leading parishioners (Bond and Gayer amongst them?) against him. The Chancery and arches cases represent the legal fallout from the resulting disputes.

Not that we should conclude with a vision of a parish torn apart by factionalism, riven with overt personal, perhaps even ideological, conflict. For we can surely discern in the very close, perhaps almost staged, vote in the vestry, as well as in Sir John Gayer's circumspect abstention, an admittedly divided parish and vestry trying to preserve at least the appearance of consensus and the outward forms of procedural civility – in Professor Kishlansky's terms, clinging to the consensual seeming niceties of selection, as opposed to embracing the adversarial polarities of election.[60] One smells a compromise, with a balancing group inside the parish perhaps prepared to back Lee but not to go to the mat with the bishop over the issue. Gayer's suspension of judgement, until the bishop could be sounded out on the matter, may well reveal a parish that had recently attracted the hostile attention of ecclesiastical authority through its internal divisions and dealings with Denison, now very anxious to stay on the right side of Juxon. Conversely, it might represent the machinations of a firmly anti-Lee and anti-Denison faction, desperate for the bishop to do their dirty work for them, thus enabling them to get their own way and still deny all responsibility for the outcome, just as they did in the Chancery case. Either way, these were scarcely the actions of an aggressively insurgent Laudian faction determined to wrest control from a puritan clique by calling in outside episcopal authority, but rather of a parish elite, divided by Denison's antics, and now squeezed between a group of their fellow parishioners (Denison supporters, perhaps one might even call them puritans), on the one hand, and the potentially intrusive presence of Laudian episcopal authority, on the other. After all, for all the divisions within the parish, things only came to a real head when outside authority, in the shape of Bishop Juxon, brought them there by refusing to accept Lee and preferring Rhodes instead. The vestry merely refused to challenge his decision, which was the straw that broke the camel's back and brought all the long-standing political and religious tensions in the parish pouring out into the open in the Stonehill Chancery case.

How that case ended is unclear but what is certain is that the victory of the

The Laudian style

pro-Rhodes group scarcely proved definitive. Rhodes was indeed instituted to the living in January 1635/36, only to be replaced the following October by George Rush, who remained in post until 1643.[61] Again there is an aura of conflict avoidance and compromise surrounding these events, with Rhodes getting the living to prove a point and satisfy the bishop and then almost immediately leaving, perhaps to avert further trouble and allow a man untainted by involvement in the previous stirs – Rush – to be appointed.

THE VERDICT

Indeed, the High Commission court itself seems to have contributed its ha'pennyworth to the process of restoring calm to the parish. Certainly, it would be absurd, with Prynne, to picture Denison as some victim of Laudian tyranny. After all, as we have seen, in going after Denison at all the authorities had been responding to local demand and, indeed, to Denison's own increasingly outrageous behaviour. Indeed, throughout, the court showed itself very keen to extract from the parish the backpay owed to Denison for the time he was under suspension. Nor should this surprise us. The High Commission was, after all, the highest *ecclesiastical* court in the land and throughout the early Stuart period churchmen of all stripes had come increasingly to acknowledge the need to vindicate the status and rights of the clerical estate against the depredations and disrespect of the laity. These were priorities which Laudian clericalism could only reinforce, even when the minister in question was as intemperate and as Calvinist as Stephen Denison. For suspended or not, Denison was still an ordained minister, whose interests and just perquisites had to be protected from lay encroachment. Moreover, as we have seen, there were erastian elements, inherent in Denison's situation as a lecturer and perpetual curate, that, at the best of times, would surely have offended what had become very exalted Laudian notions of the autonomy and status of the clergy. No doubt Denison needed to be dealt with, but the laity also needed to be kept in their place.

Denison's backpay amounted to a considerable sum, 'sixty-six pounds old money' to be precise, 'whereunto was to be added ... the allowance for this quarter from Michaelmas last to Christmas next, which was twenty pounds more'. Leading parishioners were, however, dragging their feet and the court could not find any 'principal of the parish' who did not either refuse 'or, by some dilatory excuse', defer 'to pay so much as their own part', 'their example ... working' the like effects 'with others'. The court, after 'divers monitions to the adverse party to think upon some course for the collecting or raising' of the arrears, resorted to the ultimate threat. Denison would not finally and formally be 'removed' from his post in the parish 'till his said money was paid'. If the parish wanted to be rid of Denison, and thus be in a position permanently to replace him, they would have to pay up. As for Denison himself, in the end he was even restored to the ministry, except, that is, in the parish of St Katharine Cree, where, the court concluded, surely with good reason, it was 'improbable and unlikely, in respect of the manifold grievances and affronts by him given to his parishioners by his indiscreet and intemperate manner of railing in the pulpit, that he should ever do any good amongst them'.[62]

There remained, however, the issue of Denison's monthly lecture in preparation for the reception of the sacrament. Even here the authorities were prepared to compromise. As we have seen, the lectureship was a result of a bequest and 'was settled on him for life'. It was, therefore, difficult to take away, which indeed was something that the High Commissioners declared themselves entirely unwilling to do. With Solomonic discretion, instead of parting Denison from the lecture, they parted the lecture from the parish, referring the question of which neighbouring parish (since Denison was barred from St Katharine Cree) should provide the venue for the lecture to the bishop of London. Denison and two of the 'feoffees in trust for payment of the stipend or salary' for the lecture duly applied to the bishop and his chancellor Dr Duck, who provided a list of three adjacent parishes, of which the church of St James on Duke's Place was the nearest. The parish, which was literally just around the corner, had been carved out of the greater whole of St Katharine Cree as recently as the 1620s and was thus the logical choice as 'the most convenient for the parishioners' of St Katharine Cree 'to resort unto the hearing of the said lecture on the usual day and at the hour formerly preached by the said Dr Denison'. (In fact, it seems that in the end the lecture was transferred not to Duke's Place but to St Botolph's, Aldgate, where it remained until 1643.)[63]

Denison's ministry would, therefore, appear to have divided the parish but, far from simply shutting Denison up or, still worse, driving him from the ministry altogether, the authorities seemed intent on separating the parties, restoring order and vindicating their own authority, all the while leaving Denison in possession of his just rights, perquisites and clerical status. Indeed, they seemed positively happy to allow those in the parish who retained a soft spot for their powerful preacher continuing access to his services, so long, that is, as Denison himself was kept out of the pulpit of St Katharine's itself.

THE RETURN OF STEPHEN DENISON

There the situation remained until 1640 when, in January, the first steps were taken to return the lecture before communion to the parish. When it eventually arrived in 1643, Denison came with it. Evidently, there were still some in the parish prepared (indeed perhaps even anxious) to see him return to the pulpit from which he had been so vocally denouncing his local enemies since the 1620s. Not that the resulting rapprochement between parish and minister was achieved without considerable trepidation. In a meeting of November 1643 it was agreed that Denison should turn up with the deeds regulating the finances and conduct of the lecture and, if both 'he and the parishioners' would promise 'to leave aside all old grudges', 'the said Mr Denison is to come in love and preach the monthly lecture in our church again'. Later in December it was recorded that 'Dr Stephen Denison brought in the said deeds, in love, and was received, in love, and so preached the lecture the same night, being the 29 December 1643. He was received in love by Mr Rush and Mr Scholfield.'[64]

But even as Denison came back, it may well be that Abraham and Isaac left. Certainly, at the same meeting of November 1643 that approved Denison's return, 'in love', it was noted that 'it is in question whether the round of Abraham and Isaac in the east window should be taken down' – a local debate no doubt undertaken in response to a parliamentary ordinance against idolatry, of the preceding August. From the surviving parish records one cannot tell whether or not the offending images were then removed. Certainly, while the extant glass in the upper portion of the east window dates from the 1630s, that below it, where the figures of Abraham and Isaac could once have been seen, dates from the nineteenth century.[65]

Whatever the fate of the window, the select vestry had certainly been dismantled by the time parish records resume in 1640. It was replaced by a more popular form of parish government with meetings notified to the parish in advance, in one instance after the sermon of the fast day. Decisions were taken 'by the general vestry, lawfully summoned and called together and holden this day ... by the generality of the inhabitants'.[66] Certainly in elections for parish offices, like churchwarden or overseer of the poor, upwards of ninety votes were regularly cast.[67] However, while the outward forms may have changed greatly, there was considerable *de facto* continuity in the way in which the parish was actually run – with executive committees with memberships of something like twenty, and often considerably smaller quorums, being set up to deal with particular tasks and problems. For instance, in 1643 twenty-two were deputed, out of whom any four were to assist the churchwardens in petitioning parliament about the redress of the parish's grievances concerning the rectory. Again in 1644 eight men were deputed to negotiate with Magdalene College over the lease of the living.[68] While the resulting agreement was duly consented to and ratified by 'the generality of the parish' at a meeting held the following year, twenty-eight men were nominated to actually sign the lease as feoffees for the parish at large, in a motion that was signed by over thirty parishioners, over and above the twenty-eight nominated as feoffees.[69] Likewise when the move, described above, to increase the minister's wages and raise a parish rate to pay for it fell through, fifteen men were put on a committee, with a quorum of seven, to sit daily until the problem of the minister's arrears of pay and the question of a 'competent maintenance' for the minister were solved.[70]

These relatively low numbers may suggest that one of the things involved in the disputes clustered around the rebuilding of the church, the removal of Denison and the choice of his successor was a struggle between an institutionally entrenched elite or oligarchy – the select vestry – and another group, just beneath them in the social and parish hierarchy, who wanted a piece of the action and a say in affairs and were prepared to seek it by invoking and, indeed, appealing to 'the generality of the parish' against an allegedly corrupt and self perpetuating clique. 'Puritanism', in the form of the stridently querulous voice and personal following of Stephen Denison, lent ideological edge and coherence to that pitch. What would appear to have happened with the shift from a select to a general vestry was a triumph for the vision of the dissident, Stonehill group, as they had articulated it in their bill of complaint to Chancery. There they had pictured a sort of notional golden age, a largely fictional status quo ante, prior to the oligarchic intrusion of the select vestry. And now that golden age had returned; all the objections of Stonehill and his allies to current theory and practice had been met; government operated in the name of the generality of the parish; parish affairs and office holding had been opened up to a wider constituency and yet the parish elite (albeit a slightly more broadly defined and informally self selecting version thereof) still held the crucial offices and, in effect, ran the parish. Thus was administrative order and continuity preserved. What passed for administrative continuity, however, should not be mistaken as continuity of personnel in the conduct of parish government. Thus, amongst the names of the parish notables that recur throughout the 1640s, I can find very few of those involved (on either side) of the Chancery case of 1635/36. Nor can I discern any particular patterns or alignments amongst the names of those who were thus involved. If there were long-standing factions or mutually antagonistic groups, created by the furore over the window and Denison's ouster, they appear to have left little or no trace in the records of the succeeding decade.

Some scores were settled, and some inherently unsatisfactory compromises unpicked. The most notable victim of this process was poor George Rush. If he had been a compromise candidate, chosen to still the troubled waters created by the removal of Denison and the struggle between Lee and Rhodes, like much else that had been patched together during the 1630s, his appointment was undone in the 1640s. At a vestry meeting of February 1644, it was recorded that 'Mr George Rush, curate, hath promised for to take the good will of the parish and he will resign his place up to such a man that the parish shall ... make choice of by the maior part of the parishioners'. 'At the same time and day Mr Rush declared himself willing to accept the gratuity of the parishioners at his departure lovingly and all this to be done between this and the next first of April 1644.' Since he signed both the protestation against the introduction of ceremonial and popish innovations into the church and, back in 1633, the petition supporting George Walker against Laudian attack, Rush would not appear to have been removed as part of some sort of anti-anti-puritan purge.[71]

Rush having taken a backhander to leave without fuss, the parishioners' options were now wide open – certainly open enough to allow Denison to return to the curateship as well as his lectureship had any one wanted him to. That, however, did not happen. An election was held between three candidates: Mr Yates, Mr Down and Mr Bolton. Yates won (polling fourteen votes to the other two's two apiece) only to turn the job down, although not without undertaking in the meanwhile 'to preach in the forenoon till the parish was provided for'.[72] Another election was planned in March but fell through and it was not until the following May that a choice between Mr Thomas Porter and Mr William Thomas confronted the parishioners. Porter was elected unanimously and proved to be a minister of impeccably puritan, not to say presbyterian, credentials.[73]

The parish too pushed towards the establishment of what one can only describe as an unofficial eldership, deciding, in 1645, that the 'churchwardens, for the time being, (if they please) may assist Mr Porter in conferring with and approving of such persons as intend to receive the Lord's Supper, otherwise the business aforesaid is wholly referred to the discretion of Mr Porter'.[74] Clearly the balance between lay and clerical authority in the parish was still up for grabs. Incidentally, Porter's pay continued to be in arrears and, as we have seen, an elaborate plan to regularise and increase his stipend failed ignominiously.

There is, however, no doubting the univocally puritan tone of the parish during these years, at least insofar as that tone can be reconstructed from the vestry minutes. Popular elections to parish offices, up to and including the curateship itself, a pseudo-lay eldership to help a minister of impeccably presbyterian views regulate access to the sacrament, all betokened a certain style of politics and religion. In similar circumstances other parishes had taken the opportunity to call back, in triumph, ministers driven out in the 1630s. By this point Denison must have been well into his sixties and so age may have been a factor but the failure to even mention his name in any of the elections for the living surely shows that his earlier behaviour had broken too many fences, to mix the metaphor, ruffled too many feathers, to allow him to be a viable candidate. Denison, however, kept his lectureship until his death in 1649.[75] Indeed, the parish even took steps to reorder the finances of the lecture and pay him his arrears.[76] He evidently felt good enough about the place by his death to leave money for the poor of the parish and, ironically enough, for the upkeep of the church.[77]

To conclude, given the gaps and reticencies in the parish sources, it is all but impossible to come to definitive judgements about the nature of the religious or political divisions that rent the parish during the 1630s and 1640s. We might tentatively conclude that it was Laud's decision to reconsecrate the church that converted an elaborate and expensive, but by no means exceptional, exercise in church refurbishment into a showcase for the Laudian style. Certainly, if Prynne is to be believed, Laud's predecessor at London, Montaigne, had intended to indulge in no such liturgical floor show, merely allowing the church to return to full use as the building works were completed. We might argue that this Laudian fuss altered the way in which the rebuilding project and, indeed, even the window itself, were viewed, raising the stakes for Denison and his ilk. Being a scene from the Old Testament, depicting men, admittedly holy patriarchs but still men, and not aspects of the divine or scenes from the life of Christ, could the window conceivably have been viewed as an allowable embellishment for a proudly refurbished parish church, rather than as a sign of a distinctively Laudian piety? Perhaps. But while it did not demand, the window certainly allowed a reading of itself as an architectural setting forth of, say, John Cosin's views on sacramental grace as he had explained them to Etherington in High Commission back in the 1620s.

That, certainly, seems to have been Denison's view of the matter. On Prynne's account, he had immediate recourse to the discourse of idolatry. And if, as all accounts agree, there were those in the parish who agreed with him, that was obviously not how the likes of Bond and Gayer saw things. Whether their involvement in the rebuilding process represented a positive endorsement of a Laudian style of piety or merely a proud embellishment of their parish church, according to the latest standards of material and aesthetic display, must, in the current state of the evidence, remain unclear. Certainly, even relatively late in the process of refurbishment, enthusiasm for the rebuilding of the church and attachment to, or respect for, Stephen Denison, were not mutually exclusive emotions. As we have seen above, in his will of 1631, William Avenon left both a substantial amount with which to build a memorial for himself into the fabric of the new church and a bequest to Denison. Nor does there remain any trace in either Gayer's will or Bond's career of a distinctively Laudian piety. Bond's defiantly secular funeral monument, adorned with an image of him dressed for his part in the defence of the city against the Armada is scarcely what we might expect from a lay Laudian. But, at the very least, we can conclude that there were powerful men in the parish quite happy to produce a church that met Laudian standards for the beauty of holiness.

The Laudian style

But whatever one's initial take on the window, it presumably did not take a Laudian zealot to find Denison's antics in the pulpit alarming and distasteful, as the failure even to entertain his return as curate in 1644/45 shows. Throughout the High Commission case and elsewhere, Denison appears as the insistent aggressor: denouncing the window, naming or identifying with broad hints his opponents, directly addressing, in the pulpit, rumours about his sexual conduct, all in all, making it quite clear that those who were not for him were against him. Again, his refusal satisfactorily to respond to the questions put to him in High Commission and his subsequent defiance in the face of the recurrent warnings and injunctions of the bishop of London and the High Commission, all show us a man running out of control. On the other hand, the machinations in both the arches and Chancery against the vestry, in which he was almost certainly involved, show us a man of considerable pertinacity and political will. In part, at least, what was at stake here was Denison's temperament; we have evidence for this sort of florid and intemperate preaching style and behaviour stretching back to his first arrival in the parish in 1617. He had, on his own account, consistently opposed the monopoly powers of the vestry. His behaviour during the Etherington dispute had scarcely been a model of tact and decorum and, as we have seen, he had accordingly attracted the critical comment of at least some of the London godly. Again, his horning-in on the side of dear, departed Edward Elton in 1624–25 looks like a gratuitous and heedless act of provocation to the authorities, who responded by burning his book and suspending him from his lecture. To say the least, therefore, Denison had an intemperate, combatively volatile personality and past.

But there was surely more at stake here then merely a repeat performance by Denison the powerful preacher and hysteric. For Denison was now operating in an ideological context dominated by the rise of Laudianism and he was not taking it well. His outburst against the book of sports, his denunciation of idolatry in the midst of Laud's consecration service and his later foul-mouthed assault on the window and its supporters, all bespeak a man somewhere near the end of his tether. Clearly a combination of an ideological temperature raised by the impact of Laudianism, and his own temperamental extremity, was forcing Denison over the top.

But where, in his earlier run-in with Etherington, the course of national and court politics had run in his favour, now things were very different. Then, circumstances had conspired to combine ideological instincts and reflexes basic to his nature – anti-Arminian and anti-popish ardour and mainstream puritan anti-sectarianism – with Denison's own intemperate personal style, in a potent but politically and rhetorically effective mixture. Like three lemons on a slot machine, all three elements worked together to Denison's personal and polemical advantage. Now, however, the target of Denison's ire was not some lowly boxmaking zealot but policies and symbols beloved of both episcopal and royal authority and backed by central figures in the local parish elite, the people who, in effect, employed him. Accordingly, his belligerent style and whining self-righteousness, while it might play well enough with at least some of the godly, now, in the wider world, counted against him. After all, in a confrontation with at least part of the parish elite and the court of High Commission, a popular following amongst the godly of the parish and beyond was scarcely an asset. The likes of John Bill, Rowland Thomson and Susan Price might go to their graves thinking that Denison was wonderful, but that could neither save his job in 1635/36 nor get it back for him in 1643/44.

We might even see Denison as caught by the ideological tensions unleashed by Laudianism between the expectations of his own lay puritan following – a following, as we have seen, by no means limited to the parish where he was employed nor to the social elite who ran the select vestry – and the demands of discretion and tact, as the local and national power structures, to which he owed his living, defined them. Responding, increasingly recklessly, to the former, he alienated definitively the latter. Certainly, if he was playing to an increasingly radical puritan, anti-Laudian gallery, it would seem that Denison was doing so to good effect. For, as we have seen, in 1633 Samuel Grame, the brother of Abraham, Denison's colleague in the campaign against Shaw and sometime lecturer in St Katharine Cree, was accused of saying that 'if it were in his power he would throw all the bishops of this land out of their places and put honest men in their stead'. Amongst those 'honest men', along with Richard Rolls and John Downham, Grame named Stephen Denison.[78]

In short, there could scarcely be a better illustration of the way in which the rise of Laudianism had made the church of England a far less comfortable place for the likes of Stephen Denison. And here we should remember that, for all his temperamental extremity, Denison's opinions were very far from extraordinary. Indeed, given the prevalence in various establishments, local, municipal and national, of precisely Denison's view of the world, his fate in the 1630s is not an insignificant sign of the shift in the ideological centre of gravity of the English church that had occurred since the days of his triumph against Etherington in the mid-1620s.

All this, of course, is most definitely not to see Denison as some 'moderate' puritan victim of Laudian oppression and innovation. On the contrary, Denison brought his fate down on his own head, as his increasingly extreme diatribes against the window and his local enemies reopened old wounds, in part inflicted on the social body of the parish by his own rebarbative pulpit style. Thereafter, provoked beyond measure by any signs of criticism or opposition, he consistently misbehaved himself into an impossible position, systematically ignoring the best efforts of authority to bring him back from the brink, until the High Commission almost had no choice but to remove him from the parish. Cast out of the parish but not out of the church, Denison must have suffered a considerable decline in income and status, piecing together a living from his lectureships and pick-up preaching. However, he was far from ruined – indeed he retained standing enough amongst the London godly to have his name affixed, along with those of Daniel Featley, William Gouge, John Prideaux and Richard Holdsworth, at the bottom of a probably fraudulent circulating certificate appealing for funds to relieve an allegedly distressed expatriate German divine.[79] Indeed, as the six ministers prepared to back him in the High Commission, the court's decision to move his lectureship before the sacrament to an adjacent parish and his later return as lecturer to St Katharine Cree, all testify, he retained a significant following in the parish and indeed the wider London godly scene.

While that following was not enough to get him all his old jobs back, the removal of the compromise candidate Rush and his replacement by the elected presbyterian Porter, together with the decorous discussion of the allegedly idolatrous nature of the window all reveal the parish returning to the same mainstream puritan tradition that had produced and nurtured Denison. While the clipped and laconic administrative sources of the 1640s scarcely allow us to penetrate far beneath the seemingly peaceful surface of parish politics, some things clearly remained the same. Money, as ever, was an issue and so too was church fabric – when the steeple proved unsteady in 1650 the parish again struggled to raise the very considerable sums needed to repair it.[80] The parishioners seemingly retained their habit of dividing their loyalty between rival preachers. What became of whatever elements of spontaneous lay Laudianism had lain behind the church rebuilding is entirely unclear. Bond and Gayer are noticeable by their absence from parish records during the 1640s, but then both had gone on to higher things, Bond in the next life (he died at the ripe old age of 85 in 1643) and Gayer in city politics. The parish, in fact, seems to have reverted to the sort of ideological timbre and collective life that rendered a now nearly seventy-year-old Stephen Denison only too happy to leave some of his hard-earned savings to the poor of the parish. It was, all in all, an oddly peaceful and consensual end to a notably long-standing and turbulent relationship between pastor and flock.

NOTES

1 PRO S.P. Dom. 16/261, fol. 282v.
2 House of Lords Record Office, main papers, 23 March 1624; J. Malcolm, *Londinium, revivum* (London, 1802–7), VI vols, vol. III, p. 307; C[ity] of L[ondon] R[ecord] O[ffice] Viewers's report, 1623–1636, membrane 5. For the will of Lawrence Williamson, dated 29 August 1629, see P[rerogative] C[ourt] of C[anterbury] Clarke 92; PRO Prob. 11/146/ fols 222v.–223r.; for that of Christiana Wells, see PCC Hele 146; PRO Prob. 11/50 fol.

289r.–v.; for that of John Hough, dated 6 August 1625, see PCC Clarke 113; PRO Prob. 11/147, fol. 82r.–v.

3 The Clothworkers' Company Court Orders, order dated 20 April 1631, fol. 109v. Also see their Accounts for 1630–31, fol. 19v. I owe these references to the kindness of the archivist of the company Mr D.E. Wickham. J. Stow, *A survey of the cities of London and Westminister ... now lately corrected, improved and much enlarged by J. Strype* (London, 1720), vol. II, p. 65. The foundation stone was laid on 23 June 1628. For the petition to Sir Henry Martin see Inner Temple, Petyt MS 538, vol. 51, fol. 165r, a reference I owe to the kindness of Ariel Hessayon.

4 PRO C2/Chas I/C81/63/1, petition of Stonehill *et al.* dated 25 January 1635/36.

5 *Calendar of State Papers Colonial (East Indies and Persia) 1630–34* (London, 1892), p. 82. I owe this reference to the kindness of Anthony Milton.

6 Corporation of London Record Office, Repertory 43, fol. 181r., dated 18 March 1629/30.

7 G[uildhall] L[ibrary] Ms 5570/2 (Court book of the Fishmongers' Company), pp. 791–2, dated 15 March 1629/30.

8 I owe this information to the kindness of Ken Fincham.

9 L[ondon] M[etropolitan] A[rchives] DL/C/343 (Vicar-general's book, 1627–36), fol. 137r.

10 Stow, *A survey*, vol. II, p. 65; for Woodliefe's will see PCC Barrington 23; PRO Prob. 11/153, fols 232v.–233v.; for Avenon's will, dated 30 December 1631, see PCC St John 135; PRO Prob. 11/160, fols 522v.–524r. For Gayer's arms on the font see Stow, *A survey*, p. 65. I should like to thank Anthony Milton and Julia Merritt for many discussions on this subject.

11 LMA DL/C/343 (Vicar-general's book, 1627–36), fol. 137r. LCRO Repertory 43, fol. 181r., dated 18 March 1629/30.

12 For the Fishmongers, see GL Ms 5570/2, p. 792; for the Merchant Taylors see Merchant Taylors' Company Ms 302, vol. 15, entry for 21 April 1630.

13 For the Ironmongers, see GL Ms 16988/4 (Accounts, 1630–33), p. 411 and GL Ms 16967/4 (Court book), p. 72, dated 18 November 1630. For the Goldsmiths see Goldsmiths' Company Warden's Accounts and Court Minutes, vol. 16, p. 340, dated 22 April, 1630.

14 For the Grocers, see GL Ms 11571/11 (Accounts), fol. 341r., dated 23 June 1630; for the Skinners see GL Ms 30,727/6, p. 383.

15 For the Haberdashers see GL Ms 15842/1 (minutes of the court of assistants), fol. 260v., dated 28 May 1630.

16 Drapers' Company Assistants' Minutes, fol. 237v., dated 16 May 1630. Also see Warden's Accounts, p. 53 for payment. For the Vintners see GL Ms 15201/3 (minute book), p. 15, dated 3 May 1630. For the Mercers' Company see Acts of Court, 1625–31, fol. 264r.

17 For the Leathersellers, see Warden's Accounts 1629–30, and Court Minutes, dated 5 July 1630. Due to the reorganisation of the company records formal references were not available for these citations, which I owe to the kindness of the company archivist, Ms Wendy Hawke. For the Tilers and Bricklayers see GL Ms 3043/2 (Court minute book, 1620–63), entry dated 10 August 1630.

18 For the Salters, see Salters Company Minute Book, 1627–84, p. 52, dated 13 September 1630.

19 For the Clothworkers, see Clothworkers' Company Court Orders, fol. 109v., dated 20 April 1631 and Accounts, 1630–31, fol. 19v., dated 25 June 1631.

20 GL Ms 3043/2, entry dated 10 August 1630. The full list of company coats of arms embossed onto the ceiling of the church is as follows:

North aisle	Nave	South aisle
Mercers	City arms	Grocers
Drapers	Fishmongers	Goldsmiths
Skinners	Merchant Taylors	Haberdashers
Salters	Ironmongers	Vintners
Dyers	Clothworkers	Brewers
Pewterers	Leathersellers	

I owe the identification of these coats of arms to K.E. Campbell, *A brief history and account of St Katharine Cree church* (1979) a guide book available in the church itself.

21 Goldsmiths' Company, Warden's Accounts and Court Minutes, vol. 16, p. 340; for Fishmongers see GL Ms 5570/2, p. 792.

22 For donations to St George's Southwark see, for instance, Mercers' Company, Acts of Court, 1625–31, fol. 264r., recording a gift of £20; Salters' Company Minute Book, 1627–84, p. 43, recording a gift of £5; Drapers' Company, Assistants' Minutes, fol. 237r., recording a gift of £10.

23 For the setting up of the select vestry see LMA DL/C/341, fols 262r.–263r., dated 8 May 1622.

24 For Gayer see DNB. Thanks to the kindness of Andrew Thrush I have been able to consult the biography on Martin Bond he has compiled for the History of Parliament.

25 *Calendar of State Papers, Colonial (East Indies and Persia), 1630–34*, pp. 80. 82–3, 137.

26 LMA DL/C/343, fol. 137r., petition dated June 1630.

27 Julia Merritt, 'Religion, government and society in early modern Westminister' (University of London, Ph.D. thesis, 1992) and her path-breaking article 'Puritans, Laudians and the phenomenon of church-building in Jacobean London', *Historical Journal*, 41 (1998).

28 P. Lake, 'The Laudian style', in K. Fincham, ed., *The early Stuart church* (Basingstoke, 1993). For the application of certain key Laudian texts to contemporary London church design, including, very briefly, that of St Katharine Cree, see John Newman, 'Laudian literature and the interpretation of Caroline churches in London', in D. Howarth, ed., *Art and patronage in the Caroline courts* (Cambridge, 1993).

29 For the stained glass in St James, Duke's Place see Stow, *A survey*, vol. II, p. 59.

30 For details of the consecration service see *ibid.*, pp. 60–1. Also see LCRO Repertory 37, fol. 57v.

31 See, for instance, GL Ms 2968/3, fol. 355r. and All Hallows-by-the-Tower, Ms RR/Di/1 (churchwardens' accounts, 1628–66), fol. 62r.–v., recording payments for visits by representatives of St Dunstan's-in-the-west and of All Hallows, to view recent refurbishments in a number of other London churches. I owe these references and this point to the kindness of Ken Fincham.

32 Stow, *A survey*, vol. II, p. 61, for the legal challenge to the autonomy of St James, Duke's Place, mounted by the Master of Magdalene College, Cambridge, the owner of the

living, and by Stephen Denison. The challenge failed. For the monument and verses at the east end see *ibid.*, pp. 59–60. I owe this point and these references to the kindness of Julia Merritt, who is working on a project on religion and society in early Stuart London centred on Stow's *Survey*. On the stylistic question, see Newman, 'Laudian literature and the interpretation of Caroline churches', p. 179.

33 William Prynne, *Canterbury's doom* (London, 1646), pp. 113–14. The date is confirmed by Laud's laconic note in his diary that on 16 January 1630/31 'today I consecrated St Katharine Creed church in London'. This was followed a mere seven days later on the 23rd by his consecration of another new model Laudian church, St Giles-in-the-Fields. *The works of the most reverend father in God, William Laud, D.D.*, ed. J. Bliss, 7 vols (Oxford, 1853), vol. III, p. 213. Here, then, was a concentrated demonstration, in the capital, of Laudian notions of sacred space and the liturgical and architectural forms that should best contain and shadow forth the holy. On St Giles, in particular, and these events in general, see Newman, 'Laudian literature and the interpretation of Caroline churches'. For plans to give far more expansive (and expensive) architectural expression in London to the more broadly Caroline notions of decorum, order and hierarchy that underpinned the political, religious and social values and programme of the Personal Rule see J. Newman, 'Inigo Jones and the politics of architecture', in K. Sharpe and P. Lake, eds, *Culture and politics in early Stuart England* (Basingstoke, 1994).

34 PRO S.P. Dom. 16/261/ fol. 282v.

35 *Ibid.*, fols 283r., 282v.; Etherington, *The deeds of Dr Denison*, sig. A3v.

36 PRO S.P. Dom. 16/261, fol. 283r.

37 *Ibid.*, fol. 283r. For this case see CLRO, Repertory 47, fol. 309v., 16 July 1633. I owe this last reference to the kindness of Ariel Hessayan.

38 *Ibid.*, fols 283r.–v. For the presentments against Bond and the others see Guildhall Ms 9274, fols 4r., 13v.–16r and MAO DL/C/320, pp. 415, 532, 563, 564. The names of the vestrymen for this period can be reconstructed from a lease signed by all the members of the select vestry with Magdalene College, in March 1627. The names were Martin Bond, Bartholomew Elnow, John Dyke, Randolph Owen, John Gayer, William Thompson, Robert Parsons, Martin Hall, John Weller, John Offield, William Webb, John Smart, John Wall, Richard Blackwell, Wiliam Smyth, Richard Glover, William Avenon, Nicholas Sheldon, Aldridge Halsey, John Brewer, Richard Arnway, John Atkin. See Guildhall Ms 1213, a box of parish deeds from St Katherine Cree. I should like to thank Ariel Hessayon for drawing this material to my attention.

39 PRO S.P. Dom. 16/261, fol. 144v. For Denison's suspension see *ibid.*, fol. 175r. For the continuation of his suspension but the protection of his maintenance see *ibid.*, fol. 184r.; also see *ibid.*, fol. 187r., where he was allowed 'to maintain his lecture at Great All Hallows only so long as he gave no occasion of scandal or offence'.

40 *Ibid.*, fol. 243v.

41 *Ibid.*, fol. 283v.; *ibid.*, fol. 291v., for the personal appearance of the women involved as witnesses against Denison – Mary Smith, wife of William Smith, tailor; Margaret Cordall, wife of William Cordall, cutler; Magdaline Bryan; Jean Keech, wife of Richard Keech. Denison had earlier referred in the pulpit to rumours concerning his sexual activities, telling his auditory that his accusers could 'not charge him with committing any act with any woman and that they would, they do the devil good service therein'. *Ibid.*, fol. 283r. The fact that these rumours were transmuted into formal charges and

that four women turned up in court personally to denounce him might be taken to lend them a certain credence.

42 Ibid., fol. 283r.–v.

43 Ibid., fols 283v.–284r. The names of the six ministers who supported him in court – Richard Watson, parson of St Mary Aldermanbury; John Down, parson of St Benet, Gracechurch Street; Richard Culverwell, parson of St Margaret, Friday Street; Richard Crook, parson of St Mary Swithins and William Cooper, parson of St Thomas Apostle's – are given at ibid., fol. 291v. For further parts of the verdict see ibid., fol. 292r.

44 Etherington The defence, p. 3. Etherington, The deeds of Dr Denison, sig. A2v. 'And whereas in the third page you blame me so greatly for that, in my defence, Mr Roborough is set down curate, if he had wrong done him therein, let the reader blame the register or Roborough himself, for so I found it in his deposition recorded, which I have yet, under the register's hand, to show and whatsoever he is now, he might be so then, for ought I know and to have the care of or be a curer of souls need be no disparagement to him; nay, rather it would be happy for him if he were so.' Roborough was lecturer and stipendiary curate at St Leonard's Eastcheap at the time. He did not become the incumbent there until 1641, so Etherington was technically correct in calling him a curate, although he was not Denison's curate; a position Etherington no doubt did confer on him for satiric purposes. I owe this point to Paul Seaver. For Denison's attempt to maintain the status and repute of his witnesses – 'honest men, as well ministers as other professors', 'men so honest, so religious, so truly zealous' – and in particular 'of Mr Rowborough, a godly minister and no curate' and 'Mr Stevens a bachelor in divinity' 'men of honest repute' of whom 'none (as I think) will speak evil ... but the factious whom they do oppose' see Denison, The white wolf (1641), pp. 77–8, 80.

45 Denison's lay witnesses were named as follows: Thomas Stephens, Henry Kent, Humfrey Aston, John Witham, John Smith, Marian English, Richard Murch, Gabriel Collington, Margery Godfrey, Richard Jackson, John Blois, Edward Gibbons, Robert Gibbons, Lodovic Hughes, Alice Birt, Richard Worrall, John Folkwood, Richard Burdon, John Brent, Nathaniel Bullock, John Bowen. PRO S.P. Dom. 16/261, fols 75r. and 85v.

46 Lambeth Palace Library Ms CMVII/11, fol. 25r. headed 'the certificate of St Katharine Creechurch'. Fols 26v.–29v. A table of fees agreed upon 'at a vestry holden ... by the curate and vestry men the 16th December 1604' signed by, amongst others, Martin Bond, as a churchwarden.

47 John Bloyes, John Smith, John Witham. While a John Gibbons was a party to the Chancery case, two other Gibbons, Robert and Edward, stood as witnesses for Denison. Edward had been presented in 1634 for absenting himself from church 'in Sundays in the afternoons of November', but unlike the others so charged had sought to excuse himself by explaining that he had been called away to witness a christening in another parish. George Thorpe had also been presented in 1634 for refusing to receive the communion kneeling – 'he went away not receiving to the offence of the congregation'. This may be a hint that the pro-Denison, anti-window faction was tinged with puritan non-conformity; it certainly suggests that both sides of the dispute were using the church courts against their enemies during the early 1630s. See Guildhall Ms 9274, fols 14r., 15v., 167v.

48 PRO C2/Chas 1/C81/63/1, petition dated 25 January 1635/36. GL Ms 9274, fols 13v., 15v. Also see ibid. fol. 82r. for the certificates from January 1635 of Bond and Offield having

cleared their accounts 'before the minister and parishioners'. MAO DL/C/320, pp. 415, 532, 563, 564. If anything, the dispute with Sheldon was determined in Denison's favour, with the chest with three locks and keys, one each for Denison and the two church wardens, and containing all the parish ornaments and books (but not its deeds and documents) removed, according to the canon, from the vestry to the chancel and with 'the money collected at the last communion' handed over to Denison and the overseer of the poor, John Dyke, to be 'distributed to the poor' 'with the privity and consent of Mr Dr Denison'. See *ibid.* pp. 564, 601. I should like to thank Ariel Hessayon for drawing the Guildhall material to my attention and for much advice on these points.

49 PRO S.P. Dom. 16/342/87, parts I–V. Pt. I, fols 215v., 216r., 216v.

50 *Ibid.*, pt. IV, fols 223r.–224r.

51 *Ibid.* pt. III, fol. 221r.–v.

52 *Ibid.*, pt. V, fols 225r.–226v. S.P. Dom. 16/376/107, tentatively misdated in the calendar to 1637.

53 PRO S.P. Dom. 16/342/87, pt. V, fol. 229r.

54 PRO S.P. Dom. 16/376/107.

55 P.R.O. C2/Chas 1/C81/63/1, bill of complaint by Stonehill *et al.*

56 Reply of the defendants attached to the bill of complaint, dated 1635. For the court's reprimand see C33/170, fols 278r., 301r.

57 PRO S.P. Dom. 16/261, fol. 308r., dated 8 December, 1635. Etherington, *The deeds of Dr Denison*, sig. B3v.

58 PRO C2/Chas1/C81/63/1.

59 LMA. DL/C/343 (Vicar-general's book, 1627–37), fol. 137r.

60 M.A. Kishlansky, *Parliamentary selection* (Cambridge, 1986).

61 GL Ms 9539A/1 (subscription book), fol. 62v, subscription of Thomas Rhodes to the three articles upon his appointment as perpetual curate at St Katharine Cree, dated 12 January 1635/36; *ibid.*, fol. 81r., subscription of George Rush, on his taking up that very job, dated 8 October 1636.

62 PRO S.P. Dom. 16/261, fols 308r., 284r.

63 GL Ms 9657/1 item 22, dated 28 February 1637/38. For the ultimate destination of the lectureship see Etherington, *The deeds of Dr Denison*, sig. B3v.

64 GL Ms 1196/1 (first surviving vestry minute book from St Katharine Cree, starting 1639/40), fol. 5r., for a meeting held in January 1639/40; fol. 23v. for another held on 14 November 1643.

65 *Ibid.*, fol. 23v.

66 *Ibid.*, fol. 23r. 'There was a lawful warning given by the clerk, after the sermon upon the fast day, being the 8th of June 1643'; *ibid.*, fol. 25r. 'a general vestry'; fol. 26r. 'a meeting of the parishioners in the vestry house'; fol. 27v. 'a general meeting of the parishioners'.

67 *Ibid.*, fol. 26v.

68 *Ibid.*, fol. 23r., for the nomination of the committee in 1643. Also see *ibid.*, fol. 24r. where, at a meeting of 9 February 1643/44, the same committee was reconstituted to manage certain properties left to the parish.

69 *Ibid.*, fol. 28r.; see fol. 30r. for the ratification.

70 *Ibid.*, fol. 35r.

71 *Ibid.*, fol. 24r., meeting held 9 February 1643/44. For the protestation see *ibid.*, fol. 12r.

72 *Ibid.*, fols 25r., 26r.

73 *Ibid.*, fol. 27r., results of the electoral 'contest' between Thomas Porter and William Thomas for the curate's job.

74 *Ibid.*, fol. 32r. Porter signed the 'Desires and reasons' of the London presbyterian clergy in 1645, see A. Argent, 'Aspects of the ecclesiastical history of the parishes of the city of London, 1640–1649 (with special reference to the parish clergy)', (unpublished Ph.D. thesis, University of London, 1983).

75 GL Ms 1196/1, fols 32v., 35r.

76 *Ibid.*, fol. 27v., meeting of September 1644.

77 For a bequest in 1651, see *ibid.*, fol. 82r.–v. Also see fol. 50r and PRO C5/396/96, a reference I owe to Ariel Hessayon.

78 Bodleian Library, Tanner Ms vol. 114, fols 115r.–v.

79 PRO S.P. Dom. 16/386/36, parts I and II. According to a Chancery case of 1657, Denison left an estate of some value, out of which £40 were paid for his funeral, £40 for the upkeep of his sister, Magdalene, until her death at the age of 80 in 1653 and another £20 for her funeral still leaving a tidy sum to be deployed to help the poor of the parish. See PRO C5/396/96.

80 GL Ms 1196/1, fols 83r., 92r., 95r.

Chapter 12

Retrospective: Denison and Etherington position themselves for posterity

A POWERFUL PREACHER SURVEYS THE RUINS OF HIS CAREER

The sermon notes taken by Henry Fleming from a series of Denison's sermons preached between 1637/38 and 1639 provide us with a wonderful source through which we can observe Denison as he looked back in anger and self-righteousness on the debacles of the late 1620s and early 1630s. For in these pulpit monologues he revisited the sites of his altercations with Etherington, Shaw and Nye, his trials and tribulations before High Commission and his troubles in and final expulsion from St Katharine Cree. Admittedly he did so in general terms, mentioning (if Fleming's account is to be believed) no names, dates or places but rather ruminating on the recent past under a series of general headings or rubrics, thus transforming (as he no doubt thought) his own bitter experience into nuggets of spiritual wisdom and practical advice for his auditory of the late 1630s. Of course, we cannot know or prove for certain that Denison was always self-consciously reflecting on his own experience in these sermons, but as we shall see, it is certainly far from fanciful to read many of the central themes and the more bitter, pointed and insistent remarks therein as commentaries upon the events of ten years before.

The sermons were studded with hostile references to and asides about his old *bêtes noires* – the brownists, familists, anabaptists and antinomians. Thus at one point he claimed that there were 'many' 'rigid brownists in the city' many of whom claimed, much as he had earlier claimed Etherington had claimed, 'that a bishop cannot be converted to God'. This, of course, was an opinion with which Denison would have nothing to do, for, as asked his auditory, if the ex-whore Mary Magdalene could 'be converted why may not a bishop be converted? If a bishop cannot be converted, how came the bishop of Milan, St Ambrose, to be converted? How came Chrysostom and Austin so likewise? How came Cranmer to be converted to be a martyr? How came Ridley to be converted and to lay down his life in martyrdom? How came many holy popes of Rome to be converted, for you must consider that pope in former time hath been a name that hath been given to godly men, fathers of the church, before popery came in.' Such beliefs were, however, only too typical of the rigid brownists who, Denison claimed, 'will not see any beauty in the ordinances of God enjoyed by them' [in the national church].[1]

But if Denison continued to lambast the schism of the separatists, after his experiences of the late 1620s and the early 1630s, his attention was now much more concentrated on the doctrinal heresy of those whom he termed 'false prophets'. Even the most seemingly holy men could have their errors, Denison warned, and error, if fundamental, could prove damning to those who accepted it as saving truth. 'It is plain', he concluded, 'that a man or woman may be damned for an error in judgement, if it be fundamental, as well as for an error in life.' 'So that they are in as clear a way of damnation that follow the pope or the turk as any are in the way of hell that live in sabbath breaking, in whoring and drunkenness and in oppression or any other sin.' 'So that a man is in an evident way to hell in the way of anabaptism if he do receive their abominations, yea a man is in an evident way to damnation that follows the way of the antinomians that do reject and abolish the eternal law of God and turn to libertinism, though they pretend never so strong a faith concerning justification, yet they, flattering themselves with the law of God, thinking God sees no sin in them, are in an evident way to hell and damnation.'[2]

For Denison, then, antinomians, familists and anabaptists were the classic wolves in sheep's clothing and Denison warned his flock against them in no uncertain terms, just as he had warned the London godly against Etherington in the mid-1620s. We must beware, he insisted, of 'those that seem to be good men and do deliver such and such points and we are persuaded that they are very good men and holy men, such as favour the people of God and the church of God'. For it was natural in the face of a spectacular display of external piety for us to think that 'that which they deliver is very sound and [that] we need make no question of it'. But such a conclusion, Denison warned, was dangerously mistaken. 'They come and pretend themselves to be sheep and to belong to Christ's flock and fold as well as others, though inwardly they are ravening wolves.' 'They may come with seeming honest lives', he warned, ' nay perhaps their lives may be civilly honest though not religiously and for all this he may be a wolf in sheep's skin and clothing, coming disguised.'[3]

On this subject, Denison had words of admonition for both the laity and the clergy. He told the clergy that 'it is not for ministers to go and raise some new opinions and dangerous opinions for to get a name to be magnified of a sort of ignorant people that are ready to embrace any kind of doctrine if it come under the colour of zeal'. 'The mother of all heresies', he opined, 'is pride and you shall see that those that raise new doctrine, they are extremely proud. They are damnably proud, more than any other.' Accordingly all the godly, both clerical and lay, 'must labour for humility'. But if Denison was concerned to warn the likes of Peter Shaw or Philip Nye against the dangers of doctrinal novelty and a populist playing to the crowd, he was even more concerned to denounce the factious laity who 'are ready to receive any heretical doctrine whatsoever it be, though it be contrary to that which they have been instructed in. Some are of the foolish opinion of Cicero that had rather err with Plato than hear others, so there be many that choose rather to be damned with some erroneous minister than to hear the truth from others.' The laity should, therefore, have regard not so much to the man, the personal qualities of the preacher, as to the nature of his doctrine. 'Ministers may justly tax' those professors who proved receptive to the deceiving message of these false prophets 'to be heretics (as it is the brand of an heretic) that are ready to be seduced and carried away with every vain gloss of false doctrine, especially if he do continue in it and will not be corrected'.[4]

In all this Denison was almost certainly justifying his own former conduct in his campaigns against Etherington and Shaw and their lay followers. Not only were the terms deployed in the sermon precisely the same as those he had used against Etherington and Shaw – a wolf in sheep's clothing – but many of the doctrinal issues at stake – the status of the church of England as a true church, the spiritual condition of bishops, the relationship of justified Christians to the law – were exactly the same as those with which he had been concerned during his disputes with Etherington and Shaw.

By this point, however, it was antinomianism that bulked largest for Denison as a threat to doctrinal orthodoxy. We have already found him denouncing antinomians as doomed to hell by their faulty understanding of the key doctrine of justification and their consequently completely erroneous belief that they were free from sin. The pride of such heretics knew no bounds, Denison explained. 'The sects they are so proud that they denounce all the churches of the world in respect of themselves. So the anabaptists they do despise all the world and the antinomians they are so proud that they say they are now like to Christ and the law being taken away they can have no sin in them and so are made more damnable proud by their faction then they were in the state of nature.' So great was their pride and self-love, Denison explained, that they equated 'the beauty of the house of God' not with the pure ordinances on offer in the national church but with 'the gathering together of a custom of factious persons, as the antinomians, that will follow none but those that do favour them'.[5]

On this crucial subject of human perfectability in this life Denison went out of his way to explain how his position differed from that of the familists and antinomians. Just as those groups did, Denison maintained that true believers must be 'full of the spirit'. 'Not of the spirit of delusion ... But it must be with the spirit that is the spirit of God, and this must warily be understood, for it is not meant we must be filled with the essence of the spirit of God as the spirit of God did dwell in us essentially either as the form of the manner or as the matter of the manner.' Recourse to such formal scholastic terminology in the popular pulpit was very often a sign of a certain discomfort, an attempt by the minister to negotiate a particularly ticklish or controversial point by blinding his audience with science while at the same time enhancing his own reputation for learning and judgement. Such would certainly seem to have been the case here, for having introduced these distinctions Denison made no effort to apply, explicate or explain them, although he had clearly invoked them to leave his audience with the impression that his version of the way in which the spirit of God should or could be present in true believers differed fundamentally from that espoused by both the familists and the antinomians. And to be fair to Denison here, as David Como has shown, he was addressing a rather technical, difficult but crucial area of doctrinal difference between mainstream puritans and antinomians. Thus he went on to denounce 'the blasphemy of the wicked familists' who 'dream of the spirit of God dwelling in them' in precisely the same way that it dwelt in Christ. 'It is sufficient', Denison explained, 'that the spirit of God doth dwell in Christ in that sense. Neither must we think to be filled with the spirit of God or the Holy Ghost as to have it to dwell in us personally. Far be it from any Christian to think such great blasphemy as to make himself in this respect equal with God. But we must be filled with the spirit by a metanomia, the efficient for the effect', with 'the graces and gifts of the spirit' rather than with the spirit itself.

But taken in that sense Denison was only too ready to concede that possession of the spirit was a distinguishing characteristic of the true Christian and that we should all labour to achieve the graces and gifts of the spirit. As we have seen, the means to that end were, on Denison's account, entirely conventional, amounting to little more than enthusiastic and frequent recourse to the word, prayer and the sacraments. But within these limits Denison was prepared to talk of the spirit and its gifts in a language fully as exalted as that used by Etherington or T.L. 'It is like a fire Math.3.1. He shall baptise with the Holy Ghost and with fire because where the spirit of grace is, it is light in the understanding and heat in the heart; where the spirit of grace is he is like as fire.' Moreover, where the spirit was there was liberty from sin; not, he hastened to add, as the antinomians conceived of it, as freedom from the 'inhabitation of sin but from the reigning power of it. Where the spirit of God is, there is liberty, so that a man is freed from spiritual bondage, that sin shall not reign in him at its pleasure, as it hath done, but shall find opposition where it found none before.'

Denison and Etherington again

Of course, Denison was careful to add that by the injunction '"be ye filled with the spirit" it is not meant as though we could be absolutely perfect in this being filled with the spirit but is meant we must be filled with the spirit, that is comparatively, in comparison of that we have been before' and 'in comparison of the wicked, who are destitute of the spirit'. Yet the the presence of the spirit in the godly must and would have its effects – effects, in fact, not entirely dissimilar to those described by Etherington. 'Where the spirit of God is there is love to God and to his children in respect of the grace that is in them, love to the house of God and to the truth of God and to the ordinances of God.'[6]

As ever, Denison presented his position as a golden mean of truth and moderation located between two extremes and, as before, popery continued to play the role of polar opposite to protestant sectarianism. But Denison's experiences of the late 1620s and early 1630s had served to produce another ideal type of theological deviance, another ideological marker in terms of which he could construct and defend his own position as the epitome of orthodoxy. I refer of course to the Laudianism against which he had bumped repeatedly and with such force in the early 1630s. Of course Laudianism is a term of art used by modern historians and in so far as Denison named this strand of thought, feeling and ecclesiastical policy he termed it Arminian or popish, referring once to the erroneous opinion of 'the Jesuits of the time and Arminians' that denied Rome to be the seat of a recognisably papal Antichrist.[7] But generally, in marked contrast to his anti-antinomian diatribes and asides, Denison's opposition to Laudianism has to be extrapolated and inferred from more general remarks. Thus, discoursing on the way in which sin often appeared dressed in the borrowed clothes of virtue, he lamented how 'ducking and cringing, which is mere superstition, doth not pass to be so but to be a devout kind of worshipping God'. Ostensibly this was an anti-papal remark, succeeding, as it did, a similar attack on the religious value of pilgrimages. However, given the current furore over Laudian practices like bowing to the altar or at the name of Jesus, in which Denison and his close associates had been such active participants in the recent past, it is surely not entirely fanciful to see in remarks like this sidelong blows aimed at current Laudian policy, intended subliminally to associate such policies and practices with real popery.[8]

But perhaps unsurprisingly, given his experience over the rebuilding of Katharine Cree and in particular over the east window, it was on the issue of the 'beauty of holiness' that Denison gave the clearest vent to his anti-Laudian opinions. Thus he devoted the best part of a whole sermon of 1639 to the question of 'wherein the beauty of God's church doth consist'. He asserted there that the 'beauty of the house of the Lord' 'doth not stand in the stately structure ... in the stately building of it nor in the brave images and fine building, that is not the beauty of it'. On the contrary, that beauty was to be found in the pure ordinances of God, in prayer, in singing of psalms, in reading of the scripture, in preaching, in meeting together of God's ministers and God's people, for this is to meet together in holy duties. God is the special beauty of his own house. The beauty of God is the principal beauty that is to be beheld in the house of God. Where two or three are gathered together in God's name there God will be in the midst of them. As the principal is better than the extract, so God is better than all his benefits and than all his works, so that the principal beauty that is to be contemplated in the house of God it is the beauty of God himself and Christ himself.

Typically, immediately before this passage, Denison had defined beholding of the beauty of the Lord as 'to contemplate the excellencies of God as they are made known in his house by faithful and true preachers'. The easy movement in these passages between the public ordinances of God generally conceived to preaching and thence to the meetings (both public and private) of God's people and ministers and thence to the actual presence of God in his church, rendered immanent in and through the meeting together of his people at his ordinances, is, of course, entirely typical of Denison's vision of the holy and the way it was most directly present in the world and church.[9]

We are back then with that word- and preaching-centred vision of divine worship and the divine presence in the church so familiar from Denison's earlier printed works. It was a vision that he defended in these sermons against both those (in our terms 'Laudians') who, he claimed, placed the beauty of God's house in its external structures and decoration and against those protestant sectaries (in his terms anabaptists and antinomians) who denied any such beauty to the national church and equated the house and beauty of the Lord exclusively with their own meetings and conventicles.[10]

Here, given explicit and extended articulation some seven or eight years after the event, are the grounds for Denison's opposition to central aspects of the church-rebuilding project at St Katharine Cree. Now Denison made it clear in a list of acceptable charitable works proffered to the well-meaning but confused lay person that he was far from being opposed to church repair or construction in and of themselves. His list consisted in order of 1. 'as to build free schools for children to be taught', 2. 'to give to poor scholars at the university', 3. 'to build and repair churches', 4. to fund 'lectures in barren places', 5. 'to give bibles to those that are desirous to read and are not able to buy them', 6. 'to erect hospitals and to erect almshouses', 7. 'to erect houses of store for corn for poor people against hard times', 8. 'to give dowries to poor honest virgins, to give money to poor young beginners, to lend money freely to shopkeepers without use', 9. to repair highways and bridges.[11]

The list, of course, is distinctly logocentric, dominated by the provision of education and books whereby ministers could be trained and true religion, as Denison and his ilk recognised it, could be propagated. But the rebuilding and repair of churches is up there right next to the funding of lecturers, which was surely a cause dear to Denison's heart, for even in his salad days Denison had always drawn some of his income from lecturing and by the late 1630s he was solely dependent on his lectureships for his livelihood. It seems clear from all this, therefore, that Denison's objections to the rebuilding of St Katharine Cree were particular to that project rather than general. Indeed, they almost certainly represented an ideologically based reaction against what he took to be the superstitious and erroneously Laudian values inscribed in the refurbishment programme as it had emerged by 1630. Over against that Laudian vision some seven or eight years after the event he was still asserting his own mainstream puritan view of the beauty of holiness as it inhered in pure ordinances and preaching, the godly worship and edification of God's people for which the physical church structure provided a decent and sheltered site or space.

In short, Denison's view of true religion, the church and the godly community remained centred, as it always had been, on the links between the powerful preacher and his flock, variously conceived. In so far as the physical, financial, liturgical and institutional structures of the national church enabled and even facilitated the process of edification whereby that temple built only of lively stones, the godly community, was constructed and sustained, all was well. However, as we have seen, during the crisis of the late 1620s and early 1630s, it had been precisely the mechanisms of mutual respect, control and constraint that bound Denison to his flock, at least insofar as that flock was defined by the parish that he served, that had come under most strain. Indeed, it would surely be fair to say that by 1633 those links had been almost entirely sundered. Thus when Denison returned to this subject in the late 1630s we find him modifying his earlier position, in ways that shifted the balance between pastor and flock ever further in favour of the clergy and which certainly served to limit the room for the exercise of the autonomous judgement of the laity.

This was not perhaps immediately apparent since in his diatribes against false prophets Denison reiterated his earlier insistence on the duty of the ordinary laity to check the doctrinal claims of the clergy against the word. 'All hearers' were obliged 'to do that which the apostle saith in Thessal.1.5. Prove all things, keep that which is good. True, orthodox, sound professors must prove and try all things and only keep that which is good.' So much Denison had said before, but now he added a crucial caveat, a caveat notably absent from his earlier pronouncements on this subject in print. 'Now we do not grant to people arbitrament of ministers' gifts, that we must leave to bishops.'[12] That might seem to give an altogether more authoritarian twist to Denison's position, legitimating, by implication, his recourse to the High Commission during his campaigns against both Etherington and Shaw.

Yet there was a limit to how far someone with Denison's opinions could go in that direction. Thus, he continued, 'we grant to all hearers to examine points that they have been instructed in former time in sermons and not rashly to keep everything that hath been delivered. We must try all things by the canonical scripture, by the whole canonical scripture ... and also by the analogy of faith and we must try what we hear by that portion of faith which we have received from time to time. If we find the doctrine to be contrary to scripture we must not receive it.'[13]

Now since each Christian's portion of faith might differ this might seem to be a recipe for chaos. After all, presumably both Etherington and Shaw's followers felt that they had indeed tested their mentors' doctrine by precisely these means before pronouncing it sound and taking it to heart. But if Denison's analysis of this issue had once more or less stopped here, now he pushed on adding that

> again we must try it according to the judgement of orthodox divines.[14] This was the manner of the church, Corinth.1.14.22, in the apostles' time, Acts 15, in the beginning. It hath been the wisdom of the church formerly to have counsel gathered together against heresies. It is more like to find the truth by the judgement of many when many are of the council. I say it is more likely to find the truth by many learned men better than by one, as many eyes are able to see more than one. So the judgement of most orthodox divines is a means to try that which is sound and a good means to try that which is not sound. This is a means to discover false teachers when they come alone and bring forth new doctrine as though none could do so but themselves.

Combined with Denison's injunction, delivered later in the sermons noted by Fleming, that the laity should bring their 'questions', 'their spiritual doubts' 'to the temple', 'to the house God' to be 'resolved', this would seem to put the process whereby the doctrine of the clergy should be checked against the word very firmly back under clerical control.[15] We are far closer here to the modes of clerical arbitration through which the dispute between Walker and Wotton had been handled than to the flurry of lay conventicling and articling which Denison had summoned up to deal with Etherington and initially at least with Shaw.

And yet having seemingly placed the regulation and definition of right doctrine safely in the hands of godly ministers like himself, Denison promptly proceeded to take it away again. For immediately after the passage just quoted he added, 'there are some helps required', which helps he proceeded to list. First, he claimed, 'we must be such as are well catechised in the grounds and principles of religion'. Second, 'we must be conversant and frequent in the word of God, in the canonical scripture'. Third, 'we must be practicers of the word of God, of the doctrine that we hear'. Fourth, 'we must labour for humility'. For pride was a divine turn-off and the spirit of God refused to work through 'the proud and conceited' 'as many professors are of their own knowledge. God doth resist such and doth teach and instruct the humble and meek. If we be humble and meek and so God doth take upon him to instruct us we shall be able to stand against the assaults of the devil, whereas if men be proud they are easily carried away with false teachers.'[16]

With these injunctions, of course, Denison plunged the whole issue back into a hopelessly subjective hall of mirrors, full of circular, self-confirming arguments and claims. We are back here in a world in which only the godly could decide who the godly were and only those who already possessed and understood the truth could be trusted to recognise and defend it. Indeed, we are alarmingly close to the rhetoric of the 'little ones' so beloved of Etherington and T.L. After all, one person's 'Christian boldness' (which was, as we shall see, a quality much prized by Denison) was quite likely to be another's spiritual pride; one's love of the truth and sound scriptural knowledge, another's proud conceit of their own knowledge and opinion; one's love of the truth, another's spiritual flightiness, a typically heretical pronenesss to change one's mind at the first sound of a novel doctrine. Thus, in seeking to stabilise and codify godly procedures for the definition of orthodoxy and the regulation of theological dispute, Denison ended up vainly trying to square the circle. In the process, of course, he revealed with wonderful clarity, the inherent instability of a set of assumptions and practices that mingled the supposedly objective criteria of scriptural and dogmatic truth, underwritten by some supposed consensus of learned and orthodox divines and the authority of 'the bishops', with inherently subjective, value-laden and almost infinitely glossable notions of sincerity, humility, zeal and godliness.

Here again the *de facto* instability of Denison's theory closely resembled and indeed reflected the nature of his own practice or experience. After all, he had personally experienced the downside of all this when various members of his own flock had either sided with the likes of Shaw or Etherington or repudiated his efforts to bring these supposed heretics to book. Now we can be sure that Denison, in his own eyes, was that most valuable of commodities, that most potent of ordinances, 'a powerful preacher', and yet in his own parish that powerful preaching had provoked the most adverse of reactions. How could such an outcome be explained? Here Denison had recourse to another central tenet of his printed works of the 1620s. Since the great sign of a converted Christian was a renewed attraction to and love for 'powerful preaching', the opposite must also be true; those who resisted or reacted against a powerful preacher must be in a very serious spiritual condition, indeed they were very likely reprobate. Just as Christ 'when he preached to them of Nazareth he told them that they were not worthy of his ministry because they did despise him and contemn him and were filled with wrath against him, so those men that can easily be filled with wrath and often against the ministers of God, preaching the truth unto them, they are filled with a worse thing than wine, if it be possible'.[17]

Those who resisted the word were clearly hard of heart, Denison concluded, and 'no wholesome minister is able to please, much less to regulate a hard heart'. It was simply impossible 'to convert one that is totally and finally hardened ... this is that that makes the ministry of God's ministers unprofitable and so is a great bar to conversion. It is a bar to salvation. God hath sworn that unbelievers and those that have hard hearts ... should never enter into his rest.' Thus when 'Christians come to sermons but have no feeling and reap no benefit by them', they 'presently repute it to be the coldness of the minister, when the truth is the greatest cause is of our own selves, we bring with us a hard heart and therefore do not profit by the word of God'. Thus Denison was able triumphantly to conclude that 'a minister that doth preach to a hard heart is like a silly smith that works upon cold iron, but no smith will be so silly. But the ministers do often work upon cold iron and so their preaching doth come to little effect.'[18] All of which rather let off the hook ministers who, like Denison, succeeded as much in alienating and infuriating their flock as in converting them to true religion. Certainly, viewed from this perspective, there was little doubt about who was to blame for the events in St Katharine Cree in the early 1630s. Once again the doctrine of reprobation had come to Denison's rescue. Evangelically effective in providing an anti-type of notorious sin and hardness of heart against which the averagely pious and anxious auditor could react, here it provided a perfect reason/excuse to explain why even a preacher as powerful and orthodox as Denison could have provoked so hostile a reaction in at least some of his flock. If we put these passages together with his frequent attacks on the mores of the parish and city elite (quoted above from these same sermon notes) we can watch Denison put together a totally unflattering portrait of his enemies in the disputes of the late 1620s and early 1630s.

Indeed, throughout these sermons we can see Denison seeking to provide a detailed justification for his own conduct during those disputes. For even if he had been confronted by an alliance of false prophets, proud and misguided godly lay people and rich, corrupt and most likely reprobate parish notables (and clearly not everyone thought that he had), he still had to justify his own inimitable style of pulpit warfare. He proceeded to do so through a series of paeans of praise to a quality he termed 'Christian boldness'. Commenting on the example of Mary Magdalene, Denison opined that 'this should teach us to imitate this woman in holy boldness. We should not fear the face of tyrants, though they have never such an opinion of our person or our profession. We should not fear to look on the proud as this woman did not fear to look this pharisee in the face. Thus by boldness we may much abate the pride of our adversaries.' 'You must know', he added, 'that the adversaries of the church ...

are as wolves. Now the nature of a wolf is this that if a man spy him first and pursue him he will run away but if the wolf spy the man first and pursue him and the man doth run away the wolf will spoil him. So the church's adversaries, if a man fear them, they will make him bondslaves of them but if they do not fear they will not be so bad against them.' Thus we must 'labour for assurance of salvation, it is that which the wicked papists do oppose and say it is presumption but we must labour for it ... He that is in a base place and is assured of a better preferment he cares not though he go out of the other. So the children of God will not fear to go out of this world if they were assured they should go to a better life.' 'If we do not depend upon ourselves but upon the mighty power of God only we need not fear the face of any tyrant', Denison concluded.[19] And this, of course, was almost certainly what Denison thought he had been doing in his campaigns against Etherington, Nye and Shaw as well as in his displays of defiant disobedience before the High Commission and of truculent defiance in the parish. Far from pursuing a number of personal vendettas and hobby horses he had been displaying exemplary Christian boldness against the adversaries of the church, no matter how high and mighty, seemingly godly or popular they may have been.

Denison, of course, had in some sense 'lost' those encounters, and, if not ruined, then he had certainly severely damaged his career and reputation. But that too went with the territory of Christian boldness. 'We must not', he told his auditory in 1639, 'think it too much to depart with our good name and reputation for Christ's sake ... We must not think too much to depart with our very lives for Christ, as the martyrs did.' By the same token, given the world's propensity to take against true religion and its godly carriers, Denison explained that we must be prepared to recognise the cause of the gospel in the most unlikely, humble and reviled of locales. It was a good way 'to gauge our faith and try our confidence' to see if we could discern 'the beauty in God's religion when it is most disgraced in evil times' or the 'beauty in God's servants when they are most trampled under foot'. 'Can we say that we account the reproach of Christ in suffering his name? Do we account it greater riches than the treasures of Egypt. If we can do this it is a hope [?] that we have a true faith.'[20]

Reviled in some quarters as a persecuting tyrant and a clerical pharisee for his campaigns against Etherington and Shaw, in bad odour with the authorities for the Christian boldness he had displayed with such persistence in the pulpit at St Katharine Cree, at the end of his trials and tribulations, taunted with accusations of sexual harassment and incontinence, Denison himself had lost a great deal of his own good name during his struggle against the adversaries of the church. And on the basis of the passages analysed above we can surely conclude that not only did Denison discern the beauty of true religion and of God's servants in his own debasement and humiliation, he was prepared, in effect, to dare his auditors to do the same, with the strong implicit argument being that if they could not do so, they themselves did not have a true faith.

However much Denison might proclaim his willingness to sacrifice his good name to the cause of Christ, as these claims made from the pulpit in the face of the public congregation show, he had anything but given up on re-establishing his reputation for zeal and godliness in London puritan circles. But this too required justification and he tried to provide it in a sermon of 1639 dedicated to the theme of the nature and value to a true Christian of a good name. 'A good name is better than precious ointment' was Denison's text. This was a verdict that he tried mightily to confirm as he spent a great part of the sermon denouncing those who wanted to deny the blessing of a good name to God's children. Throughout, Denison came down very hard indeed on slanderers and informers who deprived the godly of their reputations. 'Therefore let slanderers know the extent of their sin. They are thieves and brethren to murderers and in some respect worse', he declaimed.[21]

Denison's accounts of how all this worked bear the ring of bitter personal experience. Thus he expatiated on the cumulative effects of seemingly small slanders. 'An evil report being once raised though it be but little at first, it comes to be great at last. He that is slandered suffereth great damage more than any man doth in his goods. Besides if a thief take anything from a man he may make him restitution with advantage ... But it is not so with a good name, that cannot be restored. If a good name be once shut down, if it be not the greater mercy of God it will never return to right again.'[22] Denison was surely lamenting here the permanently deleterious effects on his public standing of the whispering campaign about his sexual habits that had started in the late 1620s. Equally bitter personal experience echoes through his account of those who 'innocently' pass on such tittle-tattle without either endorsing or denying it. Denison at one point posed the conundrum 'will you say those that broach evil reports without any malice, that they are murderers?' Perhaps inevitably this was a rhetorical question and the answer was immediate and unequivocal. 'Those that will defame the most cunningly they will acknowledge some good to be in the party that is defamed but that good shall come in with such a cut-throat biting that it is but a great help for them to slander them that are defamed and they come in pretence of former good they thought nothing too dear for such a man ... but he hath done this or that. These do but colour over the maliciousness of their slander.'[23] We can almost hear the worthy parishioners of St Katharine Cree passing on the 'news' of Denison's alleged sexual peccadilloes 'more in sorrow than in anger'. Even years later Denison was still trying to get his own back in the pulpit by shaming his erstwhile parishioners into repentance for their assaults upon the good name of their powerful preacher. Thus at one point he declaimed that all this 'should be a terror to those that are slanderers of others though they be never so rich and carry their heads as high as a may pole, as it were, yet they are hereby to be rebuked for they are worse than thieves'.[24]

If we can discern some of the more prominent of his enemies in the parish behind these remarks (Bond and Gayer perhaps?), in other outbursts against informers and defamers of the clergy we can see Denison settling other equally bitter old scores. Thus he attacked those that do 'persuade themselves they do God good service to inform against the ministers of God and labour to imprison the truth of God and to interrupt the preaching of God's word'.[25] In another passage he ran together the type of 'sycophant that follows the court of justice, that frames articles against the children of God which they are in no wise able to prove' with the 'parish sycophant that doth ingratiate himself with the chief of the parish to accuse men falsely'. Elsewhere Denison railed against 'gossips that prattle among others and many malicious schismatics that tear the names of others and many others that are prone to believe reproaches'.[26]

It was bad enough slandering private individuals, Denison moaned, but 'schismatics' slandered 'whole states and whole churches in comparison to their churches as the brownists do'. Others slandered ministers and in doing so weakened the ministry of God. 'Woe will be to them that slander the ministers of the gospel, be they never so mean in the church, yet woe is to them that do slander them, for as much as they hinder the going out of their ministry. Those that slander do hinder the power of their ministry, in as many as believe them. Look how many receive the scandal for truth they take away the power of the minister to do good to such and cursed be those that hinder the current of the gospel.'[27]

In these passages Denison had assembled all the various parties to that bizarre marriage of convenience between proud parish notables, gossips, schismatics and informers that had brought him low in the early 1630s. Having conjured up this melange of probable reprobates and ne're-do-wells Denison proceeded to spit defiance in their faces. 'A black saint that hath aspersions cast upon him and is made black by the wicked, such a one, being sound, is ... better than those ring leaders of hypocrisy and schism whom they so extol, whom they will make so white. A black saint that is evil spoken of is better than any of their painted white devils.'[28]

So seriously did Denison take the sin of slander that at one point he actually compared it to another of his pet hates – usury; 'those that have wronged the commonwealth by usury, those that have put others to unjust vexation and unjust charges by their false calumnies, they ought to make restitution, otherwise there is no matter of salvation to be offered to them'.[29] Once again, then, Denison had managed to associate his personal enemies with the notion of reprobation. Indeed, he arguably went even further than that, citing long passages of scripture calling down the vengeance of God on slanderers. 'O Lord recompense them according to the work of their own hands, give them sorrow of heart or hardness of heart, a special judgement upon any man. Yea persecute them and destroy them for ever. Thus you see the church of God, though charitable, yet how it remembreth God of vengeance on defamers.'[30]

And yet there was something of a problem in all this. Not only might such a drive for vindication and revenge seem petty, self-serving and certainly uncharitable, it might also be taken to fly in the face of some of Denison's own dearest assumptions. For, given the inherent hostility of the world to true religion and the godly, it was surely all but impossible for a true Christian to avoid slander. In such circumstances how much should Christians allow themselves to care about what the world thought of them and how far should they go to protect their good name? 'No Christian ought to wonder', Denison conceded, 'if the world reproach him ... A Christian may say what need I care what is spoken wickedly of me so long as they be wicked themselves that speak it.' 'Why should a wise man be moved at malicious prating', Denison asked at one point, adding that 'the slanders of the wicked is nothing else but malicious prating'. 'A Christian must not fear the reproach of men'; 'if he be reproached, he must make little of it'. But if we must accept criticism with equanimity, neither, Denison concluded with admirably stoic moderation, must we 'be too careful of the praise of men'.[31]

But such arguments should not be taken too far. For, when the godly found themselves defamed, there was more involved than their own personal pique, feelings or credit. 'Consider', Denison asked his audience, 'how requisite a good name is in respect of the honour of God, in respect of the glory of the gospel, of the benefit of others and of ourselves.' It followed, therefore, that it was not only allowable but requisite for the godly person to be 'careful of his reputation and good name', seeking to preserve the same 'by all fitting and lawful means'.[32]

Here, then, was an extremely powerful retrospective justification for Denison's very determined efforts to face down and defy his local enemies and to preserve his reputation by all the means at his disposal. Thus, he argued, we all 'ought to be ready to answer for the servants of God, yea when wicked men are, like Jonah's whale, ready to swallow the poor prophet at a bite. So when wicked men are half drunk at a feast they are ready to swallow up a man at a bite, as it were, we ought to be ready to vindicate the reputation of others and those that keep silent at that time give a kind of consent to them. Yea, we ought to answer for our brethren and to appear for them to our power in public.' 'True Christians ought as much as in them lieth [to] vindicate their brethren's good name either by word or, as much as they can with a good conscience, by oath or by their purse or by their good word or by other friends or by other means'.[33] Once again it is not hard to recognise here those six ministers who had come to Denison's rescue, purging him on oath before High Commission or indeed those lay supporters who had backed him in his campaigns against Etherington or Shaw or indeed the quiet backstairs' influence exerted by Sir Henry Martin, as he massaged Denison's case against Etherington through the courts and *The white wolf* into print.

What is perhaps most striking about all this to the modern observer is the extraordinary way in which Denison's excoriations of his various enemies and justifications of himself could have been simply reversed and used against him by the likes of Shaw or Etherington. He, they could argue, had slandered them; blackguarding them as heretics and sectaries, when they were no such thing; he had displayed a pharisaical pride in his own learning, orthodoxy and status as a powerful preacher; he had informed on them to the authorities; he and his friends had spread rumours about them; he had misled a foolishly doting lay following into potentially damning error. But Denison, no doubt, would have replied that he was attacking heresy and schism and defending orthodoxy and order, while they, by undermining a powerful preacher, were trying to silence the gospel. But that of course was a view of the situation that neither Shaw nor Etherington could be expected to share.

A SEPTUAGENARIAN'S REVENGE: ETHERINGTON COMES OUT OF THE UNDERGROUND

Nor did they. For if the late 1630s found Denison entirely defiant about his former conduct and fate, the early 1640s revealed John Etherington to be, if anything, even more uncompromising in his self-righteousness and sense of grievance. The crisis of the 1640s had many momentous consequences, amongst which, it must be admitted, we cannot number its effects on the dispute between Stephen Denison and John Etherington. However, for the two men themselves, its impact was significant enough. Denison, at least, got his lectureship back and, with the collapse of censorship and the abolition of the High Commission, Etherington regained access to the public prints and was able to use it to repudiate the sentence of the court and to reopen the dispute with Denison that had lain dormant for fifteen years. He did so in two pamphlets of 1641 and 1642. Then, two years later, he returned to print for the last time to revive his controversies with familism, on the one hand, and with anabaptist separatism, on the other.[34]

It must have seemed just like old times to Etherington as London returned to a more spectacular version of the religious turmoil of his youth. Once more, there were groups of real familists, anabaptists, separatists and independents to listen to, meet and debate with, and rabidly reactionary puritans like Thomas Edwards and his presbyterian friends to denounce them. Once again, Etherington was able to position himself amongst these contending parties, propagating, in his aggressively irenic way, his now familiar brand of radical puritan conformity. Only now the performance was topped off with an explicit statement of his own brand of eschatology, proffered, as ever, as a third way between the false spiritualising claims of the familists and the altogether more carnal notions of reform purveyed by puritan radicals.

Let us begin, however, with his pamphlets against Denison. The first of these, as we have seen, claimed to reprint a manuscript apologia written inside 'the new prison in Maiden Lane' in 1627. There Etherington recounted the details of Denison's dealings against him, presenting himself as a dutiful protestant layman who had dared, in the course of his strenuous but entirely orderly godly round, to challenge some of the more extreme and unlikely doctrines disseminated by Stephen Denison. In a postscript Etherington was at pains to explain to the reader that he had lain in prison for three years after his humiliating appearance at the Cross, only being released on the 'last court day of Michaelmas term in the year 1629'. He could have gained his liberty far earlier, he explained, had he been prepared to acknowledge his guilt to the court but this he had consistently refused to do. When he was finally released, he emerged without having made 'any kind of justification, either of the court's proceedings or the witnesses' depositions or any part of Denison's doings or acknowledging myself guilty of the things wherewith I was charged, further than I have declared'.[35]

Etherington, then, had never conceded either the justice of his punishment or the accuracy of the charges that had produced it. Yet, for all his martyr-like pertinacity and suffering in prison, his reputation was still in tatters. Denison's smear tactics had managed to convict him before the kangaroo court of godly opinion.

> Notwithstanding this, that I am now at liberty from prison, yet the scandals and reproaches of my adversaries remain still all over this land and other parts likewise by reason not only of that unrighteous sentence of the court passed on me upon those insufficient and false depositions but especially of those wicked infamous sermons and books which my accuser and prosecutor Denison hath published against me and are dispersed through the kingdom. So that not only my person but my name is odious and hateful to many, my friends, my children and all that bear my name suffer by this means.[36]

These claims receive confirmation from the passage cited above from Samuel Harlib's papers in which, as late as 1633, considerable notoriety was attributed, to 'one Hetherington' a boxmaker and his denouncer Dr Denison.

Etherington's pamphlet was designed to set the record straight and it caused enough of a stir in London to prompt a reply from Denison which Denison claimed was a reprint of *The white wolf* with an appendix replying to Etherington's pamphlet. Etherington contemptuously retorted, with the disdain of one author for another who cannot sell his books, that, far from being a genuine reprinting, this was merely a reissue of unsold copies of the first edition with a new title page dated 1641 and a few new pages added at the end. But reprint or not, Etherington was nettled enough to reply for the last time in his *The deeds of Mr Denison a little more manifested* of 1642.[37]

This was largely a point by point response to Denison's defence of his former conduct. There he had tried to soothe the godly sensibilities ruffled by his initial rough handling of Etherington in the 1620s. He had not sedulously avoided all contact with Etherington during their dispute. They had met many times on the street and he had attempted to speak with the boxmaker only to be rebuffed. He had not pressed the court for costs, nor had he demanded that Etherington be burned as a heretic. Denison then reiterated some of the central doctrinal allegations of *The white wolf* involving the sabbath, the sacraments, the book of Esdras, the status of the church of England as a true church and added a charge culled from Etherington's book of 1610 that Etherington had there condemned 'all reformers'.[38] Interestingly, none of these charges were in any very obvious sense familist. By now the real areas of debate between the two men had been all but shorn of the anti-familist and anabaptist framework that polemical convenience had lent them in the 1620s.

Etherington replied, as we have seen, with a new list of Denison's largely sabbatarian and predestinarian errors preached at Katharine Cree and Great All Hallows 'while he was reviling and scandalising me'[39] and with a point by point treatment of Denison's most recent claims. He dismissed, almost certainly with good reason, Denison's rewritten version of himself as a moderate pastor acting more in sorrow than in anger against an errant layman. On the doctrinal questions he denied that he held that the church of England was not a true church, finessed the issue of the canonicity of the book of Esdras and restricted his remarks on the sabbath in this second pamphlet – he had, after all, been explicit enough about his views in the first – to a denial of Denison's allegation that 'I will have no duties pressed on the Lord's day, neither prayers nor preaching nor coming to the sacraments but Christians left to do what they list.'[40] On the claim that he had condemned 'all reformers', Etherington replied ambiguously that 'I own no such books or words', the closest he ever came, in these exchanges, to admitting that he had changed his mind since 1610.

Interestingly, Etherington chose to stand his ground in this second pamphlet only on the sacraments, reaffirming his belief that baptism 'doth not convey grace nor confirm it to the heart of any man no more than circumcision did'. 'Grace is conferred and confirmed to the heart of a Christian by a more supernatural power than is or can be in the outward act of baptism, even by the power and spirit of God. Outward baptism I hold to be an outward seal of God's faithfulness in ... his covenant to the faithful and their seed ... it is an outward sign showing that we must be circumcised or cleansed in heart by the grace and spirit of God, through faith in Christ, if ever we be heirs of Abraham.'[41]

This was an analysis Etherington repeated on the subject of the Lord's Supper, where he denied that he had repudiated (as Denison claimed) any notion of 'spiritual eating and drinking the body and blood of Christ'. However, he went on to define those terms in such a general way as to all but empty them of any resonance or meaning peculiar to the sacrament. For he defined the process of spiritual eating as 'the spiritual enjoyment of the grace and love of God, through faith in Christ, which that sacrament of the supper doth show forth unto all true Christians'.[42]

For Etherington, then, the sacraments were still but outward signs that showed forth, symbolised or staged, but did not themselves communicate, the inner spiritual realities of God's grace. Any alternative to that position, of the sort purveyed by Denison, Etherington tried to assimilate to the opinions of 'Arminians or papists'.[43] 'But you Mr Dr your opinion and doctrine belike is that Christians, by the very acts of eating the bread and drinking the wine of the sacrament, eat and drink the grace of God. Is this your orthodoxal doctrine, sir? Is this your opinion of spiritual eating? A fit man sure, are you not, to preach the lecture of preparation to the sacrament, as you are admitted to do at Botolph's without Aldgate, and well are the people taught there the while, are they not? Let the orthodoxal reader judge.'[44]

Here Etherington was surely getting his own back on Denison for that remarkable scene in the High Commission when Denison had cynically invoked the issue of the sacraments to turn Neile, Buckeridge and Cosin against him. Now, in 1642, with the fall of High Commission, the collapse of Laudianism and the disgrace of Arminianism, the shoe was most definitely on the other foot. Now Etherington was able to pose in print before a notional godly audience in London as 'orthodoxal', and to assimilate Denison's position on sacramental grace to that adopted by Cosin and Neile in their interview of 1626/27. Much of this was, of course, sleight of hand. Denison's views on the sacraments were not the same as those of the Laudians. Indeed, Denison's sacramental theology approximated far more closely to what passed for orthodoxy amongst the godly than Etherington's own really rather extreme vision of the sacraments as mere outward signs. That, of course, had never been Etherington's view of the matter and now circumstances were conspiring to allow him to assimilate Denison to the sacramentalism of the thoroughly discredited Laudian regime.

This was a tack that Etherington pursued further through what he pictured as Denison's nostalgia for the court of High Commission and its role in repressing the likes of Etherington. Under Abbot a view of that institution as a bastion of orthodoxy and order may have seemed relatively unproblematic, even to the likes of Denison, but, in the interim between 1626 and 1642, events had turned the court, in the eyes of many of the godly at least, into one of the central engines of Laudian and Arminian repression. Etherington tried hard to present Denison as a toady and accomplice of now discredited prerogative and episcopal authority, citing Denison's 'saying in your fourth page [of his reply to Etherington's pamphlet of 1641] and your glorying in the presentation and dedication of your book to the king'. Both there and in the dedicatory epistle of *The white wolf* Etherington exhorted the reader to 'see how you play the sycophant and colloquer especially with the High Commission Court and Bishops of Canterbury and London, Abbot and Montaigne'.[45]

While Etherington might picture Denison longing wistfully for the return of the prerogative courts, for his part Etherington gloried in the change. 'And although there be now no High Commission Court, as you tell me, implying that you would complain against me again there if there were, yet, let me tell you sir, there are other courts as high and as good as that and laws also as just and good to judge of these matters unto which you may complain if you please.' Indeed 'seeing my defence will not silence you, nor all that I have suffered by your means satisfy you', Etherington made Denison an offer. Let us, he wrote, 'have all matters between us heard and considered in a fair way either before the bishop of London and some other ministers chosen on both sides or else by some committee of the parliament, if it may be obtained, that so the blame may lie rightly where it ought'.[46] Interestingly, Etherington now sought precisely the sort of arbitration of their dispute that Wotton had granted Walker at Bishop King's insistence all those years ago.

On his own account, at least, in the 1620s Etherington had been denied a fair hearing either in the High Commission court or in the semi-public sphere of godly opinion by the shenanigans of Stephen Denison, his lay followers, friends in high places and the near monopoly of access enjoyed by learned ministers like Denison to the two great public media – the pulpit and the press – whereby godly opinion was shaped. But now, in the 1640s, with the collapse of the personal rule and the High Commission, the discrediting of episcopal and Arminian authority and the cessation of state-sponsored control of the press, Etherington could appeal, over the heads of clerical authority, both episcopal and puritan, directly to the godly of London.

Etherington, then, made much of his readiness to have the proceedings of the High Commission against him laid open in print for public scrutiny and debate. He challenged Denison to be as frank about his own little local difficulties with the same court, in the process, of course, coyly reminding both Denison and the reader of the nature of those difficulties. He had been charged with abusing 'some of the chief of your parish ... and some several women', 'they of your parish publicly, in the pulpit, and the women, secretly, in your chamber'. 'I will not here name the particular abuses', Etherington

Retrospective

explained, using a modest self-restraint only made possible by the tacit assumption that Denison's alleged misconduct remained notorious in London.[47] He then proceeded to challenge Denison to accept a further trial by public opinion.

> Now sir if your cause be so good and yourself so honest and innocent as you would have all men think (which yet they do not) write down all what your accusers have charged you with and what hath been deposed against you and by what manner of persons, everything in their own plain words, and what the sentence of the court was and publish the same openly in print, with your defence unto every particular charge and deposition as you see I have done that of yours against me. Do this, I say, if your cause be good and clean and your self honest and upright. It will be no greater charge, I suppose, then the new reprinting of your wolf-sermon that so all men may see plainly and judge of the cause and you accordingly. But otherwise, if it be nought and foul and yourself justly charged, as you in your own conscience know best, then let it alone, except in the way of humble confession of your sins unto God in true repentance, if it be possible.[48]

There could scarcely be a clearer example of the use of the medium of print to construct a notion of the public and of public scrutiny before which claims to truth or honesty should be canvassed and tested. Certainly this was anything but a new phenomenon in the 1640s, as Etherington and Denison's own previous publishing careers in part attest, but equally it was not something inherent in the medium of print itself. As we have seen, in the cases of William Chibald or Wotton and Walker, in the right political and institutional contexts, print could be used to close down rather than open up debate. For, in both those disputes, the cultural capital and licensing powers of the likes of Featley and Mason had been deployed to endorse a moderate statement of the issues at stake and to deny access to the press to Walker and other of Chibald's ministerial adversaries. Then print had been used to impose a certain sort of compromise solution on the dispute, one altogether more congenial to Chibald and Wotton than to some, at least, of their accusers (the chief of whom in both instances seems to have been Walker). However, the changed and charged political conditions of the revolutionary decades rendered such a use of the medium altogether less easy. Rather they facilitated a cultural politics of openness, disclosure and petition to 'the public', an appeal, as Denison described it, from the verdict of the High Commission 'to the judgement of the reader', of the sort being pursued here by Etherington. In his pamphlets, with their proclaimed willingness to have the dispute between himself and Denison heard by parliament or a nominated committee of divines, Etherington sought to present himself as a proponent of properly constituted public authority and open discussion against the hole-in-the-corner, 'prerogative' methods of his opponent. Now clerical privilege and personal connection would have to yield before the demands of a genuinely public authority and the unyielding eye of public scrutiny (a scrutiny constituted here, of course, by the London-reading public and the wider court of godly opinion). Such appeals, through print, to a wider, and notionally impartial and fair-minded, 'public' against the doings of an arbitrary and inherently unaccountable authority were, of course, to figure prominently in the politics of the 1640s. Here, of course, the name of Lilburne and the levellers springs most obviously to mind, although such tactics were by no means a 'radical' monopoly. As the researches of Ann Hughes and Kate Peters are beginning to show, a different version of essentially the same assumptions and manoeuvres underlay the polemical career of presbyterians like Thomas Edwards, as they sought to mobilise the impulses and revulsions of decent godly folk against the extremism of the sects. Now Etherington, of course, was no Edwards and still less a Lilburne, but the political and cultural tactics of such men were arguably based, in part, on the pre-existing public sphere or spheres, the networks of news and rumour, and the ideological presuppositions about the court of godly opinion in London and the 'public' status of printed (and, of course, manuscript) appeals to that opinion, that Etherington's career and altercation with Denison illustrate so neatly for the period before 1640. Such connections, of course, are replete with ironies. For some dim memory of Etherington's past as a sect master can be picked up in precisely the sort of anti-sectarian squibs and pamphlets of the 1640s, to which genre, of course, Etherington himself was contributing in his pamphlets against familism and anabaptism. Thus the Hetheringtonians are included along with seekers, Traskites, libertines, socinians, Arminians and a host of others listed in *A catalogue of the several sects and opinions in England and other nations* of 1646. A passing reference to Hetheringtonians can also be found in *A relation of several heresies* of the same year and heretical boxmakers figured in a number of attacks on 'tub preachers' and artisanal heretics.[49]

But if the convulsions of the early 1640s opened up the streets and presses of London to John Etherington, they performed the same service to a good many other godly groups and factions. Although at this point well into his seventies, Etherington clearly took a lively interest in what was now becoming something like a free market in religious ideas and, in particular, he was able to return to the site of his two earliest polemical engagements, those with anabaptist separatism and familism. He did so in two pamphlets of 1644 and 1645, the first against familism and the second against anabaptism. Typically for Etherington, both pamphlets start with accounts of what he presented as encounters with real men and congregations. The anti-anabaptist tract had its origins in 'some little speeches had with three or four of these anabaptists about their opinions and practice', in the course of which some of them had claimed that 'they could bring men who had as sufficient gifts and authority from God to preach and baptise as the apostle Peter had'.[50]

A meeting was arranged between Etherington and the anabaptists' 'chief speaker', one T.L. Their colloquy was broken off in mid-stream, however, 'because many people stayed at his house, as they said, to hear him preach that evening' and so T.L. had to hurry away. In lieu of further personal debate the two men then agreed to exchange arguments on the subject of infant baptism, exchanges which, with a long excursus on 'what the true reformation is and shall be, are exceeding in spiritual and heavenly respects the corrupt conceits of these anabaptists', constituted the body of Etherington's pamphlet.[51]

The anti-familist tract had similar origins, Etherington claimed. He had heard 'some doctrines delivered in a house within the Spittleyard without Bishopsgate, near London, by one Mr Randall, whom I was requested (by some friends) to hear. And observing the multitude of people that followed him and how they affected with his doctrine, which I did plainly perceive was the very grounds of familism, contained in the writings of H.N., I hereupon thought good a little to inform the people thereof; whereat some were much offended and one mocked and said "see what a old man here is and what a child here is".' Despite this somewhat unpromising beginning, Etherington proceeded to cross-question some of the congregation about their beliefs.

> I asked one of them if he did believe that the bodies of men, which were dead and buried in the earth, should be raised to life again and he answered me, saying 'I cannot tell'. And I mentioning Christ's resurrection from the dead, one answered 'Christ was not then a true man but only God' and another affirmed that he [had] known Christ after the flesh. And I asked him when and where, but he would give me no answer. Whereupon I said 'see how this people are taught'. And a woman answered and said unto me 'I think if you did speak with the minister, you should not find him of their mind.' And I told her she was deceived, he thought the same things. So I left them for that time.[52]

But Etherington left only to return again, this time with position papers, prepared to initiate a debate with Randall himself. The paper was drawn up as something of a formal challenge, under the heading 'this gentleman Mr Randall doth delude the people with the deceitful doctrine of familism, which I will undertake to prove by the things he hath delivered and that he therein doth pervert the straight way of the Lord and destroy the hope of the saints, as much as in him lieth'. Thus armed, Etherington turned up and waited through Randall's sermon. 'And when his sermon was ended and that upon consideration of a point of doctrine he delivered that a man baptised with the Holy Ghost knew all things, even as God knew all things, which himself greatly admired as a deep mystery and likened it to the great ocean where there is no casting anchor nor sounding the bottom, I said unto the people "this man hath many great words and a great deal of deceit".' This intervention, perhaps predictably, did not go down well with the assembled company, 'some of them being much displeased and moved with anger at my saying'. Finding discretion the better part of valour, Etherington removed himself from the room in which the meeting had taken place and 'went down out of the house into the yard' where he attempted to foist some of his controversial papers onto one of Randall's followers and 'a friend of mine whom the man knew' informed him that 'we desired to speak with Mr Randall'.[53]

Three or four days later, through the same intermediary, a grocer named Cullombeame, a meeting between Etherington and his friends and Randall was arranged for the following Tuesday (25 Febuary) in Cullombeame's house in Thames Street. Etherington turned up and waited for two hours or so but Randall never came, at which point Etherington gave Cullombeame a paper 'wherein I had written a few arguments for proof of the forementioned charge ... and wished him to give it to Mr Randall and request him to give us his answer to the same in writing'. Randall, however, never replied, leaving Etherington to publish a controversial pamphlet essentially without an opponent or rather against an opponent constructed by himself from positions he claimed to have gleaned from Randall's sermons, glossed and compared with long quotations from Henry Niclaes' work *The joyful message of the kingdom* (i.e. the *Evangelium regni*).[54]

It is, of course, just possible that all this elaborate circumstantial detail was invented: an exercise in flyting, the construction, in the 'familist' Randall, the anabaptist T.L. and their loyal lay followings, of straw men and false pretexts, which would allow Etherington to return to the polemical lists of his youth, on terms entirely of his own choosing, while still hoping to sell books through his pose of standing in the gap against these newly topical threats to godly unity and orthodoxy. This may appear all the more likely in the case of the debate with the otherwise unidentified anabaptist T.L. Why, in the relatively unconstrained atmosphere of 1641–42, the recourse to initials? Etherington, who was otherwise obsessed with providing seemingly otiose names, dates and places in order to enhance the reality effect of his pamphlets, was only too eager to name Randall. Why, therefore, did he allow the anabaptist prophet of his 1642 tract to hide between those enigmatic initials? And these, of course, were not just any old initials. Was it, in fact, entirely a coincidence that Etherington's anabaptist interlocutor of 1641 should have precisely the same initials as the mentor of his youth or middle age?

But if the shadowy anabaptist T.L. might have been a figment of Etherington's imagination, the conjured shade, perhaps, of his long-dead mentor of the 1590s, with Mr Randall we seem to be on altogether firmer ground. For this was almost certainly Giles Randall, a radical preacher and translator of the *Theologica germania*, who was pouring out radical doctrine at the Spital during the early 1640s. Even here, however, we should beware of merely taking Etherington's account of Randall's position at face value. Nigel Smith gives a nuanced evaluation of Randall's opinions, locating him, with John Everard, in a broad-bottomed and eclectic mysticism that, Smith claims, owed little or nothing to the works or tenets of H.N. On this view, then, Randall was not a 'familist' in anything like the Marshian sense. That he was regularly accused of being one was not, perhaps, surprising, given the currency of that category as a term of abuse and dismissal amongst both Laudians and mainstream puritans during the 1630s and 1640s. That Etherington, given his own familist past and decidedly interesting relationship with the term during his altercation with Denison, should have chosen to 'prove' that Randall was indeed a follower of H.N., surely tells us something of what Etherington was doing in the two pamphlets under discussion. Through the figures of Randall the familist and T.L. the anabaptist, Etherington was redefining himself and, if not quite rewriting, then at least giving final interpretative shape to, his own chequered past and the complicated palimpsest of his former opinions.[55]

For there were more than a few echoes of the past inscribed in Etherington's account of his transactions with these men. To begin with, there are striking similarities between the sorts of meetings and mechanisms of challenge and dispute pictured here and the account given above of the workings of the London puritan underground before 1640. News of familist-style heterodoxy had clearly spilled out of Randall's congregation. Etherington, presumably as someone with a reputation for not only knowing familism when he saw it, but also with a track record of successful disputation with familists, was 'asked by some friends' to attend. Having turned up and indeed detected familism, Etherington disrupted the proceedings at Randall's sermon and drew up a list of objectionable opinions extracted from Randall's discourse that he could identify as of obvious familist provenance. What followed – the delicate negotiations between friends of the main parties, the meeting arranged on neutral ground, in this case the house owned by the grocer Cullombeame, a mutual friend of both Etherington's nameless companion and Randall himself – all paralleled perfectly the delicate negotiations and manoeuvres between Denison and Etherington or Shaw and his enemies in the 1620s.

There clearly were continuities linking these interactions with the workings of the earlier pre-1640 London godly community. Etherington was, in part, reprising his former performance as a private anti-familist and anabaptist gadfly and disputer and, in part, standing in for Denison as a heresy hunter and radical basher. The exchanges that he initiated in this role followed very much the same unwritten rules and procedures as before, only now the whole process was speeded up and fed much more readily into the public discourse of print, where it met and no doubt played off what was now a luxuriant growth of anti-puritan, anti-familist and anti-anabaptist squibs and broadsides. Thus, in explaining the sudden efflorescence of religious polemic, the upsurge of radical puritan, heretical and heterodox activity in the 1640s, we might posit merely the unconstrained working of the sort of social mechanisms and ideological exchanges that had been in operation for years before. No longer constricted by episcopal or royal authority, the processes of assertion, critique and counter assertion could now not only be conducted in the houses and conventicles of the godly, they could overflow into the streets and pulpits of the city. There the processes of articling, conference, debate and denunciation outlined above could be greatly accelerated, with recourse to print now an obvious and relatively easy option. And, once printed, these polemical outbursts, with their sallies and counter sallies, were available for response and interpretation by newly unfettered godly and, indeed, un- or anti-godly audiences.

ETHERINGTON'S FINAL SYNTHESIS, THE AVOIDANCE OF ANTINOMIANISM AND THE CONSTRUCTION OF A FAMILIST OTHER

Nor, in Etherington's case, were the continuities limited to the realm of outward forms and procedures. As one might expect from a man in his seventies, his pamphlets of the 1640s in many ways repeated positions that Etherington had taken up earlier in his career but they did so in ways that throw an interesting retrospective light on his earlier claims and development and allow us to come to a final, rather more settled, judgement on the nature of his peculiar familist/puritan/protestant/conformist synthesis.

Let us start with his final and most developed rejection of familism, for that was how Etherington was determined to characterise his attack on Giles Randall. The full title of his pamphlet, *A brief discovery of the blasphemous doctrine of familism, first conceived and brought forth into the world by one Henry Niclaes of the Low Countries of Germany about an hundred years ago and now very boldly taught by one Mr Randall and sundry others in and about the city of London*, in many ways tells the story. The middle section of the tract contained a series of comparisons between Randall's opinions and those of H.N., designed to prove definitively that Randall was indeed a 'familist'. Given Etherington's own earlier familist phase, if he was now choosing to define himself against an image of familism largely of his own creation, the particular elements of familism that he chose to dwell upon and excoriate may tell us as much, if not more, about his own position than they do about the opinions of Randall himself.

Etherington chose to attack five familist positions in his challenge to Randall. First came the doctrine that 'the perfection and resurrection spoken of by Paul ... are to be attained in the fullness and perfection of them ... now in this present time, before the common death of the body'. Together with this doctrine went an explicit antinomianism which Etherington also rejected, dismissing out of hand the notion that such as are 'baptised with the baptism of the Holy Ghost have, from thenceforth, nothing to do with the law nor with the baptism of repentance, which John preached, but away with the law and away with John Baptist, from such a one'.[56]

For 'familists', as Etherington constructed them, the doctrinal concomitant of this essentially antinomian vision of the relationship between the justified Christian and the law was the view that the second coming was in fact accomplished 'in this present time in those that are baptised with the Holy Ghost' and that 'the sting of death, which is sin' was 'quite taken away and all the great and eternal promises' were 'fulfilled in them' in the here and now. In familist doctrine, as Etherington construed it, this second resurrection, this second coming of Christ within the believer, represented a return to a pre-lapsarian union with God that had been complete. And here Etherington denounced the idea that 'every creature in the first estate of creation, because they were made by the word of God, was God'. And, finally, he excoriated the attitude to scriptural authority that rendered these erroneous opinions possible. Familists, he claimed, turned 'the holy writings and sayings of Moses and the prophets, of Christ and the apostles, and the proper names, persons and things mentioned and contained therein into allegories and give them out to be the mystery and spiritual meaning of the same ... and therein presume above that which is written and so addeth to and taketh from the sayings, writings and prophecies of the holy scriptures and deceiveth the people, themselves also being deceived'.[57]

As we shall see below, an insistence on the spiritual privileges of those blessed with the second baptism of the Holy Ghost had remained a central feature of Etherington's thought for over thirty years. Even in his avowedly predestinarian book of 1623 his descriptions of the prerogatives and powers of the little ones of God had been couched in language redolent of the familist doctrines that he was now repudiating so explicitly in his attack on Randall. In addition, Etherington's insistence, in his altercation with Denison, that repentance was a preparation for, not a part or effect of, justification, could lend itself to antinomian readings. Certainly in the person of Peter Shaw we have someone who was at least accused of using familist themes and language to formulate a full-scale antinomian critique of what passed for orthodoxy amongst the godly. But if Etherington's opinions contained tendencies in that direction he was now being very careful to close them down. In his account of his exchanges with Randall he can be seen protecting his own position from such antinomian readings through his construction and repudiation of a familist other.

He started, as ever, by stressing just how exalted the spiritual privileges of the little ones of God were. 'In the spirit', wrote Etherington, 'the faithful have, through faith, an entrance into the eternal rest of God and kingdom of the

Lord Jesus Christ and so are risen from the dead and live and shall not come into condemnation, soul nor body, and this is called perfection, the first resurrection and renovation spiritual, the first fruits of the spirit etc.'. But almost immediately he went on to stress that in this life these privileges and graces remained partial and imperfect. 'This is not the perfection nor the resurrection spoken of' in the scriptural passages cited by Randall and other familists.

> Neither is this entrance into the rest of God and kingdom of the Lord Jesus Christ the full possession promised the saints and which they look for. But they press hard toward the mark for the prize of the high calling of God in Jesus Christ, looking unto that which is before them and not casting off any of the principles or beginnings of Christ [like the law, or the 'baptism of repentance'], as to say, as Mr Randall did, away with this or away with that, nay but only not to look upon them as if that were all, but to leave and forget them in that respect, as things behind, and yet nevertheless, as Paul also saith, whereunto we have already attained, let us walk by one rule.[58]

The relationship between the justified Christian and the law was thus not dissolved but merely changed and, in some ways, even intensified.

> And although the very perfection of the law of God be now required of the saints and that they are to set the same before them as a perfect mark, as well in respect of the spiritual intent thereof, as the literal, to love and delight therein with their whole soul, and to keep it in the very perfection, not in part, or for an hour or day but fully and continually, yet do they not attain thereunto here, nor can ... but they sigh and mourn and weep because of their sins and daily failings and would fain keep it perfectly (that is the law of their mind through the spirit) but they have another law in their members, which leadeth them captive to the law of sin and of death and yet nevertheless they crying out against themselves, bewailing the same, do assuredly believe that they shall be delivered from their body of sin and death, as Paul saith ... the sting of death, which is sin, shall be taken away and death swallowed up in victory, when the Lord cometh.[59]

Thus to claim, as Randall and the familists did, that true believers – 'those baptised with the baptism of the Holy Ghost' – had nothing to do with the law was, claimed Etherington, to 'pervert the straight way of the Lord'. Not only did it deny 'those baptised with the second baptism of the spirit ' 'the use of the law of God, to delight them therein and serve the same in his mind' but it also rejected 'the estate of a broken, repentant, contrite heart', an estate that was crucial to the life of the true believer. 'The repentant contrite heart being it which the Holy Ghost purgeth and cleanseth, comforteth and reviveth daily and the baptism of repentance and the baptism of the Holy Ghost being the parts of a new birth from above, wherein he that is born anew walketh and goeth on daily weeping and yet rejoicing, dying and yet living, sowing, in tears, his precious seed, in an assured hope, one day, to reap in joy and come to a city and kingdom promised.'[60]

In this vision of the continuing interaction between the baptism of repentance and the baptism of the Holy Ghost or, if you like, between the law and the gospel, within the soul of the justified Christian, Etherington was both echoing H.N. and T.L. and approaching very close to conventional puritan piety. For Etherington, as for mainstream puritans, justified Christians were not freed from the demands of the law altogether, it was merely that their relationship to that law was transformed. Now the law was no longer a source of threatened punishment and fear, it had become, as Etherington put it, a 'delight'; a guide to conduct which justified Christians could love and seek to obey rather than a stick with which to beat themselves when they were down. Thus Etherington might insist, with William Chibald and T.L., that repentance preceded justification, but for Etherington as for Chibald, that did not mean that repentance had no role to play in the life of the justified Christian. Here Etherington parted company with genuine antinomians like John Traske, who agreed that repentance preceded justification but also held that it ended with justification as well.[61] Etherington (again agreeing with T.L.) did not push the argument anything like so far; he might, with Chibald, shift the focus of the elect saint's attention from sanctification to justification but that did not commit him to a familist or antinomian perfectionism of the sort he imputed to Randall. The most, then, that we can attribute to Etherington here is a form of anti-legalism rather than of antinomianism. His was a developed reaction against certain forms of puritan preaching, which stressed sanctification over justification, equating, as Chibald had said, saving faith with assurance and sending the believer in search of assurance off to examine his or her own efforts to obey God's law as the best evidence for the work of the spirit in the elect saint. Etherington's impatience with the legalist excesses to which this could lead was best exemplified by his repudiation of Denison's sabbatarianism. But none of that amounts to 'antinomianism', as it had emerged in the late 1620s, 1630s and early 1640s. And, of course, in his pamphlet attack on the 'familist', Giles Randall, Etherington was going out of his way to emphasise just that point; using the accusation of familism against Randall to define his own position as safely not Randall's, not familist, not antinomian.

Having established that, Etherington could then proceed to a more or less conventional account of the justified Christian's path through the process of sanctification. Now the true believer no longer experienced the law as a sentence of death but as a model for conduct, to which, thanks to the purifying effects of the spirit, he or she could respond with greater and greater success. That success could, of course, never be total in this life. Even the truest of true believers would sin, but when they did so they would express the truth and purity of their profession in a soul-searing repentance for their sins. The result was, on the one hand, a vision of the effects of sanctification as a foretaste of that union with the God in Christ that awaited the elect in the next life. As such, the condition of the sanctified saint could be described in a language so exalted that it seemed to toy with precisely the sort of perfectionism of which Etherington was here accusing the familists. But equally, that rhetoric was balanced by the knowledge that even the most godly elect saint could sin and that one of the crucial marks of elect status was a lively, even a heightened, sense of one's own sins and imperfections. In short, in Etherington and T.L.'s terms, the dialectic between the baptism of repentance and that of the Holy Spirit, between, in more conventional terms, the law and the gospel, continued until death.

THE AVOIDANCE OF SEPARATION AND THE ANABAPTIST OTHER

Etherington's position approached closest to the cliches of conventional puritan soteriology when set out against a polemically constructed version of familist heresy. But, neither in the 1610s, the 1620s nor the 1640s, had Etherington's presentation of himself merely oscillated between his critiques of a Denison-style legalist puritanism, on the one hand, and of an antinomian familism, on the other. From his tract of 1610 on, his polemical opponent of choice had always been separatist anabaptism and, at least since the 1620s, he had come habitually to locate his own position between a triad of opponents – familism, puritanism and anabaptism. Thus what looked like theological conservatism when asserted against familist error might look a good deal more radical when set out against anabaptism. That had certainly been true in 1610 and it was still true in 1644. Thus, if we want to trace the radical legacy of Etherington's (and T.L.'s) position, with its emphasis on the spiritual autonomy and prerogatives of the little ones of God, it is once again to Etherington's critique of anabaptism that we should turn.

In part, as one might expect, his anti-anabaptist tract of 1644 was a mere reprise of the position he had adopted in 1610. Baptism under the gospel, as circumcision under the law, was merely an outward sign of true profession, a means of distinguishing the faithful from the heathen, but not the true Christian, enjoying a true justifying faith, from the false or hypocritical believer. Baptism, in fact, was a mere outward sign, designed 'to set forth and signify', but not to communicate or effect, 'the circumcision of Christ made without hands, the circumcision of the heart'. According to T.L., Etherington's anabaptist interlocutor, if false Christians, hypocrites and apostates like Simon Magus, had been admitted to baptism by the apostles it was a mistake, produced by the inability of those doing the baptising to judge infallibly whether the baptised had a true justifying faith or not. This was a position with which Etherington would have nothing to do. To begin with, Christ, whose knowledge of the spiritual estate of his followers had been complete, had allowed Judas to become a disciple, precisely to show us that membership of the outward visible church and enjoyment of the common gifts and benefits conferred by that membership, should be open to all those prepared to make an outward avowal of Christian faith. But for Etherington this did not mean that no further decisions as to the spiritual status of Christians could be made other than inherently provisional and imperfect judgements based on outward appearance. On the contrary, it was axiomatic for him that there was 'a rule that Christ hath given to his church and children of wisdom to judge the heart of man by, and that it is a most true and perfect rule, whereby they can and shall know a false prophet and also a true, a true Christian and also a false but no rule for baptism. And although the words are plain that they shall know them by their fruit, as certainly as men do know a good tree and a bad tree by their fruit, yet it will not be so understood by T.L. he will ... make it but a thinking or a conceiving or a knowing probably (which is no knowing at all).'[62]

In other words, the church could distinguish infallibly between true and false believers, the godly and the ungodly, it was just that that distinction had no relevance for external baptism, which was a mere mark of outward profession not of membership of the true church. Thus, argued Etherington, when Philip had baptised those of Samaria, Simon Magus amongst them, he had 'judged rightly of them all; he saw and knew what they believed so far in that kind as made them meet for outward baptism, even Simon Magus as well as the rest, and did not lay his hands on any of them but left them so, till their fruit might make them manifest'. Thus whoever did 'believe, assent unto and gladly receive' 'the first principles of Christ' should be baptised with outward baptism, but that said nothing about his or her true spiritual state, which would only become apparent 'afterward' when some would attain 'to true repentance and remission of their sins through faith in his name and showing forth the fruit thereof' and some would not. It was only the former 'whom the Holy Ghost calleth good ground, trees of righteousness, the children of righteousness, the children of wisdom, the children of God, the called of God in Jesus Christ, beloved of God, saints by calling, sanctified in Jesus Christ.' For although 'the other evil sorts are altogether with these in the outward state of the church, partaking with them in common things, yet these only, properly and truly considered, inwardly and spiritually, are the church of the living God, his temple and tabernacle. And to this church do all the most special, peculiar privileges and treasures, graces, gifts and promises belong.'[63]

We are back here to Denison's accusation that Etherington equated the true church of the elect with the community of the godly as he defined and identified it. Judging from these passages that was precisely what Etherington was doing. T.L. had done it in the 1590s, Etherington had done it in 1610 and again in the 1620s and he was still doing it in 1644. Of course, as Etherington had explained in the 1620s, that no longer meant, if it ever had, that he thought that the church of England was a false church, but it did mean, given his rather jaundiced and distanced view of all questions of external form and church government, that he could take a somewhat sceptical attitude to the many claims to further reformation and spiritual purity being registered in the 1640s by various groups with blueprints for the reform of the visible, institutional church or churches. Again the dominant note here is one of continuity; on these issues Etherington was displaying precisely the same sceptical distaste that he had shown towards similar claims advanced by presbyterians and separatists in the 1590s and 1610s.

For, on Etherington's view, all such reformers ran the risk, with the papists, of overrating the importance of outward forms; of placing far too much emphasis on outward baptism or circumcision of the flesh, and consequently of overlooking the necessity of 'the new birth'. This was an event about which Etherington continued to speak in a most exalted language, redolent of his earlier familism. Thus Etherington could remark of the anabaptists of the 1640s that

> these and all other such like gatherers of people together, builders and planters, which come so near to their strain, in framing and settling themselves in their independent way, under the pretence of casting off all the abominations of Antichrist and practising according to the state of the churches of the apostles' times, let them and all other who, in other kinds, seem to endeavour a reformation, take heed and fear lest, while they promise and assume great things to themselves, they miss the very thing and go clean beside the way of the the true reformation, which God will have to be in this last age.

Thus in 1644, as in 1610, Etherington held that all would be 'reformers' of the visible church stood in grave danger of confusing the form with the substance, the letter with the spirit.[64]

Again, just as he had in 1610, Etherington ended his anti-anabaptist tract of 1644 with an essentially eschatological account of 'what the true reformation is and shall be, far above these anabaptists and all such carnal builders' conceits'.[65] While the process of reformation was conceived, as in 1610, as a largely spiritual one, not directly concerned with the reform of visible institutions or outward forms, this spiritual reformation was no longer associated or equated with H.N. and his works as harbingers of the last days or, indeed, with any explicitly familist version of the second coming. Now Etherington envisaged a far more conventional process of spiritual attrition working itself out against what was now a recognisably papal Antichrist, to be followed by a literal second coming by Jesus Christ, God and man, to judge the quick and the dead and institute the new Jerusalem.

APOCALYPSE SOON: THE ESCHATOLOGICAL CONTEXT OF THE LITTLE ONES

The events of the current age, Etherington explained, needed to be put into their proper apocalyptic perspective if we were to understand them aright. In attempting to do that, Etherington reproduced almost perfectly the apocalyptic schema outlined in the 1590s by T.L. Again, the great instruments of reformation were 'the two witnesses of God' whom Etherington equated, following T.L., with the two testaments of scripture. These were the sole instruments whereby the process of reformation was to be wrought and Etherington strongly denied that any human agency, 'any magistrates, ministers, men or angels', could either be the two witnesses or be regarded as equal to them.[66] There was no room left here for any eschatologically charged role for H.N., or any other human agent, in the unfolding of the divine purpose, and precious little inducement to see changes in the outward form or structure of the church in eschatologically charged terms.

If the two witnesses were the two testaments of scripture then the beast 'being risen up and placed in the dragon's throne makes war against' them, overcoming and killing them. He did so in part by 'putting out and taking away the true intent and meaning of their word and testimony, which is their light and life, and giving false and lying interpretations of the same to the people and suppressing those that testified and walked in the light and truth of them'. He finished the job by 'keeping the letter of their word from the people, that so their testimony might not be read, understood and laid up in their hearts, where they ought to be buried'.[67] Here, reproduced perfectly, was T.L.'s rather oracular rendition of the traditional protestant motif of the rise of the papal Antichrist, in the age immediately following that of the apostles, to power and dominance in the church.

Having 'lain thus slain so long in the streets of the spiritual Sodom unburied' 'these two witnesses', Etherington claimed, are now 'in their resurrection'. 'The spirit of life from God is entered into them and they are standing on their feet and walking again as was foretold, Rev.11.' The process of reformation had started, then, and it was through these purely spiritual and scriptural means that 'the Lord, with the spirit of his mouth, hath been consuming that man of sin all this while, according as the apostle Paul foretold 2 Thess.2.8'. This was a process, Etherington claimed, that had been going on for 'at least these hundred years past'.[68]

As Etherington explained (again echoing T.L.), the three and a half years during which the bodies of the two witnesses had lain dead in the streets of the beast's city, Sodom, 'are the three prophetical years and a half of the beast's reign and not three natural years and a half, as they of the church of Rome and some of our own would have it'. Nor was the death of the two witnesses complete, even during the period of seemingly complete popish dominance of the church.

> They are said to prophesy all the time in sackcloth, while their bodies lie dead and unburied in the streets of Sodom ... yet they prophesy against them all the time notwithstanding, and the judgements of God which they have spoken with their mouth against the beast and his church shall surely come upon them. Neither do nor did their bodies lie dead and unburied in the church of the saints at any time, though they were never so few or never so dispersed into the desert or wilderness, they always retained them alive and prophesying but yet in sackcloth and with much opposition.[69]

In other words, even at the height of popery, God had retained his scattered flock of little ones amongst whom the two testaments of his word had been kept alive. Here Etherington (again following T.L.) plumped for the more radical populist version of the Foxeian myth of the true church hidden under persecution in the wilderness, while the visible institutional church was given over entirely to popery. In the process of reformation, whereby Antichrist was brought down, nearly all the credit was given to Christ and the little ones of God whom he was leading into battle and very little indeed to Christian princes or ministerial reformers.

This little flock that had guaranteed the continued existence of the true church in the world was now on the march.

> He whose name is called the word of God, who hath on his head many crowns and in his mouth a sharp sword, he is come forth on his white horse and his heavenly armies following him on white horses, clothed in white and fine clean linen (who are the called of God, his chosen and faithful servants, as he saith Rev.17.14) He, who in righteousness doth judge and make war, hath been with those, his armies, fighting and prevailing all this while against the beast and those kings of the earth and their armies ... according as it was foretold ... and as at this day we see.

This was a process of reformation that was now well under way. 'All these things have already thus far passed and proceeded', Etherington explained, 'otherwise that reformation which is and hath been within those years, of kingdoms', and cities' and peoples' revolt from the beast and his church ... which we have seen, read and heard of and which cost the lives of so many thousands that testified and maintained the truth of God's two witnesses against them, had not been.'[70]

While the process of reformation was very far from complete, its progress was now palpably quickening.

> So then the two witnesses, being the two testaments of God which are his two candlesticks also that carry in them the light of his truth and power of his spirit, which the beast at his rising had killed, but are now come to life again, even the spirit and life of God's own word, whereby also he made the worlds, which name belongs only to him who sitteth on the white horse, the lamb, Jesus Christ, the branch, the stone that hath the seven eyes, which are the seven spirits of God, sent out into all the world, spoken of in Zach.3.8, 9 and 4.10, Rev.5, 6. Even the head

stone which Zerubbabel was to bring forth; he that is king of kings and lord of lords, who hath the sharp sword in his mouth. He, as he hath prevailed thus far against the beast and his armies, so he shall go on and prosper in his war, let the beast and the kings of the earth, with their armies, gather themselves against him and his armies and do what they can, the beast shall not recover out of his consumption, he must be taken and with him the false prophet, his clergy, that wrought miracles before him and both be cast alive into the lake of fire, burning with brimstone and those kings of the earth, and the rest of his armies be slain with the sword of him that sits on the white horse, which comes out of his mouth etc., as the lord hath spoken Rev.19.[71]

While he described this conflict in the most violent, militaristic and apocalyptic language available, Etherington continued to insist that this was a gradual and largely spiritual process, worked through the word and its impact on the little ones of God. By these means 'the abominations of Antichrist and his church hath been in part discovered, from day to day, to this present. And as their glory decayeth, so, accordingly, shall the face of her, the Lord's true church, by degrees, be seen, more and more, to shine in her true spiritual light and beauty, until she come nearest like unto the primitive state that she, in this last corrupt age of the world, can come, to which upon the full end and desolation of the beast and his church, will be.'[72]

Then things would be a good deal better than they were now.

> Many things which now remain obscure, even to some of God's chosen servants, hid and obscure, (though foretold in scripture) shall be known and understood. Then shall she, the true church indeed, come clean forth of that wilderness, her secret resting place, where she had been fed so long and be far more visible than now she is. She will not be divided into so many sects, as now are of those, that falsely take on them her name, having so many several independent leaders as there are independent sects and as many sects as every one that will rise up to draw disciples after him can (by speaking perverse things unto them) make. Nay, she shall be as she always hath been in such respects (and is) undivided, though dispersed, holding faith and truth without confusion or division.[73]

Here surely was being described the spiritual cacophony of the post-reformation era in general and of the 1640s in particular, as each 'independent' sect made its pitch for a monopoly of spiritual truth. Here, too, the current confusion was being compared to the next succeeding age, when, in T.L.'s parlance, the key of David would, in the hands of the little ones, unlock the last secrets of God's word; the age, in short, to which T.L. had bequeathed his book against Baro in 1592.

While the church thus constituted would remain geographically dispersed and, 'in respect of her several places of abode, be distinguished by the names of the places, yet shall she not be divided, nor any one part independent from another, nor from the whole, no more than the parts or members of one body are; nor one part say or think of another, I have no need of thee, no more than the members of one body may'.⁷⁴ The church's unity then would be spiritual as would her autonomy, springing directly from her head Jesus Christ. For the members of the true church, thus conceived,

> are free and independent from men, in all spiritual things concerning God and their own consciences, not having, in such respects, any supreme head, ruler or teacher over them but Christ their lord, nor may (so) call any man on earth Lord because one is their lord, nor any man doctor, because one is their doctor, even he, the Lord himself, who hath appointed no one in his stead during the time of his personal absence so to be over his church but his Holy Spirit only, the spirit of truth, the comforter, which he hath sent and is with his church to the world's end to rule and govern it, to teach and guide her, and all her children, in the ways of truth, as being the great moderator of all his spiritual matters.⁷⁵

All of which did not mean, however, that the church was 'therefore free from all kind of dependency on the magistrate or state'. For the magistrate retained a residual duty 'to have special care of the glory, worship, and service of God and to see that he be not dishonoured by idolatry, superstition or any blasphemous, erroneous, Antichristian doctrines'. On the contrary, the magistrate was to see that 'the church, as well as the state, be ordered and so settled in a form of government according to the word of God and so protected and defended by them that all the people may peaceably be taught in the ways of truth and salvation. So the church and children of God are bound to submit and be obedient.' It was only if the magistrates 'shall fail in their duties before mentioned and do and command things contrary, as hath been hitherto most commonly in all kingdoms and states in the world' that 'the children are free and not bound to obey but rather to suffer unto death; they are to give unto Caesar the things that are Caesar's and unto God the things that are God's'.⁷⁶

We are back here in the same mental, rhetorical and indeed linguistic universe that had produced both T.L.'s apocalyptic commentaries and that remarkable coda to Etherington's pamphlet of 1610. Here, again, is the same rather odd combination of protestant, even, in the case of the doctrine of passive disobedience summarised above, conformist, cliche, all couched in an inflamed pseudo-scriptural language more suited to the business of semi-ecstatic prophecy than the seeming banality of Etherington's ostensible message. And yet here, as in T.L.'s works of the 1590s and Etherington's tract of 1610, the overall effect is to create the sense of a subtext, a message behind the message, considerably more radical than the doctrines to which, when challenged by Denison in the 1620s, Etherington had had recourse to explain his position.

And here again, as in the 1590s and 1610, that latent radicalism centred on the little ones of God, the godly community called together by Christ and the

Retrospective

two witnesses to constitute the true church in the midst of, at best neutral and at worst hostile, secular and ecclesiastical hierarchies.

> This church, if ever it come so near the primitive state as is hoped upon good ground it will, she will be so eminent in every part where she shall be so severed and distinguished, that, if one brother trespass against another and will not be reconciled, it may be known where to go and tell it to the church, according to the rule of Christ, Matth.18, which church, if the trespasser shall refuse to hear, he is then to be unto his brother in account as a heathen and a publican. For of this church and her children it was that Christ spake when he said 'verily, I say unto you, whatsoever ye shall bind on earth, shall be bound in heaven and whatsoever ye shall loose on earth, shall be loosed in heaven' vers.18. And therefore he saith again 'if two of you shall agree on earth' (he saith not any two in the outward state of the church but two of you, meaning of his truly faithful ones) as touching anything that they shall ask 'it shall be done for them of my father, which is in heaven, for where two or three be gathered together, in my name, there am I, in the midst of them'.

Etherington had reverted here to a version of his equation of the little ones with the church as exalted as that he had first adumbrated in his familist tract of 1610.

Again, he was explicit that merely outward or formal Christians, though 'they be never so great in place and power external and wisdom natural, have nothing to do with these excellent treasures. They have no part with the spouse herself therein, it is to her and her children alone that Christ hath promised, given and will give those special peculiar graces and those keys of the kingdom of heaven ... Neither is the prince or magistrate, having the same grace, exempted from these privileges, because he is in place of authority, but rather the more to be honoured that way.'[77]

Here, then, was the same vision of the true church that Etherington had first expressed in 1610, only now, in the 1640s, he was sure that the final moment of triumph for 'the little ones' was actually at hand.

> This church, I say, shall now daily (in respect of her light of faith and truth and other graces and gifts of the spirit), increase and, by the word of God's two testaments and power of his spirit ... shall not only convince the Antichristian people and wicked perishing world of sin, of righteousness and of judgement but also, and more especially, by the same word of truth and power of his spirit, bring forth and accomplish all her own children, even the full number of God's elect, the generation of his first born, which, within the very time of this present last age, will be fully perfected, as the prophet Daniel declareth.

We have indeed returned here to the central claims of his pamphlet of 1610; Etherington may have been no longer a familist, but his opinions had not changed all that much since his youth and middle age.[78]

The 'final desolation of Antichrist' to be wrought by these means was, Etherington declared, 'now near at hand'. This presaged the last days. For a brief period the church would then shine forth, as in her first glory, before the dragon had 'raised his great persecution against her and her child'.[79] But now, as then, this glorious period would be cut short by 'the dragon, the devil, satan, who ... shall be loosed again out of his prison and go unto the kings of the earth and of the whole world to deceive the nations, that are in the four quarters of the earth, even Gog and Magog, and gather them together and bring them down in number, like the sand of the sea and compass the camp of the saints about and the beloved city and so (for a little season) greatly trouble her, even till fire shall come down from God, out of heaven and devour them'. Christ himself would return, judge the quick and the dead and the world would end, to be replaced by 'new heavens and a new earth'. Then 'the whole house of Israel, all God's elect and chosen people, of all nations and times, shall now be perfectly and fully delivered from all their captivities and troubles ... as the Lord hath promised ... And he, their lord and king, Christ Jesus, shall reign over them, in mount Sion, for ever and ever, world without end.'[80]

This was an eschatology proffered by Etherington (throughout reproducing almost exactly the tenets of T.L.) in self-conscious contradistinction to those offered by the familists, on the one side, and his radical puritan contemporaries, on the other. In his anti-familist tract of 1645 Etherington explicitly repudiated what he presented as the typical familist positions on these matters. In this, at least, his opinion had changed decidedly since 1610.

> As touching the coming of the Lord at the last day, it is not to be understood in a mystical manner, in the spirit only, as H.N. would have it, as if Christ had left or quite put off his humane person. Neither ... is the presence of his spirit to be taken for his coming, nor [is] the instruction, guidance, comfort of the spirit ... the resurrection he speaks of ... as H.N. and the teachers of familism would have it. Nay, but the Lord's coming shall be in a most open, manifest and glorious manner; so as that every eye shall see him and all shall know him to be the very same man, Jesus Christ, that was crucified and pierced at Jerusalem, he shall in person really and truly come, as the clear words of the scripture speak.[81]

Antichrist and Christ were literal historical figures and forces, not internal spiritual states; Antichrist was the church of Rome; neither H.N. nor any other human agent, entity or prophet would bring Antichrist down or judge the world; these were tasks first for the two witnesses and then for Christ himself, who would come in person, God and man, to end the world and judge the quick and the dead. Here, at least, Etherington was siding definitively with T.L. over against H.N.

But if Etherington distanced himself from what he presented as the unduly spiritualised and allegorised eschatology of the familists, he also objected to the fetishised concern with the externals of church government and worship, the reformist doings of magistrates and ministers, that he took to be typical of radical puritan eschatology. Here was an altogether too 'carnal' notion of reformation for Etherington's taste. And insofar as such notions were being increasingly linked, in radical puritan circles, with a pre-millennial eschatology, that held the reformation of the church, the calling of the saints into gathered churches and sometimes the conversion of the Jews, to be crucial preparations for the fall of Antichrist, the second coming and the thousand-year rule on earth of Christ and his saints, before the last judgement ended the world, Etherington found them doubly objectionable.

In the lists of errors attributed to Denison and other nameless ministers printed in his second pamphlet against Denison, Etherington had included a number of what he took to be erroneous opinions about the second coming and the end of the world, all of them pre-millennial in nature. Denison, he claimed, had maintained in the pulpit that 'Christ may yet personally descend from heaven to the earth before the day of judgement.' 'Others, whom I will not now name', had claimed in the late 1620s that 'the Jews should be delivered ... out of all countries, to the land of Canaan and be converted, all of them, to be true Christians and dwell in the land, in great glory with a great king of their own stock (either Christ himself or some other in his stead), for a thousand years before the end of the world.' Still others had maintained 'that Christ shall indeed come personally and raise up all the saints that have suffered or (as some of them teach) all the saints in general that are asleep and reign with them, on earth, a thousand years, before the end of the world and resurrection of the unjust'.[82] By the 1640s all of these opinions – opinions which Etherington dismissed as 'false and contrary to the scriptures' – were becoming associated with or attached to various independent and sectarian schemes for ecclesiastical reform.

Instead of these radical puritan chimeras, Etherington proffered his own eschatological vision, a vision that harked back to the views that had, according to Dr Bauckham, passed for orthodox amongst the protestant divines of Etherington's youth and young manhood, precisely the period during which T.L.'s two works of apocalyptic had been produced.[83] On this view, there was no millennium to come, merely a process of gradual spiritual enlightenment worked through the word and the spirit. The fall of Antichrist was marked by secular struggles, wars and rumours of wars, conquests and invasions that could be attached to contemporary happenings and read off against a scripturally derived timetable of events. Such events mattered, hence Etherington's references to the revolt in recent memory of 'kingdoms and cities and peoples from the beast and his church'. But what mattered far more was the spiritual process whereby the true church built only of lively stones, the little ones of God, were gathered together and united with more and more clarity and purity of belief and profession. It was the essentially spiritual triumph of these true professors, beneficiaries of the second baptisms of repentance and the Holy Spirit, that would destroy the papal Antichrist and prepare the world for the second coming. To adopt T.L.'s terminology from the 1590s, as possession of the key of David became ever more prevalent, dark things would become light, and the scripture would yield up its last secrets. In this process ministers and magistrates could claim no more than a walk-on part. With T.L., Etherington took the Foxeian tradition, with its emphasis on small groups of true believers keeping the true church alive through the depths of Antichrist's reign, and carried it forward into the period of church history dominated, on Foxe's account, by the Christian magistrate and minister. Retaining the eschatology that had passed for conventional in Foxe's day, Etherington gave it a radical tilt, ending his vision of the last days with a period of ever increasing spiritual purity and reform, in which the little ones of God would emerge, in greater numbers and as more obvious presences in the world, to exercise the spiritual powers ceded to them by Christ with greater and greater potency and success.

CONTINUITY AND CHANGE OR ETHERINGTON ACHIEVES CLOSURE

In short, basic elements both of T.L.'s works of the 1590s and of Etherington's vision of 1610 were retained in his pamphlets of the mid-1640s. He may have sifted out, hypostasised and repudiated what he took to be the errors of H.N. in the interim, but the familist influences – gradualist, spiritualising, conformist, yet very radical in their vision of how the true church actually worked to reproduce itself within the empty husk provided by the institutional church and the Christian prince – were retained.

It is hard not to believe that Etherington was seeking, in these last works, self-consciously to comment upon, interpret and round out his own earlier pronouncements on these subjects. The eschatological coda to his anti-anabaptist pamphlet of 1645 recalls nothing so much as the overtly familist conclusion of his earlier anti-anabaptist pamphlet of 1610. That this second book was written against one anabaptist T.L., just as another T.L. may have been Etherington's mentor either during the 1590s or 1610s, was very likely more than an accident. The 'coincidence' is rendered all the greater by the fact that, as we have just seen, the eschatological schema with which Etherington concluded his attack on 'T.L.', his anabaptist interlocutor of the 1640s, was taken straight from the works of that other T.L. Here, then, one T.L. was being used to confute another. This might make sense if T.L. were, in fact, the same Thomas Lemur who had hung out in separatist circles in London in the early 1590s, written, under those initials, the exegetical and prophetical works to which Etherington retained a life-long allegiance, before, around 1600, going off to the Low Countries, where he took an increasingly eccentric doctrinal path into anabaptism and beyond. Loyal to the initial insights of the T.L. of the 1590s, was Etherington, in his pamphlet against T.L. of 1645, using the first

A VOYCE

Out of the
WILDERNES
CRYING,
With many Tears and strong perswasions to the World for
REPENTANCE.

Proving by undenyable Grounds from the Word of God, that the great Day of his righteous Judgement shall certainly be in this present Age, before 61. Years after this present Yeare 1651. shall be expired.

And unfolding many great and wonderfull Mysteries of God forespoken in his word to come to passe and be fulfilled, from the rising of JULIUS CÆSAR, first Emperour of ROME, to this present time, and from hence to that Great Day of the Lord.

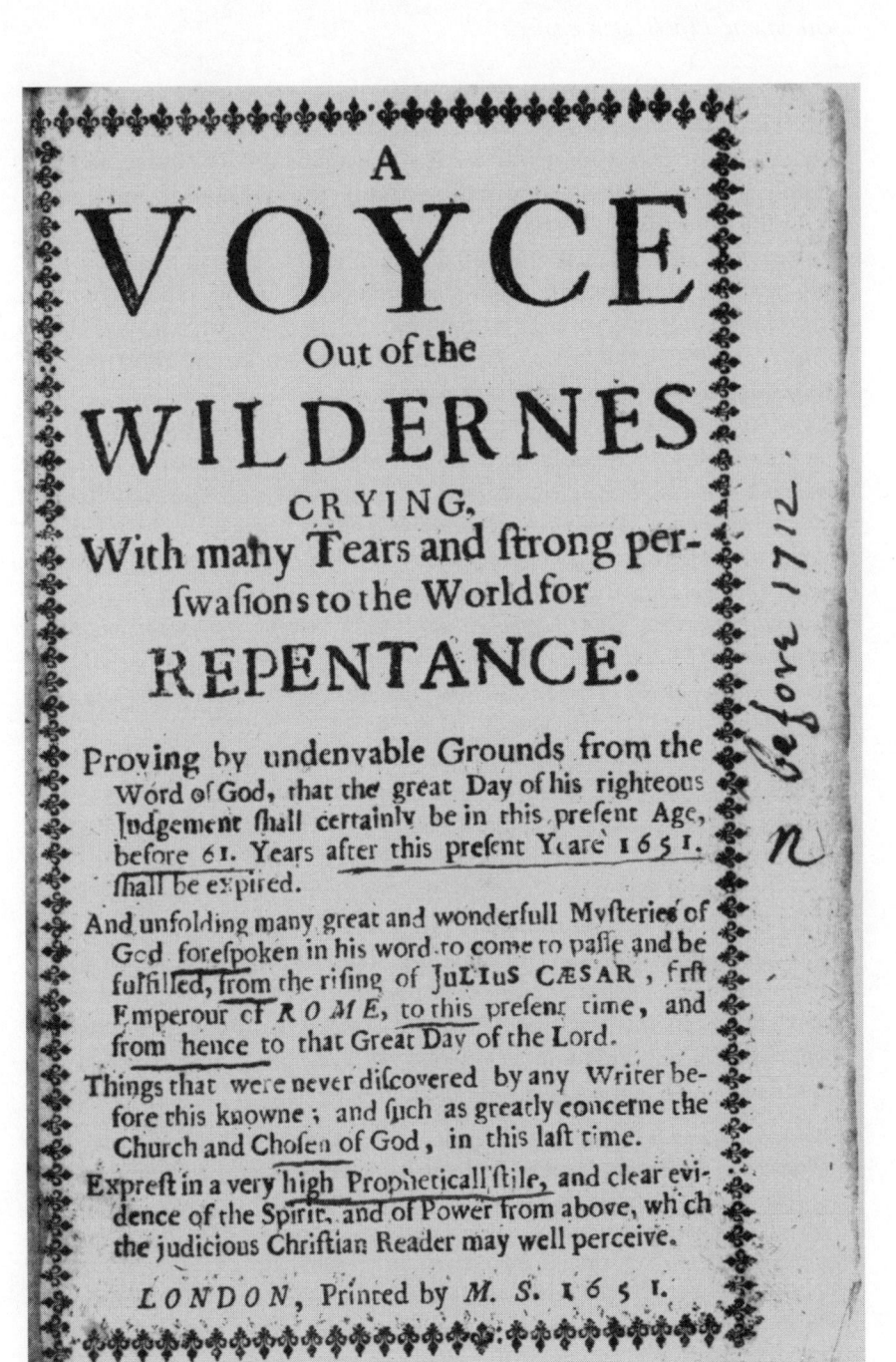

Things that were never discovered by any Writer before this knowne; and such as greatly concerne the Church and Chosen of God, in this last time.

Exprest in a very high Propheticall stile, and clear evidence of the Spirit, and of Power from above, wh ch the judicious Christian Reader may well perceive.

LONDON, Printed by M. S. 1651.

Figure 9 The title page of Etherington's 1651 edition of the collected works of T.L.

authentically prophetic English phase of his mentor's thought to confute the later flirtations with heresy and anabaptism that Lemur had allegedly produced in the Low Countries? Such speculations are, of course, fanciful; certainly, given the current state of the evidence, they are entirely unprovable. But, by the same token, it is hard to resist the conclusion that these last works were heavily coded and self-referential texts in which those in the know were being invited to interpret Etherington's earlier career and pronouncements in terms of these later works, to appreciate with Etherington, what he was clearly trying to present, at the last, as the underlying coherence and consistency of both his and the first T.L.'s ideological project.

The circle, if circle it was, was closed definitively by what appears to have been Etherington's last publication. In 1651 a pamphlet appeared with the title *A voice out of the wilderness, crying, with many tears and strong persuasions to the world, for repentance. Proving, by undeniable grounds from the word of God, that the great day of his righteous judgement shall certainly be in this present age, before 61 years after this present year 1651 shall be expired. And unfolding many great and wonderful mysteries of God, forespoken in his word to come to pass and be fulfilled from the rising of Julius Caesar, first emperor of Rome, to this present time and from hence, to that great day of the Lord. Things that were never discovered by any writer before this known and such as greatly concern the church and chosen of God in this last time. Expressed in a very high, prophetical style and clear evidence of the spirit and power from above which the judicious Christian reader may well perceive.* The volume was introduced by a dedicatory epistle to 'the parliament of England and council of state' and comprised four books, 'the first to the church of Rome, the second to Queen Elizabeth, the third to the earl of Essex, the fourth to King James'. All were attributed to one T.L.[84]

The epistle explained that since it was evident that 'God hath raised you up and appointed you in special manner as his choice servants to know his ways, to set forth and maintain the honour of his glorious name and truth unto and throughout not only this nation wherein we live but all other besides', the author had thought good to dedicate the following texts to the parliament.

> For it is, or may be, apparent to all people of the world that God hath wonderfully blessed this nation above others in these latter days, not only with temporal and earthly, but also, and more especially, with spiritual and heavenly, blessings in raising up amongst us holy men, yea prophets, whom he hath instructed from above, by his spirit of truth, to understand his word and the great things contained therein and to declare the same, not only to this nation of ours but to all the world, the like to which hath not been in these last days, amongst any other people known.

It was 'for these causes and reasons' that the author presumed 'in all humility [to] present this voice out of the wilderness (a great mystery of truth and heavenly prophecy, as I may truly call it) contained in this little book to your honours' judicious view and consideration, that you may, according as you shall see cause, receive the same in your hearts, prefer it by your word and maintain it by your power'.[85]

It was all the more necessary that the rump should do so since the world was now so rife with false prophets and phony messages. One recalls here, of course, Etherington's earlier contemptuous dismissal of independent congregations and sects, carnal schemes for further reformation and the false versions of the millennium in which they were often wrapped up.

> You have all heard, seen and known enough of the many several, differing spirits that have been and are this day amongst us and of their several opinions and practices. Some whereof, being most grossly erroneous, wicked, blasphemous and how every of them have endeavoured to possess even your honours' minds also, as well as the peoples', with the love of their doctrines and ways; wherewith you have been (as I suppose), by this time, wearied, there being no satisfaction to be found in them to any soul but rather distraction and confusion, as time will yet further manifest. Therefore now, as in a seasonable time, I beseech your honours as ye love truth and hate error and as truth only is worthy to be received, held forth and maintained let this be so dealt with by you because it is the very truth, as a short time to come will fully prove.

The epistle was signed with the initials J.E.[86]

Not only that, but the volume was graced with a further missive signed with the same set of initials (surely Etherington's) appended to the reprinted version of *De fide*. Here, at last, Etherington came clean about what he clearly took to be the prophetic powers of T.L. In these small treatises, which he begged the reader to read over a second time, was contained 'the truth of God' leading 'from the first beginnings of God, in and throughout the whole way, to the perfect state of a true Christian'. This, Etherington explained, was 'the last time wherein is so great confusion of spirits and opinions in matters of religion and distraction of mind thereupon'. To guide his chosen ones through these disturbing and confusing times God had raised up 'a prophet amongst us' and instructed 'him, by his word and spirit, in these great matters, even unto the very year wherein Christ shall come in his glory (his saints be raised and changed, this present world end and that world without end begin, wherein he shall reign with his saints forever in joys eternal)'. 'That the author of these small books was and is the man so to account with God, I dare be bold to say.'

Here was a divinely inspired prophet, a latter-day Noah, sent by God finally to open the coded messages entrusted to Daniel all those years ago. 'All these things Daniel foresaw and wrote', Etherington explained, 'but the time of the end, he understood not. God would have that secret closed up, till this very time of the end, wherein he would instruct one of those his servants that he should be purified and made white, by the blood of the lamb, in this last time. I say one especially, first, who (as I am, upon good grounds, assured) was the author of these books, which I desire the reader yet again to read and consider.' Just like Noah, so T.L. had been sent to forewarn the world of the onrushing end. 'There being as great need now as was then, or rather greater, that we should be forewarned of that great day, by which means his elect might be brought to repentance and the rest the more convinced in judgement, they being now left without all excuse.' For in large part T.L.'s warnings would be in vain; 'neither they of that church of Rome nor the greatest number of other Christian churches, so called, will believe these things', warned Etherington.[87]

Here Etherington returned to his earlier attacks of 1610 and the mid-1620s on what one might term the mainstream godly, railing against 'divers that would be esteemed religious, though they embrace this present world and thirst after the things of this life, like men without hope of a better' and who thus 'remained unwilling to hear of the appearing of Christ and the day of judgement'. It is not hard to discern in these remarks the outline of established and learned puritan divines, both presbyterian and independent. These were the spiritual successors of Stephen Denison, men who, having profited from the redistribution of ecclesiastical livings and political patronage brought about by the revolution, were now comfortably ensconced in the hierarchies of this world, and thus remained resolutely sceptical in the face of the sort of 'repent now the end is nigh' enthusiasm being peddled by Etherington and his ilk. All such, both papists and protestants, Etherington concluded, 'being carnal and earthly minded', 'will scoff at' the warnings of God's prophet T.L., carrying on in their corrupt and unrepentant ways 'without all fear of judgement' until it was too late. 'And when these things shall come to pass, as verily, in their appointed time, they shall, then shall [they] ... know that, in the days of their rebellion, there was a voice of a servant of God heard amongst them.'

Nor was this parallel with Noah a mere conceit; for Etherington it was a structurally and prophetically confirmed truth, a real equivalance through which symmetrical closure was about to be conferred on human history. For just as Noah had prophesied the flood 120 years before the event, so T.L. had prophesied the end of the world precisely 120 years in advance. Etherington demonstrated this sinister parallel by pointing out that, having identified 1666 as the year of Antichrist's fall, this placed the end of the world 45 years after that, which was 120 years after T.L.'s prophecy, as 'is manifest by the date of his book to the church of Rome and of that to Queen Elizabeth'.[88]

It would appear, therefore, that a now eighty-year-old Etherington finally felt able to publicly proselytise for the prophetic status of his mentor/hero T.L., seeking now to deliver T.L.'s saving message both to the wider godly public and to the new rulers of England. Unheeded by Elizabeth, Essex and James I, T.L. was now to be vindicated certainly by events and perhaps even by the actions of the Rump parliament itself. Here was a perfect ending for Etherington's sixty-year spiritual pilgrimage, with the delivery of the apocalyptic message of his mentor to the revolutionary government of post-regicide England. And here, too, was final vindication for Stephen Denison. For sect master or not, T.L. clearly had been regarded by Etherington, and presumably by others, as a prophet, his writings taken to be almost holy writ or divine revelation. Nor was Etherington the only person in 1650s' London who continued to hold dear the prophecies of the long-dead T.L. In 1661 another change of regime elicited a second printing of the complete works now tactfully shorn of the earlier dedication to the Rump and, Etherington presumably having died in the interim, now pressed upon the public by a new approving 'preface to the reader' by one J.W.

A veteran for over fifty years of the London puritan underground, Etherington was a living link between the eschatological excitements and sectarian seekings of the 1590s, the Arminian and antinomian controversies of the 1620s and 1630s, the eschatological excitements that attended the Thirty Years War and the very different but also rather similar world of the 1640s and 1650s. The strange ideological synthesis that his views represented contained sectarian, familist, puritan, Calvinist and conformist elements. analysed layer by layer, it represents almost an archaeological section cut through the discursive deposits left in the capital by fifty-odd years of intra-protestant debate and puritan spiritual experience and sectarian experiment. Neither sectarian nor familist, neither puritan nor conformist, neither radical nor moderate, Etherington makes a suitably enigmatic symbol for the puritan impulse during that period. Perhaps he had never been a card-carrying familist at all, certainly by the 1620s he was no sort of familist or sectary, but clearly Stephen Denison had been right to smell a rat when confronted by Etherington's calmingly provocative assurances of orthodoxy and conformity. For ministers of Denison's stamp, not to mention men of more enthusiastically conformist leanings and sympathies, let alone Laudians, there was plenty to worry about in John Etherington. Indeed, if we want to understand how the seemingly order-obsessed, orthodoxy-haunted puritanism of the period before 1640 (represented in many ways so neatly by the perhaps appropriately, if not unbalanced, then at least deeply intemperate, figure of Stephen Denison) produced the radical maelstrom of the 1640s, then the career of John Etherington and his altercation with the dyspeptically 'powerful preacher' of Katharine Cree is no bad place to start.

Denison and Etherington again

NOTES

1. American Antiquarian Society, Denison sermon notes (hereafter Denison sermon notes), fols 70r., 58r.
2. *Ibid.*, fol. 35r.–v.
3. *Ibid.*, fol. 36r.–v.
4. *Ibid.*, fols 37r.–v., 38r.
5. *Ibid.*, fols 81r., 57v.
6. *Ibid.*, fols 41v.–43v., 44v.
7. *Ibid.*, fol. 66r.
8. *Ibid.*, fol. 31r.
9. *Ibid.*, fols 55r., 58r.
10. *Ibid.*, fols 57v., 55r.
11. *Ibid.*, fols 105v.–106r.
12. *Ibid.*, fol. 38v.
13. *Ibid.*
14. *Ibid.*, fols 38v.–39r.
15. *Ibid.*, fol. 58v.
16. *Ibid.*, fols 39r.–40r.
17. *Ibid.*, fol. 45v. Also see fol. 90v. for the love of powerful preaching as the sign of a true conversion.
18. *Ibid.*, fols 10v., 18r.–v.
19. *Ibid.*, fols 76r.–77v.
20. *Ibid.*, fols 93v., 96v.
21. *Ibid.*, fol. 126v.
22. *Ibid.*, fol. 122v.
23. *Ibid.*, fol. 126r.
24. *Ibid.*, fol. 122r.
25. *Ibid.*, fol. 12v.
26. *Ibid.*, fols 109r.–v., 124r.
27. *Ibid.*, fol. 129r.
28. *Ibid.*, fol. 127r.
29. *Ibid.*, fol. 110r.
30. *Ibid.*, fol. 124v.
31. *Ibid.*, fol. 128r.–v.
32. *Ibid.*, fols 129r.–v., 128v.
33. *Ibid.*, fols 130v.–131r.

34 John Etherington, *The defence of John Etherington* (London, 1641); *The deeds of Dr Denison a little more manifested* (London, 1642); *The anabaptists' groundwork for reformation* (London, 1644); *A brief discovery of the blasphemous doctrine of familism* (London, 1645).

35 Etherington, *The defence*, p. 62.

36 *Ibid.*, p. 63. Certainly, as we have seen above, news of Denison's campaign against Etherington had reached the Hartlib circle by the mid-1630s.

37 Etherington, *The deeds*, sig. B4v.

38 *Ibid.*, sigs A2r.–A4v.

39 *Ibid.*, sigs B. Br.–v.

40 *Ibid.*, sig. B2r.

41 *Ibid.*, sig. B2v.

42 *Ibid.*, sig. B3r.

43 *Ibid.*, sigs A4r., B2v., where Etherington repeated his question to Denison: 'are you a papist, an Arminian or an anabaptist for, belike, you hold the same doctrine of sacramental grace as they do?'

44 *Ibid.*, sig. B3r.

45 *Ibid.*, sig. A3r.

46 *Ibid.*, sigs B2v., B4r.

47 *Ibid.*, sig. B3v.

48 *Ibid.*, sig. B4r.

49 Denison, *The white wolf* (London, 1641), p. 81. A. Hughes, 'Gender and politics in leveller literature', in S. Amussen and M. Kishlansky, eds, *Political culture and cultural politics in early modern England* (Manchester, 1995). Also see her '"Popular" presbyterianism in the 1640s and 1650s: the cases of Thomas Edwards and Thomas Hall', in N. Tyacke, ed., *England's long reformation, 1500–1800* (London, 1997). I owe the references to the anti-sectarian literature of the 1640s deployed here to the kindness of Ann Hughes.

50 Etherington, *The anabaptists' groundwork*, sig. A2r.

51 *Ibid.*, sig. A2v.

52 Etherington, *A brief discovery of ... familism*, p. 1.

53 *Ibid.*, pp. 1–2.

54 *Ibid.*, p. 2.

55 N. Smith, *Perfection proclaimed* (Oxford, 1989), pp. 116–18, 65–72, 136–8, 141–3.

56 Etherington, *A brief discovery of ... familism*, pp. 2–3.

57 *Ibid.*, pp. 3–5.

58 *Ibid.*, p. 11.

59 *Ibid.*, p. 12.

60 *Ibid.*, p. 3.

61 J. Traske, *Heaven's joy or heaven on earth* (1616), pp. 54–5. I owe this point and this reference to the kindness of David Como.

62 Etherington, *The anabaptists' groundwork*, pp. 9, 16–17, 14.
63 Ibid., pp. 16,17, 11.
64 Ibid., p. 24, title page.
65 Ibid., p. 27.
66 Ibid., p. 25.
67 Ibid., p. 25.
68 Ibid., p. 27.
69 Ibid.
70 Ibid., pp. 25–6.
71 Ibid., p. 28.
72 Ibid., p. 29.
73 Ibid.
74 Ibid.
75 Ibid., p. 30.
76 Ibid., pp. 29–30.
77 Ibid., pp. 30–1.
78 Ibid.
79 Ibid., pp. 31–2.
80 Ibid., pp. 32–3.
81 Etherington, *A brief discovery of ... familism*, p. 12.
82 Etherington, *The deeds of Dr Denison*, sig. Bv.
83 R. Bauckham, *Tudor apocalypse* (Abingdon, 1978).
84 *A voice out of the wilderness* (London, 1651), title page and dedicatory epistle.
85 Ibid., sig. A2r.
86 Ibid., sigs A2r.–v.
87 Ibid., a section appended to *De fide*, entitled 'to him that shall read this work, grace and truth be multiplied'.
88 Ibid., section appended to the preceding one, entitled 'the days of Noah and the coming of Christ in glory mentioned Math. 24 and Luke 27, compared and referred to the reader's consideration'.

Chapter 13

Conclusion

What, finally, then, are we to make of all this? Let us start with the easy bit. In the career of Stephen Denison we have as clear cut a vindication as we are ever likely to get of the legitimacy, and even of the relative precision, of puritanism as a term of art in the analysis of early Stuart religion. For all that the appellation was continually being defined and redefined by contemporaries, in the course of their own struggles for polemical and existential identity and advantage, the preceding account of the career and thought of Stephen Denison clearly allows us to endow the word with a relatively stable, distinctive and clear-cut meaning.

For Denison's position is surely an almost perfect exemplar of what both many contemporaries and subsequent historians have tended to understand by the word. His experimental predestinarianism and its attendant intensely introspective style of piety; his vision of the Christian community as radically split between the godly and the ungodly, with the community of the godly called together and sustained by the word preached and with the sacraments in a prominent yet subordinate position; his rabid sabbatarianism, with its insistence that the whole sabbath be devoted to the worship of God, to the exclusion of all secular activities or recreations; his drive to construct the resulting vision of true religion against an overtly Antichristian popery – taken together all these seem to be typical and constitutive puritan characteristics in early seventeenth-century England.

That phrase 'taken together' is of the essence here. For I am precisely not arguing that the espousal of any of the tendencies listed above, held in isolation from the others, can be used as a simple litmus test of 'puritan' status. This is no mere shopping list of disparate characteristics and opinions. As the preceding analysis shows, the various parts of the puritan world view were integrated by divines like Denison into an emotionally compelling and dynamic synthesis. Here was a distinctive strand of divinity and piety, of theory and practice, of thought and experience, which can be traced throughout the period. It is the emotional whole, the ideological totality, rather than the isolated occurrence of one or two of the constituent parts, which matters.

Terms like puritan are usually (and quite properly) viewed as ideal types, conceptual models or caricatures, produced as heuristic devices by the observer. As such, they tend to attain far greater coherence in the observer's mind or texts, than in the far messier world of contemporary action, polemic and argument. But as the instance of Denison shows, when it comes to puritanism there were at least some contemporaries who espoused ideological positions virtually identical to the historian's ideal type. Such people recognised themselves as a coherent group (as the discussion above of Denison's notion of the community of the godly shows), and were recognised as such by their contemporaries. Moreover, both from the inside looking out and the outside looking in, the word puritan was often used to denote this social and ideological entity.[1]

Denison, of course, was a cleric but the resulting ideological synthesis was not only of clerical provenance. Nehemiah Wallington and Denison not only moved in the same social circles, Wallington's view of the world (as it has been so memorably described by Professor Seaver) was an almost exact replication of that pumped out for thirty years in the pulpit and press by Denison. The dispute with Etherington was started by and festered first amongst certain of Denison's really rather humble lay followers. Denison called Etherington a sect master but in Etherington's account of their exchanges Denison, too, had his adoring lay following. It was, moreover, a following by no means limited to the parish elite or even the prosperous middling sort. Admittedly his most eminent supporters were the very prosperous Juxons. He was clearly in with the likes of Sir Henry Martin, well connected enough to preach twice at the Cross and to secure a DD from Cambridge. He also had considerable connections within the clerical brotherhood of the city as Juxon's will from the start of his career and the six ministers prepared to stand by him in High Commission in the middle of it both show. And yet the inner core of his supporters in the campaign against Etherington were lay people of considerably more humble status, including amongst their number joiners, clothworkers and a porter's wife.

There are also all those hints throughout the various accounts of the ructions in the parish that Denison's support did not, in the main, come from the parish elite. From the outset he had set his face against the exclusivist claims to power and authority of the select vestry. At the crisis point those parishioners prepared to back him and put their money where their mouth was by taking on the ruling clique in the courts appear not themselves to have been members of the vestry. Certainly his enemies, both in 1622 and during the crisis of the early 1630s, used the rhetoric of the lesser sort and of popular disorder and misgovernment to describe their opponents and his supporters and their programme, while conversely Denison and his allies used the language of popular consent and involvement in the government of the parish and choice of parish officers (up to and including the curate himself) to justify their claims. As we have seen above, the disputes about the government of the parish contained in microcosm debates about the nature and origins of authority that resonated with many of the great political and constitutional issues of the day, with Denison and his allies continually taking up the cause of popular inclusion and consent, of popular assent and election not elite selection, as constitutive of legitimate authority and its exercise.

All that might, of course, have been mere rhetoric, scare tactics to get the authorities to come to the aid of an embattled parish oligarchy. But when we recall that Denison's opposition to the window and refurbishment clearly did put him at loggerheads with the leaders of the vestry and some of the most substantial men in the parish (Bond and Gayer again), it begins to seem that there is more going on here than the self-serving case-making of Denison's opponents. When all this is combined with the extended sections of rant against the arrogance, irreligion and pride of wealthy parishioners and office holders to be found throughout Denison's sermons (both as printed and noted down by Fleming), then it becomes all but certain that we are dealing here with a style of religion and of personal ministerial charisma the appeal of which was anything but restricted to the parish or city elite.

It is not that Denison's constituency was in any sense class based, limited to or even necessarily concentrated amongst any one social group. Throughout, he clearly retained supporters amongst the lay and clerical elite of the city. In the early 1620s Thomasine Owefield had set up a lectureship just for him. As late as 1631, the wealthy goldsmith William Avenon was prepared to leave bequests both towards the rebuilding project and to Denison himself as the parish minister.

Rather, Denison's support crossed over what we might somewhat anachronistically term class lines. But we can surely go further than that; for Denison's was a style of pulpit oratory, of moral and social commentary, with something of an edge to it. If he had a following amongst the humbler inhabitants of the city it was very likely in part because he was prepared both to champion their claims to a say in parish government and to stand up to and excoriate the apparent hypocrisy and self-interest of the wealthier members of both the parish and, indeed, of the godly communities. In this instance, at least, the puritanism of Stephen Denison and his followers, for all his formal commitment to as austere a vision of the reformation of manners as one could wish, had, in practice, little or nothing to do with 'social control' as it is conventionally understood; that is, it served not to strengthen or legitimate the

Conclusion

grip of local elites on the conduct of parish business but rather to launch and legitimate a clericalist/populist challenge to such control.

The point here, of course, is not, on the basis of a single case, to replace one univocal, 'moderate', order-dominated, 'reformation of manners'-dominated and 'social control'-dominated model of puritanism with another equally univocal, 'radical', populist, conflict-centred paradigm. On the contrary I want both to reiterate and illustrate a point made elsewhere;[2] that the social, political and ideological valence or impact of 'puritanism' varied according to the social, political, ideological and, indeed, personal circumstances with which the ideology and its carriers were, at any given moment, interacting. In any given circumstance, the past history and current disposition and trajectory of the power relations and political narrative/s in question did as much to determine what the puritanism of any of the major players meant or was doing as anything inherent in the complex and ambivalent ideological synthesis deemed puritan.

Again, according to circumstance, different strands in that synthesis could come to the fore or seize the initiative. In Denison's case, in the particular circumstances of the mini-political system that was St Katharine Cree, the clericalist and populist elements within the ideology combined to trump its equally prominent order-centred, oligarchic aspects. Conversely in his interactions with Etherington and Shaw, Denison became the (only too willing) carrier of the authoritarian, clericalist and orthodoxy-dominated strands within puritanism, while his opponents, both lay and clerical, got to mobilise the populist, spiritualising, emancipatory, anti-clerical elements in the ideology against Denison himself; elements with which, ironically and to his considerable detriment, Denison himself came to be identified, at least in the eyes of his local enemies in the parish and of central authority, as he turned, with increasing rhetorical intemperance and loss of control, against the Laudianism emanating from the centres of ecclesiastical and political power. At one level, this may seem to be merely a rather verbose and abstract way to maintain that circumstances alter cases, but it is perhaps a necessary corrective against some long-standing trends in the literature on this subject, in which those scholars most enthusiastic in their espousal of the notion of puritanism as a relatively stable ideological and/or social or interpersonal entity have also been those keenest to ascribe a univocal, 'radical' or 'moderate', ideological, social or political valence or trajectory to the phenomenon thus defined. The latter procedure or tendency is not, however, a necessary concomitant or consequence of the former. On the current account there is nothing wrong with defined, well-maintained and self-reflexive general categories as long as they do not become hypostasised and static, their very application to particular sets of historical circumstance at worst preventing and at best retarding a scrupulous attention to the, in the widest sense of the word, 'political' particularities of the situation in question.

Anyway, on the basis of all this we can surely make a claim for Denison's style of puritan religiosity as a species of 'popular religion', albeit a rather divisive one. That is precisely not to say that his was a religious style likely to attract the devotion of the majority of 'the people' (whatever such a religion might have looked like in post-reformation England) but merely to observe that it was certainly one able to draw support from across the social spectrum and to attract to itself the enthusiastic partisanship of really quite humble lay persons. Moreover, by collating Fleming's manuscript notes against Denison's printed sermons we know enough about what Denison said in the pulpit and the press to conclude that we are dealing here with a species of popular predestinarianism. The doctrinal positions adopted in his catechism fit perfectly with what he said in the pulpit. On this evidence, at least, there clearly was such a thing as a puritan-style predestinarian and sabbatarian catechism in early Stuart England. A devotion to catechesis and religious instruction in general clearly did not have to mean permanent descent into the homogeneous soup of Christian platitude concocted by Professor Green out of his fifty or so best-selling catechisms. Certainly any one lucky or, if you prefer, unlucky enough to be catechised and preached at by the likes of Stephen Denison would have been left in no doubt that he or she had been exposed to a distinctive (puritan) style of religious belief and practice.

While it is possible perhaps to detect some differences of tone and presentation separating Denison's printed sermons from Fleming's sermon notes, the two styles of discourse were clearly rooted in the same reformed, predestinarian thought-world or tradition. Indeed, what we can conclude from the Fleming notes in particular is that Denison, and presumably a good many other puritan preachers, were quite capable of manufacturing an evangelically urgent and effective style of pulpit oratory directly out of a rigidly predestinarian style of divinity. Indeed, in the popular pulpit, in the hands of a preacher like Denison, even the doctrine of reprobation could become both an arrestingly (even titillatingly) alarming and an evangelically comforting topos. Moreover, it is clear, from the urgency of their opposition to Etherington and Shaw, that even some of Denison's more humble lay followers, like the joiners Thomson and Rogers or Susan Price, were passionately interested in and were felt both by Denison and themselves to understand and to have a legitimate stake in the theological fine print of the style of divinity that Denison was selling. 'Orthodoxy' clearly did matter to these people and they had a fine-grained and detailed sense of just what orthodoxy was and what it was not.

Given his status as a lecturer in at least two other parishes, as well as his role as perpetual curate at St Katharine Cree, it is extremely unlikely that the lay, indeed the popular, following that Denison acquired through the propagation of this style of divinity was parochially based. Indeed, we know that it was not. Of his known patrons and followers, the merchant John Juxon was not a resident of any of the parishes in which Denison officially preached. Rather, he lived in St Lawrence Pountney[3] and had a country house in Mortlake, Surrey. As we have seen, the pattern of Juxon's bequests both to individual ministers and to different lectureships indicated a series of networks that stretched promiscuously across the parish boundaries of the city. Again, Etherington may never have been, in a technical sense, Denison's parishioner; certainly, at the time of their dispute, he was described as living in Putney.[4] Even Denison's seemingly most dedicated lay henchman, the joiner Rowland Thomson, who had been so prominent in the campaigns against both Etherington and Shaw, lived not in St Katharine Cree but in St Stephen's, Coleman Street. To judge from the relatively scattered lay households in which Etherington was interviewed, it seems extremely unlikely that the 'parish community' was the organising principle around which the campaign against him was orchestrated.

George Walker claimed that he found his new parishioners in Watling Street tainted with the errors of Wotton, a lecturer in All Hallows Barking. Denison, of course, had made a similar claim about the contamination of his flock by Etherington. Walker met with a hostile response from the laity when preaching in Blackfriars, a parish with which neither he nor Wotton had any official connection and where Walker had turned up as a total stranger to fill in for William Gouge at a Wednesday lecture. Denison's campaign against Etherington was conducted from at least two (three, if we count the Cross) different pulpits to what must have been a city-wide audience, as well as in print. Similarly, the campaign against the fly-by-night lecturing activities of Peter Shaw, who was himself active in at least three separate parishes, was spread across the city.

This is not to claim that in London the institutions, offices, solidarities and symbolisms of the parish were irrelevant or marginal, even to the religious lives of the godly. As Dr Merritt and Dr Boulton have both shown, they most definitely were not.[5] After all, you do not lavish the time and money it took to rebuild and refurbish Katharine Cree on an institution about which you do not care. It is, however, with Dr Merritt, to argue two things. The first is that what might appear, from the surviving church structures, the will evidence and the memorialisation of the rebuilding project in Stow, as a seamlessly smooth expression of the integrity and unity of the 'parish community', a corporately sponsored product of consensual religious sentiment and social solidarity, was, in fact, nothing of the sort. Clearly, the parish was religiously, and probably socially, divided long before the rebuilding effort got started, divisions which the ideological and financial strains inherent in that project seriously exacerbated. But for the chance survival, in the state papers, of certain court records (most notably those of High Commission and the court of arches, the bulk of the records for which courts do not survive for this period) we would know next to nothing of these divisions. Here, as arguably elsewhere, the charitable beneficence of the parish and, indeed, city elites served to call into being and celebrate an 'imagined community', a stratified and consensual social imaginary, that bore anything but a straightforward one-to-one relationship with social 'reality'; an imaginary that had, in fact, to be continually constructed and maintained in the face of countervailing forces of considerable strength.

Secondly, it is to observe, again with Dr Merritt, that, particularly in London, the religious lives of the godly cannot be studied solely through the unit of the parish and its records and that activities like sermon gadding, which elsewhere might remain somewhat deviant and even risqué, were almost entirely normal, if not legal, in the capital. A natural consequence of the social and ecclesiastical geography of the city, they could be encouraged even by the Laudian High Commission which could complacently envisage Denison's supporters trotting over the parish boundary from St Katharine Cree to hear him preach in St James, Duke's Place. In London, then, there were real tensions and contradictions between what one might term the imagined normalities of a parochial and episcopal national church and the day-to-day lives of even ordinary Christians, let alone the godly. On this view, London, with its parishes crushed in on one another, its lively and scarcely regulated lecturing scene, its complex network of ecclesiastical jurisdictions and peculiars, its variegated godly community, spread widely across both the city itself and the social order, must have been a Laudian, indeed even a Bancroftian, bishop's worst nightmare.[6]

Here was both a voracious, indeed almost a bottomless, market for the word preached and an environment perfectly suited to turn the resulting cacophony of clerical voices and lay responses into a lively series of ongoing arguments, disputes and rivalries. Here, in the networks along which stories and rumours passed, around which various manuscripts and position papers circulated, in a variety of more or less formal debates, disputations and discussions, we can see the outlines of a city-wide puritan underground; an audience or series of audiences before which various pitches for reputation and charisma could be made and various claims and counterclaims to orthodoxy staked out and contested.

But talking thus of a puritan underground may represent both an exaggeration and a misnomer; one might almost as well talk of a 'puritan public sphere', for much of the resulting activity was designedly public in that the issues were canvassed before witnesses (both clerical and lay) in terms of publicly known criteria or principles of orthodoxy and right opinion. Only thus could fair play be seen to be done and the truth publicly be vindicated. Moreover, as we have seen, the correction, conversion and subsequent

Conclusion

devotion or allegiance of the godly laity was the ultimate sign of and seal on the ministry of a truly powerful preacher. Described more prosaicly, indeed reductively, in terms of the machinations and manoeuvres of an often intensely local and interpersonal godly politics, such displays and exchanges were nearly always calculated to construct and mobilise a variety of different constituencies of support. As often as not, therefore, 'publicity' was a good part of the point.

Before 1640, the discursive terrain and social space thus delimited remained an underground in two important senses. First, it relied for its very existence on a series of practices and assumptions that were either technically illegal (sermon gadding, 'conventicle keeping', the central role of godly opinion in validating 'orthodoxy') or which sailed very close to the wind of the legally permissible (and here much, of course, turned on what precisely was meant by a conventicle).[7] Second, the dubious legal status of these proceedings, together with the ideological exclusiveness that came so naturally to the godly, ensured that this was a world restricted, in intention at least, to the godly themselves. But while that might represent an ideologically or culturally select grouping, it could, as we have seen, be socially very heterogeneous. The socially levelling effects of puritan godliness can be seen in both Denison and Etherington's circles. As we have seen, Denison's following encompassed rich merchants like the Juxons, joiners like Thomson and Rogers and Susan Price, a porter's wife, while Etherington's 'familist' connections led him into dispute both with Denison's humble lay followers and with peers of the realm. Moreover, when doctrinal conflict and disagreement broke out, such people proved only too ready to get in on the act. Nor was this merely a matter of lay assertiveness or intrusiveness; Denison may have resented Etherington's career as a lay theological gadfly and commentator, but he was happy enough to encourage the egregious Rowland Thomson's activities as a lay elder without portfolio, just as Wotton was entirely content to work through his lay follower Spencer in pursuing his dispute with the young George Walker. Lay activism and zeal, it seems, were fine as long as they served 'orthodox', that is, one's own, purposes. Defending the witnesses who had testified against Etherington in 1627, Denison referred to them as 'honest men ... honest religious men and such as yourself confess do profess strictness in religion'; here were the 'truly zealous', both clerical and lay, whose support for Denison went a good way to demonstrationg the righteousness of his cause.[8]

What, though, does all this look like when we view it from the perspective provided by John Etherington? In Etherington we seem to have personified a tradition of lay radicalism, stretching from the 1590s to the 1650s. That, in itself, is extraordinary enough. It is a strand of lay, even plebeian, activism apparently worked out in the teeth of mainstream puritan and, in particular, of clerical hostility. Finally driven underground in the 1620s by Denison's somewhat previous, but rather accurate, impression of Thomas Edwards, Etherington only re-emerged into the light of day with the collapse of censorship during the 1640s.

On Denison's account at least, Etherington's was a conventicle-centred style of activism, run by Etherington as a sect master and centred on the writings of T.L., which were viewed by Etherington and his followers almost as sacred texts. Even allowing for a good deal of exaggeration on Denison's part, Etherington's own description of his activities as a disputatious gadfly and incorrigible edifier of his contemporaries, friends and family, together with his long-standing addiction to the insights of T.L., lets us see something of what Denison was getting at. Incorporating large chunks of Denison's own position, lapsing back into apparent orthodoxy, even conformity, Etherington's pronouncements, like those of T.L. before them, always had an insistently subversive edge or subtext to them. In his exchanges with Denison we can see many of the more radical or subversive elements in Denison's own position being mobilised against him. If this was puritanism, it was a puritanism of a very different sort from that pushed by Stephen Denison and internalised by Nehemiah Wallington.

Confronted with this paradox, one option is to cast Etherington as a representative of an underground sectarian tradition, largely separate from and antipathetic to mainstream puritanism. Such an origin for the radicalism of the 1640s and 1650s has long been suggested by Christopher Hill and more recently this is one of the three possible lessons drawn by Professor Collinson from recent work on the continuities of rural dissent. Certainly, while his account of the ideological valence of familism is very different from Hill's, even Dr Marsh has tended to present familism as an ideological enclave entirely distinct from the rigourism of the mainstream godly. On his account, familism was a creed closer to the tolerant temper and pelagian proclivities of the mass of the population than the predestinarian authoritarianism and intolerance of the godly.[9] Etherington, of course, was, at least at one stage of his career, a familist and T.L.'s thought was almost certainly suffused with familist influence and language.

Such an interpretation would have the advantage of leaving puritanism, as it has been described above, intact as a free-standing, relatively stable view of the world, positively aligned with the forces of law, order, hierarchy and (Calvinist or reformed) orthodoxy against an altogether more subversive and heterodox dissenting underworld. Connections could then be drawn between that underworld and the radical upsurge of the 1640s and 1650s, while the likes of Denison and Wallington would be preserved untouched by these developments, the spiritual ancestors only of appalled conservative puritan commentators on the cacophony of the war years like Thomas Edwards.

There are, however, a number of drawbacks to this view. To begin with, the traditional moderate/radical dichotomy when applied to the dispute between Etherington and Denison keeps breaking down. Throughout their dispute both men insisted on constructing themselves as loyal servants and defenders of the English church against the papists, on the one hand, and a variety of sectarians and puritans, on the other. This was a claim which interestingly they both assumed absolutely required the assertion of a Calvinist view of predestination against an Arminian threat, a threat that they both equated equally with anabaptism and popery. Indeed, throughout, both Etherington and Denison tried hard to portray themselves as moderates, their position located on a middle ground defined by the two extremes of popery and a variously constructed puritan sectarianism. But that, of course, was precisely the way in which the Laudians, too, presented themselves. Indeed, the similarity between the polemically constructed image of puritan deviance which all three parties invoked in order to stake their own claim to the 'middle ground' of conformist respectability and doctrinal orthodoxy is quite remarkable, as too is the gusto with which they all claimed the middle ground of moderation and orthodoxy as their natural habitat. The *via media* was clearly something they all believed in but it was also a tag and a territory that meant very different things to different people.

Other things being equal, it might seem natural to cast Etherington, the unlettered lay activist, challenging the authority of the learned clergy on the basis of his own knowledge of the bible and the inspiration of the spirit, as the radical. And yet not only did Etherington adopt a more aggressively and unequivocally anti-puritan tone than Denison, in the doctrinal disputes between them Etherington's opinions were sometimes, according to the conventional construal of the spectrum of contemporary opinion, more 'moderate', even 'conservative' than Denison's. Certainly, on the sabbath, Etherington's position was identical to that later adopted by the Laudians. Even on predestination his insistence that repentance must precede justification and regeneration might, on certain views of the issue, be described as more 'liberal' or conciliatory than Denison's austere statement of Calvinist orthodoxy. Finally, it was Etherington, 'the radical', who appealed to the ecclesiastical authorities against the 'moderate' Denison, while it was Denison, 'the moderate', who resorted to the court of godly opinion rather than the church courts in his campaign against Etherington. Again, it was the 'Calvinist', Denison, who successfully used Etherington's anti-Arminianism to persuade an ecclesiastical commission, now dominated by Arminians, to take his side against his errant parishioner.

These difficulties all speak to the dangers inherent in using the terms 'radical' and 'moderate' as hypostasised or hypostasising categories in and of themselves. In fact, these terms are only of any use when they are employed situationally, as modifiers, in conjunction with some other more substantive term of analysis, which brings with it an implicit range or spectrum of opinion

Conclusion

to which the terms radical, moderate and conservative can then speak. Thus, no one can simply be described as a 'radical' or a 'moderate' but rather as a moderate or radical puritan, Calvinist, Laudian or whatever. Thus, to take an example, if we seek to characterise the opinions of contemporaries according to the Calvinist/Arminian axis, then the spectrum implied by those categories will run from the starkest statement of absolute predestination, at one end, to a view of predestination from foreseen faith, at the other. Similarly, the conventional moderate/radical spectrum can be applied with relative ease to certain constructions of the term puritan. Those puritans who felt driven to give overt institutional form to their basic scripturalism, their drive to shepherd out the godly from the ungodly, to avoid popery and to render the fostering of a truly godly consciousness amongst the people the constitutive element in their concept of ecclesiastical order, can meaningfully be termed radical. This description would therefore encompass both those who refused on principle to conform and those who went further and developed presbyterian or congregationalist platforms of church government as alternatives to the episcopalianism of the English church. The term 'radical' would then operate in contradistinction to the appellation 'moderate' which would be applied to those puritans who (like Denison) felt able to avoid such overt gestures of disaffection and disobedience and to pursue their vision of true religion within the structures of the English church without overt complaint.

This last group would be in the majority. As a great deal of recent research has revealed, many puritans, both lay and clerical, managed to embed themselves within the power structures and hierarchies of the early Stuart church and state. With Denison, the clergy acquired lay patrons and livings, collaborated with the ecclesiastical authorities in the defence of what they took to be right doctrine and the fight against popery and generated a body of casuistry and argument to justify outward conformity to the norms and observances of the national church.[10] There was, therefore, more than a grain of truth in the self-presentation of men like Denison as loyal sons and defenders of at least what had become a common reformed construction of the church of England.

So far so good, but where does that leave Etherington or, for that matter, T.L.? Never overtly sectarian, indeed meticulously conformist in their treatment of the externals of ceremony and church government, neither man quite fits the bill as a radical puritan, still less as a separatist. Now a good deal of the resulting confusion might be attributed to the discombobulating effects of familism. Familist nicodemism, the capacity to speak in what amounted to oracular riddles, to toy with the most radical-seeming formulations and logical outcomes only to withdraw into the apparent safety of pseudo-orthodoxy and actual conformity, were all central characteristics of familist discourse and

Conclusion

they remained central characteristics of all the texts produced by T.L. and Etherington.

And yet familism as an explanation of our difficulties will only take us so far. For one thing, it is unclear how far or for how long either man was ever really a familist. Etherington certainly seems to have had an expressly familist stage, but he had repudiated the most overtly familist positions of his 1610 pamphlet by 1623, and many of the positions held in common by both T.L. and Etherington were scarcely compatible with what most modern commentators (and indeed John Etherington in his 1623 incarnation) believe/d familists believed. We are left with a residue of suggestively familistical language and a deep sediment of what may well be, in origin, familist assumption. But those elements appeared to coexist in the thought of both men with elements taken from a wide range of other ideological positions and discursive formations.

Mainstream protestant predestinarianism and apocalypticism, central elements from the Foxeian defence of the protestant church against an Antichristian Rome, equally central elements of the Whitgiftian defence of the power of the magistrate over things indifferent, great chunks of the puritan rhetoric of edification and the necessity, spiritually, to build the temple built only of lively stones as the real task of the church – all these can be discerned in the writings of both T.L. and Etherington. Nor does Etherington, on either his own or on Denison's account, seem to have occupied the sort of introverted, endogamous enclaves described by Dr Marsh as the familists' natural habitat in rural Cambridgeshire.[11] On the contrary, Etherington seems to have been a familiar figure in godly circles in London, always willing to question the doctrine and beliefs of a variety of groups and persons.

Thus, in both T.L. and Etherington it seems altogether unlikely that we are dealing with the continuation of some hermetically sealed sectarian, familist or 'dissenting' tradition, stretching, in the genes or the marriage alliances of various families, from lollardy to quakerism.[12] Rather we are witnessing a series of acts of creative bricolage, kaleidoscopic combinations and recombinations of ideological materials, drawn from a number of sources, to create the eerily sudden shifts, the tracking back and forth from the apparently orthodox, to the overtly and austerely conformist, to the vertiginously radical denial of real spiritual worth to all outward forms and ecclesiastical institutions, that characterised the works of both T.L. and Etherington.

Nor was the trajectory of either man's thought uniformly 'radical'. On the contrary, on his own account, Etherington moved from a pseudo-sectarian, seeking, youth, through what he termed anabaptism, into familism and out again into the radical puritan conformity from which he confronted Denison in the 1620s and to which he returned in his last publications of the 1640s. Thus far the trajectory of Etherington's career confirms Professor Collinson's point that the fissiparous and centripetal forces within English protestantism/ puritanism were counterbalanced, for much of the period before 1640, by centrifugal, unitive forces, pulling the godly, through all sorts of ideological, emotional as well as material considerations, back into the embrace of the national church. On this view, Etherington becomes a rather more resolved and efficient version of Randle Bate, that is, someone who, for all the 'radicalism' of many of his opinions, managed (quite successfully in Etherington's case, less so in that of Bate, who died in prison), to avoid separation and reconcile himself to the national church.[13]

In the mid-1640s Etherington could surely have adopted at least as familist a pose as he had in 1610 or indeed any number of separatist or semi-separatist positions, if he had wanted to. But he did not. Instead, as we have seen, he chose to attack both radical puritan and independent schemes for further reformation and the often frankly millenarian language in which they were couched. But he did so from a prophetic and spiritualising perspective, culled directly from the works of T.L., and the underlying subversiveness of his position continued to show through. Thus, while Etherington might oppose radical puritan reformation and the thousand-year rule of Christ and the saints on earth as excessively carnal versions of the spiritual renewal and reformation he knew to be coming, he retained his belief in T.L. as a prophet, or divinely inspired exegete and in T.L.'s vision of a truly spiritual reformation, as, in the penultimate sixth age, the spiritual powers of the little ones gradually took over and transformed the state of the church. In the process, of course, he revealed the decidedly limited and subversively *de facto*ist nature of his espousal of outward conformity and obedience to the powers that be, as, in 1651, he dedicated to the Rump parliament the collected works of his mentor T.L.

Ultimately, then, both Etherington and T.L. defeat any conventional rendition of the radical/moderate spectrum or dichotomy. They might be taken to do so largely because their positions, developed under a potentially hostile episcopal authority, and in tension with a potentially at least as hostile puritanism, were designed to do just that. Variants on a form of familist nicodemism, their spiritualising radicalism was contained within a husk of conformity and an appearance of orthodoxy that was perfectly suited to allow the carrier of these ideas to maintain a presence in, but not entirely of, both the national church and the puritan community within that church. But tempting as it might be to see that as a mere pose, a prudential masking of a real radical kernel behind an outward husk of conformity, Etherington's behaviour during the 1640s gives the lie to such an interpretation. Whatever its origins, however much initially the position espoused in print by T.L. and Etherington may have born the imprint of the hostile environment in which it was formed, there seems no doubt that by the 1620s at least Etherington's views had achieved the same stable, free-standingly coherent form with which he was to confront his public in print in the 1640s.

This means that we should probably take seriously Etherington's espousal of core puritan and protestant attitudes to justify his behaviour and opinions during his altercation with Denison. Perhaps the relatively accepting attitude towards the boxmaker's eccentricities and errors, which Denison imputed to many of the London godly, had a real basis in a genuine ideological affinity. On this reading, one of the sources for T.L. and Etherington's thought emerges as puritanism itself or rather a common stock of hot protestant attitudes, assumptions and doctrines that both men shared with the godly. Here may be the source of that sense, recorded by Denison as prevalent amongst the godly, that Etherington was 'one of us' and therefore that it was bad form to excoriate him so mercilessly from the pulpit and denounce him as a heretic to the authorities.

But if that sense has something to tell us about the Etherington, it has more to tell us about the nature of the London puritan underground. For if Etherington's career there, sustained over fifty years, is anything to go by, and if we can trust his account of his own and/or Jessup's ideological development at all, then the range of opinions in circulation in that underground, the sort of positions being canvassed and debated there, was far wider than a perusal of the works of divines like Denison would lead us to believe. Familists, separatists, oddballs like the Legat brothers, inspired exegetes and would-be prophets like T.L., all appear to have had a home there. Nor was this only a matter of persons, it was also a matter of texts. T.L.'s works were, as we have seen, intermittently reprinted during the early seventeenth century. An anonymous edition of *The key of David* was readily available to be cited by Chibald in his own defence in 1623. In order to write his attack on Randall, Etherington must have had at least one book by H.N. in his possession in 1645, along, of course, with the complete works of T.L.

Professor Collinson has written perceptively of the sort of social and ideological mechanisms and pressures, the semi-secret, yet in godly circles, semi-public debates and disputations through which the godly tried to regulate their own affairs, policing the boundary between mainstream puritanism and schism, seeking to apply spiritual and argumentative balm to 'England's incurable wound' of brownist separatism.[14] The analysis conducted above of Denison's dealings with Etherington and of the treatment meted out to Shaw and Chibald suggests that we should expand the range of concerns and issues treated in this way within the godly community, at least in London.

Nor should we see this as some sort of aberration, forced on an otherwise stable and authoritarian puritanism by a semi-autonomous dissenting tradition. As the instances both of Etherington himself and of William Chibald show, the doctrinal issues that were canvassed in these debates were not always introjected into puritanism from a separate dissenting or familist strain of heterodoxy. On the contrary, the triad linking formal doctrine, practical divinity and the religious subjectivity of the godly had a dialectically generated dynamism all of its own. On this account, puritanism could generate quite enough of its own dissent and heterodoxy from within. Again, the very sense of insiderhood, of being one of us, that served to protect Etherington for so long, and that lay behind all the intra-puritan exchanges and debates described above, was drawn from the very centre of the puritan world view. The whole vision of a community of the godly, a church built only of lively stones, and the consequent obsession with edification, that process of spiritual building, of mutual advice, admonition and, if necessary, rebuke, whereby the spiritual temple of the godly community was constructed and maintained, were of the essence of puritan religion.[15] When Etherington or T.L. spoke that language they were not lapsing into some radical dissenting code, they were deploying concepts and keywords drawn from the very centre of the discourse of puritan godliness. Again, when Etherington cited the right of individual lay persons, armed only with scripture and the insights vouchsafed to them by the spirit, to challenge the pronouncements of clerical authority, he was doing what puritan ministers told their flocks to do all the time. Even his challenge to what he saw as the tyrannical legalism of Denison's sabbatarianism could claim considerable warrant both from puritan treatments of popish or conformist legalism and formalism and from the spiritual anguish of members of Denison's own flock.

And here we return to the tensions and potential contradictions noted above in Denison's thought; tensions between lay activism and clerical authority; between the primacy of the spiritual experience of the godly and the demands of a stern, constricting and clerically defined and disseminated orthodoxy; between the autonomy and fluidity of the godly community and the outward forms, observances and institutions of the national church. Clerical careers like those of Denison and their pietistic correlatives amongst the laity like Wallington represented one way of bringing those tensions under control through the shared assumptions, the routinised subjectivities and collective behaviour patterns of moderate puritanism. But devoid of the sort of institutional structure that only a full-scale presbyterian reformation of the church could provide, there was a limit to how successful those efforts at stabilisation could be, especially since the world view disseminated by Denison and internalised by Wallington contained within itself and helped to reproduce the very tensions and instabilities outlined above.[16]

It is in this context that the question of censorship is best addressed. For as we have seen above, in the instances of Chibald, Wotton and Walker, censorship should not always be seen as an authoritarian intrusion, an official fiat, introjected into the internal workings of the godly community. We are not dealing here so much with a means whereby the government apparatus of the state church sought to control and suppress a largely puritan opposition. Rather, on many occasions, censorship worked as an extension, even a welcome beefing up, of the internal self-regulating mechanisms and impulses of the godly themselves. Here, of course, the topic of 'censorship' collides with the both influential and much reviled notion of a 'Calvinist consensus' which, we are told, united both puritans and conformists into some sort of reformed Jacobean synthesis. However, these notions of 'censorship' and 'consensus' were not connected in the ways in which one might assume from much of the recent writing on the subject. A deep sense of 'consensus' was indeed central to the workings of this system of censorship but 'consensus' here was not some monolithic body of right opinion, imposed from above through the mechanisms of official control and repression. On the contrary, it was a sense of ideological and emotional affinity, of being on the right and, indeed, on the same side – of being, in some fundamental sense, in agreement – which allowed particular disagreements, even on quite central doctrines like justification, to be organised under the sign of the doctrinally peripheral or, in Whitgift's priceless phrase, the inherently 'disputable' and hence managed and controlled.[17]

This sense of basic doctrinal agreement clearly underlay that effacement of the traditional signs and shibboleths of puritan disaffection with the liturgy and polity of the church undertaken by well-affected censors like Daniel Featley. Such men were probably almost as concerned to ease the passage of works by authors like Elton and Crompton into print as they were to geld those works of their controversial puritan bits. But this sense of fundamental doctrinal and/or religious agreement also prompted and conditioned such men's management of intra-puritan disputes like those between Wotton and Walker or between Chibald and his various critics. For if either sort of interaction were to be carried off successfully a sense of mutual trust, of ideological affinity, between the censored and the censor was crucial.

Here the role of evangelical Calvinists and episcopal chaplains like Featley and Mason was central, both in maintaining the links between the puritan community and the establishment and in maintaining the relative internal peace of the godly community itself. Featley and Mason are revealed, in some of the interactions outlined above, as acting more like literary agents or sub-editors than what one might think of as censors. Their role in regulating access to the public medium of officially sanctioned print resembled more that of unofficial referees or umpires in the doctrinal squabbles and discussions of the godly than that of spokesmen for an authoritarian and univocal 'orthodoxy'. We are dealing here with relatively delicate negotiations, bargains struck between what the censor thought the demands of doctrinal propriety and attendant political circumstances would bear and what the censored would accept.

Of course, if push came to shove, the censor held the whip hand. However, what was at stake was not so much the simple suppression of deviant opinions – these after all could be circulated alarmingly effectively in manuscript or by word of mouth, or indeed be published abroad, as both Wotton and Walker found. Rather, what was at stake was the symbolic 'public' standing uniquely conferred by officially approved print. Wouldbe authors like Walker, Wotton, Chibald, Crompton or Denison wanted to appear in print as validated players, officially sanctioned participants, in the elaborate dialectical dance whereby 'orthodoxy' was produced and maintained in the English church. And in the pursuit of that, both sides had reason to compromise.[18]

Or rather they did if they shared essentially the same view of the world – as arguably Chibald, Mason, Wotton, Walker and Featley, Elton, Crompton and Denison all did. This cosy system of give and take was most liable to breakdown when unsympathetic spirits intruded themselves into the licensing process, either directly as licensers or indirectly, as in the Elton/Crompton business, as ideologically motivated sneaks and busybodies. As theological opinion polarised in the 1620s, who licensed what became a crucial issue, as Richard Montague himself acknowledged in his famous request to John Cosin to get *Appello Caesarem* licensed 'but of no puritan'. Here we approach the inherently personalised and politicised nature of the licensing system in its most overt form. Each licensing exchange was a potential field for negotiation, conflict, compromise and confrontation and hence brought with it at least the potential to generate mini high-political narratives. Moreover, as both the Elton/Crompton and the Denison/Etherington affairs show, those narratives could both feed into and feed off the highest of high political narratives at court and in the parliament house. Here the very different outcomes of Denisons's two run-ins with the authorities in 1624/25 and 1626/27 show just how sensitive to the surrounding political circumstances the whole licensing process could be.[19]

But if there was a high politics involved in these exchanges extrinsic to the puritan community, there was also a politics entirely intrinsic to that community at work too. Issues of temperamental as well as ideological predisposition were of course important in the often fraught, face-to-face world of godly politics. As we have seen in the cases of both Walker and Denison, an irascible propensity to argument, an aggressive instinct for the polemical jugular, a tendency to invoke, at the first opportunity, the nearest stereotypes of heretical enormity, could render compromise solutions, complex and hedged agreements to disagree, almost impossible to achieve.

But there was more at stake here than the temperaments and predispositions of the particular players. On the one hand, there was the often bitter, almost structurally determined, politics of intra-ministerial rivalry and lay/clerical friction. Once initial postures had been struck and stances taken, and, in particular, once high-flown charges of ideological deviance and heresy had been laid, the personal stakes could become very high indeed. Moreover, as we have seen, the polarising attack mode, much beloved of both Denison and Walker, whereby the errors and misapprehensions of one's chosen adversary were assimilated, by a brutal process of logic chopping, to some dreadful principle of heretical iniquity (in Wotton's case socinianism, in Etherington's familism), and the more irenically moderate mode, claimed by Gataker, whereby the points at issue were distributed under the headings of the inherently disputable or the forgivably erroneous, represented not merely different temperamental or personal styles, but equally central strains in the reformed tradition, mutually dependent dialectical and rhetorical means whereby orthodoxy was produced and policed in early Stuart England. Here was the good cop/bad cop double act whereby agreement was induced amongst the godly. Thus even 'moderates' like Gataker and Featley were not allergic to the polemical mode when they took really central doctrinal issues to be at stake – *vide* Featley's response to Montague's Arminianism.

Indeed, in some ways both Gataker's assault on Walker and that of his nameless godly critics on Denison represented a sort of *petitio principii*. For if Etherington and Walker really had been familists or socinians such treatment would have been quite in order. The issue, in many such exchanges, was not so much the mode itself as the appropriateness of the target. What were involved in these disputes were not, therefore, only personal tiffs, in which the precarious holds on equanimity and reality enjoyed by both George Walker and Stephen Denison were put to the test and found wanting, but the working out of structural, ideological, emotional and doctrinal tensions and instabilities within the puritan tradition itself.[20]

The career and opinions of John Etherington exposed those instabilities mercilessly. As we have seen, at the level of ideology and argument, his position struck at what were probably the three most important means (the sacraments, the sabbath and the authority of the powerful preaching minister) whereby Stephen Denison had sought to attach the godly community to the institutions and structures of the national church. At the practical level, Etherington's career as a disputatious gadfly, a conventicle keeper and barrack-room lawyer, embodied that challenge in an intensely irritating and potentially subversive presence, that simply would not go away.

Of course, Denison's decision to do his best to make Etherington disappear definitively probably owed as much to the asperities of his own temperament as to the seriousness of the objective threat that Etherington in himself posed to the stability of the London puritan community. I am most definitely not arguing here that we should rewrite the history of pre-civil war puritanism in London, or anywhere else for that matter, in terms of a radical dissenting tradition carried by crypto-familist boxmakers. (In a career as singular as

Conclusion

Etherington's any sort of artisanal determinism seems entirely out of place.) Rather, I want to claim that Etherington's very peculiar career and, more particularly, his eerily protracted altercation with Stephen Denison, can stand as symbols, synecdoches, for wider tensions and instabilities within the puritan project as a whole. In particular, I want to argue that the peculiarities of that career, together with the rather paranoid temperament of Stephen Denison, have combined to give us a glimpse of the workings of the London puritan underground that we would otherwise, given the available sources, be largely denied.

Of course, all ideologies are in some sense unstable and contradictory, and I am not claiming that puritanism was so peculiarly so that it was simply doomed to collapse under the weight of its own contradictions. For, as Professor Collinson and more recently Dr Webster have both pointed out, the way in which the tensions inherent even in moderate puritanism played themselves out was a function of any number of contingencies. There are always a number of micro- and macro-political narratives against which all such ideological analyses need to be set. As we have seen, Denison's assaults on Etherington and on Shaw are scarcely intelligible outside the wider political and ideological context provided by the rise of Arminianism during the 1620s and many of the tensions surrounding 'antinomianism' and 'familism' during the 1620s and 1630s stemmed directly from pressure exerted on the godly by Laudian and Arminian polemical manoeuvre.

And yet it is one of the more unfortunate effects of the view of the religious history of the period that is dominated by the great debate between Calvinism and Arminianism to convey the impression of a static, monolithic, indeed, conservative puritan Calvinism under attack from a dynamic and innovative Arminianism. That same interpretative school also tends to privilege a top-down political narrative of doctrinal and polemical change, with Arminianism or Laudianism starting in the universities and at court and spreading thence out into the wider church and society. There is, of course, much truth to such a view, but adopted as a total explanation of religious change, as it sometimes has been, it does seriously underplay the dynamism and, indeed, the potential instability of the English reformed synthesis, particularly as it was disseminated in the pulpit by puritan divines and internalised by the godly laity as a style of practical divinity.[21]

Indeed, one of the things we are getting in the debates between Chibald and his critics and between Etherington and Denison is a glimpse of, as it were, spontaneously generated internal debates and disputes amongst the godly about the nature of orthodoxy. If nothing else Stephen Denison's career stands as a monument to the capacity of mainstream puritan values to generate conflict and division not only between the clergy and the laity, the godly and the ungodly, but also amongst the godly (both clerical and lay) themselves.

Of course, one might attribute a good deal of the resulting fuss to Denison's rebarbative temperament. But even then one would have to factor in the opportunities for self-serving moral grandstanding and self-assertion offered to the godly and, in particular, to the godly clergy, by puritan ideology. Telling other people off and what to do was presumably at least half of the point and spiritual one-upmanship within the magic circle of the godly was endemic to the puritan world view.

In part, the dynamic of the resulting doctrinal disputes was dialectical, a product of a sort of challenge and response mechanism operating both amongst the puritan clergy themselves and between the clergy and some of their more uppity or anxious parishioners. In part, then, it was internal to the puritan tradition and experience, representing the working out of the sorts of internal tensions and even contradictions that were examined in the analysis of Denison's position above. But in the person of Etherington, with his sectarian and familist past, we can also see those disputes as part of a wider dialogue, in which a whole range of influences and experiences were brought to bear on the process whereby 'orthodoxy' was shaped and disseminated, consumed and criticised amongst the godly. And in the hothouse atmosphere of puritan London we have precisely the right circumstances in which such volatile ideological mixtures might be concocted and consumed.

The point, therefore, as ever, is to get the balance between these various forces – between internalist and externalist accounts, between long-term discursive structures and instabilities and short-term political contingencies – right. On the basis of the necessarily indeterminate story of the relations between the two men and a pair of initials with which we started, it is obviously not possible to say anything definitive about these issues. The most that I can hope for is that the preceding analysis has served three purposes.

The first is to confirm puritanism as a central term of analysis and object of study in the period before the civil war. The second is, perhaps perversely, almost simultaneously to problematise and even to destabilise that term. I do not want to do this by distinguishing puritanism from, or even opposing it to, an underground and more authentically popular, strain of dissent. On the contrary, Professor Collinson is surely right to argue that all roads from the lollards to the 'radical dissenters' of the 1640s and 1650s (if such roads there were) must run through, not under or by, puritanism.[22] Rather, I want to incorporate the likes of T.L. and Etherington, and the ideological and social forces they embodied, into a widened sense of what puritanism (seen as both an ideology and a series of social entities or networks) was, in early modern England. That is to say, I want to modify the relatively hard-edged, Denison-centred ideological definition of puritanism with which we started this conclusion, with a more fuzzy-edged 'phenomenological' approach.

Here the social entity of the godly or puritan community is defined in terms of the social fact of godly insiderhood as it was registered, for instance, in the various reactions of the London godly both to Etherington himself and to Denison's assault upon him. On the one hand, this is to undercut or modify the relative precision of a definition based on doctrine with one based on the social networks and patterns of mutual recognition and acceptance of those who did indeed perceive one another to be in some sense brethren, at least potential members of the saving remnant of true believers and godly seekers within the wider national church and community. Of course, the one definition is and was related to the other; we can try, as both hostile and sympathetic contemporaries tried, to tease out, define and number the formal opinions and tacit assumptions that underlay this wider sense of socio-cultural recognition or mutuality. But certainly the analysis conducted above has shown that the social reality of puritan godliness contained a far wider range of opinions and positions than the relatively narrow renditions of 'orthodoxy' being peddled by Denison, Elton or Walker would lead us to expect. Precisely the leeway extended by many of the godly to Etherington or by Gataker and others to Wotton ensured as much. Only thus can we explain that ideological amphibian Etherington's remarkably succesful sixty-year career as some sort of back-street Socrates, feeding dialogically off the doubts and obsessions of the godly laity and the excesses and self-contradictions of the godly clergy. This is to put at or near the centre of our analysis a necessarily nebulous sense of insiderhood, of being one of us, based not so much on numbered points of right opinion as on diction, affect and personal and ideological association or affinity.

However, for all that it deprives us of at least the appearance of precision, such an approach brings with it considerable advantages. Most obviously, it enables us, with Geoffrey Nuttall, to give due weight to the inherently dynamic, open-ended nature of puritan 'faith and experience' and thus necessarily of successive or competing puritan constructions of orthodoxy. For, it has been argued here, such notions of orthodoxy were a product of a consistent conversation, a three-cornered interaction, between formal doctrine (as it was defined and defended, primarily by the educated clergy, in the schools, in the pulpit and in works of formal polemic), puritan practical divinity (as it was developed, out of the central tenets of formal orthodoxy, again largely by the clergy, in the pulpit and in pietistic guides to holiness) and the responses and reactions to both those levels of clerical discourse of the godly laity. Here, as Etherington's pronouncements on the sabbath showed, the confused and confusing dross of adverse affective reaction could sometimes be transmuted into the 'gold' of explicit doctrinal critique. While the godly laity were more than capable of mobilising one aspect of the puritan synthesis against another, the clergy themselves were bound by the requirements of their own ideology to respond to, to ease and, if they could, to

Conclusion

accommodate the spiritual drynesses and exuberancies, the doubts and certainties which their own doctrines and nostrums had induced or provoked in the laity.

In that conversation, godly lay persons had a considerable role to play. Nor was that role always adversarial, in tension or contradiction with the tenets of orthodoxy and affective correctness disseminated by the clergy. For every John Etherington there were probably a good many more Elizabeth Juxons or Nehemiah Wallington's, lay persons whose responses and experiences, whose godly lives and deaths, confirmed and developed rather than challenged or subverted the religious style propagated by divines like Denison. What was involved here was a lay/clerical dialogue with plenty of room for dissent and agreement, as the doctrines of the clergy were by turns internalised, misconstrued, or pushed back at the ministers by their alternately confused, alarmed or elated lay clientele.

Having presented such a view of puritanism, I want now to use the open-ended, admittedly slightly nebulous, dialogic version of puritanism outlined above, to suggest some ways in which the order- and hierarchy-obsessed world of the godly before 1640 – the world evoked so powerfully and yet so differently in both Collinson's *Religion of protestants* and Hill's *Society and puritanism in pre-revolutionary England* – was connected to the ideological cacophony of the 1640s.[23]

As the researches of David Como are starting to show, the emotional and theological roots of many of the specific doctrinal experiments and disputes of the 1640s and 1650s can be located in the reaction against the clericalism and legalism of the mainstream puritan clergy that produced figures like John Etherington or Peter Shaw, peddling their anti-legalist, antinomian messages to a godly audience alternately exhilarated, dazzled and confused by the austere puritan pietism of Stephen Denison and his clerical colleagues. Similarly, the self-regulating mechanisms, the procedures and protocols of the London puritan 'underground', which had been used to keep these spats and squabbles under wraps before 1640, presaged, indeed arguably provided the grounds of possibility for, that genuine 'public sphere' which, in the 1640s and 1650s, broadcast those disputes to all and sundry. For, by the early 1640s, the formal structures of authority ('censorship' very broadly defined) with which the order- and orthodoxy-obsessed tendencies and tenets of mainstream puritanism had co-operated to keep this underground more or less under ground, had largely collapsed. So too, under the mounting pressure of events and intra-puritan dispute, had the internalised reticencies, the self-censoring controls which the godly had previously brought to bear on their own internal bickerings and disagreements.

Now there was little to hinder the rapid transition of private disagreement into semi-public dispute and then fully public altercation, as the polemics and

Conclusion

position papers of the godly achieved something like immediate access to print. The significance of this was two-fold. Firstly, if a propensity to rush into print did not initially accelerate the speed with which news of doctrinal dispute could circulate, it surely widened and potentially depersonalised the range of networks and contacts along which such news could spread, thus exposing the divisions of the godly, as often as not gussied up for print in the polarising asperities inherent in the polemical mode, to the direct view of the wider world.

But equally important was the way in which merely stating something in print brought with it a raising of the personal and polemical stakes. For, as we have seen, then as now, the significance of print involved more than merely facilitating the transfer or circulation of argument, insult or information. For, certainly when matters of formal doctrine and personal reputation were at stake, print brought with it a certain public authority, it attached a certain aura or charisma both to the author and his opinions, which were now made 'public' in a sense that transcended their mere availability in the marketplace for books and ideas. After all, ideas could be perfectly well circulated in the pulpit, through word of mouth and in manuscript. Denison had effectively denounced Etherington for months both from a number of city pulpits and through the gossip networks worked so assiduously by his lay supporters. No doubt his stock, his public profile, went up considerably when he was allowed to finish the job at the officially sanctioned proceedings at Paul's Cross. But surely his triumph was rendered complete, the seal on his victory seemingly permanent, by the printed version of his sermon there, complete with its expensive woodcuts, its dedication to the king and its elaborate genuflection's towards Denison's allies and backers on the High Commission and in Lambeth Palace. So much would seem to be implied both by Denison's triumphalist tone in *The white wolf* and by Etherington's fifteen-year determination to get his own back on Denison, in print. Recourse to officially approved or licensed print here emerges as an exercise of very considerable cultural power. A minister's books and their fate were a very important register of his standing as a godly divine, a full member of that club of respectable arbiters and representatives of 'orthodoxy' to which all mainstream puritan divines aspired, and to which Denison, for one, clearly felt he had an innate right to belong. For Denison, of course, *The white wolf* represented the perfect recovery from the earlier shaming ritual of 1625, when Denison himself had been outed as a dangerously subversive puritan, through the bibliographic *auto-da-fé* at the Cross which had also consumed Elton's books. On this evidence, access to print and the public affirmation of one's orthodoxy and reliability that went with it, was a crucial part of the way in which reputations were made and maintained by the godly clergy during this period.

Such a conclusion seems confirmed by the Chibald and Wotton/Walker

Conclusion

affairs, recounted above. In both cases the point was not merely to have one's say but to have it instantiated in the public record of print and, in both cases, access to that most 'public' form of expression or vindication of one's views was manipulated both by the authorities and by the godly not so much definitively to decide or judge, as to close down, the doctrinal disputes in question. They did so both by determining which side could have access to print and on what terms that access was available. Thus, in the Walker/Wotton spat neither man got to explain himself in print, only William Bradshaw was allowed to comment there on the issues at stake and he did so as a supposedly disinterested umpire, an umpire who proceeded to use his considerable cultural capital as a famous puritan, to call the whole thing quits. Chibald, on the other hand, got to defend himself while his opponents were denied access to the press. But he expressed himself only in the moderate tone of surprised dismay at the aggressive misapprehensions of his critics described above, while mentioning no names and allowing his position to be glossed and mollified by Featley and Mason. Denison, in contrast, got to unleash the full panoply of the polemical mode on Etherington, as he crowed over the silenced boxmaker at the Cross and in print. After 1640/41 such subtle modulation of the publication and licensing process was nothing like so readily available, and the act of printing became an option for both sides in a dispute and as such tended to operate as an aggravating and exacerbating, rather than a moderating, force.

We can see how this worked in Etherington's rush, almost as soon as the censorship had broken down, to vindicate himself from Denison's slanders and Denison's willingness to reply in kind (with the now lost reissue of *The white wolf*). We can see the same impulses at work in Etherington's subsequent publishing career, as he sought to construct himself afresh, in the public record of print, against the great bugbears of his earlier career (familism, anabaptism and mainstream puritanism), and topped the whole performance off with that final triumphalist dedication of the works of T.L. to the Rump. Nor was this desire restricted to the likes of Etherington, who, after all, was an embittered and eccentric layman, anxious to horn in at last on the doctrinal discussions and public printed pronouncements of the educated puritan clergy. Even ministers as established in the London and national puritan scene as George Walker and Thomas Gataker were subject to similar impulses. Both men were seemingly ready, even anxious, to revive the details of their twenty-year-old dispute in print, virtually as soon as circumstances allowed. Walker having reopened the affair by using Wotton's alleged errors to attack Goodwin, Gataker clearly felt impelled to reply in kind and put the record straight by vindicating in print both himself and his old friend Wotton from Walker's accusations and innuendoes.

Under these sort of pressures, 'underground' really could become 'public

Conclusion

sphere', as charge was met with counter charge and no sooner had a position achieved relatively coherent statement, than it was printed and provoked, in turn, counter statement. Now all the long-standing principles about the need to vindicate and maintain orthodoxy in public, to square the pronouncements of the clergy with both the dictates of the word and the insights and scruples of the laity came into full play. Here, too, the socially inclusive, potentially empowering consequences of puritan ideological or affective exclusivity were made manifest, as tradesmen like Denison's henchman Rowland Thomson transferred their active membership of the godly community, which, as we have seen, had got them into intermittent trouble with the authorities before 1640, onto the wider stages of civic and national politics.[24]

Thus, in these circumstances, the resulting ideological cacophony was not only the product of a radical or antinomian fringe. On the contrary, it was as much the mainstream puritan impulses towards order and 'orthodoxy' – precisely, that is, those impulses which have played so central a role in recent characterisations of the 'conservatism' of pre-war puritanism – that, now transposed into a more populist polemical key, were acting to polarise and embitter an already divided and volatile London puritan scene. In other words, perhaps we should see Thomas Edwards as but the continuation of Stephen Denison by other means. And if there was a remarkably straight line to be drawn from *The white wolf* to *Gangraena*, there was surely a similarly direct line of descent to be traced from the likes of John Etherington and Peter Shaw to the heterodox objects of Edwards' obloquy in the 1640s. Arguably, then, 'puritan orthodoxy' came fully into its own only at the moment of its final dissolution.

NOTES

1 P. Lake, 'Defining puritanism – again?' in F. Bremer, ed., *Puritanism: trans-atlantic perspectives on a seventeenth-century Anglo-American faith* (Boston, 1993); 'Puritan identities', *Journal of Ecclesiastical History*, 35 (1984); '"A charitable Christian hatred": the godly and their enemies in the 1630s', in C. Durston and J. Eales, eds, *The culture of English puritanism* (Basingstoke, 1996). Also see T. Webster, *Godly clergy in early Stuart England: the Caroline puritan movement, c. 1620–1643* (Cambridge, 1997).

2 Lake, 'Defining puritanism'.

3 The two funeral sermons were preached in that church and he is described in his will as coming from that parish.

4 Stephen Denison, *The white wolf* (London, 1627), p. 33.

5 J. Merritt, 'Government, religion and society in early modern Westminster' (University of London, Ph.D. thesis, 1992); J. Boulton, 'The limits of formal religion: the administration of holy communion in late Elizabethan and early Stuart London', *London Journal*, 10 (1984). This is not to assimilate Dr Merritt to some sort of 'organic parish community' school of interpretation. Rather her work represents a model of how

the importance (both symbolic and social as well as administrative) of the parish can be acknowledged while yet placing tensions and divisions within the parish at the centre of one's analysis. On this see also her 'Puritans, Laudians and the phenomenon of church-building in Jacobean London', *Historical Journal*, 41 (1998).

6 P. Seaver, *The puritan lectureships* (Stanford, 1970) and *Wallington's world* (London, 1985).

7 P. Collinson, 'The English conventicle', in W.J. Sheils and D. Wood, eds, *Voluntary religion: studies in church history*, vol. 23 (Oxford, 1986).

8 Denison, *The white wolf* (London, 1641), pp. 78–9.

9 C. Marsh, *The family of love in English society, 1550–1630* (Cambridge, 1994).

10 P. Collinson, *The religion of protestants* (Oxford, 1982); P. Lake, *Moderate puritans and the Elizabethan church* (Cambridge, 1982), see esp. pp. 46–54 and chapter 10 for the development of a moderate puritan casuistry of conformity and its application to the crisis following the Hampton Court conference. Also see P. Lake, 'Moving the goal posts: construing conformity in the early Stuart church', forthcoming in P. Lake and M. Questier, eds, *Orthodoxy and conformity in the church of England, 1560–1660*. For further discussion of the same material see A. Hunt, 'Laurence Chaderton and the Hampton Court Conference', in C. Litzenberger and S. Wabuda, eds, *Belief and practice in reformation England* (Aldershot, 1998). For an excellent discussion of the way these intra-puritan debates and discussions were replayed and, indeed, started to come unravelled, under the pressure of the 'new conformity' being imposed by Laudian authority in the 1630s, see Webster, *Godly clergy*, part III.

11 Marsh, *Family of love*.

12 M. Spufford, ed., *The world of rural dissenters, 1520–1725* (Cambridge, 1995).

13 P. Collinson, 'Sects and the evolution of puritanism', in Bremer, ed., *Puritanism*.

14 *Ibid.*

15 J.S. Coolidge, *The Pauline renaissance in England: puritanism and the bible* (Oxford, 1970). And here we need to remember that 'edification' was a theological as well as a social category not always best translated into modern parlance as simple sociability, cf. Webster, *Godly clergy*.

16 Here a comparison might be in order with presbyterian Scotland where, perhaps in part through the effects of a fully reformed spiritual discipline, an intense 'heart religion' and virulently emotive expressions of both individual and collective piety seem to have been rendered compatible with a level of reformed orthodoxy (and a relative absence of theological dispute and fragmentation) very different from those maintained and experienced by the English godly during the same period. On 'the heart religion' of the covenanters and its relation to rather stern definitions of reformed orthodoxy see John Coffey, *Politics, religion and the British revolutions: the mind of Samuel Rutherford* (Cambridge, 1997), esp. chapters 4 and 5; also see Leigh Eric Schmidt, *Holy fairs: Scottish communions and American revivals in the early modern period* (Princeton, 1989) and L.A. Yeoman, 'Heart-work: emotion, empowerment and authority in covenanting times' (University of St Andrews, Ph.D. dissertation, 1991).

17 For Whitgift's notion of 'things disputable' see Lake, *Moderate puritans*, p. 210.

18 Anthony Milton, 'Licensing, censorship and religious orthodoxy in early Stuart England', *Historical Journal*, 41 (1998).

19 *The correspondence of John Cosin*, ed., G.Ormsby, 2 vols, Surtees Society, vols lii, lv (Durham, 1869–72), pt. 1, p. 33, Montague to John Cosin, 12 December 1624. We might perhaps consider giving up talk of censorship and think instead of a series of licensing exchanges or episodes, each taking place within a whole number of different contexts – legal, institutional, commercial and logistical, certainly, but also ideological and political. I merely expatiate here on insights gleaned from conversations with Anthony Milton many of which are to found in his article 'Licensing, censorship and religious orthodoxy'.

20 P. Lake, 'Calvinism and the English church, 1570–1635', *Past and Present*, 114 (1987).

21 Nicholas Tyacke, 'Puritanism, Arminianism and counter-revolution', in C.S.R. Russell, ed., *The origins of the English civil war* (London, 1973); *Anti-calvinists* (Oxford, 1987), esp. chapters 1, 2 and 3; C.S.R. Russell, *Parliaments and English politics, 1621–1629* (Oxford, 1979).

22 See the 'Critical conclusion' by Patrick Collinson in Spufford, ed., *Rural dissenters*.

23 Compare and contrast C. Hill, *Society and puritanism in pre-revolutionary England* (London, 1964) and P. Collinson, *The religion of protestants* (Oxford, 1982).

24 Thus the joiner Rowland Thomson, a veteran of Denison's campaigns against both Etherington and Shaw, came out of the puritan underground to give evidence at his trial against Archbishop Laud, see PRO S.P. Dom. 16/500/6, fol. 38r.

Index

Abbot, George, 87, 88, 89, 96, 97, 201, 224, 239, 247, 256, 276, 281, 306, 359, 360
Abbot, Robert, 200, 221
Aldgate, 250
Allde, Edward, 120, 121
All Hallows, Barking, 300, 394
All Hallows, Lombard Street, 59
All Hallows the Great, 58, 59, 62, 252, 282, 313, 358
Amsterdam, 181
anabaptism, 75, 80, 105, 113, 151–2, 153–4, 171–2, 184, 187, 262, 291, 292, 344, 356, 362, 370–2
Andrewes, Lancelot, 181
Andrews, Richard, 303
Antichrist, 80, 111–12, 114, 121–8, 141, 142, 143, 150, 166, 175, 179, 372, 373–80, 384
Antidoton or a sovereign remedy against schism and heresy (H. Clapham), 173
antinomianism, 211–12, 270–6, 279, 283, 291, 385
anti-puritanism, 36–7, 106–8, 112–13, 129–30, 183–8, 262–4, 371–2, 378–9, 384
Appello Caesarem (Richard Montague), 88, 405
arches, court of, 317, 319–23, 326, 394–5
Arianism, 172, 173, 175, 185–6, 187
Armada, Spanish, 124, 171, 177, 332
Arminianism, 16, 18, 75, 87–8, 89, 90, 99, 153–4, 201–2, 208, 213, 214, 232, 239, 240, 244, 245–6, 255, 272, 279, 280–5, 287, 291, 292–3, 314, 325, 359–60, 385, 398, 399, 406, 407
assurance, doctrine of, *see under* Chibald, William; Denison, Stephen; Etherington, John; Niclaes, Henry; T.L.
Avenon, William, 62, 300, 305–6, 332, 391

Babylon is fallen (T.L.), 120, 121, 123, 125–6, 141, 176, 177, 178
Balmford, James, 224
Bancroft, Richard, 63, 183, 184, 185, 223
baptism, *see under* Denison, Stephen; Etherington, John; Niclaes, Henry; T.L.
Barking, 222
Barkham, Sir Edward, 305
Barlow, John, 230

Barlowe, William, 130
Baro, Peter, 121, 133, 134, 135, 136, 137, 138, 141, 142, 159, 177, 213–14, 226, 271, 375
Basel, 243
Bate, Randall, 401
Bauckham, Richard, 124, 379
Baxter, Richard, 200, 221
Bayly, Lewis, 224, 225, 228, 230, 236, 242, 243, 254
Baynes, Paul, 198
Bermondsey, 86
Bernard, George, 13, 14, 20, 28, 32, 68
Beza, Theodore, 248
Bill, John, 313, 321, 322, 334
Bishop's Auckland, 283
Blackfriars, 223, 394
Blackwell, Richard, 303
Bloyes, John, 317
Bolton, Robert, 187
Boulton, Jeremy, 394
Bond, Martin, 63, 65, 299, 301, 302–3, 311, 313, 318, 319, 323, 326, 332, 335, 391
book of sports, 286, 333
Boswell, William, 279
Bozeman, Theodore, 275
Brachlow, Stephen, 105
Bradshaw, William, 12, 106, 186, 231–2, 233, 234, 235, 238, 241, 241, 243–4, 252, 254, 412
Brerewood, Edward, 270
Brewer, John, 319, 320, 321, 322
Bricklayers' Company, 56, 301
brief discovery of the blasphemous doctrine of familism, A (anon.), 366
Brough, William, 277
Bucer, Martin, 233
Buckeridge, John, 80, 284, 285, 359
Burgess, Cornelius, 277, 278
Byfield, Richard, 270

Calvin, John, 248
'Calvinist consensus', existence and nature of, 8–9, 13–5, 31–5, 68–9, 71, 90, 239–46, 404–7
Cambridge University, 4, 88–9, 132, 133, 135, 137, 176, 222, 390

416

Index

Carlson, Eric, 12
Cartwright, Thomas, 106, 175
Castleton, Andrew, 277, 278
catalogue of the several sects and opinions in England, A (anon.), 362
censureship, nature of, 218–21, 242–6, 404–5, 410–13
Chaderton, Laurence, 4, 79, 132, 133,
Chancery, court of, 316, 317–18, 322, 323, 324, 325, 326, 330, 333
Charke, William, 133
Charlemagne, 123
Charles I, 89, 254
Cheapside, 248, 254
Chibald, William, 190–214, 218–21, 230, 233, 236, 238, 241, 242, 245, 246, 247, 249, 254, 257, 270, 274–5, 276, 369, 402, 403, 404, 405, 407, 411
  on assurance, 191–4, 206
  on faith (justifying), 191–5, 197–8
  on predestination, 199–202
  on repentance, 195–6, 197–8, 204, 206–7
  on sanctification, 209–10
Clapham, Henoch, 172–3, 174, 183, 184, 185, 187, 188
Clare College, Cambridge, 176
Cleaver, Master, clerical ally of Denison, 253, 254, 256
Clothworkers' Company, 299, 301
Collinson, Patrick, 12, 16, 130, 227, 397, 400–1, 402, 407, 408, 410
Como, David, 275, 345, 410
confutation of the Rheimists' translation, The (Thomas Cartwright), 175
Conway, Sir Edward, 89
Cook, Robert, 321
Coppinger, Edmund, 2, 255
Cordall, William, 313
Cornhill, 288
Cosin, John, 87, 88, 284–5, 307, 332, 359, 405
Cotton, John, 12, 282
Covell, William, 263
Crabtree, Elias, 59, 277, 278, 286
Crashaw, William, 98
Creech, Giles, 180
Crew, Randall, 63
Croft, James, 300, 320, 321
Crompton, William, 87, 88, 89, 244, 404, 405
Crossfield, John, 303
Crossfield, Thomas, 2
Culombeame, Mr, a grocer, 364–5
Culverwell, Ezekiel, 221
Culverwell, Richard, 59, 21, 277, 278, 279, 286
Cumber, Archibald, 317
Cust, Richard, 90

Davenant, John, 282
Davies, John, 317
Davies, J.C., 12
deeds of Mr Denison a little more manifested, The (J. Etherington), 358
De fide (T.L.), 121, 133, 138, 383
Denison, Stephen, 2–3, 11–99, 246–94, 277–8, 311–35, 342–62, 389–413
  alleged sexual peccadilloes of, 312, 314–15, 360–1
  on antinomianism, 20, 270–1, 291, 343, 344–5
  assaults (verbal) on parishioners (coded), 41–5, 60, 65–6, 342–56; (uncoded), 64, 311–15
  on assurance, 18, 20, 21–8
  on the atonement, extent of, 17, 29–30, 32–5
  on baptism, 67, 69–70, 291, 314
  bequests to, 59, 61, 62
  on bishops, 342–3, 348
  on clerical authority, 54–5, 57–9, 266, 286–91, 348
  on conformity, 79–80
  on conventicles, 289, 297 n.46
  demeanour in pulpit of, 54–6
  on distinction between godly and ungodly, 22–33, 35–40, 45–8, 55–6, 66, 73–4, 355–6
  on double decree, 16–18, 19–20, 282
  on Esdras, book of, 149, 358
  on John Etherington, errors and activities of, 86–7, 91–2, 98–9, 120, 148–9, 162–3, 178, 182, 190, 247–8, 251, 253, 256–7, 264, 284–5, 287, 311–12, 358, 385, 397
  on false teachers, 42, 55, 57–8, 251, 264, 287–90, 343–4
  on God as the author of sin, 19–21, 291
  on godly community, 31–3, 37–48
  income of, 60–2, 327–8, 331
  on lay/clerical relations, 57–9, 66, 251, 266, 287–91, 343–4, 348–51
  on Laudianism, 346–8
  lectureships of, 59, 61–2, 327–9, 331
  on moderation, 45, 79–81, 346
  ouevre of, 11
  on perseverance, 18
  on prayer, 72
  on preaching, 53–8, 65–6, 347–8, 350–1
  on 'puritanism', 36–7
  removal from parish, 327–8
  on repentance, 27, 69–70, 190, 212–13
  on reprobation, 28–32, 351
  on the sabbath, 25, 31, 36, 42, 74–6, 149, 162–3, 270, 286, 343, 358

Index

on the sacraments, 67–73, 291–2, 358
  compared to the word preached, 67, 69–73
  divine presence in, 67
  frequent reception of, 67–8
  as means of grace, 68–71
  preparation for, 25, 27–8, 42, 68, 69–70, 73–4
on social order, 40–8
on T.L., 120, 144–5, 385
Dent, Arthur, 204
De reconciliatione (A. Wotton), 243
description of the true church of Christ, A (J. Etherington), 109, 110, 148, 150, 151, 152, 154, 159, 170, 171, 177, 180, 181, 265
Devereaux, Robert, Earl of Essex, 120, 124, 125, 126, 127, 177, 382, 384
discovery of the abominable delusions of ... the family of love, A (anon.), 156
discovery of the errors of the English anabaptists, A (J. Etherington/E. Jessup), 149, 155, 185
Dodd, John, 12
Dort, synod of, 235
Dow, Christopher, 277, 278, 279, 281
Downham, John, 224, 228, 243, 286, 334
Drapers' Company, 301, 305
Duck, Arthur, 64, 310, 316, 319, 321, 328
Duke, John, 303
Dyke, John, 300, 313, 318

Eales, Jacqui, 12
Eastcheap, 250
East India company, 300, 302–3
Eaton, John, 274
Edwards, Thomas, 356, 362, 413
Elizabeth I, 33, 97, 123, 126, 132, 176, 382, 384
Elnow or Ellner, Bartholomew, 303, 319
Elton, Edward, 86–9, 234–5, 244, 246, 333, 404, 405, 409, 411
Ephemerides (S. Hartlib), 176
epistle to the church of Rome, An (T.L.), 99, 120
Error on the left hand (H. Clapham), 173
Error on the right hand (H. Clapham), 172, 174
Etherington, John, 2, 86–9, 90–115, 148–66, 170–2, 174, 177–9, 212–14, 246–56, 262–94, 356–85, 396–413
  and antinomianism, 271, 367–70
  on Antichrist, 110, 166, 179, 372, 373–80
  on assurance, 100–1, 152–4
  autobiographical remarks of, 92–8, 149–53, 155, 171–2, 182–3, 247, 248, 253, 265, 283–5, 288–9, 311–12, 357–64
  on baptism, 92, 104–6, 158–61, 266, 284–5, 358–9, 368–9, 370–1
  on bishops, 92, 108, 266–7
  on clerical power, 95–6, 107–8, 164–5, 265–8.
  on conformity, 106–8, 268–9
  as conventicle keeper, 91–2, 93–5, 182
  on Denison, 95–7, 262–4, 282–3, 288, 357–61
  on Esdras, book of, 91, 92, 178–9, 358
  on familism, 107, 109–15, 149–52, 155–9, 182–3, 363–70, 378
  on 'the little ones', 92, 100–6, 156–8, 265–7, 367–8, 371, 374–7, 379–81
  on 'love', 101, 156–7
  on the power of the keys, 100, 102–3, 377
  on the power of the prince, 94, 95, 106, 376, 377
  on predestination, 92, 100, 153–4, 166, 398
  on puritanism, 106–8, 113, 179, 262–4, 372, 378–9, 383, 384
  on repentance, 100–1, 190, 212–14
  on the sabbath, 91, 92, 162–4, 253, 267–70, 275–6, 358, 398
  on the sacraments, 92, 161–2, 164, 285, 358–9
  on separatism, 94–5, 105, 107, 149, 171–2, 181–2
  on T.L., 178, 378, 380–5
  on the visible and invisible church, 100–6, 165, 370–1
Evangelium regni (H.N.), 110–15, 151, 165, 364
Everard, John, 183
Exeter, 221
exposition to the XI, XII, XIII chapters of the revelations, The (T.L.), 120, 125, 126, 128, 141, 176, 177

Facey, Jane, 140
Fairlambe, Peter, 183–4, 185, 187
familism, 75, 80, 89, 96–7, 109–15, 148, 149–52, 154–5, 156, 165–6, 173, 174–5, 178, 179–80, 182, 184, 187, 213, 251, 255, 262, 268, 274, 287, 289, 290, 291, 292, 344–5, 356, 362, 363–4, 365, 366–70, 397, 399–400, 407
Featley, Daniel, 87, 219–21, 232, 233, 241, 242, 244, 245, 246, 249, 335, 404, 405, 406, 412
Fields, John, 317
Fincham, Ken, 12, 227
Firmin, Giles, 203–8
Fish, Cornelius, 305
Fishmongers' Company, 300, 301, 302
Fleming, Henry, 11, 15, 21, 28, 31, 32, 33, 34, 41, 71, 342, 391, 393
Fosbrooke, Nicholas, 121, 177

Index

Foxe, John, 140, 202, 233, 380

Gangraena (Thomas Edwards), 413
Gataker, Thomas, 62, 87, 88, 185–6, 221, 224, 225, 226, 228, 229, 231, 233–42, 243, 245, 249, 252, 254, 406, 409, 412
Gayer, Sir John, 300, 301, 302–3, 311, 313, 319, 323, 324, 326, 332, 335, 391
Gibbons, John, 317
Gibson, John, 125
Gifford, George, 125
Glover, Richard, 319, 320, 321, 322
God's holy mind (Edward Elton), 86
Goldsmiths' Company, 301
Gomarus, Franciscus, 201, 234
Goodwin, John, 142
Goodyeare, Thomas, 229–30
Gouge, William, 221, 223, 224, 228, 243, 286, 335, 394
Grame, Abraham, 278, 279, 280, 286, 334
Grame, Samuel, 278, 334
Gravesend, 173
Green, Ian, 13, 14, 393
Greenham, Richard, 12
Gresham college, 234
Grindal, Edmund, 227
Gringltonians, 148, 291
Grocers' Company, 62, 301

Haberdashers' company, 301, 302
Hackett, William, 2, 255
Haigh, Christopher, 13, 15, 16, 32
Hall, Joseph, 282
Hall, Martin, 63, 303
Halsey, Aldridge, 313
Hampton Court Conference, 184, 227
Harley, Sir Robert, 89, 276
Harrison, William, 123
Hartlib, Samuel, 176
Hartwell, Abraham, 120–1
Haydon, John, 221
Henry VIII, 123
Heresiography (Ephraim Pagitt), 177
Herring, Julines, 12
Hetheringtonians, 2, 362
Hickes, William, 224
High Commission, court of, 4, 60, 61, 88, 89, 96, 97, 224, 225, 242, 247, 248, 249, 250, 253, 255, 256, 278, 279, 289, 298, 307, 311–15, 325, 327–8, 332, 333, 334, 348, 352, 356, 359, 360, 394, 395, 411
Hildersham, Arthur, 12
Hill, Christopher, 15, 16, 294, 397, 410
Hill, Robert, 317
Holdsworth, Richard, 286, 335

Hooker, Thomas, 205, 206, 207
Hough, John, 299
Hughes, Ann, 362
Hunt, Arnold, 68–9, 72, 82n.31, 292
hypothetical universalism, 33, 282

Ironmongers' Company, 301

James I, 120, 227, 382, 384
Jessup, Edmund, 98, 99, 149, 150, 152, 153, 172, 182, 185, 187, 402
Jones, William, 178
Jordan, Ignatius, 221
Juxon, Elizabeth, 11, 18–19, 25–7, 35, 36, 37, 39, 41, 55, 59–60, 62, 74, 75, 76, 79, 100, 313, 394, 396, 410
Juxon, John, 11, 59–60, 62, 79, 100, 315, 394, 396
Juxon, William, 316, 324, 325, 326

Kendall, R.T., 209
key of David, The (T.L.), 121, 128, 140, 141, 202, 214, 402
King, John, 201, 224, 225, 226–7, 242, 244, 245, 247, 360
Kishlansky, Mark, 326

Lambe, Sir John, 321, 322
Lambeth Articles, the, 133, 226
Lamont, William, 123
Laudianism, 68–9, 71, 80, 163, 277, 289, 292, 304, 306, 307–11, 312, 325, 326, 327–8, 332–5, 346–8, 359–60, 392, 398, 407
Law, Rose, 56, 62, 66
Lawes, Edward, 63
Lawn, Christopher, 173
lay/clerical relations, 57–66, 95, 100–3, 107–8, 164–5, 246–57, 264–8, 286–91, 297n.46, 343–4, 348–51
Leathersellers' Company, 301
Lee, Richard, 323, 324, 325, 326, 330
Legat, Bartholomew, 172, 185, 186
Legat, Thomas, 172, 174–6
Legat, Walter, 172
Legatine-Arians, 173, 181, 184
Leigh, Walter, 305
Lemur, Thomas, 174, 175, 176–7, 181
Levant Company, 302
Lilburne, John, 362
Lincoln's Inn, 185
Lincoln College, Oxford, 305
'the little ones', the, spiritual gifts and prerogatives of, *see under* Etherington, John; Niclaes, Henry; T.L.

419

Index

London,
   city of, 301
   court of common council, 300
   Lord mayor's court, 312
   puritan scene in, 179–88, 218–57, 395–413
'love, the', *see under* Etherington, John; Niclaes, Henry; T.L.

Magdalene College, Cambridge, 60, 61, 298, 302, 316, 317, 318, 323, 329
Maiden Lane, new prison in, 357
Marsh, Christopher, 97, 148, 154, 156, 157, 166, 179, 180, 182, 262, 397, 400
Martin, Sir Henry, 89, 96, 97, 276, 281, 299, 310, 316, 356, 390
Mason, Henry, 219–21, 224, 227, 232, 233, 239, 241, 242, 243, 245, 246, 249, 404, 405, 412
Mede, Joseph, 86
Mercers' Company, 301
Merchant Taylors' Company, 301
Meredith, Edward, 317
Merritt, Julia, 303–4, 308, 394, 395
Milton, Anthony, 240
Montague, Richard, 87–8, 90, 245, 263, 284, 405, 406
Montaigne, George, 308, 321, 360
Morrill, John, 16
Mortlake, Surrey, 59, 394
Morton, Thomas, 202
Munday, Anthony, 299, 301, 306

Nalton, Thomas, 277, 278
Neile, Richard, 87, 88, 283–5, 359
Newberry, Richard, 319, 320, 321, 322
New gag (Richard Montague), 87
Newgate prison, 172, 174, 186, 252
Nicholas, Abraham, 317
Nicholson, Christopher, 315
Niclaes, Henry (H.N.), 97, 109–10, 110–15, 120, 129, 130, 132, 148, 150, 151, 155–9, 160, 170, 178–9, 182, 275, 363–7, 372, 373, 402
   on Antichrist, 11–12, 150
   on baptism, 110–11, 114, 158–9
   on false teachers and the 'scripture learned', 111–12, 114, 165
   on 'the little ones', 110–11, 114, 150, 166
   on 'love', 114–15
   on popery and the church of Rome, 112–13, 151
   on predestination, 110–11, 114, 166
Norwich, 221
Nuttall, Geoffrey, 268, 409
Nye, Philip, 272–3, 274, 275, 278, 279, 282, 283, 342, 344, 352

Offield, John, 313, 318, 319
Okey, John, 174, 248, 254, 316
Oldsworth, John, 62
Olevianus, Caspar, 233
Owefield, Thomasine, 61, 315, 391
Oxford University, 2

Pagitt, Ephraim, 177
Paraeus, 233
Parker, George, 321
Parker, Henry, 320
Parker, James, 319
Parker, Ken, 12, 75
Parry, Glyn, 122–3
Parsons, Robert, 303
pastoral problems and formal puritan divinity, 33–5, 192–3, 196–7, 203–12, 275–6, 407–10
Pater Noster Row, 279
Pemble, William, 233
Perkins, William, 4, 132, 198, 202, 203, 205, 207, 233, 248
Pike, lay supporter of Denison, 250, 254, 255
Piscator, Johannes, 233
Plain and easy exposition of the Lord's prayer (Edward Elton), 86
polemical mode, use and abuse thereof, 238–42
polemical sources, uses and limitations of, 8–9, 187–8, 293–4
Pordage, John, 183
Porter, Thomas, 331, 335
predestination, *see under* Chilbald, William; Denison Stephen: reprobation; Etherington, John; Niclaes, Henry; T.L.
Preston, John, 89
Price, Susan, 96, 100, 254, 316, 334, 393, 396
Prideaux, John, 2, 335
print, significance of recourse to, 33–4, 219–21, 230–2, 362, 365–6, 410–13
profane schism of the brownists, The (C. Lawn), 173
prophesy that hath lyen hid for two thousand years, A (T.L.), 121, 177
Prynne, William, 304, 308–11, 327
Putney, 394

Randall, Giles, 363–70, 402
Randall, John, 224, 228, 235–6
Rantan, Nicholas, 305
recantation of a brownist, The (P. Fairlambe), 183
relation of several heresies, A (anon.), 362

420

Index

repentance, *see under* Chilbald, William; Etherington, John; Niclaes, Henry; T.L.
Reynolds, John, 227
Rhodes, Thomas, 323, 324, 325, 326, 327, 330
Richardson, Alexander, 221–2, 230, 237–8, 241
Roborough, Henry, 76, 78, 79, 99, 212, 249, 253, 256, 263, 316, 339n.44
Rogers, Daniel, 207
Rogers, John, 203
Rogers, Thomas, 198–9, 202, 203
Rogers, Thomas, a joiner and supporter of Denison, 249, 250, 277, 279, 315, 316, 393, 396
Rolls, Richard, 334
Rump parliament, 382, 385, 401
Rush, George, 327, 329, 330–1, 335
Ryves, Bruno, 310

St Andrew, Undershaft, 313
St Antholin's, 59
St Botolph's, Aldgate, 328, 359
St George's, Southwark, 302
St Helen's, Bishopsgate, 279, 280
St James', Duke Place, 305, 306–7, 328, 395
St John the Evangelist, Watling Street, 222, 223
St Katherine Cree,
    composition of select vestry in, 1627, 338n.38
    consecration of, 308–11
    election of church wardens, 319–23, 331
    election of curate, 323–7, 327–8, 330–1
    fabric of, 298–9
    living of, 60–1
    rebuilding costs of church, 299–300
    select vestry of, 57, 60, 63–5, 316–20, 324, 329–30
    stained glass windows in, 306–7, 311, 329
St Lawrence, Pountney, 277, 394
St Lawrence Old Jewry, 279
St Leonard's, Eastcheap, 76, 77
St Magnus the Great, 277
St Margaret's, New Fish Street, 59
St Margaret Moses, 277
St Martin's in the Fields, 278, 303
St Martin's, Ironmonger Lane, 277
St Mary, Aldermanbury, 56
St Mary, Colechurch, 277
St Mildred's, Bread Street, 59
St Nicholas, Cole Abbey, Old Fish Street, 190
St Paul's Cross, 2, 75, 86, 88, 243, 253, 264, 283, 357, 390, 394, 411, 412
St Peter's, Broadstreet, 62
St Stephen's, Coleman Street, 394

sabbath, *see under* Denison, Stephen; Etherington, John
sacraments, the, *see under* Denison, Stephen; Etherington, John
Salters' Company, 301
sanctification, 197, 209–10
Sanderson, Robert, 282
Sanford, John, 232, 239
Saxby, Thomas, 62
Seabright, Saloman, 249–50, 254, 255
Seaver, Paul, 12, 16, 76, 77, 390
Sharpe, Kevin, 13, 15
Shaw, Peter, 183, 273–6, 277–81, 316, 342, 344, 348, 350, 352, 356, 367, 392, 393, 394, 402, 407, 410, 413
Sheldon, Martin, 313, 318, 319, 322
Sheldon, Nicholas, 303
Shepherd, Thomas, 205, 206, 207
Sibbes, Richard, 59
Skinners' Company, 62, 301
Smith, James, 319
Smith, John, 317
Smith, John, the se-baptist, 105, 171, 181
Smith, Joseph, 280–1
Smith, Nigel, 364
Smith, William, 303, 313, 318, 319
Smithfield, 172
socinianism, 200–1, 223, 224–5, 229, 232, 236, 239, 340, 251, 362, 406
Some general directions for a comfortable walking with God (R. Bolton), 187
Spencer, a tradesman, protege and supporter of Anthony Wotton, 222, 224, 242, 250, 396
Spendloe, John, 59
Spittleyard, 363, 364
Standish, a lay supporter of George Walker, 249
Stanhope, Sir Edward, 184
Stephens, Thomas, 253, 256, 316
Stepney, 183
Stock, Richard, 224, 228, 229–30, 242, 243, 256–7, 287
Stonehill, John, 317, 323, 324, 326, 330
Stow's *Survey of London*, continuation thereof by Anthony Munday, 301, 305, 306, 394

T.L., 120–45, 148, 155–66, 170–1, 174–9, 202–3, 212, 213–14, 270, 271, 275, 293, 294, 364, 369, 370, 373, 374, 375, 376, 378, 380–5, 397, 399–402, 408, 412
    on Antichrist, 121–8, 384
    on assurance, 131–2
    on baptism, 130, 137, 158–9
    on the church of Rome, 121–8, 138–40

Index

on conformity, 130, 142–3
on faith, 133–4
identity of, 174–7
on 'the little ones', 128–9, 130–9, 141–2, 156, 157–8
on 'love', 131–2, 135–7, 156
oeuvre of, 120–1, 177–8, 380–3
on the powers of the prince, 122, 125–7, 129–30, 140, 142–3
on predestination, 129, 134–5
prophecies of, 121–8, 140–3, 382–4
on puritanism, 129–30
on repentance, 131, 135–7, 158–9
on separation, 130
on the two witnesses, 127–8, 140
T.L., (1641 version), 363, 370, 380–1
Taylor, Thomas, 221
Thames Street, 364
Theologica germania, 364
Thomson, Rowland, 249, 250, 277, 279, 315, 316, 334, 393, 394, 396, 413
Thomson, William, 303
Thorpe, George, 317
To the church of Rome (T.L.), 120, 128, 138, 139, 142, 144
Torshell, Samuel, 233
Townes, Robert, 277
Traske, John, 274, 362, 369
Travers, Walter, 133
treatise of justification, A (W. Bradshaw), 231
tree of regeneration, The (T.L.), 120
trial of faith by the touchstone of the gospel, A (W. Chibald), 190–214, 218, 219
Trinity College, Cambridge, 4
true Christian, The (Giles Firmin), 203
two witnesses, the, 127–8, 140, 175, 373–5, 377
Tyacke, Nicholas, 12, 304

Ursinus, Zacharius, 233

Villiers, George, Duke of Buckingham, 88
Vintners' Company, 301,
voice out of the wilderness, A (T.L. and John Etherington), 381–5

Vorstius, Conrad, 227

Walker, George, 185, 186, 200, 201, 221–46, 247, 248, 249, 250, 252, 253, 254, 257, 275, 279, 286, 331, 360, 396, 403, 404, 405, 406, 409, 411, 412
Walker, Nathaniel, 274, 277, 278, 279
Wallington, Nehemiah, 72, 76–9, 270, 390, 397, 403, 410
Walsham, Alex, 14
Walton, Brian, 277, 278
Ward, Samuel, 89, 282
Watt, Tessa, 14
Watts, William, 277, 278, 279
Webb, William, 303
Webster, Tom, 12, 407
Weller, John, 303
Wells, Christiana, 299
Wells, William, 62
Wentworth, Thomas, Earl of Strafford, 286
Whateley, William, 198
Whitaker, William, 248
White, Francis, 202
White, John, 221
White, Peter, 13, 15
Whitechapel, 98
white wolf, The (S. Denison), 4, 89–92, 98, 120, 148, 155, 180, 247, 252, 284, 290, 291, 292, 360, 411, 413
white wolf, The (S. Denison, 1641 edition), 357
Whitgift, John, 106, 183, 184, 226, 400
Whitmore, George, 305
wolf in sheep's clothing, A (G. Walker), 243
Woodmongers' Company, 305
Worcester, Peter, 250, 254, 315
Wotton, Anthony, 185, 200, 201, 221–46, 247, 248, 249, 250, 252, 253, 254, 255, 257, 279, 360, 394, 396, 403, 404, 405, 406, 409, 411, 412
Wilkinson, John, 172, 174, 175, 181
Williams, John, 304
Williamson, Lawrence, 299
Wilson, John, 279
Woodliefe, Grace, 300